REMAKING JAPAN

REMAKING JAPAN

The American Occupation As New Deal

Theodore Cohen

Edited by Herbert Passin

THE FREE PRESS
A Division of Macmillan, Inc.
NEW YORK

The Free Press
A Division of Macmillan, Inc.
866 Third Avenue, New York, N. Y. 10022

Collier Macmillan Canada, Inc.

Printed in the United States of America

printing number

1   2   3   4   5   6   7   8   9   10

Library of Congress Cataloging-in-Publication Data

Cohen, Theodore
    Remaking Japan.

    Bibliography: p.
    Includes index.
    1. Japan—History—Allied occupation, 1945–1952. I. Passin,
Herbert. II. Title.
DS889.16.C65 1987   952.04   86–33726
ISBN 0–02–906050–8

Just before I left for Japan for the first time in December 1945, a female cousin brightly chattered to me, "Now, don't you go bringing back a little Japanese girl!" I didn't. I married her and stayed with her in Japan for almost three decades. It is to her, Mitsuko, that this book is dedicated.

Under the Auspices of the East Asian Institute
Columbia University

The East Asian Institute is Columbia University's
center for research, teaching, and publication on modern
East Asia. The Studies of the East Asian Institute were
inaugurated in 1962 to bring to a wider public the results
of significant new research on China, Japan, and Korea.

Contents

Foreword

Most Americans will remember that we fought a war with Japan and won. "Remember Pearl Harbor" is still alive and kicking, although it sometimes seems more a reminder of the Japanese "trade menace" than of the Pacific war. And thanks to the continuing, if slightly dimmed, luster of General Douglas MacArthur's name, some will even recall that we occupied Japan for a while.

It is shocking, however, to discover how few remember anything about the Occupation: how long it lasted (six years, seven months, and twenty-eight days), what it did, and what effect it had on Japan's development. The American Occupation of Japan certainly ranks as one of, if not *the* proudest, achievements of postwar American foreign policy; it was, among other things, central to the development of Japan's "modern miracle." Yet it is as if it had disappeared down Orwell's memory hole. Everybody knows about the "economic miracle," but, as Theorodre Cohen says; "the roots of the miracle have been overlooked. The story of how it came about, of the Washington planners influenced by the New Deal, of Douglas MacArthur the Occupation Commander, of all the other Americans involved in its execution, and of the consequent rebirth of Japan in a new form, an astonishing Phoenix among the nations, still remains to be told." This is what the book is about.

Theodore Cohen—Ted—writes this history of the Occupation from the perspective of a major participant in some of the events he describes and a close observer of others. He held the delicate post of Chief of the Labor Division for about a year and a half, and then he was "kicked upstairs" to become adviser to General Marquat for another three years. In this latter position he was as close to the events he describes as anyone other than a direct participant could be. It is this quality of nearness and immediacy that gives such sharpness to his account.

Ted arrived in Japan from the Civil Affairs Staging Area in Monterrey, California, in January 1946. The Occupation had been underway since September of 1945, but in many key areas policy still remained to be worked out. First assigned as an adviser to the Government Section, he very shortly found himself appointed to one of the hot spots of the Occupation, the Labor Division, as its chief. In this position, he carried through two of the Occupation's three major labor reforms (the first, the basic Trade Union Law, giving workers the right to organize to strike and to bargain collectively, had already been put into effect before just before his arrival, in December 1945). These were the Labor Relations Adjustment Act of September 1946 and the Labor Standards Law of April 1947. And during his short but stormy tenure, he had to deal with two of the most "confusing, complicated, and vexing affairs of the Occupation"—the *Yomiuri* newspaper strike in the summer of 1946, in the course of which the Communist-dominated union effectively took over control of Japan's then third-largest newspaper, and the general strike of February 1947.

He was then twenty-eight years of age, the youngest chief of a major division in the Occupation. At that point in time, he was probably the only American who knew anything at all about Japanese labor. That had been the subject of his master's thesis in History at Columbia University, which he attended after completing his undergraduate work at City College of New York (CCNY). It was not surprising, therefore, that he would eventually find himself involved in the wartime planning of postwar labor policy—although if one recalls the classical Catch-22 mismatches between skill and job for which the military is famous, perhaps it *is* surprising. His appointment as Labor Division Chief was, in one sense, serendipitous, but, in another, the natural culmination of his intellectual life to that point.

That a New York boy, son of Russian-Jewish immigrants, and CCNY graduate, should rise to such high position in General MacArthur's staff was a surprise to some, and an irritation to others, it may be added. But that this could happen tells a great deal about General MacArthur himself and about his Headquarters.

Ted, however, was not alone. Among the leading players in the Occupation, four others were Jews. One cannot recount the history of the political reforms, including the rewriting of the Constitution, without constant reference to Colonel Charles L. Kades, the brilliant Deputy Chief of General Whitney's Government Section.

Wolf Ladejinsky, a Russian-born former employee of the U.S. Department of Agriculture, was the "father" of the land reform, by general assent the most successful single reform carried out by the Occupation. During the war years Ladejinsky, an expert on international agriculture, came up with a plan that formed the basis of the program the Occupation eventually decided upon. During the Occupation, he was a top adviser of the Natural Resources Section and influenced MacArthur's own determination to carry through the reform in spite of resistance from Japanese landlord interests and from American conservatives who saw it as a form of "socialism."

Dr. Alfred Oppler, a refugee from Hitler Germany, where he had held the position of Associate Justice of the Prussian Supreme Administrative Court, played the leading role in the reform of the legal system. First as Chief of the

Courts and Law Division of the Government Section, and then later as head of the Legislation and Justice Division of the Legal Section, he was better able to engage with Japan's essentially continental European-style legal system than lawyers and scholars trained in Anglo-American law.

Finally, there was Dr. Sherwood Fine, Chief Economic Adviser to General Marquat, head of Ted's own Economic and Scientific Section.

Ted's own development was not untypical for bright but poor Jewish boys of the 1930s. CCNY was their Mecca, not the Ivy League, where the tuition was too high and the social distance seemed too great. In the late 1930s and early 1940s, CCNY could boast of one of the most brilliant faculty and student bodies in the country. Ted was part of the same cohort that produced such internationally known intellectuals as Daniel Bell (Professor of Sociology, Harvard), Irving Kristol (writer, John M. Olin Professor of Social Thought at New York University, Editor of *The Common Interest*), Seymour Martin Lipset (Professor of Sociology, Stanford University), Melvin Lasky (Editor of *Encounter*), Irving Howe (writer), Everett Kassalow (former Research Director, Industrial Department, United Automobile Workers Union), Nathan Goldfinger (former Research Director, AFL–CIO), Nathan Glazer (Professor of the Sociology of Education, Harvard), Kenneth Arrow (Nobel Prize winner in Economics), Herman Feshback (Professor of Physics, MIT; former President of the American Physics Society and of the American Academy of Arts), and many others. But while they became intellectuals and labor activists, Ted became a businessman.

He shared, however, much of their intellectual and political trajectory— attracted to the radical movements of the 1930s but anti-Stalinist (and even somewhat pro-Trotskyist, especially on the question of the "nature of the Soviet Union"), strongly sympathetic to and sometimes active in the labor movement. Some of them later moved much farther to the right, a few ending up as so-called neo-conservatives. Ted never became a neo-conservative, but he was hard-headed and commonsensical in his approach to economic and political issues. Wherever he went he was instantly recognized as a man of extraordinary brilliance, sharp of wit and tongue, a propensity that in his delicate position would as often get him into trouble as out of it.

His job, as he saw it, was a twofold one: to liberate Japanese labor from the savage repression of prewar Japanese authoritarianism, but at the same time to prevent it from falling under the control of the Communists. This dual task required a delicate balance, one that was often too subtle for high military officers to comprehend.

Curiously, however, MacArthur was not one of these. In spite of his image at home as a right-wing "reactionary" Republican, he was able to understand and to maintain that balance in a way that one cannot imagine of any other leading officer of the American military at that time. During the threatened general strike of early 1947, for example, he was even more "liberal" in his early responses than Ted himself. MacArthur has been described and analyzed many times over; yet Ted, from his unique observation posts, manages to come up with new and fresh insights into one of the most enigmatic figures in American history.

After the abortive general strike, the balancing act became more and more difficult. Ted came under constant attack both from the left and from the right, from Japanese conservatives and from American conservatives (Roy Howard, the president of Scripps-Howard, for example), from Japanese leftists and from left-wing American journalists. Nor did he have the support he should have had from the American labor movement, which was more concerned with placing one of its own professional labor bureaucrats in his position than with the substantive issues involved. General MacArthur's reaction was, however, very different from the McCarthyite one that many Americans would have expected: instead of firing Ted, he waited out a cooling-down period and then kicked him upstairs to the position of Special Assistant to General Marquat, the chief of the section of which the Labor Division was a part. Ted continued to be employed by the Occupation three more years, and at the end of that time, even though McCarthyism was still far from a dead issue, he received an official commendation from General MacArthur in recognition of his services.

Ted's account of the struggle between the reforming "New Dealers" and the Republican and conservative forces sheds light on an important phase of American history. The New Dealers, so-called, were strong during the early postwar reforming phase of the Occupation. In 1946, however, even though Harry Truman won the presidency, the Republicans took both the Senate and the House of Representatives with resounding majorities. The Republican ascendancy had major consequences for the Occupation. From then on, American policy began to shift from rapid "democratization" to more cautious change, stability, and economic recovery. It is fashionable to attribute this shift in emphasis, the so-called reverse course, to the "cold war"; as Ted shows, however, relieving the American taxpyaer of the burden of providing continuing relief and rehabilitation to occupied Japan was a motive more proximate. The cold war became a factor later, after the shift had already begun.

It is in his exposition of the interaction of the diverse forces involved in the formulation and execution of Occupation policy that Ted is at his best. Did General MacArthur make Occupation policy, or did he only carry out orders from Washington? Such oversimplistic propositions dissolve in Ted's analysis of the intricate dynamics of the Occupation policy process. We see how policy is formulated in Washington, how it is transmitted, how it is received, how it is interpreted at the highest level, and then how it is received, interpreted, and finally executed by small groups or even individuals at the far end of the process. Sometimes, in the course of this lengthy process, the memory of the original policy, not to speak of its underlying concept and intent, is lost along the way.

The role of individual ideas, vested interests, ideologies, MacArthur's political ambitions, foreign policy concerns, personal relations, and conflicting interpretations in the end product—the action taken and its timing—becomes pellucidly clear in Ted's account. He gives us, in effect, a major lesson in the functioning of the American policy process.

It also becomes clear that the Japanese, even though occupied, were not simply the passive subjects of orders from the Occupation. Their input into the way Occupation policy, in many spheres, was put into effect was substantial. Many of the ideas for the land reform, for example, came from the Japanese themselves. The same was true for the reforms of the Civil Code (under Dr. Oppler's leadership). And in regard to the very constitutive structure of the Japanese legislature, the Diet, the Japanese insistence upon a bicameral assembly actually prevailed over the original American plan for a unicameral legislature.

In Japan itself, the place of the American Occupation in the creation of modern Japan is the subject of lively and extensive debate. Not so, alas, in the United States; here the interest is confined to a small group of scholars. But there can be no question that the Occupation was a major historical force, in Ted's view, a major turning point in Japanese history on a par with the arrival of Chinese influence in the seventh century and the Meiji Restoration of 1868. In fact, Ted originally thought of entitling this book "Japan's Third Turn."

But whatever the ultimate historical assessment might be, the Occupation either brought about or marked a decisive change in the course of Japanese history. Some Occupation programs remain virtually unchanged in the decades since the end of the Occupation in 1952. The Constitution, for example, has never been amended. Even the controversial Article 9 ("the Japanese people forever renounce war as a sovereign right of the nation and the threat or use of force as means for settling international disputes" [to which end] "land, sea, and air forces, as well as other war potential, will never be maintained"), which is widely attributed, and probably correctly, to MacArthur's own hand, still remains unamended despite the opposition of many conservative and even not-so-conservative people who regard it is an impermissible attainder on the sovereignty of Japan as an independent nation. Although Japanese agriculture has undergone major changes, of the same kind occurring in all the other advanced industrial countries, there has been no return, in any degree, to the semifeudal prewar landlord-tenant system. Nor has the enfranchisement of women, a major, if unheralded program of the Occupation, been reversed; on the contrary, the foundation established by the Occupation forms the basis of the continuing expansion of women's rights in Japan.

Some Occupation reforms have disappeared entirely—tried and found wanting, or too much in conflict with one or another vested interest. The American-introduced system of elected local school boards, for example, which was tried out for a while and then finally ended in 1955. Or the purges of political, business, educational, and other public leaders, which were terminated—in some cases, even before the formal end of the Occupation and, in others, just as soon as the Occupation was over.

Most of the reforms, however, have continued to undergo a natural process of evolution in accordance with the changing values of the Japanese people and the changing balance of political forces. The Occupation's dissolution of the *Zaibatsu* and its antitrust legislation have been modified, but not entirely eliminated. One of the major Occupation reforms, the decentralization of government, must be rated only a qualified success. Local autonomy has increased, in some fields more than in others, but not as much as the American reformers had intended. The Ministry of Education still retains predominant authority over the national school system even though somewhat less than before the war. The Occupation had hoped to eliminate the elitism of the university system and the brutal competitive examination system and its attendant "examination hell"; it failed. If anything the elitism has increased, and the competition has become more severe and widespread than before.

Many of these "reversals" do not appear unreasonable. Some reforms simply did not fit Japanese styles. One enthusiastic military-government officer out in the provinces had the notion that the way to bring democracy to the Japanese was through square dancing. So he started a go-go program to teach square dancing. Well, for a while some Japanese went along with it, but it was not long after his presence no longer graced the scene that the whole idea was dropped.

In other cases, we can question whether the American model, or what was purported to be the American model, was necessarily the best. In the United States, for example, because of our special historical development, we have the most decentralized educational system in the world. The U.S. Department of Education does not have the authority to tell schools what to do. Instead, we have something like 15,000 school districts of varying degrees of autonomy. There is no reason to think that this is the only alternative model to the highly centralized prewar Japanese system. There are many good alternatives that lie between the two extremes—total centralization on the one hand (as before the war in Japan, or in France, for that matter) and anarchic decentralization on the other.

That the Occupation did not accomplish everything it intended to does not negate its central place in the development of Japan as we know it today. In Ted's assessment, the Occupation accomplished two main things. First, political democratization—whatever their failings, the reforms did succeed in bringing the common people of Japan into the mainstream of citizenship. The land reform liberated the farmers (at the end of the war, almost 50 percent of the population); the labor reforms liberated the workers; the enfranchisement of women started the process of bringing women into the political, educational, social, and economic arena; and the educational reforms opened access to higher education for the common people. (Today, almost 95 percent of children of high school age graduate from senior high school, the highest rate in the world.)

Second, economic democratization—"that portion of New Deal ideology that became official fiat only in the few weeks immediately after the surrender." As Ted writes. "the freeing of the farmers from their debts and rents and the unionization and collective bargaining of millions of white- and blue-collar workers created a domestic mass market for consumer goods for the first time in Japanese history." This laid the basis for the mass-consumption society that Japan has now become.

The "burgeoning purchasing power" not only "stimulated the whole productive apparatus," but, even more consequential for us today, it stimulated the development of a powerful export economy. The strength and range of Japan's domestic market constitute the basis for its export competitiveness. It is part of the irony of history that our success in rehabilitating our wartime enemies, Germany and Japan, may have made them stronger economic rivals than they would otherwise have been.

Ted died suddenly on December 21, 1983. The two-volume edition of his book in Japanese had been published earlier in the month, but the first copy sent to him only arrived one day after his death. So he went to his grave without ever having seen a copy of his book in print. Nor could he complete its final editing for the American edition. The task fell to me, because I was his friend and had shared many of his experiences. The book, however, is all Ted's.

HERBERT PASSIN

A Personal Note

A few months before I left Japan after almost twenty-eight years, five with General MacArthur's Tokyo Headquarters and twenty-three in private business, I was approached by a Japanese publisher to do a memoir on the American Occupation of Japan. The idea was attractive. After all, if the law is what the judges say it is, then history is what the historians say it was, and here was my chance, as a controversial figure in those years, to tell my side of the story. The fact that so many of my fellow participants and wrong-headed critics were no longer in any position after more than three decades to contradict my version of events did not, needless to say, make the idea any less attractive. But self-indulgence was scarcely sufficient motivation for what quickly became much more than a memoir. Besides, there were still enough Occupation survivors left to keep me honest. Rather, what made the project a must, indeed a duty for a historian—and I had started off my professional life as a historian—was the very special circumstances of Japan under an American military occupation.

For more than six decisive years, Japan had two governments, a public one and a "secret" one. The first was, of course, the official Japanese Government with its prime minister, Diet members, political parties, and administrative appartus. The other was the General Headquarters of the Supreme Commander for the Allied Powers under General of the Army Douglas MacArthur. What the Japanese Government did, or tried to do, went on almost entirely in the open, in full view of the Japanese people, and the conventional accounts of the period have come down fully stocked with Japanese heroes and villains. What happened in General Headquarters, however, was largely unknown and has remained unknown, and so have its American heroes—other than General MacArthur— and its villains. Yet it is not hard to conclude that of the two the hidden government was by far the more crucial in determining the course of events. Indeed, an understanding of what went on in that sheltered enclave is the key to the events of Japan's historic third turn [see Prologue]. Without it, the transformation of Japan remains baffling and incomprehensible even to this day.

General Headquarters' temporary nature, fatal for historical record-keeping; the overwhelming preeminence of a commander who brooked no competition from his staff when it came to publicity; and the predominant *modus operan-di* of ''informal guidance'' by Headquarters officials in lieu of formal directives to the Japanese authorities have combined to make for a sadly inadequate written record. The MacArthur Headquarters was voluble all right,[1] but while it reported at least the gist of what SCAP and the Japanese did, it did not report what went on inside SCAP Headquarters.

To this day only a handful of rather specialized memoirs—including one on the legal reform by Alfred Oppler,[2] another on the religious reform by William Woodard,[3] still another on the political reform by Justin Williams,[4] a breezy and interesting but brief account by Brigadier General Elliott Thorpe, the head of the Counter Intelligence Section, of his six-month operation in Japan,[5] plus a rather limited number of oral histories at Columbia University and magazine reminiscences—supplement the firsthand special pleadings of the two indefatigable defenders of General MacArthur, Brigadier General Courtney Whitney[6] and Major General Charles Willoughby.[7] Those generals, moreover, devoted only a minor part of their books to the Japanese Occupation and besides were too far above the battle to know and tell a good deal of what transpired beneath them. Finally, too many of the SCAP survivors, starting out with the best of intentions, have never gotten down to the chore or have fallen by the wayside before doing so. By and large it has been, on the American side, a memoir-less Occupation, its main internal developments shrouded in secrecy.[8]

When I retired from business several years ago and was tempted to make my contribution, it was the first time I was free to do what several scholars had previously urged as my duty to history and to Japan. I started out thinking small, but the memoir ran away from me. A memoir is fine, but it is usually comprehensible only to those who know the background, unless the author is truly famous or personally exotic. Further, while I had been a principal actor in some of the important Occupation scenes, I was just a bit player in others and only an inside observer of still other developments. And what of the continuity and significance of all that had transpired?

Better to tell instead an ''insider's tory,'' an account of those phases of the Occupation, from planning to execution and results, of which I had some special inside knowledge or understanding. The result may appear somewhat lopsided. Some of the most noted Occupation reforms—the new Constitution, the educational reform, and the disestablishment of Shintō, for example—are hardly or not at all mentioned. I knew no more of them than anyone else. For the same reason, other Occupation measures, like the land reform, are mentioned only tangentially in connection with matters with which I *was* involved.

As a participant in and observer of so many different phases of the Occupation, I cannot but recognize that no matter how objective I may try to be, the reader is entitled to know just who is talking and from what standpoint. If it is an insider's story, just who is the insider and how far inside was he really? I can only reply that it is the story of a New York City boy, born and bred as far away from the Far East as it is possible to be, who fell into Japanese studies utterly by accident and then through the happenstance of war ascended rapidly to the upper levels of the real government of Japan. Some of my fellow specialists on the Far East always seemed to me to have some connection with Japan. C. Burton Fahs, who originally hired me into the Japan Section of the Office of Strategic Services just before Pearl Harbor, had a great-great-uncle who was ship's doctor on the Commodore Perry expedition.[9] Others were missionaries or the children of missionaries to the Far East, or pursued business interests out there, or received assignments from editors or opted for a diplomatic career. As one, however, whose parents were Russian-Jewish immigrants into the United States in 1903 and 1904 and who had hardly been any distance out of New York City until my 1938 graduation from CCNY, my only family connection with Japan was an uncle who hid in the forests around the White Russian town of Dubrowna for almost two years evading the Tsar's conscription, which would have brought him into the Russo–Japanese war. That is to say, no connection at all.

What happened next was perhaps best told by Dan Seligman in a *Fortune* magazine article on "Luck and Careers."

> In the mid-1930's Cohen was studying history at New York's City College and aspiring to an academic career there. He ended up spending 23 years as a businessman in Tokyo.
>
> A critical turning point was a classroom incident in 1935. Professor Louis L. Snyder had told the members of Cohen's class that each must prepare a thesis on some different aspect of modern nationalism. On the day set for final approval of the thesis topics, Cohen showed up intending to write on German anti-Semitism. But when Snyder went down the class list alphabetically, the student just ahead of him—the name was Chekanow—preempted that subject.
>
> After casting about a bit, Cohen decided to write on Japanese nationalism. This led to his getting interested in Japan, learning the language, and serving in the U.S. Occupation under Douglas MacArthur. When the Occupation ended Cohen stayed on and built a prosperous career with a Canadian import company. He and his Japanese wife are now living in retirement in Mexico. It would all have turned out differently, he reflected recently, if Chekanow had picked another subject or had somehow missed class that day.[10]

What *Fortune* neglected to mention were the details of what followed the classroom incident. Aside from five and half years' absorption in Japan as a student, both undergraduate and graduate, I went through six careers in the years that followed: teaching history at CCNY (1939–40); military intelligence in the Office of Strategic Services, where I was the Washington specialist on the nonmilitary aspects of the Japanese mandated islands in the Pacific and the Japanese electric power industry (1941–44); military government planning in the Foreign Economic Administration, where I worked on Chinese food relief and the Japanese Emperor's property and became chief of the Japan Labor Policy Section (1944–45); labor, as civilian chief of the Labor Division in GHQ in Japan (1946–47); economics, as Adviser on Economic Programs and Special Assistant to General Marquat, chief of the Economic and Scientific Section (1947–50); and then private business (1950–73), first selling wool waste and construction and materials-handling machinery to Japan, then buying all kinds of consumer goods from Japan and later all over the rest of the Far East, mostly for Canada. It was a varied and well-balanced diet, considering that the principal ingredient was Japan.

When I started on my fourth career, that of chief of SCAP's Labor Division, I was not yet twenty-eight. I never talked of that to the Japanese—with their emphasis on seniority they wouldn't have believed it anyway—but it does explain why some thirty-five years later I am still around to write these pages while most of my Headquarters contemporaries are not here to dispute them.

The twisted sequence of my careers, spending twenty-three years in "real life" in Japan after leaving Headquarters, which compelled me to live with the consequences of my own and my colleagues' actions in the Occupation, has given me a lot of time to reflect on our motives, as well as our wisdom and capacity or lack thereof, and also the changing policies of the U.S. Government toward Japan. The result of the introspection comes forth as a number of theses in this book, many of them unorthodox. The reader will meet them soon enough. But overall there is no question in my mind that the Occupation was a very good thing for Japan and any blunders have to be taken philosophically by both sides. I know of no alternative scenario after such a devastating war that would have brought about a happier result.

There is no need to bore the reader with a dissertation on sources and the difficulty of reaching them in Guadalajara or elsewhere in Mexico. Fortunately, I made preparations and amassed material before I left Japan. I should point out only that I have used the *Nippon Times*[11] as my newspaper of record, that is, for names and dates. The rest will be evident as we go along. Basically, however, the story remains a memoir. The footnotes are for scholars and disbelievers.

I should also like to acknowledge the interest and efforts of a small group in Mexico and elsewhere who assisted me greatly. It is one thing to proffer words of encouragement and show a polite curiosity from time to time. It is quite another to spend time and effort. I should like then to express my deepest gratitude to the late Murry Gabel, to Gerrard Eckstein, Colonel Warren Polking, USAF (Ret.), and the late Jay Brewer, who all spent countless hours going over and commenting on the manuscript with me; to my daughter, Jean Reiser, who helped in whatever long-distance research was necessary; and especially to Alvin Grauer, whose mature wisdom and experience in publishing were particularly helpful in organizing and orienting the work at a crucial time in its preparation.

My thanks, finally, are due to Valerie Goyzueta for typing the manuscript so expeditiously and so well.

THEODORE COHEN
Guadalajara, Mexico, 1982

Prologue

JAPAN'S THIRD TURN

TWICE BEFORE IN THEIR HISTORY the Japanese people had veered sharply from their previous course. In the seventh and eighth centuries, in response to their encounter with the Chinese, they absorbed Chinese culture, language, writing, and religion. Again in the last decades of the nineteenth century, forced to open their country to the world, they responded by embracing industrialization, a European system of government, and a modern military establishment. That road led in time to constantly expanding military ventures, ending with a disastrous war. And when the guns fell silent in 1945, the Japanese, their cities in ruins, their country under American military occupation, their old course at an impasse, were compelled to undertake another shift in national direction, the third turn in their long history.

The third turn was more abrupt than the other two. It was largely accomplished in six years, whereas the first took centuries and the second decades. It was also less voluntary, for countries under military occupation are in no position to argue. It was nonetheless just as fundamental and momentous in its consequences as the others. The Japanese people could easily have changed direction again afterward. But they did not. Instead they kept to the new course and remade their nation along the new lines, so that today it is as far from Meiji as Meiji was from Tokugawa and Tokugawa from the era of the Yamato clans fourteen centuries ago. After the Occupation, Japan could never again be the same. The third corner had been turned for good.

Not only was the new turn exceedingly rapid, it was also about as sharp as it could be in terms of Japan's previous course. For the preceding hundred years the response of Japan's leaders to every adversity and outside danger had been to build *fukoku kyōhei*—a wealthy country and a strong defense—on the sacrifices of the mass of the Japanese people. Faced with the utter devastation of 1945 and

1

a conventional military occupation, the leaders almost certainly would have insisted on continued, and even intensified, popular sacrifice. But the American Occupation would not have it that way. The American policy-makers were fearful that such a society of sacrifice, reconstructed on the backs of the under-classes—peasants, miners, factory workers, and the rest—would be inherently unstable and dangerous, just as it had turned out to be in the 1930s. To the surprise and even the bafflement of the Japanese, the U.S. authorities demanded internal justice instead. To Americans, who had just lived through a decade of depression and the New Deal, that meant especially economic justice and a radical reordering of the Japanese economic system to bring it about—in a word, economic democratization. The new Japan and, especially, its economic institu-tions were to be rebuilt in democratic form to safeguard the peace of the world.

As with the two earlier turns, however, the ultimate consequences of the third turn went far beyond those intended or foreseen. None was more important than the radical shift in the focus of Japan's economy. The Occupation au-thorities were under orders to disarm, demilitarize, and democratize Japan, and this they did. But what emerged unexpectedly from that process was the phe-nomenal development of a mass-production and mass-consumption society. For the first time, mass consumption dominated Japan's life and consciousness, and Japanese consumer goods began to move out into the world. Abroad, Japan became known as an economic animal, and at home its rigid internal class structure dissolved into an almost universal middle class.

Not all of that was unforeseen. Disarmament and demilitarization did remove the principal obstacles to the development of peaceful industry. That much was planned. But what was not was that democratization, especially eco-nomic democratization, notably the liberation of the peasantry and the freedom of labor unions to bargain collectively, created for the first time in Japan's history a domestic mass-consumer market in depth. It was the mainspring of subsequent Japanese economic development and all else that followed.

American leaders and their Occupation officials did not look ahead far enough to visualize those consequences. They were engrossed in preventing the resurgence of Japanese militarism and building democratic bulwarks against it. Nor did the Japanese see that far ahead at the time. They were happy to have their erstwhile domestic oppressors off their backs and a peaceful "cultural Japan" in prospect. But such was the logic of the third turn. The Americans got what they thought they wanted, and so did the Japanese. What they got in addition was an "economic miracle" and all that went with it.

Meanwhile, the roots of the miracle have been overlooked. The story of how it came about; of the Washington planners influenced by the New Deal; of Douglas MacArthur, the Occupation Commander; of all the other Americans involved in its execution; and of the consequent rebirth of Japan in a new form, an astonishing Phoenix among the nations, still remains to be told after more than thirty years.

Part I

THE PLAN AND THE
NEW DEAL

FOURTEEN YEARS of war. And when the battered Japanese war machine shuddered to an abrupt stop on August 15, 1945, the weary passengers alighted, looked around warily . . . and went to the movies. In a matter of days, the sparse surviving populations of the wrecked cities took to standing in long lines in the steaming heat, jamming the remaining movie houses. An exhausted lassitude took hold of the people, along with an overwhelming need for escape. And no wonder, for inside the cinema was a living world, outside a desolation.

Thirty-five years later it is very hard to recall the devastation that was Tokyo and almost all the other cities of Japan. A foreign visitor in the autumn of 1945 would alight at Atsugi airfield with its double row of propellerless Zero fighters, ride through the green, almost untouched countryside, whose only sign of war was the baggy *monpei*[1] attire of the women and hand-me-down military uniforms of the men, and then enter the final battlefields, the centers of the cities. Here, destroyed by the concentrated incendiary raids and fire storms of April and May, the only things left protruding from the rubbled earth were iron safes and concrete chimneys, silhouetted against the sky as silent witnesses to the small shops and communal bathhouses that spawned them, then died.

The safes and chimneys were only a shade more eloquent than the eerie absence of anything else. In each large city the pattern was the same: a score or two of reinforced-concrete multistory buildings, weathered but intact, scattered about near the city's center, then a concentric belt, several miles wide, of total devastation, the whole surrounded by outlying districts of crowded tile-roofed wooden homes and shops, still more or less as they had always been.

In Tokyo, 70 percent of the area of the city was destroyed, in Osaka 80, in Nagoya 90. Urban populations had withered swiftly in the last year of war, some killed in the air raids, most having fled to relatives in the countryside. Tokyo entered the war with five million residents and finished it with one million. Other cities had shrunk as well.

Transportation was limited to crowded, creaky trains, hand-pulled two-wheel "rear cars" designed to be attached to bicycles, and oxcarts. At war's end, in all of Japan there were only 41,000 motor vehicles, half of them inoperable[2] and almost all the rest powered by charcoal fumes. There were no street lights at night and very few house lights. The food situation was highly problematical if not desperate. Everyone tensely calculated how long his own family's hoarded kitchen stocks would last and when the inevitable famine would strike the cities. There were no fat Japanese. Even the sumo wrestlers carried badly sagging jowls and flabby bellies. The dogs had long since disappeared.

Unwilling to remember the recent past, unready to face the future, the people longed for escape. The nation of fanatic warriors and compulsive workers had simply run out of steam. Most felt that with the war lost, matters were now out of their hands. Let someone else take charge for a while. Meanwhile, they went to the movies.

But while they were going to the movies, two documents of transcendent importance to them arrived secretly in Tokyo. On September 18, 1945, the new Occupation Commander, General Douglas MacArthur, received the first half of the American directive to him on how to conduct the occupation. On October 22 he received the second half. The two together formed the "Basic Initial Post Surrender Directive to Supreme Commander for the Allied Powers for the Occupation and Control of Japan," better known by its serial number, JCS 1380/15. From then on there was no escape for anyone. There was to be no waiting for a peace treaty to decide Japan's future. Japan's course since its second turn, which had produced heavy industry, a modern state, and a powerful military machine, had come crashing into a dead end. The Japanese now had to figure out where they were going to go. But the U.S. Government was not going to leave that to them. JCS 1380/15 was the American master plan to transform Japanese society yet again, and to do it during the military occupation in the interests of a durable peace.

But there was much more to the directive. For the plan, military in form and language, was simultaneously, in spirit and essence, a product of Franklin Roosevelt's New Deal era. The American command, led by General MacArthur, never recognized it as such. Still less could the Japanese, isolated from American political currents for many years, imagine such a thing. Nevertheless, they could not evade the impact of so powerful a victor's current ideology on their defeated nation. No Japanese, moviegoer or otherwise, could escape his new destiny.

Unconditional Surrender

THE AMERICAN OCCUPYING FORCES debouching onto the soil of Japan through its airfields and its principal ports experienced excitement, not lassitude, optimism, not anxiety or despair. The sudden Japanese surrender had spared them two certainly bloody invasions: Operation Olympic, scheduled for October 1, 1945, to conquer Kyūshū,[1] and Operation Coronet, set for February 1, 1946, to subjugate the wide Kantō plain around Tokyo and Yokohama. After years of jungle fighting in New Guinea, the Solomons, and the Philippines, officers and men greeted a peaceful, temperate, and civilized though badly battered land with relief and enthusiasm.

To their immense surprise, the Japanese were complaisant and cooperative. The Americans settled down to adventure and new experiences while counting the "points"—so many for time in service, so many for overseas time, for campaigns, battles, wounds, and so on—they needed to bring them home again. And the high-speed, efficient MacArthur General Headquarters turned almost without missing a beat from war to peace, that is, to carrying out JCS 1380/15. Led and inspired by a commander, General of the Army Douglas MacArthur, who saw the new Occupation not as a rest at long last from arduous battle, as did so many of his American counterparts in Europe, but as a completely new career, the capstone of his life's work, the exhilarated American staff felt able to do anything it was asked to do: disarm a world power, demobilize its armies, govern it, and transform its basic institutions. Their horizons were unlimited. After all, they had won the war.

REPLETE WITH PARADOX

Within a month of the initial landings of the Occupation forces at Atsugi and Yokohama on August 30, Occupation Headquarters plunged into an unprecedented drive to remake 70 million Japanese, to that time "feudalistic" and violently "militaristic," into a democratic and peaceful nation. It turned out to be a five-year program. From all appearances it was a remarkable success. Certainly it was the most successful of the American postwar interventions, varying blends of good intentions and national interest, in the internal affairs of distant countries all the way up to Vietnam. Its very effectiveness undoubtedly had a great deal to do with American public acceptance of the interventions that followed, but in none of those did the U.S. presence succeed nearly so well. Just what was right about the Japanese episode that wasn't so right about the others is a fascinating question. America had won its right to intervene with blood rather than with financial aid, of course, but also the Japanese people themselves were part of the answer.

At the time, no one thought the Japanese occupation would set any kind of precedent. On the contrary, what was obvious to its participants was that it was unique. It was also big, important, and fundamental. It was a cause to light a fire in one's eye and to inspire the remarkable dedication that comes from feeling oneself a part of history in the making. Nothing the United States had ever attempted in any other land, or even in its own, was as grand in conception. In retrospect, one trembles at American presumption. Nevertheless, the Occupation remade Japan.

On the face of it the great project was replete with paradox. The idea of democratizing by means of that least democratic of institutions, the Army, was patently illogical from the beginning. Assigning a charismatic war hero, General MacArthur, the job of demolishing a long-standing military heritage studded with charismatic Japanese war heroes seemed equally inappropriate. Entrusting the detailed reconstruction of the internal workings of an extraordinarily subtle and complex society, certainly the least known among the major nations to America, to a corps of officials very few of whom had even a smattering of Japanese history or language clearly invited ridicule. But historic opportunity does not often provide the most suitable tools to go with the job, and Americans' faith in improvisation and in their native ingenuity, so recently proven in wartime production and combat, was strong. America had to ensure, they felt, that Japan would never again endanger and humiliate the United States with new "Pearl Harbors" or upset world peace with military aggression. In light of that mission, who worried about paradoxes or minor obstacles like ignorance?

Above all, leaders and people were determined not to repeat past mistakes. Averell Harriman, who was as privy to Franklin Roosevelt's foreign policy thinking as anyone at the time, attested many years later that the President's formulation of unconditional surrender "was very much influenced by the mistakes he thought [Woodrow] Wilson made."[2]

The American people generally agreed. Between wars they may have been dubious about Wilson's old crusade to make the world safe for democracy, but by the time World War II drew to a close they were convinced Wilson hadn't gone far enough. Instead of merely exiling the Kaiser and skeletonizing the Wehrmacht, this time the Allies would reorganize and reeducate Germany from top to bottom, even if it took a generation. Japanese militarism, believed to be even more ingrained than the German, would undoubtedly take more time and perseverance. Popular writers on international affairs and triumphant field commanders vied in this kind of extremism. The occupation of Japan, they warned, had to last at least twenty years to be successful. What qualified an admiral like Halsey or an infantry general like Eichelberger to be experts on Japanese society and the Japanese psyche is hard to say, but people listened. The cumulative effect of such repeated warnings was a national mood that accepted no limitation on what the Allies were to do in Japan or on the time it would take them to do it.

Without apparent public hesitation, American war aims were broadened by a slight verbal emendation. Where in World War I the United States was determined to eradicate militarism, at the end of World War II American leaders were resolved to eliminate also the *conditions that brought about militarism*. Now *that* was a radical and fundamental change. How could anyone say for sure what fostered militarism and how far back into Japanese history one had to go to find out? The newly "sophisticated" American public, however, quickly accepted the enlarged goal. This time the boys would not have died in vain.

In similar and even greater degree, the other Allies rejected limitations. The Australians and New Zealanders, as it turned out in the first month after the surrender, thought the Americans too lenient.[3] Together with the Chinese they hoped to start *their* reorganization of Japan by trying the Emperor immediately as a war criminal. As for the Russians, the Draconian measures the Soviet armies were taking all through Eastern Europe, then in Manchuria and North Korea, did not suggest that they would show any greater restraint in the occupation of Japan if they had their way. By comparison, the American attitude, revolutionary as it was, seemed a model of self-control. If a former enemy were to suffer by accident the practical consequences of mistaken sociological or economic analyses or of administrative amateurism, why worry about it? It would be little enough, thought the Americans, compared with aggression in China, the Philippines, and Pearl Harbor and *their* consequences.

It is quite understandable how in such an atmosphere established international legal restrictions on the conduct of occupations were modified or even brushed aside. Article 43 of the Hague Rules on Land Warfare provided that "the authority of the legitimate power having passed into the hand of the occupant, the latter shall take all measures to restore and ensure, so far as possible, public order and safety, while respecting unless absolutely prevented, the laws in force in the country." *Oppenheimer's International Law*, the accepted authority on the subject, states that "the occupant . . . has no right to make changes in the laws or in the administration other than those which are temporarily necessitated by his interest in the maintenance and safety of his army, and the realization of the purpose of war."[4] Domestic legislation by an occupation force is barred in principle by international law.

The last phrase in *Oppenheimer,* "purpose of war," however, provided the key to a precisely opposite interpretation. Previously, aside from Napoleon's campaigns, the purposes of war in the eighteenth and nineteenth centuries had been limited: changes in territorial boundary or dynasty, imposition of indemnities and reparations, or the direct weakening of a possible future adversary by restrictions on its armed forces. But now the purpose of war had been expanded to eliminating the *conditions* that bred militarism,[5] and the terms of the peace were correspondingly enlarged. Total war proclaimed by Hitler had opened the door to a "total peace."

One terse sentence in the Truman–Attlee Potsdam Declaration of July 26, 1945, was sufficient. "The Japanese Government," it asserted, "shall remove all obstacles to the revival and strengthening of democratic tendencies among the Japanese people." Obstacles? Strengthening? Tendencies? Rarely were more inspiring and less exact words used in what turned out to be a vital legal document. For when the Japanese Government accepted the Potsdam Proclamation, the boundaries of permissible Occupation legislation receded to the far horizons. The very first Japanese objection to an Allied order—on August 17, 1945, protesting Allied instructions to turn over Japanese embassies and legations abroad on the grounds that "they do not correspond to any provision of the Declaration of Potsdam accepted by the Government of Japan"[6]—was summarily squelched.

UNBOUNDED AUTHORITY?

Thereafter, the Allied governments, and in practice that meant the Supreme Occupation Commander, were the only authorized interpreters of the words of the Potsdam Declaration. In my five years in Occupation Headquarters, involved as I was in the consideration of hundreds of proposed written or oral directives to the Japanese, I cannot once remember anyone's seriously raising the question of the permissible limits of Occupation authority according to international law other than with respect to property and war crimes. Neither the Occupation Forces nor the American public were particularly aware that, apart from forbidding mistreatment of the local population, there were any legal limitations at all on an occupation's authority after an unconditional surrender.

The legal limits question was raised seriously by Americans only once, in the U.S. State Department, immediately after Japan had accepted the Potsdam Declaration. On August 29, 1945, at the top-secret meeting of the State–War–Navy Coordinating Committee Subcommittee on the Far East (SWNCCFE), which was reviewing the overall draft directive to be sent to General MacArthur, Eugene Dooman, special assistant to Under Secretary Grew and head of State's Office of Far Eastern Affairs, gave it as his Department's view that the Supreme Commander's powers were limited by international law. He denied that there was an unconditional surrender at all. It was, he said a contractual arrangement between the governments of Japan and the United States.[7] Within three days John Carter Vincent replaced Dooman and informed the Subcommittee that the new Under Secretary of State, Dean Acheson, had overruled his predecessor. State now confirmed that the surrender was indeed unconditional, even though the Japanese had undoubtedly relied upon the provisions, that is, the conditions, of the Potsdam Declaration in deciding to surrender.[8] As President Truman said when he saw the Japanese reply, "I deem this reply a full acceptance of the Potsdam Declaration which specifies the unconditional surrender of Japan. In the reply there is no qualification."[9] Thereafter, the unified view of the U.S. Government was that the United States had merely issued an ultimatum "whereby we told the Japanese what we proposed to do" but was not itself bound by it.[10]

Absent any idea of constraints, the Civil Information and Education Section of Occupation Headquarters felt free to sponsor square dancing and billiards for the Japanese as obviously more democratic than geisha dances and *kendō* sword-fighting. The Civil Transportation Section's Chief[11] had no compunctions about explaining to the Transportation Ministry (and later to a GHQ General's Committee on Relaxation of Occupation Controls, of which I was a member) that pricing second-class rail tickets at triple third-class fare and first-class at triple second-class fare was not democratic, because it did not reflect the true costs, which were only double and double respectively. The imposition one fine day of daylight savings time by the executive officer of the Economic and Scientific Section (ESS),[12] while his boss was away in the States, was even more distantly related to Oppenheimer's "purpose of war." He later explained he was intending to save electricity and stimulate production—not to make more time available for after-hours tennis—but when he did it in June 1946, "stimulating production" was supposed to be a Japanese responsibility. In reality, it had just not occurred to the efficient colonel, or to anyone in his vicinity, that international law simply did not allow him to do it in the first place.

Those kinds of action on the scene only reflected attitudes pervading the highest levels in Washington. "In this area [Japan] the authority of the military commander will be absolute and [derives from] international law, and, as such, he will be limited only by directive to him from the Joint or Combined Chiefs of Staff," one such statement ran.[13] Washington might dispute the wisdom of the Command, but never its international authority.

But if there was no international legal authority to restrain General MacArthur, and if the Japanese, after surrendering unconditionally, could not themselves protest, that did not mean MacArthur himself had unlimited authority or was a kind of American Caesar, a free agent—"proconsul" was the favorite word of the writers on Occupation Japan—who determined policy on his own. True, he fostered that illusion, and the U.S. Government backed him up on it, for otherwise who could tell how long the line of Japanese appellants to Washington against his actions might grow? It was an illusion at the time shared by almost all the Japanese, who thought democratization was MacArthur's idea in the first place (indeed, it is still shared by many, and not only Japanese). The truth, however, was quite otherwise. General MacArthur was under orders, and the orders were JCS 1380/15. In a military headquarters such an order was controlling.

THE MILITARY COMMAND

In a civilian government, policy decisions are splendid statements of intention, but the degree to which they are carried out depends in large part on how subordinate officials interpret them. But MacArthur's GHQ was not a civilian government, and as controversial as JCS 1380/15 might have been had it undergone individual evaluation, no one on the staff was asked what he thought of it. An order is an order—even more so in a headquarters with strong leadership—and combat discipline, still only weeks old in memory, was carried right over into operational planning. On the receipt of JCS 1380/15 the Chief of Staff and his colonels dismembered its 179 paragraphs and 7,500 words—the equivalent of some twenty-five double-spaced typed pages—into fragments, and parceled them out paragraph by paragraph to the thirteen staff sections for "implementation." The section chiefs and their executive officers divided their assigned paragraphs and subparagraphs among their divisions, whose chiefs and executive officers in turn broke their assigned texts even further into assignments for their branches. Sometimes the fragments were as small as a sentence or even a clause. No part of JCS 1380/15 remained unassigned to someone, and almost every branch, division, and section had some part of the directive as its "mission," even if only a phrase. And its mission was assigned verbatim—no question of interpretation—from the highest military authority in the nation, the Joint Chiefs of Staff. It would take a rash soul, indeed, with his military career dependent on how well and how fast he could implement his new mission, to disagree or quibble about it, no matter how strong his personal convictions.

When I first arrived in Tokyo a few months after the surrender, coming as I did from the constant in-fighting and intrigue of Washington, I was astonished at the dispatch with which the most momentous actions were taken. Almost every staff officer in those sections to which had been assigned the bulk of the "missions" seemed to be feverishly engrossed in preparing action papers implementing his part of the directive.

Now, an American military staff in theory has no independent authority, nor do any of its officers, no matter how high their rank, unless they have been specifically assigned operational responsibilities as well. Only the Commander makes decisions. In the first months of the Occupation, therefore, each officer with an assigned mission would prepare his proposed action—whether directive or letter to the Japanese Government, orders to a subordinate American command, press statement, or some combination of them—for the signature or approval of General MacArthur or the Chief of Staff acting in MacArthur's name. He would support his recommended action with a "memo for the record" that quoted the relevant fragment of JCS 1380/15 like scripture, set forth the facts, and explain why the proposed action was necessary and appropriate. The initiating officer, of course, had to show that no one else's mission under the directive would be adversely affected, which he would do by obtaining initialed "concurrences" from all other GHQ agencies likely to be involved. (They could not, of course, agree or disagree with the merits of the action; it was none of their business.) A fast staff officer, carrying his file around himself, could sometimes line up his concurrences in forty-eight hours. If he could convince his superior and his superior's superior, all the way up the chain of command, that JCS 1380/15 was applicable, his action was almost certain to be quickly approved. Once approved by General MacArthur or in his name, that ended all further discussion.

THE OCCUPATION PHILOSOPHY

MacArthur's GHQ was a wonderfully efficient high-speed machine for translating the directive's provisions into action. But the directive in turn was essential to the machine; otherwise it would have been spinning its wheels aimlessly. True, three weeks before the first part of JCS 1380/15 arrived in Japan, the State Department's "U.S. Initial Post Surrender Policy for Japan" (SWNCC 150/4) was radioed to MacArthur for his guidance—his message center received it on August 30, the very day he was flying in to Atsugi from Okinawa—but it was inadequate and not worded as an order. No military man could take it seriously. Its impact, consequently, was almost nil. I cannot remember anyone in GHQ ever referring to the State Department's policy paper. JCS 1380/15, on the other hand, programmed the operations of GHQ with respect to the Japanese from top to bottom.

The JCS directive was, of course, much more than an operational paper. Indeed, it was unique in the annals of world history—a military order to remake a society. MacArthur was told that "in addition to the conventional powers of a military occupant of enemy territory, you have the power to take any steps deemed advisable and proper by you to effectuate . . . the provisions of the

Potsdam Declaration," that is, "democratize" Japan. Take paragraph 25, ordering the Supreme Commander to "encourage and show favor to policies which permit a wide distribution of income and ownership of the means of production and trade." Was that a military matter? Indeed, the directive's three parts—General and Political; Economic and Civilian Supply and Relief; and Financial—covered a bewildering array of nonmilitary subjects: the use of Japanese governmental authority, the breakup of nationalist organizations, political liberalization, freedom of speech and assembly, removal from office and disqualification of undesirables, abolition of the secret police, industrial disarmament, economic and labor democratization, educational reform, and so forth, including a variety of control measures as well. How many of those had ever before—except for the contemporaneous German occupation perhaps—been the concerns of an occupation commander? Now the unprecedented was the heart of the Japanese Occupation. And strange to say, the great bulk of the Japanese people wholeheartedly embraced most of the underlying principles. For them, JCS 1380/15, even though they did not know of its existence, liberated Japan.

In doing so, JCS 1380/15 was the making of Douglas MacArthur's reputation as a civil governor. It supplied him with a comprehensive, coherent, and relevant philosophy, and a concrete program to go with it. No one, not even a man with MacArthur's breadth of vision, could have turned from the intense concentration demanded by combat planning to produce such an analysis in so short a time. With JCS 1380/15, MacArthur had answers to the questions the Japanese were tremulously asking at the end of their debacle—not only as to immediate problems, such as, "Who will rule us?" or "Will we have enough to eat?" but also the profound doubts troubling the nation's very soul: "How did we get into such a calamity?" "How can we get out never to return?" "Are we a first-rate or fifth-rate nation?" Without appearing to be able to provide the answers, how could even the charismatic General have exercised leadership? Who would have followed a leader without convincing answers? With the answers, MacArthur was a prodigious political force. Without them he could have been an actor without lines.

This is not to say that he had no ideas of his own on the conduct of his Occupation. On the contrary, it is very much to the General's credit that he took the initiative in the agricultural land reform, the only important Occupation reform not included in the directive and quite probably its most successful. He himself was also responsible for women's emancipation, including women's suffrage, neither of which had much effect on the general course of the Occupation, beneficial and important as they might have been for the future. And finally, his proposal for a unicameral legislature was dutifully tried out on the Japanese representatives by the Government Section during the negotiations with respect to the new Constitution, but MacArthur dropped it when his GHQ people reported unanimous Japanese opposition.[14]

MacArthur had been deeply worried that he might be ordered to enforce an "imperialistic" and harsh occupation. In March 1945 in Manila he farsightedly told Robert Sherwood, President Roosevelt's emissary, that if the United States could refrain from occupying Japan in an imperialistic manner and treat the Japanese justly and liberally, "we shall have the friendship and cooperation of the Asian people far into the future."[15] Now he warmly embraced the new reform directive when it arrived and made it his own, using it as a comprehensive framework comfortably consistent with his own special ideas. Less than two years later, he would call it "one of the great state papers of modern history"[16] and publicly defend some of its more controversial provisions with vigor and his own prestige.

It was fortunate that in large part the directive coincided with some of MacArthur's previously conceived notions. How much coincidence there was is impossible to tell, for MacArthur had access to both the State Department finished policy statement (SWNCC 150/4) and an earlier draft of JCS 1380/15 before he arrived in Japan and made his resplendent pronunciamentos to the Japanese. In any case, the Washington directive was controlling. MacArthur was not the independent, free-wheeling force he seemed to be.

To say that is not to belittle his role. In both style and substance, perhaps no other commander, civilian or military, could have contributed so much to the Occupation of Japan. But Under Secretary of State Acheson's declaration in September 1945 that MacArthur was "the instrument of policy, not its determinant" was necessarily true. No modern government could have permitted anything else. No passive instrument, MacArthur was allowed perhaps the greatest leeway ever accorded an American officer in peacetime, but that was precisely because his additions to the directive were so closely in tune with its objectives. Even the land reform was on the agenda of the SWNCCFC when MacArthur took his action.

The "ideology" of the Occupation came from Washington; its concrete expression was JCS 1380/15. If it was not the conventional military occupation bound by the accepted restraints of international law, neither was it, despite square dancing, "democratic" railway rates, daylight savings time, and all the rest of the overexuberance of individual Americans, a runaway uncontrolled by outside authority. The Occupation was rather a powerful reform stream running through clearly defined channels. Its commander did not seek to break the channel walls but rode the stream along its predetermined course. In the process, he became Japan's greatest twentieth-century reformer and the key performer in Japan's third turn. But who erected the walls in the first place, and by what rationale? How did those architects manage in wartime Washington to hammer out a unified position so thoroughly that it could be imposed wholesale on Japan?

2

Threads in a Maze

MODERATION REJECTED

HENRY STIMSON, U.S. Secretary of War in 1945, was a Republican. Secretary of the Navy James Forrestal was a conservative Democrat with big business connections. Assistant Secretary of War John McCloy was a Republican, too. Secretary of State Edward Stettinius was another big business recruit. Under Secretary of State Joseph Grew was a professional diplomat known widely as a staunch conservative. Those were the men charged with supervising American policy toward Japan under the forthcoming military occupation. There was not a certified liberal, let alone a New Dealer, among them. Yet the official directive the departments they headed sent to the new Occupation commander was essentially a New Deal prescription: Distribute the wealth more widely, break up the financial combines, purge big business, encourage labor unions, ban trade cartels. And in a foreign country, too. Now, how did that unlikely result come about?

HILLDRING

The "how" is a complicated story, tortuous even, and at the time the participants themselves scarcely understood it in its entirety. As one of them, I was able to piece the entire process together long afterward only with difficulty, through a number of talks with other survivors. One of those I queried, Hugh Borton, who had been one of State's principal planners then, thirty-some years later confessed himself baffled at the last-minute appearance in State's formal policy statement of economic democratization provisions. It could have been a kind of accident, considering the frantic pace at the end of the war, he ventured.[1]

14

Borton was wrong. An accident it decidedly was not. It was, rather, a demonstration of how political currents and strong personalities can make mincemeat of carefully ordered government organization charts, producing policy children that their putative fathers would not acknowledge if they scrutinized them at all carefully. That was not unique in the Washington of those days, nor possibly of these, and maybe it often did not matter much. But in Japan's case the outcome was fateful, for it determined the shape of the reborn country and its future for decades to come. The story begins one day in April 1943 with a relatively unknown, nonpolitical professional soldier, John F. Hilldring, at its center.

On that day, when General Douglas MacArthur's forces were still battling in Northeast New Guinea, 3,000 miles and scores of islands from Japan, Hilldring, one of hundreds of major generals in the U.S. Army at the time, strode into the office of General George C. Marshall, Chief of Staff, in the brand new Pentagon Building in Arlington, Virginia. Hilldring, no West Pointer, was nevertheless as "regular army" as it was possible to be. He had had a twenty-six-year career from second lieutenant in France in 1917 to the Infantry School, the Advanced Infantry School, and then through the Command and General Staff School in Leavenworth. Though white-haired and balding, he was an alert, vigorous forty-eight, at the pinnacle of every professional soldier's ambition, for only the year before he had been given his own division, the 84th Infantry, which he had just finished training and bringing to full combat readiness. Now he was awaiting orders to lead it into battle in North Africa or wherever his men were needed. Summoned to Washington, he hoped the Chief of Staff would tell him where. Instead, what he heard ended his career as a combat commander. His country needed him more, Marshall said, to take over a small new section on his special staff, the Civil Affairs Division (CAD).[2] He would have the mission of planning the nonmilitary aspects of whatever occupations the Army would have to handle in the future. Hilldring was to report to General Marshall himself once a week and to work directly with Assistant Secretary of War John McCloy. From then on he was to be desk-bound.

No one said "no" to the austere Marshall where duty was concerned. Hilldring choked back his disappointment, he told me several years later,[3] when he was Assistant Secretary of State. He snapped out a brisk "Yes, sir" and went back to say a tight-lipped farewell to his beloved division. On May 4, 1943, he became the Director of the Army's Civil Affairs Division, destined to preside over the gestation and birth of JCS 1380/15.

His first eight months on the job were tied up with North African and European problems, and it was January 1944 before Hilldring had a chance to think seriously of Japan. As he saw it, his job was to prepare a directive to the future occupying commander in Japan on civil government, both for the limited areas falling under America's control in the wake of battle while fighting raged elsewhere and for the whole country after the final victory. To do that, he needed to know what the policy of the United States toward a defeated Japan was to be. Where does one go in the U.S. Government to find a foreign policy? Obviously to the Department of State. And that is where Hilldring went.

THE OLD JAPAN HANDS

Before the war, the State Department was the only organization in the American Government, other than the narrowly focused military and naval intelligence services, that dealt with Japan on a continuing basis. Within the Department, the Office of Far Eastern Affairs and its Japan Division were the experts. Staffed with experienced, carefully selected career foreign service officers (FSOs) who had lived in Japan for extended periods and had had intensive language training, the division and office were augmented in 1942 by the repatriation on the *M. V. Gripsholm* of the American diplomats interned in the Far East at the outbreak of the war.

Foremost among those repatriated was ex-Ambassador Joseph C. Grew, a graduate of Groton and Harvard, who had been in Japan since 1932. Before that, he had been Ambassador to Turkey; earlier still, he had been Under Secretary of State under Coolidge. Grew was also a longtime friend and Dutchess County neighbor of President Roosevelt, and he still had occasional access to him. In May 1944 he was named head of the Office of Far Eastern Affairs, displacing Stanley Hornbeck, favorite of the "old China hands" in the Department, and in November 1944 he was once again named Under Secretary of State. The influence and prestige of the Japan FSOs were at their peak. If Hilldring wanted policy, the Office of Far Eastern Affairs and the Japan Division within it were obviously the proper source.

Very shortly, however, Hilldring would find that it was not so simple. As the war went on and peace drew nearer, other officials in the government, in and out of the State Department, laid claims to a role in postwar policy decisions on Japan. The ideas of Grew and his FSOs, under increasing scrutiny, came to be seen as out of sympathy with the mainstream of American thinking both in government and out. And, perhaps most immediately important, the Japan FSOs demonstrated an inability to turn out policy over the range of fields and in the detail required.

Hilldring discovered that he could not simply reel in any one policy line from any one source, especially not from the Japan Division. Painstakingly, he had to seek out and gather in the multiple policy threads wherever he could find them in that vast maze that was the wartime federal government, disentangle them, and then pull them together into a coherent, consistent, and acceptable whole. The circle of those involved in Japan occupation planning grew from a handful to a hundred, and from the one obvious office to more than a dozen in five departments (State, War, Navy, Agriculture, Treasury) plus two independent agencies (the wartime Office of Strategic Services and the Foreign Economic Administration). By the time the process was over, the FSOs were largely out of it.

It was a crucial change. Had the FSOs had their way, the democratization of Japan would never have been given to MacArthur as his primary mission. Grew, their "guru," expressed his deepest convictions frankly when, in his first briefing of President Truman in May 1945, he assured the new President that "from the long-range point of view, the best we can hope for is a constitutional monarchy, experience having shown that democracy in Japan would never work."[4] Nor would General MacArthur and his staff have instituted the far-reaching changes that remade Japan's economic structure into a mass consumer economy: the land reform, labor unions, democratization of business, and so forth. Indeed, a State Department paper of November 1944, co-drafted by Robert Fearey, who had been Grew's secretary in Tokyo, and concurred in by five other FSOs, recommended that "except as they may be specifically directed, the Occupation authorities should not attempt long-range reforms or reorganization of the internal economy."[5] As it turned out, both JCS 1380/15, the secret directive to MacArthur, and SWNCC 150/4, the public U.S. policy statement for Japan, provided for almost precisely the opposite—and modern Japanese history followed a different route.

The first diminution of the Japan FSOs' assumed monopoly over postwar Japanese affairs, including the prospective Occupation, was hardly resisted, indeed was welcomed, by the FSOs themselves. After all, regional "experts" the FSOs might be, but essentially they were, for the most part, diplomatic mechanics. An occupation, particularly one that might have to exercise military government over tens of millions of people, had to cover the whole range of administrative responsibilities: industry, materials allocations, public finance, banking, prices, food distribution, labor, farming and tenancy, local politics, civil rights and criminal law, education, and so forth. Hilldring needed information and guidance on all those subjects. The FSOs were generalists, not specialists, and simply could not supply those needs.[6]

Finally, peculiarly enough, the FSOs were very busy. The outbreak of war, far from ending Japanese–American diplomatic relations, simply shifted them to third-party channels—Switzerland and Spain—made them more arduous to handle, and raised a host of new subjects: mistreatment of prisoners and internees, remittances of money to them, violations of the rules of war, property claims, and so on. The Japan Division was overloaded with routine; its members had no time, even if they had the ability or the inclination, to deal with the future of Japan.

Problems arising from the limitations of the professional diplomatic mind, of course, extended beyond the Japan FSOs. Leo Pasvolsky, the astute adviser to Secretary of State Hull on international security matters (mostly formation of the United Nations Organization), obtained permission from his boss to establish an innocuously named "Special Research Division," later changed to an equally innocuous "Territorial Studies" (TS), to deal with postwar problems within all enemy countries and their possessions. The division had to be innocuously named, because the various regional offices in State,[7] mostly staffed by FSOs, formed the traditional backbone of the Department, and their officers were fiercely jealous of their prerogatives.

Nevertheless, Pasvolsky was able to induce Philip Mosely, a professor of Russian history at Columbia, to head his new division, and he in turn brought in two other liberal academics, George Blakeslee of Clark College and Hugh Borton, to handle the Japanese side. From then on, TS took over the main burden of postwar Japan policy-making in State. Borton, in particular, was indefatigable. In 1944 he was involved in practically every State Department paper on Japan, Korea, and Formosa (Taiwan) and drafted or co-drafted half of them.

Borton and Blakeslee were quite different in outlook from Grew; his chief aide, Eugene Dooman; and the other senior Japan FSOs, Joseph Ballantine and Earle Dickover. Blakeslee was a gentle humanitarian and idealist of the Woodrow Wilson stripe who had served at the Washington Naval Conference of 1922 and on the staff of the ill-fated League of Nations Lytton Commission set up in 1932 to contain, unsuccessfully as it turned out, Japanese aggression in Manchuria. Borton was of earthier stuff. A Quaker who had refused several offers of posts in the war agencies because of his pacifist principles, Borton had written his doctorate on peasant uprisings in Japan,[8] had guided my own graduate studies on Japanese labor at Columbia, and was well aware of and sympathetic to the "other Japan" of the poor and oppressed common people so unknown to high-ranking American diplomats. Where Borton knew the Japanese potential for sudden revolutionary violence, the diplomats were generally nostalgic for the well-ordered, peaceful land they loved, in which so much of their lives was invested—Grew spent ten years in Japan, Dooman half his life—and in which they were respected and honored in that Japanese way that would hardly have been possible in their own homeland.

To Grew and the Japan FSOs, the Japanese problem, that is, Japan's careening drive for military conquest, was not the fault of the civilian Japanese leaders, whom they thought they knew so well. The blame rested on the wild men in the Japanese Army, the insular and arrogant military officers, particularly the young fanatics lately off the farms, and their even more fanatical extreme nationalist supporters, such as the blood brotherhoods, assassination societies, and the rest. Japan had made much material and political progress in the 1920s when "liberal" civilians were in power, a time when, in the later picturesque language of Shirasu Jiro, Prime Minister Yoshida's confidante, "all over the country soldiers were very much looked down on and the fever attained such a height finally that no officer even dared ride a streetcar with his saber dangling on.''[9]

Japan could return once more to such peaceful progress provided the militarists were eliminated, their baneful influence ''blotted out'' (in Grew's words to Truman), and their organizations—including the Kempei-tai military police and the extreme nationalist groups—dissolved. True, safeguards of a constitutional nature—ensuring Diet control of the budget, abolishing the Privy Council, making the Diet superior to the Emperor, securing civil liberties and political rights, among others—would be required. But detailed American intervention in Japanese administration would be unwise and ultimately resented by the proud Japanese. With the elimination of the militarists and some U.S. encouragement, the liberal elements would come to the fore. They could be trusted by America. A 1944 State Department memo identified those elements as follows:

> There exists a fairly substantial body of moderate political influence which has been rigidly suppressed and silenced since 1931 but which it is believed can be encouraged and made the nucleus of a liberal movement. The elements comprising this body include the statesmen of the so-called Anglo-American school who held political office in the 1920's and who have been conspicuous among the personal advisers of the Emperor, a considerable sprinkling of business leaders whose prosperity was based on world trade rather than on the greater East Asia co-prosperity sphere, Christian leaders such as Kagawa, a limited but courageous group of educators and social and political reformers et cetera.[10]

Nowhere did the FSOs show a great interest in labor unions, peasant organizations, or the prewar antiwar ''proletarian parties.'' The lack of interest was not surprising, considering how many of the FSOs, expatriates in Japan during most of the New Deal 1930s, had had no experience with such organizations in their own country. The rare references to popular rather than elite Japanese movements in the 1944 State Department papers, as for example in the memorandum of May 9 advocating the ''encouragement of political parties, labor unions, credit unions, consumers cooperatives, and other organizations of the people''[11] were invariably supplied by the newcomer, Hugh Borton.

On the other hand, the FSOs were not alone. According to Borton many years later, only Under Secretary Sumner Welles had any faith in the Japanese people. All the other State Department stalwarts[12] concurred in Grew's basic doubt that democracy could work in Japan. They were supported publicly by most of the ''old Japan hands'' outside the U.S. Government, especially former news correspondents and professors, who warned against trying to go too far too fast and imposing an alien culture on the Japanese.[13]

In the absence of presidential or Cabinet leadership to the contrary, the view of the old Japan hands prevailed for most of the war. Neither Roosevelt nor Truman ever thought much about internal changes to be effected within Japan after the war. Henry Morgenthau, the firebrand on Germany, was a "burnt-out case" by the time Japanese policy reached top-level consideration, and even Secretary of War Stimson could not make up his mind on whether to reform Japan or let the Japanese do it themselves.[14] As for the Secretary of State, even his knowledge of the basic geography of the region was suspect. One story making the rounds in those days told how Stettinius[15] came late to a meeting with War and Navy Department officials, called to determine whether to invade Japan by way of Formosa or Philippines-Okinawa. After listening bemused for some twenty minutes, he turned to an aide and whispered, "Where the hell is Formosa?"

After all, there were other much more urgent problems at hand: the prosecution of the war on several fronts, war production, maintenance of global supply lines, lend-lease, price controls, the draft, and, a little later on, postwar American demobilization and reconversion to peace. Even Germany's postwar treatment had precedence over Japan's. And for most of 1944 the presidential election campaign absorbed top-level energies. No one from topside bothered State's cozy monopoly of Japanese postwar policy for almost three years after Pearl Harbor.

Within State, the Japan Division, the Office of Far Eastern Affairs, and the FSOs staffing them retained their domination. Borton and Blakeslee might press for more democratization, but they represented one of the smallest, most junior, and least prestigious units in the Department. The papers Borton wrote had to be coordinated through those innumerable committees necessitated by State's rat's-nest organization, and on the key committee, the Inter-Division Area Committee for the Far East, the FSOs sat as a bloc, numbering from a third to half of those present at any time.[16] They might not write much, those FSOs, but they could vote, and as a practical matter—for who would want to defy such an experienced group—they exercised a veto. The main weight of State's opinion remained behind the objective of restoring the old liberal, civilian elements of bygone times.

TWENTY-THREE QUESTIONS

Hilldring was not a political man. He was a professional soldier, and he could work just as well with one policy, the restoration of Japanese liberals to power, as with something much more drastic. But he needed detailed guidance rapidly. In February 1944, after talking with State's James Dunn and consulting with his own small staff, Hilldring drew up a long list of pragmatic questions on postwar Far Eastern policies. Twenty-three of them dealt with Japan. Combining them with questions from his Navy counterpart, Captain H. L. Pence, on the Pacific islands, Hilldring sent them over to State for guidance.[17]

There was little order or structure in the grab-bag of questions: Would the occupation of Japan be divided into zones or be unified? How long would it last? Would it be punitive, mild, or concerned only with safeguarding reparations? What obnoxious laws should be nullified, and what political parties prohibited? What should be done about the Emperor, Shinto, freedom of worship, labor unions, public works, social insurance—even, what proclamations should be issued? Much was omitted, and some questions were naïve. But they were a start.

Quite probably Hilldring expected answers in a matter of few weeks. As it happened, some of the replies took up to five months, and a few of his questions never did get answered. The responses were from one to four pages each in length; unsurprisingly, they contained little detail. For example, to Hilldring's query as to what political parties should be banned, State—the drafting officer was an FSO—recommended in part that "it would be politically advantageous if the military administration could conduct a study" to determine which should be banned.[18] To the query on what obnoxious laws should be nullified, State's reply—drafted by another FSO—mentioned only two laws by name, arguing that "information is not available in Washington upon which a complete list . . . can be compiled."[19] In fact, all the Japanese laws and ordinances, compiled in the official *Hōrei Zensho* through October 1941, were in the Library of Congress.

Considering that in the "wake of battle" neither Japanese cooperation nor library facilities could be expected, State was scarcely helpful when it advised the military government to stop and make studies before acting. Furthermore, the military would need local labor almost immediately, but State supplied Hilldring no answer to his queries on labor, even though there was an International Labor Relations Division elsewhere within State.

The fact was that State, steeped in its traditional view of diplomacy and foreign policy, shunned anything that smacked of operations, even to the point of disdaining its own nonregional specialized offices. The gap between State's grand policies and the concrete tasks of Hilldring's CAD was too wide. He needed a corpus of operational policies in between the two, and as the episode of the twenty-three questions showed, State—even with the FSOs reinforced by Territorial Studies—could not provide it.

Another kind of planning director might have decided to build up his own staff to supply the answers, but Hilldring was no bureaucratic empire builder— no desk empire could replace his lost division—and as a professional soldier, he shrank from formulating policy himself. Instead he decided to find help elsewhere.

THE CIVIL AFFAIRS DIVISION

The first place to look elsewhere was in the vast War Department establishment with its immense human resources swept in by the draft and the mobilization of reserves. But there Hilldring found himself stymied. True, there were two other military organizations dealing with posthostilities Japan, but one, the Joint Post-War Committee of the Joint Chiefs of Staff,[20] was focused solely on the preparation of the surrender and associated documents. The other, the Military Government (MG) Division in the Provost Marshal's Section, was equally unusable, because it was somewhat of a political pariah. In fact, its fall into political disfavor was one of the main reasons that Hilldring's Civil Affairs Division, ostensibly covering the same ground, had been activated in the first place. MG had aroused the deep suspicion of the President of the United States.

The existence of such a broad activity as military government in such a narrow staff section as the Provost Marshal, whose principal function was the activities of the military police, was a relic of World War I, when the American army had had to help provide police, fire-fighting, public utility, and other services in a small number of French and Belgian towns they had occupied. Upon the outbreak of World War II MG was reactivated, and in January 1942 the Army staff decided to set up a training school in Charlottesville, Virginia, for future military administrators. For whatever reason, or for no reason at all, the State Department was not consulted, nor was the President notified in advance.

Now, Franklin Roosevelt had his own idea as to the proper role of an American military occupation abroad, namely, to attract the world's populations to democracy by a practical demonstration of what a caring, active, democratic government could do for the "forgotten man." He had installed Paul Appleby, a New Deal stalwart from Henry Wallace's Agriculture Department, in a special office in State Department where he was to report only to the Secretary. What the President told Appleby is not certain, but Appleby, according to one of Roosevelt's administrative assistants, Jonathan Daniels, believed he had a presidential mandate "to create the staff for military government for occupied areas." "He is very anxious," Daniels noted in his diary, "to get a staff of New Dealers to organize the whole occupation effort."[21] (Appleby wanted to recruit Dean Acheson to head the program; Daniels preferred David Lilienthal.) The MG school now cut directly athwart Roosevelt's efforts, and to the President it looked as though it might have been deliberate sabotage on the part of anti–New Dealers in the military.

He could not confide his suspicions to his Republican Secretary of War Stimson, writing to him only "that the whole matter is something that should have been taken up with me in the first place. . . . The government of occupied territories . . . in most cases . . . is a civilian task."[22] However, to a sympathetic Sumner Welles, who had protested the Army's lack of coordination with

State in what was a political matter, Roosevelt related in only half-jest that a sign over the door in Charlottesville warned that friends of the Administration would not be welcome.[23] And he asked at least two persons, Daniels and William Bullitt, ex-Ambassador to France, independently to check up on the character of the school.[24] Bullitt advised him he had nothing to worry about, while Daniels, after a visit, simply thought the school undistinguished and leaderless. Provost Marshal Gullion, who had greeted Daniels's visit with the unsolicited declaration that he was himself a Kentucky New Dealer, was upset enough by the commotion to write Edwin ("Pa") Watson, the President's appointments secretary, protesting against the idea that he was running a "school for gauleiters."[25]

But it did no good. From then on the MG Division found itself frozen into operational and organizational matters only: first, the compilation and publication of Civil Affairs Handbooks and other materials; second, the operation of training schools; and third, the establishment of staging areas in which MG officers were to get final staff training and from which they would be shipped to occupied areas. The Civil Affairs Division was established in its stead for substantive planning. Hilldring had a good nose for the political atmosphere. He was not about to jeopardize higher approval by asking MG's recommendations on anything.

If there was no help from elsewhere in the military or from State, however, there remained the temporary civilian war agencies, the Foreign Economic Administration, the Office of Strategic Services, the Office of War Information, and the others that President Roosevelt had set up to conduct the new foreign operations of which the State Department elite, policy-makers above all, wanted no part. Those agencies in 1941 and 1942 had launched aggressive talent searches in the universities, and the OSS, besides, had managed to have assigned to it any number of experts who had been drafted into the army. As a result, by the end of 1942 Washington had a greater concentration of foreign area and professional expertise available to work on foreign country problems than ever before or since, and the bulk of those people were in the civilian war agencies.

Now Hilldring turned to them. Undoubtedly, he had no ulterior motive, but with his approach Japanese occupation planning moved out of the cocoon of specialized Japan "experts" and into the world of broader realities. The Civil Affairs Division of the Army was itself composed of professionals—lawyers, bankers, and brokers—as well as soldiers, almost none of whom had any special knowledge of Japan to start with. The OSS Research and Analysis Branch, on the other hand, had originally staffed its Japan Section with Japan specialists, particularly those who knew the language, but as the war went on, other types, professional specialists, joined. Among those the Army drafted and assigned to the Japan Section of OSS were the editor of the Commerce Department's prestigious periodical, *Survey of Current Business;* the statistician from the Labor Department who later became the longtime U.S. Commissioner of Labor Statistics; an official from the U.S. Manpower Commission;[26] and others of similar stature.

Those people in the new war agencies did not buy the mystique of Japan assiduously promoted by the "old Japan hands." Japan was, to them, a country like any other. Increasingly, Japan postwar planning, previously a problem in area expertise, was drawn both into the mainstream of American foreign policy as a whole and into the turbulent American domestic political currents and the political, even ideological, alignments that were inseparable from them. More important than area expertise was a policy consistent with what the United States was doing elsewhere. In the circumstances, that elsewhere meant Germany.

THE NEW DEALERS' PLAN FOR GERMANY

German postwar planning had already started almost two years before under the sponsorship of Vice President Henry Wallace. Appointed the first Chairman of the Board of Economic Warfare (BEW) in 1942, the restless Wallace was not satisfied with export licensing controls, arranging the supply of scarce materials, preclusive buying to deny the enemy his critically needed raw materials, and industrial and economic intelligence. Determined to make war on Nazi economic institutions as well as on German industry and trade, Wallace brought in as his deputy on the subject an exceptionally intelligent and hostile expert on trusts and monopolies, Max Lowenthal, former counsel of the Senate Committee on Railroad Reorganization, headed by the old progressive Democratic Senator Burton K. Wheeler.

Lowenthal created an Economic Institutions Staff (EIS) in the BEW and filled it with a host of New Dealers eager to fight the war and the peace, too, along New Deal lines. Lowenthal did not stay long, nor did his immediate successor, but Allen Rosenberg, a labor lawyer, the personable and attractive third chief of the group, did. Rosenberg was aware of the inadequacy of State's occupation period planning for Hilldring's purposes—for the General had invited BEW to participate in an abortive eight-agency committee[27] on civil affairs—and was deeply suspicious, like Lowenthal, of what he considered "reactionaries" in the State Department who would shield Nazi business collaborators. He proposed to Hilldring that the EIS could informally supply the General with the information and guidance he needed on subjects of Hilldring's choice. From this was born what amounted to an alternative, although on the surface only a supplementary, military government program for Germany in the shape of a series of studies recommending how to proceed on various subjects. Falling halfway between factual handbooks and military orders, they were called Civil Affairs Guides.

EIS was a strange organization for the federal government, its nomenclature abnormal, its connection with the agency head after Wallace tenuous, and its personnel predominantly composed of New Dealers with a sprinkling of Communist sympathizers, if not worse.[28] Not that more than a few of the staff may actually have been Communists,[29] but for me, although working at that time not in EIS but on the Civil Affairs Guides in FEA, to be rubbing shoulders with members of some invisible "in-group" who hinted at common hidden objectives was a disquieting experience. I can remember being in Rosenberg's office with one of his deputies when the news of the Yalta agreement came over the radio and being utterly baffled as they cheered excitedly at each point of the agreement—recognition of the Lublin (Communist) Polish Government, the cession of Dairen, and the other concessions to Stalin.

Predictably, the EIS program for Germany was far harsher than that being worked out in State, for the New Dealers were determined to smash German war industry, radically restructure the German economy, and punish German big business as Nazi collaborators. The regular State Department Germany specialists, on the other hand, feared the consequences of a permanent economically distressed area in the heart of Europe and a political vacuum between the West and the Soviets. It was a policy split of the most fundamental kind, one that had to be resolved on a much higher level than Hilldring's, and until it was, Hilldring was not entirely sure how much he could use some of the FEA Guides. Nevertheless, he could not but appreciate the flow of expert technical information and operational recommendations he was getting. After the episode with State of the twenty-three questions on Japan he decided to institute a Civil Affairs Guide program for that country as well, not necessarily limiting himself to the EIS.

In the late spring of 1944, Hilldring asked Lieutenant Colonel James Shoemaker, a former professor of economics at the University of Hawaii and editor of the MG Handbooks on Japan, to help line up the Japanese Civil Affairs Guides. Hilldring could not use MG's recommendations, but he could use its contacts. The gregarious, hyperactive Shoemaker had also worked for the Board of Economic Warfare and knew just about everyone in the Far Eastern field. Hilldring listed seventy guides he thought he needed, and by early summer Shoemaker had gotten EIS, now part of the new Foreign Economic Administration,[30] to agree to prepare twenty-two. Then he turned to the OSS, which signed on for twenty-five.[31] The Agriculture Department, too, agreed to do one, because it had in its employ the preeminent American specialist on Japanese agriculture, a naturalized Russian immigrant who had educated himself at the City College of New York at night while he sold newspapers on upper Broadway in the daytime, Wolf Ladejinsky. The CAD itself accepted three.

At the same time Hilldring, in the absence of top-level policy, had devised a way to get the next best thing, a consensus of the interested agencies. He organized a Committee on Civil Affairs Studies and invited State, War, Navy, OSS, Treasury, Agriculture, and FEA to become members. The committee, in turn, delegated the actual review of the Guides to working-level committees. No one wanted to reject the invitations, not even State, for who knew what might be agreed upon in their absence? For the first time, State Department officials had to express their policy views face to face with those outside the Department, even if only by commenting on outside proposals, and to defend their comments. It was an enormous step forward for the outsiders like myself. I can remember once in 1943 casually asking Borton what he was doing in State, only to be told that he couldn't talk about it because it was top secret. Cyrus Peake, his fellow professor at Columbia and good friend, had the same experience. To Peake and me, working on operational intelligence connected with impending military operations, such as the invasion of the Marshall Islands or bombing targets, it seemed a little absurd to consider broad foreign policy such a secret, but State had kept it that way. Now, the State foreign service professionals, at least those of lower rank, were occasionally smoked, as it were, out of their holes.

Furthermore, the very list of Guide subjects—electric power, property of the Imperial Household, police system, wage controls, agricultural organizations, to name a few—was in itself a kind of policy decision against the convictions of State's FSOs, who had never contemplated such detailed American intervention and thought it undesirable. But they could hardly oppose planning for what might become military necessities. The idea of a detailed control over Japan during the Occupation became generally accepted. State had brought outside agencies into operations by refusing to participate and then into operational planning by being incapable of handling the job itself. Now, to execute those responsibilities, the outside agencies were threatening to invade State's sphere of policy-making.

Nevertheless, for quite a while it was not at all clear what was happening and which way Japan policy was going. Those of us working on Japan occupation policy, particularly economic policy, in the war agencies—and at first the Guides were only a part of the work program—were not at all sure whether we were plugged into real decision-making or just spinning our wheels. We consulted with each other, wrote memos, and waited for the results. Many of us, new to Washington, wondered whether this was not the way the Government normally operated—in a fog. With no one at the top of the U.S. Government showing interest, we joked that Japan, like the British Empire, might be remade in a fit of absence of mind. If the war were suddenly to end, top officials, in a rush and for want of anything else, might just scoop our memos off our desks and declare them United States policy after all.

On a minor scale, in 1944, bureaucratic exigencies were already causing things like that to happen. One day Henry Fowler, Director of the Enemy Branch of FEA, on his way to an interagency meeting on Japan's postwar economy and knowing little of the subject—he had just transferred from the War Production Board—hurriedly picked up the only memo written on the subject in his "shop" to date. It happened to be a memo of mine entitled "General Survey of the Economic Problems Expected to Face a Military Government in Japan." He read it in his car on the way to the meeting and, in the absence of anything else, converted it into the agency's position on the subject. Such an action was a bureaucratic necessity, for to have nothing to say at an interagency meeting was to forfeit one's claim to participation in the future.

The key question was just who was going to be plugged into "the top" when decision time came for both Germany and Japan. For each country, two separate and rival occupation programs were being developed along contradictory lines, a "hard line" from the war agencies and a relatively "soft" line in the State Department political offices. After years of furious warfare against Germany and Japan, the American public was adamant on a "hard" peace. In the case of Japan, an American Institute of Public Opinion poll revealed in November 1944 that 13 percent of the American people wanted to kill *all* the remaining Japanese after the war! More than half, according to the National Opinion Research Center in Denver in the spring of 1945, thought that Japan would *always* be a menace to the peace of the world. And 85 percent of those asked by *Fortune* magazine in June 1945 would have rejected a hypothetical Japanese offer to surrender on condition that their home islands not be occupied despite the huge American casualties that were bound to accompany an invasion.[32] Opinion about Germany, while not as drastic—after all, millions of Americans were of German descent, while hardly anyone outside the West Coast knew the Japanese—was similarly suspicious of unrepentant Germans. But the State Department professionals occupied the key policy-making positions, and the war agency people, like frustrated hounds baying at the barred doors of the castle, could find no way to get in—until the whole course of events for both Germany and Japan was suddenly changed by the redoubtable Secretary of the Treasury, President Roosevelt's intimate friend, Henry Morgenthau.

THE MORGENTHAU PLAN

The Treasury Secretary cared little about Japan, but the fate of Japan had become intertwined with that of Germany. In August 1944, while Morgenthau was flying to London to consult with the British on Lend-Lease, his Director of Monetary Research, Harry Dexter White, presented him on the airplane with a State Department memo calling for German reparations from current production and the conservation of a sufficiently productive German economy to provide them. Morgenthau, a bitter anti-Nazi, was shocked and disturbed at the prospect that the United States might build up German industry for reparations or for any other purpose. On his ensuing swing through France, in numerous conversations with British and American officials, including General Eisenhower and Foreign

Secretary Anthony Eden, Morgenthau repeatedly and urgently raised the question of postwar Germany. Gradually he evolved the concept of destroying the country as an industrial power and reducing it to farming and grazing—the most Draconian concept evolved by any American official.

Before his return to Washington, Colonel Bernard Bernstein, a regular Treasury official who was acting as the head of the Finance Section in the Civil Affairs Division of Eisenhower's SHAEF (Supreme Headquarters, Allied Expeditionary Force), provided his old boss, Morgenthau, with a copy of the draft SHAEF Handbook of Military Government for Germany, which had been worked out on the basis of State's negotiations with the British. The Handbook, too, emphasized the importance of maintaining the German industrial machine and avoiding civil unrest by assuring minimum feeding levels for the population. There was hardly any mention of de-Nazification. Morgenthau was outraged.

Several days after his return home, days spent protesting to Harry Hopkins, Stimson, and McCloy, Morgenthau went to see the President on the morning of August 25 with the handbook and a memo from White summarizing its contents. Roosevelt, too, was scandalized. According to an account that appeared in Drew Pearson's syndicated newspaper column three weeks later (which had apparently been leaked by Treasury Department sources), the President threw the Handbook down on his bed indignantly. "Feed the Germans!" he said, "I'll give them three bowls of soup a day with nothing in them. Control inflation! Let them have all the inflation they want. I should worry. Control industry! There's not going to be any industry in Germany to control!"[33]

In a cabinet meeting that afternoon Roosevelt declared that only a subsistence level of food was required for the Germans. According to his Navy Secretary's diary, "as he [Roosevelt] put it, soup kitchens would be ample to sustain life—that otherwise they [the Germans] should be stripped clean and should not have a level of subsistence above the lowest level of the people they had conquered."[34] Then, after reading the handbook overnight, Roosevelt composed a reprimand to Secretary Stimson, which he sent over to him the following Monday, commencing with the words, "This so-called handbook is pretty bad."[35]

What actually happened next is not clear, but various reports circulating among us planners in those days left the impression that Roosevelt ordered Stimson to come up with an alternative program in a matter of days and that Stimson turned to McCloy, who in turn obtained from General Hilldring a full set of the EIS Civil Affairs Guides for Germany. Stimson rushed them, together with summaries, to the President, who looked them over and said, in effect, "That's more like it." Whatever the actual sequence of events, on September 29 the President's press office released a letter from Roosevelt to Leo Crowley directing Crowley's Foreign Economic Administration to make studies of what should be done about postwar Germany. That, of course, was promptly interpreted as applying to Japan as well.

Thus, sparked by Morgenthau, the President had endorsed the hard peace line, upset the State Department monopoly on postwar enemy country planning, and legitimized the Civil Affairs Guides at the highest level of government as alternative input for Occupation planning.

Meanwhile, over the Labor Day, 1944, weekend, Harry Dexter White labored continuously to produce a coherent four-page memorandum containing his Secretary's views, including the dismemberment of Germany, the destruction of all German heavy industry, the breakup of the large landed estates, forced-labor reparations—in effect using Germans as slaves to rebuild Russia—and a disclaimer of occupation responsibility for postwar German inflation, unemployment, housing, rationing, or reconstruction.[36] When Roosevelt traveled to Quebec to meet Churchill ten days later, he brought only Morgenthau of his Cabinet officers with him, and Morgenthau brought his memo. Both national leaders on September 15 issued a communiqué pledging themselves to reduce Germany to an agricultural and pastoral state, thus adopting the Morgenthau Plan. On Roosevelt's return, however, the boss was met by almost unanimous Cabinet opposition—Stimson called it immoral, the others bad policy or impractical—and with an election in the offing, he could not afford a cabinet row. He let the Morgenthau Plan simply slide slowly until after the election and, as it happened, ultimately into oblivion.

THE GERMAN DIRECTIVE AND THE JAPANESE DIRECTIVE

For at least a month, however, the Morgenthau Plan was the official policy of the U.S. Government, and during that month CAD produced the first and most severe version of JCS 1067, the Occupation directive to General Eisenhower. That was the very version used as a model for the first draft of the JCS 1380/15 directive, which Hilldring's CAD worked out for Japan. Military officers, who under General Marshall rigorously considered themselves executors, not originators, of policy, found any already approved model a great comfort. Furthermore, many of those who worked on the actual drafting of the Japan directive in CAD had previously worked on the German. It is not surprising, then, that so many of the phrases and sentences of the September 1944 version of JCS 1067 found themselves with little or no modification in the final JCS 1380/15 for Japan. And since the German directive at that time was almost a joint Treasury–CAD effort—Harry Dexter White visited CAD personally a number of times on Germany, and CAD officers, including Hilldring's then Assistant Executive Officer, Lieutenant Colonel Kades, later to be such a key figure in the Japanese Occupation, visited Treasury as well[37]—many of the Morgenthau Plan's ideas appeared as a matter of course in the draft for Japan.

I remember in the first few days of September 1945, just after the surrender, being put into a small secure room at the FEA, furnished with a draft of the economic section of the directive then being readied for Japan—it was so secret the copy did not even bear the serial number—and asked for comment. Apparently all the agency's specialists were being canvassed simultaneously in the same way. One sentence provided for the breakup of the "large landed estates" in Japan. I told my emissary[38] that the provision made no sense, because there were no large landed estates in Japan; the landlord class comprised some 900,000 small *rentier* land owners. Obviously the provision had been lifted from some draft directive for Germany; indeed, paragraph ten of Morgenthau's four-page memo on Germany, composed by Harry Dexter White, declared: "All large estates should be broken up and divided among the peasants and the system of primogeniture and entail should be abolished." This particular provision did not make it even to the first, incomplete version of JCS 1067. Happily, it did not make it to JCS 1380/15 either. Others besides myself may have pointed out the blooper to CAD.

But a number of other German provisions did get into the Japanese directive, some of them verbatim. A few, to be sure, were essentially technical.[39] But others, including denying Occupation responsibility for fighting inflation or for economic rehabilitation and specifying that economic controls be left to local authorities, were highly important, purposeful policy decisions modeled after the German directive.[40]

Of course, sometimes the same words carried quite different meanings in the different contexts. The JCS 1067 assignment of responsibility for economic controls to the German authorities where there was no central German government could well mean economic chaos, a condition Morgenthau and his men were quite ready to accept cheerfully, whereas the same wording in JCS 1380/15 was practical in Japan, where the central Japanese government survived intact. The antidiscrimination rule, which when applied to Germany with its mistreatment of Jews and Eastern Europeans meant one thing, in Japan became primarily a protection for the few Europeans who had lived through the war there. (The Chinese, that is, Taiwanese, and Korean residents who remained for the occupation needed no help. When they declared themselves victors, the Japanese police, uncertain of their legal status, were usually afraid to contest the issue.) The Japanese antidiscrimination provision also, interestingly enough, turned into an unintentional Occupation commitment to ameliorate social discrimination against the two million or so Japanese *burakumin,* or social "untouchables," of whose existence the military officers who copied the German directive were totally unaware.

The threads in Hilldring's maze had become very entangled. The foreign service establishment of the United States was clearly no longer a reliable guide to the foreign policy of the United States, at least as applied to the occupation of

Japan. American professional planning for Japan, originally carefully insulated from outside influences, had now become exposed to them. The result was the rejection of moderation and its counsel of a Japanese liberal restoration after the war.

3

Threads in a Maze

HOW THE RADICAL REFORM TOOK SHAPE

DECISIVE EVENTS sometimes pass by contemporaries without their slightest awareness at the time. In August and September 1944, President Roosevelt intervened in Occupation planning for Germany. That sharply altered the thrust of postwar American policy toward all enemy countries, and the center of power in the nation's military–foreign policy establishment shifted accordingly. Perhaps no single action was more decisive in determining the immediate postwar future of Japan.

THE THREE-DEPARTMENT COMMITTEE

The U.S. State Department foreign service specialists on Japan seemed oblivious of what was happening, somewhat like the warrior whose neck has been cut through by the slash of a samurai blade so keen that he does not realize he has been decapitated until he tries to shake his head. On November 16, 1944, the State Department Country and Area Committee (CAC) issued its third version of a paper that devoted a quarter of its text to fighting expected inflation and a third to ensuring sufficient supplies of food, clothing, fuel, and shelter for the Japanese civilian population![1]

Now, that was precisely the "soft" policy the President had just demolished for Germany. Two months later, the State planners were still presenting it for Japan. Perhaps they knew nothing of the harsh new Germany directive, JCS 1067, issued in mid-September, because it was secret, but certainly they had read the *Washington Post* and must have been aware of the Morgenthau Plan. Could they really have thought that the bitter controversy over Germany would have no bearing on Japan? Did they think they could successfully resist the President of the United States and powerful domestic political currents by convincing them that Japan's case was entirely different? If so, they overrated their persuasiveness and the prestige their expertise carried. They were courting irrelevancy.

Top-level State officials, however, were more sensitive to the bureaucratic implications. Mortified by Morgenthau's raids on foreign policy towards Germany—How had it happened that upstart Treasury officials were drawing up papers for the President on dividing Germany, Junker landholdings, "labor reparations" for Russia, and the dismantling of German industry?—they decided to join forces with the War and Navy departments to keep intruders out. Moreover, the President, perhaps influenced by the performance of State's political offices on Germany, too, decided to strengthen the State Department internally. After both moves had been made, the once predominant FSOs were bureaucratically farther away from the crucial decisions on Japan than ever before.

Treasury's intrusions had been made possible, the State Department's leaders thought, by the absence of a mechanism for political–military decisions through which all agencies had to go. That had allowed Morgenthau to approach the President directly and Morgenthau's people to play off the State and War departments against each other. Now State asked War's help in keeping Treasury out. During November, State first proposed a coordinating committee of the three departments on Far Eastern Affairs, where Morgenthau's marauders had not yet complicated postwar planning, but War and Navy preferred to broaden the committee to all political–military matters affecting the three of them. Accordingly, an exchange of letters established the SWNCC (State–War–Navy Coordinating Committee),[2] destined to be the forerunner of the National Security Council. A short time later SWNCC set up a Subcommittee on the Far East, abbreviated to SWNCCFE, which did all the real work on Japan. It met fifty-one times in the first ten and a half months of 1945. From then on, all policy papers on Japan, including the directive to General MacArthur, were to go through SWNCCFE, then SWNCC, and then to the President. Treasury was to be faced with a solid front, and State would no longer be hit with unpleasant surprises.

As machinery, SWNCC worked surprisingly well, but the effect was to destroy State's monopoly of postwar planning once and for all. Hilldring now had a regular channel through which to present the war agencies' ideas.

President Roosevelt's reorganization of State—the second in eleven months—had an equally decisive effect. Late in 1944 the President finally accepted the resignation of an ailing Secretary Hull and promoted Stettinius to Secretary with the principal mandate of organizing the United Nations. With the decks cleared, Roosevelt then moved Grew up to Under Secretary and increased the number of assistant secretaries from four to six. (When the white-haired

Stettinius presented his new seven-man team to the press in the State Department auditorium, one reporter promptly dubbed them Snow White and the Seven Dwarfs.) To the dismay of the liberal newspapers—*PM*, the *Philadelphia Record*, the *New York Post* and others—Dean Acheson, darling of the liberals, moved from Assistant Secretary for Economic Affairs to Congressional Relations and International Conferences. Roosevelt replaced him in economic affairs with Will Clayton, head of the largest cotton brokerage firm in the world (Anderson Clayton) and a Texas political protégé of the arch-conservative Jesse Jones.

The promotions of the conservatives Grew and James Dunn, the latter to be Assistant Secretary for all political affairs except Latin America; the sidetracking of Acheson; and the installation of Will Clayton to head the crucial economic affairs offices, caused the liberals to charge betrayal of the New Deal in foreign affairs. The big businessman Clayton, in particular, was their *bête noir*.

The liberals' crystal ball, for perhaps not the last time, turned out to have been badly clouded. Clayton, a proud man, was determined when he took office to establish parity for his economic division with State's territorial political offices in the policy-making process. Accustomed as he was to running a global business, he was not going to be subordinate to anyone else on his own bureaucratic level. To help him map an independent course on postwar enemy country economic policy, he brought in as his deputy Edward Mason, Deputy Director of the Research and Analysis Branch of OSS. In March 1945, Mason recruited Edwin Martin, Chief of the Japan Section in OSS, to handle the Japan side. Martin turned out to be the key figure in transforming State Department policy into one of radical economic reform for Japan.[3]

Tall, sandy-haired, cherub-faced, and highly articulate, although with a small, husky voice, Martin was a quick study, decisive and highly political-minded. As a student of political science and economics at Northwestern University from 1925 to 1929, he graduated just in time to be hit by the stock market crash and the tragedy of the Great Depression. When he came to Washington in 1935, by then an avid New Dealer, he was employed at an interagency statistical commission and then served two years with Isadore Lubin, Commissioner of Labor Statistics and one of the White House New Deal coterie. (In 1975, forty years after he arrived in the capital city, Martin told me that even after a thirty-year career in State, he still was a New Dealer. There weren't many men left then who still thought of themselves in New Deal terms.) During the war Martin rose to the top civil service level as chief of the War Production Board industrial priorities system. All his work was on the U.S. economy.

Brought to OSS nevertheless as the new Chief of Research and Analysis, Japan Section, in September to direct work on industrial bombing targets and to represent OSS on the prospective Joint Bomb Targeting Group for Japan, Martin suddenly found himself directing civil affairs studies instead. When five months later Martin moved over permanently to State, he had had a total of nine months' exposure to things Japanese. But, as a result of Clayton's insistence on equal status with Dunn, Martin suddenly found himself equal to the longtime Japan veterans Eugene Dooman and Joseph Ballantine.

Clearly Clayton did not know, or perhaps did not care, that Martin was an ardent New Dealer, for Clayton—in some ways the father of the Marshall Plan[4]—was far from the narrow reactionary the liberal press pictured him to be. The FPOs understood even less the significance of the New Dealer Martin in a post where for the first time someone jointly represented all the State economic offices (Financial and Monetary Affairs, Commodities, Trade, Labor, and so on) and therefore constituted a counterbalance to the traditionally backbone political offices. In fact, I am not sure Martin himself realized the difference his arrival made. Years later, when I asked him conversationally whether he was the one responsible for introducing into the official U.S. policy and the JCS 1380/15 directive the crucial economic-democratization provision favoring a "wide distribution of income and of ownership of the means of production and trade"— the one on which MacArthur based his land reform directive—Martin replied somewhat uncertainly, "I guess so. I was a New Dealer, and of course we believed in greater economic equality."[5]

When Dooman and Martin agreed in April 1945 to split up their responsibilities, with Dooman taking the political part of the postwar policy and Martin's people taking the economic, the die was cast. Dooman and Ballantine, supported by Grew, had been prepared to fight to the last for a liberal restoration in Japan rather than a radical economic reform, but somehow they had quietly agreed to a jurisdictional settlement that effectively ensured their complete defeat. Martin's acquiescence to their political reform program obligated them to accept his more fundamental economic reforms, which inevitably determined the character of the political reforms. So in the end Martin got what he wanted in both spheres. Perhaps Ed Martin was a consummate con man, perhaps the FSOs simply did not understand the impact of economics on politics, or perhaps the foreign service expatriates simply could not believe that such a clean-cut native Midwesterner could be—by their standards, of course—a radical.

Important as Martin's role was, however, he was by no means the only one pressing for a radical reform, nor did he begin to exert direct influence on the policy until mid-April 1945, when he first proposed the economic part of the Initial Post Surrender Policy, SWNCC 150, to SWNCCFE in accordance with his agreed-upon division of labor with Dooman. By that time work by Hilldring's Civil Affairs Division on the Japan occupation directive was already three months old. In January 1945, General Marshall had notified Hilldring of the Joint Chiefs' November 1, 1944, decision to invade Japan. Hilldring, unable to wait any longer for presidential policy and very conscious that if nothing were done in his shop nothing would be done anywhere, gave the order to his staff to prepare what was to become JCS 1380/15. His staff, however, included some very able New Dealers, such as Major Ernest Gross,[6] Lieutenant Colonel David ("Micky") Marcus,[7] and Lieutenant Colonel Charles Kades, all of whom had been engaged in drafting the Morgenthau-influenced occupation directive for Germany.[8] They firmly believed in a radical transformation of Japan as well as Germany. Even if Martin had not been a New Dealer, and even if State had opposed radical reform, quite likely CAD, with the support and ammunition furnished by the war agencies, would have striven nevertheless to mandate a fundamental democratization program. And possibly, as in the case of Germany, the decision would have had to be made at the presidential level.

As it happened, with Martin in his key position representing Will Clayton, thus indirectly enjoying the unknowing and incongruous backing of the Jesse Jones Texas Democratic machine, such a fight was unnecessary, and a good deal of the war agencies' ammunition, particularly the Japan Guides, was never expended. Unlike the studies on Germany, the Japan Guides never went to the President and never took on the overall importance of the German Guides. In quantity they did not amount to much either. I do not remember that more than a dozen were completed and put out to the theater in time. Of that number some were outpaced by events. The "Electric Power" Guide, for example, proved unnecessary when the Japanese engineers remained in place, while the Guide on "Imperial Household Property," which had assumed a hostile, uncooperative Emperor, had to be rethought.

Two of the Guides, however, did have a powerful impact on the course of the occupation, the one on labor and the other on agriculture. Both outlined programs that in fact were followed in detail, initiating two of the three principal occupation actions—the third being the breakup of the big business combines— that constituted the backbone of the radical reform. Not only did those Guides provide concrete substance for the more general policy statements, but by granting freedom to the Japanese worker and farmland to the peasant, they demonstrated the American official commitment to the welfare of the Japanese rather than to punishment à la Morgenthau. Most important, they showed the United States would be going beyond the liberal elements of the 1920s, an elite minority after all, to appeal to 80 percent of the Japanese population, the hitherto disaffected workers and peasants. By giving both those groups a vital stake in a new democratic, antimilitarist regime, they were to be induced to become, in their own interest, the prime American allies within the country.

In the execution of both those Guides, the personal element loomed large. Their respective authors subsequently became key officials in Japan, charged with carrying out their own recommendations, I in the case of the "Trade Union" Guide as Chief of the Occupation's Labor Division in 1946 and early 1947 and Wolf Ladejinsky in land reform as Special Adviser to the Chief of the Natural Resources Section. There could thus be no divergence, misconstruction, or dilution—at our level anyway—in the field. There was a further personal element in that MacArthur was much taken with the slight, gray-templed Ladejinsky, a pipe-smoker like the Supreme Commander himself, with a soft-spoken, charming, continental manner and intriguing Russian accent. MacArthur supported him all the way.

Ladejinsky and the Land Reform

It is easy, of course, to exaggerate the personal element, for without Ladejinsky or me some kind of land and labor reform would still have been carried out. Before any official Washington policy on land reform ever reached Tokyo, the Japanese Government had begun to draft a modest farmland redistribution law, and on December 9 General MacArthur issued his famed Directive #411, formally ordering the government to present GHQ promptly with a massive program for rural land reform. This was almost a month before Ladejinsky arrived, quite literally, in the Japanese rice fields; his C-54 overshot the runway at Atsugi, and the passengers had to wade through the paddy mud to dry land. Similarly, within the State Department's Office of International Labor Relations, the office that supervised U.S. labor attachés abroad, Julian R. Friedman had worked for months independently and without much recognition on a policy for workers' organizations in the forthcoming military occupation.[9] Nevertheless, the shape of the reforms as they took place and indeed the roles that Ladejinsky and I, both "outsiders," played were products of our respective Guides and the Japanese Guide program.

Even though Ladejinsky had not yet arrived in Japan, MacArthur's land reform directive was not unrelated to him. On the contrary, the Supreme Commander's action was prompted by a memo on the subject knowingly incorporating Ladejinsky's ideas, which was prepared by Robert Fearey, then on the Political Adviser's staff in Tokyo, in the fall of 1945. Fearey knew and admired Ladejinsky in Washington from the time he had served as State Department representative on the interagency working-level committee (together with me, representing the Foreign Economic Administration, and others) that considered Ladejinsky's Guide. When Political Adviser George Atcheson sent Fearey's memo to the Supreme Commander in late November it struck a responsive chord. A few days later, according to Fearey, two colonels from SCAP came bursting through the door with the news that MacArthur "was very taken" with the memo and wanted Fearey to work with his staff on a land reform directive along those lines.[10]

Fearey did not, but other agricultural nonexperts did. Years later, Arthur Behrstock, then a captain in the Civil Information and Education Section, recalled to me how MacArthur called in Colonel Ken Dyke, the section chief, and asked him to prepare a directive on rural land reform. Dyke told Behrstock that

MacArthur was going to justify his proposed action by JCS 1380/15's call for a wider distribution of the means of production. When Dyke asked why his CIE Section was chosen, and not the staff section charged with agriculture, he was told that the Natural Resources Section was too slow. MacArthur had been greatly impressed by the speed with which CIE had turned out the Civil Liberties Directive[11] the month before, and besides, the general wanted appropriately inspiring words, which the "NRS farmers" could not supply. Behrstock, Chief of CIE's Planning Staff, which had not one agricultural specialist in the group, rapidly produced a draft, and MacArthur never changed a word.[12]

Among the Washington planners on the other side of the Pacific, there was general agreement that some kind of land reform was essential for a lasting democratic order in Japan. But there was less unanimity regarding whether an alien military occupation should impose it from outside. According to Fearey, Borton and Blakeslee within State favored land reform. The older FSOs opposed the idea, fearing it might interfere with critical food production and arguing besides that a passive, inarticulate peasantry might not cooperate, that is, that the Japanese peasants were too stupid to want their own land. Ladejinsky's Guide took the issue outside of State. The Guide's proposal for compulsory sale of absentee *rentier* lands cheaply to village land committees, with resale on easy terms to working farmers, focused the otherwise formless general discussion on to a yes-or-no operational plan. Because the plan was derived from the ideas of agricultural economist Nasu Hiroshi's prewar Land Reform Institute, it could hardly be dismissed as "alien." Nothing hindered a prompt decision any longer.

Indeed, the interagency working-level Guides committee quickly approved the Ladejinsky Guide, after a heated discussion had first ended with rejection of my FEA proposal for a moratorium on farm rents instead, and so did the top-level committee as well. But at SWNCC the action stalled. Anticipating a critical food shortage, SWNCCFE split off and settled the food production and distribution recommendations of the Guide first as SWNCC 98, "Control of Food and Agriculture in Japan." The more controversial land reform[13] was set aside when on November 15 SWNCCFE decided to get a report from the field before doing anything.[14] Three weeks later MacArthur issued his land reform directive. Ladejinsky's ideas had first reached him by way of Fearey. In another three weeks, Ladejinsky himself was on the scene.

The land reform turned out to be one of the Occupation's great successes, with lasting credit to Nasu, MacArthur, and Ladejinsky and enduring benefit to the farmers and the country. But would it have come about without Hilldring and his Civil Affairs Guides? In the late afternoon of the day following the abrupt Japanese surrender, Ladejinsky and I, both temporarily civilian advisers at the Civil Affairs Staging Area (CASA) in Monterey, California, stood together on a bluff overlooking the steep slope of the camp and Monterey Bay in the distance. CASA was in convulsions. The work for which its officers had been preparing for so long was suddenly at hand, and we watched a group of officers below us hurriedly departing by bus for the plane to Manila and then to Japan. We were both reflective, for the great adventure was beginning without us. We were due to leave instead in the opposite direction the following day for Washington. Ladejinsky was morose, convinced his contribution was over. "I envy you," he said abruptly to me. "But why?" I asked. "Well, you'll go over to Japan and help lead the labor reform. You'll be famous," he answered. "But what about you?" said I. "Oh, they'll never let me be an American official abroad with my Russian accent and birth," he replied despondently. "They just wouldn't listen to me there." And perhaps "they" never would have from the beginning, hidden as he was in the massive Agriculture Department, an introverted and hypersensitive immigrant amidst all the extrovert native American farm types, if James Shoemaker had not discovered and recruited him for Hilldring's Guides program. And Japan's postwar farmland reform could have been very different.

THE "LABOR" GUIDE

The Trade Unions and Collective Bargaining Guide affected final U.S. policy more directly. Finally approved by Hilldring's Inter-Agency Committee in June 1945, it became the only one of the whole Guide series whose recommendations the SWNCC accepted almost verbatim and sent out to SCAP.[15] It was also the only Guide that was approved, even though informally, by an extragovernmental body, in this case the AFL and CIO. And it was the best example of how Hilldring managed adroitly to get rapid governmental unanimity behind an Occupation policy that originated outside the State Department.

The "Trade Unions" Guide started out, however, along quite different lines. Shortly after FEA contracted to provide Hilldring with twenty-two civil affairs Guides on Japan in the fall of 1944, it became apparent that its resources were inadequate. Bowen Smith, Deputy Staff Director, an immensely likable Baltimore newspaperman who was in charge of the Japan Guides for FEA, asked me, along with several other non-EIS members, to help. I proposed doing the "Trade Unions" Guide, pointing out that I had spent three academic years studying the subject and had turned out a 200-page master's thesis at Columbia in 1939 entitled "The Japanese Labor Movement 1918–1938." Imperfect as my knowledge was, it was far superior to anyone else's in Washington. Smith conceded my credentials but apologetically told me that the "Trade Unions" Guide had already been assigned to the EIS Labor Division and its chief, George Wheeler. Instead I went on to produce a civil affairs Guide on the "Property of the Imperial Household."

A few months later Smith was back about the "Trade Unions" Guide. Could I defend the draft before the interagency working-level committee?

Wheeler had left, on his way to assume the position of Director of the Manpower Division in the American Zone Military Government in Germany. His assistant, David Denson, who had done the drafting, would shortly follow him. I agreed, and we visited Denson, a stubby, nearsighted, fussy fellow, too harassed by the administrative requirements of his forthcoming trip—he was too busy even to take his overcoat off—to do anything more than turn over his draft to me. When I read it at my leisure, I was appalled. His paper was written in a Leninist class-struggle jargon that would have suited the Communist *Daily Worker* better than a U.S. Government document. All of it was in the most general terms, betraying no special knowledge of Japan.

Denson did not stop at an economic role for labor unions. His Guide draft, as I remember it, proposed that newly organized workers' groups, including factory committees set up by whoever might be found to organize unions, be recognized *prima facie* as democratic and utilized to sweep away "fascist" bureaucrats. The groups might, for example, take over food distribution responsibilities where existing Japanese government agencies were deemed undemocratic. That recommendation may have seemed reasonable at first glance and, in fact, it turned up in Martin's first draft of the economic section of the State Department Initial Post-Defeat Policy for Japan, dated April 18, 1945. But it also paralleled the Communist line in Italy at that time and caused some astonishment. The Communists' organizational energy and discipline would surely produce a disproportionate number of qualified "democratic" workers' groups for them. It took no great leap of the imagination to visualize whose friends might be getting scarce food for political purposes. It was hard to resist the suspicion that the Guide intended it that way.

I asked Smith whether he had read the Guide draft. He had not. I told him I could not defend it but would present it to the committee for its views. As I expected, the committee's views were just as critical as mine. After listening silently to their horrified reactions for half an hour, I proposed, to unanimous agreement, to withdraw the document for redrafting. From now on, with Bowen Smith's relieved blessing, it became my assignment.

While I was finishing up the new version of the Guide in the ensuing weeks—it was submitted to CAD on March 2—I must admit I felt some trepidation as to how the active Left in EIS would react to my primary emphasis on economic trade unionism. And would the law-and-order conservatives elsewhere be upset by the ideas of encouraging union organization, permitting strikes (except those affecting Occupation Force security or objectives), and completely excluding the police from labor affairs? Then in the early spring of 1945, the new Enemy Branch Chief, Henry Fowler, set up a Labor Division to deal with policy for occupied Germany and Japan and named Irving Brown of the AFL Machinists' Union as its chief. That changed everything.

Brown, a swarthy, hard-drinking labor intellectual with a master's degree in political science from New York University, was an extremely aggressive anti-Communist. That was why Fowler, whose own background was that of a lawyer with Goldman Sachs, a Wall Street investment house,[16] brought him in. Fowler had just finished a stint as counsel to the War Production Board's Labor Division, where the American labor movement's representatives, men like WPB Vice Chairman Clinton Golden of the CIO Steelworkers and Joseph Keenan of the AFL, had educated him on Communist infiltration into American unions. Fowler feared the same kind of penetration in Germany, Austria, and Japan and wanted the proper policy to stop it. When Keenan and Golden both recommended Brown as his Labor Policy Division Chief, Fowler was enthusiastic.[17] As my neighbor with whom I shared a wartime car pool, Brown knew something of my work on the labor Guide and also my anti-communist convictions. He asked me to join him as Chief of his Japan Labor Policy Section.

From that time on, my Guide was among friends and protectors. The Wheeler–Denson political approach was out.[18] Brown went through my Guide draft with me, pronounced it just right, and recommended no changes from its emphasis on economic unionism, collective bargaining, the right to strike combined with voluntary dispute-adjustment machinery, and the elimination of police from Japanese labor affairs.

As an intimate of many union leaders in both the AFL and the CIO— although an AFL man, he had participated in the United Auto Workers' organizing drive at Ford and had been cruelly beaten up by Harry Bennett's security guards, along with Walter Reuther and Richard Frankensteen—Brown had the trust of both federations, and Hilldring knew it. Hilldring had developed a healthy respect for American labor's political clout in the course of his assignment as military adviser to the U.S. tripartite (labor–management–government) delegation to the International Labor Conference of 1944 and earnestly wanted the unions' support. Even though it was extragovernmental, labor opposition could greatly embarrass the forthcoming occupation. Hilldring arranged for Brown to attend the meeting of the Inter-Agency Committee on Civil Affairs that considered my Guide. With him standing by as a visible symbol of AFL and CIO support, the committee approved the document, again without change.

With seven agencies unanimously supporting the Guide, it was not surprising that when Philip Sullivan of the Division of International Labor Affairs in State was assigned to draft the SWNCC paper on "Treatment of Japanese Workers Organizations,"[19] he simply copied out most of the Guide's recommendations, changing the wording only to reflect the change from a previously anticipated military government to a Japanese Government functioning under an American Supreme Commander. On December 28 the paper was approved and sent out to the theater, arriving just about in time for my appointment as Chief of the Labor Division in GHQ at the end of January.

It was a pleasure to see my own words ordering me about—a fact I never talked about in Japan when I cited "Washington" policy to justify my actions—but the peculiar coincidence by no means made labor policy a one-man show. Not many months later, when conservative critics of the Occupation labor policy, such as General Willoughby, our G-2 Intelligence chief, and Roy Howard, the head of United Press and some twenty-six Scripps-Howard dailies, condemned that policy as the product of a "leftist" labor division and its "leftist" chief, they were in ignorance of the facts. Perhaps no Occupation policy other than demobilization of the military had more general acceptance within the U.S. Government in the planning stage. It would have seemed disastrous to all concerned to let the Japanese workers go communist. The American federations insisted that a healthy, free, democratic Japanese labor movement was the best safeguard against communism and pointed to their own experience. Seven U.S. departments and agencies agreed with them; no one opposed.

The Collapse of the Old Japan Hands

Meanwhile, Martin was busy "democratizing" the overall State Department economic policy. His initial reception was somewhat frosty. When he first submitted his section of SWNCC 150 to SWNCCFE, a bristling General George Strong, formerly Army G-2 and the War Department representative—Martin would later call him "a peppery old gentleman"[20]—labeled Martin's submission an "utterly impracticable, academic approach" that "showed an utter lack of knowledge of the Japanese government and Japanese psychology."[21] An unabashed Martin persisted, however, producing a series of revised versions in April and May. His May 3 version put forth the revolutionary proposal that Military Government "favor a wider distribution of ownership, management and control of the economic system." And when that was accompanied in the first overall Occupation policy statement (SWNCC 150, dated June 11) with a restatement of Borton's earlier (since 1944) principle that "Military Government encourage the development of democratic organizations in labor, industry and agriculture",[22] two New Deal principles of economic democracy were established as occupation goals.

A further revision, SWNCC 150/2, of August 12, called for Military Government "to show favor to" as well as "encourage" democratic organizations. Citing that addition, repeated verbatim in the directive, I was later able to remove a trade union building from the Occupation Army requisition list. In the same document a paragraph was added specifically denying any exemption to Imperial Household properties from actions needed to carry out Occupation policies.[23] Labor union property was to get preference over the Emperor's in the new dispensation!

To the rapidly changing thrust of Occupation policies, Joseph Grew was increasingly unable to object. First, his promotion to Under Secretary, as well as his frequent role as acting Secretary, left him with little time for the wording of new policy papers being hammered out in SWNCCFE. Meeting Dooman and Borton in the State Department's executive dining room one day in mid-April 1945, he asked what had happened to all the Japan policy papers that he had approved as Director of Far Eastern Affairs six months before.[24] Second, his outspoken refusal to condemn the Japanese imperial institution in numerous speeches made after his repatriation and his friendship for the Westernized Japanese aristocrats, displayed in his diary published in 1944, had earned him increasing mistrust in the liberal and even the not so liberal press. After one of his speeches the *New York Times* reproached him for recommending that "we sponsor an autocratic theocracy."[25] At his Senate confirmation hearings on December 12, 1944, he was attacked for having opposed the scrap iron and oil embargo against Japan before Pearl Harbor. Robert Sherrod, *Life* magazine's distinguished Pacific war correspondent, wrote the Secretary of State asking whether American officials, meaning Grew and his followers, were not deluding themselves with their "spare-the-Emperor appeasement."[26] Under that barrage, Grew had little time or inclination to worry about Martin's machinations in economics.

To the Under Secretary, the "Emperor question" was the heart of the Japan problem. Deeply worried, even obsessed, by the prospect of an American bloodbath if wartime "prejudice" against the Emperor were allowed to prevail, Grew stood fast in his conviction that the Emperor was the key to surrender. If the Japanese, whom Grew considered "a fanatical people capable of fighting to the last ditch and to the last man," were to believe that their surrender meant "the destruction or permanent removal of the Emperor," the "cost in American life would be unpredictable." In the rebuilding of the country afterward, moreover, only the Emperor could hold the country together and prevent anarchy. Repeatedly, Grew hammered away at his main theses: "Japan does not need an Emperor to be militaristic nor are the Japanese militaristic because they have an Emperor." It was urgent, he pressed the new President, Harry Truman, to tell the Japanese public that America did not insist on the destruction of the Emperor system. He even submitted a draft statement along those lines,[27] which ultimately became the Potsdam Declaration. Truman agreed to Grew's plea in principle, but General Marshall, Navy Secretary Forrestal, and War Secretary Stimson, meeting the next day, thought the time inopportune for "certain military reasons not divulged."[28] The reasons were, it turned out later, the impending atomic bomb tests at Alamogordo.[29]

Right or wrong, Grew's pro-Emperor campaign brought him not only public obloquy but intense criticism from within the Department, particularly from the "old China hands." The latter had seen the Japanese from a different vantage point, that of an invaded and despoiled China, and were bitterly opposed to all their leading elements—the Emperor, the military, the big business combines, and the rest. They found powerful support from Assistant Secretary Dean Acheson. In a series of top-level intradepartment meetings, Acheson contended that the Emperor "was a weak leader who had yielded to the military demand for war and could not be relied upon."[30] Facing such strong opposition on what was to him the crucial issue, Grew was in no position to take on another unpopular battle against radical reform. Nevertheless, he was still a power in the Department, and with his backing Dooman and the Japan FSOs were still able to hold their line politically and act as somewhat of a brake even in economic matters.

The Victory of the Radical Reformers

The rough balance between the "Japan crowd" and the coalition of radical economic reformers and the "China crowd" supported by Acheson was suddenly upset in the summer of 1945. On July 3, with the United Nations officially established, President Truman, who had wanted to appoint James Byrnes as his new Secretary of State ever since the day after Roosevelt's death, finally did so.[31] Byrnes, returning from Potsdam, offered the Under Secretary's job on August 11 to Dean Acheson in place of Grew, and that tumbled Grew's FSO dominoes. In the next few weeks, John Carter Vincent, senior "old China hand," replaced both Dooman on SWNCCFE and Joseph Ballantine as head of the Office of Far Eastern Affairs. Earle Dickover, another old Japan FSO, gave way as chief of the Japan Division to Hugh Borton. When Secretary of War Stimson asked Byrnes to name a political adviser to General MacArthur, his choice, recommended by Acheson, fell not on a Japan veteran—Dooman had been confidently expecting the assignment—but on George Atcheson, whose Far Eastern diplomatic experience had been Chinese, including handling the 1937 Japanese bombing of the U.S. gunboat *Panay* on the Yangtse and a tour as Embassy Counselor in Chungking in 1943–45. It was almost as though the surrender of the Japanese had triggered a rout of the old Japan hands in State as well. Although the old guard did not leave immediately—Dooman's last SWNCCFE meeting was August 29, and Ballantine stayed well into September—once Acheson was appointed, the die was cast.

In general, the radical reformers had no quarrel with the political section of the SWNCC paper drawn up by the FSOs and the Borton–Blakeslee shop.[32] Nor did they disagree with the formula worked out hurriedly upon the Emperor's acceptance of the Potsdam Declaration that the Occupation was simply to use the Japanese Government, not support it. But what mattered to the radical reformers was the restructuring of economic institutions, not the political arrangements. With Acheson's support, Martin introduced two vitally important provisions in the August 22 draft (SWNCC 150/3): first, a purge in business of "individuals who do not direct future Japanese economic efforts for solely peaceful ends,'' and second, a commitment to dissolve the ''industrial and banking combines which have exercised control over a great part of Japan's trade and industry.'' Together with the other policies Martin had previously inserted to favor democratic labor and farm organizations and also a wide distribution of income and the ownership of production and trade, he and his allies had succeeded in putting the essentials of a New Deal-style radical reform in place. On August 20 the War Department radioed MacArthur the text of SWNCC 150/4, and on September 6 Truman signed his approval.

That left the much more important companion document, the Joint Chiefs of Staff directive to the Supreme Commander. The open State Department policy attracted worldwide attention (except in Japan), but the top secret directive would actually control the Occupation. Early in August, Brigadier General William Crist, enroute to become MacArthur's G-5 (Civil Affairs), passed through the Civil Affairs Staging Area in Monterey, California, clutching the draft, entitled ''Blacklist,'' that Hilldring had initiated the preceding January. Prepared in its latter stages by a committee of Hilldring's CAD and officers of the Joint Chiefs of Staff—together they were called the Joint Civil Affairs Committee (JCAC)—the directive was so secret that Crist would not allow any civilians on the premises, including advisers like Ladejinsky and me, to see it. But the surrender and the radical reformers' victory had outdated ''Blacklist.'' Revision was urgent.

Once again, the political portion offered no difficulty. Such problems as there were—for example, the transposition of the wording of the de-Nazification of the European theater to Japanese conditions—raised no controversies. After inserting verbatim the provision against intervention in case of democratic violence, little remained but detail.[33] On September 1 the political section of the directive was ready under the number JCS 1380/5. By September 17, both the Joint Chiefs and the President approved it and sent it on its way.

The economic portions were something else again. The really serious policy issues had not been fundamentally settled until the latter part of August. The decisions had to be nailed down in the form of concrete orders. To save time, the SWNCCFE members decided to meet jointly with the JCAC members on the directive rather than wait first for JCAC's finished product. As the Joint Chiefs' officers were contributing little, that meant joint working sessions of Martin, Vincent, and their men together with the Civil Affairs Division drafters, particularly Major Gross. (According to Martin later on, Gross, then a major, was the principal drafter.)[34] All three were, in greater or lesser degree, New Dealers.

As it happened the three, plus Under Secretary Acheson too, were united not only in support of reform but also in their lack of confidence that the job could be left to the broad discretion of military men. They set out, therefore, to nail the policy down by concrete orders and to close every loophole through which their intent could be frustrated in the field, intentionally or not. The result was, as Martin put it, that in the first part of September SWNCCFE "expanded considerably" the policy of SWNCC 150/4.[35]

The economic purge, for example, was expanded from those relatively few who *in the future* would not direct Japanese efforts to peaceful ends to those who *in the past* had been "active exponents of militant nationalism and aggression," and then it was expanded again by instructing the Supreme Commander to assume, in the absence of contrary evidence, that all persons who had held "key positions of high responsibility since 1937, in industry, finance, commerce or agriculture" to have been "active exponents of militant nationalism and aggression." That was a sweeping assumption if ever there was one, taken almost verbatim from the directive for Germany. The Joint Chiefs of Staff wanted to omit the assumptions and leave the determination up to the Supreme Commander, but State insisted, and the far-reaching assumption was restored.

Similarly, the directive instructed the SCAP to require the Japanese Government to submit plans for dissolution of the business combines—the Joint Chiefs made that "large" business combines—and ordered him also to dissolve the industry "control associations," to abrogate measures that limited free entry of firms into industries, and to terminate Japanese participation in international cartels. While accepting the recommendations of the Guide on "Trade Unions and Collective Bargaining" in summary form—SWNCC 92/1 was not yet written—Martin, Gross, and their men went further. The Supreme Commander, the directive now said, could prohibit strikes "*only* when you consider that these would interfere with military operations or directly endanger the security of the occupying forces" (italics added). The Guide proviso allowing the SCAP to prohibit strikes prejudicial to the objectives or needs of the Occupation was omitted. Apparently, the radical reformers thought the formulation too subject to abuse.

By the time they had finished, the paragraphs on economic democratization—a subject that had been summarily ruled out by the original Japan FSO planners—were 60 percent longer than those on the operation of the economic system. The heavy emphasis on inflation control was reduced to a stricture to the Supreme Commander "to direct the Japanese authorities to make every feasible effort to avoid such inflation." Economic controls were to be the responsibility of the Japanese. Democratization, however, was the direct responsibility of General MacArthur. In the set of economic objectives of the Occupation put forth in the directive, a new one stood out prominently: "to encourage the development within Japan of economic ways and institutions of a type that will contribute to the growth of peaceful and democratic forces in Japan."

On September 20, the economic and financial sections of the directive

encompassing all the basic radical reform elements, except for farmland redistribution, were ready and approved by SWNCC. It still took another month to
get by the Joint Chiefs of Staff's objection to the wording of the economic purge,
for the President to approve the document, and for the Joint Chiefs to dispatch
them, as JCS 1380/8. On November 3 the complete combined directive, com-
prehending all political, economic, and financial provisions, was sent to the field
as JCS 1380/15.

THE NEW DEAL WAVE

Hilldring had finally seen his job to fruition. More than two years after he
started, he had traveled just as far ideologically, from a liberal restoration to a
radical reform, as Douglas MacArthur had geographically, from New Guinea to
Tokyo. Unlike MacArthur, however, he could not have foreseen his destination.
Instead of one continuous policy thread he had had to unravel and retwist many
Washington skeins in order to trace them to journey's end. At almost every
juncture some personality—White, Morgenthau, Fowler, Clayton, Martin,
Ladejinsky, Brown, Byrnes, Acheson, and even I—had made a vital mark. Was
it then solely the accident of personalities that formed the American policy for
the Occupation of Japan and that framed General MacArthur's directive?

The fact is that there were just too many key officials who agreed with the
radical reforms and who pushed them forward for JCS 1380/15 to be an accident. Those men represented a well-nigh universal mood of the country, which
would have brooked no less. Indeed, had the moderate reformers, Grew and his
group, won out instead, *that* would have been more accidental. For once Japan
planning left Grew's shop, the planners had to accommodate to the buffeting
currents of American political life and to the deep-rooted beliefs of the American
people. In 1945, the two most crucial for the shape of the Occupation to come
were, first, the fear that the wily Japanese would somehow wriggle out of the
consequences of their defeat and, second, the New Deal conviction that political
reforms were inadequate and only fundamental economic changes could be
effective.

"Their racial characteristics are such that we cannot understand or trust
even the citizen Japanese," the gentlemanly and otherwise enlightened Henry
Stimson had lamented in defending the removal of the Japanese from America's
West Coast in 1942.[36] Three years of war later it was still a fair statement of
American opinion. The trauma of Pearl Harbor persisted, combined with doubts
that American diplomats were up to matching the tricks of the enemy. In government offices, civilian officials doubted that the military had the background and
political understanding to withstand the expected Japanese maneuverings. The

Navy member of SWNCCFE felt that the purge of "flagrant exponents of militant nationalism and aggression" as proposed by the civilians was insufficient. He wanted them all arrested and interned.[37]

"Can Japan Win by Losing?" was the intriguing title of one magazine article.[38] The only way to make sure they wouldn't was to close all the loopholes, turn a deaf ear to Japanese blandishments, and steel ourselves to be "hard." All the complex issues of an Occupation Japan became transmuted, regardless of their intrinsic merits, into tests of "hardness" versus "softness," "thoroughness" versus "half-measures," "realism" versus "naïveté." It was no contest. The very moderation of those who espoused limited reform, keeping the Emperor and restricting intervention to political and constitutional matters, hindered their efforts in the end. The very radicalism of their opponents—going to the roots of Japanese society—was perceived as proof of their seriousness and assured their success.

The direction of the radical reform, however, was provided by the ideas and experience of the New Deal, so recently the overwhelmingly dominant influence on American life. Political democracy had long been an undisputed article of faith with everyone. But widening the ownership of the economy, encouraging labor unions, breaking up overly big business, eliminating—read purging—"the malefactors of great wealth," strengthening family farm ownership, all by government action—those were New Deal policies. JCS 1380/15 was in great part a New Deal document. MacArthur, who disliked the New Deal in the abstract, admired it in the reality of JCS 1380/15.

In the postwar atmosphere, where distrust of the Japanese and faith in beneficent government economic activism combined to produce a national desire to punish the Japanese with one hand and improve their lives with the other, public opposition hardly arose. The kind of radical reform for Japan embodied in the JCS 1380/15 directive and the SWNCC 150/4 policy was suddenly politically possible within the United States. A handful of dedicated planners, beginning with Hilldring, were convinced that that kind of reform was essential for the future peace of the world. They produced a political, economic, and social reform plan unparalleled in the annals of military occupations.

Now the question was whether the Occupation commander, Douglas MacArthur, with his staff and his army, could carry out the plan.

Part II

MacARTHUR AND HIS
MEN

EIGHT THOUSAND MILES from the Washington planners, the wiry, black-haired First Cavalry Division captain and his battleworn squad picked their way down the ladder of the troop transport anchored in glassy Tokyo Bay on the morning of September 2, 1945. Awaiting them below was a launch to take them to the Yokohama pier, from which the division transport officer was to issue them newly landed vehicles. With those they were to make a circuit around to the south and then west of Tokyo, reconnoiter the countryside, then head for the center of the bombed-out capital for the purpose of listing habitable buildings their Division might requisition as billets. War was war, and peace was peace, but on that cloudy, humid morning the squad was somewhere in between. No one could predict their reception by the populace, even though the American air landings at Atsugi airfield over the past three days had been uneventful. After the wartime fire bombings, the people were bound to be unfriendly. Rumor had it that kamikaze air units were just waiting to reopen World War II and that individual American soldiers or small units would be ambushed in narrow roads by diehards resolved to frustrate the peace. Part of the squad's mission was to test those stories.

As the launch chugged across the bay, placid after the typhoon of the week before, the patrol marveled at the size of the American armada anchored there. Led by four full-size battleships plus aircraft carriers, there were hundreds more, cruisers, destroyers, auxiliaries, transports, mine sweepers, some 260 vessels in all. As it happened, their course took them close to the majestic bulk of Admiral Halsey's flagship, the USS *Missouri,* where scores of small craft flying the starred flags of generals or admirals clustered at the foot of its gangplank. Above, on the towering deck, the sounds of honored guests being piped aboard could be heard. It was shortly after 9 A.M. Unknown to the cavalry captain and his squad, the surrender of the Empire of Japan to the massed forces of the United States and its allies was about to take place.

To almost all of the hundreds of high-ranking officers of the new occupying powers formed in rows on three sides of a square cleared before the signing table, the ceremony was a time for celebration, the conclusion of a hard and painful war. To the Japanese who had come aboard to sign, the one-legged Foreign Minister Shigemitsu Mamoru and his aide, the Harvard-educated Kase Toshikazu,[1] both attired in formal diplomatic striped trousers and morning coat, and to their military counterparts in boots and swords, it was a conclusion too. It was the crushing end to Japan's long-held imperial dream and marked the entry into a period of passivity, "to bear the unbearable," in the words of the Emperor.

But to General MacArthur, the newly appointed Supreme Commander for the Allied Powers, it was even more a beginning, the commencement of an effort different from any before, and no less strenuous. MacArthur, consciously and purposefully, was about to stride into the vacuum that Japan had become in defeat, to fill it, and in the process to become the object of a defeated nation's infatuation for its victorious occupier unparalleled since Alexander the Great.

MacArthur had been contemplating his new assignment almost continuously for days. He had spent almost the entire flight from Okinawa to Tokyo three days earlier pacing up and down the aisle of his four-engine C-54 "Bataan," gesticulating with his corncob pipe and thinking aloud to his fellow passengers about the reform measures he would take in Japan. And on his arrival in Japan he was handed an advance copy of SWNCC 150/4, the State Department Initial Post Surrender Policy for Japan. The Japanese hardly knew him except as a military adversary. When the signing ceremony was completed and MacArthur in summer tans, with open-necked shirt and the scrambled-egg garrison cap of a Philippine field marshal, rose to speak, those of the Japanese party who understood English listened with the utmost concentration to his every nuance for clues as to what would befall them.

"Today, the guns are silent, a great tragedy has ended," the new Supreme Commander for the Allied Powers intoned. He went on movingly to remember the dead and praise the living. He reported to the parents of America that their sons had done their job well and faithfully. In more somber but passionate tones, he denounced war as a soldier, warning dramatically that another world conflict would threaten the survival of humanity. "We have had our last chance. If we do not devise some greater or more equitable system Armaggedon will be at our door."

Then he turned to the Japanese. Just before the signing of the instrument of surrender he had declared that he would conduct the occupation in a spirit of justice and tolerance. Now he proclaimed his faith that Japan would again become a great nation. "The energy of the Japanese race, if properly directed," he affirmed, "will enable expansion vertically rather than horizontally. If the talents of the race are turned into constructive channels, the country can lift itself from its present deplorable state into a position of dignity."[2] As far as he was concerned, it was to be a peace in the reconciliatory spirit of Appommatox, not Morgenthau.

The American people at home did not hear his words, for the Truman White House had arranged for the President to address the nation immediately after the surrender ceremony, just when MacArthur was speaking.[3] Some of the Allied officers on the deck of the *Missouri* were deeply moved. One of them, an Army colonel named Philip LaFollette, formerly Progressive Governor of Wisconsin, was so touched that he changed his lifelong low opinion of the General and became one of his warmest admirers. "I honestly believe that Gen. MacArthur is the greatest living American and that is not hero worship on my part, I assure you," the veteran politican was to tell a correspondent two years later.[4]

The most deeply affected, however, were the Japanese listeners. They and their people faced the bleakest of futures, unsure of even the food needed to ensure their survival, their self-confidence destroyed—in the early Occupation days they tended to disparage themselves as a tenth-rate people—and all the guidelines they had followed for fourteen years cast aside. But now, at their lowest point, the American victor, instead of gloating or boasting, was offering them hope and declaring his confidence in them as a people, even if they had none themselves. For the first time, MacArthur was to the Japanese more than just another American general. He was on his way to becoming a Japanese national leader.

In the meantime, on that momentous September 2 the First Cavalry squad had arrived at South Pier and drawn a jeep and a weapons carrier. With a machine gun mounted in the latter and each man alert and with weapon at the ready in both, the squad set off to make its reconnaissance. Steadily meandering hour after hour through the pot-holed back roads of the villages west of Yokohama and Tokyo the Americans met hordes of curious children, shabbily dressed men who watched them quietly, oxcarts, bicycles and their attached rear cars, but no motorized traffic and absolutely no women. Eight hours later, with the sun setting, the procession began its last leg, eastward toward Tokyo's center. Still no hostility was visible. Arriving in the vicinity of the town of Chōfu at dusk, however, the captain was reluctant to enter the shattered capital in the dark. He ordered a night bivouac in the broad dirt yard of a rambling, unpainted wooden two-story schoolhouse.

As the mess corporal heated the C-rations over cans of sterno in the gathering darkness, the weary, relaxing soldiers suddenly heard the faint sounds of a motor vehicle in the distance. At its gradual but unmistakable approach, heralded by the grinding whine of an engine traveling in low gear, they reached for their weapons, only to gape in astonishment as a battered old charcoal-burning truck turned into the schoolyard. Its back was loaded with kimono-clad women smiling and bowing at them. A stocky man dressed in an old Japanese army uniform minus insignia jumped down from the seat beside the driver. He asked for the captain and identified himself with several bows as interpreter and representative of the Recreation and Amusement Association. The women, he said in pedantic English, were volunteers "to satisfy the lust of the Occupation forces." He suggested politely but hopefully that perhaps it would not be necessary to molest the virtuous women of the neighborhood.

The soldiers who clustered around had been fighting, some of them almost continuously, for three years in jungle after jungle in the South Pacific, experiencing a minimum of civilization in all that time. They listened with disbelieving ears. Surely, it was an offer too good to refuse. But the captain abruptly burst their bubble. Not one to be taken in by a possible subtle trick of a cunning enemy, he refused the offer and ordered the truck and its passengers away. It was, the captain later reminisced, the only time in his wartime military service when he thought he might be facing a mutiny. As the Supreme Commander for the Allied Powers was beginning to supplant the Emperor in the eyes of the Japanese on the deck of the *Missouri,* his men were beginning to learn the reality of Japan on a quite different level.

It was only the beginning. For the next five years and more, occupiers and occupied were to meet on every possible level, with almost every conceivable variety of encounter, from the sacred to the profane, the sublime to the ridiculous, the serious to the absurd, and the dignified to what often seemed burlesque. The Occupation of Japan was the most massive culture clash in modern history. Two societies, that of the occupiers and that of the Japanese, each built on premises alien to the other, existed side by side. The results of their interaction were unpredictable, for despite their long and arduous labors, the one thing the Washington planners could not plan was the chemistry between several hundred thousand occupying Americans and 70 million Japanese. The results were, nevertheless, to be crucial to an Occupation that proposed radically to reform Japanese institutions, mores, and ways of life for their own good.

The instruments became as important as the "determinants," to use Dean Acheson's words. Whether commanders, staff, or troops, they could convince the Japanese by their good sense, determination, and force of example. Or they could destroy all their government's fine words by their actions. And of all of them, by far the most overwhelmingly dominant was General Douglas MacArthur.

4

Douglas MacArthur and Japan

ON OCTOBER 11, 1946, more than a year after the Occupation had started, an editorial in the *Jiji Shinpo* declared: "Practically every Japanese holds it a supreme fortune to find General MacArthur as the Supreme Commander for the Allied occupation forces in Japan. . . . No wonder that a booklet containing General MacArthur's biography has proved the postwar best seller here, selling to the extent of 800,000 copies." Then the editorialist, Dr. Itakura Takuzō, somewhat perturbed, went on to comment:

> The Japanese people have long been plagued by the mistaken idea that government is something to be executed by some deity, hero or great man . . . after the surrender Japanese teachers have traditionally been bent on inspiring the children with this habit of blind worship for the ruler . . . —a tendency constituting the worst enemy of democracy. . . .
>
> The proper way for the Japanese people to repay General MacArthur's sincere efforts for democratizing this country and his wise administration is not to worship him either as a deified personage or as a great man, but to rid themselves of the subservient way of thinking and make efforts, with high self esteem, to grasp the actual authority of government themselves. Then, and only then, the Supreme Commander will rest assured that the object of occupation has been achieved."[1]

THE EXPANSION OF SCAP'S AUTHORITY

Dr. Itakura's position, correct though it was, was exceptional at that time and place. In the early Occupation years, MacArthur bestrode the land like a Colossus, and the Japanese called him "father." Some Japanese, the *Nippon*

53

Times reported on September 28, 1946, prayed for a chance "to see the general in person while I am still alive and hear his voice over the radio." Others worshiped him as "a living god," the reincarnation of the Emperor Jimmu.[2] Even allowing for the multiplicity of Japanese gods, that niche was still a pretty high status for someone who took his orders from the Joint Chiefs of Staff and the President, mere mortals, after all.

When I first arrived in Japan at the beginning of 1946, I was astonished at the degree to which the Occupation had become personalized. Every Occupation action, every policy, every decision was MacArthur's. His name appeared countless times in the newspapers, those of his immediate subordinates, themselves men of great power and influence, hardly ever. All the Washington policies, so diligently hammered out in 1944 and 1945, were ascribed to MacArthur. In four months, the General had, in effect, displaced the U.S. Government as far as the Japanese people were concerned. On January 31, 1947, when MacArthur had to call off a threatening general strike, the *Mainichi* newspaper apologized to him on behalf of the Japanese people for causing him so much trouble in the kind of language until then reserved for the Emperor. The General had displaced him, too.

Years later all that, especially the Japanese psychic dependency on Mac-Arthur, receded in the mists. Americans at home had never understood it; it looked to them like another MacArthur propaganda production. Deeper thinkers sought the explanation in the Japanese belief in yielding to superior force when inevitable, the bamboo bowing to the typhoon while the oak came crashing down. It was all a fake, the American public said. As if in verification, an American reporter, Gordon Walker of the *Christian Science Monitor,* unearthed a copy of the final order from the extreme nationalist East Asia League (*Tōa Remmei*) instructing its followers to obey every Occupation directive promptly and completely so the Americans would quickly conclude force was unnecessary and withdraw their Army. The same final order advised the Japanese people to align themselves thereafter with world Jewry, which had now proved its invincibility by triumphing over Hitler. Afterward the Japanese, riding the crest of a seemingly endless recovery wave, often felt ashamed of their past subservience and preferred to forget the whole thing.

But at the time, the attitude of awe and veneration was palpable. Letter after letter from ordinary citizens, intercepted at random and translated by our GHQ Allied Translater and Interpreter Service—I read them constantly in the spring of 1946 in my capacity as Chief of the Labor Division—showed how solidly grounded the feeling was among the Japanese people. Roger Baldwin, pacifist founder of the American Civil Liberties Union and never enamored of military uniforms or intimidated by high authority, spent seven weeks in Japan early in 1947, mostly amid Japanese fellow anti-authoritarian activists. He reported to the War Department that General MacArthur personally was the Occupation's number one asset.[3]

Indeed, before long MacArthur's predominance over Japan seemed the most natural thing in the world, and it would have been difficult for the Japanese—or the Occupation people, for that matter—to imagine the Japanese Occupation under the leadership of anyone else. His command seemed foreordained.

Yet it was anything but. To be sure, the principles that the Occupation would be unitary, not zonal as in Germany, that the Commander would be an American,[4] and that it should be the "Theater Commander [who] should be duly authorized to receive the unconditional surrender of Japan on behalf of all the United Nations at war with Japan"[5] had been laid down by the State Department in 1944. But it had not been at all clear who that theater commander would be. The Army and Navy were running separate campaigns, the former in the Southwest Pacific, the latter attacking due west from Hawaii. Had President Roosevelt accepted the Navy approach to Japan by way of Mindanao in the Philippines and Taiwan instead of the Army's (that is, MacArthur's) proposal to proceed via Luzon and Okinawa, the theater commander and hence the first SCAP would have been Admiral Chester W. Nimitz. Even after the President, in a dramatic confrontation between a lone MacArthur and the top Navy braid in Hawaii in July 1944, had ruled tentatively in MacArthur's favor, the Navy kept appealing the decision.[6] As late at March 1945, after his return from Yalta, Roosevelt was still undecided. He asked Robert Sherwood who *he* thought the Supreme Commander should be, and when Sherwood, just back from meeting with MacArthur in Manila, enthusiastically recommended the General, Roosevelt merely nodded.[7] After all, he had once called MacArthur one of the two most dangerous men in the United States.[8] When the President died the following month, the final decision still had not been made.

The Joint Chiefs of Staff directive to MacArthur to prepare a plan for the military occupation of Japan to accompany the "Olympic" and "Coronet" invasion operations was strictly a military request. When MacArthur's appointment as Supreme Commander finally came, that was strictly a military matter, too, the tail pinned on the rear end of the war, unrelated to any considered appreciation of the civil and political problems to come.

When President Truman named MacArthur on August 11, he had no clear idea of what the Supreme Commander's job would entail. MacArthur did not see the reform-minded Initial Post-Surrender Policy paper until at least two weeks later. Even if he had, there was an immense difference between being Supreme Commander primarily to receive the surrender and running the defeated country for an extended period thereafter. Truman's words appointing MacArthur pointed to the more limited assignment:

> In accordance with the agreement among the Governments of the United States, Chinese Republic, United Kingdom and Union of Soviet Socialist Republics to designate a Supreme Commander *for the purpose of enforcing the surrender of Japan,* you are hereby designated as the Supreme Commander for the Allied Powers. . . .

> From the moment of surrender, the authority of the Emperor and the Japanese Government to rule the State will be subject to you and you will take such steps as you deem proper *to effectuate the surrender terms.*[9]

Technically, MacArthur was SCAP only for the purpose of accepting the surrender of the Japanese armed forces and putting the surrender into effect. Even if Truman missed that technicality, he seems not to have recognized the irony of appointing a politically ambitious anti–New Deal general to enforce an essentially New Deal program. Of course, the frantic week of August 6 to August 13, encompassing two atomic bombs, Russia's entry into the war, and Japan's acceptance of the Potsdam Declaration, was no time for deliberation or calm, reflective analysis. A blizzard of paperwork—orders, communications, arrangements within the U.S. Government, radio messages to the military commands and among all the Allied Powers—and a torrent of meetings kept all the principal officials of the United States from the President on down racing to keep up with events, and sometimes working all night. In such circumstances, when the Joint Chiefs recommended General MacArthur for military reasons—after all, surrendering forces have to surrender to someone, and who better than the ranking officer and commander of the victorious forces?—Truman's approval was automatic.[10] Both JCS 1380/15 and SWNCC 150/4 were still in the future.

Once Truman appointed MacArthur, circumstances—and MacArthur himself—conspired to aggrandize the General's position far beyond merely receiving a surrender. In the immediate postwar period, the leaders of the United States felt obligated to give the appearance of full Allied, especially Soviet, participation in the occupation of Japan—while maintaining American *de facto* supremacy won by force of arms—or else to surrender Western claims to a voice in the Russian occupations in Eastern Europe established by Soviet arms. Pragmatically, the U.S. leaders developed a simple but effective three-step formula: First, grant the Allies participation in "policy" (through the Far Eastern Commission); second, reserve all "operational" matters to the Supreme Commander, an American; and third, consider everything important to be operational. Thus Dean Acheson, certainly no friend of General MacArthur, vigorously endorsed the suggestion of Justice Robert Jackson, the U.S. Nuremburg Trials prosecutor, that the Supreme Commander alone should establish the Tokyo War Crimes Tribunal, appoint the judges—on nomination of their respective nations—and recruit the prosecuting staff. "I incline," Under Secretary Acheson said, "towards the desirability of having Gen. MacArthur do the whole thing, *particularly as this preserves the principle of his authority*" (italics added).[11] In the face of challenges by the Japanese, questions from the Western Allies, and maneuvers by the Russians, the U.S. Government firmly supported their Supreme Commander's authority. They could not help themselves, and the General's power inevitably grew.

How the process worked was shown by two Japanese Foreign Office maneuvers and what happened to them. On August 16, only two days after the Emperor's surrender rescript, the Foreign Office, as though it were negotiating, not surrendering, sent a message to the United States advising the best way to occupy Japan—"also in the interest of the Allies," they said—namely, no troops in Tokyo or other such cities; self-disarmament by the Japanese forces themselves as "the best and most effective method"; allowing the officers to retain their swords as a matter of honor; and the quick dispatch of food and medicine, as well as speedy transport home of Japanese troops overseas.[12] The next day, the Foreign Office rejected Allied instructions to turn over Japanese embassies and legations in neutral foreign countries to the custody of the Allies, arguing that such instructions "do not correspond to any provision of the Declaration of Potsdam accepted by the Government of Japan."[13]

Washington referred the first message to MacArthur in Manila. He denounced it angrily as "fundamentally violative" of the Potsdam Declaration and contrasted the Japanese request for favorable treatment for their men with the death marches of Allied prisoners of war taken in Bataan and Singapore in 1942.[14] Whatever the humanitarian aspects of the Japanese request, President Truman felt that bargaining with the unconditional surrenderers was no way to start an Occupation.[15] He ordered a cold, formal reply stating: "Such information as the Japanese Government requires to carry out the surrender arrangements will be communicated by the Supreme Commander at appropriate times determined by him. . . . This return [of the dispersed Japanese soldiers] will be arranged through the Supreme Commander." Any Japanese channel to Washington outside of MacArthur was closed before the Occupation even began.

The second Japanese maneuver ended up by strengthening MacArthur even more. When the U.S. State Department, stymied in diplomatic channels, asked the General as Supreme Commander to order the Japanese to transfer their diplomatic stations, MacArthur asked the Joint Chiefs of Staff for a clarification of his powers. The reply, drafted by SWNCCFE and signed by the President, told him on September 6, "you will exercise your authority as you deem proper to carry out your mission. Our relations with the Japanese do not rest on a contractual basis, but on unconditional surrender. Since your authority is supreme, you will not entertain any questions on the part of the Japanese as to its scope." It is hard to imagine a more unequivocal statement on the subject. When, at MacArthur's request, it was made public,[16] the Japanese were utterly silenced.

To the Western Allies, the Truman Administration was more courteous but just as firm in supporting its Supreme Commander. A British complaint to the effect that Truman's September 6 message to MacArthur on his authority had been issued without consulting the Allied Powers[17] was met only with soothing words. When Foreign Secretary Ernest Bevin asked Secretary of State Byrnes about dispatching a British political representative and staff to Tokyo,[18] Byrnes instructed the U.S. Ambassador to reply that MacArthur would have to approve first.[19] Indeed, JCS directive 1380/15, para. 4h, specifically prohibited the independent operation of any other U.S. Government or United Nations agencies in Japan without SCAP's approval. Eventually all the neutral missions in Japan were either shut down or accredited to SCAP.

THE SOVIETS

The most serious challenge to MacArthur came, of course, from the Russians. Even before hostilities had ended, Foreign Minister Molotov, in a meeting with Ambassador Harriman on August 11 in Moscow, accepted America's decision to name MacArthur as Supreme Commander for the Allied Powers. But, Molotov said, the U.S.S.R. thought there should be *two* Supreme Commanders, the other being Marshal Vassilevsky, head of the Soviet Far East forces. Harriman, the most controlled of men in dealing with the Russians, brusquely rejected the suggestion, refusing even to relay the proposal to Washington, and walked out of the meeting. By the time he had arrived back at the U.S. Embassy, Molotov's secretary was on the phone advising that the Foreign Minister had consulted with Stalin and that there had been a slight misunderstanding. The Soviet Union was accepting MacArthur as sole Supreme Commander.[20] Molotov's bluff, probably Stalin's too, had been called.

The next Russian try came less than a week later. In a brief message to Truman, Stalin asked that the northern part of Hokkaidō, Japan's northernmost main island, above a line from Kushiro to Rumoi and including both cities, form a Russian occupation zone, adding, "I greatly wish that my modest suggestions as stated above would not meet any objections."[21]

Stalin was asking for a Soviet area outside of MacArthur's jurisdiction. Moreover, although it contained only a tiny percentage of Japan's population, the dividing line Stalin was asking for cut a huge slice out of the only trunk railway line on the island, giving Russia the means to strangle the Hokkaidō economy without having to support it. The next day Truman shot back coolly: "It is my intention and arrangements have been made for the surrender of Japanese forces on all the islands of Japan proper, Hokkaido, Honshu, Shekoku [sic], and Kyushu, to General MacArthur."[22] Stalin's reply sounded pained: "I have to say that I and my colleagues did not expect such an answer from you."[23]

A much more serious threat was the Soviet attempt to intervene in the conduct of the Occupation and to cut MacArthur's powers by insisting on an Allied control commission in Japan, on which each member would have a veto, that would give the Supreme Commander his orders. The United States refused, conceding only an Allied policy advisory commission in Washington. The tug-of-war went on for four months, during which Molotov repeatedly raised the question at meetings with Americans, and Stalin himself took up almost all the time at two long meetings with American Ambassador Harriman at the dictator's Black Sea hideaway in Gagri to discuss it. The Americans were too lax, Stalin complained. For example, they were not punishing the Japanese for anti-Soviet newspaper stories. Specifically, Lieutenant General Derevyanko, the Soviet Mission Chief in Tokyo, complained to MacArthur's Counter Intelligence Chief that the Japanese papers were reporting that Soviet soldiers in Manchuria had stolen watches and other personal belongings from Japanese prisoners of war.[24] If the Soviets could not join in control, the Soviet dictator told Harriman, then they could withdraw completely and let the Americans run Japan as they liked,[25] rather than stay as a "useless piece of furniture." Implicit was the threat that the Russians would then expect a similarly free hand elsewhere.

Byrnes and the Americans refused to be outfaced, and Stalin eventually decided that a formal Russian presence, equal to the American, at a continuing conference table in Tokyo was better than nothing to remind the Japanese that the U.S.S.R., too, had won the war; to provide a future propaganda platform; and to serve as a useful contact point with the local Communists. On December 30 Byrnes and Molotov agreed upon a four-power U.S.–China–U.S.S.R.–British Commonwealth Allied Council for Japan (ACJ), with no mention of "control" in the title. Although by that agreement the American Supreme Commander had to "consult and advise" with the ACJ before issuing orders of substance to the Japanese, "the exigencies of the situation permitting," his decisions were, in any event, to be controlling. Only where an ACJ member disagreed with a prospective SCAP order to change the constitutional structure or the Japanese Government as a whole was SCAP to await a decision from the elven-nation Far Eastern Commission in Washington.[26]

It is hard to imagine an arrangement that, while maintaining a façade of international direction, could more effectively have safeguarded MacArthur's authority and freedom of action, for a commander with his fingers on all the levers of power would hardly need to resort to formal orders. The General, already undisputed master of Japan for four months, however, greeted the announcement with one of his own, making it clear that he had not approved of the Byrnes–Molotov terms. In fact, he declared, he had opposed them up to October 31, after which his advice was not sought.[27] It was a curious affair, a general telling the world that he opposed his country's policy. His statement was only slightly tempered by his subsequent remarks that he would dutifully carry it out nonetheless.

The fact that no one in Washington rose to call him to account, as Acheson had in September, is a measure of how powerful he had grown in the interim. By the time the Allied Council actually met in Tokyo three months later, MacArthur was able not only to welcome them "with utmost cordiality" but also to inform them that their "functions would only be advisory and consultative" and that he would not share any of the "heavy" administrative responsibilities or executive authority with them.[28] And indeed, I cannot remember in my five years with the Occupation any SCAP policy or program that was ever modified by any Allied Council action at its biweekly meetings. As far as the conduct of the Occupation was concerned, the ACJ was a fifth wheel. There was nothing either its members or their home governments could do about it.

At the very time that the Soviets had put so much effort into securing a foothold by way of participating in a "control commission," they deliberately passed up an opportunity to send troops for occupation purposes. The U.S. Government, faced with pressure to bring the boys home, needed Allied troops to help bear the burden of the 600,000-man occupation first believed necessary and invited the Soviet leaders to send a contingent. The first American plan, drawn up on August 28 pursuant to SWNCC 70/5, "National Composition of Forces to Occupy Japan Proper," called for 175,000 Russian troops (five divisions, five air groups) to join 315,000 American, 135,000 British Commonwealth, and 60,000 Nationalist Chinese soldiers after three months. The Joint War Plans Committee revised those figures downward with time, but the lowest for the Soviets was 70,000, combined with 145,000 Americans, 65,000 British Commonwealth, and 60,000 Chinese.[29]

MacArthur was in accord with the principle of Soviet participation. Impressed by General Marshall with the urgent manpower shortage in the U.S. Army, he was also willing to accept contingents of 30,000 men each from the other three powers, but on condition that half the total force would be American and that no allied country be given an Occupation zone. He would integrate the contingents at lower levels. There is no indication that his second condition was ever accepted by the JCS, for when the British Commonwealth Forces—largely because of Australian enthusiasm[30]—offered 20,000 to 30,000 men, they were assigned to their own zone, Western Honshū (Chūgoku), with their headquarters at Kure near Hiroshima. They stayed there till the Occupation ended. Rumor at GHQ had it that the Chinese, who had pledged three divisions, were going to occupy Shikoku. But, bedeviled by an intensifying civil war, they never sent a single soldier.[31]

In any case, the Russians refused to play the game. When Harriman apprised Stalin on October 23 at Gagri of the U.S. intention to invite Soviet as well as British and Chinese troops for Japanese Occupation purposes with the proviso they be under General MacArthur's command, the dictator wryly replied that to preserve MacArthur's freedom of action, perhaps no non-American troops at all should be stationed in Japan.[32] When Harriman later tried repeatedly to remind Molotov of the American invitation, the Soviet Foreign Minister stonily declared that Stalin's statement represented the position of the Soviet Government.[33] Nothing MacArthur himself did averted the arrival of Russian troops, any more than he prevented a Russian co-SCAP, a Soviet occupation zone in Hokkaidō, or a Russian veto in a control commission.

Nevertheless, somehow the Supreme Commander was credited with keeping the Russians out of Japan. No matter that it was Harriman, Truman, Marshall, Acheson, Byrnes, and McCloy who rejected Soviet pretensions and that Stalin and Molotov themselves declined Soviet troop participation, the Japanese were sure it was MacArthur who had protected them. Apparently it pays to advertise. Washington was still working quietly in 1945 and early 1946 under the burden of trying to achieve Russian cooperation in the United Nations and elsewhere. MacArthur in Tokyo, however, was free to articulate his opposition to international communism, and when the rumors of how the Russians were kept out of Hokkaidō swept Japan, it was only natural that MacArthur became the hero.

MacArthur's Resolution

It was of a piece with MacArthur's good fortune in being named the SCAP by virtue of being the Theater Commander that simultaneously the Washington planners came up with a radical democratic reform for him to preside over and consistently expanded his SCAP powers for international reasons, even though they did not really like him much. One essential element in the General's rise to overwhelming authority was, as in other critical junctures in his career, his sheer good luck.

From MacArthur's viewpoint, those particular strokes of good luck could not have come at a better time. Sixty-five years old and already retired once in 1937 from the U.S. Army, with the end of the Pacific war he would be facing his twilight years. Any presidential aspirations awakened by scattered supporters in 1944 would have no outlet for three more years, and how was he to stay in the public eye that long? He could tamely take over the chairmanship of some big American corporation, lending it his name and prestige,[34] or become the head of some noncontroversial, subordinate government agency, like General Omar Bradley with the Veterans' Administration. Either road led downward. But to be peacetime Supreme Commander on behalf of eleven victor nations—an international first—and to redirect and recreate the life of a nation of 70 million, that would be a career worthy of its prologue. And by 1948, who could tell what might happen after all?

Good fortune to MacArthur, the quintessential activist, was not a gift to be enjoyed but an opportunity to be exploited. In Europe, combat commanders quickly gave way to administrative types, Eisenhower to Clay, for example, but MacArthur's first priority was to harden his almost accidental selection into irreplaceability. The way to do it was to run an Occupation so brilliantly successful that no one would dare to remove him.

On MacArthur's flight from Okinawa to Atsugi, Colonel Bonner Fellers, then his military secretary, told me some eight months later, the General paced up and down the aisle of the *Bataan,* ticking off the reforms he thought essential. Almost none of them were immediate concerns: raising the status of women, reorganizing the educational system, encouraging labor unions, abolishing the secret police, and so forth. He was flying into a sea of several million armed and hostile soldiers, but he had dismissed that danger from his mind relegating the details of their disarmament and demobilization as well as the installation of his troops to his staff. It was the long-range problems that engrossed him, and he had every intention of being around while they were being solved.

The initial period of deployment of his forces and consequent enforced political inactivity must have been a time of suspense and nervousness for MacArthur. Suspicious that his Washington enemies were already using his lack of motion to begin working for his removal, he was even more sensitive to press criticism than usual. Less than two weeks after the formal surrender, he surprisingly responded to only scattered comments in the American press that he was being too "soft" on the Japanese with an official press release admitting his own impatience, defending his restraint so far on the basis of security and military expediency, and pledging: "The surrender terms are not soft and they will not be applied in kid-glove fashion."[35] A few days later he was in the headlines again, this time congratulating his forces, and implicitly himself, on the smoothest occupation deployment in history as a result of which the United States could cut its Occupation force requirements by two-thirds in the next six months. Finally, with his forces in place and his political directive (JCS 1308/15) in hand, he set out to remake Japan and to make all America, and the world, aware of it.

From the end of September he abruptly loosed a series of triphammer blows, coming with such rapidity that the Japanese officials and leaders, whose natural inclination was to "roll with the punches," to agree to each measure, contain it, and then implement it in the way least harmful to themselves, simply had no time to adapt. Thick and fast came the directives: Remove the censorship system (September 29); establish civil rights, release political prisoners (October 4); give women the vote, encourage labor unionization, abolish child labor, liberalize education, end thought control, disperse ownership of the economy, and democratize the economic institutions (October 11); dissolve the four largest *zaibatsu* holding companies (November 6); distribute agricultural land to the farm tenants (November 7 and December 9); arrest eleven major war-crimes suspects (November 17), then fifty-nine more, including almost all the nation's leaders for the preceding seven years (December 15); freeze the Emperor's assets (November 20); and abolish State Shintō (December 15). Even licensed prostitution was ordered abolished by directive. On January 4, as a climax,

MacArthur ordered the purge from positions of influence of all who had held important positions during the war, a clean sweep of Japan's leadership.

Political circles in Japan were left reeling, but the war-dulled people unexpectedly set on a new and radical course by an occupying general were enthusiastic, particularly about the General. Almost everything MacArthur was doing was just what he had been told to do by his superiors, but he was doing it with such vigor and flair, with such a volley of press releases, that it all appeared to be his own program. The fact that his directive, JCS 1380/15, was top secret furthered the illusion. Even the Initial Post-Surrender Policy, SWNCC 150/4, which President Truman had signed and made public to inform the world of what the United States was doing, somehow received very little publicity in Japan. The _Nippon Times,_ for example, never mentioned it even once. The other newspapers were also remiss, so far as I know.

Meanwhile, MacArthur refused to leave Japan. Receiving repeated informal invitations from both the President and Congressional leaders to return home for a hero's welcome like Eisenhower's, MacArthur politely but firmly declined, pleading his work in Japan was too important. He immersed himself ever more deeply in it, to the point where he and the Occupation were almost indistinguishable. Both to the Japanese people and to other countries, his prestige had become just too valuable for the United States to dispense with. He was there to stay.

A more diffident general might have taken the same actions in a more modest manner, allowing top members of his highly disciplined and effective staff to share public credit with him or even alluding to Washington policy once in a while. But that was not MacArthur's style. He could not rely on the Administration to support him publicly—after all, it had blacked out his postsurrender speech on the _Missouri_—only by his own public relations could he reach America and the world. Important Headquarters measures were therefore taken in the name of the Supreme Commander, not the United States, and were accompanied by thunderous press statements emphasizing the revolutionary and epochal features of each successive action. In the heady days of the autumn of 1945, the word went around Headquarters, not entirely a joke, that the Supreme Commander had to be presented with one epochal achievement a week. Since characteristically the "achievements" were liberal and New Dealish, MacArthur succeeded within a matter of months in confounding American liberals, who also knew nothing of the directive under which he worked. The conservatives and ultra-conservatives, on the other hand, trusted MacArthur no matter what he did.

Among those most confounded were the American liberal press and the liberal correspondents attached to MacArthur's Headquarters. Journalism is a profession of cynics. They could not understand, first, how any rational human being could possibly believe that his every action could be so historic and, second, how a previously "reactionary" general could suddenly become a flaming liberal. Many of the correspondents did not like him personally—they thought him immodest and egotistical—but as professionals they were prepared to discount personal feelings. Nevertheless, also as professionals, they were inclined to suspect him of dissembling. "On a clear day you can see Mac-Arthur," one of them snorted. The Australian W. MacMahon Ball, the British Commonwealth Member of the ACJ, put it another way. Exasperated at having his mildest—as he thought them—criticisms in the Council met with a fierce, unyielding defense by MacArthur's deputy there, he could only sigh, "It's not that they do so little, but that they claim so much." Mark Gayn, a free-lance journalist, in his 1945 book, *Japan Diary,* which in translation quickly became the Japanese leftist intellectual's bible on the Occupation, denounced the subsequently successful land reform as a failure even though it was just then getting under way. He could not believe MacArthur no matter what he said or did.

Liberals had serious doubts about MacArthur's political integrity. If Mac-Arthur really were a fake, then his reforms could not be relied upon to be genuine. If each reform were presented as largely accomplished already, the Supreme Commander could not be counted upon for the unglamorous, arduous, and detailed follow-up. On the contrary, once having made his public-relations point, MacArthur might more easily be diverted by eventual counter-reform pressures. Indeed, MacArthur could circumvent his orders, whatever they were, in the first place if he did not believe in them. But in fact, the doubters were wrong on all three counts. MacArthur took military obedience seriously. His profound belief in his destiny as a world figure was genuine. And in 1945, regardless of what he may have professed earlier, he was not an antidemocratic reactionary but essentially an old-fashioned patriotic populist. His critics often simply confused his ideas with those of his political supporters back home.

For MacArthur it was the most natural thing in the world to believe in his star. "When George Dewey sailed into Manila Bay on May 1, 1898," Mac-Arthur told the young Theodore H. White in his Manila Hotel penthouse just weeks before Pearl Harbor, "it was manifest destiny working itself out. By God, it was destiny that brought me here! Destiny!"[36]

Splendid Isolation

That kind of declamation could be taken as pure histrionics. MacArthur's life actually, however, was as different from the ordinary U.S. Army officer's as possible. His continued unparalleled eminence and excellence had always set him apart from his peers. As the son of a general, a Civil War hero, who had earned the Congressional Medal of Honor and risen to the highest rank in the Army, MacArthur was used to the prerogatives of command and took for granted a wide acquaintance with many of his country's leaders. At West Point, he had received grades that have never been equaled since. At thirty-eight, he had become the youngest general in the Army, rising to be Deputy Commander of the Rainbow Division in France in World War I. Injured twice and gassed once, he had nevertheless refused to leave his division under fire, earning thirteen decorations for gallantry in action, seven citations for extraordinary valor—those who called him "Dugout Doug" in World War II could have known nothing of this—and twenty-four decorations from foreign governments. In his early forties he was already Superintendent of West Point, and at fifty he became the youngest Chief of Staff in the Army's history. With the end of his term as Chief, the highest position in the U.S. Army, he was sent to the farthest outpost of American possessions to reorganize the ragged Philippine constabulary, all but forgotten at home. When he retired from the U.S. Army in 1937 to work solely for the Philippine Government, his career seemed over.

Then the Japanese struck south, and once more MacArthur found himself at the center of events. It was a bitter potion. Sacrificed together with his men to a Europe-first strategy and facing death or long captivity, he was plucked again from the maelstrom, and by war's end he was a five-star general, the victorious commander of an immense force. Once more at the edge of retirement, he was given, or himself grasped, responsibility for remaking a nation of 70 million, the most powerful foreign post ever accorded to an American in peacetime. Others, like the correspondents, might doubt him, but each time his career was at its nadir, his unshakable faith in himself had been vindicated by events. What else could one expect him to believe?

The very speed of his meteoric career and the early ages at which he attained each successive rank, distinction, and position—those were the days before the young Air Corps generals of World War II—could not but set him apart from all the other generals. Eisenhower, Bradley, Van Fleet, McNarney and fifty-five other World War II generals of the graduating class of 1915, the ones on which the "stars fell," were lieutenants when MacArthur was a brigadier general. In 1945, when the Japanese Occupation began, a whole generation of regular Army majors and colonels regarded him as the father figure of their academy days. During most of the Occupation period he outranked his nearest Headquarters subordinates by no less than *three* ranks.

Naturally, the American military in Japan stood in awe of him. Colonel Hugh Casey, his engineer officer, waiting in a PT boat off Mindanao in early 1942 for a dawn rendezvouz for the flight to Australia, adamantly refused to give the order to open fire on what appeared in the distance to be an approaching Japanese destroyer, despite the pleas of the Navy skipper. In the end the "destroyer" turned out to be MacArthur's boat. "If that had been 'the old man' and I had fired," Casey said, "I would much rather it had been the Japanese destroyer after all."[37]

The General, for his part, could never forget that some of the most eminent

Army figures were much his juniors. He took their rise beyond certain levels, like that of Dwight Eisenhower, his former aide, as an implicit rebuke. His explosive reaction in 1947 to Eisenhower's ingenuous statement that a military man should not become President of the United States was provoked (according to General Marquat, to whom he exploded at the time) by his certainty that Eisenhower had really aimed the statement at him. Chief of Staff General George C. Marshall, only a colonel when MacArthur himself had been Chief of Staff, was the only highly placed Washington figure to whom he could bring himself even to half-apologize. In September 1945, when Marshall rebuked him for not clearing his statement that an Occupation force of 200,000 should be adequate for Japan, MacArthur radioed: "Your War 65406 [code number of the radioed rebuke] distresses me. There was not the faintest thought that my state-ment . . . would cause the slightest embarrassment." As for all others, age, rank, and an unparalleled sense of mission set him, by circumstance and choice, far above them.

His remoteness was institutionalized by MacArthur in his Headquarters administration. He made himself virtually unapproachable. No telephone was ever installed in his sixth-floor office in the Daiichi Building. Access to him was only through his military secretaries, and only General Whitney, the Chief of his Government Section, was able to come up without an appointment. His working hours, from 10:30 in the morning to 2:30 in the afternoon and again from 5:15 in the evening to 10:30 or later at night, were completely apart from the normal routine of the Headquarters, which was from eight in the morning till noon and from one to five in the afternoon. His closest section chiefs, Marquat, Whitney, and Willoughby, had to work both schedules if they wanted to retain control of their sections and their cherished access to "the Old Man." His hours, like his Filipino field marshal's cap and his residence in the U.S. Embassy, served to set him even farther apart from ordinary humanity.

The only Japanese who could see him were the Emperor and the Prime Minister. The rest of the Japanese and Japan were seen at second hand. For more than five years, with the rarest of exceptions, the only thing MacArthur saw of Japan physically was on the automobile route between the Daiichi Building and his quarters at the American Embassy, a distance of about a mile. He took no inspection trips within Japan, and his ventures outside the country were few and brief. He took no time off. "The only thing the 'Old Man' takes off," Marquat quipped, "is his shoes."

He was equally aloof from Washington officialdom whenever such aloofness served to reinforce his higher status. Assistant Secretary of War John McCloy visited him in October 1945 to ascertain his view of the Russian position on the proposed allied council for Japan. To coordinate, McCloy held a trans-Pacific telex conference with Acting Secretary of State Dean Acheson. Another Su-preme Commander would have welcomed the opportunity to present his views directly to the Acting Secretary, but MacArthur disdained to be present, sending his Deputy Chief of Staff, Major General Richard Marshall, to represent him as an observer. As the Supreme Commander for eleven nations, he would not involve himself officially in the give and take of subsecretaries.

When the State Department, at Secretary of War Stimson's request, sent MacArthur a personal political adviser, the adviser soon found himself advising by means of memoranda passed through the Headquarters Chief of Staff. The Political Adviser's Office was shortly afterward militarized as the GHQ Diplomatic Section, and the political adviser became simultaneously chief of the new section, in which capacity he ranked below the deputy chief of staff as well. At the very same time, the political adviser was informally writing President Harry Truman directly and being asked by the President to continue to keep him informed.[38]

BEHIND THE BAMBOO SCREEN

Seemingly always ready to talk to the world at large, the General, it appeared, was willing to talk with hardly anyone individually. During the Pacific campaigns, his office diary showed, he had met thirty or more times with twenty-three officers from March 1942 to August 1945, and there had been many more informal meetings never recorded.[39] In Japan he spoke regularly with only his personal aides[40] and five others: Whitney, Marquat, Willoughby, the current Chief of Staff, and, the day before many biweekly Allied Council meetings, his deputy there, the Chief of his Diplomatic Section. Outside of those routine contacts, he entertained such visiting VIPs as publishers, politicians, and Cabinet members at dinner in the Embassy residence. But that was the extent of his socializing. He never socialized with even his top staff; they were supposed to be too busy. The only social overture to the General's staff was an invitation one day to a drum concert by eleven-year-old Arthur MacArthur in the Embassy residence. Those invitations were as highly prized as a central place in the reviewing stand at the Kremlin on May Day. General Marquat looked in at my office on his return from the concert. "The kid was pretty good," he said.

In general, MacArthur's private life was very private, devoted entirely to his second wife, Jean, and his son, the only family he had known in his adult life. Jean, whose selfless devotion to the General could hardly have been surpassed, was free to travel, visit curio shops, attend diplomatic receptions, and go to Army football games with other generals' wives, like Mrs. Marquat, but never with the General. His private life was carefully shut off from view.

About certain events, not necessarily private, that showed MacArthur in a favorable light, he was curiously reticent. Never averse to press exposure on big issues, perhaps he felt that talking of lesser ones would leave him open to attack as a publicity hound. One day, as he strode across the sidewalk from his car to the Daiichi Building with General Whitney in his wake, a discontented Japanese civilian tried amateurishly to kill him, the only attempt on his life in Japan of which I am aware. The would-be assassin was quickly seized by the Military Police. Arriving at his sixth-floor office a few minutes later, MacArthur ordered his assailant to be brought to him for a cup of coffee and a discussion of his grievances. The man was then released without publicity. From then on he was a fervent MacArthur admirer. Later the same day, Whitney was moved to tears as he told his section top staff about the incident.[41] Nothing of it was ever revealed to the press.

Similarly, there was no publicity when MacArthur moved to help thousands of American soldiers who were prevented from marrying the Japanese girls with whom they had fallen in love, with whom they were often living secretly, and by whom they had sometimes fathered children. The Oriental Exclusion Act then in force prevented them from bringing such wives home, and the Command therefore refused to permit the marriages. Informed of the situation by Roger Baldwin, whom I had briefed before he went up to see the general, MacArthur wrote to Congressman Frank Fellows of Maine. Fellows managed to relieve the situation through legislation, but MacArthur himself never took credit for that. For the Supreme Commander, unlike several of the officers under him, race prejudice did not exist. President Quezon of the Philippines was his son's godfather, and I can testify personally that there was no anti-Semitism in his makeup. Perhaps his conception of himself as a universal world figure left no room for such particularism.

MacArthur's method of operation from behind the bamboo screen was undeniably effective in practice. He asserted on several occasions that this remoteness was in accordance with his reading of ''Oriental'' psychology, and perhaps he was right. There were Japanese precedents. Undoubtedly it also suited his predilections and the need of a man in his late sixties to conserve his energies. But certainly neither the Russians nor anyone else could treat him as just another American general.

In his insistence on keeping his mind free for ''big problems,'' he relegated internal administration to his successive Chiefs of Staff, not always with happy results. While MacArthur's Olympian decisions commanded instant obedience, some of them would certainly have benefited in quality from a more diversified input. Still, there were few bad decisions. On the whole his methods worked.

Perhaps what offended critics most of all was his highly vocal self-confidence that what he was doing was at all times right. Of course, self-confidence is the essence of military leadership, for who will follow a doubting leader into danger? In military matters MacArthur had repeatedly, although not invariably, been proved right and found his belief in his own judgment vindicated.

In civil government, however, that kind of self-confidence sounds like conceit and a corresponding contempt for others. It was hard for the journalists to swallow. And yet one might ask whether it, along with his faith in their future, was not just right to inspire the Japanese in their time of despondency after the war. In the end, when with the Occupation drawing to a close MacArthur was fired by President Truman for insubordination, he provided the long-time military-dominated Japanese with their greatest lesson in democracy: No military man, no matter how great he may be, is above a democratically elected government.

A MAN OF CONTRADICTION

If MacArthur's personality disconcerted his critics, his political ideas—those of a "reactionary" at home turned crusading reformer in Japan—utterly baffled them. They were thinking in twentieth-century terms, while MacArthur's education and background were essentially of the nineteenth century. Far from being a convinced ideological rightist, the General was a political primitive with wide open spaces where his reactionary principles were supposed to be. An engineering officer who had spent much of his boyhood in Army posts on the populist prairies, he had little urban and no industrial experience that might have prepared him for the great American and European social conflicts after World War I. (He did, however, have startling insights into Asian peasant thinking.) He received his formal education in the humanities and social sciences at West Point at a time when conventional history in America was a narrative of Presidents, parties, and elections; when political science dealt with constitutions, Montesquieu, and clean government; and when presidential primaries, referendum, and recall were the popular reforms of the day. Any economics taught was severely classical, and every cadet learned to venerate America's national heroes. It was they personally, and not abstract social or economic forces, who had made things happen. Significantly, in later hours of stress, MacArthur once told me, his thoughts turned to George Washington. Later I realized how deeply affected he was by the parallel, in military terms, of himself as a latter-day Washington. Both generals initially retreated before insurmountable odds—to Australia, Pusan, Valley Forge—all but abandoned and written off, but courageously maintained their faith, turned the tide, and emerged victorious in the end.

At the turn of the century, gentlemen and officers were not taught Marxism, labor movements, or revolution. They were taught the classics, and MacArthur knew his ancient Greek and Roman history very well indeed. His library of several thousand books, much of it inherited from his father, was abandoned in the Manila Hotel in the move to Corregidor on Christmas Eve of 1941. After the war, American Counter-Intelligence Corps agents discovered a large part of it intact in the Nagoya home of a Japanese general and returned it to MacArthur in Tokyo.[42] Together with subsequent additions it is now on view in the MacArthur Memorial in Norfolk, Virginia.[43] There is nothing there on Marx, Lenin, Fabian socialism, or proletarian revolutions, nor much of twentieth-century ideologies of any kind. The Supreme Commander faced his twentieth-century problems without the usual ideological baggage of the twentieth century.

There were great advantages to being a self-made political thinker, principally an extraordinary flexibility in unorthodox circumstances. That is not to say MacArthur had no core of fundamental beliefs. In the early 1930s he was inclined to lump liberals, pacifists, and Communists together rhetorically, but then they were all trying to cut Army appropriations, and he was Chief of Staff. Through most of his life politics meant wire-pulling, personal advancement, and getting funds and supplies appropriated in a succession of different arenas, not the clash of political ideas. When some of his top officers turned more authoritarian as a result of the Depression, the New Deal, and the war, MacArthur, possibly because he was removed from the Washington political stage in the Philippines, seems to have been strengthened in his fundamental democratic convictions. General George Kenney, his Air Corps commander, recounted one dinner with the General's staff in Manila in the months before the war. MacArthur's brilliant Chief of Staff, Lieutenant General Richard Sutherland, son of an ultra-convervative Supreme Court Justice who was one of ''the nine old men'' attacked by President Franklin Roosevelt, insisted at length that in wartime democracy had to be abandoned. No, MacArthur said reflectively, democracy worked best and would always work, because the people were allowed to think, talk, and keep their minds free and supple.[44] His vision for a postwar Japan, as pronounced to his fellow passengers on the August 30 flight into Japan, was passionately democratic. Afterward, when from time to time he received authoritarian advice from some of his subordinates (Willoughby, Bunker, and others), he simply brushed it aside.

It was as an essentially pragmatic but convinced democrat that the Supreme Commander could embrace the Washington radical reform directive for Japan, a document so different from his pronouncements of a decade and more earlier, and make it his own without any qualms. In its enforcement he was equally pragmatic. When Japanese unions in 1946 resorted to production control strikes, a kind of sit-in strike reminiscent of the CIO auto workers' sit-downs of 1937,[45] the General was free of the kind of preconceived notions about the sanctity of private property that would have required immediate repression. He preferred instead to accept my recommendation to leave the matter to the Japanese courts. When the Japanese Socialist Government in 1947 proposed to nationalize coal mines, he was prepared to stand aside, provided only that they mine more coal. Only someone unmired in conventional categories could have denounced the Japanese big business combines as ''private socialism.'' That was an obvious "contradiction," incomprehensible to the conservative second-generation post-war Washington leadership, heavily larded with bankers, of 1947–49. But then they never understood MacArthur's vision for Japan anyway.

There were also some disadvantages to being self-made. Like any self-made man, the General had huge and utterly unpredictable gaps in his knowledge of modern society, particularly of his own country in the New Deal era. His protracted absences from home did not help. Aside from a few months in 1937 during which he married his Jean, he lived out of the United States from 1935 to 1951. One evening in the summer of 1946, General Marquat, the head of the Economic Section and my immediate chief, dropped into my Labor Division office. He had just come from seeing the "Old Man" and wanted me to settle a disagreement. According to MacArthur, Marquat said, U.S. law required a worker to be a member either of the AFL or CIO. "And I claim he doesn't have to," Marquat added. "Who's right?" I could only conclude that the Supreme Commander had been reading the *Chicago Tribune* a little too assiduously.

His opinion of stock markets was another example. Intellectually he appreciated their economic function in mobilizing equity capital for private business. Nevertheless, we in the Economic and Scientific Section tried for well over a year in 1948–49 to get his permission to reopen the Tokyo stock exchange at Kabutochō. MacArthur simply knew from his own practical experience that stock exchanges were gambling dens. What he thought of public gambling was best illustrated by a phone call General Marquat received from the Chief of Staff one day when I happened to be in Marquat's office. The Chief, General Paul Mueller, had noticed an advertising balloon floating over GHQ and wanted to know the meaning of the characters in the trailer. When I translated for Marquat that they publicized the national lottery, Mueller exclaimed in a horrified bark that rattled the receiver, "Get that the hell out of here, or the Old Man will order it shot down!"

THE OVERSEAS SUPPORTERS

Nevertheless, it was the same pragmatism, not theory, plus the lifetime military strategist's habit of anticipating an adversary's moves, that induced him constantly to place himself in the other fellow's position. The General had long ago concluded that if he were a peasant he would want his piece of land and would die to defend it. That had been apparent to him during his father's campaign against Aguinaldo's Filipino rebels. Similarly, his common sense told him that if he were a worker he would be sure that only a union with his fellow employees could adequately protect him against his employer. Considering how far he was from being, or even seeing the intimate life of, a peasant or a worker when 70 percent of his own life was lived as a general or the son of a general, those were heroic feats of imagination and empathy. His common sense, however, was by no means infallible. After depriving the government workers of their rights to collective bargaining in 1948, he could still be shocked that they insisted on following their leaders, who had bitterly opposed his action. But then his *amour propre* was involved. For someone supposedly arrogant and egotistical, his reading of oppressed humanity was sometimes startling.

Unfortunately, MacArthur was a political miser who hoarded support from wherever it came, and after Pearl Harbor it came to him not only from solidly respectable folk but from some very sinister elements, too. Fervently patriotic groups of Midwestern ethnic Germans and big city ethnic Irish saw in the war in Europe a repetition of the World War I struggle against their "old country," Germany, in alliance with the hated British occupiers of Erin, as well as a humiliating reminder of how they or their parents had been stigmatized as traitors during the earlier war. They constituted the backbone of the powerful pre–Pearl Harbor isolationist movement. After December 7, 1941, they could no longer oppose American participation in the new conflict, but they could clamor for priority for the war against Japan, the only country that had actually attacked America. The top American commander fighting Japan, Douglas MacArthur, automatically became their hero.

Those ethnics' viewpoint was understandable, and their preference for the Pacific arguable. But swimming alongside the honest isolationists in the swirling, confused currents of anti-Roosevelt Depression politics were some very odd and savage creatures: partisans of white Christian supremacy for whom fighting Oriental Japanese was more congenial than battling white Germans; followers of Father Charles Coughlin's rabble-rousing campaigns against the banks and Jewish "international money changers"; the fascist Silver Shirts; elements of the pro-Nazi German–American Bund; and all kinds of Roosevelt haters. All the rightist splinter groups, almost to the last man and woman, became rabid partisans of Douglas MacArthur. Perhaps they remembered his early brand of anti-Communism, but now they saw him as another Roosevelt victim, deprived of men and munitions as part of a nefarious New Deal conspiracy to save Godless Russian Communism. They promptly adopted MacArthur as one of their own.

It mattered little to them that MacArthur's basic philosophy, his ideas on freedom, democracy, and racial and religious tolerance differed radically from theirs, nor did they bother to ask. The German ethnics did not want to know that in 1919 MacArthur had flamboyantly assured the Prince of Wales that America could come right back and beat Germany again, if necessary.[46] The anti-Soviets among them passed by in silence the message in February 1942 from the besieged general on Corregidor that the "world situation at the present time indicates that the hopes of civilization rest on the worthy banners of the courageous Red Army."[47] The ex-isolationists and extreme radical right fringe retained the MacArthur image they thought the hero of the times should have, that of an audacious military leader fighting *their* war and refusing to knuckle under to Roosevelt and the New Deal.

For his part, MacArthur, 10,000 miles away, did not bother too much about the background of his admirers. Completely absorbed in a grueling war punctuated with moments of peril and high tension—from 1942 to 1945 his forces made eighty-seven amphibious landings in hostile territory—and burdened always with immense problems of logistics and supply, he had no time. Mail from his admirers back home was spotty and slow. (In 1948 our Economic Section's chief clerk handed me a letter from Lane Bryant, the maternity dress house in New York, dated 1942 and addressed "Brig. Gen. MacArthur, Brisbane, Australia."

The mail was also one-sided and adoring. Two of his closest military aides, Bonner Fellers (1944–46) and Laurence Bunker (after 1946), were themselves ultra-rightists. They played an active role in the American Commonwealth Party and the John Birch Society after the war and were unlikely to disparage any of the General's right-wing correspondents. MacArthur, for his part, embittered by what he considered Roosevelt's deceitful promises of help for his battered men on Bataan, was ready to accept assistance from the devil himself to make Washington send him what he needed to win the war. He never rejected the radical right, usually acknowledged their admiring letters, and was inevitably tarred with their brush. Any number of Americans simply assumed that he, too, was a fascist or at best an incipient fascist.

Indeed, the vehemence, vituperation, and emotionalism of his supporters, even after the war, was frightening. It did not take much to trip the wire. When Dean Acheson went so far as to rebuke their hero implicitly in September 1945 by calling him an "instrument" and not a "determinant" of policy, twelve Senators, all of them from the Midwest and border states, and a third of all the Republicans in the Senate, were ready to impeach the new Under Secretary of State for that "insulting" remark. (As Acheson had not yet been confirmed, the best they could do was to vote, vainly, to recommit.)

Dean Acheson may have won his personal fight, and handily, but the lesson was not lost on more vulnerable lower-rank officials. No civil servant wanted to tangle with MacArthur and face a congressional buzz saw. Supervising the Japanese Occupation from Washington became a ticklish business. The cable traffic between Washington and Tokyo was only a fraction of that passing between Washington and Germany. In 1947, Colonel Charles Kades, then deputy chief of SCAP's Government Section, visited Washington and was offered the post of Deputy Assistant Secretary of State for Occupied Germany. To familiarize him with his responsibilities he was shown the enormous detail that he would have to supervise and declined the appointment.[48] Nobody would have tried to manage MacArthur that way.

Not only details but anything that might cause controversy or offend the

Supreme Commander was treated with caution. Often the War Department simply neglected to transmit critical comments. In early 1946 the U.S. Labor Department and State's International Labor Relations Division sent the War Department two reports critical of the new Trade Union Law of December 1945 for forwarding to GHQ in Tokyo.[49] As chief of MacArthur's Labor Division at the time, I would undoubtedly have received them and been asked to comment on them to the Supreme Commander, but in fact I never saw the reports till twenty-eight years later. I can only conclude that the War Department simply had never passed them on.

Hugh Borton, then chief of State's Japan Division, had the same experience at the other end of the same line. Investigating a failure of the Tokyo Headquarters to acknowledge a certain Far Eastern Commission decision, Borton discovered the War Department officials involved had decided not to irritate the Supreme Commander by forwarding him a decision he might not like. They would not budge even when Borton pointed out that by international agreement SCAP was the executive arm of the FEC and the United States was duty bound to forward all FEC decisions to him. Almost thirty years later Borton was still flabbergasted.[50]

Conversely, for the first few years of the Occupation MacArthur's recommendations to Washington were treated with the utmost respect, a circumstance of the greatest value to the Japanese, on whose behalf he was asking for food and monetary aid. Just the fact that the General was supervising them was enough to obtain immunity for a while from conservative attacks on the radical reforms of JCS 1380/15. MacArthur's right-wing supporters swallowed programs in Japan, such as encouraging labor unionization and breaking up big business combines, on which they would have gagged in the United States. Just as it was preposterous to suspect General MacArthur of wasting taxpayers' money on foreigners, it was inconceivable to them that MacArthur was a radical. Still, by lending MacArthur their political coloration, the extremists among his followers frightened away almost everyone else and, incidentally, made MacArthur's own credibility suspect when he pushed genuine democratization programs in Japan.

SELF-SACRIFICE AND LOYALTY

In all this, in Tokyo as in Washington, people counted more to MacArthur than their professed principles. That was one reason, perhaps, why he did not delve too deeply into the political beliefs of his supporters. Always excepting himself, of course, he suspected that most people displayed political principles as flags of convenience. Personal loyalty, especially if salted by self-sacrifice, was at the apogee of his values. Of his top GHQ staff officers during most of the Occupation, four—Marquat, Willoughby, Casey, and Akin—had come off Corregidor with him in their boats, and Whitney had been his lawyer in the Philippines before the war and a family friend. MacArthur appointed Marquat, an anti-aircraft officer with no economics background, as chief of the Economics Section to hold the fort until a replacement could be found, because it was a crucial post and he trusted no one else available to be loyal. A year or so later, the Pentagon asked whether Marquat could be released to become an anti-aircraft officer of the Army. MacArthur refused, and although his dreams of a third star were thereby blasted, Marquat never emitted a murmur of his profound disappointment.[51] Later, when Washington tried repeatedly to replace Marquat with a big business type, MacArthur absolutely refused to let it happen.

Loyalty, to MacArthur, had to work both ways. He could claim none if he gave none. When Brigadier General Frayne Baker made the last of a series of missteps as MacArthur's Press Relations Officer, the Supreme Commander asked Marquat to find a place for Baker in the Economic Section. "One more general on my neck," Marquat groused to me. I suggested he appoint Baker as foreign business and investment adviser, for I had developed a foreign investment policy and felt someone with impeccably conservative credentials could best get it approved and moving. Marquat brightened at the idea and named Baker, who had no other visible qualifications and who accepted my draft gratefully.

A year and a half earlier I had learned for myself about MacArthur loyalty, for he refused to bow to considerable pressure to fire me as being too "leftist"— encouraging labor union organizations was not popular in some quarters, especially when the unions struck—and "promoted" me instead to be an economic adviser. My lack of any kind of reproof or public comment—indeed, I defended his action to liberal visitors (Roger Baldwin, Father Boland, and various labor representatives) as realistic and politic—was sufficient for him to continue to support me steadfastly against occasional outside attacks and internal cirticism for the next three years.

The importance MacArthur placed on personal loyalty had its drawbacks, of course. Within GHQ, protecting the Supreme Commander—not the President or the U.S. Government, be it noted—became a legitimate reason for a proposed action, carrying no less weight than the merits of the case. Not even the most fervent protestations of loyalty were enough to protect an officer from his own mistakes or inadequacies, but they must have influenced the Supreme Commander's judgment. The divided command in Korea, for example, which facilitated the Chinese breakthrough in November 1950, could be plausibly attributed, at least in part, to MacArthur's reciprocal loyalty to his recent chief of staff, Major General Almond (who had called his boss "the greatest man alive") and his consequent decision not to integrate Almond's Tenth Corps into Lieutenant General Walton Walker's Eighth Army (Walker was a Bradley–Eisenhower man). Certainly, Courtney Whitney's preeminence in the Occupation derived in large part from MacArthur's confidence that no one protected him more loyally.

"CONSTRUCTIVE PARANOIA"

MacArthur's reliance on such personal loyalty was his best defense against the conspiracies he was sure abounded against him. His view of human nature predisposed him to look for conniving. He had had plenty of experience with that, beginning with his father's career and his mother's incessant letter-writing to the powerful on behalf of her son. In a Headquarters where it was taken for granted that Roosevelt had deliberately starved MacArthur of supplies in the Pacific theater for domestic political reasons, any outside criticism was assumed to be only the tip of an iceberg. Censure on the basis of honest conviction or principle seemed to the General, if theoretically possible, highly unlikely in real life. When I visited him to say my farewells in October 1950, his opening words to me were, ''Who's been out to get you, Ted?'' It was not enough for him that the labor program I had pushed so hard as Chief of his Labor Division was unpopular among conservatives and positively threatening to Japanese reactionaries. MacArthur could not believe that mere disagreement on principle could generate such heat. There must have been some sort of personal conspiracy against me, and he could never figure it out.

Sure that criticism of himself was usually personally motivated, MacArthur did not hesitate to attack his critics personally too. Attack, in any case, was more congenial to him than defense, even when a convincing defense was at hand. When the Soviets notified the Command that they were going to question Occupation labor policy in the next day's session of the Allied Council in July 1946, MacArthur refused to reply to their questions, to which he had very good answers. Instead he ordered Ambassador Atcheson to denounce their statement as bearing ''the familiar signmarks of propaganda'' and to attack labor practices in the U.S.S.R. Indeed, Atcheson captured the headlines, where a more reasoned response would have barely made the newspapers' inside pages.

MacArthur's suspicions of adverse criticism extended particularly to the press. Very early in the Occupation, stung by two brief adverse Reuters reports emanating from London and Moscow, the latter merely quoting the Russian press, MacArthur sent a special message advising General Marshall in the Pentagon that Reuters apparently had mounted a ''campaign'' against American policies in Japan. The American Ambassador in Britain was accordingly directed by the Secretary of State to bring the matter to the attention of the British Government.[52] There the matter rested.

Again, an article published in *Newsweek* purporting to reveal rivalries within GHQ on the purge of Japanese nationalists was met by a 750-word formal statement by the Supreme Commander himself on purge policies,[53] a much prompter and fuller statement than high-ranking officials in State Department were ever able to get out of him on that or any other subject.

His reactions to press criticism were not just offended vanity. MacArthur feared his truth would never catch up with his enemies' lies if he gave his adversaries too much of a head start. Where an incipient conspiracy existed, he had to break it up as soon as possible. One might call his attitude constructive paranoia.

Any unfavorable comment on the Occupation usually drew orders from MacArthur to his subordinates to give him a full reply to the charges plus an analysis of the man who was making them and why. Thousand of man-hours were spent at the upper levels of GHQ preparing those replies. In one case, that of the Kauffman report, a hostile private review of Occupation activities made by an American corporate lawyer in 1947, a score of top-level personnel were involved in the rebuttal, from the Chief of Staff's office down. Typically, its wild distortions of fact were inexplicable to MacArthur until we told him that Kauffman was a lawyer for the Libby-Owens-Ford Corporation, which had a substantial interest in Nippon Sheet Glass Company, a monopoly then being broken up by the Occupation. Kauffman's report then became clear to him.

Concern to forestall criticism was even greater, if possible, than combative replies after the event. The red carpet was repeatedly rolled out for important visitors, particularly editors and favored journalists. For only one Australian correspondent, a man named Courtenay, who had been particularly laudatory of MacArthur during the war, division chiefs in the Economic and Scientific Section (ESS) in 1947 were directed to turn out a series of nine memos on different aspects of Japan's economic situation. A group of ten visiting journalists in mid-1947 was treated to briefings on twenty-six subjects by ten staff sections, including several divisions within each section—the ESS enlisted the aid of seven of its divisions in the project—over a period of eighteen days.[54]

The most effective public relations ploy of all was the MacArthur interview. Here the General's carefully cultivated and legendary remoteness afforded him the opportunity of allowing the privileged visitors to come behind the bamboo screen as a mark of favor. Each meeting, furthermore, was thoroughly stage-managed to demonstrate the Supreme Commander's deep concern for, and if possible his mastery of, the subject his interviewer was most interested in or, if not, a sign of special confidence in the form of a morsel of inside information. The same treatment was accorded senior staff who were about to depart and who might possibly talk or write publicly thereafter. The surprised and flattered visitor, deeply aware of having met history face to face, was almost inevitably converted into or confirmed as a MacArthur admirer. To Roger Baldwin, whose entire adult life had been devoted to pacifism and civil liberties, the Supreme Commander delivered a forty-minute monologue on the importance of civil liberties in the new Japan and the desirability of a Japanese civil liberties union. To a dazzled Wolf Ladejinsky, his land reform specialist, MacArthur spoke for a half-hour without interruption on agricultural land reforms since antiquity, from the Greeks of Solon, through the Romans of Marius and the Gracchi, and up through the situation in the Philippines in the 1900s, when his father had been military governor. Ladejinsky was not up on Greek and Roman land reforms. My particular nugget when I left MacArthur for the last time, at his euphoric high point of the Korean War, was a preview of his intended governmental arrangements for a united Korea. In only one case that I know of, that of a departing chief of his Industry Division, Joseph Reday, who later provided the basis for a critical article on the Occupation economy for *Fortune* magazine (April 1949), did the tactic fail.

It was all very contrived, but it was MacArthur against the world. It was indeed almost impossible for "outsiders" to appreciate MacArthur's Bataan trauma, which lay behind so much of that attitude. In the early months of World War II what he had always anticipated and feared took place. Washington, that is, President Roosevelt and Chief of Staff Marshall, deliberately misled him to make him and his men fight harder, and then abandoned them.

On January 2, 1942, Marshall radioed him, "A stream of four-engine bombers, previously delayed by foul weather, is en route with the head of the column having crossed Africa. Another stream of similar bombers started today from Hawaii staging at new island fields. Two groups of medium bombers of long-range heavy bomb-load capacity leave next week. Pursuit planes are coming on every ship we can get."[55] A few days later, Roosevelt radioed Manuel Quezon, the Philippine President, "I can assure you that every vessel available is bearing to the Southwest Pacific the strength that will eventually crush the enemy and liberate your native land. Vessels in that vicinity have been filled with cargoes of necessary supplies and have been dispatched to Manila."[56] But MacArthur got nothing, and his men were left to rot in Japanese prison camps. His very soul was seared. From then on he was still part of the U.S. Government, still subject to its orders, and still supplied and supported by the massive Army machine, but he was never again to trust or rely upon the Administration.

Now coming into Japan, he had to rely on his staff and his troops, for Douglas MacArthur himself was only one man, and not even a Japanese low-rank god.

5

The Corridors of Byzantium

SHORTLY AFTER THE JAPANESE SURRENDER, Lieutenant Colonel Charles E. Kades, then Deputy Executive Officer of the Army Civil Affairs Division in the Pentagon, was asked by his chief, Major General Hilldring, if he would like to be assigned to General MacArthur's new SCAP headquarters in Tokyo. Hilldring wanted Kades in Japan to keep him apprised, informally of course, of the progress of the Occupation. Kades was not at all sure that he would like the assignment. In the first place, as a lawyer he was looking forward to going into private practice, not staying in the Army. In the second, although "back channel" communications were not exactly illegal, the commander being reported on would sometimes get sticky about it. When Kades had been in Italy in 1944, the British military government had learned of his out-of-channels communications to Hilldring. Some of them had divulged discrepancies in implementing the civil affairs directives. Without warning Kades had suddenly found himself assigned to the first few waves of troops invading Southern France and subsequently languishing in an isolated Rhineland village. He certainly didn't want that again, or worse. Besides, he told Hilldring, he didn't feel quite right about serving in a MacArthur headquarters. With all its reported favoritism, sycophancy, and scheming, it had the reputation of being altogether "like a Byzantine court."[1]

Kades's remark was more than the expression of a personal distaste for a style. It amounted, in the circumstances, to an alarming indictment. He was speaking about the Headquarters that was supposed to carry out the radical democratization reform, the program on which Hilldring and his associates had been working so hard. Neither CAD nor State originally had much confidence in MacArthur's liberalism or in that of his top subordinates. Now, if the Headquarters organization was also a nest of personal intrigue besides, with its top officers working at cross purposes, what chance would the directive have of being force-fully and coherently executed?

Such fears quickly turned out to be groundless, for if MacArthur's head-quarters was Byzantium, it was the vigorous Byzantium of Justinian, not the decadent court of the later rulers. George Atcheson in November 1945 had bitterly criticized the exclusiveness of MacArthur, his Chief of Staff, and "other members of the Bataan Club who act as his privy council or *genro*,"[2] but by January 1946 the "club" members had dispersed: Only four of the eleven officers who left Corregidor with MacArthur for Australia still remained on his staff. Atcheson had stopped complaining to become a fiercely loyal supporter.

Others who, like me, came directly from the continuous infighting of the Washington agencies found the decisiveness and dispatch of the early SCAP operation a revelation of how expeditiously a government could govern. Kades was probably the most agreeably surprised. Allowing himself to be persuaded by Hilldring, with the help of a promotion to full colonel—the last full colonel appointed in World War II—he entered Japan on the third or fourth plane into Atsugi. By the time I arrived, he was securely ensconced as top assistant to General Whitney, Chief of the Government Section, and had already become one of the shrewdest and most effective operators in Byzantium.

THE DUAL STRUCTURE OF SCAP

Overemphasized, personal loyalty can tear an organization apart with sycophancy and intrigue. But, as the effectiveness of MacArthur's wartime staff showed, with strong leadership it can also stimulate healthy competition and creativity. MacArthur never allowed favoritism to interfere with performance. Setting a personal example that was hard to match, he was intolerant of any deviation from his high standards of excellence, dedication, and hard work, especially among his favorites in key positions. They, in turn, insisted that their subordinates perform, too. A leader who knew and showed what he wanted left little room for underlings to maneuver on policy. The fact that MacArthur saw very few subordinates regularly narrowed the ground even further. The disper-sion of the old South Pacific campaigners caused most of the old intrigues to disappear.

The most important circumstance, however, in restraining destructive in-trigue was MacArthur's steadfast upholding of the Army command structure. Even when he agreed informally with a section chief's proposal, that officer still had to run the paper work through the Chief of Staff. At the same time, Mac-Arthur never disowned any staff agency action taken in good faith in discharge of its assigned responsibility. The basic principle of Army staff work was that responsibility is divided, not shared. The command "mission," as established by directives from higher authority, was split and then split again among the several staff agencies. Just as responsibility for formulation of action proposals was delegated downward, so approval always had to be sought from higher authority. Where a mission involved more than one staff agency, actions initiated by one agency had to be "coordinated" by means of concurrences from the others, and irreconcilable disputes had to be settled by the Chief of Staff or the Supreme Commander.

There was no lateral movement. Unlike the Japanese, who sought a general consensus, or the Americans in Washington, who were accustomed to anyone at all trying to catch the President's ear on any problem at all, especially under Roosevelt, no one would be consulted or heard from under MacArthur's Army system unless his assigned mission was involved. For example, the officers of G-4's Petroleum Division might think encouraging labor unions ill-advised or communistic, while the Labor Division might consider G-4 Petroleum's actions designed selfishly to reinstate the American oil companies in postwar Japan. But neither opinion was solicited or heard. Responsibility and, therefore, staff activity were compartmentalized, and if a function was in someone else's compartment, not all the grousing in one's beer at the officers' club bar could break down the compartment walls.

To give a more trenchant instance, Colonel Kades was a New Dealer, while Colonel Laurence Bunker was an ultra-conservative, later to become a national officer of the John Birch Society. Bunker outranked Kades in seniority. But Kades was Chief of the Public Administration Division and later Deputy Chief of the Government Section in charge of Japanese political democratization, while Bunker was General MacArthur's military aide. Kades consequently was a powerful figure in the Occupation, whereas Bunker influenced the course of the Occupation not at all.

The crucial elements in determining who ran the Occupation after General MacArthur were, first, the assignment of functions and, second, access to the Supreme Commander; the first had a lot to do with the second. Lieutenant General Eichelberger was the second-ranking American officer in Japan, but reporters who interviewed him and his successor, Lieutenant General Walker, at their Yokohama headquarters found the pickings slim. Eichelberger and Walker commanded the Eighth Army only, not Japan or the Japanese. The most publicized American in the country after MacArthur was the American representative to and Chairman of the Allied Council for Japan. Every two weeks Ambassador George Atcheson, and later William Sebald, would do battle with the Soviet representative, usually ending up in the newspaper headlines. But ultimately both were simply spokesmen on a short leash, with no more effect on SCAP programs than the Allied Council itself.

Finally, according to the organization chart, the most important officers were clearly the Chief of Staff, then the two Deputy Chiefs of Staff, and then the

Assistant Chiefs of Staff—G-1 Personnel, G-2 Intelligence, G-3 Operations, and G-4 Supply. In reality, however, only G-2 had any direct and substantive importance in the governing of Japan, and even the Chief of Staff was essentially a traffic cop, assigning missions and approving or rejecting actions. Meanwhile a lowly captain headed all price control and rationing, including critically short food distribution; a major was in charge of trust-busting; and a lieutenant colonel had responsibility for all newspapers, schools, and religious institutions. The Tokyo GHQ at the time had as many as twenty generals, and for a while it took two of them to run Special Services, responsible for the PXs and troop recreation.

Indeed, the GHQ framework was a historically unique improvisation, neither detailed in Army manuals nor taught at Leavenworth. It was an ingenious solution to an emergency suddenly created by the combination of the surrender and the receipt of an unexpected and breathtakingly broad democratization policy for Japan. In Spring 1945, MacArthur, anticipating an invasion, expected to have to administer the Japanese civilian population on progressively expanding beachheads and to concentrate on maintaining public order and essential services, as well as preventing starvation, disease, and unrest. In response to his request to the Pentagon for a suitable officer to head a new G-5 Civil Affairs Section, the Army in July despatched Brigadier General William Crist, an old China hand.[3] Suddenly neither the plan nor the man seemed adequate; besides, the Japanese Government was now SCAP's tool. MacArthur ordered Lieutenant General Sutherland, his Chief of Staff, to draw up a new organization plan, and Sutherland assigned the job to a group of his staff colonels, headed by Raymond C. Kramer, a New York department store executive in civilian life. In a few days the small group drew up a plan that was to last six years and govern Japan efficiently during that time. Its key: to convert G-5 from a staff section to an entire new GHQ for SCAP, operating side by side with the existing AFPAC (Army Force Pacific) combat command.

Whether intentional or not, the scheme also solved the paradox of democratizing a country by means of an inherently undemocratic Army machine. It simply short-circuited the bulk of the theater brass right out of the democratization process. The SCAP GHQ, initially comprising nine sections (Economic and Scientific, Civil Information and Education, Natural Resources, Public Health and Welfare, Government, Legal, Civil Communications, Civil Intelligence, and Statistics and Reports), was staffed mostly with reserve officers with broad civilian experience, while the AFPAC GHQ was mostly regular Army. General MacArthur was Commander of both GHQs, either as the SCAP or as CINCAFPAC (Commander-in-Chief Army Forces Pacific)—later FEC (Far East Command) and CINCFE (Commander-in-Chief Far East) respectively—and he had the same Chief of Staff for both. The plan provided, however, for two Deputy Chiefs of Staff, one for each GHQ, and the organizations from there on down were separate. Just as Japan had two governments, the Japanese and the Occupation, so the Occupation had two headquarters.

For the most part the coexistence of the two GHQs was smooth. Nor was the separation absolute, for the AFPAC/FEC general staff sections had limited functions for SCAP too, like G-1 for immigration, G-2 for civil intelligence, G-3 for repatriation of Japanese stranded abroad after the surrender, and G-4 for receiving Japanese military supplies and returning them to the civilian economy. But for the most part the separation was maintained. That was a boon, because both GHQs, while intertwined and interdependent, were fundamentally at odds in background and outlook.

In GHQ AFPAC/FEC, military rank counted for much, and the G sections were very important. In SCAP's GHQ, however, American civil servants, including many officers who had converted to civilian status, quickly came to outnumber officers on active duty, and the channels were far less rigid. The military often resented civilians—SCAP divisions found they could get AFPAC/FEC concurrences easier if their proposals were hand-carried over by a regular officer in their organizations—and civilians chafed at unnecessary military restrictions. When the two did collide, literally in a traffic accident and the subsequent fracas, a GHQ court-martial convicted the civilian involved of insubordination on the theory that any military man, even a private, outranked a civilian, who had no rank at all. When the military collided with civilians on matters of policy, like soldiers' "black marketing," the curtain of misunderstanding sometimes seemed impenetrable. The SCAP civilians and officers looked down on the AFPAC/FEC sections as engaged in no more than glorified housekeeping. For their part, a good many of the regular officers in AFPAC/FEC privately looked on Japan as only the scenery outside one more Army post; its progress and prosperity, which so engrossed the SCAP people, were largely irrelevant to the real Army job of physically occupying the land.

Still, physical occupation was routine. Governing Japan was anything but. The success of the Occupation would stand or fall on the quality of the key SCAP officials. U.S. policy was hostage to them. What sort of men were they?

At the very top of the SCAP pyramid, just below General MacArthur and his alter ego, the Chief of Staff, stood the Section Chiefs, each with a vast domain. They were, however, by no means equals, for the scope of the sections varied greatly, and even more varied was their access to the source of all power in Japan, General MacArthur. Of the constellation of SCAP and AFPAC sections, three chiefs stood out as most powerful in terms of function and access: Brigadier General Courtney Whitney, Government Section (GS); Major General William F. Marquat, Economic and Scientific Section (ESS); and Major General Charles Willoughby, Assistant Chief of Staff, G-2 Intelligence. Each had extraordinarily broad functional responsibility, long years of service with the "Old

Man,'' and undisputed personal loyalty to him, for he had made them. But each was very different from his fellows.

COURTNEY WHITNEY, LOYAL RETAINER

Courtney Whitney, a pink-faced, bald Manila lawyer with a small reddish-brown mustache, was an extremely astute operator for whom Douglas Mac-Arthur was the sun, moon, and stars. A reserve Air Corps colonel, Whitney happened to be outside the Philippines when the Japanese attacked in December 1941. In early 1943 he was in Washington, preparing to go to Kunming, China, as intelligence officer of the Fourteenth Air Force, when MacArthur, whose prewar attorney he was, asked for him to be assigned to his command. On Whitney's arrival in Brisbane, MacArthur assigned him to organize and coordinate the activities of the Philippine guerrillas. With a typical Byzantine touch that skirted the edge of the command structure without infringing on it, the general told Whitney to report directly to the Chief of Staff, not to the G-2, Willoughby, or to the Counter-Intelligence Chief, General Thorpe. Whitney was effusively grateful,[4] for apparently he already regarded Willoughby and Thorpe as rivals. It was an indication of the special relationship between the two men, one that would continue into the Occupation and indeed for their rest of their lives.

MacArthur trusted no one as much as "Court." He had brought him from his work miles away with the guerrillas especially to wade ashore by the Commander-in-Chief's side at Leyte beach and to appear in the historic photographs of MacArthur fulfilling his pledge to return. Whitney would also accompany MacArthur at the Inchon landing in Korea. The day before the signing of the Japanese surrender on the deck of the *Missouri,* MacArthur borrowed Whitney's fountain pen and "forgot" to return it. After the signing ceremony was over, the new Supreme Commander gave it back, remarking that the "Mac" part of his signature had been written with it, and Whitney could have the now historic pen to leave to his children. Whitney's eyes filled with tears, he recounted later, at MacArthur's personal thoughtfulness at such a crowded moment. Eventually he had the pen framed and hung on his wall.[5]

Even during the war, Whitney's reputation as a "can do" type was widespread. Colonel Joseph Rauh, a staunch New Dealer, advised Kades, a fellow New Dealer, when their paths crossed on a Pacific island at the end of the war, to hook up with Whitney, who was known to be conservative. "He gets things done," Rauh said.[6]

But Whitney had never had a regular place in the AFPAC Headquarters. In the fall of 1945 he was still unattached, wandering around the commander's offices on the sixth floor of the Daiichi Building and doing special jobs for the

"Old Man." Then suddenly in November a suitable top-level slot opened, or was opened for him, Chief of the brand-new Government Section.

The current Section Chief, Brigadier General Crist, the officer originally dispatched to MacArthur in August to be G-5 Civil Affairs, was finding the going hard. Charged under Kramer's plan with military government in Korea and "the internal structure of civil government in Japan,"[7] Crist, an outsider in a very introverted headquarters, seemed unable to get even the "political" purge, surely within his purview, past the Deputy Chief of Staff. MacArthur, his head filled with grandiose reform projects, was getting impatient, and Whitney was available. Crist was reassigned. On November 11, 1945, Colonel Courtney Whitney became the Chief of Government Section, a post in which he was to influence the course of the Occupation profoundly. He would leave it only to accompany his beloved chief home when Truman relieved MacArthur in April 1951.

According to Kades, Whitney, a shrewd lawyer at home, was unaware of the realities of Japan. But he learned fast. In late 1946 Kades, ruminating to me on how far Whitney had come in such a short time, shook his head disbelievingly and said, "Why, do you know that when Whitney was first appointed Chief of GS, he asked me what our first problem was. I told him the purge, and Whitney said he could not see why there should be a purge of war leaders just because they were defeated. If we had lost, Whitney said, the same grounds could have been used to purge us. Gee!" Kades added, "he had an awful lot to learn."[8]

In Headquarters infighting, Whitney had no peer. Early on, General Willoughby, his archrival as G-2, tried to have the SCAP sections report to the Chief of Staff through one of the G sections in the same way as the AFPAC sections. That would have put GS under G-2 and Whitney under Willoughby. Whitney would have none of it and offered to resign first. The Chief of Staff, knowing how close Whitney was to the Commander-in-Chief, chose not to precipitate a crisis and turned down the plan.

On another, more spectacular occasion, Willoughby insisted that his G-2 organization was the most qualified in GHQ, because of its intelligence resources, to implement the purge of extreme nationalists ordered by the JCS 1380/15 directive. When the subject came up at a general staff meeting, Whitney innocently asked Willoughby to give his estimate of the purpose and value of the purge. Willoughby could not pass up the opportunity to enlighten his peers. He started his discussion moderately enough, but as he went on he became more and more emotional and critical of the entire purge idea. He ended up with a blistering denunciation. When he had finished, Whitney, in his best trial manner, after a long silence turned to the Chief of Staff. "I submit' " he said, "that anyone who is so opposed to a program is the wrong man to implement it." That ended the argument. The purge implementation was assigned to GS.[9]

Whitney's appointment electrified the section and kept it on its toes from then on. Their boss was quickly promoted to brigadier general, and with his access to MacArthur—he was the only section chief who could drop in on the SCAP without an appointment—the section members felt themselves close to God, an elite company, somehow above the other "operating" sections, as I was told during the brief time I was a GS member. Indeed, with Whitney's backing and Kades's clever manipulating, GS was a power to be reckoned with, with no compunctions about taking over other sections' turf—the police reform, the economic purge, and so on. The section's greatest hour came in February 1946, when the Supreme Commander, impressed with its work on the purge, designated it "a committee of the whole" to draw up a model constitution. Translated into Japanese and modified in minor ways in conferences with Japanese representatives and in the Diet, it became the fundamental law of the land and still is. GS turned out to be the Japanese constitutional convention, Whitney its James Madison, and its members the Alexander Hamiltons, John Jays, and so forth of Japan. Indeed, GS was the only SCAP section that produced its own history, *The Political Reorientation of Japan*. In a way, that was Whitney's best tribute to MacArthur.

Marquat: The School of Hard Knocks

Marquat, the second of the trio and the Chief of the Economic and Scientific Section through almost all of the Occupation, was altogether unlike Whitney in personality. No polished lawyer, he was a warm-hearted, shortish, balding man who wore a mustache to give a touch of elegance to an otherwise homely face. Marquat had come up through the school of hard knocks. In his youth he was for a short time a professional boxer, then a reporter for the *Seattle Times*. At the age of nineteen he secured a scoop by getting to interview the reclusive Henry Ford by the unusual expedient of presenting himself openly and formally at Ford's private railway car with spats, cane, boutonniere, and calling card. Ford, whose guards had been beating off reportorial snoopers in all manner of disguises, was so impressed with the young man's politeness and candor that he granted him an interview, which Marquat made sure to have photographed as evidence for his editor that his story was not a fake. Story and photograph stopped the presses and made the front page.[10]

Volunteering for the Army in World War I, Marquat obtained a commission through Officers' Candidate School and found himself in the field artillery trying to shoot down the newfangled airplanes. In those days the gunners aimed ahead of the moving planes as though they were ducks, but the field artillery was not as maneuverable as shotguns, and the planes were sometimes faster than ducks. Marquat was the first in the U.S. Army to devise mathematical formulae for rapidly computing a plane's future position allowing for speed, wind factors, and so forth and aiming the guns accordingly. (After he became an anti-aircraft general, he collected slide rules as a memento of that period in his life. They were the only presents he accepted from the Japanese. At one time his Tokyo office safe held twenty of them.)

After World War I, Marquat returned to journalism, becoming a humorous feature writer. For one article he tried unsuccessfully to sell five-dollar gold pieces on a downtown Seattle street corner for a dollar each, then wrote sorrowfully about man's distrust of his fellow man. A week later the FBI visited him. Someone else had taken advantage of the stronger faith his article had produced among readers by selling fake ten-dollar gold pieces for five dollars each. The FBI wanted to know if he was part of the preliminary set-up for "the sting."

One day he saw a notice in one of the service papers inviting ex-officers to return to the Army. He took the competitive examination, passed, and returned as a regular officer. For seventeen years he languished in the rank of captain in an Army without much money and zero growth. Most of that time he spent coaching service athletic teams and devising improvements in anti-aircraft aiming methods.

Finally posted to the Philippines to join MacArthur's staff in the late 1930s, Marquat was a major when Japan attacked the Philippines. When MacArthur left Corregidor by PT boat in March 1942, he took Marquat along with him as one of the small group intended as the nucleus of his new headquarters in Australia. In three and a half years of continuous campaigning, Marquat reached the temporary rank of major general and aircraft officer of AFPAC.

Where Whitney battled to balloon his section's (and his) sphere of jurisdiction, Marquat did not have to. Kramer, in assigning the functions of the various sections, was sure that he himself would be the new economic chief. He therefore combined in one section all the functions and responsibilities that in the parallel Germany headquarters were dispersed among three: economics, labor, and finance. Then he added science. All of industry, foreign trade, price control, rationing, antitrust activities, and economic statistics were included. Kramer's agglomeration was huge, numbering some 500 economists, engineers, businessmen, and assorted other staff members at its peak. It supervised three Japanese ministries—Finance, Commerce and Industry (later International Trade and Industry), and Labor—plus the Economic Stabilization Board and the Bank of Japan. Its responsibilities reached into every cranny of Japanese everyday life, and its Chief was pulled into almost every problem of significance.

Kramer turned out to be right. MacArthur quickly named him Chief of the Economic and Scientific Section. He made a fast start. After only a few weeks he had induced the four big Japanese *zaibatsu* holding companies to dissolve themselves voluntarily. But in 1942 Kramer, as a troubleshooter, had written an unflattering report on Colonel Harry Vaughan's performance as Provost Marshal in Brisbane, Australia, and now Vaughan was President Truman's aide. When the War Department nominated three colonels on MacArthur's staff, Whitney, Kramer, and Ken Dyke (Chief of the Civil Information and Education Section), for their brigadier star, the White House reviewer—who else but the President's military aide?—deleted Kramer's name. Kramer picked up his marbles in December 1945 and went home to resume his business career.

Kramer was a hard act to follow and while searching for a successor in the theater, General MacArthur appointed Marquat, his affable, wise-cracking anti-aircraft officer with no aircraft around to shoot down, to take over the Economics spot temporarily. (A few months later, MacArthur asked Marquat temporarily to wear a third hat as well, as the first Chairman of the Allied Council.) No one of appropriate stature in the economic field turned up for the ESS job, not even in the various visiting missions. Abandoning the search but reluctant to risk the imposition of a hard-to-handle outsider from Washington, MacArthur made Bill Marquat, a man with no technical training, qualifications, or experience for the job, but of unfaltering loyalty and shrewd native intelligence, his permanent economics officer.

Marquat was a man of unassailable common sense, an extraordinarily hard worker in a headquarters where hard work was common, a fast learner, able to get along with almost everyone, and loyal to MacArthur. Shrewdly deprecating himself, he allowed visitors and staff to think they could lead him around and use him. But as Brigadier General Elliott Thorpe once told me admiringly,[11] Marquat would figuratively seat the visitor in a plush chair, light his cigar for him, and then slip the rug out from under him so deftly that the visitor wouldn't realize it for months. Very few people were able to deceive him, and of those who tried even fewer realized they were unsuccessful. His faculty of anticipation was fueled perhaps by worry, for he was a chronic worrier, but that made him a leader who organized work on problems before they arose.

Of all his personal qualities, perhaps the most admirable were his kindness and compassion. He was always helping someone, whether his gardener's cousin, his aide's Japanese wife, or his Filipino driver. On several occasions, when I tipped him off, he prevented the racially prejudiced G-1 from forcing the discharges of American officers and civilians who had married Japanese women. He distrusted the Military Police, not for themselves but because he distrusted excessive personal control from whatever source, and the MPs were too readily available to insensitive persons in authority. (For that reason he also sympathized with my fear, as Chief of the Labor Division, of MP intrusion into Japanese labor affairs.)

Disdainful of stuffed shirts, Marquat was always muttering imprecations against West Pointers who thought themselves superior to others. After one telephone call from a visiting general who had interrupted a staff meeting to ask a personal favor, Marquat returned to the meeting grumbling, "God damn generals! In my army there'll be no generals!" Of course, if anyone else tried to denigrate the U.S. Army, Marquat would turn on him violently. He was too proud of the position he had achieved in the Army to suffer easy criticism of it in silence.

His two great loves were baseball and comic "one-liners." Those of us who worked with him were subjected to a constant stream of corny humor, for example: "A debutante is a tomato with lots of lettuce." "My clock can navigate the stairs; we wind it up on the second floor and let it run down." And so on.[12]

At the age of fifty-four he played second base on the ESS softball team and led the league, consisting mostly of young soldiers, in batting. As nonprofessional baseball commissioner for Japan, he had a constant stream of sports figures coming through his office, including Lefty O'Doul and Joe DiMaggio. He sponsored and supported the organization of the two big professional baseball leagues in Japan, an arrangement that continues to this day, and was instrumental in bringing the first postwar American professional baseball team, the San Francisco Seals, to Japan in 1949. Bill Marquat was a man with extraordinary authority and immense responsibility thrust upon him, but a very human human being all the same.

General Willoughby: Charles the Terrible

Major General Charles Willoughby, G-2, the third of MacArthur's top trio, was quite different from the other two. He played a negative counterpoint to almost every one of their positive themes. He was the only one of MacArthur's men who was born a subject of a foreign ruler, who spoke English with a foreign (German) accent, who had no civilian work experience or adult career, and who finally was resolutely opposed to the main democratization objectives of the Occupation. In the political infighting in GHQ he lost on every important issue, especially when he tangled with Whitney, and so in the end he had little influence on the main course of the Occupation. The only Japanese agency he supervised was the police, but Whitney and GS were put in charge of police decentralization. In Europe, CIC under G-2 took charge of de-Nazification and de-Fascization; in Japan, the parallel purge was implemented by the Japanese Government under GS. Willoughby is remembered for no particular achievement. Why then rank him with the other two?

Things did not look the same then as they do in retrospect. At the time Willoughby was one of the powers of the Occupation, and everyone knew it. After reaching Australia from Corregidor, MacArthur had kept intelligence split into two organizations: Willoughby's G-2 dealing with strictly military intel-

ligence, and Elliott Thorpe's civil intelligence and counter-intelligence operations. The dual intelligence organization lasted all through the war and into the
early months in Japan. Guarding the Emperor was Thorpe's job, and so were
unearthing hidden caches of treasure and war material, rounding up war crimes
suspects, questioning Japanese-held political prisoners, and supervising the Japanese police. But in February 1946 Thorpe left. Willoughby inherited his Civil
Intelligence Section, his Counter-Intelligence Section, and that section's Civil
Censorship Detachment (CCD) with more than 400 persons. He also controlled
the Allied Translator and Interpreter Service (ATIS), 500 strong, and supervised
the 441st Counter Intelligence Detachment with ninety officers and men.[13] All
these were attached to G-2 and under Willoughby in one way or another. For
example, the Director of the Civil Intelligence Section, Colonel Rufus Bratton,
had the office next to Willoughby's even though theoretically outside of G-2 as
such. Within a short time, Willoughby had more than one-fourth of the entire
GHQ (both AFPAC and SCAP) staff working directly or indirectly for him.

Nor was that all. G-2 also had control of the American employee security
files and, through the Public Safety Division of Civil Intelligence, the Japanese
police files too. His own CIC operatives practiced surveillance of Occupation
personnel, went through their wastebaskets, and recorded their visitors.[14] We in
sensitive posts always assumed our phones were tapped or easily could be. The
combination of CIC and police was formidable, even though, so far as I knew,
unauthorized. In December 1950, for instance, when I had left GHQ, a Japanese
policeman arrived at my house in Tokyo to ask me a list of questions. Over tea in
the living room I could read upside down the questions and the CIC letterhead on
the paper he was holding.[15] It was a rash Occupation functionary who, no matter
how high his official position, would cross General Willoughby.

The key to his preeminence was, of course, his long service with and
loyalty to MacArthur. He had been MacArthur's G-4 Supply and then G-2 in the
Philippines and had been, together with Marquat, one of the indispensables the
general took with him from Corregidor to Australia. He had subsequently produced the intelligence estimates on which MacArthur's Pacific campaigns had
been conceived. Though he made mistakes,[16] and though Chief of Staff
Sutherland disliked him,[17] some of his intelligence predictions were uncanny for
their accuracy,[18] and MacArthur retained considerable confidence in him.
Willoughby repeatedly displayed a fanatical loyalty. Once in the early days of
the Occupation he complained about "unjustified criticism" of his General in
the U.S. press. When a correspondent asked if he considered all criticism of
MacArthur unjustified, he replied, "Certainly."[19] There was reason for the
"Old Man" to be loyal in return.

By any standards, Charles Willoughby's career was singular. Born in 1892
in Heidelberg, Germany, son of a baron, Freiherr T. von Tscheppe-Weidenbach,
and an English lady, Emma Willoughby, he emigrated to the United States at the

age of eighteen, was naturalized as an American, Americanized his given name from Karl to Charles, adopted his mother's maiden name, and even organized an ROTC unit at Gettysburg College in his senior year. Two years later he joined the U.S. Army, to remain there for thirty years (as of 1946), serving in the chase after Pancho Villa on the Mexican border in 1916 and with the First Division in World War I, and attending and teaching in the Infantry School and the Command and General Staff School at Fort Leavenworth. His whole life was military. True, he had spent nine years, from 1921 to 1930, in diplomatic circles as military attaché in Venezuela, Colombia, and Ecuador, where he became an expert, by his own account,[20] on communist infiltration and subversion in Latin America. At Leavenworth his specialty was the Soviet armed forces "order of battle."

None of that was *civil.* Indeed, his background handicapped him in understanding what ordinary civilians thought, hoped, and felt. Born an aristocrat, he lived in America as a member of the upper classes, whether as a college man at a time when only a small elite went to college or as an officer in the Army. It is not surprising that he believed not in democracy but in a natural aristocracy, among which he counted himself. Fascism and Nazisim were mass movements led by riffraff demogogues, but Franco's brand of traditional authoritarianism was congenial. On a visit to the Spanish dictator after he departed from Japan, Willoughby called him "the second greatest general in the world"[21] after MacArthur, of course. He never became attuned to American life. Marquat was "the baseball general," and Whitney brought MacArthur the college football scores every Sunday morning in the fall, but Willoughby had no interest in sports. Instead, he cultivated the image of an Old World intellectual, a fancier of European political philosophers congenial to his own views and of military historians. He himself wrote poetry, which he once discussed with Kades and me at lunch in the Imperial Hotel mess.

His fellow officers naturally considered him affected and snobbish and called him "Sir Charles." His manner confirmed their opinion. A bulky man with an incongruously soft voice, capable of extravagant courtesy and charm—he was unfailingly polite to me and several times gave me lifts to GHQ in his car—most of the time he "appeared to be looking out," as a fellow officer once put it in a memorable quote, "as though over a high board fence."[22] When crossed, however, he was given to temper tantrums. He was reputed to have flung a glass ashtray across the room at a subordinate on one occasion. Whitney inspired respect among his aides, Marquat affection, but Willoughby inspired fear.

As an aristocrat Willoughby could not be expected to concern himself with the theoretical squabbles of Marxists. Unread in Marxism, he did not care to distinguish among various shades of radical thought. That would have been pardonable in a military intelligence officer, but it was a crucial flaw in a political security chief. Seeing no difference between a pro-Soviet Stalinist and an anti-Soviet democratic socialist or a Trotskyite, he was bound to miss the practical implications regarding the likelihood of Soviet espionage, sabotage, and the like. Nor did he ever understand why people became radicals, for he knew radicals only from the outside, as policemen know criminals. It was a severe drawback for a civil intelligence chief.

In a country where Marxist terminology was the common coin of intellectual exchange and whose trade unions all professed to be socialist at the very least, Willoughby was out of his depth. To him, socialism was just a station on the way to communism. Democratic socialists were not allies in the fight against the communists but subverters of the established order. They made radical ideas respectable and thus weakened society's capacity to resist communism. Only Japanese conservatives could be trusted. In a secret memo in September 1946, Willoughby denounced those "attempting to discredit the present Yoshida Cabinet and thereby promote the interest of the Japan Communist Party."[23] For him, there was no middle ground between the conservatives and the communists. His outlook ran directly counter to the main thrust of U.S. policy and JCS 1380/15.

WILLOUGHBY'S CONSPIRACY

On the surface the three powerful generals got along famously. To each other, they were "Charles," "Bill," and "Courtney." Below the surface was another matter. Marquat, with a job almost too big to handle, was by no means a bureaucratic empire-builder; he had gladly turned over reparations operations to a new Reparations Section. Whitney, sure of his relationship with the "Old Man," was more aggressive, always interested in new big projects, and he was not averse to acquiring them at Willoughby's expense. Willoughby, on the other hand, in spite of having inherited a large civil intelligence–police empire from Elliott Thorpe, had to watch its importance and influence steadily dwindle.

In mid-1946, moreover, the course of the Occupation was going counter to Willoughby's deeply felt ideas, and no one was asking him what he thought, for the channels had been shifted elsewhere. In June and July, when the Labor Division threw a roadblock against Japanese police intervention in a Communist-led union's attempt to capture the *Yomiuri* newspaper and cited Washington directives prohibiting police activity in labor affairs, Willoughby was outraged. The Yoshida government was facing increasing opposition and massive labor parades and demonstrations, but the demonstrators were not reined in. The traditional bulwarks against communism were being eroded, as Willoughby saw it, by irresponsible Occupation reforms and reformers. He had been able to do nothing against the reforms as such, but the reformers were something else again.

Thus was born the biggest intrigue of GHQ's short history, an ultra-conservative general's revolt against a liberal Occupation by means of character assassination. From August 1946 until May 1947, Willoughby put seven full colonels,[24] his top civilian aide,[25] his Civil Intelligence Division, his Special Activities Unit, and a number of CIC operatives to work on the project of discrediting as many reformers as possible and intimidating the rest. By the time he was finished he had fingered five civilian members of Marquat's ESS, five (one an ex-member) from GS, and two others as dangerous leftists who should be discharged forthwith. "I maintain," he said in the final memo putting forward his accusations, "that subversive elements are employed in this headquarters. . . . We are vulnerable, exposed to proven international espionage and local maneuvers."[26]

The ultimate product of the G-2's process was a bulky secret report entitled "Leftist Infiltration into SCAP," containing more than a hundred closely packed pages of names, dates, and details, plus tables and charts. In its finished form it comprised three sections. The first presented summaries of the dossiers of eleven American SCAP civil servants charged with being "leftists"—G-2 never used the word "Communist." Only ten were actually on the MacArthur SCAP staff; the other was a telephone repairman. The second section was a list of 199 GHQ American civilian employees who themselves (six) or whose parents (193) were born in Russia and its East European satellites, including Poland, Austria, Hungary, and Rumania, but excluding East Germany. Almost all those listed were Jewish. The third section was an in-depth study of one of the first ten.

I must confess that at the time I had no inkling of Willoughby's project or my inclusion as one of the "leftists." It was all a closely guarded secret, about which only those who worked on the project in G-2/CIS, MacArthur, the Chief of Staff and one or two of his colonels, Whitney, Marquat, and, I presume, the G-1 knew. True, Willoughby's subordinates were acting strangely. Colonel Rufus Bratton, his Deputy, averted his eyes when we passed in the corridors in the Imperial Hotel. Spinks, his top civilian aide, with whom I had lunched in Washington during the war, always seemed distant and anxious to get away when we happened to meet. Intrigues are often sooner sensed than seen. But the idea that the infiltration of a whole group of "leftists" was placing GHQ in great danger, from which it was necessary for Willoughby and his section to save the Supreme Commander, was beyond my imagination until more than thirty years later, when I came across Willoughby's papers in the MacArthur Memorial in Norfolk, Virginia, in 1978.

It is, of course, in the nature of security officers to be suspicious, to think the worst of everyone, and to give more weight to security needs than to fairness. But the Willoughby Papers confirm that, as Whitney and Marquat believed all along, the G-2 was not really serious about uncovering Communists, but was more intent on labeling as "leftists" those he thought too liberal. Besides the final report, the papers include also the miscellaneous memos and penciled notes he sent his subordinates telling them what to do. Taken together, the documents make it clear that Willoughby chose as targets people whose activities, including official duties, seemed to him dangerously radical. What he wanted from the CIS was evidence that his suspicions were correct. Sometimes his choice of target was contradicted by the files. For example, subject ''F''[27] was reported to have received a four-way security clearance from Washington, that is, four federal agencies cleared him—and no wonder, for his father was a confidential adviser to the FBI on Communist infiltration—but, the CIS summary said, ''his activities in this theater have been of such a leftist nature as to warrant his inclusion in this study.''

Even earlier, on August 15, 1946, when the project was just getting under way, Willoughby, in a memo to Colonel W. S. Wood,[28] was dismayed to find his people had only four ''leftist'' cases instead of the nineteen they had led him to expect. Two days later Wood, presumably after more discussion with Willoughby, penciled a note to Colonel Duff: ''Here is our opportunity to prove that 'Research and Analysis SID' [Special Intelligence Division] can provide an answer to any question received. Turn this over and let me have something which will fulfill Gen. W's requirements. This must be done rapidly so give it priority. Let me know when I can expect the first case—use Cohen [that is, yours truly] as #1. If not already there, place Miss [E] on your CIC Civ. Emp. suspect list.''[29] I, of course, had upset Willoughby by my handling of the *Yomiuri* affair. Just that day Subject ''E'' had offended him by attending a Tass cocktail party at the Tokyo Press Club in company with a correspondent from *U.S. News and World Report* whom Willoughby considered a leftist. A month later, the G-2 was surprised that there was still no dossier summary on me, the derogatory information on me being so meager. He decided to combine my case with ''C2's.''[30] So much for systematic intelligence selection.

Considering the objectives and methods, it is not surprising that Whitney's and Marquat's sections were heavily targeted. Indeed, of the ten SCAP staff members cited, seven appeared to be connected with the three programs that disturbed the G-2 the most: the purge, the *zaibatsu* big business breakup, and the labor reform.[31]

Next to target selection, presentation for maximum impact was Willoughby's highest priority, far ahead of accuracy, a word not found in his instructions. For instance, CIS made no attempt to check the references supplied by the ''subjects.'' Each civil servant had to provide four, and among my total of forty-odd references were such undoubted anti-Communists as Irving Brown, the AFL European representative, and Kathryn Lewis, John L. Lewis's sister. Not one was contacted. Instead we find Willoughby coaching his subordinates on ''dolling up outside folder with nice lettered title . . . substitute our time-honored yellow tabs . . . a neat staff study.''[32] Or he recommends the use of a typewriter with a smaller typeface: "By using 'elite' we saved a full page. . . . Brevity is worth seeking, for psychological effect."[33]

It was not only external presentation that concerned the G-2, but the "proper" arrangement and interpretation of the data to prove his point, what Willoughby shamelessly called "G-2 deductive analysis." In dealing with a dossier summary on subject "G," a young woman employee, a naturalized American whose Austrian-Russian parents were musicians who, buffeted by anti-Semitism and hard times in Europe, had found a haven in Japan, the G-2 pronounced himself dissatisfied with the bare facts. He personally reconstructed a lurid scenario and ordered Spinks, then Chief of the Special Activities Branch, to "work this into your report on the [G] case." In part his scenario went this way:

> At this time, we run into a small Jewish clique, associated with the Symphony Orchestra, partly State supported. One Jew recommends the other; so here we find strange characters drift into Tokyo, many of them via Shanghai, where they work mysteriously and precariously. Shanghai, that focal point of intrigue and espionage, then and now. And we begin to catch glimpses of motives and money and purposes. One of this musical "clique" is one M. [name deleted]. He also comes under the icy purview of the Jap Kempeitai; they move slowly and relentlessly, these people. Then we run across the crazy-quilt of the Sorge case.[34] Sorge, the international spy, working for both the Russians and the Germans. A story, in itself. The "musical group" is drawn into his net.[35]

There was no evidence, of course, of any connection between the parents and Sorge, the Kempeitai, or anyone else. But having once entangled the daughter in the convolutions of his 1946 imagination, Willoughby could indignantly ask Spinks—and through Spinks, the Chief of Staff and MacArthur—"why we, the U.S. should reach for and employ these murky twilight zone suspects."[36]

In the end Willoughby's intrigue was a complete failure. Whitney refused even to discuss the individual cases, categorizing the whole affair as "an attack on Government Section."[37] From time to time Marquat would go over to the Daiichi Building to look at more "evidence" and come back muttering about "those damned G-2 flatfeet." Mostly he wrote soothing words, bided his time, and admitted nothing.

Indeed, neither Whitney nor Marquat could bear to accept Willoughby's charges for reasons of internal GHQ power politics. For if Willoughby had the authority to supervise official actions of SCAP officials for security reasons in their business with the Japanese, he would in fact be usurping the established section chief's authority and fragmenting the SCAP staff. The charges themselves were a reflection on Marquat and Whitney that neither could abide. Willoughby's use of evidence given by Japanese, usually those adversely affected by the enforcement of SCAP policies, against Americans enforcing the policies was a dangerous game, something that even Willoughby recognized. "We should develop U.S. records and lay off the Japs for a while," he instructed early on.[38]

In the end it was the poor intrinsic quality of the evidence, combined with MacArthur's relaxed attitude toward charges of "leftism," that doomed Willoughby's efforts. After all, even at face value, his report was pretty tame stuff: three persons affiliated with the Institute of Pacific Relations, two persons suffixing loyalty certificates with statements that they had signed them pursuant to the provisions of law, two members of the Washington Bookshop, one attending meetings of the American Peace Mobilization, and not a single "big-C" Communist. Perhaps a few merited further investigation, but out of a few thousand GHQ civilian personnel, that was not much. A danger to SCAP? MacArthur simply let the report gather dust. Three years later, he awarded me, one of Willoughby's principal targets, the Army Civilian Commendation for Meritorious Civilian Service, citing, among other things, my loyalty. Perhaps he just knew his Sir Charles too well.

MacArthur, a longtime and highly vocal anti-Communist who believed democratic reform was the best antidote to communism, was a hard man for the simple-minded and the single-minded to stampede. The Byzantine intrigue did not succeed in halting democratization. That was done by the later changes in U.S. policy.

The Quiet Officers

Compared with the three generals, the other staff section chiefs exerted surprisingly little influence on the course of the Occupation. True, the SCAP chiefs knew their business. Colonel Alva Carpenter, head of the Legal Section, was an excellent lawyer. Colonel Hubert Schenck, Chief of Natural Resources, was a geology professor at Stanford, and General Crawford Sams, head of the Public Health and Welfare Section, was a public health doctor with an outstanding reputation. But they never got involved in the broad issues of the Occupation. Carpenter, for example, supervised the Class B war crimes trials (individual violations of the rules of war), while the Class A trials, dealing with conspiracy to commit international aggression, were handled by the International Military Tribunal for the Far East. Schenck could have involved himself in the land reform, but he left it to Ladejinsky, his adviser. The Civil Information and Education Section was exceptional. Early in the Occupation, its chief, Colonel Ken R. Dyke, a former vice president of the National Broadcasting Company, was a powerhouse, demolishing thought control, revising textbooks, disestablishing Shinto, encouraging and guiding the press and radio, purging the schools, and bringing over a prestigious Education Advisory Mission to draw up a plan to restructure Japan's education system, which the Japanese accepted and implemented. But when Dyke left in May 1946, his successor, Marine Lieutenant Colonel Donald Nugent, turned out to be an unimaginative, stodgy administrator, and the CIE spark died.

The two successive American representatives on the Allied Council for Japan had even less influence. George Atcheson, the old China hand, appointed over the old Japan hand Eugene Dooman as Political Adviser, made his greatest impact when, goaded beyond endurance by the sniping of the Australian W. MacMahon Ball at the American Club of Japan (ACJ) one day in October 1946, he burst out that the Japanese Government and Occupation now had identical objectives. Because that ended the need for formal SCAP directives, other than routine ones—why would it be necessary to order the cooperative Japanese around?—it opened an era of "informal guidance," a kind of off-the-record pressure. Even though Atcheson changed from a critic of MacArthur to a strong supporter, he remained an agent and was never consulted on policy. Nor was William Sebald, his attractive successor, a noted Japanese law scholar who had translated the Japanese civil and criminal codes in the 1930s and returned to Japan as a Navy lieutenant commander.[39]

Indeed, even the successive Chiefs of Staff, powerful though they were in GHQ, left no mark on SCAP programs. They were men who construed their functions in limited military terms and who in fact developed little intimacy with their boss. Once in the spring of 1948, General Marquat tried to persuade the Chief of Staff, Major General Paul Mueller, of the desirability of some measure by pointing out that to act otherwise might injure the "Old Man's" chances of being elected President of the United States "But," Mueller answered naïvely, "he isn't running for President." "Yes, I know," Marquat said, "but just the same I wouldn't want to be the one who hurt his chances."

Major General Edward Almond, who succeeded Mueller, was related to Vice President Barkley by marriage. Even so, he was not much more sophisticated in civilian matters. One time, when the electrical workers' union persisted in causing scattered and rotating five- and ten-minute power cutoffs in defiance of General MacArthur's call to sacrifice for economic stabilization, Almond asked Marquat for a report on the percentage of industrial production lost as a result, to be secured if necessary by telephoning all the factories in the country. Marquat, certain that the Chief had no idea of the statistical magnitude of the task, simply reported: "General, have you ever tried to make a phone call in this country? Nine out of ten times you can't get through." That stopped Almond cold.

Washington's planners, directing a radical democratization reform in Japan, had not been very optimistic from the beginning about the general to whose lot it fell to carry it out. They would have had to be even less sanguine about his organization, filled as it was with personal loyalists antagonistic to Washington, protective of their chief, and with no record of social vision. And yet the results were surprising and impressive. Carefully cutting the strictly military off from Japanese affairs by an ingenious double headquarters and a rigid insistence on military channels, MacArthur also separated most of his politically reactionary and ultra-conservative loyalists[40] from SCAP policy by giving them ornamental but essentially meaningless positions. Meanwhile he hewed to his democratic line. It was no accident, for he appointed capable and dedicated democratizers to his critically important SCAP sections: Whitney, Kramer, Dyke, and Marquat. His other section chiefs were at least competent and dutiful, and sometimes considerably more. MacArthur inspired and led them, but he also controlled them, for he was the source of their status and authority. When Willoughby conspired to overturn his policies by massive "red scare" intrigue, he handled him calmly, patiently, and with minimum damage.

It was all rather Byzantine to be sure, but then Byzantiums are never completely out of date, are they?

6

The View at Mid-Level

POLICY PROCLAIMS, but details decide. If the generals, with their foibles and rivalries, dominated SCAP Headquarters, they could not run Japan. The mastery of detail needed to manage a populous, industrialized, complex society and to transform it along democratic lines as well was beyond the reach of one Supreme Commander and nine, or later thirteen, section chiefs. Only a large number of specialists could do the job. When planning the Occupation of Japan, Washington officials were worried about MacArthur and the intrigues of his intimates and would-be intimates. They never gave a thought to the quality of his staff.

Yet in the event, the Occupation carried out its democratization program well. The principal programs—the purge, the new constitution, the land reform, and so on—were all managed by SCAP officials, not by military officers. Every one of them was below the level of section chief. The true executive aristocracy of the Occupation was composed of the division and branch chiefs in GHQ SCAP. Usually of field grade (major to colonel) or the civilian equivalent (CAF 13–15), they were the most important individuals, as measured by day-to-day influence on the course of events. In the Occupation hierarchy they and their subordinates were perhaps at mid-level or somewhat above, but to the Japanese they were at the top. They were the backbone of the American effort.

After more than three decades, in which almost every Occupation name has receded into the mists except that of General MacArthur, the critical importance of the SCAP staff has been forgotten. But at the time, its capacity to handle the immense variety of the detailed jobs required to implement Occupation policies was crucial, and the Command knew it. Late in August 1945, just a week after the surrender, the Chief of Staff, Major General Richard Sutherland, radioed Washington urgently for help. He asked that twenty "economists" be rushed out to Tokyo by September 10. The War Department was baffled; no one knew what kind of economists he wanted, or for what purpose. (I didn't care. I

99

was anxious and ready to go—all I had to do was get my shirts out of the laundry—but hardly anyone else was.) Three days later the panicky requisition was canceled, but the urgent need remained. A staff was assembled rapidly, if not frantically. By April 25, 1946, 1,550 American officers and civilians, plus hundreds of enlisted men, Japanese, and third-country nationals, were working for GHQ SCAP. By January 1, 1948, the number had risen to a peak of 3,200. From division chief to clerk and from colonel to second lieutenant and all those in between, Japan had received a functioning new super-government to rule over its existing one in record time.

Legally, of course, it could not be called a government. It was a staff, and in a military headquarters a staff does not govern. It prepares actions for the decision and signature of the commander. How then could a group of individual American officers and civilians have become so powerful?

In the first place, the job of governing a nation of 70 million, even using an existing Japanese Government as an administrative arm, was too big and varied to fit the military staff scheme. It was simply not feasible to run more than a fraction of the decisions through the Supreme Commander or Chief of Staff at the top or, for that matter, through the section chiefs. Which textbooks were militarist, and were the rewrites satisfactory? Which industrial plants were to be earmarked for possible reparations selection? What transactions of the *zaibatsu* subsidiaries should be allowed, and which companies were to be designated subsidiaries? What were "key" positions of "high" responsibility for which and from which people were to be purged? And so on. From the beginning, therefore, SCAP directives permitted "technical" communication between the SCAP staff members and their opposite numbers in the Japanese Government to explain SCAP directives and guide implementation. The Command almost immediately placed a good part of its business outside of command channels.

Moreover, while in theory "technical" means anything that is not mandatory, there are ways to convey shades of meaning. The SCAP practice of "not objecting" rather than actually "approving" Japanese proposals—MacArthur was not one to accept responsibility unnecessarily—was particularly suitable for indirection. If I, as Chief of Labor Division, were to advise Welfare Ministry officials, as I once did, that I could not recommend SCAP nonobjection to a proposed Imperial ordinance unless it was modified in certain respects, the chances were very good that the Japanese would modify it. I could truthfully testify that I had ordered nothing. Similar "technical" formulations obtained the same results elsewhere in SCAP. And as the work of the Occupation proceeded and the area of "technical" contact grew, a body of noncommands with the force of commands grew along with it.

Proposed legislation, whether sponsored by SCAP or not, was scrutinized in numberless small meetings between Japanese and "SCAPanese" for conformance with policy and directives. Before the budget came up for "nonobjection" by General Marquat as Chief of ESS, hundreds of hours were spent by Finance Ministry officials answering the searching questions of Eugene M. Reed, Chief of the Public Finance Branch, and his staff. Informal meetings proliferated on every subject, and very little of what was said by SCAP officers in those meetings ever reached the section chief, let alone General MacArthur.

LARGE RESPONSIBILITIES

In the second place, the small number of SCAP officials as compared with the huge domain of SCAP responsibility afforded each official an unprecedentedly large piece of the action. The SCAP staff of 1,500 in 1946 or 3,000 in 1948 may have seemed oversize, if one ignored the size and complexity of the nation they were administering. In fact a visitor to downtown Tokyo in the Occupation years could not fail to be impressed with the ubiquitous American presence: the conspicuousness and numbers of American pedestrians, the predominance of American vehicles, the numerous sizable buildings with American flags, American street names, and the PXs and American theaters. Symbolic of the American preeminence downtown was the duo directing traffic at the Hibiya intersection right next to General Headquarters. An MP and a Japanese policeman gave simultaneous traffic signals, or almost simultaneous, because the policeman was always a fraction of a second behind the MP. Central Tokyo was almost an American city.

But the appearance of a multitude of Americans running Japan was deceptive. Even at their peak the number of Allied (almost entirely American) officers and civilians living and working in Tokyo amounted to only 10,000, two-thirds of them outside of the SCAP staff.[1] They were a physical presence, to be sure, but they had nothing to do with actually running Japan. Furthermore, the SCAP headquarters itself included substantial organizations that were outside the governing process proper: the Allied Translator and Interpreter Service, the Civil Censorship Detachment, the Counter Intelligence Corps operatives, the Statistics and Reports Section, and the War Crimes Tribunal with its prosecutors, defense counsel, judges, and court personnel. Finally, half of those employed in the SCAP agencies that did govern Japan were internal administrative and clerical staff. The SCAP staff who themselves participated personally in the governing process, making the pertinent decisions and recommendations, amounted to no more than about 500 in April 1946 or some 900 in January 1948.[2] They were a meager band indeed to administer an activist, radical reform program in all phases of politics and economics, and part of the social sphere as well, in a country as large and intricate as Japan.

No wonder one man could dominate the entire Japanese press, another direct a SCAP campaign to break up the biggest business concentrations in the country, a third supervise distribution of all imported food, a fourth control all the hospitals, and a fifth dominate the movie industry. In December 1946, Noel Busch, writing in *Life* magazine, declared that I, as Chief of the Labor Division, "combine[d] in himself the powers of Lewis Schwellenbach, William Green and the N.L.R.B." It was not exactly true, but the jurisdiction of my division did extend to the equivalent in the United States of the Labor Department, the U.S. Conciliation Service, the U.S. Employment Service, the War Labor Board, the Wage-Hour Administration, National Labor Relations Board, and the various state bureaus of labor standards, workmen's compensation, and so on. Everyone had his own big job.

Finally, in any military headquarters "big shots" are usually bigger, and in Occupied Japan that was particularly true. It was not just a question of dividing an extremely broad grant of power to SCAP among a relatively small number of officials but, equally important, the absence of checks and balances, judicial review, and voter approval, which normally restrain any civilian administrator. Unlike Washington, the military command structure was streamlined, with no overlapping agencies and departments, each with its own constituency that had to be conciliated. In the United States, the Treasury Department contended with the Federal Reserve Board over monetary policy and with the Bureau of the Budget over appropriations. In SCAP all three were concentrated in the Public Finance Branch of the Finance Division under one branch chief.

Instead of organizational checks, "directives from higher authority" served as the ultimate control. It was one of a superior officer's most important responsibilities to see to it that his subordinates stayed within the directives. He might delegate the checking, but the responsibility remained his nonetheless. A SCAP official trying to push his own ideas beyond or in opposition to directives without his chief's knowledge could endanger his boss personally with *his* superior. And that was almost the ultimate offense. The system could not abide breach of trust between "officers." If discovered, the offender would shortly lose the confidence of his superior, then the normal range of his authority, and finally, quite possibly, his job.

In practice, however, higher officials were inclined to go along with the man who had the assigned mission, especially if the matter was the least bit "technical." For almost two years the Labor Division had a free hand to institute labor reforms in accordance with very broad policies in the higher directives. In that period, we sponsored three major pieces of legislation, all of which, although with some modification, are still on the books. I do not believe General MacArthur or General Marquat ever read a line of any of them. They simply trusted the staff.

As the Occupation progressed, the chances of keeping important informal actions quiet diminished. The Japanese, although they had surrendered unconditionally, retained considerable and increasingly friendly access at various levels of SCAP. Prime Minister Yoshida could and did complain to General Mac-Arthur. Lower Japanese officials could question the validity of informal SCAP advice and guidance to higher SCAP levels. General Marquat met weekly with the Ministers of Finance, Commerce and Industry,[3] and Economic Stabilization, and biweekly with the Governor of the Bank of Japan. Any one of them could "innocently" ask for clarification at any time of a staff action they did not like. That would have prompted an investigation and resulted in a reply. Outside of Tokyo it may have been easier, but in GHQ it was hard to conceal rogue actions. Each SCAP official knew that. He had to be sure of his ground in advance.

Those arrangements, unplanned and unwritten, did not, of course, constitute a full-fledged adversary system. Americans were understandably reluctant to overrule Americans, and the Japanese knew it. The Japanese were equally reluctant to antagonize SCAP officials in a position to make their lives difficult later on. But neither did the arrangements amount to absolutism or a bureaucratic dictatorship. The Japanese were used to the idea of dual governments and to the involved negotiations and delicate adjustments required by them. The Kyoto Imperial court had existed in parallel with the Genji rulers, the Hōjō regents, and the Tokugawa shoguns for centuries. The willful Finance Minister Ishibashi Tanzan[4] and the stubborn Economic Stabilization Director-General Zen Keinosuke[5] were irritants in the functioning of the new duality, but they were exceptions. In general, things went smoothly, and the SCAP staff's authority was rarely challenged. For five years, from a handful of buildings in downtown Tokyo, they ran Japan.

THE BACKGROUND AND QUALITY OF THE STAFF

It is fair to ask, since so much depended on them, who they were and where they came from. Help at this level was on the way even before the call went out for the "twenty economists." Some two score officers, who had been assembled in the Army's Civil Affairs Staging Area (CASA) in Monterey, California, where they had been engaged in "wake of battle" planning exercises as an S-5 staff, were quickly flown out to Manila in the few days after V-J day. Arriving in Tokyo in the first two weeks of September, minus a few lost along the way,[6] they were absorbed into GHQ, either in the G-5 Military Government Section or in the other staff sections being set up during September. ESS Chief Kramer grabbed one young captain who had had experience in a family business—his family owned the biggest chain of bakeries in Minnesota—as his Price Control and Rationing Division Chief and another officer, a major who had served with the New Jersey Mediation Service, as his Labor Division Chief. (Both, incidentally, had held corresponding positions in the CASA S-5.) Kramer gave them the broadest authority, telling his first Labor Division Chief,

William Karpinsky, that he was the labor expert, not Kramer, and that he was to go ahead and do what was necessary with Kramer's full support. Other CASA luminaries were assigned to other sections.

The most obvious and available resource for staff recruitment was passed over, namely, the 2,900 graduates of the Military Government School in Charlottesville, Virginia.[7] Three years earlier, President Roosevelt had become suspicious that the school was anti–New Deal. Now, General MacArthur was unwilling to accept hundreds of officers whom he did not know into his close-knit headquarters. Some who had graduated early may have made it to GHQ in Tokyo by way of CASA or other routes, but those shipped directly to MacArthur at war's end wound up either in Okinawa or in Military Government of the Yokohama-based Eighth Army, which promptly assigned them to the forty-six prefectural military government teams all over Japan to check compliance with SCAP directives and policies. They were firmly kept out of Tokyo.

Instead, the Chief of Staff launched an intensive "in-house" recruitment effort. Notices were placed on the bulletin boards of all Occupation units inviting officers who thought themselves qualified for civil affairs to apply for transfer to GHQ and to come down to Tokyo for interviews. With several hundred thousand men in the Armed Forces stationed in the Japan area at war's end,[8] an enormous reservoir of lawyers, bankers, economists, industrial technicians, and almost everything else was close at hand. Most were only too eager to rush home to career, sweetheart, or family. But many were unready to settle down so quickly or were not eligible to go home because of insufficient "points" (calculated for months of service, overseas service, purple hearts, and so on), and they thought service in their specialty even in bombed-out Tokyo would be more congenial than vegetating in a nonfighting combat unit in an equally bombed-out small town in the country. From a radius of hundreds of miles, those interested made their way by whatever transportation they could arrange and flocked into GHQ in October 1945.

In a large room, later to be the preserve of the Government Section, a number of tables were scattered around with hand-lettered signs, such as "Finance Division," "Fisheries Division," "Labor Division," and so on. Behind each table was the newly appointed division chief, often comprising in his own person the total division staff as well. Uniformly hungry for anyone he could find with experience to help him out, he was predisposed to accept all comers. If a deal was made, the candidate was "hired" on the spot, the processing completed rapidly, and the newcomer at his job the next day, sometimes before proper furniture to accommodate him could be secured. Interviewees frequently received two or more job offers and were in the novel position, for officers in a "combat zone," of choosing their own spots. Occasionally an officer with sufficient service to permit him to leave for home would prefer to stay in his new spot as a civilian with higher equivalent rank, which meant better billets, transportation, and other privileges than he had ever had as an officer. An ex-lieutenant earning $3,600 a year, including pay and allowances, and now hired to be a CAF-12 civil servant at $6,500 dollars a year ($5,180 plus 25 percent overseas differential), would remove his insignia and rank from his uniform, happily assume his new "assimilated" rank of major, draw a vehicle from the motor pool, and condescendingly visit his former commanding officer, a captain.

It was a rough-and-ready procedure, but it worked. Some of the recruits were of exceptionally high caliber. Several sharp Federal Reserve Bank economists in uniform joined the former manager of the National City Bank branch in Shanghai to become the bulwark of the Finance Division. Lawyers were snapped up for the Government Section, for the legal offices of various other sections, and for war crimes matters. Industrial technicians, forestry and fishery experts, agronomists, mining engineers, and even radio broadcasters and labor organizers came forward. Within a month a staff of a few hundred had been assembled. Often laboring far into the night, they were able to begin the application of directive JCS 1380/15 at high speed.

Early on, the War Department in Washington was brought into the staffing process. Calls went out from General MacArthur for a series of advisory missions from the United States on different subjects, and from almost every group some incidental recruitment was done. In November 1945 a foreign trade group was sent to the theater, including several businessmen who had lived in Japan before the war. Almost all of them were then hired to staff the new Import–Export Division. In December a "democratization" mission was sent out for a six-month tour to help the Government Section. It stayed on to constitute the bulk of the GS civilian component. The members of the Corwin Edwards mission on Japanese combines arrived in January with supplies of cigarettes to defray personal expenses and departed leaving behind not only the cigarettes but a new chief of the Antitrust Division. The Stuart Rice statistical mission in April bequeathed almost its whole personnel to staffing the Research and Statistics Division of the ESS, while the Labor Advisory Mission arriving in the same month supplied a deputy chief to the Labor Division. The Civil Service mission, among others, also provided people.

In effect, SCAP delegated selection of a good part of its higher ranks to experts. Once the War Department, in collaboration with whatever other Washington agencies, chose the mission head, he, usually a man of eminence and wide acquaintanceship in his field, could be relied upon to select the best people for his mission, and many of his selections were equally suitable for GHQ staff afterward. The liquidating war agencies in Washington supplied a great many people, but a surprising number were drawn from private industry, campuses, and even labor unions.

For the first year and more, urgency ruled each day. Building a new super-government from scratch left little time for deliberation in selecting individuals.

At the upper echelons it was possible to bring over a proposed chief of the Economics and Scientific Section as the head of a temporary foreign trade mission, look him over for a time on the spot, and reject him as being of insufficient caliber. But for hundreds of individuals comprehensive checks were very difficult and, when recruited directly from the theater, impracticable. As Chief of the then five-man Labor Division, I was visited late one afternoon in February 1946 by a Women's Army Corps corporal who had arrived from Manila the day before. After a twenty-minute interview confirming her Washington Labor Department experience, I hired her as a desperately needed statistician. She was processed that afternoon by our section personnel officer and started work at 8:30 the next morning. That may have been a record.

Clearly there was some danger in entrusting policy to such hastily chosen and untested instruments. But the alternative would have been not to get the job done at all, for GHQ could not afford to lag behind events or the Japanese Government. The potential hazards of such haste to both U.S. policy and the Japanese population turned out to be minor. The staff assembled in that hasty fashion turned out to be MacArthur's strong right arm.

Adjustment of the SCAP people to thinking on a much larger scale than ever before was matched by the need to adjust to their newly elevated, albeit temporarily, station in life. To begin with, the salaries were outsize. As a division chief, I earned more than a U.S. senator, a congressman, or the under secretary of any Cabinet department. My branch chiefs earned almost as much as an Assistant Secretary of War.[9] Upon arrival in the theater, the top three civil service ranks, equal to lieutenant colonel and colonel, were entitled to a sedan with driver for both official and recreational purposes. Later on, those in such grades having families with them were provided with private houses and servants.

Most unsettling of all was their new official power, far more than they had ever exercised in their past experience. The upward leap was, of course, unavoidable. Since the top levels of Stateside officialdom, law, business, and politics were not about to desert posts and careers for temporary stints abroad, the top-rank jobs in the Japanese Occupation had to be filled with those in third- and fourth-rank jobs at home. That did not mean they had third- and fourth-rate minds; on the contrary, there were many first-rate minds among them. But even the brightest still had to adjust to maintain his balance.

It was easiest for the younger officials to accept their new exalted status as part of the fortunes of war and keep their feet on the ground than for their more mature and settled elders. The Occupation, with its severe wrenches from the normal, was, like war, a young man's game. Even so, it was sometimes too much. Early in 1946, a young enlisted man wandered into our Labor Division office on the advice of a GI buddy. After he had been brought in to me by my executive officer on the basis of his special qualifications—he had been a wages specialist for the City of Los Angeles—I snapped him up to fill the vacancy left by an officer departing home on points. I sent him up to the floor above to see our section personnel officer, a warrant officer (ranked in between a sergeant and a second lieutenant) with instructions to get himself processed and report back promptly. Three hours later I had heard no more from him. I phoned up to him at the personnel office to find out what had happened. My new man replied that he was waiting for the personnel officer to get to him. "He's only a warrant officer," I exploded, "You're going to be a major. You don't have to wait for him." I got the personnel officer on the phone and told him crisply that I needed the man. Could he get him processed and back to me in a half-hour? "Yes, sir," he replied, and he did. But clearly, something had to be done to improve my new man's self-image, for the change from a private in a combat unit in rural Japan to a national executive was just too abrupt. My solution was to order a sedan for him and tell him to ride around Tokyo for the next day and a half visiting officers' installations and getting accustomed to being and acting like a major. That did it. When he returned, he was ready to talk back to officers and do his job.

The older men, however, tended rather to see their sudden authority as the well-merited culmination of a successful career. A colonel who was made Chief of the new SCAP Construction Division took up skiing at the age of fifty as an activity commensurate with his new eminence. Another, suddenly appointed division chief, ran his office like a dictator, emptying the files into the trash one night because there was too much paperwork and walking Afghan hounds in the almost dogless streets of Tokyo as an indication of his social status.[10]

The adjustment problem worked two ways. The Japanese, faced with an intrinsically strange milieu and isolated from the outside world, found it difficult to judge the individual American's "real" status. Was he a truly important man in his own country, or was it only the circumstances of the Occupation that made him look that way? To the hierarchical Japanese it was a grimly serious problem. They could not be sure, and so they tended to play safe. The Kansas City stockbroker in uniform who for a time was in charge of all Japanese public finance, the small-town California newspaper publisher who became czar of the Japanese press, even the young lieutenant industrial officer of the Tokyo Military Government Team teaching Mitsubishi Steel the "latest" U.S. metallurgical practices, which he had learned in engineering school only a few years before— all were accorded a personal deference that would have been laughable in other conditions. After the Peace Treaty, there was much embarrassment among Japanese of importance when they discovered that they had misjudged a number of their objects of solicitude, mixed with a scarcely concealed rancor at having been taken in by nobodies. But that was hardly the fault of the SCAP staff.

Gift-Giving and Morality

In 1946 and early 1947, SCAP people happily welcomed the efforts of Japanese Government officials and businessmen to get to know them by way of entertainment, for there was little else available outside of the drinking at the Officers' Clubs, and their families were still in the United States. While the ESS was one of the special targets because of the life-and-death power of so many of its divisions,[11] I do not know of any part of GHQ, especially the Occupation offices in the field, that was excluded from such overtures. Some American correspondents in the early months tried to run down rumors that the Provost Marshal himself had been given a tour of the best brothels and a taste of the merchandise. Nor were the beneficiaries only military. Mr. Ando, head of Ando-gumi, surely one of the most polished and courteous gangsters in the world, once proffered Lee Martin a beautiful pearl necklace minutes after being introduced to her, simply to honor her for being the first American woman correspondent he had ever met.

Entertainment and gifts were, in Japan, a way of doing business, and each company or government office had an entertainment fund. Geisha parties for Occupation officials were standard, complete with ballroom dancing in stockinged feet on *tatami* mats, the playing of prewar records, and such exotica as opera sopranos rendering "O sole mio," arias from *Madame Butterfly,* and "You Are My Sunshine." Almost every mid-level Occupation staffer learned to do the "Tankō Bushi" coal miner's dance with the geisha, as well as the "Beisubōru" (baseball) dance.

Not knowing the tastes of the Americans, the Japanese devoted themselves to a serious study of them. At one small party (small because of a tiny budget) given for four of us by the two labor bureaus of the Welfare Ministry in February 1946, three of the bureaucrats plied us with whisky, beer, and sake while asking questions about our hobbies and likes. Gradually, as the Japanese became drunker, our responses became more imaginative. When all but one of the Japanese were *hors de combat,* apparently asleep under the table, we said our farewells to the last surviving host. We had not gone more than a hundred meters in our jeep when one of us discovered he had forgotten his overseas cap. We turned around, and he was back within minutes at the room we had left. There were our "drunken" hosts, suddenly sober, sitting around the low banquet table and comparing notes on their departed guests. I don't know who fooled whom more that evening.

Whatever else the Americans' tastes were, the Japanese were sure that women would always be warmly welcome, and many of the parties came complete with stayover girls, often termed "*daruma*[12] [pushover doll] *geisha.*" The opportunities for blackmail seemed to me to be too dangerous. In the Labor Division I instituted a rule that officers had to arrange their own romances. Still,

American officials staying overnight in the field sometimes found it difficult to reject their new companions, who tearfully explained that they might be blamed for offending the Americans if they were not allowed to stay. A few heads were turned by the sexual abundance, but not many. Often the beneficiary was in no position to deliver in return. One economist, a senior analyst in the Research and Statistics Division of ESS who could no nothing for anyone, went around Japan savoring the hospitality of the various prefectural governments, with women supplied at most stops. When he reached Ōtsu in Shiga Prefecture[13] one day, his hosts told him that theirs was a poor prefecture and they did not have enough money to give him a proper party. "That's okay," he replied magnanimously. "You supply the women and I'll split the costs with you fifty-fifty!"

Gifts were another way of seeking favor, but the practice ran into a cultural impasse. The Americans usually could not appreciate the true value of the old art objects offered and, worse still, did not know that by Japanese custom they were thereafter obligated to the giver. Once that obligation was denied, the eagerness to present gifts evaporated. Two representatives of Tokyo-Shibaura, electric machinery and appliance manufacturers, tried to give me a console radio–phonograph in March 1946 after I had stated in writing that looting factories was an improper way for their Korean former contract (forced) laborers to compensate themselves for the hardship and indignities they had suffered during the war. I told my visitors that I could not accept the set as a gift but would be happy to pay the wholesale price. They never returned. Pure helpfulness was not what they had in mind.

Bribery, whether direct or camouflaged, was not very common in GHQ, nor was it successful. The level of GHQ morality turned out to be surprisingly high. For some, perhaps, a deep sense of involvement in a historic mission blocked out thoughts of seriously looking for bribes; for others, perhaps, the language barrier got in the way. For most, it could have been simply that as SCAP officials they had nothing to sell. After all, SCAP Headquarters was ordinarily involved not in operations but in issues and in supervising a Japanese Government. The burden of maintaining administrative honesty while approving subsidies, loans, price increases, licenses, and so forth fell much more heavily on the Japanese Government, for which it was a serious and widespread problem. For SCAP it was only minor.

True, where SCAP entered directly into economic controls, suspicious cases did arise. As special assistant (as well as economic adviser) for more than three years to the Chief of ESS, I heard accusations that a few of our commodity specialists received favors in return for export and import approvals and rather more charges of partiality toward private American businessmen. On the other hand, our Foreign Trade Division's Claims Branch was convinced that American traders were out to victimize the defenseless Japanese. The most serious charge of bribery I heard, after the Occupation, was that one of our Industry Division officials had received, after he left GHQ, a valuable parcel of land in Azabu, near downtown Tokyo, in return for dropping a shipyard from the reparations removal list. In fact, he did get that land. Ultimately, all shipyards were dropped, so the bribe, if that is what it was, was wasted.

Speaking from my own experience, however, no "black mist" enveloped GHQ, regardless of what later scandal sheets insinuated. Only one of the allegations made against ESS personnel in my five years with the section was proved. Some divisions, like the much-partied Antitrust Division, went out of their way to avoid favoring their benefactors. Perhaps the best proof of honesty at the upper levels was the fact that nothing specific of the extensive intra-GHQ discussions of the forthcoming dollar–yen exchange rate leaked out, and the fortunes that could have been made were not. Generally speaking, SCAP was clean.

PERSONAL IDEOLOGIES AND OCCUPATION POLICY

Lack of sympathy with the Occupation mission on the part of staff members was another danger. In Germany sabotage of mission, or at least foot-dragging by responsible Occupation officials, had already become public in various areas. In Japan, MacArthur's spirited and unambiguous leadership made those tactics risky for officials at the higher levels. Few dared cross the Supreme Commander. In most cases professional officers could be trusted to obey their orders to the best of their ability. But there were those who filtered their understanding through their world outlook. No orders could have been more unambiguous than SCAP's Command Letter of November 1945 to the Eighth Army forbidding any involvement in labor disputes. Still, a Military Police lieutenant strode into a collective bargaining session at a Tōshiba Electric Company plant[14] one day in October 1946, evicted all but twenty negotiators, and closed the doors to all others until the strike was settled.

The civilians recruited for GHQ were less disciplined. Some of them had been posted to Japan before the war and remembered fondly how things had been then. The electro-communications specialists hired for our Civil Communications Section, for example, found it hard to understand why democratization required a purge or breakup of the large telecommunication companies, which would interfere with the recovery of their industry—as if the reason for the Occupation was to improve telecommunications in Japan. Some of our industry specialists in ESS felt somewhat the same way; the democratizers were interfering with their job. Perhaps the most critical were the representatives of the big oil companies in G-4 Petroleum, selected for their technical expertise. They were certainly competent, but they could not refrain from sympathizing with their private Japanese oil company counterparts in such matters as the domestic price of gasoline, which, after all, was none of their business.

It is not surprising that such individuals, meeting with like-minded conservatives nightly in the incestuous atmosphere of Officers' Clubs—there were hardly any other on-limits amusements in the first year and a half—would reinforce each other's convictions that radicals had surreptitiously taken over GHQ. (Of course, they were not aware that radical reform was official U.S. policy.) Welsh, the Chief of the ESS Antitrust and Cartels Division, came in for his share of obloquy, but it was the labor issue, with noisy union parades flaunting red banners in the streets and highly publicized strikes, that was most likely to set them off.

Perhaps that was the reason I, as chief and then former chief of the Labor Division, seemed to attract their ire disproportionately, particularly after they had had a few drinks. In May 1950, Major General George Eberle, G-4 Supply, wrote to General Marquat apologizing for two of his petroleum advisers who had been overheard calling me a Communist. "I am sure you know how much I regret this inexcusable affront to a member of your section," he said.[15] Neither of the two had ever met me. On an earlier occasion, in 1946, an onlooker at the nightly poker game in the Daiichi Hotel[16] cellar bar regarded me fixedly for perhaps twenty minutes, then suddenly announced he was going to kill me because I was a Red, and stalked out. He turned out to be an industrial technician. I did not know him either. In any event, the Army command structure made those extreme reactions irrelevant even if personally uncomfortable.

The danger from Communist personnel in GHQ could have been much greater—on that one point Willoughby was correct—for such people acted in organized fashion, and surreptitiously. In a liberal reform Occupation, moreover, they managed to cast themselves as particularly dedicated liberals and blend in with the other reformers. One highly placed adviser to the Government Section, for example, tried hard to persuade me that a general strike shutting down the country was no different from an ordinary strike, only bigger. Unfortunately, it took a measure of political sophistication to tell the difference between a liberal or independent radical on the one hand and a Communist on the other. Most of our higher officers had never knowingly met a Communist in their lives and could not tell one from a cornstalk in Iowa.

Recruits for GHQ SCAP in the theater, that is, from among combat officers, were gentlemen and presumed trustworthy, and the Pacific war, especially in places like New Guinea, was as far from politics as one could get. In Tokyo, the recruitment process was too rushed to permit any reliable security review. As for Stateside recruitment, anyone already working and cleared for government service was presumed to be acceptable in GHQ. But that was hardly a guarantee. (In 1943, when my security clearances had to be confirmed in connection with a mission to Moscow, the security officer for the "cloak-and-dagger" Office of Strategic Services was much upset to discover that I had been handling confidential and secret documents as an OSS analyst for almost three years without any formal clearance on my record. I was then cleared formally.) After the new recruits went to work, very few of their division chiefs ever gave serious thought to the possibility that some might be Communists. The chiefs didn't have the time; besides, they thought they knew and could trust their own people.

With all those loopholes, the number of Communists in the Japanese Occupation was remarkably small. Most American Communists were personally more interested in Europe anyway, and perhaps the higher priority the party assigned to the infiltration of the Military Government in Germany exhausted their available manpower. With my background and labor mission, I was preternaturally suspicious of Communist infiltration, and at no time could I count more than five or six of them in GHQ. Three were in the Civil Information and Education Section, where it would not have surprised me to learn they had a cell going. In April 1946 Ken Dyke,[17] the section chief, relieved two of them assigned to stage and films and then abolished CIE Labor Education, where one young and personable lieutenant was suspect because he had been one of Harry Bridges's Longshoremen's Union organizers at a time when the Communists dominated that union. Similarly, the Government Section terminated the contract of one analyst recruited from the FEA Economic Institutions staff after only three months when it discovered his Communist connections and those of his wife. For my part, as Chief of the Labor Division, I refused to extend the temporary assignment of a lieutenant when I found he had been a paid organizer for the Communist-controlled United Electrical Workers–CIO. I just could not imagine the Communist leadership wasting union money on non-Communists. All of this, be it noted, took place in the spring and summer of 1946, well before Willoughby launched his drive against "leftists" in GHQ.

Then there was that senior adviser to General Whitney. He lasted for more than a year. Whitney staunchly defended him against charges of being a Communist on a number of occasions, but finally, to settle the matter in his own mind, called him in and asked him to sign a prepared statement affirming that he had never been a member of the Communist party. When the adviser refused on the grounds that it would abridge his civil rights, Whitney had him separated and sent home. That left only three questionables. As General MacArthur said to George F. Kennan, they didn't mean much.

Not counting the Willoughby "leftist infiltration" exercise, GHQ did very little about subversives until the loyalty program ordered from Washington reached the theater. And then, in 1948 and 1949, a whole new wave of names and lists of associated names cropped up. A division chief in ESS and some less prominent officials were sent back home. (After a Stateside investigation, the division chief was restored a year later to GHQ at his old rank.) The continuous loyalty-security process and the informants it seemed to attract ultimately made GHQ an unpleasant place to work. Marquat was called over from time to time to G-2 to see the results. He reported to me that I was noted in the files as a regular habitué of the Mimatsu Dance Hall in spite of the fact that, alas, I was no dancer. He also disclosed that we had a few spies in ESS, including our Labor Education Branch Chief, who to Marquat's infinite disgust was reporting to the Chief of Staff over Marquat's head.

Whatever its merits elsewhere, I could never convince myself that the Washington loyalty program ever did much good in Japan, except to reassure the squeamish. On the contrary, the program had a chilling effect on relations between the SCAP people and Japanese intellectuals, who usually were socialists. Association between them was likely to raise questions for the unsophisticated security officers in GHQ. Sometimes an affair did not have to be political to start with. One American middle-level official had been asked by a group of college students, one of whom worked as security guard at the official's residence, to hold weekly discussions with them in English. Inevitably the discussion turned to current events, and the official was reported as running a Communist cell in his home.

In spite of all the unpleasantness, however, the 1948–49 Washington loyalty program did not change the Occupation reforms, for it came late, when all the main projects were already in place. The nonideological economic recovery fervor that dominated GHQ at that time was invulnerable to charges of that nature.

THE RUSSIANS

Of course, the Americans were not alone as occupiers. Ten other nations were also involved, but most of them were concerned at first with recovering or setting up embassies and with related housekeeping and then with strictly national interests. The British focused on commercial affairs and getting back prewar British properties; recovering patents, copyrights, and designs together with the interim fees for using them; resuming the operation of British shipping, banks, and insurance companies; and securing airline landing rights. The Nationalist Chinese were even more narrowly interested in commerce, although on an individual basis. Almost every member of the huge Chinese mission was understood to be running his own private enterprise in some aspect of the black market, including PX supplies, for their official salaries were inadequate. Even the Australians and New Zealanders, outspoken though their representative might be in the Allied Council for Japan, were principally concerned with commerce. Some of the smaller countries were preoccupied only with reparations.

But the Russians—well, that was different. Surely Stalin had not insisted with so much vehemence on a meaningful share in the Japanese Occupation just to settle for a ringside observer's seat. It was only logical that the Soviets would try to use that seat to influence domestic politics in Japan. From the beginning, however, things just did not work out for the Soviet mission. When the fiery local Communist leader Tokuda Kyūichi rejected the Comintern choice, Nozaka Sanzō, to take over the Japan Communist party (JCP), his followers stood by him, and the Soviets were without their expected leverage. Then MacArthur fenced in the Soviet mission members as completely as he could without a diplomatic incident. Americans were not allowed to travel farther than 25 miles from Moscow? Very well, the Soviet mission members were not allowed more than 25 miles from Tokyo. The Soviets, further, were not allowed any official activities other than one justice and a prosecution group in the International War Crimes Tribunal. They got no representation among defense counsel, but then probably they did not want any. In any event, they were never able to find an excuse for exceeding the 25-mile limit or for mingling with the Japanese even within Tokyo.

In fact, the Russian ties with the JCP seem to have been weaker than the Americans would have dared hope. None of the Japanese ex-Communists who have written memoirs of those days have ever referred to orders from Mamiana-chō (site of the Soviet Embassy) to Yoyogi (the JCP headquarters) in the way that American ex-Communists[18] have talked of the heavily accented orders from a succession of Comintern "international reps," dictating to the "ninth floor" of 50 East Thirteenth Street, Manhattan, where the American Communist Party Central Committee was housed. The Japanese relationship was entirely different. When the Soviet-backed Nozaka and the local leader, Tokuda, clashed on the Emperor question, the Party followed Tokuda. That would have been inconceivable had the Soviet mission dominated the Japan Communist party.

Many years later, Takano Minoru's reminiscences to me confirmed my impression of the distant Soviet relationship with the JCP. Invited to the Soviet Embassy several times in 1946, Takano, a left-wing socialist opponent of the Communists, was puzzled by the invitations but accepted out of curiosity. At the Embassy, Derevyanko's aides quizzed him repeatedly in the presence of the Russian general about various personalities within the Japanese labor movement. Many of them must have been known to the Soviets through the JCP. Takano speculated that the Russians must have been fishing for corroboration and more information. "It seemed," he said, "that the Soviets were looking for potential agents or candidates outside the JCP. Maybe they did not trust Comrade Tokuda."[19]

If there was little or no official contact between Americans and the Russian mission men in 1946, the same could not be said of social contact. For almost a year after their arrival in Japan, the Russian majors and colonels were billeted together with Americans and sundry other nationalities—Australians, New Zealanders, Indians, and Chinese—of equivalent military and civilian rank in the Daiichi Hotel in Shimbashi. The eight-story modern, boxlike concrete structure had 650 tiny guest rooms—so tiny, we used to say, that if one entered a room too fast he might find himself going out the window—one dining room, two bars, a roof garden, a branch post exchange, and a service staff of 1,200 Japanese. For a short time in 1946, it was one of the unique hostelries of the world, unmatched in its concentration of governmental power, its clashing of national uniforms and outlooks, and the unorthodox sexual behavior of its residents. Until dependent wives and families started to come over, practically all of the American GHQ division chiefs, assistant chiefs, and branch chiefs resided there, plus two section chiefs as well.

Most of the residents being Americans, the hotel had an unmistakable American flavor. The nightly American high-stakes poker game in one corner of the lobby, presided over by hard-bitten, laconic, cigar-smoking Regular Army colonels, lent a certain stability to the hotel's social life. The officers' club bar in the lobby, thronged before dinner by those trying to throw off the pressures of the day, was a clearing house of information on the day's events. But after dinner, the drinkers preferred the cellar bar, which also had a ping-pong table. The near silence of the lobby was then punctuated only by the occasional rustling departure of some officer's kimono-clad date slipping down the main stairway from the rooms above and the muted sounds of revelry from below.

Here the few Russians were in their element, congregating at the same tables every night and thoroughly enjoying themselves. To the Americans' songs—"Bluetail Fly" and "Roll Me Over in the Clover"—the Russians would respond with the "Volga Boatman." One Soviet major delighted in holding the final bravura high note for an unbelievable ninety seconds, to the fervent applause of the Americans. In other ways, too, the Russians would concede nothing. One Soviet lieutenant colonel, watching a double-jointed American touch his forearm with his thumb bent backward, blurted out, "Anything American can do, Russian can do." He then slowly bent his thumb way back until, with a loud crack that startled everyone in the room, he broke his thumb.

It was not only in the bar that Russians and Americans joined forces in drinking. At one notable party in the third-floor room of an American colonel, the American and two Russians took to parading up the hotel corridor in single file uproariously singing a martial tune that ended with the words that appeared to be "On to Budapest!" Afterward, sitting relaxed at the open window, the American colonel, glass in hand, lost his balance and slowly toppled out into the night. "He is my friend! I save him!" one of the Russians roared and promptly jumped out after the American. The American landed in a high hedge two floors below, momentarily unhurt, until an instant later the Russian crashed down on top of him, a boot heel in his friend's eye. Next morning at breakfast, the American sported a black eye, a plaster strip, a hangover, and a determined silence. The Russians were nowhere to be seen.

It was a camaraderie of men who had faced great personal danger but now could relax and, being far from home, were receptive to kindred spirits whatever their uniform. Nevertheless, there were always sharp differences in outlook looming beneath the surface.

Common political ground was impossible to achieve. Returning from a drive in the country one sleepy Sunday summer afternoon, I found one of my Labor Division officers in the cool Daiichi Hotel cellar bar deep in a drunkenly solemn discussion with a Russian officer on the nature of democracy. The American insisted on pointing out at great length the deficiencies of a one-party system and the Soviet election process. The Russian officer listened patiently and then rejoined that the Americans could not call themselves democratic if General MacArthur would not allow the Soviet officers to travel more than 25 miles outside of Tokyo. The American, perhaps too drunk to remember the 25-mile limit on Americans in Moscow, gravely acknowledged that the Russian had something there, but he considered election procedures in the Soviet Union more important. The Russian then said that when the weather was hot, nothing was more important than to go more than 25 miles outside of Tokyo. And so on, back and forth, until one gently fell asleep and the other carefully picked his way out of the bar.

The representatives of the various countries that officially made up the Occupation lent color, variety, and some measure of international sanction, but that was all. A few non-Americans held positions in SCAP. Brigadier O'Brien, the Chief of the ESS Scientific Division, was an Australian, and so was General Whitney's secretary. Further, the Allies shared in the prosecution of the war criminals and in judging them, and a number of countries had reparations missions. But they were divorced from the Occupation mainstream.

THE FOREIGN CORRESPONDENTS

Outside of GHQ SCAP, only one group of nonofficials had any effective influence: the foreign correspondents. In a headquarters that was super-sensitive to what the American people would be reading about them with their breakfast coffee, the care and feeding of the reporters received high priority, even if the reporters didn't particularly care for the heavy-handed way it was sometimes done. Later on, correspondents with families were assigned to requisitioned Japanese houses on the same basis as Occupation staffers, but even as early as the Spring of 1946 the correspondents obtained their own building in downtown Tokyo, at number one "Shimbun [newspaper] Alley," as they christened the narrow, block-long street. For a long time it was the only on-limits alternative to military facilities for Occupation people; certainly it was the only place to get a sandwich at night. The correspondents were usually billeted there, and military off-limits rules did not apply. They could have anyone as their guests, a privilege that suddenly seemed a little chancy when two correspondents discovered that the elevator boy was meticulously keeping a record in his school notebooks of every nocturnal arrival and departure. He claimed that no one put him up to it— he just liked to keep records. But the notebooks could well have wrecked half the Press Club members' happy marriages until the two reporters wheedled his notebooks away from him, put them to the torch, and threatened him with dismemberment if he ever kept such records again.

The foreign correspondents were in Japan to gather news, and copy under some of the most prestigious by-lines were filed at one time or another from Tokyo, often composed on the Press Club typewriters. But many of the reporters held strong and diverse political opinions themselves, and their writings, intentionally or not, exerted political pressure on Occupation operations.

Miles Vaughn of the United Press; Burton Crane, economic reporter of the *New York Times;* and Walter Simmons of the *Chicago Tribune* were the chief American conservatives, while Mark Gayn of the *Chicago Sun,* Gordon Walker of the *Christian Science Monitor,* and Joseph Fromm of *U.S. News and World Report* represented the liberals and left. Russell Brines of AP, Ernest Hoberecht of UP, Hessell Tiltman of the *Manchester Guardian,* Keyes Beech of the *Chicago Daily News,* and Howard Handleman of International News Service were politically neutral or moderate. At the beginning of the Occupation the liberal critics occasionally stung the brass, but thereafter it was overwhelmingly the conservatives whose words drew the most notice, especially when like-thinking officers around MacArthur managed to bring clippings of their dispatches to the SCAP's attention. It was assumed that conservative reporters had the ear of their publishers, and the 1948 elections were not far away.

Many of the conservative American reporters had done tours in Japan before the war—like the State Department foreign-service officers, living as Americans in prewar Japan tended to make them conservative too—and they considered themselves experts on the country. Those correspondents retained their old sources and connections, typically among the prewar political and business giants, who were now mostly purged, resentful, and not at all averse to spreading poisonous stories about liberal Occupation officials through their American friends in the press. The journalists agreed that such Occupation officials were young and callow, doctrinaire, and impractical reformers or worse. When Roy Howard, then perhaps the most powerful press lord in America, came to Japan in early 1947, he was briefed by his man on the spot, Miles Vaughn, and then recommended to General MacArthur in a private interview that the radical Occupation labor policies be drastically changed. Unlike the liberal reporters, who had visited me frequently, Vaughn, in more than a year, had never once called at the Labor Division. Sometimes, such a visit could be more damaging than complete avoidance. I do not suppose Burton Crane would have approved of "my" policies in any case, but when I asked him to get his shoes off my coffee table, that eliminated any tendency to soften his dispatches about Occupation labor programs.

My lack of diplomacy was regrettable, of course, but the power of the *New York Times,* real or imagined, was a fact of GHQ life that could not be ignored, as officials tried to stay on the good side of the correspondents. The sharp decline in American press coverage of Japan in 1947 and 1948 did not visibly reduce the Occupation's concern. Perhaps the Japanese press was easily handled, but the American press was a power to be reckoned with in Occupation circles until the end.

THE SCAP STAFF IN RETROSPECT

Even so, the Occupation power on a daily basis resided with the SCAP staff in the first instance. They were indispensable, and they intruded almost everywhere in Japanese Government operations. Numbering less than one out of every 15 or so Allied officers and civilians in Tokyo, less than half of 1 percent of the total occupying force, they called most of the shots on the government of the country—not without limitations, not without supervision, and not on their own authority, but with enormous influence nonetheless.

With all their influence, the SCAP staff had nothing to say about relations between the Occupationnaires (including themselves) and the Japanese public. That subject was entirely within the purview of AFPAC/FEC, and in the Army's view it was none of the SCAP officials' business how the Army was run. The separation was unfortunate. While SCAP was preaching democracy, AFPAC/FEC enforced a contrary military discipline on a considerable number of Japanese. GHQ, in effect, spoke with two voices. The result was a galloping case of schizophrenia.

7

Men, Women, and Martinets

IF THE JAPANESE had not themselves occupied China, the Philippines, and other Southeast Asian countries so recently, perhaps they would not have faced the entry of American troops into their own country with such dread. Despite military censorship,[1] the Japanese public was quite conscious of its army's misbehavior, even its atrocities, in the lands they occupied. Arrogance toward inferiors was normal practice in Japan and certainly understandable toward subject populations. But enough of their soldiers had returned home to their families with vivid and often boastful tales of brutalities toward terror-stricken Chinese and Filipinos to convince the Japanese at home that occupation armies were dreadful and uncontrollable once let loose in a conquered land.

"Bear the unbearable and suffer the insufferable," the Emperor had told his people in his surrender broadcast. Of the terrible trials to come, not the least was the oncoming occupation army. Unable to see why the American soldiers would be any gentler than their own, the fearful Japanese awaited the inevitable. In the two weeks before the entry of the Americans, the radio repeatedly warned women to go to their families in the countryside, and on August 29 men with megaphones passed through the streets of Yokohama with houses still standing to repeat the warning and urge all females to stay indoors when the Americans arrived. Japan prepared for the onslaught.

A LIGHT FROM A NEW WORLD

To their astonishment, nothing of the kind took place. Weary of fighting and of long years in jungles or primitive areas of the Solomons, New Guinea,

119

and the rural Philippines, the ordinary American soldier was delighted to be at peace in a civilized, although terribly battered, country. He had nothing against the inhabitants of Japan, not recognizing at all in the Japanese he saw there— women, children, and even male civilians—the warriors he had been battling for years in the islands. Indeed, he was astonished at the apparent amiability and cooperativeness of the Japanese once he landed in Japan. Almost none of the Japanese, for their part, had ever seen any American fighting men close up. They knew only the stately and deadly B-29s sowing flames from the night sky, not the men who piloted them and released their bombs. Perhaps it would have been very different if the invasion had taken place and fighting had raged in the country lanes or rubbled cities where the individual combatants could be seen. As it was, after almost four years of war the individuals on both sides had nothing against each other when they finally met.

The first few weeks saw both sides thoughtfully reconsidering their basic attitudes. The GIs, wandering around with intense curiosity, gave their extra chocolate and chewing gum to the Japanese children, who, once they overcame their shyness, were ready to sing choruses of *"Haru ga kita"* ("Spring Has Come") and *"Chō-chō"* ("Butterfly") for their conquerors. Japanese adults were coming to the conclusion that "they" were not so bad. Almost all were endlessly curious and wanted to know more of the outside world from which they had been so completely isolated by their militarists. The American visitors were now windows on that world. In the meantime, clearly, the Occupation forces were neither punishing them nor living off their substance, as they could see with their own eyes.

Although the immediate power balance between conquerors and conquered would seem to indicate the exact opposite, it was far more important for the Americans to impress the Japanese favorably than vice versa. The success of the Occupation and the acceptance by the Japanese of American objectives depended on it. In an occupation that claimed to be liberating the people from the bad old days, it was imperative that the occupiers act like liberators. By Japanese standards, and especially in light of initial Japanese fears, they surely did.

Perhaps what made the greatest impression on the Japanese were the everyday courtesies of Americans whose counterparts in a status-ridden society were so different. When American soldiers stood up in a crowded trolley or bus to offer their seats to Japanese women, the Japanese passengers were stunned. In Japan men did not publicly defer to women.[2] On one occasion it took several minutes of "you first" motions to persuade a Japanese cleaning woman to pass through a Headquarters corridor door before an American officer. One can imagine the story she told her family that night. On another occasion in Kyoto an old country woman with a handcart of fruit, surprised by the clang of an oncoming trolley car on which I was a passenger, upended her cart, spilling fruit over the tracks. The trolley managed to come to a stop in time, and as the woman set about painstakingly picking up the fruit, two impatient GI passengers jumped down from the car and to the astonishment of the other passengers helped to gather up the fruit and speed the trolley and themselves on their way. In the fog of grievances that so many lowly Japanese (and most were lowly), had against their social superiors, the Occupation troops' behavior shone through like sunshine from a new world.

It was not only a question of egalitarianism. In Japanese society, where spontaneity, at least in public, was rare, the spontaneous behavior of the Americans brought admiration. One evening, while two of my labor officers and I were returning by jeep from the outskirts of Tokyo, we spotted a red glow in the sky. Hurrying to the scene, we found a growing conflagration. Firemen whose unreeled hoses were not long enough to reach the water supply were standing around uncertainly, and onlookers watched impassively. My officers jumped out and began furiously to drag inflammable material from the fire's path, creating a firebreak, shouting and gesticulating all the while to the onlookers to help, which they eventually did. The fire was contained, and the crowd was deeply impressed.

On another occasion, a GI jumped into a river to rescue a drowning Japanese boy, while the civilian crowd, possibly nonswimmers, did nothing. The newspapers reported the incident with admiration and asked why a Japanese had not jumped to the rescue. Again, walking one Sunday afternoon in Tokyo's Ueno Park in the spring of 1946, I saw a middle-aged Japanese man slump to the walk, apparently overcome by hunger. Numerous Japanese pedestrians walked right around him while an American ran to fetch a policeman. Of course, there were good Japanese reasons for not offering help—putting someone under an obligation without his consent, risking long-term involvement with the victim, and so on. Kindness in traditional Japan, especially toward strangers, had to be tempered with caution. But now the Japanese, inclined to believe that "traditional behavior" was somehow responsible for their defeat, were in the mood to question. The Americans' actions offered an alternative pattern, more immediately "rational," and what is more, it had proved more successful.

Throughout the entire Occupation there was a uniform strand of generosity on the part of the Occupying forces, at least until the Army prohibited it. Army mess rations were so huge—4,000 calories daily—and canned "C" rations or boxed "K" rations so easy to acquire that Americans usually brought food along on visits to Japanese. Many an American, striking up an acquaintanceship with a Japanese man or girl, came to call on his or her family out of curiosity and then proceeded to supply such rations regularly, introducing many Japanese to the unfamiliar taste of ham and eggs and processed cheese. Local liaison men and interpreters whose duties brought them frequently to GHQ were also helped by friendly Americans. Later on, perhaps, the incidents were remembered in a prosperous Japan with a tinge of embarrassment or shame, but at the time the gifts were lifesavers, which the recipients never forgot. In true Japanese fashion the gratitude and the friendships engendered by such help lasted for many years.

The contrast between such spontaneous generosity—easier when one has something to give—and their own dark rejection in the turmoil of war, when friends and even family deserted them, led many Japanese to despair of their own people. A Japanese girl on a train once told me that after her parents were killed in an air raid, none of her family would take her in. "That's the way the Japanese are," she said. A twelve-year-old who had lost a hand in a fire-bombing and, rejected by everyone, had subsisted since by shining shoes with the remaining hand commented particularly bitterly in GI patois: "Japanese no fuckin' good!"

Each experience with Americans was as different as the individuals involved, and perhaps the Japanese generalized mistakenly or tended to read too much into what were often casual gestures. Indeed, some ugly incidents also took place. Two soldiers tossed an overinsistent prostitute into the canal at Sukiyabashi in the heart of Tokyo, where the poor girl, unable to swim a stroke, drowned. A GI on guard duty killed some Japanese youths looting U.S. Army property—why hadn't he shot to disable if they were running away? Americans were also guilty of occasional rapes and drunken brawls.

But the overwhelming majority of encounters were pleasant, and there were so many American soldiers all over Japan—600,000 to begin with and well over 100,000 for most of the Occupation—that a very large number of Japanese were able to gain firsthand favorable impressions of the Americans somewhere along the line. Those experiences could not be dismissed as propaganda, and their impact on a people grasping at straws was stunning. Personal fraternization, demonstrating a freer and kindlier way of life, certainly a different one, convinced the Japanese that the more abstract ideas of GHQ were worth listening to. It was the secret weapon of the early Occupation.

Curiously, the fraternization phenomenon was as unexpected as it was unplanned. In Germany, the initial U.S. policy of strict nonfraternization had proved unenforceable and, moreover, had raised a storm of protest from labor and liberal organizations in the United States. Washington would not, therefore, order a nonfraternization policy in Japan. But neither would it go to the opposite extreme at such a distance. Washington left the question up to General MacArthur.

The State Department SWNCC 150/4 stated: "Association of personnel of the occupation forces with the Japanese population should be controlled *only* to the extent necessary to further the policies and objectives of the occupation."[3] The directive, JCS 1380/15, put it another way: "With this end in view [i.e., demonstrating to the Japanese that militarism does not pay] and to insure the security of the troops, a policy of non-fraternization may be applied to Japan if and to the extent you may deem it desirable."[4]

Those orders suited General MacArthur perfectly. It was hard to see how security or proving that militarism did not pay would be served by keeping the Americans and Japanese apart. Anything but a prude, and loyal as always to his men, MacArthur was grateful for their immense contribution to victory and deeply conscious of the trials they had undergone. They needed companionship, he thought. Fraternization with Japanese women was inevitable. Why harass them? "They keep trying to get me to stop all this Madame Butterflying around," he once told his aide, Major Faubion Bowers (an outstanding expert on Japanese Kabuki theater), "I won't do it. . . . I wouldn't issue a non-fraternization order for all the tea in China."[5] He was convinced of the beneficial effect of greater contact between Americans and Japanese. Seeing the behavior of the ordinary American soldier gave the Japanese, he said, "the opportunity for comparison between the qualities of the old and the new . . . more particularly, from close-hand observation of the American soldier standing in their midst, reflecting as he does those fine traits of character, outgrowth of the American home."[6] As a result, fraternization in varying degrees became the order of the day for the Americans.

In the British Commonwealth Occupation Forces area matters turned out otherwise. Perhaps it was an echo of the long-time British establishment dread of their colonials' "going native." "You must not enter their homes nor take part in their family life," General John Northcott told his men.[7] But then, the American Command understood how much the Australians hated the Japanese at that time and how much they feared that their underpopulated continent might be swamped by Asian immigration. At any rate, the BCOF area was a relatively minor corner of Japan. GHQ paid little attention to BCOF internal policies.

SINGLE MEN IN BARRACKS

Whatever its technical meaning, everyone understood that "fraternization" for the most part involved relations between American men and Japanese women. It could not be otherwise. At the beginning of 1946, Occupation men outnumbered women by a ratio of a few hundred to one. Three months later, after a substantial influx of professional and secretarial women plus the introduction of civilianized WACs from elsewhere in the theater, the GHQ telephone directory still listed 3,760 men and only 453 women among the officers and civilians, a ratio of eight to one. In the field outside Tokyo it was many times more lopsided. Many of the American women, moreover, were beyond the romanticaly attractive age. For ordinary enlisted men, it goes without saying, the only female companionship available was Japanese. International dating became the norm.

Both sexes found an exotic attraction for each other. The Japanese girls were surprised by the deference and gentleness of the American men, while the

American men were equally surprised by the deference and gentleness of the Japanese women. The result was that in 1946 a good part of the GHQ men, perhaps 40 percent by my observation at the time, had regular Japanese girl friends. After American wives and families began to arrive in numbers in 1947, the percentage fell, but even then I doubt that it went below 20 percent. The commingling reached near the top levels of the Headquarters itself. Two successive deputy chiefs of the Government Section had secret Japanese girl friends, and one married his. In the Labor Division, five of the top seven members were similarly involved, and two married their sweethearts. Even the Army Judge Advocate's chief civilian legal adviser, who drafted the exceptionally severe personnel control and "black market" regulations, turned out to have had a Japanese mistress all along.

In the difficult and complicated situation that prevailed—the Japanese women were enemy nationals, Orientals were forbidden entry into the United States to settle, and social ostracism was the common reaction to interracial marriages in most of the United States at the time—there were undoubtedly many blighted affairs. To the Americans, dating was a game in which both parties had to take care of themselves and knew it. To the Japanese women, however, casual dating was new, love and marriage deadly serious, and virginity a prerequisite to marriage in a good family. The bittersweet "Chō-chō" or "Butterfly" song the Japanese women sang, chiding the man with his many girl friends—"he alights on every leaf"—was rarely taken seriously by the Americans. How many new Madame Butterflies were created can only be guessed at. One Occupation official I knew abandoned his lovely sweetheart when he learned she had contracted intestinal tuberculosis, because he thought he might catch it. True, he paid her hospital expenses, while her father callously gathered up her clothes and sold them on the day she went to the hospital because she would shortly die anyway and would not be needing them any more. Other tragedies had more pedestrian causes—the arrival of a wife, the passing of an infatuation, or rotation back home.

The visible consequences of the broken unions were around for years. Their Eurasian children were regularly rejected by an insular, racist Japanese society that really had no place for foreigners, let alone those of mixed parentage, and could not digest them except in show business, modeling, interpreting, and similar occupations. The plight of the offspring of Japanese girls and black soldiers was particularly poignant, for their parentage was more immediately obvious. Besides, the Japanese always felt uneasy in the presence of blacks, who were so strange to them. Not all the children had terrible lives. The fatherless son of the Daiichi Hotel front desk manageress went through Nippon University and became a successful businessman. But most had a very hard row to hoe. Occupations can leave as many hostages to fortune as wars can take.

Stories can also be told of exceptional love and constancy. An American wire service correspondent, married to a Japanese girl before the war, learned in America that she was dying of an incurable illness. He just managed to make it to her bedside after the surrender before she died. In tribute to her he wrote a fictional account of their affair, which, published in Japanese under the title "Tokyo Romance," became a runaway bestseller in the early months of the Occupation.

Indeed, most marriages that took place between Japanese women and American men—excluding those of immature, infatuated young soldiers or Japanese bar girls scheming to get rich quick—stood up much better than comparable all-American marriages. The difficulties involved in getting married against Army disapproval and the prospect of future social rejection eliminated the casual, impulsive wedding and fire-hardened the marriage relationship. Couples had to be sure they cared deeply for each other before they tied the knot.

In the end several thousand Japanese–American marriages took place, including those of the future Dean of the Graduate School of Washington University in St. Louis, a future vice president of Booz, Allen, Hamilton (International), and a number of future business executives with such firms as International Telephone & Telegraph. One Japanese wife, after naturalization, even became a Democratic party district leader in St. Louis and a national official of Americans for Democratic Action. In later years the children of those couples constituted a special bond between the two nations, together with the ubiquitous Japanese grocery stores to be found outside almost every large Army or Air Force base within the United States. When the time came, the Japanese wives could live without their children, but not without their food.

Neither the Japanese nor the American authorities appreciated the seriousness of the situation. To the Japanese it was simply a familiar biological problem. The Home Ministry knew from the Imperial Army's recent experience in China how fearsome the uncontrolled sex drive of a conquering army could be. What the government wanted was to divert the Americans from the respectable Japanese women. Right at the beginning of the Occupation, officials called on the operators of the bombed-out night clubs and bars, *machiai* (houses of assignation), and brothels to mobilize all their available female talent in the various branches of the intimate entertainment industry—bar hostesses, geisha, pseudo-geisha, prostitutes—for service under one umbrella organization, the Recreation and Amusement Association.

The RAA was formed with extraordinary speed and showed a remarkable ability to secure facilities and building materials in short supply. Within weeks it was operating beerhalls and similar establishments for GIs, sometimes with considerable ingenuity. For example, in the center of Ginza, where all but a handful of buildings had been destroyed by the war, the RAA operated a hostess-beerhall for enlisted men in the second subcellar of what had become a vacant lot. It was appropriately called Oasis of Ginza. Next door, the U.S. Army Medical Corps set up a prophylaxis station to deal with venereal disease.

The RAA stood ready to provide female companionship for a wide range of activities, from the equivalent of church socials, models in kimonos for photographic competitions, innocuous military unit dance parties, beerhall hostessing, all the way to prostitution. They had few illusions that the demarcation lines were absolute, but the girls were usually of that minority of "unrespectable" women anyway, and the purpose was patriotic: to keep Japanese blood lines pure and the family system intact. In the words of a popular Occupation song, "to save our nation's maids, they said, you've got to keep those Yanks in bed."

The most startling monument to that philosophy was the International Palace, or "IP," opened by the RAA in late 1945 for Occupation personnel only in Funabashi, between Tokyo and the neighboring city of Chiba. Probably the largest brothel in the world at the time, its assembly-line style made it known to some as "Willow Run," after the giant bomber factory built by the Ford Motor Company during the war (and, unbeknownst to most of the GIs, from the Japanese term for the prostitution quarters, the "flower and willow world"). The entering soldier or sailor would leave his shoes, Japanese-style, at the entrance and would then pick them up, cleaned and shined, at the other end of the long barracks-like structure when he left. News photographs of this marvel in the American press with long lines of GIs waiting outside shocked a number of parents and occasioned several letters to the War Department and the chaplains. Then a congressman arrived on a survey and discovered the IP. That was enough to persuade the Command to shut it down after only a few months, thereby puzzling the RAA officials who were proud of their efficiency and rapid service. Surely it surpassed the cumbersome system of "comfort girls" the Japanese Army used to dispatch overseas. Thereafter centrally supplied, open prostitution was out.

More discreet hostess cabarets, separate for black and white servicemen— just as the Army itself was segregated in those days—took their place. The RAA, having soon learned that American race mixtures and alcohol often ended in brawls, supported segregation. The cabarets were set down near the units, and the engineer and port units, mostly black, were located away from the others, mostly white. A black soldier entering a white cabaret was met with country and western music and unfriendly stares; a white who opened the door of a black cabaret, hearing blues and boogie-woogie, would receive a clear signal that this was not his turf. The RAA dispensed "beer and broads" evenhandedly to both.

The initial attitude of the American Army authorities toward sex was as pragmatic as it was toward alcohol. From the beginning, the Army made strenuous efforts, long before powdered milk became available, to provide individual liquor rations to the officers and local beer to the men through their clubs. I could never understand that order of priorities until one day in the billiard room of the Tokyo Red Cross Club (located in the Bankers Club building) I saw a young sailor seated with head in hands, apparently hung over from a binge the night before. After a while he removed his hands, opened his eyes, and discovered to his horror that he was blind, presumably from drinking the methyl alcohol. His uninterrupted screaming for long minutes till he was led from the room impressed me deeply. When my Labor Division sponsored a conference of Eighth Army labor officers from all over Japan the following month, we agonized for a long time on which brand of liquor, Tomy's or "45," was safer for our guests. Suntory whisky, considered the best and safest—"Aged in Wood Especially for the Occupation Forces," its label said—was in short supply.

Similarly, questions of morality did not enter into the original official Occupation attitude. The Kipling gem about single men in barracks not being "bloomin' plaster saints," quoted to me at lunch one day by Colonel R. D. Palmer, commanding officer of the Eighth Cavalry Regiment, was generally accepted by those in direct contact with the problem. If the Army tried to bar sex one way, the men would get it another. Why bother to control it or them, as long as they hurt no one?

Restrictions on the movement of Occupation personnel were at first dictated only by commonsense necessity. Japanese restaurants were off limits because of the extreme food shortage. Special rail cars or half-cars were set aside for Occupation personnel to avoid ugly incidents in the frightful crush of bodies in the immediate postwar months. The relatively empty white-striped cars marked "*Shinchū-gun*" ("occupying forces") may have struck some Japanese as unfair, but enough of them remembered that in China the Japanese too had had their own rail cars. Otherwise, Occupation personnel were generally free to go where they liked and with whom.

That policy was eminently practical from the Army's viewpoint and clearly successful from SCAP's, whose basic directive said: "Your officers and troops . . . should so treat the Japanese population as to develop confidence in the United States and the United Nations and their representatives."[8] The original relaxed policy toward fraternization nevertheless was bound to change, as the battle-hardened generals who could not take "spit and polish" discipline seriously after the war were replaced by martinet types determined to advance their careers through exemplary garrison administration. Their aim was not to win a war or a peace but to maintain a disciplined force without such debilitating problems as venereal disease or entangling alliances with Japanese women. The key officers in the new dispensation were Major General Paul Mueller, the Chief of Staff, and Brigadier General William Beiderlinden, the new G-1 (Personnel), both exceptionally narrow and anticivilian. We used to joke that they didn't understand why the Army needed so many civilians to run the world. Both were contemptuous of the Japanese, whom they considered only a distraction and a complication. Their solution was to put as much distance as possible between the local population and their Army.

True, in the first several months of Occupation there had been excesses, intolerable in more settled circumstances. For example, in the Yūrakuchō Hotel, a lieutenants' and captains' billet in the heart of Tokyo, the morning group showers were usually graced by a few Japanese maidens who had stayed overnight. In Palace Heights, a company-grade officers' compound of quonset huts, some of the stay-over girl friends brought their families, including grandmothers and children, to stay with them on a semipermanent basis, roommates permitting. During the freezing winter of 1945–46 hardly any standing shelter was left in the city. The families camped out on the floors of the cramped two-man rooms, and the acrid smell of their hibachis filled the halls. No one could reasonably expect an army to function in such conditions for long.

IRRITATING CONTROLS

The Army's corrective regulations systematically put one place after another off limits to either the troops or the Japanese. First, Army clubs and messes were barred to Japanese guests. Then, bachelor officers' quarters for both men and women were prohibited to Japanese women, and so were Army vehicles. At the same time theaters, movies, subways, banks, rivers, beaches, hospitals, and finally hotels and inns were put off limits to Occupation troops. Then followed large areas of Yokohama, all side streets in Kyoto, and most of the Izu peninsula, with its splendid scenery and hot-springs hotels. The G-1 was clearly searching out and eliminating every place in Japan where Americans and Japanese of opposite sex could meet and enjoy each other's company. Fraternization was not exactly illegal; there was just no legal place to fraternize.

In January 1947 the G-1 barred Occupation personnel from staying overnight in Japanese homes or traveling more than 100 miles from their stations without travel orders or special permission. No exception was made for officers or mature, responsible civilian officials. SCAP was willing to trust them with matters of great national importance, but when it came fraternization they were no different from those young GIs the Army, standing *in loco parentis,* felt it had to control. The G-1 simply could not understand those who rejected the Army world—Army clubs, theaters, dances, bars, athletics—in favor of associating with the Japanese. As far as he could see, sex was the only reasonable explanation for such an unnatural preference. Any other social contact was simply prelude and had to be suppressed.

The result was easily foreseen. Repressing sexual fraternization by Army order was as practical as nailing shut the lid of a boiling kettle. "My father told me never to give an order unless I was certain it would be carried out,'' Mac-Arthur had confided to Faubion Bowers in rejecting the nonfraternization policy.[9]

The G-1 had a different father. To catch the off-limits violators, the MPs had the Japanese police set up informant networks, but the Japanese rarely took the matter seriously. Officers even smuggled girls past MP checkpoints in the trunks of Army sedans. GIs seeking sex just went deeper into the vast off-limits areas, which the MPs never visited at all. As ordinary socializing became too dangerous and difficult, soldiers were driven from innocent dating and companionship with respectable Japanese girls into the arms of streetwalkers and from movies, inns, and ordinary homes into dangerous places where the risks of venereal disease and victimization were far greater.

The officers in charge went through elaborate contortions to uphold the quaint idea that sex had nothing to do with it. At one 1949 session of the Generals' Committee on Relaxation of Occupation Controls, of which I was a member, General Beiderlinden, profusely denying that he was dictating morality, explained that Japanese inns were off limits for health and public order reasons. A few days later the Chief of the Medical Section testified that health reasons had nothing to do with it; he presumed it was a question of public order. The Provost Marshal, in turn, stated that Occupation personnel in Japanese inns were not a threat to public order; he had always thought it was a health problem.

It took the internal Army establishment a little less than a year and a half to convert official Washington policy tolerating, even encouraging, fraternization into a policy of suppressing it. It took only two months longer to expand legitimate Army black market controls, intentionally or not, into a means of enforcing the separation. In January 1946 the WAC officer who briefed new arrivals to the theater could reply to a question as to whether it was all right to sell PX cigarettes for yen that, ''Well, strictly speaking it's not legal, but everybody does it.'' By March 1947, however, a new FEC Circular, No. 26, defined black marketeering as ''to enter into, carry on, or perform any contract, agreement, or obligation to buy, sell, loan, extend credit, trade in, deal in, exchange, transmit, transfer, assign, dispose of or receive'' any American goods between ''authorized'' (mostly American) and ''unauthorized'' (mostly Japanese) personnel. American goods were loosely defined as any goods produced in or transported through the United States, carried by U.S. Government transportation, or intended for American personnel. Those definitions looked like a *Roget's Thesaurus'* entry and often defied common sense. A lieutenant in Sendai was court-martialed and convicted of black marketeering, that is, ''disposing of'' American goods to unauthorized personnel, because he had served two Japanese girls PX sardines and Coca-Cola. The Army Review Board threw out the conviction with an almost audible snort.[10] The circular made no distinction between large-scale commercial activity and individual bartering for souvenirs or simple gifts. Nor did it distinguish between stolen or illegally diverted government supplies and private property.

And so pregnant girls guilty of receiving baby clothes purchased at the PX by the prospective fathers[11] or Japanese fishing companions who had received old magazines, toothbrushes, playing cards, and so on from their American friends[12] were on the same legal footing with a black market ring dealing in penicillin, sulfa, cigarettes, and American dollars[13] and were arrested and incarcerated, too.

Not only was the full weight of the Japanese police, the Army Criminal Investigation Division, and the Military Police applied to suppress what in civilized circumstances was only normal, but a year later the Army establishment issued another regulation for confiscation of the goods themselves. The Army had gotten itself into a jam. In the name of fighting the black market, young and inexperienced MPs at the busy Sannomiya Station in Kobe, had removed watches from the wrists of Japanese pedestrians after first courteously asking them the time, wherever the watches had English names (like Alprosa, Roamer, and Medana, all of which were Swiss). They confiscated so-called American Ronson lighters, made, of course, in Britain,[14] and even seized gloves at Ginza 4-chōme, the crossroads of Tokyo, because their size was marked as "S," "M," or "L."[15]

As the confiscated goods mounted up in the Provost Marshal's offices in Kobe, Yokohama, and Tokyo, the Yokohama Provost Marshal finally asked GHQ what to do with them. Colonel Franklin Shaw, the Judge Advocate, was horrified to find out what had been going on, for the seizures were unauthorized and illegal.[16] Hurriedly he conferred with General Beiderlinden. Both men decided to regularize the seizures to protect the Army. SCAP Circular #23 was the result.

Innocently entitled "Contraband," a term that had previously been restricted to smuggling cases, the new circular retroactively authorized everything that had already been done, from searches without a warrant and summary seizures of any goods held in contravention of the earlier black market circular up to the confiscation of vehicles in which they had been transported or houses in which they had been kept. (So the Army CID, we may infer, had also seized a car and a house.) To avoid any questions of American constitutionality, the Judge Advocate General (JAG) lawyers cleverly issued the new circular not under the authority of the Far East Command, which was part of the U.S. Government, but under the aegis of SCAP, representing eleven occupying powers with different constitutions. Unfortunately for them, that gave the SCAP sections their first chance to comment, sometimes in acid terms. General Marquat objected that "black marketing" was the business of his Economic Section, not of G-1 and the JAG, and indeed it later turned out that in one case the Army

CID agents had seized a stock of wearing apparel of Japanese manufacture from a Japanese![17] But even Marquat's sound military argument did not move the Chief of Staff. He approved the circular without delay.

It was an ugly business, this search and seizure in disregard of legal protections and Japanese sensibilities. General MacArthur was proudly declaiming that "the Japanese citizen no longer cringes in the presence of police or other public authority; his home has become his castle, free from unwarranted intrusion, observation or violence."[18] The Japanese police, the victims, and the witnesses to the raids knew better. Pedestrians edged away from MPs on the street. By gossip and rumor, in urban areas at least, the word got around that associating with Occupation personnel was perhaps not the safest thing in the world. The Americans also got the point; association with Japanese was not safe for them either.

THE WOUNDED AMERICAN IMAGE

Nowhere was military insensitivity more strikingly demonstrated than in the campaign against prostitution and streetwalking, during which Japanese women who happened to be out at night were indiscriminately rounded up. Between August and November 1946, 2,400 women, according to the hospital records,[19] were picked up in the streets of Tokyo by squads of MPs and Japanese police, pulled into the backs of waiting trucks, and transported to the red-light district's Yoshiwara Hospital, where they were given veneral disease checks by physical inspection, sometimes with snickering MPs nearby. On the successive nights of August 28, 29, and 30, 1946, 840 women, including girl night school students and late factory workers going home—some of the raids were made on the Yūrakuchō station platform—were picked up. By the time the victims were released, the last train home had gone, and they were forced to spend the night in the hospital, with no opportunity to notify their worried relatives. It was a humiliating experience. A twenty-six-year-old girl named Fujita Setsuko, pulled in on one of the Nagoya street sweeps in May 1947, swallowed potassium cyanide in the Aiichi Prefectural Hospital rather than submit to physical examination there. She left a note asking her mother to have an autopsy made on her body to prove she had died a virgin.[20] In Kyoto, Major General Swing's dragnet caught an Imperial princess driving alone in an International Welfare Association jeep at night. She was released upon self-identification at the local police station.

In protest in the fall of 1946, thirteen national women's organizations, including the Women's Christian Temperance Union, the New Japan Women's Federation, and the women's sections of both major labor federations, delivered a petition addressed to General MacArthur, with a copy to me as SCAP Labor Division Chief, asking him to discontinue the practice. I very much doubt that he ever got the original. Whatever the reason—maybe they were just ineffective—the roundups stopped. The Japanese fear for their women at the hands of an Occupation army, however, had been rekindled. How many were reminded of the initial warnings of the Japanese authorities on August 29, 1945, to keep their women indoors or out of town?

Inevitably the harshness of some of the measures was blamed on anti-Japanese racial prejudice within the American Army hierarchy. General Beiderlinden, the key man, was undoubtedly racially prejudiced. Why else would he hound at least two marriages of Americans[21] to Japanese, legally witnessed by the American consulate pursuant to the War Brides Act in 1948, by trying, although unsuccessfully, thanks to General Marquat, to get the Americans fired from their jobs in GHQ? And why would the G-1 condone the official British policy of not allowing Nisei American civilian GHQ employees at their requisitioned Kuwana rest hotel while welcoming whites of exactly the same status?

But some of the severe actions against the Japanese, the street sweeps of "prostitutes," for example, predated Beiderlinden's advent as G-1. In reality, Beiderlinden was essentially trying to please the Chief of Staff, just as Colonel Shaw, bucking for general, was trying to please Beiderlinden. And all three were trying to avoid criticism about black markets and maintain Army discipline in the way they had learned, meanwhile protecting their careers from the dangers they saw. Any possible Japanese reaction was not one of those dangers.

In general, very little of the black–white racial antipathy among so many Americans of the time transferred itself to the "yellow" Japanese, hence the dimensions of the "fraternization problem." Furthermore, the disproportionately punitive discipline of the Army was applied to Americans as well, for example, a colonel court-martialed and dishonorably discharged for selling nine dollars worth of PX cigarettes, and a civilian suspended for three days for using an Army business sedan for recreation instead of changing to a recreational car. It was in the nature of the Army to discipline its men quickly and drastically to discourage other infractions. But applying barracks discipline unthinkingly to a whole country produced a quite different impact.

Certainly the credibility of the Occupation authorities was diminished when they preached the importance of civil control over the military and condemned as horrible examples the intrusions of the now-dissolved Japanese *kempei-tai* military police and their jurisdiction over civilians. Upon final Diet passage of the new Constitution, high-ranking Government Section officers, led by the deputy section chief, gave a congratulatory party in a Japanese restaurant—the officers' club would have been inappropriate, they thought—for top Japanese officials involved, including State Minister Matsumoto. The guests were astonished to see the powerful Americans reprimanded by two twenty-year-old

MPs, who entered, broke up the gathering, and gave out delinquency reports because restaurants were off limits.[22] The fact that the MPs were just following orders was irrelevant. The Japanese present and those to whom they quickly recounted the incident could never again quite so easily believe that in the United States the military in general, and the Military Police in particular, were subordinate and had no jurisdiction over civilians. With thousands of American civilians mixing with the Japanese, there were other encounters or near-encounters with MPs in front of Japanese witnesses that seemed to point up the hollowness of the Occupation's pretensions.

True, the personalities and prejudices of the three officers who happened to be in charge—a vindictive Beiderlinden, a crustily anticivilian Mueller, and a toadying Shaw, rather than other, more understanding and sympathetic officers—had a lot to do with such an extreme course that so directly conflicted with the Occupation's broader mission. But that the three could go so far unchecked was attributable to a serious defect in Colonel Ray Kramer's otherwise ingenious Headquarters organization plan of September 1945. To get a fundamentally undemocratic Army machine out of democratization, Kramer split off the SCAP functions in a separate SCAP Headquarters. However, he assigned no responsibility for Occupation–Japanese personal relations to SCAP, leaving them by default to G-1 Personnel in AFPAC/FEC. That included implementation of JCS 1380/15 paragraph 4e, which provided that the Japanese should be treated so "as to develop their confidence in the United States." A regular Army staff section engrossed in troop allotments, assignments and replacements, travel, billeting, leaves, dependents, and troop discipline, having little knowledge of or interest in the Japanese population, was simply incapable of following that guideline, or even of realizing its incapacity. Without assignment of some collateral responsibility on the SCAP side of GHQ, moreover, G-1 had no need to consult with those formally charged with democratization, who, though dismayed by the Army's actions, had no way to bring the issue before the Supreme Commander.

Nevertheless, MacArthur should have known. At the beginning, he was intensely concerned that his men make a good impression on the Japanese. Unfortunately, he neglected to follow through.

In accordance with his long-standing method of operation, designed to screen out all but the big problems, MacArthur left internal administration completely to his Chief of Staff, not remembering that in an occupation, personnel control could never be solely internal. That was how he could remain ignorant of a program that was swiftly eroding the original image to the Japanese of a new kind of democratic army, solicitous of the Japanese population as the Japanese never were of the occupied Chinese. So the Japanese gradually became convinced instead that, well, all armies are fundamentally the same. The generals

MacArthur relied upon let him down, of course, but the consequent Occupation schizophrenia on civil rights and liberties was his responsibility nonetheless.

Not until late in 1949 was the situation corrected. In February 1948, George Kennan, head of Secretary of State Marshall's Policy Planning Staff, visited Japan and returned to Washington with a bagful of recommendations designed to increase the independence of the Japanese Government in anticipation of an eventual peace treaty. It took Kennan until October 1948 to have his ideas incorporated into a new National Security policy, NSC 13/2. Because MacArthur was in general agreement with the document and with Kennan's purposes, he—although not Kennan—saw nothing novel about it and did not bother to circulate it within GHQ. But the paper did prompt him to have the Chief of Staff appoint a "General's Committee" on the relaxation of Occupation controls. That committee brought Japanese–American personal relations out of the recesses of G-1 into the light.

The General's Committee had only two generals: its chairman, Major General Alonzo P. Fox, the Deputy Chief of Staff for SCAP, and Brigadier General George Kyser, Fox's assistant. No doubt the Chief of Staff, like Kennan, had in mind Japanese Government–GHQ intergovernmental relations as the committee's focus. But its other members included Major Jack Napier, representing General Whitney, and me, representing General Marquat. With Fox's benign tolerance and Kyser's amused cooperation, the two of us persistently questioned every Army General Staff section head, especially the visibly uncomfortable General Beiderlinden, as to why this or that control was necessary. Under Secretary of the Army Tracy Voorhees, visiting Japan at just that time, also wanted to know why Japanese inns were not earning tourist dollars from the troops to reduce congressional appropriations for Japan. (I must confess to having put him up to it in advance.) The combination of those pressures, plus Fox's final report, did the trick.

In September hotels and inns were placed back on limits, the ban on overnight stays in Japanese homes ended, and both the black market and contraband circulars were rescinded. A new SCAP circular, #23 of 1949, declared its aim as being "to minimize restrictions on the movement and activities of Occupation personnel to the maximum practicable extent, in order to promote an attitude of friendly interest and guidance towards the Japanese people reflective of democratic ideals and devoid of unnecessary control." That accurately described the original Occupation fraternization policy, which had generated so much high regard in the first place.

It was, alas, late in the day. The martinets had poisoned half an Occupation, as it turned out. They had defaced the image of a friendly America as personified by its officers and men and its civilian personnel. They had simulated cynicism as to America's professions and suspicion as to its motives. A good deal of the original good will had been squandered.

The Legacy of the Encounter

On a people-to-people basis, especially one-to-one, the encounter of the two peoples with each other was, despite the martinets, a huge success. Both nationalities vastly broadened their respective horizons.

Americans suddenly became aware of alternative ways of doing things: bowing instead of shaking hands, pointing at one's nose instead of chest to denote oneself, counting on one's fingers by closing one's fist instead of opening it, driving on the left, and so on. A surprising number of Americans who had taken love and marriage for granted all their lives were suddenly impressed with the value of family-arranged marriages. (The Japanese went the opposite way.) Americans who were indignant at "debt-indentured" geisha and hostesses sometimes virtuously hastened to buy their contracts (they didn't cost much) and "free" the girls, only to find the transaction was not so simple. In one case a future missionary, at that time a lieutenant in our Antitrust Division, captivated by a winsome lass at a party given by Japanese industrialists, waxed indignant over her servitude. He paid her debt after the party and gave her the receipt. He never expected to see her again. The next day she appeared at his billet, her belongings in a *furoshiki* bundle, to ask where she would now live and how much he would give her regularly for her maintenance. I advised him to make a lump-sum settlement. Willy-nilly, Americans socializing with Japanese became conscious of the Japanese concept that personal responsibility outweighs personal freedom. They were deeply impressed.

All such experience was food for introspection. One grizzled civilian Southerner sagely remarked after some hours spent in an Army club bar one Saturday afternoon that somehow in Japan the barflies always got around to talking philosophy and sociology. In thirty-five years of frequenting Stateside bars, he had heard nothing but "broads and baseball." Gradually and grudgingly, the American soldiers and civilians acquired, for the most part, a respect for Japan and the Japanese. In an Army bus late one night I heard a GI rebuke his buddy who had referred to the Japanese contemptuously as "gooks." "You got it wrong, man," he protested, "In this country we're the gooks, not them." Hundreds of thousands, actually more than a million in the end, who served at one time or another on Occupation duty in Japan learned to respect and like the Japanese. At the least, Japan acquired a valuable ally in American public opinion for the next decades.

For the Japanese, the impact of the cultural confrontation was even sharper. An intensely insular people, for the first time in some 1,200 years they suddenly had to cope with a massive, if only temporary, foreign influx. Everything the Americans did was food for thought, from democracy to hair styles. Imprisoned, as it were, in their constricted society and narrow islands, the Japanese yearned for foreign manners and things, if only to feel liberated. *Avec* dating, that is, boy *avec* girl, was enthusiastically adopted. Boogie-woogie was the rage, and the prewar Florida Dance Hall was reopened, this time a block away from the Daiichi officers' billet, to booming Japanese-only business. Americanisms and psuedo-Americanisms, like "hubba-hubba" or "right away" in Army slang and "pink mood," meaning "sexy," swept Japanese speech. "Democracy" covered it all. The cultural traditionalists were unhappy. In 1948, for example, Tsuru Shigeto, later president of the prestigious Hitotsubashi University, spoke to me in bitterly pessimistic terms about the survival of traditional Japanese culture. But he need not have worried so much. The Japanese foreign "faddism" and its deeper meaning, the open-mindedness of the Japanese to foreign improvements, surely constituted one of Japan's strongest weapons for survival in the face of an intrusive world. As it happened, fundamental Japanese values changed far more slowly than styles or manners.

Through it all, a lasting friendship developed between the American people, as exemplified by the Occupation personnel, and the Japanese. Even when the Japanese in later years came increasingly to doubt the wisdom of American government policies, their friendliness toward individual Americans never slackened, as those of us who continued to reside in Japan can testify. It was the heritage of the Americans' conduct in Japan during the Occupation.

For the success of Japan's historic third turn, the good personal relationships between occupiers and occupied were crucial. Had not the Japanese people been convinced in those early postwar years of the essential decency and good will of the Americans they saw and knew, had they perceived the Americans instead as arrogant, brutish, condescending, grasping—that is, like their own militarists in relation to the Chinese in China—would they have accepted the Americans' ideas or radical democratic reform so readily? Not likely. For the Japanese to believe that what General MacArthur was telling them to do was for their own good, his own men had to display a sympathy and sensitivity toward the Japanese on a human level. That the Occupation people did so in spite of certain of their military superiors may not in itself have been enough to change the character of postwar Japan. But a contrary behavior could well have doomed the American democratic transformation effort. The ordinary Americans who made up the Occupation Forces, no matter how subordinate or insignificant their official roles, were crucial to Japan's third turn.

Part III

A QUESTION OF PRIORITIES

THE SOLEMN MIDNIGHT BOOMING of the deep-throated temple bells— mingled with the determined revelry of lonely Occupation soldiers in their billets and clubs—ushered in 1946, the Year of the Dog, according to the Japanese calendar. The dog was supposed to be the symbol of unquestioning loyalty. His year turned out to be anything but. The Japanese were in a mood to question everything to which they had been loyal, that is, everything Japanese. Driven by an accumulation of resentments against the snobbery, restrictions, and injustices of the old order, shocked by the devastation its irresponsibility had brought about, and inspired by both the person and the message of General MacArthur, the Japanese turned to "democracy." Their infatuation with it, if only for that year, should have changed the calendar. Unquestionably, 1946 was the year of *minshu-shugi*, democracy.

MacArthur and his men did not disappoint the Japanese in either energy or drive. The American "democratization express" thundered on through 1946 at full speed, heedless of the perilously weakened economic roadbed below, delivering democratic gifts to the applauding multitude—a new constitution; women's suffrage; sweeping educational, police, land, and labor reforms; the dissolution of the big three *zaibatsu* financial combine holding companies; and the purging of 200,000 of Japan's erstwhile leaders and luminaries. The list seemed endless. MacArthur and his men were implementing the detailed specifications for radical reform demanded by the Washington directive with unprecedented speed and thoroughness.

Yet the principal beneficiaries of the new democracy, at least those in the bombed-out cities and towns, were in deep distress. They could not eat, live in, or wear the new democratic reforms. The prospect of starvation frightened the cities, and the devastated industrial economy lay prostrate. Japan in 1946 could neither produce nor pay for what its people needed to live on. Once the initial numbness of the surrender shock wore off and the series of one-time cash payments ceased—war damage insurance claims, war contract cancellation indemnities, severance pay, bonuses for the August 1945 *o-Bon* (The Buddhist All-Soul's Day) and the December year end—the urban Japanese had at last to face the bleak desperation of their position. No more false dawns, no more windfalls. With their savings quickly depleted, their borrowings from family and friends exhausted, and their food stocks used up or being rapidly consumed as the food rations were cut and cut again, their incomes were simply inadequate to buy the necessary food on the black market. A study of Tokyo workers' households in April 1946 showed that they were spending from 40 to 170 percent more than they earned, depending on their occupation,[1] and yet they could hardly cut their expenses, because two-thirds was going for food alone. The overriding question was: How would they survive?

In the circumstances, was not the Occupation in its hectic, seemingly single-minded democratization drive coming perilously close to offering the Japanese circuses without bread? Many Japanese were beginning to give up on political questions. The April 1946 survey showed that many of those who had been the most avidly interested in the future of the Emperor institution in November 1945 now felt that such ideological issues could wait until the livelihood of the people was stabilized.[2] Why could not the Occupation wait as well?

Even more to the point, wouldn't the drastic changes required by an effective democratization program disrupt the functioning of what was left of the economy? The heavy passage of "the democratization express" might well weaken the railbed even further and end in disaster for all—the Japanese, the Occupation authorities, and the very democratization reforms themselves. The economy could be downgraded only at the Occupation's peril.

Meanwhile half a dozen nations gathered around the prostrate figure of Japan to lay claim to whatever they could of its remaining substance in order to restore their own war-torn lands. The Japanese, desperate for food to supplement their own inadequate production, looked about to find a world in the throes of the worst global food shortage in decades and without a friend to help them out of their hunger. How far should the United States assist them, or should Washington give precedence to its allies? Should America support the reparations claims of its wartime friends, and to what extent? Democratization versus economic recovery, and economic recovery versus competing international claims—it was all a question of priorities.

The Washington planners knew that in actual governmental operations priorities often meant more than principles. Hence they tried to assign them in advance. Fearing MacArthur and his officers might sacrifice the Washington radical reform measures to economic "emergencies," they insisted especially that democratization take precedence over economics. In West Berlin, Colonel Frank Howley, the American commander, had knowingly employed Nazis to run his public utilities—they ran them best, he said—and General Patton had publicly said that the Nazis were just another political party like the Republicans and Democrats. If the sending of the directive could help, nothing like that was going to happen in Japan.

The JCS 1380/15 directive bluntly told the Supreme Commander not to assume any responsibility for economic rehabilitation or the maintenance of any particular living standard or even the operation of the financial system.[3] Responsibility for domestic production and inflation control, it added, was a Japanese problem.[4] One could not make priorities any clearer than that.

The directive was, of course, good politics, too. Why should the American occupiers open themselves to blame for the economic chaos that had been caused by the Japanese militarists' war and that the Occupation could not quickly ameliorate anyway? The Supreme Commander was not to intervene directly in the functioning of the economy unless and until the Japanese had clearly failed. On the other hand, he *was* to take direct charge of disarmament, democratization, and reparations.

The Washington planners were right to worry that they could not completely control Douglas MacArthur. They were wrong to fear that he would downplay democratization. To their surprise and even disbelief, they discovered that MacArthur could not have agreed more with their priority for democratization. He was intent on going down in history as Japan's great democratic reformer. As a master of military timing, he knew that momentum was all. If democratization were not accomplished speedily, it might never be accomplished at all. True, radical economic democratization might bring economic shocks. All the more reason to get them over with right away, together with all the other peacetime readjustments, rather than try later on and upset a fragile economic recovery.

However, he could never accept the directive's cavalier dismissal of economic recovery as a Japanese responsibility. Without economic recovery, democracy would never last. To MacArthur, leaving economic direction to the Japanese in practice—as opposed to what might be done for appearances to advance political aims—was irresponsible. A necessarily weak Occupation-period government could not possibly deal with the enormous postwar economic turmoil. Furthermore, cashing in on Japan's obligations to the international community might be morally unexceptionable, but it was economically foolish. Only months before, the General was trying to destroy Japan, but now he adopted an extremely protective attitude. The future of Japan and his own future were going to be intertwined. History would judge his success in Japan by the shape the country would be in when he left it, and any footnotes explaining his failure as a consequence of Washington directives or the State Department's concern for the rest of the planet would appear only at the back of the book.

MacArthur could not change the policy. He understood the pressures involved in its composition and indeed praised it exceedingly.[5] Nor would he disobey it. But he could and did change its priorities. Washington ordered democratization first, reparations second, and recovery third, if at all. MacArthur agreed on the first even when it clashed with economic recovery. Otherwise, recovery took precedence, no matter what the directive said. In four specific cases—food relief, reparations, the economic purge, and inflation—the Supreme Commander made his priorities plain. Those priorities shaped the third turn as much as the directive itself.

8

Defending Japan Against the Allies

STARVATION AND DE-INDUSTRIALIZATION

NOT FOR CENTURIES, not even in the midst of the great bombing raids of April and May just past, had Japan faced a more frightening menace than the prospect of postwar starvation. Air raids, like typhoons and earthquakes, were quickly over. But the prospect of months of debilitation and ultimate death for hundreds of thousands, if not millions, with children and the aged going first, was a dread that did not go away. The specter of starvation stalked the land.

STARVATION

When I first arrived in January 1946, the Japanese authorities were forecasting spot famines by summer, and some Japanese, the future Prime Minister Yoshida Shigeru among them, even expected that as many as 10 million might die of starvation or malnutrition.[1] The Americans did not disagree. The cautious George Atcheson, General MacArthur's political adviser, conceded over the Japanese radio in April that "there will undoubtedly be some starvation."[2] Whatever the Occupation attempted, and however the Japanese faced their postwar future, feeding empty bellies had to come first.

Japan's predicament was readily understandable. The country as a whole normally produced 85 percent of its staple food requirements and still had the same capacity. But only the rural areas could be regarded as self-sufficient. The nonagricultural half of the population in the cities, towns, and mines was in a very precarious position. Farmers were reporting a 30 percent decline in the rice crop and a 50 percent drop in spring wheat and barley. Imports from the Japanese Empire were no longer available to make up the shortage. Before the war, as a rule of thumb, each Japanese was supposed to need one *koku* (five bushels, or 150 kg., of rice and other grains) a year. Now the official grain collections were enough for barely three-tenths of that, and the rationing system was beginning to break down. Hordes of hungry city dwellers jammed creaky trains to scrounge through the countryside for unreported food withheld by farmers.

By June 1946, each inhabitant of Tokyo received in his ration only 150 calories a day from Japanese sources,[3] a tenth of what he needed to keep him alive and about 7 percent of his prewar intake of 2,260 calories a day.[4] Then 7 million repatriates started flooding back from all over East Asia to share in what little there was. Clearly, without massive help from somewhere, disaster lay just ahead.

But from where? Wars traditionally bring starvation in their train, and World War II was no exception. Moreover, 1945 was an exceptionally bad year for world agriculture. Food production in the export rice bowl of Asia—Burma, Thailand, and Indochina—was down by 15 percent, with exports off by much more. The Philippines, historically an exporter of sugar, was reduced to importing it. In Europe the yield was only three-quarters of normal, and many nonfarm Europeans subsisted on less than a thousand calories a day.[5] All over the world people were hungry. Japan, as one of the aggressors who had brought on the war and the subsequent hunger, had little moral claim to the meager world supply, certainly far less than its victims and, from America's viewpoint, the victorious allies.

As Japan's occupier, the United States had to represent Japan's needs. As leader of the free world and the only great power with a food surplus, however, America had to apportion the food available fairly. In striking a balance, the Washington planners had relegated Japan to the end of the line. True, international law required the occupier to maintain public order and safety,[6] and that took food. Indeed, the U.S. indictment in the Nuremberg war crimes trials charged the Nazis with deliberately leaving subject peoples to starve. In the postwar negotiations leading up to the 1949 Geneva Convention, moreover, the United States fully supported the principle, embodied in Article 55, that "to the fullest extent of the means available to it, the Occupying Power has the duty of ensuring the food and medical supplies of the population" even to the point of bringing in whatever was necessary "if the resources of the occupied territory are inadequate."[7] Furthermore, disease and unrest stemming from starvation would imperil the occupying forces themselves. There was never any question within the U.S. Government, therefore, that Japan would get food. The issue was how much.

During the planning period and immediately after hostilities ceased, the U.S. answer was: the barest minimum. Western leaders were deeply worried about the world as a whole. "The world will pass through a period of great strain before we see the next harvest," Prime Minister Attlee warned President Truman. Truman, in turn, warned his countrymen: "If we let Europe go cold and hungry, we may lose some of the foundations of order on which the hope for world-wide peace rests."[8] In such an atmosphere the State[9] and War[10] departments agreed in an April 1945 SWNCCFE meeting to incorporate a "standard of living clause" in the postsurrender policy for Japan under which Japan would not be permitted a standard of living out of line with neighboring countries.[11] Considering the abysmal level in much of nearby China, that was pretty low. In the end, the clause was not incorporated, but the JCS 1380/15 directive ordered SCAP to limit Japanese food relief to only "the extent . . . needed to prevent such widespread disease and unrest as would endanger the occupying forces or interfere with military operations . . . such imports will be confined to minimum quantities of food . . . fuel, medicinal and sanitary supplies."[12]

But what was "minimum"? In a world in which Britain was limiting its food imports to leave more for other countries and the United States was restricting the use of grain for making beer and liquor, cutting wheat supplies to local bakers and processors, calling for one meatless day a week, and earmarking 25 percent of all wheat flour for export,[13] Japan's claims could not expect much attention. The definition of "minimum" in the JCS directive was crucial. If Washington had its way, mass starvation might be avoided, but the Japanese people would be on the edge of it for many months, if not years.

More Food or More Soldiers

Fortunately for the Japanese, their chief occupier had other ideas. What happened elsewhere did not concern him; it was Japan that was his responsibility and his fate. How could a nation on the edge of starvation be remade in a democratic mold? How could he prevent the extremists on both sides of Japan's political spectrum from taking advantage of continuous hunger and anxiety? Truman's impassioned appeal to sacrifice for the rest of the world—"we cannot ignore the cry of hungry children. Surely we will not turn our backs on millions of human beings begging just a crust of bread"[14]—left MacArthur unmoved. He was going to defend Japan, whose forces had starved his veterans on the Bataan death march, as a mother bear guards her cub.

At first, no one had to decide the crucial question of how to define the JCS minimum. MacArthur's unexpectedly rapid troop reduction from 600,000 to 200,000 men in the fall of 1945 produced a special dividend in the food supplies left behind. From depots in Japan, from elsewhere in the Far Eastern theater, and even from the Army Quartermaster in the United States, SCAP officials managed to obtain a total of 800,000 tons of all kinds of military-style food in the first year of the Occupation[15] and turn it over to the Japanese Government for distribution to the people.

The food, of course, was somewhat different from what the Japanese were accustomed to. Now they had to contend with such problems as cooking wheat flour so as to be edible—steaming it like rice, they discovered, produced stomach aches—dividing twenty-eight ration cans among sixty-two recipients, educating the consumers to *eat* the corned beef hash instead of feeding it to the chickens, or the flatulence, especially noticeable in crowded trains, induced by large quantities of peas and beans in the diet. "The new ration makes one so ill-mannered," one lady apologized to a visitor upon an unexpected eruption.[16] But there was no starvation, and U.S. Army foods saved the day. Indeed, in Tokyo in June 1946 77 percent of the ration consisted of U.S. Army surplus.[17] One can imagine the crisis had there been no such food available. The unhappy side effects of the special diet were only transitory, for the *ad hoc* Army surplus supplies were running out.

Months before, the GHQ had put together a budget request for U.S. food relief for 1946–47. A first wild estimate under pressure called for 3.7 million metric tons of staple grain imports. (Prime Minister Yoshida, depending on his experts, wanted SCAP to bring in 4.5 million tons.)[18] But the highest previous figure, in 1942, the peak of Japanese military success, was only 3 million.[19] So the increasingly expert ESS staff "scientifically" recalculated requirements based on minimal daily caloric intakes per capita. The result was a request for $280 million (more than a billion in 1983 dollars) in food, fertilizer, petroleum products, and medicines, including 2 million tons of staples in wheat and wheat flour, just about equal to Japan's 1936–40 annual average.[20] Minimal? Well, it was two and a half times the Army surplus that had averted famine the first year. Its cost exceeded the combined budget of three federal departments: Commerce, Justice, and Labor.

It was not entirely the fault of the experts, who had purposely left in a number of safety margins; had accepted the low official Japanese harvest estimates, which in fact understated the truth by 20 percent; had ignored a ghost ration population; and had failed to adjust for the lower calorie requirements of children and the aged. Our economists had expected to negotiate downward with the Washington agencies in due course.

MacArthur never gave them the chance. He cabled their figures to Washington as his absolute best. Working late one spring night in 1946, I was drafted by Marquat to help edit a secret cable he was preparing, on MacArthur's instructions, to the congressional Appropriations Committee asking for more food or more soldiers. To ex-President Hoover, the visiting chairman of Truman's Famine Emergency Committee, MacArthur asserted in May that without food relief the nonfarm population would not have enough food to sustain life.[21] The old gentleman was deeply impressed, as he told General Marquat shortly afterward.

When the most eminent soldier of his generation invoked military necessity, few Congressmen would rise to dispute him, and since Congress could not send more troops, it had to send more food. When the implacable foe of the Imperial Army declared to Hoover that he was not advocating "the slightest element of preferential treatment" for the Japanese, who could believe he was? When he evoked the image of Japan as a "vast concentration camp under the control of the Allies," who if they didn't feed the inmates would be repeating the horrors of the Bataan death march, recent memories of war crimes were too strong to oppose. MacArthur, most of all, was not part of the Administration, but an anti–New Dealer and hence a foe of wild extravagance. Who he was was even more convincing than what he said. He got the money he asked for.

The next year the General upped the ante to $330 million, and the following year to $497 million. The Japanese daily ration could now be raised step by step. By May 1948, the nonfarmers' daily food intake had almost trebled from the dark days of June 1946, back to more than 2,000 calories.[22] About 92 percent of the staples came from the U.S. ration.[23] Meanwhile, stocks within the country zoomed from almost zero to more than 3 million tons by April 1949.[24] By that time the Japanese could not eat the food as fast as the United States was shipping it in.

MacArthur may have overstated the need, but he wanted to make sure. Even more important, he understood that a bare minimum might keep the Japanese alive, but it would probably wreck his Occupation politically. In one of his statements to Congress, MacArthur had warned that "starvation . . . renders a people an easy prey to any ideology that brings with it life-sustaining food."[25] At least one man agreed wholeheartedly: Tokuda Kyūichi, leader of the Communist Party of Japan.

Some twenty-five years later, one of Tokuda's closest intimates, Hasegawa Kō, reminisced with me about Occupation days. When Tokuda first emerged from prison in October 1945, he told Hasegawa that the Party had to concentrate on exploiting two principal fields of popular grievances: first hunger, then labor unrest.[26] Takano Minoru, Tokuda's left-wing Socialist rival, confirmed that attitude to me independently. Tokuda had told him that controlling food was the key to controlling Japan, and the Communists would accordingly concentrate on infiltrating the food supply system.[27] It had never entered Tokuda's mind, however, that the Americans would actually bring in such massive food shipments for the starving Japanese.

But they did. After the food started to arrive in enormous quantities, it was the American ideology of democracy that prevailed. No more "Food May Day" demonstrations occurred at the Imperial Palace, and the Communist wardens, sent by the Party to exploit the grievances of those standing in the rice ration lines, gradually disappeared. Half of Tokuda's offensive was defeated before it really got started. The other half carried Japan to the brink of revolution in an aborted general strike at the end of January 1947. Had sufficient American food not been available to blunt the worst hunger pangs and allay the deepest anxieties of the people, who can tell what would have happened at that time?

The extra food that MacArthur obtained for Japan, mostly at the expense of reducing allocations to American allies, cost upwards of $100 million a year more than the JCS "minimums." Perhaps that was not morally defensible. Perhaps he overdid it. But the food saved Japan for democracy at a critical time. MacArthur's priorities were sounder than Washington's. And none of the Allies complained.

REPARATIONS

Thunderous statements and dire warnings served MacArthur well as he shouldered Japan to the head of the international food line, but they could be of little use in staving off an equally dangerous threat, albeit delayed, to the future of the Japanese people: the dismantling and removal of a substantial part of Japan's industry as reparations. That called for another strategy.

At war's end America's Pacific allies loudly demanded compensation for the havoc Japan's armies had inflicted on them. Morally, those claims were hard to deny. Legally, the Japanese had already accepted the obligation to pay "just reparations in kind" when they accepted the Potsdam Declaration and its paragraph 11. Both the State Department's SWNCC 150/4 policy statement and JCS 1380/15 confirmed the policy of reparations from Japan's industrial plants, and the directive even gave reparations priority over fighting inflation. The top people in the Administration, President Truman, Secretary of State Byrnes, and Reparations Commissioner Edwin Pauley, all supported the idea. The American public, still outraged over Japan's depredations, considered the policy simple justice. But once again, luckily for the Japanese people, their Occupation chief, Douglas MacArthur, came to disagree.

I doubt that the General realized at first just what the JCS directive meant for Japanese economic recovery—our ESS staff meetings in early 1946 gave no such indication—or was aware that the American reparations policy had been developed in Washington by the process of elimination. Postsurrender Japan, it was obvious to the planners, was not going to be able to pay in money, because it would be bankrupt. Reparations out of current Japanese production were also ruled out; at the end of World I England and France had exacted just such reparations from Germany, which, unable to sustain itself under such a burden, had borrowed from the United States to make ends meet. Those debts were still unpaid. The United States, not Germany, had ended up paying much of the reparations, and the planners were determined not to repeat the mistake. That left only those Japanese factories still standing as a possible source to recompense the claimant nations.

The idea was superficially attractive. Japan as a peaceful nation would no longer need much of its heavy industry, which had been built for war purposes. Why not ship the excess to Japan's victims? Japan would be disarmed industrially and at the same time its victims would receive its assets to compensate for the damage they had suffered.

The claimant nations cheered. They were avid to get their hands on something, anything; they would worry about its usability later.[28] The Soviets were all in favor. An international policy of transferring industrial plant from vanquished to victors as reparations would go far to legitimize their own brutal removals of Japanese-built factories from Manchuria into the interior of the U.S.S.R. to the extent of almost $1 billion, by Pauley's estimate. (The figure equaled nearly half of all U.S. aid to Japan over the next six years.) The Soviets claimed the value to them of the seizures was only $97 million.[29] If that was true, it was a singularly wasteful method of payment. But at the beginning no one thought so.

In Washington plant reparations seemed a brilliant idea, but in the theater, as the SCAP staff studied the implications, it made no sense at all. Japanese industrial plants, individually designed to begin with, depended on supplementary fixed facilities: docks, rail spurs, a suitable power supply, and so forth. They also needed economical raw materials and a trained labor force. Often they were integrated with nearby factories that provided them with semiprocessed products to finish or vice versa. The East Asian claimant nations had few of those assets and no money to build supplementary support systems. Only machine tools and thermal power plant sets[30] offered much possibility of usefulness. Perhaps in the more homogeneous Europe, plant transfers might have been practicable. In the East, shifting factories about like pieces on a chess board defied reality.

But a hostile and punitive world allowed for no calm reflection on the program's premises. Edwin Pauley, the hard-driving former oil man, former Democratic Party treasurer, and close political friend of the President, a man with fire in his belly and not much moderation in his soul, never questioned the premises. He was going to force implementation come what might. As Reparations Commissioner for Germany as well, Pauley had had several run-ins with the Soviets and was determined to play harder ball than even they did. When the Soviets called their $2 billion removals from Manchuria, the territory of an Allied power, simply "war trophies," not reparations, Pauley angrily radioed Secretary of State Byrnes in Paris to claim all Italian and West German industry as British and American "war trophies," thereby excluding them from reparations availability to the Russians.[31] His staff was not exactly moderate either. At least that was the impression I got from talking in Washington with Martin Bennett, a capable engineer, who was Pauley's chief of staff. Pauley's regional adviser, Owen Lattimore, advocated the nationalization of all *zaibatsu* properties and the internment in China of the Emperor and his heirs.[32]

Pauley started like a dash man out of the blocks. In November and December 1945, he visited Japan, Korea, and Manchuria. By December 6, he was already announcing his main conclusions to General MacArthur, President Truman, and the press. He proposed to remove all Japanese steel capacity above 2.5 million tons—the Japanese Empire had possessed 13 million—all of Japan's aluminum and magnesium plants; half the coal-burning electric power capacity; a large number of chemical plants; the machines and equipment from all the ordnance, aircraft, ball- and roller-bearing plants; and twenty out of twenty-nine shipyards. He also wanted all the gold held by the Bank of Japan shipped to the U.S. Mint in San Francisco. Because he was, he told Truman, "inclined to think that . . . under the policy now being pursued by the Japanese, the giant corporations will take over the country," he wanted first to remove those factories belonging to Mitsui, Mitsubishi, Sumitomo, Nissan, and the other *zaibatsu* combines.[33] A detailed report followed on May 11, 1946.

In Washington, the supporters of plant reparations in State, Edwin Martin, the radical reformer then chief of the Japan–Korea Economic Division; John Kenneth Galbraith, director of the Office of Economic Security Policy; and General John Hilldring, then Assistant Secretary of State for Occupied Areas, now set up an Inter-Allied Reparations Committee under the Far Eastern Commission and called for completion of the whole program by the end of 1947.[34] Although the United States wanted no reparations, Martin's division drew up an American claim against Japan for bargaining purposes with the Russians. Incomplete, the bill came to more than $126 billion.[35] An impatient Pauley could complain (to Will Clayton) that he was "discouraged by the progress of reparations to date."[36] But in late May and early June, the FEC approved a series of interim removals based squarely on his report. It looked as though Pauley had won.

The FEC decisions softened Pauley's Draconian proposals, but not much. For example, instead of 80 percent of Japan's steel capacity, "only 50 percent of its pig iron and 40 percent of its open-hearth steel facilities[37] were called for. All of the designated reparations were, of course, in addition to the loss of Japan's huge industrial investments on the mainland. Japan's industry was to be devastated much more effectively than by all the air raids on the grounds that much of it wasn't needed anyway. SCAP was instructed to select the plants to be removed.[38]

In a series of eight directives on August 13 and 14, 1946, SCAP designated

505 plants, including Japan's newest and best, to be held ready for reparations.[39] It was almost a year to the day after the Emperor's rescript announcing the surrender.

So far, aside from a relatively mild disagreement with Pauley's idea of taking over the *zaibatsu* program under reparations—MacArthur pointed out that a special *zaibatsu* mission was already in Tokyo—the Supreme Commander had not objected to Pauley's program. In January 1946, his Industry Division had recommended, and he had approved, the designation of some 700 industrial installations as subject to possible reparations removals.[40] Most of them were redesignated by the August directives, but the action was more show than substance. Signs were posted on the factory compound walls, and guards were stationed at the gates, while the plants continued functioning as before. The Industry Division, moreover, forwarded to the War Department materials related to "retention levels"—what Japan was to be allowed to keep for a peaceful economy. The radios were kept humming with refinements and additions. When Navy Secretary Forrestal visited in July 1946, MacArthur's complaints were limited to reparations delays and uncertainties that inhibited Japanese recovery, not the reparations policy itself.[41].

But somehow, there was little of the fire that GHQ had displayed over other programs, and certainly no initiatives. Indeed, in the ESS meetings, which I began attending in February 1946 as Chief of the Labor Division, the exchanges between General Marquat and the successive Industry Division Chiefs, Major O'Hearn and Joseph Reday, dealt not with how to speed up the program but how to answer Washington's queries and avoid criticism for noncompliance. Gradually SCAP's speed in replying diminished. The ESS comments on Pauley's December 18 report took only six weeks to prepare after the mission went home. But it took SCAP four and a half months to comment on his revised report of May 11, and Pauley had to ask twice in writing for the comments.[47]

Marquat had accepted the first report as gospel, but now disagreements crept in. While not objecting to the principle of plant reparations, SCAP repeatedly argued for more liberal treatment of Japanese industry. "In about ten cases, SCAP either comments that my findings are premature or arbitrary or otherwise that a decision should not yet be made," Pauley complained to Secretary Byrnes at the end of 1946.[43] Meanwhile Marquat, coming down from his meetings with MacArthur in the adjoining Daiichi Building, would put on his inscrutable look while quipping that it would be a long time before any factories left Japan's shores. It was plain that the Section, which meant MacArthur, was not pushing very hard.

In truth, the more MacArthur contemplated Pauley's plan, even with State's modifications, the more clearly inconsistent it seemed with the rest of his directive from Washington, especially democratization. Reparations *per se* and even the combination of plant reparations and industrial disarmament could be reconciled with the SCAP mission. But Pauley's interpretation could not. The Reparations Commissioner proposed to turn the Japanese clock back to 1932–36, the last peacetime five-year period before the outbreak of the China war. And that, reasonable on the surface, amounted, as MacArthur saw it, to a mini-Morgenthau. Postwar Japan had 10 million more mouths (including repatriates) to feed and a hundred devastated cities to rebuild. Its merchant marine and empire were gone, its foreign exchange resources nil, and its leading prewar exports moribund. Now to remove a healthy part of its industrial plant as excess might well lengthen the odds against its recovery insuperably, and democracy, as well as social stability, might not survive the ensuing public distress and suffering. It was far too risky.

MacArthur's Delaying Tactics

A hard-bitten skeptic, MacArthur did not believe anything productive was "excess"—his Scottish ancestry, Marquat joked—especially not when judged on such theoretical grounds as conditions almost fifteen years and a war in the past. The Japanese, MacArthur was sure, could find ways to convert, or reconvert, industry to peace, but not if it were removed. (Indeed, in a few short years the Kure naval shipyard was building tankers for export, Nippon Gakki was making Yamaha pianos again instead of airplane propellers, and Nippon Kōgaku had turned from bomb sights to Nikon cameras.)

We on the ESS staff could joke about how badly Indonesia needed an aluminum plant for its aircraft industry or the great care in cargo-handling for which Rangoon was famous—a recent shipment of cement had been left exposed on the docks in the rainy season—or the incorruptibility of the Filipino and Chinese officials who would be receiving the reparations equipment. But to MacArthur all that was irrelevant. Pauley's, and therefore the American, interpretation of paragraph 11 of the Potsdam Declaration endangered the economic recovery of Japan and hence the consolidation, even the survival, of his democratization. Pauley had different priorities. MacArthur, with his emphasis on democratization and recovery, would not go along.

Whatever his private opinion, however, MacArthur was reluctant to appear as enemy Japan's partisan. For a commander to oppose his own government's policy, especially when incorporated in international agreements, was a tricky business, to be spoken of circumspectly if at all. The only practical course was to stall, while appearing not to, until the passions of war cooled. It took almost four years, and in the end the game plan succeeded brilliantly.

At times the game seemed risky. The War Department radio communiqué announcing the FEC's decisions in June, even though expected, could not fail to shake MacArthur and Marquat. But the two generals kept their composure even while designating the 505 plants. The pace of international action is often glacial, and for a group of nations it is easier to decide in principle than actually to divide the spoils. If the United States stayed out of the division—America wanted no reparations from Japan—there would be no strong leadership. The others could well lapse into unproductive, protracted discussions.

Pauley, with the same premonitions, redoubled his efforts. When the British wanted to allocate reparations shares first before deciding what to remove, he,[44] and his State allies, brushed them aside. To the Navy Department's prudent suggestion that Occupation costs, not reparations, should be a first charge[45] he would not even listen. Both ideas would only delay matters. Busily he badgered everyone at State's top levels—Clayton, Hilldring, Dean Acheson, Deputy Assistant Secretary Willard Thorp, and even Secretary Byrnes—charging State's officials with neglecting, changing, and attenuating his report to the President. He even tried to maintain, somewhat inconsistently, that basically MacArthur agreed with him.[46]

Under Pauley's incessant prodding, State in September 1946 proposed to begin immediately with transfers of up to 15 percent (later 30) of each of Pauley's categories.[47] But again nothing happened. Pauley waited another month and then declared publicly that if the FEC claimant nations could not agree, the United States would begin the reparations process unilaterally.[48] How that could be done if the United States was not itself a reparations claimant was not explained. Still, as a former disburser of campaign funds, Pauley had many Congressmen beholden to him, and he began lobbying Congress hard. After all, Congress could tie Japan aid appropriations to reparations progress, and that could be painful to MacArthur's Command. More than SCAP inertia would be required.

At that juncture, General Marquat came up with a new strategy, somewhat on the order of throwing the sleigh's passengers to the Siberian wolves one by one to save the rest. Everyone had agreed that the one category of facilities clearly in excess in Japan was machine tools, which in 1946 numbered many times what had been in use in 1930. They, of all the facilities in question, could be economically moved and reinstalled. Marquat, therefore, proposed a program of "advance interim removals," limited just to machine tools and, further, only to those in government arsenals. That, he added, could be started right away. The reparations claimants would be so busy claiming and ensuring their rightful share of the "loot" that they would have to let up pressure on the balance, including the rest of the "advance" shipments. MacArthur agreed, and the War and State departments, whether they recognized the tactic or not, saw no reason to oppose the proposal.

The scheme worked beautifully. The United States invited all the reparations claimants to send missions to Tokyo. International action and protocol being what they are, the first reparations mission, that from the Philippines, did not arrive until January 1947, and it was not until May, twenty-one months after the end of the war, that all the other nine missions had appeared on the scene. The reparations mission people received red-carpet treatment. They were provided with Army Post Exchange privileges, which gave them access to an abundance of American consumer goods that they could never hope to get in their own war-ravaged countries at that time, and they were permitted to attend Army movie theaters and use Army recreation hotels. Few of the reparations representatives were in a hurry to get home. From June to September 1947, as the days passed, our Industry Division and the local Military Government officers shepherded the various reparations missions' personnel from one facility to another, inspecting no less than 104 machine tool plants, 61 large and small shipyards, 54 ball- and roller-bearing factories, and 107 miscellaneous installations, all in four months.[49] That was better than three a day, including Sundays. No one could possibly accuse SCAP of not cooperating in Japanese reparations.

In October, with great fanfare, SCAP designated some 19,000 metalworking machines in seventeen military and naval arsenals for advance removals. It took four more months to have them allocated by public drawing, have the claimants inspect, accept, or reject each machine individually, and then have them packed. A reparations packing school was organized. The first shipments went out in January 1948, and it took seven more months for the program to be completed.[50] Fifteen percent of all Japan's machine tools were shipped out. The Chinese received half, the Philippines one-fifth, and the Netherlands East Indies and the United Kingdom all the rest. The total value was put at some $20 million,[51] about 2 percent of what the Russians took out of Manchuria—in one-fifth the time.

Three years had passed since V-J Day. At that rate, it would be well into the twenty-first century before the main part of the announced removal program would be accomplished, and meanwhile there was little pressure by claimants to get into the main part.

Stalling, however, could not bring about a formal revision of the program, and in the absence of official assurances it was hard to see Japanese industry making needed investments in threatened plants. In February 1947 SCAP and the War Department colluded in bringing over Clifford Strike, president of F. H. McGraw, consulting engineers, as a reparations adviser. Advisory commissions from outside the Command had been used regularly to help implement directives; now Marquat and Strike went one step further: They organized a mission to change the directive. Strike gathered together a group of engineers from the leading American consulting engineering firms under the name Overseas Consultants, Inc., and the War Department contracted with them to assess the reparations program anew—as though reparations had become primarily an engineering matter, and no longer moral, legal, diplomatic, or even economic.

Thus was the angle of view cleverly shifted, and from the new viewpoint plant reparations were ridiculous and always had been. It surprised no one, least of all Marquat and MacArthur, when in February 1948, after six months in the theater, the engineers recommended virtual abandonment of the program. In the same month Pauley, now downgraded to Special Assistant to the Secretary of the Army, resigned and went back to the oil business.

With the prestige that American engineers had in the immediate postwar years, especially with the conservative Eightieth Congress, it was not hard for an Administration more concerned with Japan's becoming self-sufficient than with disarming it to accept the Strike report as national policy. The American representative in the FEC admitted that the new policy contradicted previous international commitments to the Allies, but those commitments had been given before the United States started to support Japan's economic recovery. Any deficiencies caused by reparations would now have to be made up out of the U.S. pocket. The Allies had a right to reparations from Japan, but clearly not from the United States.

Equally to the point, as MacArthur had envisaged, international conditions had changed too, and drastically. Nationalist China, the principal intended reparations beneficiary, was reeling from Communist offensives and rapidly becoming a risky place to which to ship factories or anything else. Indonesia was in the throes of revolution too. On May 24, 1949, the Communists took over Shanghai. Eleven days earlier, the United States officially announced the end of the Japanese reparations program.

Before the program was ended, MacArthur was no longer alone in opposing it. Defense Secretary Forrestal, Under Secretary of the Army Draper, and Secretary of State Marshall's Policy Planning Staff all objected strongly to plant reparations. However, their objections did not arise until near the end of 1947 and early 1948. For almost two years before that, when there was real danger, MacArthur was the principal and, on the top levels, the only obstructor. He never, of course, got credit for his farsightedness, even from the Japanese. When someone sabotages his superiors' express orders, even in a good cause, the best public relations organization has to hold its tongue. MacArthur's subtle sabotage of plant reparations turned out to be one of the best-kept secrets of the Occupation, mostly because MacArthur himself kept quiet. By doing so he succeeded in saving Japanese heavy industry, and with it Japan's potential for its successful third turn. He had successfully defended Japan from America's allies.

9

The Purge of Japanese Business

It was these very persons, born and bred as feudalistic overlords, who held the lives and destiny of the majority of Japan's people in virtual slavery, and who, working in closest affiliation with its military, geared the country with both the tools and the will to wage aggressive war. . . . These are the persons who, under the purge, are to be removed from influencing the course of Japan's future economy.

Douglas MacArthur
January 1947[1]

We have neither been offered nor have we found evidence of instances where prominent business and industrial leaders conspired with anyone to plan or initiate the war. . . . It's quite different from Germany. There the industrialists held the stirrups while Hitler mounted the beast. If the bankers and commercial leaders here held the stirrups it was at the point of a gun.

Joseph B. Keenan,
Chief Prosecutor, Tokyo
War Crimes trials
October 1947[2]

ON JANUARY 4, 1946, the Supreme Commander for the Allied Powers directed the Imperial Japanese Government to remove or exclude from public office in Japan all those who had been "active exponents of militant nationalism and aggression." Since 1943 the Allies had been de-Fascizing Italy, and since early 1945 they had been de-Nazifying Germany. Now, the Americans were going to purge Japan. To carry out the pledge of the Allied leaders at Potsdam to "eliminate for all time those who had deceived and misled the Japanese people into aggressive war," the Supreme Commander and his men launched a drive that would screen 700,000 Japanese and bar 200,000 of them from public or important private positions. Of all the hammer blows struck by Douglas Mac-Arthur in the first months of the Occupation, this was the most shattering. The entire ruling elite, which had governed for fifteen years of Japan's imperialist wars, would be replaced by a new one.

All through 1946, the purge rolled on, broadening and intensifying its impact. No area was sacrosanct. Government Section memos to the Japanese Government directed its extension first to political parties, then to government-owned enterprises, to semiofficial control associations, to local governments, even to neighborhood associations, and then on to schoolteachers, publishers, and other media managers. Time and again the purge caused political havoc. Five cabinet ministers were purged just before the first postwar Diet election in April 1946.[3] Hatoyama Ichiro, in line to be prime minister, fell immediately after the election. Five more cabinet ministers were purged just before the second election in 1947,[4] as were hundreds of Diet members and political party executives.

Americans in GHQ and back home applauded—MacArthur was really getting to the root of the matter, wasn't he?—and passed over the occasional absurdities of purging a Quaker pacifist[5] and a liberal labor scholar[6] as a small price to pay to rid Japan of the likes of the Black Dragon society, the assassination-prone Blood Brotherhood, and the odious military hierarchy. SCAP never relented, and the operation forged swiftly and smoothly ahead.

BIG BUSINESS AND RESPONSIBILITY FOR THE WAR

When the time came to apply the purge to Japan's economic leaders, however, the pace slowed to a crawl. More accurately, the purge sputtered, stalled, and seemed unable to get started again. The "political purge," managed by the Government Section, had struck Japan on January 4. The "education" purge, administered by the Civil Information and Education Section, had gone into action on May 6 with Imperial Ordinance #263. But almost a year after the surrender, nothing but rumors had surfaced about the "purge" of business, the mission assigned by the Chief of Staff to the Economic and Scientific Section. It looked as though GHQ simply could not make up its mind. Indeed, within the headquarters a furious controversy had boiled up. In theory, in a military headquarters a directive exists to be obeyed, not debated. But those assigned the mission of implementing paragraphs 23 and 40 of JCS 1380/15, which mandated the purge in commerce, industry, finance, and agriculture, simply could not obtain concurrences from all the other staff agencies whose missions were affected. Without concurrences, there could be no action.

"Purge businessmen?" any number of SCAP officials demanded indignantly. "What for?" Yes, they had cooperated with the Japanese war effort, the argument continued, but so did American businessmen. So would any patriot. And if some did participate in imperialist aggression, why penalize those who didn't? Furthermore, if you eliminate the most able economic leaders in the nation, how can you expect the economy to recover? And if it doesn't, not only will Japan remain dependent indefinitely on American tax money, but the country will be vulnerable to a radical, that is, Communist, takeover. Regardless of the explicit wording of the directive, the reluctant SCAP officials could not believe that American policy intended that. Besides, the Japanese businessmen they knew either personally or in an official capacity were nice fellows. Imperialists? That must be somebody else.

If two such eminent personages as the Commander-in Chief and the Chief War Crimes Prosecutor could disagree radically about the responsibility of Japanese business leaders for the war (as witness the headnotes to this chapter), how could unanimity among lesser officials be expected? In the cases of de-Nazification and de-Fascization, the Washington rationale was readily apparent, but for Japan it derived from sophisticated politico-economic concepts plus a knowledge of recent Japanese history not shared by everyone. To the radical reform planners it was self-evident that no democratization could be safe from obstruction or even sabotage without the removal of the old-line business leaders, but many of those in the theater with a narrower focus, or just those who thought along other lines, found it difficult to understand why.

In point of fact, the economic purge was a last-minute innovation in planning for Japan. As late as August 22, 1945, a week after the surrender, even after the radical reformers had replaced the Grew–Dooman moderates in State's summer revolution, the purge of Japanese businessmen in State's current policy paper, SWNCC 150/3, was still confined to "those who do not direct future Japanese economic efforts for solely peaceful ends," an entirely different conception. Another week had passed before the purge of "active exponents of militant nationalism and aggression" was extended to posts of "substantial private responsibility" in SWNCC 150/4, and it was even later that JCS 1380/15 applied the purge to "positions of important responsibility or influence in industry, finance, commerce and agriculture."

Whatever the planners' individual motives, the overwhelming influence on the actual wording of the Japanese purge was the German precedent. When a parenthetical supplement to paragraph 23 in the final Japanese directive provided that "in the absence of evidence . . . to the contrary, you will assume that any persons who have held positions of high responsibility since 1937 in industry, finance, commerce and agriculture have been active exponents of militant nationalism and aggression," that was the Army CAD repeating verbatim the words of JCS 1067 to General Eisenhower.[7] When the Joint Chiefs objected to the assumption, saying that the Occupation Commander in the field had better access to the facts, State replied that it was a matter not of fact but of policy. The State Department won out. "Policy," of course, meant the policy for Germany.

The supplement sounded somewhat like Humpty-Dumpty's pronouncement: "When I use a word, it means just what I choose it to mean." If someone had held a key big business position, he was construed by the directive to be an active exponent of militant nationalism and aggression, even if in fact he was nothing of the sort. Whatever Joseph Keenan might think of the evidence, the U.S. Government as a matter of policy judged Japan's top business leaders culpable as a group in having helped bring on the war.

But even accepting that judgment, room for interpretation remained for the theater. Just what was "a key position of high responsibility" after 1937— concretely, what firms, and what posts in them—and from what "positions of important responsibility or influence"—again, what organizations, what jobs— were the purge subjects to be excluded? If the great bulk of the businessmen were considered implicated and purged accordingly, the economy could be devastated. If, on the other hand, the purge was restricted to only a few score, its democratizing impact might be lost. Once again, MacArthur had to decide his priorities, democratization versus economic recovery. Mixed in with those priorities was another not mentioned by the directive: simple justice.

The purge advocates within GHQ saw the heated denials of the war role of Japanese business as far off the mark. Government and business in Japan did not operate at arm's length, as in the United States, they declared. The Japanese military had taken business into its confidence and had asked for, and received, its whole-hearted cooperation. In China, at the behest of the Army's Asia Planning Board, the Mitsui and Mitsubishi trading companies in 1938 had consented to import and distribute Iranian opium in order to pacify the occupied Chinese cities through drug addiction.[8] (In Japan, of course, opium dealing was strictly forbidden.) In New York and other Western cities, the economic purge advocates charged, the same Mitsui and Mitsubishi had engaged in military espionage, including attempts to obtain the drawings and specifications of the new DC-4. In Manchuria, the Nissan–Hitachi combine under Aikawa Gisuke had built up the giant Manchuria Industrial Development Company with the friendly support of the Japanese Army to the point where the entire Nissan "konzern" (Hitachi, Nippon Mining, Nissan Motor Car, and others) began to rival the Mitsui and Mitsubishi combines in size. Aikawa, also an adviser to the Manchukuo Government, and his brother-in-law, Kuhara Fusanosuke, who had turned over the business to go into politics, were by no means simple businessmen but partners, and very friendly partners too, with the Japanese Army.

The same could be said of the dozens of other Japanese firms that had squeezed out native Chinese and Western business on the mainland with the backing of the Japanese Army on the spot and preferential treatment from local puppet authorities. Within Japan itself scores, if not hundreds, of private factories had been built even before Pearl Harbor with bank loans secured by discounting the proceeds of military contracts far into the future. (The Finance Ministry allowed such financing up to 90 percent of the value of the contracts.) That, too, was a kind of joint business–military venture, wasn't it? And what of the unholy partnership that produced hundreds of thousands of imported "contract" Korean and Chinese slave laborers for the Japanese coal mines, thereby assuring the operators a stable and docile work force and releasing Japanese workers for other war industry or military service?

No, the business purge advocates said, Japanese big business as a whole was more than just business. A great many businessmen were just as much a part of Japanese military imperialism as their Army's quartermaster corps. At the very least the business leaders had prospered mightily for many years as a result of their partnership with the military. They could hardly complain if now they had to suffer the consequences of military defeat.

PUNISHMENT OR PREVENTION?

The only workable purge procedure was by categories, which raised the question of individual injustice. An America seemingly unconcerned with fairness arbitrarily punishing erstwhile enemy leaders solely on the authority conferred by military victory could hardly inspire a new democratic order designed to correct the old injustices. A few years later, when George Kennan, who had been head of the State Department Planning Staff, denounced "the indiscriminate purging of whole categories of individuals [as] sickeningly similar to totalitarian practice,"[9] he was simply reacting, although in an exaggerated way, as anyone used to American due process and antipathetic to the notion of collective guilt would. Still, how else could it be done?

At my first and only Government Section meeting on January 7, 1946, the day after I arrived in Japan, General Whitney addressed us on the implementation of the political purge directive (SCAPIN 550), which had been issued the preceding Friday. He openly admitted that all of us would undoubtedly be receiving complaints about condemning people by categories. But, Whitney said, there was no other feasible way to screen hundreds of thousands of cases. A case-by-case review would take far more years than the Occupation would last. Even the economic purge, with cases only in the thousands, as I discovered when

I transferred to ESS a few weeks later, could never be handled fast enough by tribunals inquiring into the evidence with all procedural safeguards. In any event, once GS set the procedural fashion, the other purges followed suit.

The purge advocates, notably Colonel Kades, then the Chief of the Public Administration Division of GS, argued that there was no point in even mentioning justice and courts. The purge was not a criminal proceeding, nor was it punitive in the legal sense. Those who thought so, he said to me in 1946, were confusing it with the war crime trials. The purge proceeded from paragraph 6 of the Potsdam Declaration, the pledge to "eliminate for all time" those who had deceived and misled the people into aggressive war, and that meant to eliminate them from positions in which they could do so again. The War Crimes Tribunal, on the other hand, derived from paragraph 10, which declared that "stern justice will be meted out to war criminals" and then defined the crimes according to existing international law. The two categories were entirely different. The purge was not just a shortcut. That, of course, applied to the economic purge as well.

Indeed, whereas in Germany de-Nazification threw 100,000 persons into jail and fined, sentenced to labor, canceled the civil rights of, or confiscated the property of a million more,[10] the purge in Japan restricted itself only to removing or barring affected persons from certain kinds of employment. No one could call it legally punitive.

Of course, the loss of a high position and exclusion from similar positions just because one was in the wrong job at the wrong time might be unpleasant and even bitter—a victim could derive little solace from the thought that he was not being punished in the legal sense—but, the purge defenders said, it was no worse than removing young men, whether Americans or Japanese, from *their* jobs by drafting them into military service, where their very lives were at risk just because *they* happened to be of a certain age at a certain time. Considering the importance of the program to the future democracy of Japan and a peaceful world, the purge directors did not think they were at all out of line.

If Kades is to be regarded an authority on his boss's intentions, hence those of General MacArthur himself, the only aim of the Supreme Commander was to put the Japanese "old guard" out of action for a period of years—five, ten, or possibly fifteen—not for all time, as Potsdam required. Kades assured me privately that the old leaders could not be expected to change their way of thinking at their stage of life. As Whitney told Prime Minister Shidehara on January 25, 1946, the purge was not "punitive" but "preventive," just "a necessary precaution against the resurgence of Japanese expansionist tendencies."[11]

Within GHQ the arguments of the Government Section could be accepted (of course, they were not audible outside), but what made the purge so devilishly hard to apply equitably was that in essence it was a modified de-Nazification program and did not fit very well. For example, the definition of its targets, "active exponents of militant nationalism and aggression," was a clumsy mouthful, lacking "zing" and public relations appeal. Anyone could hate a Nazi, but who could get excited about an "exponent"? Beyond that, each of its five key words was freighted with ambiguity. No wonder there was internal disagreement on interpretation. Where General Eisenhower's Washington directive was clear—purge Nazis and Nazi sympathizers—the Japanese directive, which was modeled on it, was anything but. The reason for the defect was not simply careless drafting. The trouble was that although the two purge programs were parallel, even sometimes to the point of identical wording, the histories of the two countries were not.

In Germany, the question of who was a Nazi or a sympathizer was relatively straightforward. Because the Nazis had built such a network of supporting organizations both inside and outside the government and had insisted that Nazi partisans belong to them, it was relatively clear, once the facts were in, who was a Nazi sympathizer. Because the Nazis had themselves purged government, judiciary, schools, banks, press, and so on of their opponents, JCS 1067 to Eisenhower could safely assume that important and key officials in industry, finance, and elsewhere were Nazis or sympathizers.

That kind of formula, however, did not fit the realities of Japan. True, the ultra-nationalist societies, with their shrill blather about the Yamato master race, were the most Nazi-like, and in fact 3,000 such ultra-nationalists were purged. But the Imperial Rule Assistance Association and the Imperial Rule Assistance Political Society, together roughly similar in scope to the Nazi Party, held no torchlight processions, engaged in no street brawls, and intimidated no one with physical violence. Set up *after* Japan had embarked on its aggressive career, nine years *after* the invasion of Manchuria, and three years *after* the invasion of China proper, they were umbrella organizations into which almost all the old-line political parties and politicans were absorbed.

The network of Japanese organizations supporting military rule and imperialism consisted mostly of old traditional societies that had been mobilized for the immediate purpose, to be sure, but that had long antedated the militarist capture of government power: the Shintō shrines, the Martial Arts Society, the Red Cross, and others. No one could claim that those organizations had brought about the militarist regime. Even the officials of the Industrial Patriotic Society (*Sampō*), the Japanese equivalent of the Nazi Labor Front, for the most part had been appointed automatically to quasi-military ranks because they were foremen, supervisors, or managers of factories to start with. The special "Thought Police" had a section devoted to control of ultra-nationalists—unthinkable in Germany—and any removals of antimilitarists and nonmilitarists from the civilian government were sporadic and very incomplete. That is why a Quaker pacifist could find himself governor of Hokuriku Region in 1944 and why even General Suzuki Teiichi's War Planning Board contained several socialist economists.

The poor fit of the already altered German garment on the Japanese body required further alterations in the theater. Even in the case of the political purge, those changes could not but cause delays. For example, the driving force behind Japan's imperialism had been its Army. Yet JCS 1380/15, modeled on JCS 1067, had no specific provision for purging even high-ranking officers, because U.S. policy in Germany was to differentiate between Nazi officers and the professional German officer caste. GS therefore had to fall back on the general provision to purge 39,000 out of 40,000 members of the dread *Kempei-tai* military police,[12] who had been regularly used as a kind of Gestapo, because the directive did not purge them as such.

All this GHQ interpretation took time. In Germany the de-Nazifiers went into action as soon as any substantial piece of enemy terrain was securely occupied, but in Japan GS had first to educate, overcome, conciliate, or even bypass other SCAP agencies that disagreed with the GS interpretation. When Whitney took over the Government Section in November 1945, he asked Kades what the most important task facing the section was. Kades had to reply, ''the purge.'' He showed his chief the GS draft directive, which purged all career Army and Navy officers down to the rank of major and the naval equivalent. Whitney, like others after him, exclaimed in some surprise that if the Japanese had won the war and followed the same policy, then he, Whitney, would also be purged. Kades had to explain that while the U.S. forces, including Whitney, were subordinate to the civil authority, in Japan the military services had been dominant, especially in foreign policy. Whitney then accepted the premises of the purge.

Shortly thereafter, Whitney had to fight off the attempt of General Willoughby, the ultra-conservative G-2, to take over the purge program and narrow its application. Then Kades had to contend with the office of the Chief of Staff, who wanted to broaden its scope. Major General Richard Marshall, Deputy Chief of Staff, wanted to know why the Government Section halted the purge at the rank of major. Kades explained that below that rank, the junior officers had not had enough independent authority and responsibility to be blamed for deceiving and misleading the people. Marshall was incensed. From his personal experience, he declared, the captains and lieutenants were the most fanatical. He insisted they be added to the list, too, or they would mislead the Japanese people in the future. Kades, in a hurry to get the purge going after four months' delay, agreed to include captains and lieutenants.[13]

The Purge Debate

If the ''political purge'' presented such difficulties, one can easily imagine the far more complicated problems of definition in the economic purge. Did ''key positions of high responsibility in industry, finance [and] commerce'' apply only to managing directors and presidents, or did the phrase also extend to majority stockholders, directors, auditors, and the managers of important branches like Shanghai or of huge manufacturing complexes? Did they apply to posts only in the industrial, financial, and commercial giants or in all companies? If "big" companies only, by what would "big" be defined: capital, assets, sales, share of market, essentiality of products, or all of these? If the purge of public offices took four months to get started, and of teachers eight months, it was no wonder that the economic purge took even longer. But an even more directly important retarding factor had nothing to do with definitions. It lay within the GHQ organization.

The Chief of Staff had assigned the economic purge to ESS. But the section contained no single substantive division that could implement a mission that covered industry, finance, commerce, and even agriculture. The nimble executive officer, Colonel Ryder, therefore assigned the job to the ESS Legal Division, a small group of five or six lawyers, whose principal responsibility was to service the other divisions, much like the legal department of a big corporation, without any mission of its own. In their usual work the lawyers' job was to devise legal procedures for accomplishing what the other divisions wanted done. Now they had to decide on the "guts" of the economic purge—how far down into the economic system to go—and to do so with no division mission to guide them and few positive convictions of their own. Their only desire was to draft the necessary papers in such a way as to please everyone, both in ESS and in the other sections that claimed an interest. The lawyers just wanted to stay out of trouble.

If anything was incapable of pleasing everyone, it was the economic purge. The definitions of "key positions" and "high responsibility," to say nothing of "militant nationalism" and "aggression" in business, went right to the heart of the question of who was responsible for the war, and consequently who should lead the country in the future. There could scarcely be a more "political" question—or a more emotional one, for that matter. So long as the definitions remained open, so, as a practical matter, did the larger question. Now it had come to roost in the minuscule ESS Legal Division.

The lawyer in Legal Division charged with drawing up the economic purge papers, Harry Straitiff, a largish, equable man, did his best to avoid the deeper implications. For months, Straitiff ran around GHQ with four lists, seeking concurrence from everyone who asserted a legitimate interest in his action. His first list was of important wartime companies and other economic organizations and institutions, and his second enumerated "key posts of high responsibility" in them that if occupied in the past would disqualify the occupier for the future. The third and fourth lists named, respectively, parallel postwar organizations and the posts in them from which the purged officers would be barred. If only Straitiff could get agreement on his lists, regardless of the differing rationales of the people who concurred, he could do his job without touching off a battle in GHQ over the underlying split in basic philosophy.

It was not that simple. First of all Straitiff, in his eagerness not to offend anyone, had brought an inordinate number of SCAP agencies into the picture, thereby multiplying the chances of discord. The issues had started out as theoretical, but by the summer of 1946 many officials in their daily work had come to know the Japanese potentially affected, and they neither looked nor acted like nationalist extremists. That was happening not only in ESS. The G-4 (Supply) Petroleum Division, professional oilmen on temporary assignment in Japan, found that the Japanese oil executives were "their kind of people." Some of the Civil Communications Section officials had worked in Japan before the war on technological assistance contracts—for example, International Standard Electric with Nippon Electric—and had been well treated by the very executives now potentially subject to the economic purge. Both G-4 and the Army Engineer Office feared disruption of their missions if the Japanese executives they worked with were removed from their jobs. Parochial interests and personal sentiments threatened Straitiff's efforts. Finally, Straitiff brought Willoughby's three sections, G-2, Civil Intelligence, and Counter Intelligence, into the discussions along with the Government Section, which all but guaranteed that their conflicting visions of Japan's future would make agreement unreachable.

Surprisingly, in view of the depth and rancor of the disagreements in principle in the Economic Section, Straitiff's method worked there. Once it became clear that his purge lists did not include operational managers but only covered the top level, that is, financial management, the edge was taken off any confrontation. At the intrasection meetings the Finance and Industry divisions, heavily recruited from private companies and banks, argued for the shortest purge lists possible to avoid handicapping production and industrial recovery, while Antitrust and Price Control, with their leavening of New Dealers, pushed for the longest to ensure a thorough democratization and bring in new blood to revive production. But when it came down to the actual lists, there was little argument. Faced with a Washington directive, somebody had to be purged, and if not company presidents, chairmen, managing directors, and the like, then who? With gutted factories and severe raw materials shortages, the best top management could do little in the short run to stimulate production. From that standpoint they would not really be missed. Antitrust, on the other hand, had no real interest in purging production managers. In Japan, few top corporate executives functioned also as production men. The meetings were surprisingly amicable. They took time, but Straitiff finally got his ESS concurrences.

Outside of the section, however, the amiability did not hold. Straitiff ran into difficulties, discord, and even scarcely veiled ideology. Although I had only a peripheral interest as Chief of the Labor Division, for hardly any labor leaders were subject to the purge, I had been attending many of Straitiff's meetings. I remember asking him in early August 1946 what progress he was making. Straitiff was despondent. He seemed to have reached a dead end in his efforts to reconcile all parties by individual meetings. He had decided, he told me, to call a general conference of all concerned. If they could not agree, he would throw in the towel.

On August 15, 1946, then, at three in the afternoon of a sweltering day, some twenty-five representatives of different SCAP agencies assembled round the huge table in the Daiichi Building fifth-floor conference room. General MacArthur, whose office was on the sixth floor, was out to lunch. Unlike the ESS conferences, this one was tense and formal. Too many conferees felt they were being given their last chance. Straitiff, presiding over the meeting and going by the book, called on the Far East Command general staff sections first. I could not understand what legitimate interest any of those sections, except G-2 (Intelligence), might have, but G-1 (Personnel) and G-4 maintained their missions would be injured by a rigorous application of the economic purge. The G-3 (Operations) said, to his credit, that it was none of his business and he didn't know why he'd been invited. G-2 was opposed. Then the special staff agencies were called on in alphabetical order. Almost everyone was critical of Straitiff's lists for one reason or another. Civil Communications, represented by Deputy Chief J. D. Whittemore, formerly a vice president of the Chase National Bank,[14] was forceful but typical when he said that without key people in the communications industry could not carry out his mission of restoring the Japanese telecommunications network. To my surprise, the Government Section said very little. If a vote had been taken, Straitiff's lists would have been defeated by perhaps four to one.

The most dramatic statement came from Colonel Harry I. T. Cresswell, Chief of Counter Intelligence. Cresswell, a leathery old Japan hand who had been the U.S. military attaché in Tokyo at the time of Pearl Harbor,[15] was clearly agitated all through the meeting, containing himself under great pressure as the others spoke. Given his chance, he burst into impassioned speech. In the coming war with the Russians, he declared vehemently, the Japanese industrialists would be our best friends in the country; how could we purge them? The economic purge was a tragic mistake. Unless it was dropped, America itself would be endangered.

When Cresswell abruptly stopped and sat down, his face still working, there was a stunned silence in the room. Many of the other sections, opposed to the economic purge policy, had been trying at the meeting to narrow its scope and so to kill it, but they had done so by indirection. Cresswell's action was radically different, and we knew it. We had just witnessed the end of a military career. It was not the act of a disciplined soldier to proclaim an oncoming war with a current ally, to defend an existing enemy, and to argue for disobeying a directive from the highest military authorities in the country, the President and the Joint Chiefs of Staff—all publicly, in a formal meeting, in front of a score of witnesses. A few days later, Cresswell was removed from Counter Intelligence and made Chairman of the Board of Awards and Decorations. While leaving the meeting, I asked Major Jack Napier, the Government Section representative, what he thought of the whole affair. Certainly not the way to do it, he commented.

Quite possibly Colonel Kades, who had been watching Straitiff's floundering for some time, had already decided on his next move. Straitiff's carnival had now provided him with the opportunity. Five days later, on August 20, General Whitney, Kades's boss, handed the Japanese Government representative a statement approved by General MacArthur that directed the Japanese to submit a plan for broadening the existing purge to the economic area. With that statement the economic purge was neatly lifted from the hands of ESS and its Legal Division, as well as from the scrutiny of all the other sections. "Sure," Kades said airily when I queried him about it, "there never was an "economic' purge. It was all one purge from the beginning and it was always our [that is, Government Section's] business."[16]

The fact was that when Napier returned to Government Section with his report of what had just happened, including Cresswell's emotional outburst, Kades went immediately to see General Whitney. Kades pointed out that after almost a year ESS was still nowhere near taking the necessary actions; instead a number of Headquarters sections with only remote interests were blocking the program. The only way to accomplish an economic purge fast, Kades said, was to transfer it to the section that already had all the machinery set up, that is, Government Section. Whitney, never reluctant when it came to enlarging his own jurisdiction, quickly agreed. It is a measure of Whitney's special position with MacArthur that he was prepared to ask the Supreme Commander to overrule the Chief of Staff's assignment of missions. No other general, not even Marquat, would have dared.

When Whitney went to see General MacArthur on the subject that evening, he found the General, vulnerable to the charge of boot-dragging on paragraphs 23 and 40, receptive. As usual, MacArthur was more sensitive to attacks in the United States from the suspicious left than to those from the adoring right. Finally, he profoundly agreed with the whole conception of the economic purge.

With MacArthur's assent to the transfer of the economic purge to Government Section, the program went into high gear. Kades and his men took over Straitiff's lists intact and used them to review and judge the Japanese Government's reply. Three months after the dramatic meeting in the G-4 conference room, on November 21, 1946, the Japanese Government announced the lists of companies and key positions in them whose occupants were subject to the purge. In early January of the following year, 1947, the relevant Cabinet orders were issued. At that point, the whole controversy burst out into the open.

AMERICAN BUSINESS REACTION

Cresswell's prompt transfer undoubtedly inhibited open dissent on the part of the Regular Army officers in GHQ, but it could not prevent individual SCAP officials from privately predicting to American reporters that there would be dire consequences. After August 20, as the Japanese Government worked on the purge categories, the wildest rumors spread. An article in *Newsweek* in January 1947 warned that the economic purge would remove 30,000 businessmen from their jobs and bar 250,000 more from high economic positions.[17] With only 100,000 corporations, including small enterprises, in Japan altogether, and only 1,100 firms on SCAP's restricted list of large companies[18] I had to wonder where this army of business executives was supposed to come from. Responsible Americans, however, hearing such reports and visualizing a stripping of all executive talent from Japan's economy, were alarmed.

Among those alarmed were American big business and banking circles, including high-ranking American officials who had come to temporary government service from business and had increasingly displaced the radical reformers of 1945. By 1947 three secretaries (Forrestal, Snyder, and Harriman) out of twelve in the Cabinet and two undersecretaries (Draper and Lovett) were professional investment or commercial bankers. Unlike the New Dealers who had so influenced the contents of JCS 1380/15, they valued private businessmen highly. Navy Secretary Forrestal, for instance, told Treasury Secretary Snyder in March 1947 that "the world could only be brought back to order by a restoration of commerce, trade, and business and that would have to be done by businessmen."[19] Now SCAP was proposing to purge the businessmen in Japan. What would become of Japanese economic recovery?

The American business leaders in government and out did not approach the problem from the base of the German de-Nazification directive, had not been involved in 1945 Occupation planning, and knew little of recent Japanese internal history. Although several had held very responsible posts at war's end, I doubt that they had ever studied or remembered JCS 1380/15, which still controlled Japan. That was yesterday's business, and they were busy with today's. (That is by no means as strange as it sounds. In late 1947 Defense Secretary Forrestal severely criticized FEC 230, the American position on Japanese financial combines. Six months earlier, he or his deputy had approved it in writing!) To such executives, the Japanese economic purge sounded like an aberration in American policy.

Especially hard hit by the purge reports were those Americans who were reaching out to reestablish their prewar Japanese business connections. They began to pay attention for the first time to what the American military was doing in Japan. Indeed, Americans who had met their Japanese business counterparts in person before the war found it difficult to picture them as aggressors, for they were no fiery orators, blustery militarists, or violent assassins, as the purge directive seemed to imply, but rather civilized, soft-spoken gentlemen who were exquisitely polite to foreign visitors and sometimes privately deplored their homegrown militarist wild men. These business people had "deceived and misled the people of Japan into embarking on world conquest"? On the contrary, Under Secretary of State Grew and his conservative counsellor, Eugene Dooman, had staunchly defended Japanese big business as the element most likely to serve as a bulwark against militarist resurgence. Conservative Japanese financiers and industrialists were warmongers? That, their American counterparts thought, must be the invention of doctrinaire radicals—or worse—within SCAP Headquarters, fanatics who had taken the bit in their teeth and were "deceiving and misleading" General MacArthur.

The idea of staff subversion soon found expression in the American press. Perhaps it was easier and safer to attack the ruler through his courtiers, or perhaps the critics actually believed the courtiers were to blame. *Newsweek's* foreign editor, Harry Kern, appeared obsessed by the nightmare of GHQ staff run wild, for in June 1947 he returned to the attack on the economic purge as part of a three-part, seven-page article.[20] His scenario had General Whitney conniving behind General MacArthur's back and then taking advantage of his close relationship with the Supreme Commander to get the latter's *post facto* backing.[21] That was hardly likely; Whitney was no Svengali, and MacArthur no Trilby, and there was no imaginable reason why a conservative corporation lawyer, utterly devoted to MacArthur, would entrap his chief in what Kern labeled a radical and irresponsible action.

Newsweek alleged that military rivalries played a role, but could not name the rivals. By January 1947 Whitney had sole control of the economic purge, and General Marquat, who had formerly had responsibility, was happily, as far as any of us near him could see, out of the picture. So was Willoughby. There was just no ulterior motive to be discovered. Later on George Kennan, after several hours alone in his Imperial Hotel room with General Willoughby, but never with Whitney, was to ascribe the economic purge to a "dogmatic impersonal vindictiveness for which there were few examples outside the totalitarian countries themselves,"[22] an explanation that explained nothing. None of the critics went back for the explanation to the basic directive. Somehow it was easier or more satisfying, even though less truthful, to blame the economic purge on MacArthur's staff.

The myth of the runaway headquarters persisted. Big business and conservative visitors earnestly tried to set MacArthur straight. Roy Howard, president of the Scripps Howard newspapers, complained to the SCAP about it in February 1947. James Lee Kauffman, attorney for Libby-Owens-Ford, harped on the theme of the radicals and the economic purge in a widely distributed report, which Under Secretary of the Army Draper forwarded to MacArthur in October

1947. In March 1948 Paul Hoffman, then president of Studebaker Corporation, protested to the Supreme Commander (as Whitney had said to Kades) that as president of an industrial corporation in wartime he, too, could have been purged on the same grounds by the Japanese had they won the war. They all assumed they were telling MacArthur something new that his staff was keeping from him.

MacArthur's Own Views

In a reply to *Newsweek,* published in February 1947, MacArthur declared that he personally had decided every case of disagreement among his staff sections. In other words, the purge policy was his. "I have aggressively furthered this objective [that is, of the economic purge]," he asserted, "not alone because to do so is in compliance with the basic directive by which my course as Supreme Commander is bound, but because any other course would be to ignore those very causes which led the world into war, and by so doing to invite the recurrence of future war."[23]

Cynics discounted MacArthur's assurance; for him to speak otherwise would be an admission that he had lost control over his own Headquarters. Still, all of us in GHQ knew that none of the top generals would dare take a public position on any important issue without first ascertaining what the "Old Man" thought, certainly not with a presidential race in the offing, and most especially not Whitney, who had every opportunity to check his views—he saw MacArthur every day—and who was most sensitive of all to the U.S. domestic political implications of every MacArthur action.

The refusal of outsiders to believe such a plain denial was probably rooted in their unshakable estimate of the Supreme Commander as an ultra-conservative. On the contrary, with his deep populist suspicions of big business and financial combinations anywhere in the world, MacArthur found it hard to believe that the Japanese big business leaders had not given in to the temptations of Imperial economic power. He did not need the evidentiary proofs of explicit conspiracy sought by Keenan and his lawyers to tell him how things really worked beneath the surface. After all, he had watched the Japanese businessmen at work in the Far East on and off for almost fifty years. "Japan's economic overlords," he declared, had striven "to the end that a large part of the earth's surface might be brought under [their] economic bondage . . . and that Japan might weld from conquered nations and peoples of the world a vast totalitarian empire, designed further to enrich them."[24] Civilians they might be, but they were just as guilty as the military.

The General was scornful of the charge that he was ignoring the adverse effect of the purge on economic recovery. That was an exaggeration, probably for selfish motives, he said. "The details of the purge program," he assured the worriers, "have been carefully evolved so as not to disturb the ordinary businessman, nor the technicians whose skill and brains did not influence formulation of the policy which directed Japan's course towards aggressive war. . . . In my opinion, and I believe in the opinion of truly responsible Japanese as well, the action will not unduly disturb the development of a future peaceful industrial economy."[25] The man who had impressed Navy Secretary Forrestal in July 1946 with the urgent need for economic recovery, who had fought for ample food, and who had quietly sabotaged industrial plant reparations to protect the Japanese economy was not likely to overlook the possibility of damage to recovery by his business purge. He just didn't think it would happen.

"But even, if this should prove not the case," he asserted, "even if . . . this cleansing of the economy is destined seriously to handicap industrial revival for lack of essential leadership—or even if such revival is wholly impossible without the guidance of those several thousand persons involved who directly contributed to leading the world into a war taking a toll of millions of human lives and effecting destruction of hundreds of billions in material resources—then, in that event the interests of those other hundreds of millions of people who want and seek peace leave no alternative than that Japan must bear and sustain the consequences."[26] MacArthur could have made no more unequivocal statement of his priorities, democratization above economics.

Back home, his position was politically impregnable. The American liberals would not attack him, because they agreed with him. The conservatives could not, because the American public knew he was a certified conservative. With his personal prestige at its height, the Supreme Commander stood pat. Notwithstanding the repeated attempts to put pressure on him from the outside, the business purge went swiftly forward. In a little more than a year, it was all over. On May 10, 1948, Headquarters ordered most of the Japanese purge machinery, including that covering the economic purge, dismantled.

The results were neither as drastic as predicted by the purge's opponents nor as widely beneficial as promised by its advocates. In all, only 453 persons were actually removed from their posts under the terms of the economic purge, and an approximately equal number resigned in anticipation.[27] Those resigning were almost all included also in the 914 persons who were "provisionally designated," that is, barred from taking key posts.

The economic purge, then, affected only 1,555 business people (after deducting those reinstated)—MacArthur had earlier guessed "several thousand"—a far cry from the 30,000 businessmen to be removed and the quarter million more to be barred that *Newsweek* magazine had predicted. No doubt some personal anxiety or mental suffering affected the 5,000 or so businessmen who were screened and passed, but then the whole urban population was afflicted by the consequences of Japan's military disaster in many ways. Following a "depurge" some five years later, many of those excluded returned quickly to positions of national economic leadership. Shōriki Matsutarō, deposed as president of the *Yomiuri* newspaper, founded Japan's first television station and established "Yomiuriland," Japan's earliest version of Disneyland; Kawai Yasunari, purged as Welfare Minister, became president of Komatsu Heavy Industry; most strikingly, Hatoyama Ichirō, though purged personally by General MacArthur, later became Prime Minister. Meanwhile, in the context of an entire national economy, 453 removals and 450 resignations in advance were not much.

Drastic effects on their companies were even harder to discern. Production did not fall. Indeed, from November 1947 until November 1948 the industrial production index rose 58 percent. There is no telling, of course, what might have happened to production had the economic purge not been applied. But certainly the attitudes and methods of those next in line who replaced the purged leaders hardly departed from their predecessors' ways. After all, they had been trained in just those old ways all their lives and would have succeeded in due course to the new positions anyway. Where companies were split by the Occupation, the new officers, like Niizeki Yasutarō, a former division chief of Mitsui Bussan, fought just as hard to recombine them as their purged superiors would have. The only perceptible difference was that the new men did not have the national prestige of their predecessors or their personal treasuries of social IOU's, accumulated over the years, which had given the purged officers so much influence and power across the entire economic spectrum.

That was the key to what MacArthur saw as the imperative of the economic purge. On the one hand, an "old boy" network of recalcitrant reactionaries at the key points of the Japanese economy could have sabotaged SCAP's democratization programs, whether trust-busting, labor relations, or anything else. (Indeed, we in the Labor Division regularly received reports of outbursts by "old guard" industrialists who wanted to defy the new labor unions at all costs and vehemently said so.) That was an unacceptable danger to the Supreme Commander.

On the other hand, if the business purge brought little concrete benefit, failure to purge could have brought psychological disaster. Who among the Japanese people would have believed that Japan had really changed if the same old crowd was still running the country? The big businessmen of the Imperial era were too closely identified in the public mind with war, suppression of popular liberties, and collaboration with militarism. To have permitted them to reappear once again in the newspapers, magazines, and newsreels and on the radio, still at the helm, but this time in the name of democracy instead of the Emperor and the Greater East Asia Co-Prosperity Sphere, could easily have destroyed SCAP's credibility and generated a corrosive cynicism toward the new democracy. To Douglas MacArthur, with his priorities, the economic purge was inescapable.

10

The Dilemma of the Great Inflation

For four years after the war, the great inflation hung over Japan like some immense, brooding presence. It affected every household one way or another, bringing satisfaction to the countryside, despair to the cities. No one could make decisions or face the future without being aware that things were costing more every day, that savings were shriveling, and that future astronomical school fees, marriage expenses, and even funeral costs could destroy the most careful plans. A factory girl, after several years of work, received a retirement allowance of a thousand yen, which she set aside to pay her wedding expenses and buy a *tansu* chest of drawers for her new home. Before long, it wasn't enough to buy an umbrella. Wages, no matter what they were or how much they were raised, were never enough. Words disappeared from the language. "*Entaku,*" a one-yen taxi, became a ludicrous anachronism overnight. By 1949, when inflation was finally contained, the price level had risen 150 *times* in four years. No one could take his mind off the inflation for long.

"Hands Off" the Inflation

A constant awareness of the great inflation also pervaded the two governments of the country, the Japanese Government and the GHQ SCAP. Every SCAP section supervised some part of the Japanese Government's operations—police and prisons, public health, courts and procurators, schools, agricultural extension work, and so forth—and the budgets for each were continuously dissolving in the flood of price increases. Every one of our ESS divisions, with the exception of the Scientific, spent a good part if not most of its time dealing with the inflation or its direct consequences. The same was true of the Natural Resources Section, with its mining, fisheries, and farming interests. The Civil Information and Education Section and the Ministry of Education applied themselves toward implementing the U.S. Education Mission's recommendation to restructure the schools on the "six-three-three" system (six years of primary school, three of middle school, three of high school), but there was not enough money. Indeed, the teachers wanted to use whatever there was to raise wages so they would not have to sneak off the job to scrounge for food in the countryside. The Government Section proclaimed the independence of the judiciary, and the Diet passed laws to make it so, but in 1947 Supreme Court Justice Kuriyama wended his way discreetly to my office as General Marquat's Special Assistant in ESS to beg me on behalf of the Chief Justice to intercede with our Finance Division to get judges a raise in salary so they could survive. Certainly the Occupation authorities would have to do something about the inflation, if indeed not make its control a centerpiece of the entire economic policy toward Japan.

But the directive given MacArthur said hands off! The Washington planners' reasons were sound: fear that the Occupation authorities would be diverted from the more important goal of democratization and a reluctance to assume responsibilities for a crisis not of America's making and quite possibly beyond the Occupation's capacity to repair. We knew from intelligence reports in the last wartime months that prices within Japan had already begun to soar, and we all expected that the frightful destruction and havoc attending Japan's defeat would aggravate the rise. In those days almost everyone looked upon inflation as an unmitigated evil, a kind of loathsome economic disease that had to be extirpated on principle. The planners were no exception. "Serious inflation will substantially retard the accomplishment of the ultimate objectives of the Occupation," they proclaimed in JCS 1380/15.

I believed that too at the time. In the rush of events, none of us had much opportunity to examine whether that proposition was really correct when one of the Occupation's explicit goals was to reduce the disparity of wealth in Japan. Nothing redistributes wealth more brutally and effectively, short of a revolution, than a roaring inflation that wipes out creditors and liberates debtors. The planners, however, passed over the possible use of inflation as a device to achieve the egalitarian objective. Perhaps there just wasn't enough time to recognize the opportunity and work out an appropriate policy. Instead the directive left inflation to the Japanese, and then only as something to be fought. "You will direct the Japanese authorities to make every feasible effort to avoid such inflation," the directive continued, but "assume [no] responsibility for the economic rehabilitation of Japan" and "no obligation to maintain . . . any particular standard of living."

As it turned out, the inflation was unavoidable, and it functioned in at least one key area, agricultural land tenure, as an indispensable democratization tool.

It served, furthermore, to mask the harshness of postwar life and to maintain hope among the distressed, and hence social stability, while the economy slowly recovered. It sparked a three-year battle over whether to emphasize controlling it or living with it. Whatever the directive said, it was just impossible for General MacArthur to leave it to the Japanese.

To begin with, no directive could persuade him that the management of a roaring inflation was a secondary matter. On the contrary, he became increasingly convinced that if mishandled, the inflation could wreck his Occupation and his place in history. Besides, a dependent and harassed Government, afflicted among other things by the Occupation purge, and not master in its own house, could not possibly be strong enough to fight inflation. Too many immediate SCAP interests, furthermore, were involved at every turn for the Japanese Government to proceed independently. Nor could MacArthur allow it to in any event, for any serious mistakes would reflect badly on SCAP. Finally, the Washington-imposed limits were contrary to human nature. In an all-powerful, activist headquarters, the SCAP officials ''concerned'' just could not keep their hands off.

Alarmed by the near-doubling of the Bank of Japan note issue[1] in the four and a half months after the surrender, the ESS Finance Division, many of whose staffers had ties with big business,[2] urgently recommended a complete currency conversion to curtail the money supply. General Marquat, then Chief of ESS for only two months and completely new to economics, was impressed by the experts and carried their recommendation to his chief. MacArthur, uneasy about the inflation limitations imposed upon him by the directive, told the Finance Division to go ahead, provided the operation was seen publicly as a Japanese effort. From then on the pattern was set: aloofness plus general guidance in public, but strong and active intervention from GHQ.

THE NEW YEN ISSUE

On February 16, 1946, then, the Japanese Government suddenly announced the conversion of all existing currency into brand new Bank of Japan notes. When the public brought in their old yen, they received new yen in exchange, but only up to specified limits—300 per individual plus 100 for each dependent, and varying amounts to businesses. The balance of their old yen was deposited in blocked accounts, frozen except for carefully limited monthly withdrawals. The object: to contract the note issue at the expense of the less depressed and the temporarily affluent, like black marketeers, and to dampen price rises until more basic anti-inflationary measures could be taken. The result: the note issue fell from some 62 billion yen before the conversion to only 15 billion afterward; 47 billion yen were ''blocked'' out of circulation.[3]

The operation went off smoothly, but although the voice was Jacob's, the hand was Esau's. All the way from the design to the delivery of the money, the Americans were deeply involved. The obverse side of the new ten-yen note had a double motif, the Diet Building at the left and a phoenix design on the right. The sketch submitted by the Japanese authorities originally was passed to Government Section for concurrence, and the GS democratizers noticed that the Diet Building, symbol of the new democracy, covered only 30 percent of the banknote area, the phoenix 70 percent. They ordered a roughly equal allocation of space. Furthermore, the rules regarding withdrawals from the blocked accounts were thrashed out in Finance Division, as were the means of storage, delivery, and security. One of the main depositories of the new currency was a huge vault whose entrance was from my Labor Division office in the Central Agricultural and Forestry Bank, part of the building that ESS had taken over. Working late in the evening of February 15, I was astonished when a dozen Japanese workers with wheelbarrows, accompanied by a U.S. lieutenant, showed up to remove hundreds of millions of new yen through the massive door set in the wall not 20 feet from my desk. The next day, my Labor Relations Officer had to dissuade the fledgling Communications Workers' Union from striking to stop the currency conversions in post offices.[4] The Occupation, in one manner or another, was calling the shots all the way.

One incident more than any other demonstrated the extent to which the conversion project was American—despite the plain wording of the Washington directive. As soon as the project was decided upon, the Bank of Japan started printing the new notes at a feverish pace, but as the date for the conversion approached, the Finance Ministry officials began to fear they would not have enough. They asked our Finance Division for a delay but were refused. If the Japanese did not have enough of their own currency, the Finance Division officials said, they could supplement it with the stock of ''B-Type'' yen, printed by the United States during the war for use by an American military government in the wake of the expected invasion.

The Finance Minister and his subordinates were mortified. Japan, having lost its sovereignty, now was not even able to print its own money! In a last-ditch meeting with General Marquat, Finance Minister Shibusawa Keizō offered to sacrifice himself for his country. If GHQ insisted on Japan's issuing American-made money, he declared, he would resign, accepting responsibility. Marquat looked at him fixedly for a long moment and then told him, ''This is an Occupation. You can't resign!'' The urbane Shibusawa was speechless. Years later he could not forget how incredible that seemed to him at the time. When one fails in Japan one accepts responsibility by resigning. Not accept responsibility? How could that be? ''This is an Occupation. You can't resign!'' he would repeat to me in 1951, shaking his head in amused bewilderment.

As it happened, the ''B-Type'' yen were used only in a few locations on

Kyūshū,[5] but otherwise the operation was a failure. In only seven months, the artificially contracted note issue climbed back to the preconversion level, then increased by 50 percent more by the end of the year.[6] Meanwhile, the wholesale price index almost doubled in the two months after the conversion—the money supply had risen only 40 percent from its low by then—and then prices rose by half again by December.[7]

The only concrete results of SCAP's first venture in controlling the money supply were the democratic pictures of seventh-century Prince Shōtoku, Japan's first land reformer, on the 100-yen note and the 1930s Diet Building, symbol of prewar liberalism's last gasp, on the 10-yen denomination. But from then on GHQ's intervention in Japanese Government inflation operations was established and, what is more, established under the leadership of the ESS Finance Division.

The role of the Finance Division was only natural—after all, its business was money—but it was also unfortunate. Perhaps under normal circumstances it would have been different, but in an Occupation where the occupiers lived in a protected enclave, the Finance Division members, dealing only with high-ranking Finance Ministry and banking officials, could not fully appreciate how the ordinary Japanese citizen was faring. The Labor Division, meeting workers every day; Industry, visiting blasted factories; or Price Control and Rationing, having to contend constantly with malnutrition and lack of consumer necessities, had broader experience bearing on the inflation. For the Finance Division people, their own figures constituted the fundamental reality; what I in Labor Division considered reality was known to them but not felt, a kind of distant abstraction. A knowledge of the details of the labor and other democratization missions might have tempered their thinking. But JCS 1380/15, classified "top secret," lay in a safe in our Administration office under combat security conditions, with no one without a "need to know" allowed access to it. Finance, like other staff agencies, generally did not need to know missions other than its own. Unrestrained by an awareness of competing Occupation objectives, they assigned inflation-fighting their highest priority.

My first contact with that kind of thinking was at an informal conference on fighting inflation early in 1946, which I attended as Chief of the Labor Division. For the first but not the last time, the Labor Division was asked to sponsor wage controls as labor's contribution to the common effort. I was astonished. Even by the imperfect statistics then available, we knew that workers' real income had been reduced by more than 75 percent,[8] and it was hard to see how much more they could be cut. If the Finance Division's object was to ensure that everyone sacrificed, wage controls were not needed. If equality of sacrifice was the goal, it was some other sector's turn.

When I explained this to the group and added that imposing wage controls in such circumstances would certainly destroy the Japanese workers' confidence in either our good will or our good sense, thereby endangering a major phase of

SCAP's democratization effort, I was met with incomprehension and with knowing nods that meant, well, what can you expect from a chief of the Labor Division? As it happened, one of those present, probably the most prestigious, was the special financial adviser Frank Tamagna, a man of especially wide experience (he had worked in China and had fought in the anti-Fascist underground in Italy). It was he who called off the dogs. He reminded everyone that the JCS directive left counterinflationary measures to the Japanese Government, not SCAP, and therefore SCAP-sponsored wage controls were out of order. For that matter, so were SCAP-sponsored currency conversions, but then there had been no opposition. The request was dropped.

After the meeting, Tamagna confided to me that he was afraid inflation control would be clamped on the economy too soon. I must confess that I did not understand him. But he was right. There was no means, other than inflation, for the Japanese Government to maintain its fiscal integrity by paying off its debts and charges yen for yen while being really unable to do so. There was no other way of hiding dangerously irreconcilable claims for scarce resources than paying them all and postponing conflict until improving supplies moderated the intensity of the rivalries that otherwise could well have torn the nation apart. And there was no substitute for the inflation in fortuitously helping make the agricultural land reform a resounding success.

The Land Reform

From the beginning MacArthur had been convinced that the peasants, then half the population of Japan, could be won to democracy and would forgo the extremism of so many of their sons—the violently nationalist young officers typically came from rural families—if they could be provided with land of their own. His SCAPIN 411 ordered the farmland redistribution plan, and his Headquarters experts, headed by the U.S. Agriculture Department's Wolf Ladejinsky, worked for a period of two years, supervising the remarkable double-faceted transfer program carried out by a network of elected village land committees. The committees first bought land parcels from almost a million *rentier* landlords, then resold them at low prices and on favorable credit terms to working farmers. Farm tenancy was virtually ended, and with land came economic liberation.

Yet lack of title to land was only one of two serious problems afflicting the Japanese peasantry. The other was the mountainous prewar debt borne by each farm family. It amounted to about a thousand yen[9] in a year, say 1938, when the total annual agricultural production, not income, per family was only 738 yen in all.[10] Once before, in the 1870s and 1880s, the Japanese farmers had lost their land because they were unable to carry their debt. Without heroic measures to reduce their debt after the war, the same might very well have happened again.

But the inflation neatly resolved the problem. By 1948, in real terms the farm debt was worth less than 1 percent of its 1934–36 value and was easily paid off or reduced to the status of a minor nuisance.

Equally important, the great inflation helped solve the problem of financing the land transfers. I well remember Ladejinsky showing me his land redistribution program only two days before the war's end at the U.S. Army Civil Affairs Staging Area in Monterey, California, where we were both civilian advisers. When I cautiously asked the ultra-sensitive Ladejinsky how the extremely poor tenants could afford to pay anything at all for land, let alone the presumably respectable price the Japanese Government would pay the owners— of course, the United States would not countenance outright confiscation— Ladejinsky flew into an angry diatribe against unreasonable doubters, including me, but did not answer the question. The great inflation answered it for him a few years later. Because of the rapid depreciation of the yen during the time lag between the land committees' purchase from the old owners and the new owners' payment to the committees, it was possible for the government, in real terms, to buy dear and sell cheap, meanwhile showing no loss on the books. Thus were normal capitalist principles confounded and economic democratization advanced by the great inflation.

In concrete terms a Japanese working farmer could acquire 2.45 acres, or one *chō* (equal to one hectare), of paddy field for the equivalent of twenty-one dollars if he did not pay for it until March 1949, whereas the former owner, if the village land committees paid him in March 1947, would have received ninety-six dollars. But in yen, the owner got 9,500, and the buyer paid 7,500. The Government made up the difference as a subsidy. By far the greater part of the real subsidy was a gift from the inflation.[11] And to get that ¥ 7,500, the working farmer had only to sell a fifth of *one* crop from that one *chō*.[12] Before the war, he had had to pay half of the crop each year for his rent alone. It was now a rare peasant who could not acquire the land he was cultivating outright and, free of the burden of interest on former loans, derive an adequate livelihood from it.

The same farmer, incidentally, would respond to his economic liberation by setting new records for productivity. Operating his land for the first time as he saw fit, not as some officious absentee landlord dictated, and with sufficient financial resources to do so properly, he performed a technological revolution on the farm. He used protective polyethylene sheeting to advance the sowing season and retard the harvest, applied insecticides as never before, added fertilizer when it was needed, not just when he had the money, cemented his irrigation dikes, and so forth. And he harvested a series of ''bumper'' crops in the 1950s that first astonished his countrymen and then became the new standard. The unexpected increase in domestic food supply gave a powerful boost to Japan's balance of trade just when the country needed it most. The increasingly prosperous countryside was able simultaneously to help expand the postwar domestic consumer market, which played such an important part in Japan's economic miracle. The Occupation land reform was a key achievement of the third turn. It assured the tranquility of the countryside for decades to come. And it came about thanks, in large part, to the great inflation.

TWO SCHOOLS OF THOUGHT

The application of the inflation, judo-style, to help achieve the land reform, however, was a freak. It was not intentional, so SCAP was never faced with a choice between fighting inflation and rural democratization. In the cities, however, the choice was obvious and painful. To the finance specialists, the only true way to fight inflation was to reduce the rate of increase in the money supply, because inflation was the consequence of too much money chasing too few goods. That meant bringing the budget into closer balance by restricting government subsidies, whether to producers or to consumers, and holding down government wages. But the democratization reform had stimulated and encouraged the organization of new democratic labor unions, which were agitating, protesting, bargaining feverishly, and even striking for higher wages and insisting, as consumers, that subsidized consumer prices be kept low. Monetary control and labor democratization were incompatible. Strict monetary control measures would leave little room for labor democratization to show results. Allowing such room would explode the budget and stimulate the inflation.

Within GHQ the question hinged on "realism." The monetarists in the Finance Division accused the Labor Division of not being realistic. Printing money could not create goods. Higher government wages or subsidies that enabled higher private industry wages were only illusory, because the purchasing power of the payments would surely diminish as more money went bidding for the same goods. A compliant government surrendering to its claimants was therefore deceitful and fraudulent, promising everyone what he wanted and then having the inflation do the dirty work of stealing away part of the value indiscriminately in the dark. An honest government would admit it did not have the resources to meet even justifiable demands, then would cut the claims courageously, openly, and intelligently in the budget. Realistic as to money, we countered, the approach was unrealistic as to people, for the resources were too limited and the sacrifices demanded from them too harsh.

By the end of the war, both blue-collar and white-collar workers and their families had borne the brunt of their nation's suffering. The peasants' homes were still standing undisturbed; the workers', on the other hand, had been bombed out, their belongings often consumed in the flames. On the farms production was down, but that meant the cities had less to eat while the peasants increased their own food consumption, as wartime crop collection controls weakened.

When peace came, the workers had no means to produce enough to support themselves, for their factories had been devasted, and fuel and raw materials were lacking.

Even where workers were still employed, truly productive work was rare. Shipyards, for example, were regularly idle half a day. With the collapse of motorized traffic, human beings became beasts of burden. I remember seeing one man drag a two-wheel "rear car" loaded with a few sheets of glass across the bombed-out desert of Tokyo. How much could the shipyard worker or glass hauler add to the value of his factory's product to enable the factory to pay him a living wage? The same was true of the office employee whose company was working at half-speed. And how could any of those stumbling companies and people pay enough taxes to support the teachers and government administrative employees?

Everyone could see the consequences with his own eyes. Workers or members of their families went to the countryside in droves for cabbages, sweet potatoes, *daikon* radishes, or black market rice, not in return for money, which they did not have, but in exchange for their remaining possessions—kimonos, clocks, picture frames, souvenir ashtrays, cheap cameras, and the like. Movable wealth was indeed on the move—from the relatively unproductive sector of the economy, the cities, to the most productive population, the farmers. But the workers' possessions were not inexhaustible. Shedding clothes to buy food was first compared to the snake's shedding of its skin, then to the peeling of an onion, because it was accompanied by tears.

In those circumstances survival, not holding back inflation, was paramount for the city population. That was precisely the view taken by JCS 1380/15, which did not mention money supply, balanced budgets, or any other fiscal or monetary measures to restrain inflation, but did mandate a series of direct controls: on production and prices, on black markets, and "to ensure a fair and equitable distribution of relief supplies," mostly food. The planners' purpose was to create a shelter from the raging inflation storm so that, as MacArthur would later put it, the weaker members of society would not perish. At the same time, in the allocation of industrial materials they sought to pin-point essential industries and ensure that they, too, would survive in competition with luxury goods production.

In the United States the planners of the wartime government had followed the same policy, enforcing consumer goods rationing, price controls, and industrial allocations while ignoring a wildly unbalanced budget. So why not Japan now? That way constituted an alternative to Finance Division monetarism. In the short run, until supply caught up more closely with demand, the GHQ direct-control proponents asserted, a policy of living with the inflation while trying to slow it down was more realistic than trying to stop it head-on with "realistic" budgets tailored to pitifully inadequate resources.

It was a question of democracy as well. The monetarists complained that uncontrolled inflation mindlessly preempted decisions on the distribution of resources that should be made overtly by a cabinet responsible to the Diet and the electorate. But I saw another kind of democracy on display in my office almost daily. In October 1945, General MacArthur had called for encouragement of labor unionization as an essential part of democracy, and the workers responded by organizing all through 1946 at a prodigious rate. Exercising their new democratic rights, they were demanding, not begging, that the employer or the Government do something about their economic distress. As a steady stream of labor leaders called at the Labor Division, I was struck not only by their determination to improve the workers' lives but also their faith that in the new democracy it was possible to do so through their new institutions. Indeed, through the whole year the unions successively negotiated wage increases, usually peacefully but sometimes by strike action. Their confidence in the institutions of the new Japan grew. Of course, in the circumstances the workers' gains were transitory, for advancing prices eventually swallowed them up, and the unions had to demand, negotiate, and even strike again, maybe to repeat the process yet again. But in the meantime the workers could see that unions worked, they gained a temporary respite, and the Government gained time to put the economy back on the tracks. Government action to dry up public and private funds could end all that and drive the unions to politically radical solutions. Nor was there any guarantee dissent would be confined to pacific channels. I remember warning one of the Finance Division officials that a balanced budget might bring violence into the streets. Don't worry, he replied, we're not that close. But what if the Occupation did decide really to try?

The two schools of economic thought contended within GHQ for almost three years, each trying to win the approval of the ESS Chief, General Marquat. Marquat had no business or economic experience, but he had a lot of bureaucratic agility and common sense. Courted by both factions, he baffled them by taking up both options at once.

Perhaps an economist would have found it awkward, but not a general. While the monetarists scorned the ineffectiveness of direct controls in the face of a flood of newly printed money, Marquat insisted on tightening direct controls anyway. When the advocates of direct controls denounced budgetary penny-pinching as politically and socially dangerous, the general kept lecturing the Japanese Ministers on the need to balance the budget. (His advisers noted that the Japanese in the discussions always said "balance the budget" in English, as though the Japanese equivalent had atrophied from disuse.) Marquat listened attentively as his Finance Division reported on the budget discussions that went on twelve months a year with the Finance Ministry officials. Those officials, also convinced monetarists, needed no prodding to do what came naturally. They agreed wholeheartedly with the Finance Division demands for constant budget cuts, as though the two sets of financial officials, whose countries were still legally at war, had now formed a private alliance against the high spenders of both governments.

I remember Marquat every December solemnly asking Bank of Japan Governor Ichimanda to estimate the year-end note issue, which the Governor invariably predicted wrongly. On other days, Marquat might diplomatically castigate a minister for inadequate materials controls. In one meeting, he dramatically drew the Minister of Commerce and Industry to the window to show him two movie theaters under construction across the street while factories complained they could not get materials to rebuild. (In fact, 320 movie theaters had been constructed in the first year after the war.)[13] Essential industries came first, he announced. The minister softly replied that the SCAP Civil Information and Education Section was pressing for more theaters to show the American way of life through imported films.

There were times, however, when no one could carry water on both shoulders, and then Marquat's aides, who at first were never sure that the general really understood the issues before him, nervously watched as though he were an amateur, blindfolded stunt man on a high wire and hoped he knew where he was going. It gradually became clear that on the issues of inflation, he did. He respected the statistics the financial experts showed him to prove inflation was a function of money supply, and money supply a function of the budget deficit.[14] But he also appreciated the human element and the vital need to keep up the hopes and spirits of a distressed working class if Japan were to be kept stable. How he maintained his balance, and the priorities he and MacArthur held—for Marquat conferred with the "Old Man" on all important issues two or three times a week—were first demonstrated in May 1946 in a dispute over government workers' wages. To me, it was the key inflation decision of the early Occupation.

In some countries government wage levels are administrative matters of no great moment, but that was never true of Japan at any time during the Occupation. The 2.5 million government employees—administrative and custodial staff; teachers; the workers on the trunk railroad lines; the postal, telephone, telegraph, camphor, tobacco and salt monopoly workers; the policemen; and others—constituted some 20 percent of the total nonagricultural work force. They accounted for 30 percent of all organized labor at the end of 1946. Their wage scale strongly influenced private industry wages, mass purchasing power, and the national budget. Indeed, every year that I can remember, the annual government wage revision set off at least a minor crisis in GHQ, and in 1947 the Communists managed to bring the country to the brink of revolution over the issue. If inflation was to be restrained by monetary means, the government policy would have to start with its workers' wages.

Early in February 1946, the process began with a visit to my office by former Viscount[15] Kanō Hisaakira, then Vice-Director General of the Central Liaison Office, into which the Foreign Office had been transformed during the Occupation. Kanō was a short, slight, balding, and self-assured international banker. Perhaps his self-assurance came from his noble lineage, perhaps from his stay in England as representative of the powerful Yokohama Specie Bank and the unofficial voice of the Japanese banking community in the City, as well as his position as Vice Chairman of the Bank for International Settlements and member of the Executive Committee of the International Chamber of Commerce. In those capacities he was acquainted with scores of highly important figures, from Brendan Bracken and Harold Macmillan to T. J. Watson, to name but a few.[16]

I, as a young civilian in a spartanly furnished Labor Division office—at that time I did not even have a separate room—could not have looked very impressive to him. Moreover, labor departments in Japanese firms were usually minor service appendages, while the Japanese Government had had only one bureau—no ministry, of course—dealing with labor affairs for years.[17] Kanō politely handed me a two-page Japanese Cabinet proposal to revise the salary scale of government officials and workers. Our Finance Division, he advised me, had already concurred, and he felt I would have no difficulty with it either. He would wait for my approval.

Unquestionably, it was high time the government took up the matter, for the government workers' complaints had already hit the streets of Tokyo. As early as January 19, 1946, for example, several hundred railway workers had forced their way into the Railway Ministry Building after a march from the Prime Minister's residence. They staged a five-hour sitdown strike in the lobby and entrance, compelling the Railway Minister himself to come and listen to their grievances.[18] And on January 28, the teachers *en masse* had personally confronted the Governor of Tokyo in his office, demanding higher salaries. And no wonder. There had been no overall national government wage increase since the end of the war,[19] and prices were sky-rocketing. A veteran government railway worker with seventeen years of service and a family of five was earning only 150 yen monthly,[20] that is, ten dollars a month at the military exchange rate and only three dollars a month at the black market rate.

Kanō's plan provided for only a 30 percent increase for the lowest levels, but it went up on a sliding scale to 100 percent increases for the top government officials. When I asked Kanō for the government's justification for such a regressive scale, he replied that during the war the upper levels had taken smaller percentage increases in wages than the lower levels out of devotion to the war effort. Now, with peace, it was time to return to normal. It was necessary if only to restore incentives for promotion.

I was shaken by the Cabinet's isolation from actual conditions, as demonstrated by its apparent expectation that 30 percent would do any good. Its sense of normality and timing was equally disconcerting. But most shocking was its readiness to tell the lowest-level workers that their government could not afford to pay them more than a 30 percent increase, but could find the money to pay their superiors, including probably those who had formulated the plan, double their current salaries. How did the Cabinet think the workers would react? The proposal smacked of the traditional authoritarianism of the old regime, with its arrogant assumption that the docile workers would accept whatever their betters deigned to grant them.

I told Kanō that what the government wanted to pay its workers was its business, but I could not recommend SCAP approval of any plan that offered less relief to those who needed it more. I would not ask General MacArthur to be a party to such a blatant inequity. I asked the cabinet to reconsider its proposal.

A few days later the Viscount was back with a "revised" plan, which was, however, identical in its essentials. Within a few minutes I had rejected that one too. Kanō, however, refused to listen and persisted in his arguments. I stood up to show the meeting was over. Kanō stood up too, still talking away. Finally his cavalier attitude toward me, that of the nobleman to the nonentity, together with the callous injustice of the cabinet plan, got to me. I had to do something to impress him with the importance of the Labor Division in GHQ and with my own determination. Accordingly, I interrupted him in mid-sentence, told him he was repeating himself, and asked him to leave, escorting him to the door. His sudden silence and shocked expression showed clearly that, sophisticated and experienced as he was, he had not been shown the door from anywhere for a long time, if ever. But that day he was.

Undiplomatic though my action was—I never repeated the discourtesy to any Japanese official—it got results. Several weeks later the Shidehara Cabinet proposed a revised plan, a progressive sliding wage scale with 30 percent increases for the top positions up to 100 percent raises for the lowest. Because of the delay, the increase would be retroactive until March. I concurred immediately. Then we ran into the Finance Division, the money supply philosophy, and the Japanese budget.

First of all, the Finance Division objected to retroactive settlements. Retroactivity, I had to explain to them, was quite normal in wage negotiations anywhere in the free world. Otherwise the employer would have a strong incentive to delay. Second, Finance declared, the increase would be "inflationary," for the cost of almost doubling the Government wage bill could not possibly be met from anticipated revenues. The new money, which would have to be printed by the Bank of Japan to pay the workers their raise, they told me, would only cause prices to rise, rob the wage raise of its value, and defeat the objective. I would have to be realistic about it.

Realism was certainly relative, I thought. The acting chief of the Finance Division, who preached to me of realism, was a portly, bespectacled reserve Army lieutenant colonel who in peace time had been a Kansas City stockbroker.

He had not been out of the U.S. military enclave since his arrival in Japan, did not have the faintest idea of how the government workers or indeed any of the Japanese urban population actually lived and was not much interested in finding out. At the very time he was talking to me of realism, government workers were reporting to a wage survey that their income was only 37 percent of their expenditures. How realistic was it to expect government workers to starve quietly or disaffected officials to run the government effectively? Discussion got us nowhere. Nor could the ESS Executive Officer get us to compromise. We were talking on two different planes of reality. The matter had to be brought to the Chief of Section for a formal decision.

At that time I did not know Marquat very well, and bringing it to him was somewhat like throwing dice. He had been on his job for only five months, and I had no idea of how he regarded labor problems. Still, with prices continuing to rise sharply I felt that we could not afford a "safe" compromise at some in-between figure that would be all too quickly outdated. On May 15, Lieutenant Colonel David Jennings and I squared off before the general in our "floor show."

The presentation on both sides was technical, with Jennings going into budgetary and money supply figures, while I compared cost-of-living indexes with wage rates. Jennings held up the government railways as a prime example of his thesis, asserting that a wage increase there would require either freight and/or passenger rate increases, or a vastly increased subsidy from the general account without corresponding revenues. After some 30 minutes we both fell silent. The general thought a bit and then said, "Ted, have the railway workers been doing a good job?" Seeing my puzzlement, he quickly added, "Have they been working real hard?" "Yes," I answered, without the faintest idea of whether that was in fact true. "All right then," he said, "they deserve the raise. Give it to them."

Jennings sat there stunned, his mouth open. What had *that* to do with inflation? Without a word, he gathered up his papers and left. The general, of course, was a lot slyer (and wiser too) than we thought. Having decided even before the meeting to approve a wage raise—how could one hold a wage line in a roaring inflation?—he saw no point in quibbling on the amount. But he did not want to discourage or offend his financial experts by overruling them on technical grounds when he was not an economist himself. So he simply shifted the ground under our feet. Only a major general who was not supposed to know much about economics could afford to look so "dumb"—as Marquat once said to me later, "I may be dumb but I'm not stupid"[21]—when it served his purpose.

Later on, I began to realize that Marquat appreciated very well the advantages of feigning ignorance to his top staff, for invariably they would fall all over themselves trying to teach him the ropes, hopeful that when they did they would have a major general and chief of section on their side. Meanwhile, there was no better way of assuring their loyalty. In a staff section with so many expert prima donnas with independent stature outside, that was a great advantage. Long afterward I was able to appreciate his adroitness that day. Meanwhile, we notified the Finance Ministry of GHQ approval, and on May 24, the wage increase was announced, just in time to save hundreds of thousands who were at the end of their tether, and also quite possibly just in time to preserve the public tranquility.

The course of the Occupation regarding inflation followed the example set that day. In the long series of decisions GHQ was to make thereafter, Marquat saw to it that practicalities took precedence over theories and, of the practicalities, human response was among the most prominent. The point at issue in May 1946 was wages, but it could have been any of a dozen other questions, whether import or export pricing, food subsidies, industrial financing, or tax policy. Inflation control was desirable, but social stability was imperative. Moderate the inflation, yes, but keep counterinflationary policy moderate too. Unbalanced budgets and rapid monetary expansion were his deadly foes, Marquat proclaimed, thereby convincing his monetarists that "in his heart" he was with them. But a balanced budget to him was not a precondition to start with but a goal to be achieved gradually as the economy improved.

And in that he succeeded. Presiding but not commanding, he imposed his pragmatism on his experts. The results showed his good judgment. In the consolidated budget for 1946–47, government revenues were only 58 percent of expenditures, but by 1947–48 the percentage reached 88, and in 1948–49, 92.[22] The following year, after industrial production, say in March 1949, had quadrupled as compared with January 1946, and doubled compared with mid-1947,[23] and when Japan's reserve food stocks were climbing rapidly, it became possible to balance the Japanese budget for the first time in two decades.

Long before, in the course of Marquat's pragmatism, SCAP's priorities had emerged. First of all, inflation was too important to be left to a weak Japanese government as the Washington planners had instructed. SCAP had to intervene energetically and forcefully. But neither would SCAP allow inflation-fighting to block out social and economic reforms, alienate large segments of the population, or risk social turmoil. Protection from the consequences of the inflation was, for the short run, more important than halting the inflation itself. And finally, inflation control was only one part of the economic recovery program and not necessarily the most important part.

In time the Washington agencies with other priorities considered the SCAP approach too relaxed. In terms of MacArthur's priorities and ideals, however, the policy was far better balanced. It worked. I wonder, however, whether it would have if General Marquat had not been there all the time, acting as the balance wheel and keeping SCAP's economic policy steady as the country recovered. The general policy itself was as much MacArthur's as Marquat's, but it had to be applied in complex cases, and that was Marquat's contribution. It was a remarkable, though unsung, performance. (When Marquat died in Washington in 1960, not one representative of the Japanese Embassy came to his funeral.) It was especially fortunate for Japan and its successful third turn that Marquat brought a badly needed steadiness to the direction of the economy, for the war's end and the destruction of national regimentation, for the first time in the country's history, brought Japanese society face to face with a new, unsettling, and potentially revolutionary national force, an active and demanding labor movement.

Part IV

JOURNEY INTO THE UNKNOWN: THE OCCUPATION AND THE JAPANESE LABOR MOVEMENT

UNLIKE EARLY WESTERN MAP-MAKERS charting the mysterious Orient, the drafters of Occupation directives did not mark parts of their documents "Terra Incognita" or warn "Here Be Dragons." They might very well have, because a substantial part of the area they charted for General MacArthur was truly unknown ground. Granted, some of the SCAP's responsibilities were not novel. Demobilization of the enemy, the arrest of its leaders, and control of its financial institutions, for example, all had ample precedent. However, no American military commander had ever tried to remake the political and economic institutions of another nation. That was unknown territory. The democratization program most fraught with peril was labor reform.

More than any other program, the labor reform was open-ended. In ordering SCAP to "encourage . . . the development of organizations in labor . . . on a democratic basis," Joint Chiefs of Staff directive JCS 1380/15 launched the Occupation's labor mission on a journey that had no fixed destination. The democratic labor organizations established as a result of that instruction presumably were to chart their course by themselves, since control of their internal affairs by either SCAP or the Japanese government would have been clearly inconsistent with the entire concept of worker democracy. Thus, in the case of organized labor, SCAP was not expected to produce finished political or economic institutions but rather to assist in the development of indigenous ones. No one could predict how those organizations would turn out, or even if they would end up democratic.

The Washington-based "radical reformers" believed in free trade unionism for the Japanese as part of their faith in the democratic instincts of a people whose history was anything but democratic. Others viewed union organization in Japan as an inevitable development to be accepted gracefully if not enthusiastically; for the United States to ban labor unions in Japan at a time when every Western democracy had them would be anomalous. Still others saw labor organizations primarily as counterweights to big business and a possibly resurgent military. All those schools of thought, at any rate, had to concede that unions in Japan would work only if they responded to the needs of their constituents. But what would those needs be? Unlike Germany's labor movement, which had had a long history, solid organization, and well-known leaders before being destroyed by the Nazis, Japan's labor unions had too short a past and had been too thoroughly intimidated by the prewar government to provide plausible insights into how they might develop under freedom. From the outset, then, labor reform was a gamble.

Yet the outcome of the gamble was crucial. Japanese wage-earners and their families made up almost two-fifths of the population in 1945. In Tokyo, they lived or worked in close proximity to the centers of Japanese state power—the Diet, the Prime Minister's residence, and the ministries. Nationally, they held in their hands the levers of the economy, from locomotive engines to electric power switches to telephone switchboards. Workers were concentrated in cities, where they could easily be organized. Not only were they literate, they were often well educated, and many of them displayed a flair for leadership. If their new labor organizations fell into the hands of antidemocratic extremists, democratic government could not long survive in postwar Japan. The road to revolution ran through the labor unions. In those circumstances, the labor reform was vital not only to the success of the entire Occupation but to its stability.

11

Labor Emerges as a National Force

NEVER HAD THE TOKYO SKY been so sharply blue and the air so clear as in Jaunary 1946. Little smoke wafted from factory chimneys, and there were virtually no motor vehicles emitting exhaust fumes. Bombing and fire debris had been cleared from the streets of Tokyo, but little rebuilding had taken place. The capital of the vanished empire consisted mainly of vast areas of devastation. From almost everywhere in the almost silent city, Mount Fuji, 70 miles away, was clearly visible. The clear sunlight and mild winter air were merciful to the hundreds of thousands living in shacks, corrugated iron lean-tos, and abandoned packing crates.

At nightfall, however, Tokyo turned chill and damp. The vast numbers of homeless who spent their nights indoors—in the labyrinthine passageways of the Tokyo and Ueno railway stations—found the cold penetrating their layers of worn clothing. Others lived under the clattering elevated railway lines, where the smell from their charcoal fires permeated the archways. Around Shinbashi and most of the other large national railway stations, where restaurants, shops, and amusement centers once competed for precious space, wheat and vegetables were sprouting. That strange city crop, winter wheat, also grew in narrow unpaved strips along the sidewalks of the West Ginza. It seemed to anticipate the approaching famine.

Industry was at a standstill. Nevertheless, the people of Tokyo were busy. Housewives with babies on their backs lined up quietly for hours to obtain rice, sweet potatoes, or such household necessities as rough, gray toilet paper, claylike candles, or small electric bulbs. The scene was sometimes enlivened by impromptu theater. One returnee from the Tule Lake internment camp in America, later to be a Labor Ministry adviser, harangued the queued housewives to the

189

effect that their hair was covering their babies' eyes and was therefore harming the eyesight of the next generation of Japanese.

There were other street sights. Hundreds of hawkers squatted on the downtown sidewalks, each selling a little pile of merchandise: fading photographs of prewar American and Japanese movie stars, simple electric hot plates for cooking, and aluminum tableware and cutlery scavenged from fallen American planes. In the first postwar employment census on December 1, 1945 (and again in the April 1, 1946, census)[1] hardly any of those salesmen reported themselves jobless; they proudly responded that they were engaged in commerce.

Many people spent an inordinate amount of time in trains, jammed into unbelievably crowded cars, sitting on coach roofs, or clinging to engine "cowcatchers," on their way to scrounge for food in the countryside or on long commutes to and from cold and cheerless offices or mostly silent factories. The press of bodies was almost unimaginable. When a baby carried on her mother's back was crushed to death on a train without the mother's being aware of it, a furious spate of letters to the editor erupted in the Tokyo dailies over who was responsible. When a judge who felt morally constrained to eat only officially rationed food died of malnutrition, a similar furor ensued. The indignation somehow tempered the awful bitterness of defeat. The people's spirit had not been cowed.

Indeed, optimism began to permeate the media. Tokyo's newspapers, down to four and sometimes two pages of print a day, were avidly read. On determinedly cheerful radio stations, friendly information quiz shows blossomed. NHK, the state broadcasting company, revived its Philharmonic Orchestra under the direction of the German-Jewish Joseph Rosenstock, a long-time resident who had moved back to Tokyo from his wartime internment cottage in the Karuizawa mountain resort. A new and catchy nonsense song carried endlessly on the air was "Moshi, moshi, ano-ne" (Hey, Hey, There!) set to the tune of "London Bridge Is Falling Down" by American officers partying in the Daiichi Hotel billet on Christmas Eve of 1945. The lyrics consisted mainly of repetition of the most easily remembered Japanese expressions. One version was played by a symphony orchestra with full chorus and fanfares of trumpets.

The New Labor Movement

The streets echoed to a different music: the slogans and songs of labor demonstrators. First in tens, then hundreds, and then thousands carried their bigcharacter posters and scarlet banners while singing the "Internationale," "Solidarity Forever," and "Wave Scarlet Banner." Those unfamiliar sights and sounds alarmed both the American military, to whom red flags meant violent revolution, and the conservative Japanese Government and its supporters. They were alarmed by the placards that, while thanking General MacArthur for democracy, demanded higher wages, special allowances, and more prompt distribution of rations in a strident, threatening tone. The message smacked of class warfare. To upper-class Japanese, the marchers certainly were not the compliant workers they had taken for granted for as long as they could remember. They represented a new phenomenon—individuals demanding their "rights." Where did they come from, these aggressive masses who had been invisible for so long, and where were they going? Conservatives, and not only conservatives, feared for the stability of their country.

To many, especially from afar, General MacArthur must have seemed a magician. Only six months before, on October 11, 1945, the General had been visited by the new Prime Minister, Shidehara Kijurō, in striped trousers and morning coat, calling to pay his respects. The Supreme Commander turned the ceremony immediately into a business meeting. He handed the surprised Shidehara a one-page letter listing five basic "reforms in the social order of Japan," which the Japanese Government was to institute "as readily as they can be assimilated." The second point called for "the encouragement of the unionization of labor." By Japan's first postwar May Day, May 1, 1946, some 2.7 million persons had joined 7,000 unions.[2] Apparently, all MacArthur had to do was whistle, and the Japanese obeyed.

Contrary to a common misconception, however, the Japanese labor movement was not born after the war. It was reborn. It was not created *ex nihili* by sophisticated American labor experts during the Occupation but was one of the innovations of the late-nineteenth-century Meiji Era. To be sure, it was weak and subordinate to other elements of the power structure, but it had its own traditions and even its martyrs.

Japanese labor unions had a half-century of history, from their beginnings in the rikisha men's strike of 1883 and the organization of the Shūeisha Printers' Union in 1884 to their forced dissolution and replacement in 1938 by a completely government-controlled labor front (*Sampō–Rōhō*),[3] modeled after the Nazi Patriotic Labor Front. They reached their prewar high point in 1936 with 420,000 members. Although that 1936 figure meant only 7 percent of the non-agricultural work force (10 percent, if only men are included) was organized, the situation was not much different from that of the United States, where only 10 percent of the nonagricultural work force was unionized prior to Roosevelt's New Deal reforms.[4]

Moreover, by the mid-1930s Japanese unions represented a significant political force. They were the principal sponsors of the Social Masses Party (*Shakai Taishū-tō*), which garnered 1 million male votes (no woman's suffrage existed then) in the elections of 1937 and elected 37 out of 466 representatives in the lower house of the Diet.

The veterans of the prewar labor movement did not wait for MacArthur's order to the Prime Minister before resuming their activities. Huddled nervously but hopefully around their radios to hear the Emperor's surrender broadcast, they decided even before the American Occupation Forces entered Japan, that since they were to be "liberated" they should begin to act.[5] Their experiences with the industrialists and military officers had steeled their will. They had no intention of waiting for the occupiers to tell them what to do.

During the first week of September 1945, Matsuoka Komakichi, the long-time president of the Japan Federation of Labor (*Sōdōmei*), the largest of the prewar labor federations with some 85,000 members in affiliated unions, called on his old union brothers and then visited factories that *Sōdōmei* had organized. He urged management to accept *Sōdōmei* organizing efforts on the grounds that Communist organizers were not far behind him. If management gave the green light and the factories had a sufficient number of employees, Matsuoka then dispatched the organizers.[6] Yonekubo Mitsuaki, the conservative president of the Japan Seamen's Union (*Kaiin Kumiai*), concentrated on regaining the hiring halls and seamen's hostels from the wartime labor front and on rebuilding a union that had had 107,000 members before the war. Left-winger Shimagami Sengoro's Tokyo Transport Workers Union (12,000 members prewar) was officially reestablished on September 28, 1945. All of this activity preceded MacArthur's meeting with Prime Minister Shidehara.

The revival of the prewar labor movement was no simple matter. First of all, memories of old personal and ideological feuds had not died. Takano Minoru, the principal figure in the far left non-Communist National Council of Trade Unions, told me he agonized for two weeks over whether to join with or fight his bitter prewar rival, Matsuoka, whom he had condemned as too conservative, too friendly with employers, and too authoritarian. Also remembering, however, that the unions' failure to unite before the war had made it easier for the military to crush them, Takano swallowed his pride and called on Matsuoka at home on September 15. The tall, graying, aristocratic Matsuoka—no one could have suspected that he was originally a lathe operator in a steel mill—greeted Takano in the vestibule of his son's house, the only structure still left standing on a block of rubble in a residential section of Tokyo. Takano explained that he and his colleagues wanted to join forces with Matsuoka in *Sōdōmei*. "Oho!" replied Matsuoka, "So now you, the former troublemaker, want to work with us!" Takano could only reply, "Please forgive me!"[7] Takano was then invited both into the house and into *Sōdōmei*. On October 10, 1945, the day before MacArthur's conversation with Shidehara, more than twenty prewar labor leaders, representing almost all the largest legalized unions, met in the Kuramae Hall in the Shinbashi area of Tokyo to reconstitute the *Sōdōmei* federation formally. Takano was elected vice president in a new attempt at unity.[8]

It was ironic that on that same October 10 the two top prewar Communist leaders remaining in Japan, Tokuda Kyūichi and Shiga Yoshio, were freed from almost two decades of imprisonment in Fuchū Prison.[9] Hundreds of other Communists were released from prisons around the country at the same time. The action resulted from the implementation of SCAP Directive 93, issued on October 3, which removed restrictions on political, civil, and religious liberties, under which Communists had been imprisoned for almost two decades. Thus, in that two-day period the tableau was completed. At center stage, the Occupation ordered the Japanese Government to free imprisoned labor leaders and to permit the organization of a free labor movement. Behind them, moving in and out of the wings, were Communist as well as democratic-minded labor leaders, vying with each other to carry the colors of the Japanese working class. The deadly serious rivalry between the moderates and the revolutionary Communists was destined to have a critical influence on the success of the Occupation and the future of Japan.

TOKUDA UNLEASHED

The battle was immediately joined by the Communist Tokuda. As soon as the stocky, hook-nosed, balding, fifty-one-year-old Okinawan, clad in a light green prison uniform and straw hat, stepped through the gates of Fuchū Prison, he delivered a fiery speech to the few hundred comrades who had gathered to greet him. He displayed no signs of fatigue or of physical weakness.[10] In all probability he had used his eighteen years of imprisonment to study and reflect on Lenin's march to power in the Russian Revolution. His first public utterance was a fiery declaration in the spirit of Lenin's famous call to action at the Finland Station in Petrograd on his return from Swiss exile in 1917. He was launching his own campaign to win power in Japan. It soon became clear that one of his main goals after remaking the shattered Japan Communist Party (JCP) in his image and assuring his unquestioned control over its apparatus, was nothing less than using the JCP to capture the Japanese labor movement. He would come very close to his goal.

The non-Communist labor organizers had had almost a two-month head start. Matsuoka's energetic program of organizing from the top—gaining recognition from employers afraid of a Communist alternative—bore fruit. *Sōdōmei* was particularly successful in organizing industries such as tobacco manufacturing and textiles, where the work force was largely female and there was a rapid turnover as young women quit to get married. Its organizers recognized that if they succeeded in signing up the relatively few skilled male workers in those plants, the women would follow automatically. Even after they joined, women had little say in union affairs. When I visited a cigarette plant in Tokyo together with Matsuoka, the sole woman member of the union's executive board served us tea.

Matsuoka's call to his prewar colleagues to participate in the organizing drive produced an impressive turnout. Even though most Japanese labor unions before the war had relatively low membership figures, there were almost a thousand of them.[12] That meant a good many Japanese, perhaps as many as several thousand, had served in some capacity with a labor union. They constituted a powerful, if generally overlooked, organizing resource right after the war.

At the same time, Yonekubo successfully negotiated a closed-shop agreement with the always friendly shipowners, compelling all seamen to join the revived Seamen's Union if they wanted work. The close prewar relationship between the union and the shipowners had survived the war, even if the bulk of Japan's merchant fleet had not. The shipowners had originally organized the union as a hiring hall in 1921 and only afterward turned it over to the seamen. In 1933 the shipowners had financed the construction of the Buddhist temple at Kompira-san on the island of Shikoku (where the patron saint of sailors was enshrined) and helped to install the then union president, Hamada Kunitarō, as chief abbot.[13] Thus it was mutually acceptable for the union in 1945 to claim it represented all seamen when it had only a few thousand members and for the owners to claim it represented a functioning industry when almost all their ships lay rusting at the bottom of the Pacific. Despite that blatant disregard of reality, the closed-shop agreement held up. Seamen hoping for work loyally joined their old union, and one prewar union hierarchy returned to office.

In the face of such competition, Communist activists, spurred by Tokuda, set a furious pace. His nickname, "Tokkyū," a combination of the first syllables of his surname and given name, appropriately meant "special express train." He worked as if possessed. He reportedly never went to bed before two and arose at dawn during the entire fall of 1945.[14] The time lost in jail had to be recovered.

Tokuda was convinced that the food shortages and the economic plight of the working class were the keys to successful revolution in Japan. At the end of October 1945, he estimated the number of Communists in Japan at two thousand to three thousand, with only a tenth of that number in Tokyo.[15] Nevertheless, he threw almost all Party activists, no matter who they were or where they lived, into organizing unions or food protest rallies, preferably a combination of both.

He insisted that every Communist, no matter how high his office, had to be a union organizer, and he set the example. While organizing the Party's administrative structure, relaunching the Party newspaper, *Red Flag* (*Akahata*)—its first postwar issue appeared the week after his release from prison[16]—serving as member of the government's Advisory Commission on Labor Legislation, and negotiating with the Socialists, he simultaneously undertook to organize the National Railway workers at the Shinbashi station in central Tokyo and the adjoining Shiodome freight yards. He harangued them, passed out leaflets, appointed deputies, formulated demands on behalf of the workers, and then headed delegations to present the demands to the appropriate authorities. Tokuda was convinced that labor had to be organized from the bottom up, at the workplace, and he set out to do just that. He rejected Matsuoka's approach—organizing from the top down—in the belief that unions established in that manner would not be reliable in a revolutionary situation.[17]

I shall never forget my first encounter with him. Shortly after my arrival in Japan in January 1946, he came to SCAP's Labor Division, which was then housed in the Daiichi Building, four floors below General MacArthur's office. He was accompanied by about ten silent and somewhat timid workers, whom he introduced as the representatives of the National Union of Locomotive Engine Drivers from Shinbashi Station. He immediately proceeded to deliver in his powerful voice a long speech to Captain Costantino, Chief of the Labor Relations Branch, who officially received the delegation. He announced that his colleagues had decided to call a "national" railway strike because of the harsh conditions of their lives. An unimpressed Costantino bluntly replied that such a strike would not be permitted by the Occupation, because it would adversely affect the security of Allied troops. He added, somewhat more mildly, that it would also jeopardize the lives of the cold and hungry Japanese people by delaying, in midwinter, rice and charcoal deliveries. Costantino asked how workers could do such a thing to fellow workers. After listening intently to the translator's words, in a Hawaiian Nisei accent not readily understood by Japanese, Tokuda delivered to his own delegation another lengthy oration, repeating Costantino's remarks, without attribution, about the great hardship such a strike would impose on the Japanese people. Then, without waiting for agreement from his companions, he told Costantino that the union members had heroically decided to suffer rather than harm their fellow proletarians. The strike was off. Tokuda gave a virtuoso performance, switching his position 180 degrees without a break and without consultation and carrying his followers both ways with ease. He was using our office to rehearse them in how to approach the GHQ and to organize them on behalf of the JCP. Although he won nothing from us at the time—not even an argument—he made a very important gain. One of his ten companions was Ii Yashiro, an inexperienced union official, who one year later would put on his own virtuoso performances with me, General Marquat, and several Japanese cabinet ministers, as the leader of the revolutionary general strike movement.

Tokuda pushed his closest Party comrades into union organization "from the bottom." Itō Kenichi took on the steelworkers, Mizutani Takeshi the Hokkaidō coal miners, and Kobayashi Tetsu the schoolteachers. Shiga Yoshio, Tokuda's principal deputy, made a vain effort to block the Seamen's Union's control of the merchant marine. Of the seven men on the Communist Party Politburo in 1946, five were assigned to union organizing duties. Only one was permanently exempted from such activity: Nozaka Sanzō, the Comintern's (Communist International's) man. The postwar Japan Communist Party was Tokuda's creation, and he intended to keep it that way.

THE COMINTERN "REP"

The Comintern—and behind it Stalin—clearly intended Nozaka to take over the Japan Communist Party in Japan after the war. Known also by his Party name, Okano Susumu, he had escaped from arrest in 1931. Obtaining permission from the Japanese police to visit a doctor, he had gone to the Soviet Union instead. There he became a Comintern "apparatchik," living for stretches in Moscow and leaving his wife and children there (perhaps as hostages) when he was absent. He took the "Japanese seat" on the Comintern's Central Executive Committee when Katayama Sen died in 1933, served as the international representative to the American Communist Party between 1934 and 1938, and proceeded in 1943 to Mao Tse-tung's Yenan caves, where he indoctrinated Japanese soldiers captured by Mao's forces and trained them to be Communist agents. Like Togliatti in Italy, Ulbricht in Germany, Gomulka in Poland, and Pauker in Rumania, Nozaka was one of a small group of Communist expatriates nurtured by the Comintern in the Soviet Union while "the heat was on" back home and slated to return to the homeland to take charge of the revolution when the time was ripe.

Japan's sudden surrender made it difficult for Nozaka to follow that scenario. It took him four months by foot, horseback, oxcart, train, plane, and ship to travel from Yenan to Japan.[18] By that time Tokuda was undisputed master of the Party. The JCP gave Nozaka a formal "welcome-home" demonstration at Tokyo's centrally located Hibiya Park, a seat on the Central Executive Committee, and lots of favorable publicity, but despite—or quite possibly because of—his boast that he had 200 former Japanese war prisoners on their way home to work as "trained union organizers,"[19] he was excluded from labor activities. The slender, sleepy-eyed Nozaka was relegated instead to public relations and election campaigning. He spoke soothingly and effectively about how the Communist Party wanted nothing more than to be the *aisareru tō*, the party loved by the people. His 200 agents were quickly absorbed into the Party, which already possessed a large number of sophisticated, locally trained activists. Tokuda remained the boss.

MACARTHUR'S SPONSORSHIP

The extraordinary vigor displayed by the Japanese labor movement once repression ended in August 1945 clearly demonstrated that the movement was neither created nor revived by General MacArthur and his staff. Yet it would not have emerged so easily or rapidly as a significant national force without SCAP sponsorship. True, the concept of a union—*kumiai*—was as Japanese as could be. In prewar Japan there had been a wide variety of groups using the word *kumiai* in their titles.[20] However, the prevailing view in prewar Japanese society was that organized labor was a disturbing element. Industrialists were accustomed to fighting and crushing unions, using the police to eliminate those obstacles to "harmonious" groups relations. Even workers were dubious as to the propriety of unions. As the managing editor of the *Yomiuri Hōchi* newspaper said at the end of the war, the traditional Japanese policy had been: "It's okay to kill them; let 'em have it!"[21]

Thus until General MacArthur declared publicly to Shidehara that labor unions were indispensable "in safeguarding the workman from exploitation and abuse,"[22] bitter opposition was all too likely, and unionism was still not entirely respectable. I doubt that workers would otherwise have flocked into unions in such numbers or with such enthusiasm. With MacArthur's endorsement, however, 600,000 workers voluntarily joined unions by the end of January 1946, a million more joined in the six weeks from February 1 to March 15, and yet another million in the succeeding six weeks. That sizzling pace has never been equaled in labor history anywhere. By the end of 1946, a total of 4.5 million Japanese—ten times the prewar peak—were union members.

MacArthur's statement to Shidehara alone did not do the trick. MacArthur had publicly pointed the way; SCAP's Labor Division provided the detailed markers and constant encouragement on the journey. Of course, even before the start of the Occupation, the Japanese Government had disbanded the Labor Fronts and ended labor conscription. In December 1945, with minimum SCAP pressure, the Diet passed the long-sought Trade Union Law, affording unions legal status. Nevertheless, nothing could equal personal contact in convincing the Japanese workers, their employers, and their political leaders that General MacArthur and the United States supported the labor movement. In 1946 the Labor Division, of which I was head, threw itself into the job of making friends with the Japanese workers and their leaders.

Before the war, Japanese labor union representatives had found it almost impossible to obtain a hearing from their own government. GHQ, with all those foreign faces, large bodies, military uniforms, and English sounds, must have been even more forbidding. For all that, Japanese workers could feel somewhat at home in one corner of GHQ—the Labor Division, particularly during 1946 and early 1947, when it was composed of kindred spirits. Most of its officers and advisers were in civilian life either trade unionists,[23] officials of the U.S. Labor Department, or employees of other U.S. Government agencies dealing with workers. The Chief of our Field Liaison Branch, an infantry major, had worked in a coal mine, and his father had been fired for joining the famous Boston police strike of 1919. Our executive officer, a lieutenant colonel, had been discharged by the National Broadcasting Company for organizing radio artists. Thus, whenever a Japanese unionist recounted his problems to a member of our Labor Division, he could expect a sympathetic hearing. His American listener could relate such problems to his own experience.

As Chief of the Labor Division, I deliberately attempted to demonstrate openly that we respected Japanese unionists and considered them our friends. A few days after I became Chief, I invited to my office, one at a time, a number of prewar labor leaders who were not Communists for a get-acquainted visit. Only one, an extreme radical,[24] refused to come on the grounds that he had nothing in common with a "capitalist representative." (At that moment I had a grand total of perhaps two hundred dollars in the bank.) The others were much more open-minded. When Katō Kanjū, an anti-Communist leftist in prewar days, arrived, I told him what a great honor it was to meet such a valiant antimilitarist and proceeded to recount incidents from his life. Katō, who had been only a minor figure in the prewar labor movement, was stunned that the "American Government" had been following his career so sympathetically and in such detail. Thanks to a card index of hundreds of Japanese labor personalities, which I had compiled when researching my master's thesis on the Japanese labor movement and had kept up to date, I was able to talk to *Sōdōmei* president Matsuoka about his onetime Sunday school teaching, to Tokyo Transport Workers leader Shimagami Zengorō about his union's strikes in the 1930s, and to Nishio Suehiro about the Comintern's efforts in Europe two decades earlier to enroll him in its apparatus.

In factory visits around the country every Sunday during the first part of 1946, I emphasized SCAP's interest in labor. In Nagano Prefecture I asked a mill's young female employees about their rations and learned that they included silkworms for protein. At the Ashio copper mine near Nikkō I was taken by the president and general secretary of the local union deep into the mine on a narrow ore cart. When our retinue from GHQ—me, two or three other Labor Division officials, an interpreter, and a GI driver—drew up in an Army sedan to a plant that had probably never seen any Americans before and asked to consult with other union leaders or ordinary workers, we generally made quite an impression.

In Tokyo, too, I deliberately adopted an uncompromisingly pro-labor line and publicized it among the Japanese. In recognition of the food shortage, I refused to eat at parties the Japanese hosted for GHQ officials. (The Communist Tokuda adopted the same stance a few months later.) When the president of Nippon Iron and Steel Corporation, Nagano Shigeo—who later became chairman of the Federation of Economic Organizations[25]—asked me to "teach" him about labor problems because such problems had not existed in Japan before the war, I responded icily that while he might be correct, workers certainly had had employer problems. When the operators of the Jōban coal mines asked GHQ to exempt them from the ban on female mine labor because their seams were too narrow for men to enter, I asked them whether they would like their own wives to go down into the mines. Granted that I was sometimes a little abrasive—I was younger then and more easily outraged—but I had made it a matter of fundamental policy to demonstrate the sympathy of the Occupation and General MacArthur for the Japanese workers.

Labor's response to the GHQ attitude was electrifying. Union representatives trooped into Costantino's office to report on their progress and discuss their problems. One employer, fearful that his workers' tardiness in organizing might get him into trouble, asked for help in expediting the formation of a union. Costantino advised him merely to announce that he was not opposed to a union and then to stand back.

The most spectacular visit was that paid by three geisha in the early spring of 1946. They wished to inform General MacArthur of their new geisha labor union. Accompanied by an elderly manager with a white goatee and an old Japanese Army uniform, the ladies wore colorful and ornate kimonos, perched on 6-inch-high *geta,* sported towering hairdos festooned with trinkets and little bells, and had applied makeup that made their faces deathly white except for their red-rimmed eyes. Taking tiny steps, they paraded in leisurely fashion through the building to my office. They created a sensation, as offices emptied into the hall to witness the spectacle, and accomplished in five minutes what almost four years of Japanese military attacks had failed to do—put a good part of General MacArthur's headquarters out of action.

The impact of GHQ's pro-labor attitude on the Japanese union leaders was impressive. While moderates such as Matsuoka were bound to be pro-Allies, many others in the non-Communist left, who might have merely tolerated the Occupation, became unexpectedly pro-American. Despite their Marxist upbringing, which preached that Americans, as representatives of a capitalist country, had to be oppressors of the working class, they accepted our motives. Takano, Katō, and Suzuki Mōsaburō (later to become the longtime leader of the left socialists) all became convinced that the American Government was sincerely democratic. Sometimes that faith could become embarrassing. Being friendly to labor meant, to some extent, being used by labor leaders. In one case I obtained the then brand-new streptomycin for a labor leader whose son was critically ill with tuberculosis. The son recovered. Another time, I prevented the Army from requisitioning a building being used as a union headquarters. The requests sometimes startled us. The Labor Division once hosted a dinner in the Daiichi Hotel to introduce the labor leader Katō and his wife to John Murphy, head of the New England Regional Council of the AFL. In his formal remarks, Murphy assured the Katōs that the American labor movement fully supported Japanese trade unions and would do anything it could to be of help. Mrs. Katō, a staunch advocate of birth control—known as ''the Margaret Sanger of Japan''—spoke up. She pointed out that the lack of rubber imports had created an acute shortage of birth control devices and asked if the AFL could help by shipping large quantities of condoms to her. Murphy, a Boston Irishman who was properly supportive of his Church's ban on birth control, turned a bright scarlet and was left speechless.

The most common way labor leaders "used" GHQ was to visit the Labor Division in order to gain prestige among their followers. One day Matsuoka, accompanied by twenty followers, arrived to present me with a scroll addressed to General MacArthur, thanking him on behalf of Japanese labor for American food relief. Even though our meeting took all of ten minutes, part of it in the corridor, his lieutenants had seen that he was on friendly terms with General MacArthur's labor chief. Everyone did that. The Communists, however, were the most blatant. They clearly wanted to show that they were the American's chosen vehicle for the democratization of Japan and should therefore be heeded by the Japanese people.

Many Japanese could not understand that democratic governments tolerated their enemies, and they were baffled by the American decision to release Japanese Communists from prison. They were receptive to Communist hints about some sort of secret Communist accord with the Occupation authorities and implications that they enjoyed MacArthur's support. Popular credulity was heightened by news that two prominent Occupation officers, Herbert Norman of Counter Intelligence and John Emmerson of the Political Adviser's Office, interviewed the Communist leaders in Fuchū Prison in early October 1945 and took Tokuda and Shiga, still prisoners, in a U.S. Army sedan to GHQ Headquarters in Tokyo for further questioning. Unaware of Nozaka's staggering difficulties in returning from China, the Japanese also attributed his homecoming to the good offices of the American occupiers.

The Communists nurtured such popular beliefs. Senior JCP officials visited GHQ repeatedly. While some called regularly at the Government or the Civil Information and Education Section, the Labor Division received most of them. It was quite common for a Communist labor leader to visit the Division on his own initiative, to speak to no one more senior than the chief clerk, and then to tell his Japanese constituency, "I was just at GHQ and we have to organize the coal mines." MacArthur's prestige was transferable, if one was clever enough.

The gaunt, lined face and quiet, low-key style of the JCP's second in command, Shiga Yoshio, helped him to ingratiate himself with the GHQ staff. He could tell lies with charm and equanimity. The Party must have been aware of that, for he was the Labor Division's most frequent Communist visitor. A typical Shiga performance took place in my office at the end of January 1946. He called on me to complain about the "terrible working conditions" of the Japanese seamen being trained to man the American LSTs (landing ship, tank) scheduled to repatriate the 7 million Japanese, military and civilians, stranded in other Asian countries by the sudden surrender.

The repatriation ships were operated by the Shipping Control Authority, Japan (SCAJAP), headed by a famous submariner, Admiral Mommsen. They had an ambiguous status in international law: Even though they had been U.S. Navy ships, they were not then under American law, and although manned entirely by and carrying only Japanese, neither were they under the jurisdiction of the Japanese Government. SCAP's authority did not extend to the high seas. To minimize the possibility of complicated and prolonged legal suits, Admiral Mommsen wished to complete maritime repatriation as fast as possible, and he sought the help of the Labor Division in rapidly recruiting crews. We ordered the Japanese Government to give the LST seamen a ration of six *gō* of rice and rice substitutes a day; ordinary civilians were then receiving two and a half *gō*.[26]

If Shiga's charges were true, however, the whole repatriation program could have been jeopardized. It occurred to me that Shiga might be exaggerating the situation to induce SCAP to take remedial action. He could then claim credit for improvement in the crews' conditions and gain a selling point in the JCP's efforts to wrest control of the Seamen's Union. It was hard, however, not to believe a man who had just spent sixteen years in prison for his principles. I asked my subordinates to check his charges.

A few days later I found myself quite by accident at the Mitsubishi Heavy Industry's Yokohama shipyards. I noticed some strange-looking craft anchored at a dock in the distance, and I was informed that they were two LSTs that future members of the repatriation crew were using as dormitories while in training. As I boarded one unannounced and without advance warning, I observed that heaping, steaming bowls of rice mixed with barley were being brought on board. A food carrier told me that each trainee received two such bowls three times a day. The hold of each LST was filled with rows of *futon* bedding and was quite airy and warm. Compared with the ordinary citizenry of Yokohama or any of the other devastated cities that terrible winter, the seamen appeared very well off indeed. I subsequently learned that of the 11,000 who had been recruited by January 25, 1946, only had 219 quit before going to sea.[27]

When Shiga called on me again to repeat his litany on the plight of the LST trainees, I told him what I had seen and bluntly called him a liar. He took the reproach blandly. I realized then that anyone who was willing to spend so many years in prison for his beliefs would have no trouble telling a white lie or doing much worse if it advanced the cause.

In reality, our conversations with known Communist leaders were usually at cross purposes, for at heart we were enemies. They believed that the source of all wisdom was to be found in their own scripture. They needed nothing from us other than intelligence about SCAP's intentions and the respectability gained from visiting us. Even so, they appear to have feared the effects of exposure to us on any but the most tested Party stalwarts. In retrospect, I can understand why whenever the Communications Workers president, Dobashi Kazuyoshi, who had secretly become a Party member in late 1945, visited my office, he never brought fewer than four companions, two of whom always took notes. The non-Communist labor leaders, however, regarded contacts with us in GHQ as a valuable source of knowledge about what was going on in labor movements outside Japan, from which they had been insulated for so long.

THE ENLIGHTENMENT OF THE UNIONS

Mere encouragement was far from enough. The value of trade unions to the Japanese workers went far beyond its function as a morale booster. A young woman textile worker whom I met at the foot of Mount Fuji asked me, "The employers have their unions, the merchants have their unions, why shouldn't we workers have our unions?" As we saw it, the real function of a union was to engage in collective bargaining toward a collective agreement with management. If that was to be accomplished with a minimum of industrial strife, Japanese workers had to learn as much as they could about the complex process, and employers had to agree to bargain with them. Left to their own devices, Japanese unions and employers over time might very well have worked out satisfactory arrangements. In the interim, however, there was a real danger of unnecessary emotional confrontation. The Labor Division had to help matters along.

With the prodigious efflorescence of all kinds of labor unions—1,000 before the war, 16,000 in November 1946, and 22,000 in May 1947[28]—hundreds of thousands of new union officials suddenly emerged. It was essential to start them on the right track. We made available to them the hard-earned experience of Western trade unions. The Chief of our small Labor Education Branch, who had worked as a labor education director in the UAW, could write an instruction booklet on the functions of shop stewards or the conduct of union meetings almost overnight. We also imported sample American union constitutions, bylaws, collective agreements, and the like. The Japanese were, as always, avid students. They cooperated with unexpected enthusiasm by sponsoring labor schools and seminars throughout the country. Sometimes, thousands would attend those meetings. The Japanese were also fast learners, particularly in strike organization, faster than our labor educators gave them credit for. By October 1946, more than a million workers were covered by collective bargaining agreements.[29]

Introducing employers to collective bargaining was a more difficult task. The large private enterprises, their assets depleted by the war, their top leaders threatened by purges, their factories often operating at a loss, and their customary paternalism in shambles, were demoralized. "The employers frankly admit," a 1948 publication of the Federation of Employers' Organizations put it, "that [Japanese companies] had . . . become incapable of devising means to overcome economic difficulties, amid . . . the unforeseen changes and confusion . . . and they further admit that they had been unable to exercise their . . . management rights properly."[30] When Nippon Iron and Steel Manufacturing Company president Nagano asked me to teach him about "labor problems" in the spring of 1946, he was not merely flattering me. His request had an edge of panic to it.

In Japan, when in doubt, organize. Employers responded to the spurt of union organization with associations of their own. The first was established in April 1946, and by August there were twenty-five.[31] For big businessmen from the prewar period, previously secure in their niche at the top of Japanese society and accustomed to directing their employees as they saw fit, it was difficult to adjust to the new atmosphere. Many of them found defeat at the hands of foreigners easier to accept than equal status with their workers. From time to time we received reports that the "old guard," fulminating privately at their meetings, had threatened to smash unions and, as before, to call in the police to suppress "radicals." Had such attitudes prevailed, the whole new labor relations system might have been destroyed.

Fortunately, however, there were also younger and more flexible business leaders. Under the leadership of Moroi Kanichi, President of Chichibu Cement Company, they organized their own group, the *Keizai Dōyū-kai,* or Economic Comrades Association (now known as the Committee for Economic Development). They too visited the Labor Division from time to time in order to obtain data and advice from our Labor Relations Branch. They made quite an impression on Costantino, the branch chief, for he had been a CIO organizer and wished that his American businessmen adversaries had been as wise and reasonable as their Japanese counterparts. If *Keizai Dōyū-kai* represented a minority of the business community, it nevertheless had a profound long-term influence. Its members were the first to combine traditional paternalism with collective bargaining, thereby producing the blend that has since become the hallmark of Japanese labor relations. In spite of the public impression that we were hopelessly pro-labor (an image I admit to having fostered), the Labor Division also worked constructively with employers.

With several million workers organized into unions and with some already engaged in sound collective bargaining, the democratization of the Japanese labor movement was well under way by the end of the summer of 1946. We could not yet tell, however, whether labor reform would succeed. Although General MacArthur could inspire Japanese workers, and his Labor Division could encourage them as well as provide concrete help, we—as outsiders—found it difficult if not impossible to convince them that their brand of "revolutionary trade unionism'' was bad medicine. SCAP's influence in this area was ultimately limited.

Our propositions were clear enough. We pointed out first of all that for Communists, free trade unions were temporary devices that existed primarily to bring about revolution and the construction of a Communist state. If they were victorious, the Communists, unable to abide challenges to their power from any source, would convert independent unions into instruments of their ''workers' state.'' That had happened after every other Communist takeover, and it was reasonable to expect the same in Japan. Economic unionism, on the other hand, was forever. It represented workers' interests under any government or social system.

Meanwhile, we declared, revolutionary unionism was a menace to internal union democracy. The very strengths of a trade union in its battles with an employer, namely, its unity and internal discipline, were most susceptible to misuse by a union leadership to suppress political disagreement.

For a small group of Americans to try to convince millions of Japanese, or even thousands of their leaders, of the immediacy of such an intangible future danger was all but impossible. The Occupation rule forbidding us to criticize the Soviet Union as one of the occupying powers handicapped us further. Criticism of local Communists carried little weight, for the new Japanese Communist leaders had just emerged from long periods of imprisonment pure as the driven snow and innocent of all the past Communist inconsistencies and betrayals—the Nazi–Soviet Pact, the Moscow Trials, and the gulags—that had rocked the Communist parties in almost every other land and of which the Japanese were hardly aware anyway. No one could easily believe that honest working-class people like their beloved ''Tokkyū-san'' (actually a lawyer who had been a probationary prosecutor for the Justice Ministry) and Shiga Yoshio (a journalist by profession) would eventually destroy the Japanese labor movement, not after all their years of sacrifice for ''the workers.''

LABOR UNIONISM AND POLITICS

The greatest obstacles to persuasion were the historical background and cultural heritage of the Japanese workers. American labor people, such as the AFL and CIO advisers sent to us, were flabbergasted. To the Americans, political unionism, that is, unions as partners of a party, was an antidemocratic and un-American concept, and Marxism a snare. Most informed Americans agreed. General Whitney, on receipt of the Far East Commission's December 6, 1946, Principles for Trade Unions, was on his way to tell General MacArthur about them when he met me in the Government Section general office. He was surprised and relieved to hear from me that the Occupation had been permitting

Japanese unions to engage in political activities as now required by the FEC. He had taken it for granted that I would have been discouraging that. Our civil intelligence agencies were profoundly suspicious of all the new Japanese unions, taking their Marxist language for Communism or near-Communism—"leftism," General Willoughby called it. But to me, who alone among GHQ Americans had studied the labor movement in the context of Japanese history, the resurgent postwar unions' immersion in both politics and Marxism had its roots deep in the Japan of Meiji, Tokugawa, and even before.

How could it be otherwise? For fifty years the Japanese prewar labor movement had been intensely political. In the three decades before World War I, every single trade union had been organized by or with the sponsorship of socialists of one stripe or another (Fabian, Christian, Marxist) or by anarchists or syndicalists, their foundation as much exercises in political theory as workers' response to immediate circumstances. The socialists, particularly, never saw any conflict between trade unionism and politics. When universal manhood suffrage was enacted in 1925, the socialist labor leaders leaped enthusiastically into electoral politics—in the next seven years they organized fourteen "proletarian parties," only two of which lasted more than a few years[32]—while usually retaining their trade union posts as well. Thoughtful labor leaders (notably Takano Minoru) regretted the process in retrospect as a dissipation of labor energies in sectarian political rivalries, but with the Occupation the labor union–socialist political dance resumed.

In 1946 only one of all the union officials I met, Kanemasa Yonekichi, the West Japan *Sōdōmei* chief, spoke against unions in proletarian politics. For some of the proletarian politicians, there was an undeniable attraction in being a minister, Diet member, or even local Assemblyman. (Mrs. Katō, herself a Diet member, displayed her ambition for her husband to be a minister almost every time I met her.) Moreover, after the war, with government so intimately involved in every crucial economic decision, simple trade unionism and collective bargaining were clearly inadequate. Favorable decisions on rations, prices, taxes, railway fares, and distribution of consumer goods all required labor voices in government. In 1947, the unions got them. Thirty-nine trade union officials captured Diet seats in the 1947 elections, and *Sōdōmei* president Matsuoka, one of the most steadfast opponents of Communist unionism, became Speaker of the Lower House. (Incidentally, he never had more fun.) We in GHQ learned that telling them about the dangers of political unionism was like talking to a brick wall.

The "Marxist"—and that does not necessarily mean Communist—character of the Japanese labor movement was even more natural, for the central Marxist propositions about class society—class struggle and exploitation of lower by the higher—seemed to fit the Japanese workers' own historical experience. In the immediate postwar years, when the workers were rejecting their traditional role as underlings, Marxism, with its glorification of the working class, was there to comfort them. Marxism was espoused by the vast majority of Japanese intellectuals. Indeed, in postwar Japan one could justly say that Marxism, in Raymond Avon's words, was the opium of the intellectuals.[33]

The American workingman, with his New World heritage that scorned European feudal classes, thought of his union as a voluntary association of free individuals who joined together to unite their economic powers. Although a worker, he was sure he was just as good a man as the boss. They both put their pants on one leg at a time, didn't they? In confronting management, union negotiators might concede the boss was richer, but never that he was better.

The Japanese worker, on the other hand, received his heritage from a society that had been divided for hundreds of years into castes, not only socially but legally as well. Tokugawa Japan assigned different legal rights and obligations to the four feudal classes: warriors, farmers, artisans, and merchants. Meiji, Taishō, and Shōwa Japan scarcely changed the workers' position in society. It is not surprising that at war's end, the Japanese worker could not bring himself to assert equality, American style, and to make claims upon his employer by right as an equal human being.

Still, Japanese Marxism may not have been so pure. At the tenth anniversary celebration of a Nagoya knitting firm (with which I did business many years later), I ran into Suzuki Mōsaburō, the leftist president of the Socialist Party. The Socialists, like the conservative Liberal Party, had sent the company huge floral wreaths, voicing their best wishes in honor of the occasion. When I twitted Suzuki for being so friendly with the "class enemy," he looked uncomfortable and replied, "But still, we're all Japanese."

With all the Marxist talk, the traditional Japanese concept of a worker owing loyalty to the employer who in turn owed him protection from a harsh world prevailed over the Western idea of a simple exchange of so much work for so much pay. Workers often accepted reduced or delayed wages when their company was temporarily up against it, while many a factory kept its workers on the payroll with little for them to do. After the bitter fifty-seven-day strike at Toshiba Electric in the fall of 1946, the union lent the company money to tide over its difficulties. The Kantō Electric Power Distribution Company, fighting a strike of its employees, nevertheless invited the pickets in on one cold and rainy day in 1946, when I happened by, to serve them hot tea. When the strike ended they would all be family again. Meanwhile, the workers would have been offended had the company behaved heartlessly.

Occasionally, to Western amusement but not necessarily understanding, labor–management confrontations took on the appearance of a kind of Marxist *chambara* (ritualized sword-fighting) theater, with the substantive issues relatively moderate, the rhetoric extreme Marxist, and the style uncompromising and absolute. When the time came, even dignified professors tied on *hachimaki* headbands and snake-danced in the streets, while a clash between two rival mine unions over the supply of mine timbers by boat turned into a feudal naval battle off the Miike coalmine shore. Culture determined style in labor affairs, even if the economy dictated content and politics set the alignment of forces.

Whatever the incongruity of the feudal–Marxist mixture, the critical point was that it helped to camouflage the Communists. If everyone talked like a violent Marxist, what was so special about the Communists? Maybe it was only they who really meant the warlike rhetoric, but how were the others to tell? On repeated occasions like May Day, Socialists, Communists, and trade unionists marched together, shouting the same slogans and defying the same "capitalist" foe. It would take a great deal to break the bonds they formed. Speeches and lectures from Americans could not do it. The Japanese workers would have to learn for themselves, and the year 1946 saw the beginning of the process.

The rivalry in that year between Communists, feverish and fiery, and the anti-Communists, somewhat more relaxed, was by no means unexpected. What no one had counted on was the extremely swift pace of labor union organization. With SCAP favor toward labor unions on record, every individual industrial grievance, disagreement, or dispute was sufficient to set up a new *ad hoc* labor union if one did not already exist. Neither the moderates nor the Communists had the organizing capacity to handle the avalanche. Unattached unions with brand new faces were mushrooming faster than either *Sōdōmei* or the Communists.

The moderate, economically oriented *Sōdōmei* federation did not mind. But for Tokuda and his Politburo, it was critical to mobilize "the masses" *behind* the Communists, not alongside them, to obtain control, not simple affiliation. So Tokuda, ever flexible, abruptly changed his entire approach in early 1946. Organization "from the bottom" was too slow in competition with Matsuoka and the independents. He set out to infiltrate as well as to organize. Service, adoption, and secrecy were his tactics.

COMMUNIST INFILTRATION

The incredibly burgeoning new unions all needed many things, and the Communists set out to make themselves indispensable by supplying them. Did a union leader need a mimeograph machine, a bicycle, paper for leaflets? Suddenly he discovered that a previously unknown comrade who had been hanging around headquarters knew where to get them. When messengers were short, volunteers appeared from nowhere. The same applied to placard painters, guards, editors, and especially those needed for any kind of onerous or time-consuming work under difficult conditions. With the party's resources and discipline, the Communists could make life much easier for brand-new labor leaders.

In the same way, independent, inexperienced leaders, often hardly known personally to most of their members, discovered unknown supporters who praised and encouraged them at every turn. Dobashi, the handsome president of the All-Communications Workers Union, had been an aspiring movie actor. His ego responded well to "stroking," perhaps too indiscriminately, the Communists found out, when he tried to lead his union into the moderate *Sōdōmei* Federation as well as their own *Sanbetsu* Congress. He was not the only one. Rather than try to install their own men as titular leaders of the unions that they successfully infiltrated, the Communists preferred simply to co-opt politically naïve but popular leaders already in office, to flatter them, "educate" them politically, surround them with party help, and eventually bring them into the Communist Party or at least under Communist discipline. That method also served to conceal their role effectively.

Secrecy was indispensable. Well-orchestrated maneuvers by secret Party cells or Party "fractions," that is, the secret organization of all the Communists in a union, had to give the appearance of the spontaneous opinion of the working masses. Party affiliation, therefore, had to be legitimately deniable if necessary, and the definitions of Communist were accordingly cynically variable. Shiga Yoshio, the number two Communist, told John Emmerson in November 1945 that there were only 600 Communists in Japan[34]—no cause for alarm. But Hasegawa Kō, then directly in charge of party organization, told me that in October 1945 there were two thousand to three thousand. Shiga was not lying; he was just omitting candidate members, ardent sympathizers, and others under party discipline, even though they were often more effective and more important than the cardholders. Similarly, the Party carefully guarded the identity of the party fraction leader in any union. He was never in the top spot, even though he might run the union. Most often he was a relatively unobtrusive secretary or secretary general, just as Joseph Stalin had once been.[35] Invisibility lent a degree of invulnerability.

The Communists typically went after second- and third-rank union headquarters office jobs that no one else wanted. There they were free from public scrutiny but possessed unsuspected leverage. Thus a union executive board might decide questions on its agenda, but it was the union secretariat that prepared the agenda and worded the resolutions. The secretariat also usually decided such apparently unimportant but sometimes crucial details as the time and place of meetings. At the *Yomiuri* newspaper, for example, one critical union meeting was called for 11 P.M., great for the Communist-dominated compositors and printers, who worked late anyway, but inconvenient for the anti-Communist business department employees, who had to get home before the last trains had gone. Placard calligraphers and leaflet mimeographers could "improve" phraseology without anyone's being the wiser. Even messengers could make an enormous difference by not being able to locate non-Communist officials at critical times, say for a strike vote. Finally, lowly guards could make a difference by barring anti-Communists as troublemakers from union meetings while the Communist fraction ran the assembly its way. It was remarkable what occupancy of minor jobs could accomplish.

THE RISE OF SANBETSU

When one considers the initial handful of Communists, their progress in the first eight months of 1946 was prodigious, particularly in their organization of a national federation claiming 1.6 million members, the Congress of Industrial Unions, or *Sanbetsu*.

Shortly after their release from jail in the fall of 1945, Tokuda and Shiga had tried a shortcut to labor leadership. At the invitation of Takano Minoru, they agreed in writing to enter Matsuoka's *Sōdōmei*. Perhaps they had real hopes of subverting it. Perhaps, like Lenin when he was too weak to fight, Tokuda's aim was to recruit and disrupt from within. The maneuver, whatever it was, never came to pass. When the Communists applied to enter the Socialist Party, too, they were rejected. Some Socialists distrusted them from long experience; others, like Takano, feared Tokuda's advocacy of selective compliance with Occupation orders, meanwhile "setting fires where he could," as irresponsible and dangerous. The Communist pair thereupon withdrew their application to *Sōdōmei* in a huff.[36]

Instead, on January 6, 1946, the Communist Party issued an uncompromising message to the Socialists, castigating many of their old leaders as "social fascists" and imperialists during the war and proclaiming four revolutionary goals, one of which was the establishment of a "national congress of industrial unions," *Sanbetsu* for short.[37] On February 21, at the invitation of the National Newspaper Union, a dozen brand-new unions met to form a committee for the establishment of *Sanbetsu*. The project had someone's highest priority.

From the beginning, concealment and camouflage were guiding principles. Kikunami Katsumi, a prewar foreign correspondent and writer for the *Asahi*, who presided at the first meeting as newspaper union head and also served as chairman of the committee and then of *Sanbetsu* itself when it came into existence, consistently denied he was a Communist. As late as May 1947, he was still denying it, though admitting he had long been "an ardent supporter."[38] (Hasegawa and Takano both swore to me years later that Kikunami had held a party card since early 1946). In public the sponsors justified their new rival federation as essential to promote unionization along industrial lines, just as the American CIO's departure from the craft unions of the AFL had done. That, of course, was the rationale for the name they chose—the English abbreviation, NCIO, was similar too—but it made little sense, because craft unions of the original AFL stripe did not exist in Japan, and the rival *Sōdōmei*'s unions were all industrial too. Still, certain Americans in GHQ found the idea attractive. Lieutenant Wyman Hicks, the Chief of the CIE Labor Education Branch and a prewar organizer for Harry Bridges's longshoreman's union (CIO), furnished Kikunami with a copy of the American CIO constitution and lots of other material besides. With the benefit of all the information that has since become available, there can be no doubt that *Sanbetsu* was from the beginning "a Communist project," in the words of Takano many years later. Indeed, the ambience of its headquarters was so Communist that one non-Communist union president could later complain that "unions other than those supporting the Communist Party could not join *Sanbetsu* without a feeling of embarrassment."[39] But in the midst of 1946 it was not at all that clear, certainly not to me and the SCAP Labor Division.

The Labor Division was, after all, a staff, not an operational, agency, and it had no independent investigative capabilities. G-2's Civil Intelligence Section and the Counter Intelligence Corps were useless to us; they lumped all "leftists" together, sometimes including the Labor Division itself under that label. The Japanese police were out of labor surveillance, we hoped, and their successor in labor affairs, the Welfare Ministry, had little to offer. In the end we had to rely upon anti-Communist friends in the labor movement to keep us informed, and they were not always able to penetrate the Communists' veil of secrecy and deception. Sometimes, too, our own intuition, developed from experience with American Communists, failed.

But that is getting a little ahead of our story. In August 1946, when I was invited to address the inaugural convention of the *Sanbetsu*—I had addressed the *Sōdōmei* inaugural just a short time before,—I knew that Communist influence in *Sanbetsu* was strong but did not know how strong. I suspected president Kikunami of being a Communist and knew that deputy secretary general Hosoya Matsuta was one. But I did not know that of the officials to be elected in the succeeding days, the other vice president besides Dobashi,[40] the secretary general,[41] and at least five other executive board members[42] were all Communists. But even if I had known I would still have come to warn the conference, as I did, against excessive politicization, to advise it of SCAP's attitude, and to try to affect the direction they were taking.

Most of the Communists of those days were only recent recruits, and their adherence was not at all hardened in concrete. (Indeed, in less than a year the *Sanbetsu* Communist fraction leader, Hosoya, would himself leave the Party and organize an anti-Communist group.) Even more important, Communist labor influence at that early period in postwar Japan was largely confined to union leadership, and to central leadership in particular. At the local level, Communist influence was usually negligible. There was no guarantee at all that the national leaders could carry their unions with them along the party line. In the railway union, for example, most of the ordinary railway station locals, especially in the

west, were headed by father-figure conservative stationmasters, who only recently had prided themselves on being servants of the Emperor. It was far too
early to write off Japanese unions just because some of their leaders were
Communists.

Besides, in the spring of 1946 no Communist-dominated union had yet
experienced its moment of truth, that critical time when the discrepancy between
the members' immediate welfare and the leaders' political goals clearly emerged.
When it did, the workers would have to choose which would do more for them, a
sweeping Communist revolution or prosaic day-to-day economic trade unionism
under the shelter of civil rights—and which would be safer. The Washington
planners, the great American labor federations, General MacArthur himself, and
his Labor Division were all confident that given the truth and freedom of choice,
the workers would choose democratic trade unions and reject the revolution's
siren song. But the choice had to be real, or it would never endure. That meant
the workers had to be protected in their choice by law, secure from any outside
intervention, whether employer, government, or police. In the context of a
military occupation, they had to be protected from the Occupation Forces as
well, and that could be ensured only by the Supreme Commander's authority.
The first line of protection, the institution of a solid system of democratic labor
legislation, was easier, the second, much harder. But neither was at all certain.

12

Help, but Hands Off!

LABOR AND THE LAW

In 1946, IT SEEMED THAT almost everyone in the Occupation General Headquarters was engaged in some sort of legal reform: drafting, editing, revising, advising, or building a monument of laws and more laws. The December 1945 Japanese Diet session had enacted labor, land, and election reform laws. The summer–fall 1946 session, the longest in Japan's history, approved a new constitution and ninety-four other laws, and the winter–spring 1947 Diet passed ninety-five more.[1] GHQ was involved in almost every one of them.

Involved, yes—but how? Japanese history has perhaps no greater mystery than the process by which Occupation reform intentions became law. That was no accident. SCAP, for its part, was intent on publicly establishing the *Japanese,* not foreign, character of the new legislation in order to ensure its public acceptance and hence durability. The Japanese Government was just as interested in demonstrating that it was master in its own house and hence presented the new laws as its own effort, with the least possible indication of American pressure. Informal legal consultations between the two sides rarely were recorded. The result was to obscure reality, and nowhere more than in the crucial labor reforms. Even today, standard Japanese legal compendiums begin their legislative histories of the Occupation period labor laws with their presentation to the Diet. In reality the picture was quite different. By the time the Diet got the bills, their content and passage had already been decided. And in those decisions the key agency was the SCAP Labor Division.

A TWENTY-SEVEN-YEAR-OLD LABOR CHIEF

It was a heavy responsibility for a small group, numbering only a handful during most of that time. In America and Europe, labor law had evolved over more than a century. Who were we, then, by no means legal authorities in our own country, to try to accomplish the same rapidly in Japan?

The Joint Chiefs of Staff directive did not allow General MacArthur to wait. He would have to do the job with whatever staff was available. Other SCAP agencies might turn out new or revised detailed law codes destined to remain in place permanently—an education law, a police law, a code of criminal procedure, a banking law—but our first aim was more limited: to establish basic legal protection for the Japanese workers, not least from actions of their own government. Other legislation, covering the whole range of government assistance and protection for the *individual* worker, could come later under Japanese leadership, including organized labor. Help from the law, yes, but hands off the labor movement—such was our imperative. And for that kind of mission, a small, hard-hitting division, not to be distracted by side issues, was just right.

The first Chief of the SCAP Labor Division, until January 1946, was Major William Karpinsky, a former professor at Monmouth College and mediator for the New Jersey State Mediation Service who was, on top of that, a product of the Army Military Government School. The Chief of our Labor Relations Branch was a trained labor lawyer with experience as a union organizer, first with the Steel Workers Organizing Committee and then with District 50 of the United Mine Workers. He was joined after some months by another lawyer, who had represented the Hotel and Restaurant Workers Union and others in collective bargaining and drafting labor contracts. Our wage specialist was from the City of Los Angeles, and our working conditions expert was from the U.S. Labor Department. For a few months in 1946 we also had the benefit of a dozen labor experts from the United States. Three of them participated in the drafting of the Japanese Labor Relations Adjustment Bill, and six others worked on other pieces of legislation.

Finally, while I, as the second division chief from January 1946 to May 1947, was no technical labor expert, I did have a combination of other qualifications unique for those times: intensive study in the United States of the Japanese labor movement before the war, a reading knowledge of the Japanese language (rare in GHQ outside the Allied Translator and Interpreter Service), and almost two years of work in Washington on Japanese Occupation planning, including a stint as Chief of the Foreign Economic Administration's Japanese Labor Policy Section.

Even so, my appointment at age twenty-seven and a half as civilian labor chief was largely happenstance. Eager, once hostilities ended, to get out to Japan as quickly as possible, I tried to join a labor advisory mission then being organized, but its appointed chief, a University of Kentucky professor (who never did make it), seemed to be in no hurry. Instead I joined a ''democratization'' mission sent to help General Whitney's Government Section become the planning staff for GHQ, an idea that never did come to fruition. It did not matter, for the day after my arrival on January 6, 1946, I approached Karpinsky, whom I had known briefly at the Civil Affairs Staging Area in Monterey, California, the preceding summer, to see if I could switch to his outfit. With only three officers, one of whom was slated to leave shortly, Karpinsky needed no convincing. He arranged the next day through General Marquat, his chief, to borrow me from a rather reluctant Whitney till the end of the month. Karpinsky also was in a great hurry to get home, but General MacArthur would not release him until he found a competent replacement. Karpinsky, therefore, went to work to sell me as his successor. In addition to my paper qualifications, Karpinsky could point to my connections with American labor through my friendship with Irving Brown, European representative of the AFL, and two of the non-American members of the Far Eastern Commission, Herbert Norman, representing Canada, and Sir George Sansom, the British member. That might come in handy some day.

Most important, however, was MacArthur's determination to fill all important vacant posts in his headquarters from within the theater so quickly that Washington could not send him someone with outside obligations and hence divided loyalties. Indeed, unknown to MacArthur, the AFL and CIO, with the concurrence of the War and Labor Departments, had already divided up the Occupation labor chief posts, Germany to the AFL and Japan to the CIO. They never got the chance to implement the agreement in Japan. Deciding I was his best, or safest, bet in the circumstances, MacArthur appointed me Labor Division Chief at the end of January 1946. Karpinsky was delighted to leave for home the following week.

He left behind two ticklish legal problems: first, a brand-new but seriously flawed Trade Union Law, and second, an alarming new strike tactic, ''production control.'' Either, mishandled, could derail the Occupation labor mission.

The Trade Union Law was a historic milestone, finally granting legal recognition to independent workers' organizations after more than two decades of fruitless agitation. On October 4, 1945, General MacArthur, apprised that the newly appointed Prime Minister Shidehara wanted to pay his respects, converted a courtesy call into a working meeting by presenting Shidehara with five basic reforms to be carried out as fast as Japan could assimilate them. The second was ''the encouragement of the unionization of labor.'' Then MacArthur passed the word to his staff that he wanted appropriate legislation before Christmas.

A completely baffled Shidehara, a career diplomat who hardly knew what a trade union was, resorted to a traditional Japanese ploy: When in doubt, appoint a commission. His was a whopper, 130 men of ''wisdom and experience,'' scholars, company presidents, government officials, social workers, prewar labor leaders, and politicians, including the Communist Tokuda Kyūichi, just released after seventeen years from prison. That unwieldy group chose a steering committee of thirty-one, still including Tokuda, and it, in turn, selected a working committee of five, three Welfare Ministry officials and two scholars, to draft a Trade Union Law. Considering the cumbersome machinery—steering committee, full commission, Cabinet Legislative Bureau, and the Diet—and Karpinsky's surveillance and clearance, their speed was phenomenal. One week before Christmas, MacArthur had his Trade Union Law. He greeted it warmly.

In a society where the absence of a prohibition was not enough to establish legality, the importance of a law that specifically recognized trade unions and collective agreements cannot be overestimated. The new law also exempted unions from taxes and certain kinds of claims[2] and, in a sharp break with Japan's past, brought labor relations administration out from under the old-line bureaucracy, which had considered workers only as objects to be managed, into the hands of a series of autonomous, tripartite Labor Relations Committees (LRC), prefectural, central, and maritime. Although appointed by the prefectural governors, the welfare minister, and the transportation minister respectively, the labor members of the committees were nominated by labor unions, the employer members by employer organizations, and the public members by the other nominees combined. It was a considerable achievement.

Defusing a Defective Law

But the law also had grave defects. Unions had to register and submit their constitutions for approval or modification, together with lists of officers. They also had to maintain membership lists. Finally, according to article 15, the courts could dissolve unions that "frequently violate laws and ordinances and disturb peace and order" upon application by an LRC.

When I took over from Karpinsky at the end of January 1946, I was surprised to see the degree of government supervision and shocked at article 15. Karpinsky never bothered to explain or justify the law to me, except to point with pride at its Japanese, not American, character. He did say that he had warned the Japanese against any police role in labor affairs, but otherwise he saw his own function as expediting and educational: He had spent two days in the basement of the Diet building giving lectures on American, British, and Australian labor law to the legislators and officials involved.[3] Captain Anthony Costantino, his labor relations officer, who remained behind, could shed no additonal light. Karpinsky, he told me, had not let him or anyone else from GHQ in on the legislation, relying instead on the considerable wisdom of Dr. Suehiro Izutarō, Chairman of the Commission, and avoiding any dispute that might delay the bill. Whatever Karpinsky's reasons, however, the fact remained: The law was dangerously defective.

Requiring labor unions to register and supply lists of officers and possibly members to government agencies was bad enough, especially in light of the history of government interference in the independence of labor, but a union could still decline to register without any penalty other than a loss of tax and claims exemption. Government modification of union rules was worse. And what about dissolving unions? How could that be squared with the freedom of association essential to democracy? In Japan particularly, where for decades police plainclothesmen would attend union meetings, rise midway through the proceedings, disperse the gathering, and send everyone home, and where the Home Ministry had dissolved numberless organizations in defense of the "national polity," such a measure had all the earmarks of a restoration of the old regime. True, tripartite LRCs, one-third labor, were not expected to act like policemen, but under pressure who could be sure? Article 15 apparently was aimed at labor-boss gangs and even *yakuza* gangsters posing as labor unions to acquire tax and claims exemptions, but the provision could be applied to objectionable but genuine unions. I could agree that disruptive or otherwise undesirable actions might have to be restricted, but to have the government break up the unions themselves would be intolerable.

In Washington, both the State and the Labor Departments reacted much the same way as I, sending Tokyo blistering criticisms by way of the War Department.[4] The criticisms somehow never arrived—perhaps some officer was afraid of arousing MacArthur's wrath—and I myself saw them only much later. It made no difference. Quite independently, I had resolved to nullify article 15 one way or another. The other unwelcome provisions could wait.

What could I do, however, when the law itself, only a month old, was a widely hailed democratization reform produced by Japan's first postwar Diet and was acclaimed by the SCAP into the bargain? Open repeal or modification was out of the question. The law, however, had not yet gone into effect; an Imperial ordinance specifying the effective date and other procedural details was required. It seemed the ordinance might be used to undermine the unwanted provisions of the law. When Dr. Suehiro and his working committee brought the ordinance to my office, expecting routine clearance, I surprised them by pronouncing the ordinance—not the law—defective.

Under their draft, I told them, a bona fide union could be dissolved, an effect contrary to the intent of the law, whose purpose was to encourage unions in accordance with General MacArthur's instructions to the Prime Minister. The ordinance therefore had to be amended, and I was prepared to suggest an amendment. A dissolution order under article 15, I proposed, should require a court finding that the "frequent violations" and "disturbances" had been authorized either by the members or by the officers empowered to do so by the union constitution. I did not say so, but clearly no general meeting of the members would ever authorize violations of law *per se,* and no union officer, if his organization's charter contained a proper disclaimer, could legally do so either. In brief, no union could then be dissolved, no matter what the law said. Article 15 would be defused.

Suehiro, the former dean of Tokyo Imperial University Law School and perhaps the single most eminent legal scholar in the country, saw immediately what I was driving at. A gnomelike man about 4 feet, 8 inches tall with twinkling eyes, who looked like an elderly gardener in his baggy trousers, dark blue shirt, and gray, crewcut hair, he was too diplomatic to tell me bluntly that it was the law, not the ordinance, that I found displeasing. Instead, he simply pointed out that it was contrary to Japanese legal practice to include substanative provisions in a procedural ordinance. Only the Diet could substantively modify a law. I replied with a straight face that I was not changing the substantive content of the law, but merely seeing to it that the procedures in the ordinance ensured its enforcement in the light of its intent. In any case, I was not going to recommend to General MacArthur that he permit the ordinance and then three months later see a union dissolved under its provisions. Perhaps, I suggested, we could meet again Sunday morning, when we would not be distracted. Meanwhile, I asked the working committee to devise some other procedure, if it could, to protect bona fide unions from dissolution.

The Sunday, February 17, 1946, meeting in my office in the nearly empty Forestry Building[5] resumed where the earlier one had left off. I was accompanied by Costantino, while Suehiro was supported by Yoshitake Keiichi, then head of the Welfare Ministry's Labor Administration Bureau and later Labor Minister; Togashi Seiichi, head of his Investigation Section; and Dr. Ayusawa Iwao, a former official of the International Labor Office in Geneva and recipient of a Ph.D. in labor economics from Columbia University in 1928. The Japanese working committee had no alternate suggestion, and I would not accept its original text. Our meeting went on for several hours, but neither side would yield to the other. We were at an impasse.

Wearying of the repetitiousness of the brilliant arguments on both sides, I turned the meeting over to Costantino and wandered into our now deserted division general office to clear my head. There in a corner I noticed a large box of Army ten-in-one food rations. A solution immediately became apparent. An Army travels on its stomach. Both Costantino and I had eaten hearty breakfasts. I was sure the Japanese delegation had not, having had to arise in the six o'clock darkness at the latest to get to our office by 8:30, and there were no eating establishments open on Sunday morning in the center of the bombed-out capital.

Surreptitiously, I took my lunch while Costantino continued the meeting across the hall. Then we exchanged places so he could take his. We had sternly to suppress our impulse to be hospitable in the interest of higher principle.

Dr. Suehiro, for his part, was not fortified by principle; he had made it clear that he thought the article in the Trade Union Law was a mistake. His bureaucratic colleagues, Yoshitake and Togashi, were worried mostly about breaching the distinction between legislative substance and administrative procedure and then being overruled by the Cabinet Legislative Bureau. Ayusawa, a romantic pacifist who had presented his father's samurai sword to Karpinsky in an emotional moment as symbolic of Japan's eternal dedication to peace evermore, lived the farthest away and was most striken with hunger pangs. In those conditions—sympathy for my aim plus the physical strain—they saw no reason to hold out. By mid-afternoon the Working Committee conceded the "logic" of my case. It agreed to include my wording in the Ordinance, and the Cabinet Legislative Bureau be damned.

Sure enough, several days later two outraged representatives of the Cabinet Legislative Bureau visited me to object strenuously to legislating in place of the Diet. When I was able to point out that the great Dean of Tokyo Imperial Law School, under whom they had studied and whom they all revered, had agreed to the change, they could hardly insist that it was illegal. My proposal was accepted, and it became article 17 of the Imperial ordinance.

Three years later, when the Trade Union Law was amended for other reasons, the authority to dissolve unions was abolished. Meanwhile, our casual twisting of Japanese law set no precedent. No other member of the Labor Legislation Commission, and certainly no Diet member who had voted for the law, even noticed what we had done. A serious Washington complaint was taken care of, even though it never reached Tokyo. Most important of all, no union was ever dissolved, nor did anyone ever again propose the government should have the power to do so. Unknown to the public at the time, the episode has gone unrecognized to this day as well.

PRODUCTION CONTROL

Settlement behind closed doors of that sort, however, was never possible when the unions began "seizing" their workplaces. On the contrary, "production control," or *seisan kanri,* immediately became a sensational public issue. Were such tactics legal? Did they violate property rights? To the unions, production control was a daring but legitimate technique. To management, it was impermissible. What was the Occupation going to do about it?

Early in December 1945, a Communist-organized union at the Mitsui Bibai coal mines in Hokkaido stopped work to back up its demand for more pay but found the management unperturbed. At the low controlled price for coal, the management preferred to leave it in the ground. The union promptly went back to mine coal, but on the "self-control" principle, that is, excluding management from the process. The union, in fact, exerted every effort to increase production sharply. A bewildered mine administration quickly capitulated, raised wages, recognized the union, and even agreed on a permanent labor–management council to help run the mines.[6]

The workers on the private railway lines around Tokyo[7] were no less ingenious. About the same time as the Bibai mines incident, the Tokyo Rapid Transit Company's supervision section threatened to let the passengers ride free if management refused to meet its demands.[8] It fell to the Keisei rail line union to make the threat good. On December 12, 1945, passengers arriving at Ueno Station in Tokyo were surprised to find union placards saying, "To express our gratitude for your kind patronage, we have started a 'Kindness Free Service.' However, we solicit your understanding, as cars are not operated very frequently because a number of coaches are now under repair. Labor Union Keisei Electric Railway."[9] Fares were not collected that day or on the ensuing days, even though at the beginning the disciplined passengers felt uneasy about not paying. A few days later other signs inside the cars assured the public that in view of the dangers of defective railway cars, presumably management's fault, union members in the workshops were voluntarily laboring overtime to get the rolling stock into proper condition. Railway management was as baffled as their coalmine counterparts. It, too, capitulated.

To the Occupation authorities, both affairs were bemusing, the kind of labor actions that could never take place in the United States. The Japanese, with their traditions of class differences and feudal battles, plus the added Marxist conception of class conflict, looked upon strikes as a form of surrogate warfare that could take any shape the fertile imagination could devise. Thus Japan had a long history of go-slow strikes, work-to-rule strikes, strikes where chorus girls kicked half as high or telephone operators cheerfully informed callers that they were on strike but working as usual, and strikes of limited duration, from a few minutes to several days. Leaders selected tactics according to their acceptability and effectiveness, avoiding stodgy, conventional formulas.

Unsurprisingly, the immediate sequels to Bibai and Keisei were equally novel, but there, too, the unions deliberately focused on infringing management's prerogatives. In early January 1946, for example, doctors and nurses at the Central Red Cross Hospital in Takagi-chō in Tokyo decided to strike by way of *lengthening* their work day by four hours.[10] And on January 17, the newborn Electric Power Workers Union, striking the Kantō (East Japan) Electric Power Distribution Company "took over" the business management of the company.[11]

The rhetoric was somewhat exaggerated. In fact, as the union representatives told us when they visited our office, the union had merely drawn a chalk line on the floor around the executives' offices and forbidden them to cross the line without union permission. Since an electric distribution company's office work is routine, the line was seldom crossed, and operations continued normally. Only the red flags and signs announcing "production control" at the building entrance signaled anything out of the ordinary. Considering that the action substituted for a previously scheduled strike of 1,200 workers at the Utsunomiya regional office, no one could assert the new tactic was more disruptive. A walkout would have tied the company into administrative knots even though "production control" sounded far more threatening. The company quickly settled.

Whatever the variation, the new tactic, with its implications of forcefulness and audacity, swiftly captured the imaginations of disaffected workers. In January 1946, although disputes were few and strikes fewer, 67 percent of all those who did "strike" did so by way of "production control." [12] Walkouts seemed to have been almost forgotten.

To the worker, production control seemed a "natural" way to avoid undue pressure on a tottering economy and interference with the production and transportation of the necessities of life. The new union leaders were eager to prove themselves responsible people. Finally, where so many enterprises were operating at a fraction of capacity for lack of fuel or raw materials, a work stoppage would not penalize management much. On the contrary, it could help the owners by relieving them of the obligation to pay wages on time. Often enterprise management preferred to hoard materials for price rises rather than for use in production. For them, a standard strike would be a welcome excuse to close their doors.

Resorting to production control, however, shifted the battle from the economic to the public relations arena. The idea was to shame management before the nation, to demonstrate the employer was unnecessary, or better still, to show the public that, unencumbered by "feudalistic" ways, unions could do management's job better. More ominously, it might prove that socialism, which most unions formally espoused, worked better than capitalism. Perhaps the public would end up afterward asking for "socialism."

RIOTS AND DEMONSTRATIONS

Some employers and uneasy conservatives grew panicky. An unqualified respect for private property was the foundation of their world, and once workers encroached on property rights without penalty, who could tell how much further they would go? Japanese history was full of episodic eruptions of mass violence,[13] from the countless peasant uprisings, some running into the hundreds of thousands of violence-prone rebels each, in the earlier Tokugawa epoch, to the first production control effort during the great Kobe dock strikes of 1921,[14] which required the dispatch of soldiers to reinforce the police in mass arrests and discharges. Now it looked as though anarchy, and with it mass violence, were returning to Japan. Where would it all end?

The streets of Tokyo offered no comfort. The 600 members of the National Railways labor union who marched on January 19 across downtown Tokyo to the Prime Minister's residence, waving scarlet banners, chanting labor songs, and demanding wage increases, and then sat for five hours in the lobby, were disquieting. Indeed, the Transportation Minister himself was obliged to see them and promise faithfully to do his best.[15] How long had it been since a Minister of his Imperial Majesty had condescended to discuss substantive matters seriously with ordinary workers or their leaders?

Two days later a crowd of 3,000 persons, incited by a group of activists, Communists among them, took over the warehouse of the Itabashi Government Arsenal and distributed rice, soy beans, rubber shoes, charcoal, and other items free of charge to residents of the neighboring wards.[16] "Robbery!" the police and the Home Minister charged.

And on January 28, 1,500 teachers, previously the meekest of the meek, for generations instruments of Imperial indoctrination, demonstrated in Hibiya Park across from the Daiichi Hotel, where the GHQ general officers were billeted. The hectic meeting considered, although it did not approve, a resolution calling for the "people's control of food," a transparent reference to the Itabashi warehouse case. Then came a march, once again with red flags flying, placards waving, and slogans resounding, to the Tokyo Metropolitan Government offices, to demand in person from Governor Fujimune a fivefold increase in their commodity price allowance.[17]

But perhaps the most unnerving was an in-house encounter at the Nippon Kōkan (Japan Steel Tube) plant in Kawasaki, the industrial flagship of the Asano *zaibatsu* combine. There on January 30 negotiations seeking to halt the continued implementation of a plan to discharge 15,000 employees—some thousands had already been fired—came to a stormy impasse. Angry workers' representatives accused management, including the president, the fifty-seven-year-old Harvard-educated Asano Ryōzō (class of 1912), of being war criminals and would not allow him and his assistants to break off the talks and leave. When Asano and his men, including his vice president, the diminutive English-speaking Komatsu Takashi (M.A. Harvard 1911), tried to push their way out, a scuffle ensued in which Asano and Komatsu were manhandled. Komatsu managed somehow to break away. He rushed to my office and excitedly reported that he and Mr. Asano had been seized by the throat and robbed. As he calmed down, questioning revealed only that some coats and a walking stick were missing. No one had been hurt. The union representatives' version, when we reached them, was predictably even milder. I assumed the incident would soon blow over.

The Japanese Cabinet, however, reacted quite differently. Asano was famous and wealthy, was head of one of Japan's handful of dominant *zaibatsu* combines, and was known personally to most of the ministers. Asano's report reached the Cabinet about the same time Komatsu reached me, but I am sure the Cabinet did not call the union for its version. Asano's, however, must have been quite alarming.

If a notable like Asano could be manhandled by his own workers, Japan's social fabric was in danger. The Cabinet was reeling from SCAP's purge directive only three weeks earlier—five of its members eventually had to resign—but if it could not handle SCAP, it could still show an ability to handle its own working class. And that went for production control as well.

THE FOUR MINISTERS' DECLARATION

I could not say of my own knowledge that the cabinet in its next move was responding to the "attack" on Asano, but Vice Home Minister Ōmura confirmed only two days later to the press that the cabinet decision to denounce "labor excesses" and production control was indeed prompted by the Nippon Steel incidents.[18]

I do know that on February 1, the day after the incident, Shirasu Jirō, the Cambridge-educated confidant of the Foreign Minister, Yoshida Shigeru, came to the GHQ Daiichi Building carrying a statement of the four ministers concerned with labor affairs—Home Affairs, Justice, Welfare, and Commerce and Industry—which roundly condemned labor violence and seizures of property.[19] Shirasu was looking for General Marquat, the Chief of the Economic and Scientific Section. He wanted Marquat's approval of the statement.

As it happened, the general was out. His executive officer, Colonel Ryder, asked Shirasu to wait in the anteroom and meantime called me in for the Labor Division's recommendation. As we were going over the document, Marquat walked in and perched on Ryder's desk, disdaining a formal meeting. I, who had just become Labor Division Chief the day before, tried to explain the ramifications of the proposal.

Clearly, I said, the proposal was aimed at production control. But production control included a variety of actions, some of them only symbolic, while others had caused no damage and hence were not actionable. We were all against illegal actions, but what was illegal? Normally such a question was decided by the courts on a case-by-case basis, not by general Cabinet declarations.

The concept of "ownership rights," I added, was deceptively simple. It had evolved in the West over many years and had been modified numberless times. Its limits were still ill-defined. Again, the proper place for their determination was the legislature or the courts, not the Cabinet. Meanwhile, the arrest and prosecution of Japanese labor leaders for production control would stir up bad feelings in Japan, and criticism, if not ridicule, from the United States. Arrest workers for producing more coal, improving rail car maintenance, or working extra hours without management permission? It would never play in Peoria. SCAP approval could involve General MacArthur in responsibility for a Japanese antilabor program. For example, the Cabinet evidently envisaged police action; who else would take those "decisive measures" against "unlawful actions?" That would contravene Washington official policy (SWNCC 92/1 paragraph 4k) that Japanese agencies that had "functioned in such a way as to obstruct free labor organization"—and there was no question but that the police had done so—"should [have] their powers in respect to labor revoked."

Finally, I referred to a U.S. Supreme Court decision just before the war with respect to a United Auto Workers sitdown strike. I did not remember the instance well, I said, but recalled that the Court had ruled that in certain conditions the union action was not illegal. Of course the U.S. Supreme Court had no jurisdiction over Japan, and the issues of the case were complicated. Still, why put General MacArthur into a possible conflict with the laws of his own government?

Marquat was convinced. He called in the waiting Shirasu and told him that SCAP would not support the Four Ministers' Declaration. Disturbed and crestfallen—he had counted on a quick affirmation by a military man on an issue of law and order—the elaborately casual Shirasu then had to admit that it was too late. The Cabinet had already issued the statement an hour before, he said, and would be highly embarrassed if GHQ disassociated itself from its position. That annoyed Marquat; the Japanese authorities had taken him for granted, a "patsy," as it were. The government had issued the declaration on its own initiative, he retorted, and now it would have to accept the responsibility. GHQ would not attack the statement, but neither would it hide its nonsupport.

The Cabinet's action to halt production control collapsed abruptly in a flurry of mixed signals. That very evening, the Director of the Criminal Affairs Bureau of the Justice Ministry, unaware of GHQ's disapproval, threatened to apply the full weight of the provision of the Criminal Code dealing with violence, intimidation, and infringement of private ownership to such illegal actions as labor's participation in management functions.[20] The next day, however, Vice Minister of Home Affairs Ōmura told the *Yomiuri-Hōchi* evening edition that the authorities were not going to make an issue of production control at the moment. Indeed, he added carefully, he did not think police presence at labor disputes was helpful, because they might hamper the sound growth of the labor movement in Japan.[21] Then on February 8 the Home Minister issued an instruction to the prefectural governors advising that "orderly production control" was not covered by the four Ministers' declaration after all, that its legality was not precluded, and that its occurrence stemmed in "not a few cases from lack of understanding and cooperation'' by employers, who were to be given ''proper warning'' on this point.[22]

Thereafter, production control blossomed. In the first nine months of 1946, 43 percent of all those engaged in acts of dispute used production control. In April, May, and June, it accounted for 69, 76, and 68 percent.[23] Production control tactics were used in the Yubari and Takahagi coal fields, in the Shibaura Rolling Stock Company strike, and in the Tokyo Metropolitan Government offices, where the tactic was called ''business control.'' With the passage of time it became more and more usual, even standard.

Even the combative Yoshida, when he became prime minister, was more fatalistic than belligerent. ''The Government finds it difficult to justify [production control] as a recognized form of labor dispute,'' his Cabinet's statement complained. ''It is likely to destroy the industrial structure of the country.'' But the answer was not suppression. The Cabinet recommended labor–employer management councils to increase production instead.[24] The new Home Minister merely instructed the police ''to watch carefully over instances of production control to detect infractions of law such as forgery, impersonation, or trespass.''[25]

And no wonder. From the economic point of view, production control was a boon: It kept enterprises operating while labor and management battled. Man-hours of work lost in labor disputes in the first half of 1946, when production control was most popular, were negligible, perhaps a twentieth of 1 percent. The advantages of that kind of labor pressure over American-style strikes, where everyone suffered from the disruption of production, were so marked that I and others, including Dr. Suehiro, speculated on whether Japanese labor would institutionalize it. (I even wondered if it could be transplanted to America.) A number of administrative cases explored the legal issues. The Transportation Minister,[26] who had accepted delivery from the Shibaura Rolling Stock Company while it was under production control, ultimately agreed to pay the union for the product; the Commerce and Industry Minister reluctantly permitted his Coal Board to pay the union production control managers of the Takahagi Coal Company.[27]

A thoughtful study by Dr. Suehiro on the legal theory that production control was carried out by the union in trust for the owners was widely discussed and accepted by legal scholars. Suehiro set forth certain rules: The production control managers could make only routine disbursements; they could not raise wages or otherwise use funds to effect the purpose of the strike in anticipation of a successful outcome; they could not make capital investments; and so on. Within those limits, Suehiro said, union management acts were legal during a genuine labor dispute.

The principal objections were, of course, the violation of private property rights and the possibility that temporary production control could harden into the permanent occupation of private facilities. But "normal" work stoppage strikes in fact, if not in theory, infringed property rights more than production control, for they shut private plants down, while production control allowed the installations to continue operations and, furthermore, to be run in accordance with the policies previously set by the owners themselves. In reality, all production control *per se* really did was to freeze operating policies, suspend investments, and prevent owners from closing their establishments down altogether. Used as a strike tactic, production control was surely the lesser infringement.

The fear of a gradual slide from temporary to permanent workers' control was more emotional than realistic. The life blood of any business is bank credit, and in Japanese law only officers specified in the company charter can bind the company. Union production control managers might as "trustees" use the proceeds of sales to pay company debts, but new loans, even "rollover" credits, would be hard come by if a possible repudiation loomed down the road. As long as the legal system remained intact, the gradual conversion of production control to confiscation was only a fantasy.

Toward the Labor Relations Adjustment Law

Indeed, the problem with production control was precisely that it was too weak a labor weapon. Once management grew accustomed to its hostile outward trappings and accepted a temporary loss of face, it learned to live with it, sometimes for extended periods of time. The more aggressive unions, on the other hand, became impatient with its failures to bring quick results. The Communists quickly rejected the idea, even though at Mitsui Bibai they had originated it. At the height of the production control controversy, on February 7, 1946, one week after the Four Ministers' Declaration, four Communist leaders, Tokuda among them, met with four moderate leaders of the *Sōdōmei* labor federation in a public symposium with Welfare Minister Ashida Hitoshi, one of the four who had made the statement, present. Tokuda held forth in grand style on the need for society to limit the rights of private property. But although he justified the workers' assumption of management functions when an employer locked them out, he did not otherwise advocate production control or even use the words "*seisan kanri.*"[28] At the Fifth National Communist Party Congress later that month, the Party leadership presented the faithful with four guiding principles, seven slogans, and eleven platform planks. Not one of them dealt with production control.[29] Like Prime Minister Yoshida, Tokuda preferred permanent labor–employer management councils, with implied union access to the company books. One can imagine why. Production control had no such attraction.

Nor did it remain popular with the workers. After mid-1946, production control went down rapidly.[30] Soon it was dead, and with it a promising innovation in labor relations.

For all the hackles production control had raised, it was only a matter of strike tactics. Far more important was what to do about strikes themselves. The Washington planners had viewed the right to strike as an integral part of the collective bargaining process. Still, too many strikes lasting too long would not help that process, especially in an impoverished Japan. Consequently, SWNCC 92/1, "Treatment of Japanese Workers' Organizations," had provided that "the Japanese Government should establish conciliation machinery for industrial disputes that cannot be settled by direct and voluntary negotiations." In postwar Japan that was urgent. The four ministers had demonstrated, by their exaggerated reaction to a minor incident, the traditional Japanese authoritarian view of labor disputes primarily as breaches of law and order, which it was the government's function to put down. The class-struggle ideology of the unions, on the other hand, often obscured the reality that strikes for economic objectives ultimately had to end in settlements, just as wars, no matter how bitter, are followed by peace treaties. In principle, strikes were not the business of the Japanese Government, except where military security was involved, but with the Japanese antagonists so far apart, only outside help could bring quick progress.

American Army agencies, absorbed in their own missions, added to the danger. When an Army lieutenant in charge of transforming the Takarazuka Theater into the Ernie Pyle for Americans telephoned me one day to ask me to order the workers installing his snack bar not to strike, I could put him off. But when the Chief Engineer complained to the Chief of Staff that a strike at Tokyo Shibaura was delaying dependent housing construction and that Army wives and children might have no place to stay, the affair was not trivial. As Labor Division Chief, I could counsel self-restraint when I got the chance, but I was usually the only one doing so, and I was on a subsection level. The Labor Division would have to get going on implementation of SWNCC 92/1 before someone did something foolish.

In his drive to get the Trade Union Law passed in the first postwar Diet session, Major Karpinsky had had to accept deferment of labor disputes legislation until the new year. Labor representatives on the Labor Legislation Commission did not crave such legislation; they feared any government machinery might limit their freedom. They wanted protective legislation instead. Suehiro's group had promised Karpinsky a disputes law in 1946, and the labor people had promised a protection bill in the session after that. And so, late in January 1946, Dr. Ayusawa turned up in our office bearing a massive sheaf of papers that he said was the draft of the new labor disputes bill. Karpinsky hardly examined it. He turned the papers over to me and Costantino. Several days later, he was on his way home.

Now Japan undoubtedly had many people, some of them on the full Labor Legislation Commission, with direct collective bargaining experience even under the repressive conditions before the war, but the five members of the working committee were not among them. They were scholars and bureaucrats, and they came up with a superficially attractive but totally unworkable scheme.

The biggest defect was their provision for multiple appeals from the decisions of the Labor Relations Committees assigned to mediate disputes, from the prefectural LRC, through a new set of regional LRCs, to the Central LRC. The conception was totally unrealistic, for interminable appeals would prevent speedy settlements instead of enhancing them. Neither Costantino nor I could envisage distressed workers waiting patiently while the machinery whirred on. We could, however, see frayed tempers, public disputations, politicization, and wildcat strikes.

There were other defects too: a difficult legal language the workers would never understand, a reliance on mediation to the exclusion of other settlement methods, and especially authority for the LRCs to intervene in disputes without being asked by either party. In traditional authoritarian Japan, everything was the government's business; the dividing line between public and private was hardly visible. But in a democratic Japan, the line had to be clear and the barrier erected on it high. If Japanese labor was to be free and collective bargaining genuine, government had to stay out of labor disputes as much as possible. Suehiro's scheme would put it squarely in. We asked the working committee for the appropriate modifications.

Our comments made little impression, for a few weeks later, when Suehiro and Ayusawa turned up proudly with their new draft, the language was simpler, the bill shorter, and the main concepts unchanged. Either we were not articulate enough or even the gifted Suehiro and Westernized Ayusawa were too deeply rooted in the Japanese outlook. Meanwhile, we had become host to a Labor Advisory Mission from the United States, and I asked its specialists to join Costantino and me in drafting a model law to demonstrate our points to the committee. Much as we wanted a thoroughly Japanese law, there seemed to be no other way.

And so one Sunday morning in April, five of us[31] huddled around a table in a Forestry Building office. Article by article, we constructed a model. Each of us had his turn in discussion, until the group was in agreement. Then I would summarize the conclusion and draft the corresponding article of the law on a small pad for the group's confirmation. We all agreed to ignore American precedents and problems that were irrelevant in Japan. No questions of plant elections for sole bargaining agent appeared in our model, no code of unfair labor practices, no definition of bargaining "in good faith," for which there was no comprehensible equivalent in Japanese anyway. Instead, we first drafted a statement of principle—that the prime responsibility to settle disputes remained always with the parties themselves, and the government's job was only to help when called upon. (We hoped that, printed in hundreds of thousands of copies for all sorts of purposes, as laws have to be, this bit of labor education would sink into the legal psyche of the nation, and so it has.) Then we devoted one chapter each to conciliation, to mediation, and to arbitration in turn, ending each section with a reminder that any other settlement methods could be explored simultaneously. And finally, we added a chapter restricting strike actions on the part of both management and labor where they endangered the public welfare. This last chapter was to bear the brunt of the mountainous wave of labor opposition to come, a wave that almost inundated all the rest in the public mind.

In point of fact, the restrictions could scarcely have been milder. Policemen, firemen, and prison guards, along with government administrative employees and those operating safety equipment like pumps in coal mines, could not strike. However, workers in government-owned enterprises, that is, employees of the tobacco, salt, and camphor monopolies, and of the telephones, telegraph, post office, and trunk railways, could. And so could such government employees as teachers and custodial workers who were not engaged directly in administrative work. For workers in industries where stoppages could endanger the public, which the Japanese working committee had termed "public welfare works," a thirty-day cooling-off period with compulsory mediation was provided. Even then the mediation recommendation was not binding. The model law drew the line on strikes not according to who the employer was—government or private—but on what kind of work the employees did.

The initial reaction from Suehiro and the rest of the working committee was enthusiastic. Instead of writing a new bill using our model as a point of departure, they adopted ours with minor changes. Our draft was so uncharacteristically short for a Japanese law that it almost gave its authorship away, but I had included enough phrases from Suehiro's draft to retain a pure Japanese flavor when it was translated. Whatever the criticisms of its provisions later on, no Japanese ever accused it of being an "American" law. The working committee got the full Commission and the Minister to approve, and the Welfare Ministry, after holding a series of public hearings on the bill at my request—an innovation that never caught on elsewhere—presented the bill to the Diet.

UNINFORMED OPPOSITION

Once again, the Cabinet Legislative Bureau objected. What astonished us more, however, was the outburst of condemnation from labor. The only explanation I can offer, even today, is that the Communists succeeded brilliantly in confusing and stampeding unsuspecting non-Communist labor leaders and politicians.

As it happened, the Welfare Ministry announced the Labor Relations Adjustment Bill on April 23, 1946, only a week before the first postwar May Day celebration. The observance was to be an emotional occasion—Socialists, Communists, assorted leftists, and trade unionists all celebrating the demise of militarism and their new labor freedom together. A joint committee was in the process of choosing twenty-one May Day slogans so that signs, banners, and placards could be prepared. In the spirit of unity, each group uncritically accepted the others' suggestions—or at least the non-Communists were accepting the Communists' slogans uncritically. When the Communists proposed to denounce the "repressive" Labor Relations Adjustment Bill, none of the others felt strongly enough about it to object. The slogan was adopted unanimously, and when it was ratified by a million workers on May 1 all over the country, it became too late for the Socialists or others to study the bill and dissociate themselves from the slogan.

The fact was, of course, that hardly anyone had read the bill at the time. The evening that I visited the Katōs in Gotanda with the Socialist Central Executive Committee meeting upstairs, I asked Katō Kanjū his position on the bill. He replied that he was against it as repressive. When I pressed him beyond generalities, he admitted he hadn't gotten around to reading it himself. The Socialist Party had decided to oppose the bill, and he assumed the party had studied it. I suggested he read it himself and decide.

Curiously, Shiga Yoshio, the number two Communist, had the same story a few weeks later when he came to my office alone to notify me that he was taking Tokuda's place on the Prime Minister's Labor Legislation Commission. I asked him what he thought of the new legislation, and he too said it was repressive. When I asked him to be specific and pointed out its pro-labor features, he squirmed and said that well, personally, he thought it was a good bill but the party was against it and he was under party discipline. The following week, Dobashi Kazuyoshi, the Communications Workers' president, came by. Pursuing my educational campaign, I asked him his opinion of the bill. When he too called it repressive, I said that it couldn't be too repressive because Shiga, the Communist, had told me that personally he thought it was a good piece of legislation. Dobashi and his five companions were stunned.[32] Needless to say, neither the communications union nor the Communists changed their position.

All through the summer, labor organized rallies and protests against the bill. The Transport Workers, Railway Workers, Government and Public Workers, and the Steel Workers joined in attacking the "anti-labor Labor Relations Adjustment Bill." By then they were calling it the "reactionary Yoshida Cabinet's" bill, although the Yoshida Cabinet had not been installed until almost a month after the bill was made public. On July 10, 50,000 demonstrators led by the Transport Workers' Shimagami Zengorō and the Railway Workers' Katō Etsuo denounced the bill at the Imperial Palace Plaza.[33] On July 26, the Government and Public Workers announced their decision to enforce "business control" in their offices in opposition to the bill,[34] and on August 5, 50,000 steel workers went out on a one-day strike for the same reason.[35] It was like a lemming march to the sea. The detailed charges made against the bill—for example, that it would prohibit strikes—were usually inaccurate, and the general charges were often pure fantasy. It would, the Government Workers said, deprive them of "the right to live." The bill, it appeared, was still unread by its critics.

Even Matsuoka Komakichi, leader of the moderate *Sōdōmei* Federation, was stampeded. At a meeting of the Labor Legislation Commission, of which he was a member, he remarked apologetically that he personally was not opposed, but he had to vote against it because workers generally, and his federation, too, were antagonistic.[36] Undoubtedly, by that time he and many others knew that GHQ was sponsoring the bill—how else could it appear during a cabinet interregnum?—and they had faith that the Labor Division would do nothing to hurt them. But they were politicians and would not oppose the bandwagon. With GHQ behind it, the bill would pass anyway. Why worry?

The depth of the mindless campaign was reached when a left-wing Socialist Diet member, Arahata Kanson, a respected veteran of prewar labor struggles and his party's most eminent theoretician, mounted the rostrum of the Diet House of Representatives to debate the bill in September. From the gallery I watched him struggle to carry up two huge bundles wrapped in *furoshiki* scarves and place them on the speaker's lectern. Before starting to speak, he triumphantly unwrapped them, disclosing thousands of petitions, each allegedly signed by fifty to a hundred trade unionists, and all against the bill. Those mountains of petitions were the sum total of his argument. He did not debate the bill's provisions at all.

The conservative majority in the Diet, that is, the Liberals and Progressives, paid no attention to the leftists. After a three-and-a-half-hour debate they voted the bill through in ho-hum fashion on September 5. If the labor elements were so opposed to it, they thought, it obviously must be what they themselves should want. On September 20 the House of Peers followed suit. Three weeks later a delegation of conservative Diet members on the Welfare and Labor Committee came to see me, smugly satisfied with the new law. A steel workers' strike was scheduled in four days, but the new law would stop that, they chortled. What provisions? I inquired. No one knew; they thought *I* knew. Evidently, they hadn't read the bill either.

Meanwhile the bitter controversy achieved one positive result. For several months it dissuaded the Yoshida Cabinet from introducing its own labor relations legislation. Judging from the strike bans it had proposed (and SCAP had rejected) once it woke up to the permissiveness of the Labor Relations Adjustment Law, the Communist tactic had served a useful purpose after all. Despite American authorship, with minor modifications, the Labor Relations Adjustment Law has remained—at least for private industry—the law of the land ever since.

THE LABOR STANDARDS LAW

But if SCAP's role in the labor relations legislation went unrecognized, the very opposite happened with the Labor Standards Law, the third leg of the Occupation labor reform. Conventionally, the authorship of that law has been attributed by both Americans and Japanese to SCAP. "Take the Labor Standards Law," the Libby-Owens-Ford attorney James Lee Kauffman declared in an October 1947 report that was widely circulated in U.S. Government and Wall Street circles. "This forces on an impoverished Japan the same high standards enjoyed by American labor."[37] Forces? Well, not quite. The same standards as the American? Also not correct. The improbable truth was that the Japanese Labor Standards Law was the product of Japanese drafters, led by a former "thought control" policeman, not a radical at all, but one who became the Liberal Party—that is, conservative—Governor of Kumamoto Prefecture and a one-term member of the Diet's Upper House. Furthermore, its models were primarily International Labor Organization conventions, not American practice. The story of what really happened also explains its attribution to SCAP and particularly to me.

My connection with the enterprise dated from the summer of 1946, when the recently arrived Chief of my Wages and Working Conditions Branch, Golda Stander, came breathlessly—she was often breathless—into my office carrying a sheaf of some sixty-odd double-spaced pages in English. It was the draft of a labor protection bill, and she asked whether I was aware of its existence. Glancing over it, I was surprised and impressed to see its scope and detail. (In finished form it was to total 138 articles and 298 paragraphs, four times the length of the Labor Relations Adjustment Law.) It covered a bewildering array of protection minutiae, from labor contracts to personnel rosters.[38] It was more than a law; it was a labor code for all industry. I had no idea anything like this gigantic effort had been mounted anywhere. I asked where it came from.

Stander took me into the Labor Division general office, where a smiling, diffident, shabbily dressed man with a rosy-cheeked kewpie-doll face surmounted by a crew cut was sitting quietly in a corner. He was Teramoto Kōsaku, Chief of the Welfare Ministry Labor Standards Section. He had a group, Stander told me, that had been working on the project for several months, and he now wanted to discuss it with us. Teramoto, on being formally presented, added mildly that the paper had been prepared in fulfillment of Welfare Minister Kawai Yoshinari's pledge to the labor unions that a labor protection bill would follow the passage of the Labor Relations Adjustment Law.

The Labor Division was far short of the manpower and expert knowledge of Japan required to turn out a code like this. Moreover, it was not part of our mission. Still, anything that would give the workers the stake in a democratic society that they had not had in an undemocratic one was all to the good. With the Japanese providing the initiative and the expertise, there was no reason for SCAP to object—quite the contrary. "By all means, go ahead," I said to Teramoto, and asked Stander's branch to give him all the help he needed.

As it turned out, Teramoto needed little help. He was a careful, capable administrator and a consummately clever bureaucratic maneuverer. He himself had conceived the idea of a comprehensive labor protection code only a few weeks after the war's end, when it would have seemed rather far down on Japan's list of priorities, if indeed a wrecked economy could ever afford it. But Teramoto thought that was exactly the right time, when ultra-conservative obstructionists would be demoralized, when liberal employers would see that it was necessary to promise the workers a better life in the future, and when many enterprises were so badly off that almost nothing would make things worse. Finally, he might be able to get SCAP's help, if we were serious about democratizing the country. It was remarkable foresight.

But then, Teramoto was a remarkable man, one who defied stereotyping. All but his closest colleagues thought him a standard establishment conservative, a policeman after some eight years with one policy agency or another. But he was an unusual policeman.[39] He had served, for example, in the feared Special Higher ("thought control") Police, charged with enforcing the Peace Preservation ("dangerous thoughts") Act of 1925. But his service had been in Section V, which was responsible for the surveillance and control of nationalist extremists with a penchant for political assassination, not with Koreans (Section 1), labor unions (Section 2), Communists (Section 3), or foreigners (Section 4).

A few weeks after the war's end, Teramoto found himself the first Chief of the Labor Control Section of the Welfare Ministry. Asked by the Minister[40] to codify the provisions of the various Factory Acts suspended during the war and now ordered restored by the Occupation and to determine accident compensation scales for Occupation Force employees, he decided to codify all labor protection rules in one law. He started with his own small staff on a comparative study of labor legislation all over the world and then got the Prime Minister's Labor Legislation Commission involved, thereby enlisting the support and prestige of some of Japan's leading industrialists.[41] He also got the Communists and labor people on the commission to participate. He had almost universal backing. Even the Welfare Minister, who considered Teramoto undisciplined, had to go along. But Teramoto had secured a good bit of his approval from opposing elements on the commission by subtly insinuating that GHQ "wanted it that way." What if they discovered it was not altogether true?

One morning, when I stepped out of my office into the corridor outside, I found a nervous Teramoto unobtrusively waiting in a corner. He had not wanted to make a formal call on me. The preceding day, he and Welfare Minister Kawai had had a sharp argument on penalties for employers imposing involuntary servitude. Teramoto wanted them high, up to ten years in jail, the Minister low, but Teramoto had told Kawai that he was only representing my viewpoint. (In fact, I did not even know of the controversy.) This time, the Minister, who was nobody's fool—he later became president of Komatsu Heavy Industry and built it up to rival Caterpillar in construction machinery—had decided to protest to me personally and would visit me that afternoon. "Please confirm my story or I and the bill will be in deep trouble," Teramoto requested. I told him not to worry. I would do nothing to disrupt the progress of the bill. The Minister did come by that afternoon, while Teramoto waited on tenterhooks behind a tree on the sidewalk outside, but Kawai said nothing about the issue, so I had nothing to deny. It was an anticlimax, but afterward, it dawned on me that Teramoto must have been telling everybody for some time that his handiwork was a GHQ bill and *had* to be passed. No wonder American and Japanese conservatives blamed me.

In point of fact the only concrete instruction we gave the Japanese was to advise them to ensure an effective factory inspection system. Even when Stander came to me with a Japanese provision for "menstrual leave," saying it existed nowhere else in the world and adding that as a woman she thought the idea was unnecessary and frivolous, I told her to stand aside. It was a Japanese bill, and if that's what they wanted, there was no justification for SCAP's intervening.

In the end, the Labor Standards Law, passed by the Diet in March 1947, came to be the most universally appreciated (by workers) of the three fundamental labor laws of the Occupation period. It provided the most comprehensive protection for workers ever known in Japanese history.[42] Article One summed it all up: "Working conditions must meet the needs of a worker living a life worthy of a human being." With a copy of the law procured from the nearest bookstore in his hand, an employee could directly confront his employer and demand compliance or redress on threat of reporting him to the Labor Standards Office. I know, because some years later, when I was in private business in Tokyo, that is exactly what one of my employees did to me. The law was a great success.

THE POLICE

It was surely ironic. For a year before the Diet enacted that masterpiece by Teramoto, the onetime policeman, I had launched a campaign to eliminate all ex-policemen from labor affairs. SWNCC 92/1 specifically required that "Japanese agencies which have . . . functioned . . . in such a way as to obstruct free labor organization and legitimate trade union activities should be abolished or all their powers with respect to labor revoked and all individuals who have been directly connected in a responsible capacity with the obstruction or repression of trade union organization or activity should be declared ineligible for employment in labor agencies'' (para. 4K). That, of course, meant above all the Japanese police. Policemen had to be removed from all labor agencies. The Japanese swiftly called it the "police purge."

The rationale was clear enough. How could labor leaders, with their bitter past experiences, have any confidence in the new reform legislation if they saw their administration in the hands of their traditional enemies? In theory, of course, the police had always just been following orders. They could obey the new orders as well as the old. But no trade unionist would ever believe it. The police point of view had always been that unions, labor agitation, and strikes were sources of disorder to be controlled. Almost a year after the end of the war, on August 5, 1946, Tanikawa Noboru, Director of the Police Bureau of the Home Ministry, testified before a Diet committee that the police were desirous of a healthy development of labor unions and were therefore "controlling individual cases with care."[43]

Tanikawa's assumption that labor unions needed police restraint was not a wartime phenomenon or even a twentieth-century one. It had its roots in two and a half centuries of totalitarian Tokugawa control over every aspect of Japanese society. Prior to Japan's opening to the West, police spies infiltrated everywhere to spot any evidence of discontent, often unknowingly spying on each other, and all citizens had to belong to the *gonin-kumi*, five-man groups of neighbors who kept tabs on and were responsible for each other for the benefit of the authorities. Much of that surveillance was continued into Meiji and onward through neighborhood *kōban* police boxes, which kept registers of all residents, their occupations, relations, and valuable property that might be stolen. (When I was having a friendly chat with a neighborhood policeman in my living room in the 1950s, he asked for the serial numbers of my cameras and all the electronic equipment in the house.) The policeman was the neighborhood protector, a surrogate father, and therefore the natural arbiter of disputes among neighbors and keeper of the peace.

It was in this way that policemen got into labor disputes. The police were the only prewar government agency to compile statistics on labor disputes and strikes. (When the Labor Division ordered the police out of labor affairs in late 1945, there was a hiatus of several weeks in government labor data until the Welfare Ministry could take over.)

But the policemen were not neutral. Usually it was the discontented workers who caused them trouble, and it was their friendly employer who gave them gifts at the summer *o-Bon* Festival for the Dead and on New Year's Day. Labor leaders were "troublemakers," and police files were full of information on them. (That never stopped. As late as 1951 the police, though forbidden by the

Occupation to do so, were still collecting such data.)[44] And then, in 1925, with the passage of the Peace Preservation Law, the new Special Higher Police, dedicated to combating the enemies of the *kokutai* "national polity," established Section 2 to keep tabs on labor unions. That made their hostile attitude official. The police had a long past to live down, and neither Washington nor I thought they could.

Accordingly, in March 1946 I asked the directors of both labor bureaus of the Welfare Ministry to my office, presented them with a statement of Occupation policy forbidding the use of ex-policemen in labor administration, and asked them to prepare an implementing plan. Two days later they asked for clarification. I explained that SCAP was not asking anyone to be discharged or penalized, just transferred to nonlabor jobs whether in or out of the Welfare Ministry, and that applied to labor field officers as well as the Ministry staff. They thanked me politely and left. Then for several weeks I heard nothing.

The delay was puzzling, for up to then Yoshitake, the Labor Policy Bureau Chief, had worked closely with us as a member of the Labor Legislation working committee, and Yoshida Tadaichi, the Manpower Bureau Chief, had also enthusiastically cooperated. But not now. I assigned our special projects man, Leon Becker, a young and aggressive former warrant officer (later a Supreme Court judge in New York), to find out what was wrong. It took him a month to get an implementing plan from the Japanese, but it was so vague as to be worthless. The mystery deepened. Finally we decided to ask for a list of all the ex-policemen in the two labor bureaus. When Becker finally brought it in, I discovered to my astonishment that almost every bureau, section, and branch chief dealing with labor affairs, except for Manpower Director Yoshida, was on it! The two labor legislation working committee members from the bureaucracy (Yoshitake and Togashi), the Director's deputy (Nakanishi Minoru), and even Teramoto, pushing hard for the Labor Standards Bill, were all ex-policemen! No wonder they were all stalling. We had been asking them to fire themselves.

It was then that I became aware of the old Home Ministry system, whereby every career bureaucrat aiming for appointment as prefectural governor had to serve some time in the police to broaden his experience, and of how wide the scope of the police force was, embracing factory inspectors and firemen. When the Welfare Ministry was split off from the Home Ministry in 1938, many officials with police experience came along as a matter of course. Clearly I could not justify, nor would I want to insist on, a purge that did not distinguish career police officers from Home Ministry career men. Then I got caught up unwittingly in a battle between General Whitney's Government Section and the Public Safety Division under General Willoughby's control over the application of the recommendations of Lewis Valentine's Police Advisory Mission to SCAP.

When Valentine, a former New York City Police Commissioner, left late in the spring of 1946, he had urged police democratization, decentralization, and improved efficiency. Whitney insisted on priority for decentralization and democracy, Willoughby on efficiency. My purge, and the SWNCC paragraph ordering it, was additional support for GS's Colonel Kades, who advocated democratization, and suddenly it came into the purview of the Chief of Staff's office. One afternoon, when I had been summoned to a meeting in the office of Major General Lester Whitlock, Deputy Chief of Staff for SCAP, on an entirely different matter, Whitlock leaned over to me and said softly, "Don't worry. The police purge will go through." Startled because I did not know the powers upstairs even knew about our problem, it came to me that we had become a football in someone else's game. Luckily for us, our "supporters" won out.

And luckily for General MacArthur, too, because when the Far Eastern Commission issued its "Principles for Trade Unions" on December 6, 1946, paragraph 13 provided that "no police or other government agencies should be employed in spying on workers, breaking strikes or suppressing union activities." The State Department apparently had not informed MacArthur in advance. I happened to be in the Government Section talking to Kades when General Whitney came hurrying up to me with the radio message containing the FEC statement in his hand. "We've taken care of this, haven't we, Cohen?" he beamed, pointing at the paragraph. And by that time we had.

We had painstakingly revised and refined our requirements. The general rule stood: no ex-policemen in labor administration. But we excepted several categories.[45] The necessary ordinance was issued on November 30, just six days before the FEC labor policy. And while the ordinance did not change much in the Ministry at the time, it did have a much greater impact in the field, where prefectural labor offices were reluctant to dispense with ex-policemen[46] or where local police hesitated to surrender their labor jurisdictions.[47] And when, at the end of 1947, the Occupation dissolved the Home Ministry, the police purge ordinance spared the new Labor Ministry from having to harbor former Home Ministry bureaucrats. Too many of them had been policemen.

JAPANESE INITIATIVE

The "purge" of ex-policemen was as far as I wanted to go in involving SCAP in labor administration. Surely administration was a Japanese, not an American, responsibility. But the Labor Advisory Mission, with its leavening of U.S. Labor Department people, recommended a Labor Ministry—every other modern country had one—and my subordinates pointed out that such laws as the Labor Standards Law could not be enforced without it.[48] The employment service, furthermore, had to be reoriented from providing labor for war industry to providing jobs for workers—on the advice of a Daiichi Hotel bar girl, we changed the wartime name of the labor exchanges from Labor Encouragement (*kinrō*) to Employment Security (*Shokugyō Antei*) offices—and labor relations agencies had to be staffed as well. All were worthy objectives, no doubt, but I was certain that the further we got into administration the more likely we were to make a bad mistake. It was only my realization that without a labor ministry the unions would be deprived of a channel to the cabinet that persuaded me to lend active SCAP support to the idea. Even then, the Japanese had to take the initiative.

At first they did. Only a few months after the war's end, Shidehara's Labor Legislation Commission recommended an independent labor ministry, and the Yoshida Cabinet, too, decided formally, on May 28, 1946, to establish one.[49] But then the Cabinet's attitude turned wildly erratic. For two months the Welfare Ministry's General Affairs Bureau Chief came up to see me unasked at least once a week on the project. The next three months he turned up only once. In late September there was a sudden surge of activity, but after mid-October the project seemed entirely abandoned. As I was not pushing it, none of this troubled me greatly, but I simply could not figure out what the government's policy really was.

As I finally pieced the facts together afterward, policy had nothing to do with it. The initial slowdown was the work of Finance Ministry and Home Ministry bureaucrats. The former, responsible for budgets and tables of organization throughout the government, found it difficult to accept the apparent costs of such a rapid expansion. The Home Ministry people feared for the security of the police labor files the new ministry would inherit. Then why the September eruption of interest? It seems that a sudden rumor, attributed to the Government Section, went the rounds to the effect that I was preparing for General MacArthur's approval a directive ordering a Labor Ministry, and implicitly rebuking the Cabinet for not having established one before. Then that interest flamed out, too. On October 16 George Atcheson, the U.S. Chairman of the Allied Council for Japan, exasperated by the repeated aspersions cast on Japan's democratization record by W. MacMahon Ball, the British Commonwealth member, burst out in an *ad hoc* assertion that in fact the Japanese Government's aims had become "virtually identical with American aims." After that, there could be no more formal SCAP directives—what was the need? Indeed, two days later the Chief of Staff instructed all SCAP sections to desist from them. (Informal directives could still be transmitted personally by the Deputy Chief of Staff for SCAP where necessary.) When the Japanese officials learned they had no Labor Ministry directive to fear, their urgency evaporated. But why abandonment altogether in view of their initial commitment made with so much fanfare? A casual conversation with Dr. Suehiro put me on the track.

All through 1946, Suehiro had been growing steadily in stature as a result of his work as Chairman of the Central Labor Relations Committee, and he was universally regarded as the obvious choice as Japan's first labor minister. Visiting me one day in October, he fell to chatting about his service as a legal adviser to the Japanese delegation to the 1919 Versailles Peace Conference. At one point, Suehiro said, the delegation realized it was very short of local staff and hurriedly brought over several second and third secretaries from the Japanese Embassy at London. One of them was Yoshida Shigeru, now Prime Minister, who was assigned to assist Suehiro. "Then I guess he must call you *sensei* (master)," I suggested to Suehiro. "On the contrary," he replied, "the Prime Minister avoids seeing me so he won't have to remind himself of those days." Yoshida, an inordinately proud man even for a Japanese, just couldn't subject himself to the unpleasant chore of regularly showing deference to one of his Ministers. Not until the September 1947, under a Socialist-led coalition Cabinet, was the Labor Ministry finally inaugurated, just in time to start administering the new Labor Standards Law.

It took only sixteen months to pass the three basic labor reform laws, the Trade Union Law, the Labor Relations Adjustment Law, and the Labor Standards Law, and the establishment of a Labor Ministry followed six months later. Meanwhile, the centuries-old practice of police supervision and control of labor affairs was ended. In that remarkably short time, legal and administrative practices and institutions that had evolved over decades, and in some cases centuries, were discarded and replaced by new ones that remain hardly altered—except for government employment—to this day. Subsequent legislation—the Employment Security Law of 1948, the revisions of the Trade Union Law of 1949, and so on—was all relatively minor compared with the legal revolution of 1945–47. Even the traumatic SCAP civil service reform of 1948 and 1949 left most of that revolution undisturbed. The attitude of Japanese society, as expressed officially in its laws, toward one-third of its productive population, the workers—and by extension their families too—underwent a radical transformation and an enduring one.

But that does not mean the new laws were American products. "Japanese labor legislation," a brochure of the Sophia University Socio-Economic Institute issued to newly arrived executives of foreign corporations doing business in Japan in 1972, declared, "is basically a foreign import. The laws as they stand are biased in favor of labor." Technically, the two-part statement was correct, but how misleading!

True, in the sense that tempura, tatami, industrialization, Japanese written characters, and Buddhism are basically foreign imports, so was Japanese labor legislation. But to say only that is to distort reality, for it was the Japanese who decided which foreign import to use and how to modify and apply it to their country. Two of the three basic labor laws were drafted by Japanese with little American participation or detailed precedent, while the third was essentially a statement of principles plus a framework for future Japanese practice to supply content. The elimination of police from labor affairs arose from the history of

Japan's labor repression, not from vague American parallels. And finally, the Labor Ministry was, from the first, a Japanese project. More accurately, and with greater insight, one could describe Japanese postwar labor legislation as the Japanese response to the opportunities presented and pressures applied by the Occupation.

The remark about pro-labor bias was also true. That bias was deliberate, and it was necessary. How else could one quickly overcome the antilabor bias of previous decades, the authoritarian attitude of government and big employers toward their "inferiors"? The new laws overcompensated to build labor up, to be sure, but in so doing they did not cripple Japanese industry with strikes or overburden it either, if Japan's subsequent export record is any guide. On the contrary, taken together, the labor laws with their "bias" produced not only a more just society but a higher real income for one-third of the population, turning them into substantial rather than marginal consumers and helping create the domestic mass consumer market that powered Japan's phenomenal postwar economic growth. The material stake the laws gave to a working class previously called upon constantly to sacrifice acted as a powerful social stabilizer as well.

At the time many, including high-ranking Occupation officials, were dubious, even fearful. The Occupation Labor Division, in constructing the labor part of MacArthur's monument of laws, was declaring its commitment to free democratic trade unionism and labor relations. Whether the rest of GHQ, and even General MacArthur himself, would stand by those principles in a crisis had still to be tested. We did not have long to wait. The test came in the summer of 1946. Its venue: the *Yomiuri* newspaper.

13

Travail of a Newspaper

THE *YOMIURI* REPELS THE REDS

IT WAS the most confusing, complicated, and vexing affair of the Occupation. Before it was over, the Commanding General of the Eighth Army, the Tokyo Provost Marshal, the International War Crimes Tribunal, six GHQ staff sections[1] and General MacArthur himself were involved—to say nothing of two newspaper managements, two contending labor unions, three Japanese ministries, the police, and the prime minister's office. At issue, ostensibly, was the responsibility of the management of a newspaper for its editorial policy. The reality was that the Communists took over the *Yomiuri Shinbun,* the third largest newspaper in Japan (2 million daily circulation),[2] and General MacArthur wanted them out. But the Communists had wrapped themselves in the cover of a labor union, which, under the new Trade Union Law and under U.S. policy and directives, gave them a measure of protection. Did that mean they could be dislodged only by abandoning the new labor guarantees?

As Chief of the SCAP Labor Division, I thought the only enduring solution would be to rely on the good sense of the Japanese workers themselves to expel the Communists from the union leadership. Short cuts could be dangerous. But leaving the problem to the workers would require patience, sophistication, and a faith in democracy that many in GHQ and the Japanese Government professed but few really felt, at least with regard to the Japanese workers. The Labor Division's position was not an easy one to understand. Too many were prone to interpret a defense of labor rights in the circumstances as crypto-Communism. General Willoughby, our Intelligence chief, decided I was a Communist. Back home, the conservative press exploded. "Are we exporting revolution?" the *Saturday Evening Post* thundered. It went on to remark that "thus, presumably in constructive defiance of General MacArthur, the mysterious Mr. Cohen wit-

240

tingly or otherwise was trying to force Communist control on a Japanese newspaper by using a warmed-over version of the worst features of the Wagner Act.''[3] Equally misunderstanding, the Communists hailed me as a hero.

THE START OF THE CONFLICT

The affair started in October 1945, when the staffs of all the metropolitan newspapers were in revolt against the wartime authoritarianism from which they, more than any other professional group, had suffered. Any number of newspapermen had been banned from journalism, arrested, imprisoned, and worse. Some were still in jail. As late as September 29, 1945, for example, Miki Kiyoshi, a leftist writer and *Yomiuri* correspondent, died in prison, the consequence, it was generally believed, of brutal beatings. Newspapermen organized "democratization groups" and demanded loudly that the management fire militarist collaborators, especially at the top. Of the "big three" newspapers, the *Asahi*'s publisher, Murayama Chōkyo, acceded by discharging the managing editors of the Tokyo, Osaka, and West Japan regions as well as his editor-in-chief and two chief editorial writers.[4] And at the *Mainichi,* all the directors resigned at the end of August.[5] But at the *Yomiuri,* sixty-year-old president and owner, Shōriki Matsutarō, stood firm.

There, forty editorial writers and staff members demanded that Shōriki resign as responsible for the wartime policies of the paper and hence for the disasters militarism had brought. Shōriki denied any special personal responsibility. All the staff members were equally responsible, he declared. Then, denouncing the forty as "rebels," he summarily fired five of their leaders, including Suzuki Tōmin, one of his chief editorial writers, in a humiliating session in the presence of all the newspaper executives. The mortified writers and editors, fuming at their treatment, simply took over the paper. They refused to leave. With the others they continued to put out the paper, but now without paying the slightest attention to orders from above. That was October 27, 1945. It was the first "production control" strike.

Shōriki's imperious behavior was in character. The hard-driving, bullet-headed publisher was no consensus manager but a strong-willed individualist. In 1924, having become Chief of the Criminal Affairs Bureau after a thirteen-year career with the Metropolitan Police Board, he was persuaded by a group of rich friends to leave the police and take over the then unimportant, struggling *Yomiuri.* Whether police authoritarianism ever left Shōriki is questionable.[6]

A dynamic innovator, he remade the paper to appeal to ordinary folk, while the *Asahi* and others attracted the intellectuals. For the first time in Japan, he introduced full-page color comics, a radio page, and a Sunday evening edition. He brought over a series of world-famous sports figures, the boxer Georges

Carpentier in 1930, Babe Ruth and the New York Yankees in 1934, and Bill Tilden in 1936. The *Yomiuri*'s circulation zoomed to 1.7 million, number three in the nation. Shōriki's energy never flagged. Always he commanded attention and respect.

But Shōriki was also a fiery nationalist, a last-ditch military supporter, and an exponent of racial pride. He made the *Yomiuri*[7] into the spokesman of Japanese military imperialism. He had been a director of the Imperial Rule Assistance Association, which replaced the old political parties, and of its parliamentary wing, the Imperial Rule Assistance Political Society, councillor to the Cabinet Information Board under Prime Minister General Tōjō Hideki and again in 1944 under Prime Minister General Koiso Kuniaki, whose personal adviser he also was. No other prominent newspaper figure was as identified with the old order as Shōriki. If the *Yomiuri* democratizers were serious, Shōriki had to be their first target.

Personal feelings entered into the conflict. Shōriki had dominated—indeed, overwhelmed—his staff professionally. He had also "bullied" them. One of their prime complaints was that the paper had stopped providing tea or hot water to make tea during working hours. That was a severe blow to their dignity.[8] Clearly, Shōriki did not respect them or even accept his normal responsibilities as their employer. On October 12, at a meeting of department heads, the economic chief raised the question of why the prison death of Miki, a regular *Yomiuri* feature writer, had not been reported in his home paper, while the *Mainichi* and *Asahi* had given it widespread coverage. After all, even if he was a leftist, Miki was a *Yomiuri* man. Miura Shigeo, the news editor, replied that it was undesirable to create friction in Japanese society, and Chūman Yoshimi, the managing editor, added that the traditional policy of beating Communists "even unto death" was unchanged—even for a friend and colleague. The reformers were sure that Shōriki was behind the decision.

Most outrageous of all, Shōriki and his coterie were determined to ignore all the political implications of Japan's defeat. At an editorial committee meeting on August 29, 1945, Takahashi Yūzai, vice-president and chief editor, declared that the public change in Japan's course occasioned by the "war termination" was only temporary, and the editors were expected to act accordingly. When Shōriki read a piece in the *Yomiuri* about SCAP's proposed dissolution of the *zaibatsu* financial combines, he flew into a rage and ordered that no such articles were to be written in the future. Takahashi followed that up with strict orders from Shōriki against any allusion in the paper to the war responsibilities of the military, *zaibatsu*, or bureaucrats. At about the same time, the SCAP Civil Information and Education Section (CIE) was holding conferences with newspaper editors and publishers to promote exactly such coverage.[9]

But while the standoff continued, the reform group cleverly shifted the legal grounds under both of them. Responding to MacArthur's order to Prime

Minister Shidehara to encourage the unionization of labor, they converted their "reform study committee" into a "strike committee." Suzuki, its chairman, thus found himself the head of a provisional labor union of *Yomiuri* workers. That transformed Shōriki's discharges of the five rebels, retroactively to be sure, into firing workers for labor union activities in defiance of General MacArthur. Socialists and Communists rushed to support the brand new union, denouncing Shōriki bitterly at a series of outdoor mass meetings, and other labor unions in the process of organization cabled their best wishes. The case became a national *cause celèbre*.

Throughout, however, Shōriki remained adamant and unreconstructed. He was going to tough it out in his job, just as General Tōjō, whose suicide attempt had just failed, had said he was going to do by giving "strong testimony" in the War Crimes trials.[10]

To forestall police action, the infant union quickly applied to the Tokyo Metropolitan Government for arbitration under a 1926 law on labor disputes, which had been a dead letter since its enactment. The police made no move, and the union rejected the first panel of arbitrators as unfriendly. A second arbitration committee was organized and accepted, and was at work when electrifying news came. On December 3, 1945, SCAP ordered Shōriki, together with fifty-eight others to turn themselves in by December 12 as war criminal suspects, thus joining General Tōjō, his erstwhile cabinet, and collaborators in prison.

Even under that smashing blow Shōriki did not give in. By threatening to close down the paper altogether and throw its employees out on the street, he managed to retain enough bargaining power to work out an agreement through the arbitration committee. He would sell 30 percent of his stock, leaving him 70. The union was recognized as sole collective bargaining agent for the workers. No one was to be discharged for his previous labor activity, and Suzuki and the other four "rebels" were reinstated. A wage, hour, and working conditions agreement was to be negotiated separately. A respected liberal, Baba Tsunego, who had been ostracized by all publishers since 1942 at the suggestion of the *Kempei-tai* Military Police, was to be brought in as the new publisher.[11] An administrative council of *Yomiuri* men would advise on editorial, business, and personnel policy. Finally, the union's agreement[12] was required for hiring, firing, rewarding, punishing, or other significant personnel action.[13] The first and simplest phase of the dispute was over.

THE SLIDE TO THE LEFT

As Shōriki settled himself into his cell in Sugamo Prison to fume and plan his testimony, Baba settled himself into the publisher's chair—and the editors who had been running the paper during the strike continued to run it as before.

But now every day the paper turned more to the left. In that period, it was only the Communists who called for the overthrow of the Emperor system, but the *Yomiuri*'s editorials and commentary constantly featured that issue. An editorial of January 6, 1946, for example, called for the overthrow of "the Imperial Household clique Shidehara Cabinet," a phrase borrowed from *Akahata* (*Red Flag*), the Communist Party paper, and advocated a "people's front government" of Communists, Socialists, and "liberty-lovers." But the Communist editors outdid themselves in reporting the return of Nozaka Sanzō, the Japanese Communist who had been boarding at Mao Tse-tung's table in Yenan.

At the beginning of 1946, hardly anyone in Japan had ever heard of Nozaka. He had left the country a minor functionary and had been away for fifteen years, working mostly in secret. But the *Yomiuri* hailed him as a potential savior of the country, calling him "*chibisuke*" (delightful little guy) of the revolution and "man of the hour," devoting a lead editorial to "The Return of Mr. Nozaka," publishing a photograph of him on the train to Tokyo, carrying an interview with him and the Communist leaders at Yoyogi party headquarters, and reporting even his trivial activities. A Hibiya Park "Welcome Home Nozaka" rally, which I attended along with (by my estimate) 2,000 others, was reported by the *Yomiuri* as 50,000 strong.

It was curious for a supposedly nonpartisan newspaper to give so much space to a relatively unknown politician of a minor party at a time when newsprint was extremely scarce. A number of news dealers thought so, too. They refused to handle the *Yomiuri*, because it was so full of Communist propaganda.[14]

If the prison-bound Shōriki was helpless to alter the *Yomiuri*'s Communist course, his successor, Baba, was hardly more able to do so. He sat in the publisher's chair, but no one paid him much attention. Approached at age seventy-five to save the paper, Baba, a *Yomiuri* columnist for five years (1934–39) but never an executive, had not wanted the job and certainly not the dispute. Personally courageous, he was not a hard-driving man. "His teeth lacked snap," one of his friends, Fukuda Ippei, said.[15] But Shōriki's vice-president, Takahashi, had implored Baba to save the livelihood of its employees, and Baba had accepted on condition that the current dispute be completely settled before he started on his duties. In his own mind he was assuming a public trust. "It was wrong for the president or shareholders to regard it as their own possession," Baba said. "It should not be the private property of the workers—it is a public organ. I firmly believe that a newspaper is the property of its readers."[16]

Baba's philosophy was fine, but thoroughly unrealistic on a newspaper where so many of the key jobs were held by secret Communists: managing editor and chief editorial writer, vice chief of the editorial bureau, chief of the composing room, chief of the survey division, and member of the editorial committee.[17] Many of those executives doubled as union officials. Suzuki Tōmin was union president as well as managing editor, and the Communists held at least seven of the thirteen posts on the union executive board.[18]

Baba did not know that, nor did almost anyone else. The *Yomiuri* Communists either had hidden their sympathies during the war or had been converted in the short time since its end. Gradually their actions gave them away. For example, several of the union leaders took part in Tokuda's May Day food fracas at the Imperial Palace gate.[19] But the Communist Party guarded its secrets jealously. Years later, Masuyama Taisuke, the Communist secretary of the union, recalled that Suzuki wanted to run in April 1946 for the Diet as a Communist candidate, but the Party leaders told him nothing doing; he was more valuable, as a professed non-Communist, where he was.[20] In July 1946 Major Daniel Imboden, the Chief of the SCAP CIE Press Division, denied in response to my direct query that Suzuki was a Communist, pointing out that he was a fine man with a German wife.[21] His superior, Lieutenant Colonel Donald Nugent, the second Chief of CIE, admitted to me at the same time that "as far as the *Yomiuri* individuals are concerned . . . I know only Suzuki by name and I can't even name any of the others involved."[22] It was as though politics wasn't their business—that was the Government Section's responsibility—and they, studiously neutral, were handling the affair solely on the basis of "professional newspaper principles."

The Communists, of course, were operating as a disciplined political force. Katayama Satoshi, *Yomiuri*'s survey bureau chief and then a new Communist Party member, told later what happened when he decided to argue with the Party that the masses did not go along with its anti-Emperor line. As he recounted the episode, he went to the second floor reception room of Party Headquarters at Yoyogi. Then,

> Shiga [Yoshio, the Party's second in command] came out. [He asserted] strongly . . . that anyone who did not accept the overthrow of the Emperor system could not participate in the People's Front. This was the first shock to us. If we advocated this too strongly, cooperation between the Socialist and Communist parties would not progress in Japan. I though this was very unreasonable.[23]

Katayama went back to the *Yomiuri* to follow the Party line with a heavy heart, but he did not break ranks. Nor did many others.

In the 1,700-man *Yomiuri* organization, the handful of card-carrying Communists (estimated by the anti-Communist leader Mutō Santoku at no more than twenty-three[24]) used iron discipline to impose their line on a large mass of confused postwar intellectuals, very few of whom knew enough of the Communists' record elsewhere to be disillusioned. A hold so dependent on secrecy and discipline was inherently fragile. Still, as long as the union's Communist leadership steered clear of the Occupation authorities, no one within the paper would challenge them. But the Communists would not stay clear.

CONTROL OF EDITORIAL POLICY

At first it was only a matter of slanting news items in violation of the Press Code.[25] Of the big three newspapers, *Yomiuri* was indisputably the most flagrant offender. The SCAP Press Division repeatedly called its infractions to editor Suzuki's attention. Suzuki explained them away as accidents or inexperience, one-time occurrences that would not happen again. But they did. Press Division Chief Berkov paid a special visit to the paper with his successor-to-be, Imboden, to emphasize the seriousness of the situation, but to no avail. When Baba, the publisher, complained to the new chief, Imboden, a few weeks later that his editorials were not being published, Suzuki explained carefully that that was because the compositors (who were dominated by their Communist leaders) did not agree with Baba's ideas. Imboden, a professional newspaperman who had owned a paper in San Luis Obispo, California, was shaken. Why, he said to me, the compositors even replaced Baba's editorials with their own![26] To Imboden, the whole affair was only professional irresponsibility.

On May 3, 1946, the *Yomiuri* editors printed a scurrilous account of living accommodations for the Allied judges and attorneys for the forthcoming war crimes trials. "Dance Hall at the Legal Village," "Ichigaya Legal Village Revelations," "There Is Also a Bar and Dance Hall," its headlines blared. The article added that the most beautiful women in Japan were there to serve the judges and lawyers. The story was not news; it was, in fact, a rewrite of a four-day old *Mainichi* story headlined "Death Party," based on the disclosures of one of the Japanese cooks. A livid Imboden had immediately and angrily condemned the piece, and that paper's publisher quickly and profusely apologized. Now, three days later, it seemed that *Yomiuri* was spitting in SCAP's eye.

Imboden, infuriated, summoned Suzuki yet once again. Suzuki could only reply that the article was the work of an inexperienced reporter named Ino, who did not know the *Mainichi*'s story was false. Besides, Ino had just been discharged. (That was not true: Suzuki had sent him out of town until the heat was off.)[27] Unappeased, Imboden recommended to Brigadier General Ken Dyke, the CIE Section Chief, that both *Yomiuri* and *Mainichi* be suspended.[28]

That medicine was too strong for Dyke. Why advertise a SCAP failure and anti-American attacks all over the world by suspending two out of the three biggest newspapers in Japan? That would not do. Instead, Dyke went over to see General MacArthur, told him the story, and secured his approval of the principle that henceforth the responsibility for editorial policy and content would rest solely with the owner of a paper and his appointed management, regardless of author, editor, or printer. Imboden reported the new rule as an addition to the Press Code at his next press conference. The new principle clashed directly with the *Yomiuri* editors' contention that, in accordance with their union contract with

Shōriki the previous December, neither ownership nor management had the exclusive right to dictate editorial policy. CIE said they did, and exclusively so. A confrontation was inevitable.

Only a week after Dyke's departure from Japan, it came. A slanted front page news article in the *Yomiuri* of June 4, 1946, tied government food policy— and inferentially SCAP relief food distribution—to the support of rural landlords against their tenants. "The Government's attitude essentially is to defend the landlords," the story said, clearly fracturing the sixth and seventh paragraphs of the Press Code.[29] A memo from Imboden demanding Suzuki's immediate replacement could not get out fast enough. But only publisher Baba could take the action, and Baba, long disappointed at the continuing labor ferment and his inability to control the paper, had retired to his villa in nearby Zushi. On June 7 he offered to resign.

The ensuing impasse was broken, improbably, by a man who had no staff responsibility for the case and did not even know there was an impasse: Brigadier General Frayne Baker, the GHQ Public Relations Officer. When Baba resigned, the little coterie around Prime Minister Yoshida became alarmed. How could they fight Communist encroachment on the publisher's rights if there were no publisher? On June 11, Shirasu Jirō, Yoshida's favorite English-speaking intermediary, took a list of the six leading Communists on the *Yomiuri* staff[30] to General Baker, whom he had been cultivating for some time. Shirasu casually discussed the *Yomiuri* case and convinced Baker that Baba was a good fellow who badly needed outside encouragement to stand up against the Communists. Then, almost as an afterthought, he handed over the list of six Communists. Baker was flattered to be consulted. As PRO, his job was to issue press releases and arrange accommodations for foreign correspondents, and he had little to keep him busy. A genial, white-haired North Dakota National Guardsman, he was a good fellow himself, a born politician who loved to arrange deals and manipulate people. Of course, North Dakota politics were somewhat different from radical Marxist politics in Japan, but Baker was not fazed by, or possibly not even aware of, the difference. He agreed to help. The two arranged for Baba to visit Baker the next morning.

For Baba, hemmed in on all sides, scolded by Imboden, manipulated by Suzuki, and ignored by the *Yomiuri* staff, the SCAP call was the first indication that GHQ understood his position. He traveled up to Tokyo from the seaside suburb of Zushi the next morning, June 12. His hopes were reinforced by Baker's warm greeting on his arrival. Imboden, in the same building, had not been advised, but the sympathetic Baker outranked him, and Baba unburdened himself. He confided that he had decided to quit because his staff would not obey him. Who particularly? Baker inquired. Baba hesitantly named four persons, all of whom were on the list of six. Baker, brimming over with his "inside information," opened his desk drawer, pulled out the list, scrutinized it at length, and asked, "Aren't there more? How about these?" and pointed to the other two names.[31]

Baba, keyed up and excited, took this as a GHQ order to fire all six. Suddenly rising from his seat, he told Baker that he would do it. But, he asked, could he depend on GHQ support in case of trouble? Baker, by now a little out of his depth, responded nevertheless that he could. Enormously emboldened, Baba went directly to his office, where he called a directors' meeting and asked for Suzuki's resignation "in accordance with a GHQ suggestion." Then he called a meeting of department heads and asked for the resignation of the other five. Baba's teeth had suddenly begun to snap.

THE BATTLE JOINED

Pandemonium broke loose in the *Yomiuri*. The different departments, some pro-Suzuki, some anti-Suzuki, met to consider what to do. One meeting, called by the Suzuki faction, started at midnight, fine for the Communist-led compositors and printers who worked the night shift, but not for the anti-Suzuki party, who had to go home before the trains stopped running. Emotions ran high. Suzuki, carried away in one meeting, vowed to lay down his life if necessary.[32] Baba came on the public address system tearfully to remind the staff of their long mutual association and to blame the discharges on the Occupation authorities, who would otherwise close down the paper. The heated meetings continued.

But only two meetings mattered. On the morning of June 14, Suzuki, agonizing over his personal responsibility if 1,700 persons were thrown out of work, consulted with the Party leaders at Yoyogi. That afternoon he met with publisher Baba. Suzuki's answer was "No!" He would not resign. The battle was on.

The Communist tactic was to sit tight as before, rejecting the discharge order as violating their agreement with Shōriki, which required the union's "acknowledgement" of significant personnel changes. The union also came up with a series of economic demands to make it more of a "normal" labor dispute and to provide grounds for protection under the Trade Union Law. Union activists sought at every opportunity to engage Baba in lengthy public disputation whenever he emerged from his office, even accompanying him to the bathroom. When the new editor, Yasuda, sat in Suzuki's chair in his absence, a printer jumped on the desk and threatened to stop the presses. A director was seized by his collar, a woman reporter was "insulted" and "thrust back," and another director was "confined" to his office by thirty pro-Suzuki people, one of whom "nearly struck" him with an abacus, according to the subsequent police report.[33] Lots of sound and fury, in other words, but little real violence.

Meanwhile the discharged six reported punctually every morning to work as usual and occupied their regular desks during the day. "Trespass!" Baba charged. "Never," said the six. "Legally, we were never discharged." Management hired guards, mostly recruited from *Yomiuri* news distributors, to keep the six from entering the building. The Union called on their own members to escort the dischargees past the guards. At one shoving match a window was broken, but nothing more. SCAP's Civil Intelligence Section even reported a slackening of the strife, if not the tension.[34]

Up to this point the Labor Division had stayed out of the controversy. If the affair was a genuine labor dispute, SCAP had no business interfering. If it was a question of editorial prerogatives or the Press Code, that was CIE's problem.[35]

But in the early afternoon of June 21, the day CIS would report that "no violence took place," I was startled to hear the sound of police sirens passing directly beneath my Forestry Building window. Peering out, I saw several truckloads of police racing for the *Yomiuri* Building a block away. I dashed downstairs and ran over to the newspaper, where a crowd was swiftly gathering. A cordon of police surrounded the building, while across the street another line of police kept the spectators back. At short intervals pairs of policemen would emerge from the narrow building entrance, each pair hustling a civilian between them. They would rush him over to one of two waiting police trucks and heave him into the truck bed like a sack of flour. A spectator who shouted, "Don't be so rough!" was himself suddenly seized and thrown aboard.

I crossed the street through the police lines but could not get up the narrow stairs; the downward traffic was too heavy. Retreating across the street, I watched the spectacle for a while, then returned to my office with a sinking feeling. While we were doing our best to remove police from labor affairs in accordance with SWNCC policy, only a block away truckloads of police were arresting dozens of workers in a labor dispute with no pretense of having to restore law and order. I could not believe they were doing that on their own initiative. Who was it in GHQ violating U.S. Occupation policy, and did anybody besides Labor Division care?

As I expected, phone calls to various desks in GHQ were of no avail. No one seemed to be responsible. Later reports gave us the quantities: 150 policemen arrested fifty-six *Yomiuri* employees, including four of the six whom Baba had discharged. After forty-eight hours, the four were charged with trespass.[36] Fifty-two nontrespassers were released after several hours without charges. Excited unionists reported that the police had gone through the building, lists of names in hand, arresting all those they could find on the lists, seizing them even while at work at their desks. The number of arrests was the largest ever at one time in a labor dispute in Japan's history, including even the bad old militarist days. To arrest fifty-six persons in order to catch four, or even six, certainly smelled strongly of intimidation, not normal law enforcement.[37] The new democratic police were outdoing the old.

Clearly, if I as Labor Chief could not quickly and publicly demonstrate that the massive police operation did not represent U.S. policy, I might as well go home. General Marquat, my ESS chief, was in the States at the time, and his executive officer, Colonel Ryder, carried no weight with the top brass. The hard-bitten colonel in charge of police affairs, H. E. Pulliam, and his ultra-conservative boss, General Willoughby, were not known as friends of labor rights and might even have been behind the raid, for all I knew. Imboden denied authorizing it. In any case, staff work could take weeks. Meanwhile the union would be smashed, its leaders in jail, its followers intimidated. The precedent could be devastating for the future. I decided that I would have to go it alone, no matter what the personal risk, in a military staff where staff coordination was all.

The Police

Technically, staff concurrence was required only in case of a staff action, not for information requests. Accordingly, I summoned the responsible police officials to my office three evenings later to explain. Police officials in Japan were authoritarian figures, accustomed to being obeyed instantly. They were not used to civilians, let alone foreigners and young ones at that, questioning their actions. And those officials were not minor figures: the Chief of the Criminal Affairs Bureau of the Metropolitan Police Board (ironically, Shōriki's old position), the Chief of the Criminal Investigation Section of that Bureau, and the Chief of the midtown Marunouchi Police Station. I had nothing against them personally, but I was determined to show by my line of questioning that GHQ as a whole did not condone their action. They, for their part, seethed with resentment at being called on the carpet for doing their duty, especially when they were sure that it was what SCAP wanted. As I learned later, they had first refused Baba's requests for help, acquiescing only when they heard from him later that CIE's Major Imboden had told one of his representatives ''to secure police protection by all means.''[38] Why, then, was the Labor Division now attacking them?

And I was. What prompted the mass raid? I asked. Was there a breakdown in law and order at the time? Why mobilize 150 men to arrest six? And why arrest fifty-two when only six were trespassing? Why did the police not get a court order forbidding the six from entering the premises, so that they could then act according to a judicial decision instead of deciding the merits of the controversy themselves? There was no legal provision for such a court order, they replied. Oh yes, there was, I countered, and cited it.[39] Or why not apprehend the six at their homes, I asked, instead of stirring up such a commotion at the paper?

Had they been spying on labor affairs, and if not where did the list of the fifty-six come from? My manner was as severe as some of my questions were one-sided.

The police officials did not take it lying down. They had answers for every question, and they all proceeded from their assumption that in labor affairs, as in anything else, they and not the courts had the initial responsibility to determine what was a crime—even when the point at issue was the definition of a labor contract. They conceded no special privileges for labor unions. Furthermore, they resented my interrogation and showed it. Although the Director of the Criminal Affairs Bureau promised to consider arrest warrants in the future, his section chief muttered *sotto voce* in Japanese as he went through my door, "Mr Cohen is not the only official in the Occupation."

In that he was certainly right. When the Metropolitan Police Board complained to the Tokyo Provost Marshal, Brigadier General G. S. Ferrin, that I was interfering with the police in the performance of their duties, Ferrin sympathized and complained to Major General Clovis Byers, the Eighth Army Chief of Staff, who passed the complaint on to Lieutenant General Robert Eichelberger, Commandant of Eighth Army, who raised the subject in turn with General MacArthur himself. It was the biggest fuss kicked up over a series of questions—for technically I had taken no action—I had ever heard of. But the results were worth it. Despite all the sympathy from "other officials," the police were not eager to risk another face-losing dressing down.

There were no more arrests without warrants in labor cases for the duration of the Occupation. On July 11, when four anti-Suzuki leaders asked for police protection so that they could publish the paper the following day, the police told them there could be no police protection "until violence has been committed."[40] The effect of the episode on labor unions was also salutary. Once word swept through excited labor circles that "SCAP" had scolded the police, no one could believe the rumors that GHQ had engineered the raid.

THE UNION

Suddenly, the Labor Division became a center of the *Yomiuri* storm. With the CIE and General Baker now identified as their enemies, the *Yomiuri* union decided to try to use me as an "ally." They stepped up their visits and turned over their representation to the national union president, Kikunami Katsumi, a short, stocky, massive-browed former *Asahi* correspondent in London, with deepset eyes and a deliberate, intense English speech. I shortly came to know that Kikunami was the son of a Methodist grocer and that his American nephew had been killed in action with the Japanese-American 442nd Regimental Combat Team in Italy. I did not know that he was a secret Communist Party member,[41] but I had gradually come to the conclusion, Imboden's contrary assurances about

Suzuki notwithstanding, that the union leadership had close Communist ties. Kikunami avoided contesting our assertions that were unfavorable to him—that editorial content was management's prerogative, for instance—and concentrated instead on drawing from me quotable statements that unions were entitled to protect their members from capricious discharge, that no police or employer action could impair the constituted authority of union officials, and so on. Kikunami was intensely interested in labor principles where they would serve his own purpose.

The anti-Suzuki faction was, on the other hand, satisfied with the police. It contended that the four union officers still unreleased from jail had been automatically removed from their offices because they could not carry out their functions in jail. I was shocked by the faction's short-sightedness. But its members resented the Communists' manipulation of the union for political purposes, they were afraid the newspaper would go bankrupt, and increasingly they felt themselves the true majority. What difference did a little illegality make? Labor solidarity was important, I argued. American workers, far less class-conscious, always stood behind any arrested union member as a matter of self-preservation. How long could unions withstand union-busting by police with management acting in concert if simple arrests—particularly for trespass—automatically disqualified union officers? The anti-Suzuki people were as unimpressed with inconvenient labor principles as Kikunami.

Unfortunately, that seemed to be everyone's attitude, except for a Labor Division battling to consolidate the democratic labor reforms. I was sure that in a fair contest—and the Labor Division could ensure its fairness—the anti-Communists would win out. But meanwhile, the Trade Union Law was only six months old, its prime new institution, the Labor Relations Committees, even newer. To bypass them now in the most publicized labor dispute in the country could doom them to ineffectuality in the future.

Again and again I returned to the point in a June 26 meeting with Nugent and Imboden called to coordinate our respective positions. The Labor Division stood by CIE's position on management's exclusive responsibility for editorial content; we did not oppose the six discharges; and we did not even deny the trespass charge. Still, I told Nugent, legal procedures had to be observed. Baba should have secured a court order to evict the six, and the police should have secured arrest warrants. The Labor Relations Committees were the proper tribunals for interpreting the issues involved.[42] I had no doubt, I said, that Baba would be upheld, for the law was absolutely clear. "The thing has got to be done in accordance with legal formulae," I insisted.

"There is no disagreement between us as far as we are concerned," Nugent rejoined. For the first time he divulged that MacArthur himself had personally told him "to clean up" the *Yomiuri*. (For some reason that sentence did not appear in the stenographic record.) Nugent was going to do it. Nevertheless: "We are not going to put a hand in a labor dispute. . . . The labor disputes are a matter for the Japanese to decide. . . . Beyond [the application of the Press Code] we intend to make no official statements. . . . We will try to refer them to you on matters of labor dispute."[43]

I guess I was too optimistic when I expected Nugent and Imboden to rely on the operation of a Trade Union Law they had never read, on Labor Relations Committees that they had never heard of before, and on my assurances that everything would come out all right if they left the decisions to the Japanese. Nugent could never delegate responsibility for a personal MacArthur order to others.

The very next day, Baba called a meeting of the *Yomiuri* workers and invited Imboden. After Baba's speech urging the workers to reject their "leaders," Imboden strode onto the platform, shook hands with Baba to continued applause, and then lectured on accuracy in reporting. Within minutes the meeting voted 800–200 to expel the six listed Communists from the union and deprive them of their union posts. The episode was frustrating for us to handle. With employer and SCAP watching their every move and the unspoken threat of closing the newspaper in the air, how could one be sure the vote reflected the workers' true sentiments? Furthermore, how could Japanese labor agencies operate, if SCAP officials pressured their decisions? Even if the Labor Relations Committee was going to uphold Baba in the end, who would believe theirs was an unbiased decision? More immediately, the public could see a rift opening within GHQ between CIE and the Labor Division.

A SHOT AT CLARIFICATION

Once more clarification was in order. In a two-hour meeting with Imboden I reminded him that, whereas Nugent had pledged to stay out of the labor dispute, he, Imboden, had jumped right in. Whatever Imboden had actually said, the circumstances clearly had given the workers to understand that CIE was on Baba's side in a labor dispute. To settle for good any doubt as to SCAP's position, I proposed a joint meeting for Imboden and me with the parties directly concerned. He could lay down the CIE line on responsibility of management in editorial content, while I would stress the requirements and limits imposed by the labor laws, particularly stressing that editorial content was outside a union's legal scope of activity. Imboden agreed. We selected my office as the venue. I would invite the union leaders and he the publishers. I prepared a written statement for the next day's meeting.

The idea sounded good, but the execution was awful. First, Imboden did not show up, sending a young lieutenant authorized only to take notes. That changed what was to be a coordinated SCAP stand into a unilateral Labor

Division show. Second, when I asked the union to send representatives, it named six union officers, including Suzuki, plus its national chairman, Kikunami. Baba replied that he would come alone. That meant he was outnumbered seven to one. Third, four of the union's six chosen representatives were in jail across the street. Since I had maintained that the police action did not depose them, I ordered that they be brought to the meeting from jail. Fourth, relying unwisely on Imboden's assurances, I did not realize that all the union people present were Communists. Finally, Baba told the police that he would be late for the appointment—he came an hour late—word of which had not reached me, and in fact he had not expected a meeting at all but only a few questions from Costantino.

One can imagine Baba's feelings when he walked into my office to be faced by seven Communists, six of whom he had just fired and four of whom were supposed to be in jail. A presumably hostile Labor Division was there, but the supporting presence of Imboden was missing. "The whole stage setting," he said later, "was made in a manner as if it was intended to indict me."[44] My clearly unhappy reaction to his tardiness—"So you finally made it," I muttered in a low voice, aware that he had been in his office a block away for at least an hour—and the strained atmosphere in the room added to his resentment. Yesterday, he had been SCAP's hero. Now he was the goat.

Except for Imboden's absence, the essential part of the meeting went according to plan. On behalf of CIE I first stated the now familiar Dyke–MacArthur dictum that only the publisher was responsible for editorial content. (The CIE lieutenant declined my invitation to state his section's position.) At the same time, I said, under the law hiring and firing practices were a proper concern of a union, which was entitled to take every legal step it could to protect its members from capricious discharge. Where the two interests impinged on each other, it was the responsibility of both union and management to work out an agreement protecting the worker's right to his job and the employer's right to set editorial policy.

Then I read my prepared statement. Employer domination of a union was illegal, I said, and so was any arrangement made by an employer-dominated union. The constituted authority of a labor union could not be lessened or abrogated by employer acts to disrupt the union organization—a clear reference to the 800–200 vote to reject the old leaders in the presence of both Baba and Imboden—by the discharge of union leaders, or by having them jailed. (That statement was in complete accord with the principles of U.S. labor law.) I then added my hope that Japanese labor relations agencies set up for the purpose would be used by the parties to the dispute. Costantino, my Labor Relations Branch Chief, added that the courts were also available for redress.[45]

Baba remained silent through the meeting as the union leaders asked questions and conferred among themselves.[46] The union leaders for their part were euphoric, not over what my statement said, for it denied their case, but over the circumstances. And those certainly were unusual.

When the union delegation arrived, four of them came into the Labor Division general office handcuffed and chained together with clanking leg irons, clad in black-and-white striped prison kimonos, and escorted by several prison guards. I was aghast. The prisoners had not been convicted of anything. The charge was a relatively minor one of trespass, and that was legally in plenty of doubt. Maybe some were Communists, but at the time that was legal. Why were the police, then, treating them like hardened criminals? Angrily, I ordered their fetters stricken and told the guards to wait outside the building. I asked someone to offer them cigarettes and turned to talk with someone else. When I turned back, the prisoners had disappeared.

While the Labor Division people fanned out through the building in search of the missing men, I was thinking that I needed a jailbreak like a hole in the head. The logic of nonrecognition of police actions in union affairs pursuant to SWNCC 92/1 had dictated their invitation to an employer–union meeting and their temporary release, but if the union leaders took advantage of the situation to escape, my case would be lost within GHQ—and so might I. Fortunately, it did not take long to locate the prisoners upstairs in General Marquat's empty office, where they had mistakenly wandered. At any rate, the unnecessarily harsh police treatment—they had been held incommunicado for a week, one had a bad chest bruise, and now they had showed up manacled like a chain gang—could only elicit sympathy for them. That atmosphere followed them into the meeting room.

SELECTION OF THE ANTI-COMMUNIST LINE

The contrast in my treatment of the two sides that Saturday morning of June 29 obscured the defeat the Communists suffered in substance. Unexpectedly, I became their "powerful ally in GHQ," especially after the charges of trespass against the four imprisoned leaders were dropped three days later. But their main strategy, that of deliberately confusing their hold on the *Yomiuri* with labor rights, had been derailed. I was willing to defend labor rights even at personal risk against the actions of Baba, the police, and Imboden, but I had insisted on separating that issue from the contents of the *Yomiuri* in a way that CIE would not. The union leaders could seek redress for management's antilabor "sins," but successful as they might be in that, they could not retrieve their editorial control. That fight was over.

That was not the way it appeared at the time. Baba,[47] the Tokyo Procurator,[48] and General Willoughby's special analyst, Nelson Spinks,[49] all interpreted the meeting as reopening an issue the Communists had already abandoned after the police raid. However, they were all mistaken.[50] Far from reopening the possibility of the Communists' recovery of control over the newspaper's contents, the meeting had closed it.

Kikunami could launch attacks in all directions. The national union demanded that the Central Labor Relations Committee reinstate the six dischargees on the basis of the Shōriki contract. It initiated lawsuits against adversaries on all sides,[51] mobilized outside union delegations to come thronging to the national union's headquarters and show their fervent support,[52] and even started two more strikes at the *Yomiuri,* lacing them with violence. But the union could not break down the wall between editorial and labor rights. Furthermore, the Communists now found themselves on the defensive with the union membership. By the summer of 1946, what had started out as a labor–management conflict turned into a battle for leadership of the 1,700 *Yomiuri* workers.

This time, however, there was no police or SCAP interference. The day after my Baba–Suzuki meeting, the Deputy Chief of Staff for SCAP, Major General Lester Whitlock, called Nugent, Imboden, Ryder, the Acting ESS Chief, and me in for a rare Sunday "coordination meeting." The gentle, white-haired Whitlock shook his head gravely at me when I arrived first, saying he was not criticizing my actions but could not bring himself to understand "releasing prisoners from constraint." Once we were assembled, he bluntly told us all to shut up and let the Japanese handle it. We had no doubt it was the Supreme Commander speaking. I was delighted. If everyone in GHQ would refrain from interfering, the *Yomiuri* employees themselves would get a chance to demonstrate who they wanted to lead them, and that, after all, was to me the crux of the whole affair.

Left alone, the workers quickly did. When publisher Baba on July 9 transferred forty-one of the Suzuki faction out of the city to solidify his hold on the paper, an enlarged union executive refused to heed excited Communist calls for a strike, preferring conciliation. When the persistent national president called a strike anyway and threw up picket lines around the building, the local union responded by a vote of 1,500–300 not to comply. The five-to-one anti-Communist margin was even larger than the open vote before Imboden and Baba two weeks before, and this time it was undeniably the workers' own decision. Pro-Suzuki members began to resort to desperate actions bordering on sabotage.[53]

THE SIGNIFICANCE OF THE *YOMIURI* AFFAIR

It was touch-and-go from day to day whether the *Yomiuri* could keep publishing. Excited anti-Suzuki men kept running up to CIE to report on the next day's prospects, sometimes every few hours. Three memos to Imboden on July 13 record that callers had visited him at 11:10 in the morning and 5:30 and 7:30

in the evening (the last two at his hotel) to report that, yes, the paper would be coming out, then glumly, no it would not, and then again, elatedly that, yes, it would after all.[54] On July 18, nonstrikers from other departments assaulted the composing room and bodily evicted the sit-in Communist compositors without, however, disturbing the trays. Baba immediately followed up by discharging the thirty-one sit-down strikers.

All through those events, Imboden obediently kept his silence. But on the next day, in an off-the-record remark at his regular press conference, he wondered aloud how a strike by a minority could be legal.[55] A day later, visiting the paper, he told the nonstrikers, in words that became the Sunday *Yomiuri*'s headlines, "You are the true democrats." And two days after that the *Yomiuri* reported a visit of the CIE Executive Officer to Baba's office, complete with photographs and the caption, "Lt. Col. Summers encourages workers."[56]

The spate of intervention incidents threatened to taint the process, rough and unruly as it was, by which the anti-Communists were independently winning their battle. I showed the reports to General Marquat, who passed them on to the Chief of Staff with a request that anyone who needed to talk to one of the parties in the dispute be required to coordinate with ESS.[57] The Chief may have known next to nothing about labor relations, but he respected staff jurisdiction. His subsequent order stopped all other intervention from then on.

That was fortunate, for the Communists maintained their activity with redoubled energy. Picketing continued. Several nonstriking printers and compositors reported that they were followed home and threatened, one with assassination. Electric light poles near the homes of other nonstrikers blossomed with picturesque denunciations and epithets: "silly dog," "worst enemy of the workers," "traitor," "poorest dog of the capitalists who sold his conscience for dirty money," and so on.[58] The national union threatened a countrywide strike. But the anti-Communists held firm. When the nationwide newspaper strike finally did come about in October, no one at the *Yomiuri* itself walked out.

Indeed, weeks before the October fiasco, the *Yomiuri* employees had decided to withdraw from the national union. They disbanded the old union by majority vote, thus disposing of the troublesome old Shōriki contract, and started anew, independent and unaffiliated. By the end of the summer the Communists were out in the cold. In the first such postwar case, workers given their free choice after an experience with a Communist leadership voted against them. It was an exciting event, encouraging to me and those others in the Labor Division who had bet they would do just that. And it vindicated both the Washington planners and the American trade unions in their advocacy of labor democratization in Japan.

That left the final battle: for the integrity and consolidation of the new democratic labor institutions. In this, Kikunami unwittingly did us a favor. In one of his scatter-shot attacks after the Baba–Suzuki meeting in my office, the national union president had demanded that the CLRC order the original six reinstated, later broadening the demand to include the subsequent discharges and transfers. Because of the anti-Suzuki faction's objection to Dr. Suehiro, the CLRC chairman,[59] the case was referred to the Tokyo LRC. I was not surprised by the LRC's decision, but I was impressed by its cogent, forceful reasoning; it was, after all, an inexperienced local group. Its August 3 decision was to deny the union petition on the grounds that the protection of the Trade Union Law extended only to union activities for the purposes provided in the law, namely the improvement of working and economic conditions. Hence the original firing of the six editors for obstructing management control over editorial content was legal. Shōriki's contract providing for a management committee was similarly invalid with respect to editorial affairs. Baba's July transfers and discharges, on the other hand, were not necessary, the committee said, to maintain editorial control and were in violation of article 11 of the Trade Union Law. Management was directed to consult with the union according to its contract to regularize matters.

The new *Yomiuri* union, however, was not interested in protecting its Communist enemies, and the old union had been dissolved. Further, the thirty-one discharged employees had agreed to accept voluntary retirement to protect their severance pay rights, which they did not want to risk in a losing fight. As a practical matter, the legal conflict was over. Once again the Communists had lost.

A general public diverted by the drama of police raids and GHQ intrigue hardly noticed the vital precedents established *en passant:* the right of job security, the sanctity of collective bargaining agreements, and the protection of union activities. Even in such a complicated and politicized affair, the labor rights the U.S. Government was trying to inculcate came out intact and healthy.[60]

The LRC recommendations, generally accepted unquestioningly as fair by the public, formed the substance of the principal labor settlements of the period. Without them, it is doubtful that a petulant and inexperienced cabinet could have survived the autumn of 1946 without some violence and repression. The *Yomiuri* case, as the Committee's baptism of fire, converted the provisions of a new law from words into a working institution and laid the groundwork for the LRC role in the fall. It would not have happened, however, if the Communists had not attacked along every line they knew. Baba would surely have disdained to submit the issue to the LRC.

In all this, General MacArthur refrained from direct intervention. True, he had agreed to Dyke's recommendation to make management solely responsible for editorial content, and he had personally told Nugent to "clean up" the *Yomiuri.* But he had also instructed us all, through General Whitlock, to stay out of the labor aspects of the affair. Here he was consistent with his later actions in refusing to ban a national railway strike and delaying his public decision on a general strike until the last minute. The Supreme Commander himself had more faith in the good sense of the Japanese workers than many of his subordinates, and in the *Yomiuri* case he was vindicated.

I thought the outcome vindicated me, too, but the circumstances were too complicated and my strategy—giving the Communists enough rope to hang themselves—too subtle. Few outside the Labor Division, moreover, had any interest in labor democratization. The Japanese police complaint against me by way of General Eichelberger arrived just about the time my chief, General Marquat, arrived back from the States on July 13, all unknowing of what had gone on in his absence. After a brief session with the SCAP Chief of Staff, Marquat passed on the Chief's instructions in a formal memo: From now on, the Labor Division was not to start strikes![61] A few weeks later, however, when he had had a chance to review the facts, Marquat sent the Chief of Staff a memo for the record supporting me and blaming everything on CIE.[62]

Unquestionably, Marquat had discussed the case meanwhile with General MacArthur. The Prime Minister and General Willoughy, the G-2, also discussed the matter with the SCAP. On two occasions Yoshida alleged to MacArthur, on the basis of the *Yomiuri* case, that I was a Communist. The first time the Supreme Commander made no comment; the second time, he told Yoshida never to mention the subject again.[63] Willoughby's charges to the same effect, plus his recommendation to fire me, got similarly short shrift. On my departure from GHQ some four years later, the Supreme Commander would praise my "loyalty."[64]

Those personal attacks and a faint aura of radicalism that I exuded thereafter to certain unsophisticated GHQ officers were more than compensated for by the solid achievements of the affair: police withdrawal from labor relations for the duration of the Occupation (and indeed thereafter), a warning to employers not to intervene in internal union affairs, strengthening the new labor relations agencies, and the rejection of the Communists by the *Yomiuri* rank and file. And in December 1946, when the Far Eastern Commission, in its Principles for Japanese Trade Unions, insisted that "employers should not be allowed to take part in . . . the conduct of trade unions" and that "no police . . . agencies should be employed in . . . breaking strikes or suppressing union activities," the Supreme Commander had nothing in his Occupation record to be apologetic about.

14

Labor in Turmoil

THE FALL OF 1946

OVER AND OVER AGAIN in the fall of 1946 I could not but be awed by the boundless faith of the Japanese upper classes in the limitless capacity of the Japanese lower classes to tighten their belts. Japanese feudal thought had regarded the peasants like sesame seeds, to be squeezed and squeezed again, until not a drop of oil was left in them. Industrial Japan substituted a more responsible paternalism. But a feeling of paternalistic obligation, however genuine, was no substitute for knowledge. The two groups, upper and lower, lived side by side, but the upper rarely thought of the lower in human terms or seriously tried to comprehend its hopes or aspirations. In terms of mutual comprehension, they really constituted two nations.

On a visit to the silk-reeling mills in Okaya in Nagano Prefecture, for example, I was distressed by the spectacle of twelve-year-olds, their hands constantly immersed in water at 140 degrees Fahrenheit, tending the filaments. One little girl told me her hands ached so badly that often at night she could not sleep. When I asked the mill owner how he would like to have his daughter work under such conditions, he looked at me in confusion, sure he had misunderstood me. Pain and hardship for workers had always been part of the natural order for him, and he had never thought of the mill girls and his daughter as the same kind of creature. Similarly, when the coal mine operators of the Jōban district complained to me about rules prohibiting women from working underground, and I asked them how they would like their wives to work in the coal pits, they were certain I was a Communist. Prime Minister Yoshida, when I asked him once at a party whether he had a single friend who was a worker or peasant, simply walked away.

260

THE TWO NATIONS

The upper classes thought they knew the lower, because they, too, ate *mochi* rice at New Year's and visited shrines on *shichi-go-san* (seven, five, three) day when their children were seven, five and three years old. But in fact they did not know them, and could not. The social barriers were too high, and their lives—before the democratization and its consequent mass consumer revolution that homogenized so much of Japan's way of life into a ''middle class''—were too different. The estrangement of the ''two nations'' might not have mattered so much in more stable times. But right after the war the authority of the traditional ruling classes was badly eroded, the distress of the urban workers was worse than at any time in recent memory, and for the first time strong trade unions offered a ready instrument for massive protests.

There was one other critical element: the Communists. Tokuda and his men were out to transfer the venue of national decisions from the halls of the Diet, where their party was weak, to the workplaces and the streets, where they were strong and getting stronger. Their weapons were labor disputes, strikes, demonstrations, and parades in which they could control the agenda and visibly mobilize thousands who could not be ignored. Nothing offered them a better issue than the cold insensitivity of the authorities to the workers' plight. The government played right into the Communists' hands. Labor neglected became labor in turmoil. In 1946, three great waves of conflict broke heavily against the industrial shore: In August and September, the seamen and railway workers threatened to halt all transport in Japan; in the following month, an ''October Offensive'' mobilized hundreds of thousands more against scores of mines, factories, newspapers, theaters, and hospitals; and in November, electric power came under the gun.

In strictly economic terms, when all the sound and fury subsided and the man-days lost to industrial production were added up, the damage was minuscule. But the effect on public life was profound. The government was humiliated and made to look weak. The Communists, despite their disdain for economic as against revolutionary unionism, became stronger than at any other period of Japan's history. General MacArthur stood aloof, and so did most of his men, allowing the internal forces in Japanese society to fight it out. And indeed, by the end of the year the relatively peaceful Japan of July had become a country of conflict, divided into two irreconcilable camps, with the citizenry at large waiting tremulously for the next big battle.

To the workers, the government appeared insensitive to their plight, and here the cabinet lineup in no way inspired confidence. Prime Minister Yoshida was no more interested in labor than in economics—a matter to be left to his *bantō*, or steward, in the old feudal sense—and to him the tumult was essentially political. The trade union leaders were Socialists and Communists, which made them his political enemies almost automatically. The Economic Stabilization Board Director General, Zen Keinosuke, was a professional management advocate, director of the Industrial Organizations Association, a former employer representative at both the Geneva International Labor Organization and the Japanese Central Labor Relations Committee, and well known for leading the opposition to the enaction of any law that recognized trade unions in the 1930s. Finally the Finance Minister, Ishibashi Tanzan, kept publicly insisting that the inflation was about over,[1] and all controls, including those on the production and distribution of food, should be dismantled as soon as possible. Since the low-priced food distribution system was the safety net for countless unemployed and underpaid workers and their families, the workers were alarmed. How could such a government with such ministers really care about them?

And indeed, we at ESS were also shocked by Ishibashi's proposal to end all controls in spite of the fact that the inflation was becoming more menacing.[2] But Ishibashi, who had been editor of the prestigious *Oriental Economist*, was a fervent believer in the "free market." We were even more shocked by his bland assumption that if things did not go as well as he optimistically predicted, the workers would continue to sacrifice as usual.

The Railway Strike Threat

It was this kind of faith, no doubt, that led the cabinet at the beginning of August to announce the discharge of some 130,000 out of the 550,000 Imperial Railways workers. The railway was overstaffed, to be sure, for only six years before the job had been done with 330,000. The system was losing money. Raising freight rates would raise prices across the board; not raising them would require government subsidies, which, without matching revenues, meant printing money. But 5 million people, 37 percent of the nonagricultural work force, were already jobless, the Welfare Minister reported,[3] and how would so many discharged employees find work? How long, moreover, would their severance pay last in a roaring inflation? These days much is being made of the historic Japanese responsibility of employers for employees and the principle of lifetime employment. Forty years ago the government was quite ready to disregard that "tradition."

The railway administration obviously did not realize it was playing with fire. Director General Satō Eisaku (later prime minister and winner of the Nobel Peace Prize) had just returned as a repatriate only a few months before and had no personal feeling for the situation of the workers, hundreds of whom had thronged the Railway Ministry lobby in January for five hours and forced the minister to talk with them. Satō knew the railway had a labor union, the General

Federation of Government Workers Unions, and was aware that with 400,000 members it was the largest in the country. Without police labor intelligence, however, which was forbidden by Occupation order, he had no one to report to him on the degree of Communist penetration.

In point of fact, the vast majority of the union members were still not Communists, and the locals in West Japan and in the country areas were usually anti-Communist. But higher up in the layered General Federation hierarchy, the JCP members, became more numerous, and most numerous of all in the national headquarters. Indeed, the JCP was poised to take control, especially if it could seize on the right issue to mobilize non-Communist support.

So far, the railway administration had not given it to them. Pushed by Labor Division, the government had almost doubled government workers' wages in May, and in June I had prevailed on General Marquat to instruct the government to pay the expected 1946 year-end bonus in monthly installments in advance.[4] The railway workers, sharing in those distributions, were quiescent until Satō, pushed by Ishibashi and the Finance Ministry, announced at the end of July that two out of every nine railway workers would be dismissed.

SATŌ GIVES IN

The Communists responded like a wounded bear. On August 3, arguing passionately for defiance, they swung the union's Central Executive Board behind a call for a nationwide rail strike.[5] Director General Satō fell back before their vehemence. Temporizing, he quickly reduced the number of discharges to only 75,000 and announced that only those without family responsibilities— youths and unmarried women—would be laid off. At one stroke he had given up three-fourths of the projected savings to the railway, for youths and unmarried women were by far the worst paid. His concession would curtail railway expenditures only 2.5 instead of 10 percent.[6] What was left was hardly worth a national strike. But as a matter of face, Satō could not concede more, at least not without negotiations. An implacable Central Executive Board, however, quickly set the strike date for Sunday, September 15. Afterward it would decide whether to extend it beyond the day or to repeat it.

For the next month, government and union moved steadily and ever more ominously to the brink of a direct clash. At first I refused to take an actual rail strike seriously. Clearly, General MacArthur would have to prohibit such a stoppage as endangering the security of his forces, for most Army freight moved by rail, and troop movements depended on the rail network. JCS 1380/15 had specifically authorized such a ban. Moreover, a rail strike, if protracted much beyond a day, could devastate an economy in which interurban buses, commercial aircraft, and private cars were absent, long-distance trucking was minor, and coastal shipping handled only 3 percent the volume of rail freight.[7] Indeed, all staple food, including U.S. relief food, was distributed by the railways. How could the SCAP allow a stoppage? Nor was it likely that the government would want a rail stoppage either. But the union—ah, that was different. The Communists might just want to produce a little chaos to discredit the government.

And yet the Communists were not finding it all that easy to mobilize half a million workers who had not been consulted. The western locals were almost all opposed, and so were some powerful eastern locals.[8] The Women and Youth sections were all in favor, but of course they were the only ones slated for firing. Just four days after the strike call, the *Sanbetsu* Federation inaugural convention in Tokyo roared its unanimous support of the rail strike, and Kikunami, its Communist president, immediately organized a sympathy strike committee of *Sanbetsu* unions, with memberships totaling 700,000, who would strike along with their railway brethren. But in the General Rail Workers Federation, deep disagreement prevailed.

To Tokuda, numbers were not as important as organization. His problem was how to mobilize the union if need be without a majority. Perhaps it was from his incessant prison reading that he drew the solution from Trotsky's Bolshevik-dominated Military Revolutionary Committee that made the October Revolution on behalf of an overwhelmingly non-Bolshevik Petrograd Soviet. Within days, the Communists on the rail union's Central Executive Board proposed a similar union ''Struggle Committee,'' which was quickly loaded with the most militant Communist adherents, secret or public. For chairman, they secured the most militant of all, Ii Yashirō, the sharp-witted orator and agitator from the midtown Shinbashi station. Superficially, the Struggle Committee looked like the familiar strike committees in the West, but there the committees operated under the orders of the regularly elected union officers. In Tokuda's scheme, however, the Struggle Committee displaced the regular union officers for the duration. So much for union democracy. Now Tokuda and the Politburo could run any rail strike campaign from the Yoyogi headquarters of the Japan Communist Party.

At the same time, the Struggle Committee organized squads of strong-arm enforcers under the name Youth Action Corps, or *Seinen Kōdō-tai*. The YAC, ostensibly arms of the union but actually under direct Communist Party Politburo orders, had first made their appearance in August 1946 among the younger merchant seamen, who were resentful of the passivity with which the old-line Seamen's Union officials met a wave of maritime dismissals. The officials called it realism: There were few berths, because most of Japan's merchant marine lay on the ocean bottom. The young sailors did not see it that way. Heedless of their elders, the union's Youth Section, which the Communists dominated, organized their own small groups, boarded all the remaining vessels in port, and persuaded their crews to strike. They were extremely effective. At one time 3,600 vessels were tied up in port, and the Prime Minister himself had to appeal to the striking seamen to keep the peace.[9] Transplanting the idea quickly to the railway union, the Communists set up YACs to guard union meetings from outside harassment, maintain internal order, and act as bodyguards for sympathetic union officials. In time of a showdown, they could make all the difference in pushing wavering workers into striking.

But with all the forces the Communists could gather together—*Sanbetsu* support, sympathy strike, Struggle Committee, Youth Action Corps—the agreement of the union members with the strike call remained questionable. Reports of dissent poured in from all over the country. In a last effort to unify the workers behind them, the Central Executive Board members called an extraordinary convention in the city of Uji-Yamada on September 5 and 6, only ten days before the scheduled walkout.[10]

To the Communists' surprise and disappointment, however, the anti-Communists elected an antistrike convention chairman, rejected a motion of appreciation for the work of the Central Executive Board, and instead entered a motion calling on the board to resign en masse. Only a piece of luck and a tactical maneuver saved the Communists. The anti-Communist chairman allowed himself to consider a Communist delegate's remark to be disrespectful. When the meeting did not agree, he walked out, taking with him three western antistrike delegations to a chorus of jeers and catcalls from the Communists. That left the convention without a quorum, but with a Communist pro-strike majority among those who were left. They quickly reconstituted themselves as a "rally," endorsed the strike, and went home. The strike had been "saved" by the narrowest of margins. Still, a strike with half the delegates not even talking to each other, with only a week left, seemed impossible.

It is curious that on the one hand the leader of the Struggle Committee, Ii, returned to Tokyo disheartened at the lack of mass support and convinced the whole affair would have to be postponed, while the government, completely baffled by the internal squabbling of the extraordinary convention, remained convinced of the union leaders' firm hold over the membership. Ii knew better. Even the Communist stranglehold on the Eastern Regional Council wavered; it voted on September 11 to support the strike by only a six-to-five margin instead of the usual two-to-one edge for Communist causes.[11] The enterprise was on shaky grounds indeed.

But the shrewd Tokuda suspected, or knew from inside sources, that Railway Director General Satō was equally uncertain. Tokuda and the "senior comrades" encouraged Ii to persevere, and Ii, always the fighter, plunged back into the fray with spirit revived. To all appearances, both sides were racing inexorably toward a direct clash.

The reality, I am convinced, was otherwise. Both sides, it seemed to me, expected General MacArthur to prohibit the railway stoppage. *I* certainly did. General F. S. Besson, our Civil Transportation Officer, was also opposed to permitting a strike, even though, as he advised me, the union had offered to run cars and trains especially for the Allied Forces, and the strike, after all, was to be of only one day's duration. But, Besson said, even to run only a few trains and cars for that day would disrupt schedules for a week, while signals, communications, switchpoints, and so on would have to be kept operating throughout.

At the beginning of September, moreover, we had received a precedent, when General MacArthur approved a directive to the Japanese Government, initiated by G-2 and concurred in by both General Besson and me, forbidding an announced seamen's strike from applying to vessels engaged in Japanese repatriation. The directive was public, and both Transportation Ministry and railway labor unions were well aware of it. The Labor Division had previously warned union leaders, and Tokuda, too, that SCAP would not permit either a strike in repatriation shipping or a national railway stoppage. The latest directive confirmed our warnings.[12] And on September 8 Costantino repeated the advice to railway union visitors to our office.

But suddenly the standard prohibition ceased to apply. On September 9 I told General Marquat, my ESS Chief, that his Labor Division was preparing an order prohibiting a railway strike for the Supreme Commander's signature and that both General Besson and General Maris, the G-3, had informally concurred. He told me to wait until he got MacArthur's view, went up to see the "Old Man" that evening, and the next morning, to my astonishment, told me that the General had decided to keep his hands off. MacArthur would be making no statement for the time being.

To this day I do not know MacArthur's reasoning. Perhaps he thought a one-day strike on a Sunday not worthy his intervention. Perhaps he shied from the complications of enforcement—provost courts, military police, and the rest. Perhaps he did not want his action to be used to decide the substantive issue of discharges. Or perhaps, consistent with his stand on the *Yomiuri,* he had more confidence in labor restraint in this case than I did. But I have always thought he simply did not want to appear as a strikebreaker to the American labor federations at a time when he was still in the running for the American presidential elections two years ahead.

MacArthur's decision not to intervene changed everything. Although we did not publicize it, the Transportation Ministry had to be advised. The government–union confrontation was no longer theatrics with General MacArthur cast as the last-minute savior, but deadly serious. The first official reaction, two days later, was a cabinet proposal brought by Asakai Kōichirō, Vice President of the Central Liaison Office, to General Marquat to introduce a bill into the Diet authorizing the government to prohibit strikes inimical to the security and objectives of the Occupation. If General MacArthur did not want to protect his Occupation publicly, the Japanese Government would be pleased to do it for him! There was never any chance that the SCAP would agree to such a condescending proposal, and Marquat, after seeing MacArthur with my memo on September 13, summoned Asakai and told him the cabinet's initiative was rejected.

THE SECRET AGREEMENT WITH SATŌ

That left it to Tokuda and Satō with only two days to go, and in the eyeball-to-eyeball confrontation that followed Tokuda blinked first. For Tokuda wanted not a strike but a victory. A strike might bring the Occupation far more directly into the government labor relations process and might greatly restrict the Communists' freedom of action in the future. And, of course, if Uji-Yamada was any indication, there was a good chance that the railwaymen might not heed the strike call at all. The result was a cloak-and-dagger episode that remained secret until recounted a quarter-century later by Katsura Takashi, a public member of the Central Labor Relations Committee.[13]

On the Thursday afternoon preceding the strike, which was to start midnight Saturday, Katsura got a call from a student of his—he gave lectures to adults in the evening—asking him to meet someone important after closing hours in his Central Labor Relations Committee office, after first making sure his secretaries were gone. Katsura assented, and some time after six was visited by a stranger who led him several blocks away to an old black car parked under the elevated railway near Shinbashi station. Inside, obscured by the shadows, was Ii Yashirō, who apologized that "the boss" could not come because he was being watched constantly. Ii said that Tokuda wanted Katsura, who was from Yamaguchi Prefecture, to introduce him, Ii, to Satō, also from Yamaguchi. Katsura did not know Satō very well but had met him, and they both set off in the battered, charcoal-burning vehicle for Satō's house.

The two and their driver soon got lost in the dark, not unusual for Tokyo's nameless, winding streets, and it was very late before they found the house. Called to the entrance by a maid, a courteous, kimono-clad Satō, who was convalescing from a gallstone attack, invited them in, remarking drily that he could not afford to be seen conspiring in the street with a known Communist. Once in, Ii launched into a strident speech demanding that Satō rescind the mass dismissal notice because a railway strike would be catastrophic for the nation. Satō considered silently for a few moments and then, to Ii's utter surprise, agreed. Satō's only condition was to keep the meeting secret. Now that it was clear to him that SCAP would take no action, Satō was more afraid of a strike than the Communists. Tokuda had blinked, but Satō hadn't noticed. Pressing his luck to the limit, Tokuda had won.

But the episode was not over. Because of Satō's condition of secrecy, the comedy had to be played out to its denouement publicly.[14] The next morning, Ii and twenty-two members of his Struggle Committee went to the Railway Ministry, confronted Satō in his office, and belligerently demanded withdrawal of the mass discharges. Satō had repeatedly rejected that demand before, but this time, to all the committee's amazement (except Ii's), he accepted. An agreement was drafted and endorsed by both sides within two hours.

But Ii's day of surprises was not yet complete, for on his return to union headquarters to have the agreement formally signed by the Struggle Committee, he was met by an irate Kikunami with some 200 members of the Youth Action Corps. The settlement might be a victory, but it was a betrayal of the *Sanbetsu*'s sympathy strike committee. Kikunami demanded a joint meeting of both committees. There on the second story of the ramshackle building, space was cleared and chairs pushed back and piled on tables to form an amphitheater. The YAC men crowded around and started to seize the Struggle Committee members, including Ii, by their clothing, neckties, and even hair to prevent the signing. Ii's supporters retorted with yells of *"Taihen da!* It's an outrage! They're dragging Ii off!"* In the fracas the Socialist union president, Suzuki Seiichi, disappeared. The YAC, it turned out later, had kidnapped him to prevent him, too, from ratifying Ii's agreement. The chants, scuffling, and crashing of furniture brought dozens of policemen to the scene from nearby Harajuku police station, together with a few puzzled American MPs.

Suddenly an excited unionist turned up with a rumor that the Transportation Minister had overruled Satō. Ii, Kikunami, and their followers, united once more, stormed back downtown to confront the Minister at the Diet building in raucous and impolite terms. The Minister, however, quietly confirmed the agreement, whereupon Kikunami added the further demand that a provision of the Satō-Ii agreement allowing the railways to fire incompetents with the union's consent be eliminated. No discharges at all, Kikunami demanded. Negotiations resumed, continuing far into the night. Satō finally capitulated on this point too. A frustrated Kikunami, with no more demands, had to agree to the revised settlement at 4 A.M. He would never get a chance to test the 700,000 members of the sympathy unions (steel, machinery, chemicals, and so on) even on a Sunday. It was now safe to release the union president to ratify the new agreement. And we at GHQ, learning that the strike had been called off, were left groping in the dark to figure out just what had really happened.

On their rarified level, the cabinet ministers may not have realized the implications of Satō's humiliating surrender. (Neither did most of GHQ.) But in that other nation, that of the Japanese workers, the impact was stunning. To start with, the Japan Communist Party leaders had gained control of the largest union in Japan less than a year after their release from prison. For the first time in Japanese history, a labor union had forced the government to back down. Suddenly, the Communist revolution became believable. Ii Yashirō, years later, in writing his memoir as leader of the general strike movement of February 1947,

combined it with the September railway "strike" as though the two were inseparable phases of the same campaign. If so, MacArthur's incredible luck at the
time—no embarrassing intervention, but no strike either—had its somber consequences. The massive general strike movement of February 1947 would hardly
have been attempted if the rail strike had been stopped the previous September.

THE OCTOBER OFFENSIVE

In less than two weeks, a new opportunity arose. Satō's surrender had been
more stimulus than settlement for the Communists. This time the opportunity
came to Hosoya Matsuta, old-time Communist (since 1929), who was Deputy
Secretary General of *Sanbetsu* and, more important, leader of the disciplined
Communists known collectively as the party "fraction" within that federation.
Hosoya got his orders from Yoyogi, and all party members were required to
follow him.

By the fall of 1946, labor unrest was endemic. The resources of individual
workers had been mostly exhausted, and wages had fallen far behind prices. The
rapidly proliferating unions were busy negotiating wage increases in dozens of
industries and hundreds of factories and mines. It was now the Communists' idea
to bring all those disparate negotiations under one banner and one leadership and
to convert all their varied economic demands into an assault on the government.
Thus was born the "October Offensive." The newly inaugurated *Sanbetsu* high
command held a hurried series of strategy sessions with its constituent unions'
leaders in Tokyo's Shiba Park Hall, and on October 3 Hosoya was able to
announce a concerted drive of twenty-one *Sanbetsu* unions and 750,000 members to overthrow the Yoshida Cabinet by means of large-scale coordinated
strikes.

Now three-quarters of a million workers constituted an unprecedented
force in a country whose biggest previous strike had involved 30,000 dockyard
workers twenty-five years before. And indeed, beginning with the first of October, with the clamor and clangor of a Chinese opera, strikes broke out in
succession everywhere. For several days the only voice on the air came from the
U.S. Army's station. On October 19, the 80,000-man Electric Power Workers
Union started cutting off current on a rotating basis to homes and factories.[15]

Labor was in upheaval, and it seemed that industrial Japan was being swept
away. An elated Hosoya exulted on October 9 that by the fifteenth the "October
Offensive" would reach its climax, that Japan would be immobilized by a
general strike to bring down the cabinet and that a "people's democratic government"—presumably on the model of Eastern Europe—would follow.[16]

Nothing of the sort happened, for the "October Offensive" was in large
part illusion, the figures inflated, the objective of overthrowing the cabinet

unshared by the participants, and *Sanbetsu* control a bit of sleight-of-hand. In the first place, of the 750,000 *Sanbetsu* workers, only 190,000 actually went out on strike at any time during the month.[17] With the average strike lasting only thirteen days, only 80,000 were simultaneously on strike on a typical day, and more than half of those were accounted for by only one strike, that at the Mitsui-related Tokyo Shibaura Engineering Works. Overthrow the government and establish a democratic people's republic? Hosoya never came close.

Second, whatever the Communists' objectives, the workers and local unions actually engaged in strikes did not share them. Of the 104 strikes that took place in October, the most political was the newspaper strike; it also failed the fastest.[18] Elsewhere, the Hokkaidō coal strikers won their strike in six days, signing a new contract in spite of the presence of a *Sanbetsu* head office representative sent to encourage them to fight. The 39,000 Tōshiba workers, who had begun their strike the day before the first "October Offensive" strategy session was held and received more *Sanbetsu* "encouragement" than almost any other union, settled fifty-seven days later for a wage raise tied to increased company receipts.

At *Sanbetsu* headquarters, Hosoya might be "overthrowing" the Yoshida Cabinet, but on the spot the workers were fighting for higher take-home pay. The economic strikes never did become political. Even Hosoya's boasted coordination—the point of the pre-"Offensive" strategy sessions—turned out to be a fiction. The unions might proclaim their solidarity with each other, but they bargained independently and settled their disputes separately. The puppetmaster made himself highly visible, but somehow his strings were not connected.

At the same time, the unions surprisingly displayed a degree of maturity and organizational sophistication comparable with much older unions in America. The Tōshiba workers set up a strike headquarters of 700 men and women, divided into twelve departments, from finances and liaison to public relations and publications.[19] They sent emissaries to all the neighboring factories and unions to collect strike funds.[20] They reported every few days to GHQ. To keep up morale they arranged marches, joint meetings with other unions, picnics, theatricals, arts and crafts instruction, flower arrangement classes, and lectures. They published reams of reports, comparative wage studies, special bulletins, a regular strike newspaper, schedules of events, and financial statements.[21] None of those publications, it should be noted, dealt with politics. When the strike was over, the Tōshiba workers demonstrated their sense of responsibility by lending the balance of their strike fund to the company to help tide it over its difficulties. The coal miners showed an equal sense of responsibility. When *their* strike was over, they worked twice as hard as before. Daily production soared by 70 percent, and coal production for the month of October for Hokkaidō exceeded the prestrike target by 20 percent, notwithstanding the time lost in the strike.[22]

THE PROPOSED STRIKE BAN

The Communists failed to persuade the workers to act revolutionary,[23] but they certainly convinced the ministers they were succeeding. On October 11, the day the Hokkaidō coal strike broke out, the prime minister, speaking to the Diet, denounced political strikes, declaring that they would get no legal protection.[24] Three days later, with the prime minister out of town and the Hokkaidō coal strike under active mediation by the local governor, 600 miles to the north, the Commerce and Industry Minister, Hoshijima Jirō, and Zen Keinosuke, Director General of the Economic Stabilization Board, visited General Marquat's office accompanied by the government's top liaison official, Asakai Kōichirō, to talk about industrial production. Once in, they handed the general a proposal to prohibit, by means of an Imperial ordinance, all strikes in "critical" industries, namely, coal mining, electric power, and food distribution, under penalty of fine or imprisonment.[25]

From almost every point of view, the strike ban proposal was repugnant to SCAP's mission, arrogantly brushing aside everything the Labor Division had been preaching. It constituted not only a return to prewar methods of forcibly repressing labor unrest, but it contradicted the strike provision of JCS 1380/15, conflicted directly with the newly passed Labor Relations Adjustment Law, and substituted an Imperial ordinance for Diet legislation, one of the undemocratic prewar practices that the Government Section had purposely deleted from the new constitution.

Nor had the ministers done their homework. That quickly became evident when I, called hurriedly to the meeting, questioned them. If, as the bellicose, bullet-headed Zen insisted, the emergency was too dire to allow time for the Diet to act, why hadn't the cabinet taken steps to designate coal mining a "public welfare work," thereby invoking compulsory mediation and suspending strikes for thirty days? Why designate food distribution, an industry where no strike was in progress or in the offing? Had the ministers checked with General Whitney on the use of an Imperial ordinance in place of a Diet law? What had the cabinet done to pressure the operators as well as the union to settle? And so on. The two ministers had no answers. It seemed that panic, or something more sinister, rather than serious reflection had produced the proposal.

The Zen solution never had a chance, especially after the Hokkaidō Governor, the conservative Masuda Kaneshichi, succeeded in ending the coal strike two days later. Within days, almost all the other work stoppages ended, too. On the last day of October I handed Zen and Asakai a letter, signed by Marquat, rejecting their strike ban proposal out of hand. The persistent Zen tried again two weeks later, only to be rebuffed once more by the general. The Yoshida Cabinet's attempt to suppress strikes sank into obscurity, only to create a front-page sensation thirty years later, when the Foreign Office declassified the "Asakai papers." Zen had failed to show his colleagues how to handle SCAP, let alone the "October Offensive." It was perhaps no accident that that was his last cabinet post, while Masuda, the Hokkaidō Governor, rose to be Labor Minister, Construction Minister, and Chief Cabinet Secretary.

Unfortunately, the pragmatic, judicious Masuda at that time remained in Hokkaidō. In Tokyo more volatile, political-minded men were in charge. By rejecting Zen's proposal, SCAP had saved the government and the country from violent police–labor conflicts sure to follow any attempt at enforcing the strike bans. But in the fall of 1946, when times for workers were so hard, nothing could save a government that implicitly denied the merit of labor union demands by simply labeling them political, even if some of them were. A Yoshida government that had justified the *Yomiuri* police raid[26] and secretly tried twice to prohibit strikes found it too hard to stay neutral or even, for that matter, stay out of nongovernmental labor disputes. In November and December 1946 the cabinet thoughtlessly got deeply and needlessly involved in a wage dispute between the country's 80,000 electric power workers and the nine monopoly power companies.

True, at 1,600 yen monthly, the electric power workers ranked among the highest paid in Japan. True, they were led by Communists out to defeat and embarrass the government if they could. True, finally, they wanted a raise to the then astronomical figure of 2,600 yen. In contrast the Tōshiba workers were making 525 yen, those of the other electrical equipment companies about 750 yen.[27] But the power companies (one generating and eight regional distribution monopolies) were legally independent. They received no subsidies and maintained their own accounts. Their workers were not government employees. They were, moreover, relatively prosperous; the electricity production index was triple the industrial production index.[28] War damage had been minor, while inflation had diminished capital charges, water power was free, and coal for their thermal plants was cheap. Both union and companies had already started negotiating.

Still, when both Zen and Hoshijima came separately to their respective regular meetings with General Marquat, they were indignant at the extravagance of the union's demand. The cabinet had decided, they told us, not to allow the companies to grant such an exorbitant increase. Indeed, the government would decide just what that increase could be. When that decision got out, the electric power companies quickly, silently, and gratefully retired from the collective bargaining arena. The government had impulsively pitted itself directly against a labor union, exactly what the Communists wanted.

The union first ordered suspension of bookkeeping operations, then instituted a wave of five-minute electricity cutoffs at suppertime, and then suspended power for several hours to 300 factories in the Osaka–Kyoto area and 46 plants in Tokyo and Yokohama. Finally, at the end of October, the union announced that "to cope with the deteriorating electric supply picture" it would reduce power to large consumers 30 percent and suspend power to medium users two days a week, just as though neither the electric companies nor the Ministry of Commerce and Industry existed.[29] In fact, the union was merely announcing a contingency plan already worked out by the company. But to the outraged ministers, it seemed that the union leaders were taking over the industry.

The Justice Minister immediately threatened the union with criminal penalties, including jail terms, for violation of the Criminal Code and Electric Power Enterprise Law, and called a national procurators' conference on measures to enforce those laws. To a public long inured to the almost daily *teiden* or power stoppages imposed by the company for conservation reasons—indeed suppertime cutoffs were so common that some quipped they were being compelled to eat literally in the *yami,* (which means both "black market," and "darkness,")—the threat seemed inordinately vindictive.

Even so, had the government restricted itself to quashing the usurpation of governmental powers and encouraging a settlement through the Central Labor Relations Committee, to whom they had earlier submitted the case, the cabinet would have been on strong ground. But the ministers also wanted to dictate the terms of the settlement. In originally invoking the CLRC mediation, the cabinet had declared that the "government awaits its fair judgment,"[30] but when the CLRC mediation proposal came, the ministers didn't think the judgment was fair and rejected it. Thereupon CLRC Chairman Suehiro charged the cabinet with insincerity and called for its resignation.[31] Two days later ESB Director General Zen declared that the government was planning measures to institute a national wage control.

Apparently that was too much for Zen's colleagues (as well as a complete surprise to us at GHQ), for in one more week the government changed its mind once more and approached CLRC Chairman Suehiro to try again, this time in person. Simultaneously it announced that it was returning the negotiations to the companies. Suehiro's new plan turned out to be essentially the same as the old, but public opinion was strongly against the government, and this time the cabinet made no objections to the companies' acceptance. It even approved a moderate rate increase to support the settlement. On December 2 the dispute was formally ended.

In retrospect, one of the most remarkable features of Japan's autumn of troubles was a nonevent—the almost total absence of U.S. Occupation Forces intervention in any way. The restraint showed by the Supreme Commander in the expected national railway strike served as a powerful example to those who knew of it. But in the field no one did, and even in the Headquarters the highest-ranking officers were prepared for swift action if anyone defied the Occupation.

It was a time of worry for me and the Labor Division. The labor applecart, and the entire democratization campaign with it, could easily have been upset by some imprudent military action.

The "October Offensive" inevitably imposed strains on GHQ itself. The Tōshiba strike raised more American hackles than any other, for Tōshiba was making equipment for the Army's dependent housing projects under construction, and the strike was throwing all kinds of schedules, including military dependent travel, U.S. housing availabilities, and so forth, out of kilter. Any number of other military contracts were also affected. Every few days the Labor Division would get acrimonious calls from military officers asking, in effect, who won the war anyway. It seemed ludicrous to me that U.S. policy hinged on such relative trivia as the supply of fuses or electric switches for the wives and children of American officers, but it was no laughing matter. As one tense meeting in General Marquat's office on some Eighth Army complaint related to the Tōshiba strike was breaking up, I remarked jokingly to the general that perhaps we should synchronize our watches as in the movies. Marquat did not think it funny.

THE TELEGRAM

Nor was it. A military machine is like a steamroller. It cannot be finely tuned, and once launched into motion it is not easily stopped. The day before the October newspaper strike was due to begin, the union local in the port of Numazu, south of Mount Fuji, telegraphed its Tokyo headquarters asking how to distinguish between authorized orders issued by the local U.S. military detachment and the commands of individual American soldiers. Tokyo cabled back to forward any suspicious orders for national union verification. It was a legitimate query and an apparently logical reply, but it was insensitive to the military viewpoint. When the Civil Censorship Detachment, which saw all cable traffic, rushed a translation of the exchange to Major General Willoughby, that ultra-conservative G-2 Intelligence officer took it promptly up to Major General Paul Mueller, the Chief of Staff. Undoubtedly prompted by the G-2, the Chief decided the Tokyo telegram to Numazu was defiance of the Occupation.

When I got back to my office late that afternoon I found a message citing the telegram and directing me to get over to the Chief's office as quickly as possible. I left my Labor Relations Chief, Captain Costantino, to clarify matters with the Newspaper and Radio Workers Union and rushed over to the staff conference room in the Daiichi Building across the alley to find a deadly serious council of war in progress.

Several generals were in attendance. General Willoughby had just outlined the situation. The Chief asked Colonel Rufus Bratton, Willoughby's Chief of

Counter Intelligence, for the disposition of the Counter Intelligence Corps units and directed that a CIC team be dispatched immediately to Numazu. He also ordered the Provost Marshal to furnish Military Police teams to work with the CIC and further directed G-3 Operations to work out a plan for the tactical troop units to support the MPs. The Chief of the Legal Section, Alva Carpenter, was told to set up a Provost Court and start drawing up indictments and arranging detention facilities. The conference sounded for all the world like D-Day minus one for a full-scale attack of the U.S. Army on the Newspaper Union. When General Muller got to me, I suggested that perhaps the union had not really meant defiance by its action. After all, I said, it could be that the Tokyo telegram was sent by a minor official without authority. What if I could get the union to withdraw its instructions? The Chief ordered me to get in touch with the union and report back "soonest." Meanwhile the operation was to be held in abeyance.

On my return to Forestry Building, Costantino was talking in my office to two subdued and apparently frightened Newspaper Union officials who had had no idea of the commotion their telegram had caused. Of course, the union was not challenging the Occupation, they said, and Kikunami, its president, was not even aware the cable had been sent. We gave the union two hours to countermand their instruction, and in much less time than that I was able to telephone the Chief of Staff's office with the text of the canceling cable ordering strict compliance with every U.S. military order in future. The offensive stood down.

I did not know whether General MacArthur had been consulted. I could not understand how General Marquat was kept out of it, and General Whitney, too, but there was no doubt in my mind that the action was within an ace of going forward, ordered by a Chief of Staff, who obviously did not understand the implications of what he was doing, abetted by an almost wholly military staff who were not going to contradict him. The Labor Division not only had to pacify the increasingly distrustful brass, but we had also to make sure the Japanese labor unions understood the danger of provoking Army intervention.

YOSHIDA AND LABOR

The Japanese Government policy that emerged from the tumult of the 1946 autumn labor "offensives" was unmistakable hostility toward organized labor. Not all the ministers, however, relished the situation. After all, millions of people were now unionized. Some cast about for other solutions. (A troubled Justice Minister Kimura Seiichi came up with a bizarre confidential invitation to me, passed by way of his son, to become Japan's first labor minister!) But Yoshida ran the show, and he could well counter that the Communists had started the antagonism and were out to "get him." That was doubtless true. Unfortunately, in his repugnance he did not take care to separate the Communists from the rest of the trade unionists, who were overwhelmingly economically oriented.[32] It was consistent with his position, therefore, that in a radio broadcast on New Year's Day 1947, he called the union leaders a gang of rebels, *"futei no yakara."* The Kyōdō News Service reported in late January that out of 863 letters received in recent weeks by the Prime Minister's Office no fewer than 481 considered Yoshida Shigeru to be an enemy of the working classes.[33] In the years that followed, Yoshida emerged as a genuine national hero to his people. In January 1947, he was much more a national villain.

But in this evolution of urban public opinion, the electric power labor dispute, and particularly Suehiro's call for the resignation of the cabinet, was the turning point. Before that, the Socialist leaders could oppose political strikes too, as had Nishio Suehiro and Mizutani Chōsaburō when they assured Prime Minister Yoshida in September of their opposition to a railway strike on those grounds. On November 11 the moderate *Sōdōmei* rejected a joint front with the Electric Power Workers and National Teachers unions because the latter groups were Communist-led. Even as late as November 16 Nishio could declare that the Japanese workers were interested not in overthrowing the government but in higher wages.[34]

But as the seeds of Suehiro's blast sprouted, even the Socialist *Sōdōmei,* which had called on *Sanbetsu* to purge itself of Communist elements, joined that same *Sanbetsu* on November 30 in sponsoring a series of "overthrow the Yoshida Cabinet" rallies all over the country,[35] and two weeks later half a million workers, even more than the May Day assemblage, thronged the Imperial Palace Plaza to call for the government's resignation.[36] It had become unfashionable, even treasonous, for a worker of any political stripe not to oppose Yoshida. The time was ripe for a massive Communist assault on the government.

No one was more aware of this than Tokuda Kyūichi, whose dream after seventeen years of imprisonment and fifteen months of furious work now seemed to be nearing fulfillment. By mid-November, his Communists had progressed from being fringe agitators in July to the apparent leaders of the working class. Tokuda defended the "October Offensive"—at the time it needed defending—by explaining that, win or lose, the workers were being revolutionized. "The Japanese *Sanbetsu,*" he declared at an *Asahi* symposium, "was correct. Every momentum in the labor movement should be taken up by the labor leaders to lead it to a higher plateau, that is, the attainment of a political objective set by the present stage of the class war."[37]

Just what he was driving at in that turgid Marxist prose may have been obscure to his listeners. It soon became clear to them and to the Japanese people. For as one strike climax had succeeded another in the fall of 1946, the tension mounted. December might be relatively quiet, but it was a calm before the storm. The climax was not far off. It came with the general strike movement right after the New Year. The target date was the first of February 1947.

15

Japan at the Precipice

THE GENERAL STRIKE

A GENERAL STRIKE in midwinter in a war-shattered country is a fearful prospect. As January 1946 entered its final days, the Japanese people suddenly became aware that that was exactly what they were facing. For on February 1, 1947, some 6 million workers, perhaps two-thirds of all those employed outside the farms, forests, and fisheries, were scheduled to set down their tools, leave their workplaces, and shut down the entire national economy unless the government accepted a set of labor union demands. With selected exceptions, all electricity supply, telegraph, telephone, and mail services would cease. Trains, subways, and trolleys would stop running, and with them 95 percent of Japan's transport. Factories, mines, schools, and offices, including a good part of the government apparatus itself, would close. Theaters and newspapers would be shut down. Hospital services would be curtailed. Even during the worst days of the war, Japan had not experienced such a paralysis as now threatened the land. The ''two-one'' (February first) general strike movement had brought Japan to the edge of a precipice.

The uncertainties were endless and frightening. How much food would be available, and would there be a rice panic? Would charcoal rationing continue? If not, how could people cook what rice there was? Would homes be dark and radios silent? No one knew if doctors would be able to get to patients or the patients to get medicines, if any stores would be open, or how many people would be seen on the downtown streets or in the local shopping areas. Nor did anyone have any idea of when the strike would end.

Ostensibly the dispute had started as a government workers' wage negotiation and still was. The unions' demands, though steadily augmented, were still relatively clear. But they applied to only 2.6 million government workers, and the unions of the other 3.4 million in private industry, who had joined the government employees, were pressing their own demands on a large number of diverse employers. And the demands kept expanding. Only a few days before the "two-one" deadline, on January 28, 1947, a rally of 400,000 workers on the Imperial Palace Plaza adopted eighteen additional demands. Even if the government acceded to its own employees' claims, would those employees remain on strike anyway in sympathy with their private industry comrades? A solution seemed impossible.

There was a political element, too, and it was perhaps the most important. The unions were demanding that Yoshida resign. If he did, what would prevent them from vetoing or deposing his successors by the same kind of strike pressure? With no one to govern except on the strike leaders' sufferance, revolutionary unionism would replace the ballot box and representative democracy. The Occupation's "democratization express" was heading for derailment. No one who knew Douglas MacArthur or his directives could believe for a minute that the Supreme Commander would tolerate such a result. And yet publicly MacArthur kept silent. What were the Japanese to think? They were sliding helplessly, they feared, down a slippery incline to what some of them called social dissolution.

Economic Issues

In later days, some of the participants would attribute the causes of the general strike movement to the operation of "social forces." Katō Kanjū, the left-wing Socialist leader (labor minister the next year), told me a quarter-century later that the general strike was "the logical culmination of the proletarian movement in response to the economic pressures on the working class."[1] Others saw other "social forces." But historical forces are, after all, made of human beings, and abstractions usually explain very little just how things happened and why people behaved as they did. Bad as economic conditions were, vigorous as the labor movement was, and unnecessarily irritating and inept as the government had been in labor relations, the general strike movement of 1947 was still the conscious, purposeful work of Tokuda Kyūichi, his collaborators, and the Communist Party machine of Japan.

As the biggest typhoon begins with deceptively gentle breezes, the gigantic offensive to bring down the Japanese Government started merely as an effort by some government workers' groups to obtain a wage raise. Unfortunately for them, when they approached the officials of each ministry, the officials explained, most of them sympathetically,[2] that their particular ministry had neither the authority nor the money. Besides, everyone agreed that the government wage system was preposterous and had to be reformed.[3] On November 9 the cabinet had established a new tripartite Wage Commission made up of government, labor, and public representatives. But for more than two months no one at all was appointed.[4] The government officers to whom the unions talked counseled patience and prudence, while the two teachers' unions, a smaller one connected with the moderate *Sōdōmei* and a larger one affiliated with Communist-led *Sanbetsu,* fiercely disputed whether it would be unprofessional of teachers to strike.

Economic conditions, however, made patience difficult. Statistically, food prices from August to November had abated, but they were still not back to the level of May, when General Marquat and I had arranged for a substantial wage raise to government workers. Even then, the new wages were still far below private industry. Possessions, sold progressively to make up living cost differences, were approaching exhaustion. Then the upward food price spiral resumed, and the cost of living jumped 50 percent from November to February 1947.

As economic pressures mounted, so did personal tragedies. A village schoolteacher, till then a man of moral rectitude as befitted a model for his pupils, was caught stealing rice from a farmer's field one night and was arrested. Unable to face his pupils and their parents, he preferred to commit suicide.[5] The *Sanbetsu* Teachers Union publicized the incident widely.

Finally, winter was on its way, with its special demands for charcoal to heat the flimsy shacks of the workers, for warm clothing, and for medicines. In a population weakened by months of malnutrition, sickness took a heavy toll that winter, and more of the sick died. Between November 1946 and January 1947, the death rate rose 32 percent. The population of the still devastated cities suffered more than those in the rural areas.[6]

Unable simply to wait, four government unions—the *Sanbetsu* Teachers with 320,000 members, the All Communications Workers with 380,000, the Administrative Employees with 85,000, and the Public Workers with 320,000—formed a Government Employees and Public Workers Joint Struggle Policy Committee under a moderate *Sōdōmei* trade union leader, Urabe Toshio, from the Public Workers. In late November 1946 they presented the Home Minister with their unified demands.

In retrospect it is remarkable how modest the demands were: a mere 700 yen (ten dollars) monthly average with a 500 yen minimum, plus 100 yen for each dependent, all after taxes.[7] Meanwhile the workers wanted a year-end bonus amounting to two months' wages, quite within traditional limits, but at the new scale. The advance bonus payments that I had arranged were simply forgotten. At this distance, such details look trivial, but they should be kept in mind as a measure of the demands put forth once the Communists took over. Up to the beginning of December, the moderates were still running the show. The affair was still essentially an economic negotiation.

ENTER THE COMMUNISTS

At this point the Communists began moving in, and the manipulation began at once. "A Communist," Lenin had written, "must be prepared to make every sacrifice and, if necessary, even resort to all sorts of schemes and stratagems, employ illegitimate methods, conceal the truth, in order to get into the trade unions, stay there, and conduct revolutionary work therein."[8] Exactly the prescription for the government workers' takeover.

"Conceal the truth?" As far as the public was aware, three of the four unions making up Urabe's committee were led by non-Communists. Only the Teachers Union had Communists as president and secretary general. The Administrative and Public Workers, true, were essentially non-Communist. But the powerful All Communications Workers was where the Communists had everyone—including me—fooled. Its president, Dobashi Kazuyoshi, had proposed only the previous summer that his union join the moderate *Sōdōmei* federation, and he signed the first no-strike pledge in postwar labor history. Dobashi a Communist? Impossible.[9] In the Railway Union, the Communists made no attempt to replace the Socialist union president with a Communist but worked to have all union executive powers turned over to their Struggle Committee, loaded with Communists, instead. When the railwaymen applied to join the joint government workers committee, the non-Communists saw no reason for alarm. They thought they outnumbered the Communists four unions to one. In reality, with the railwaymen, the Communists had neatly and surreptitiously taken over the committee, three unions to two.

Immediately, à la Lenin, came the "stratagems." The committee's name was changed from "Joint Struggle Policy Committee" to "Joint Struggle Committee." No one noticed, but now the committee was suddenly in charge of operations, negotiations, and everything else. Then the committee was reorganized; the three Communist-dominated unions were each provided with four seats, while the two non-Communist unions received only three each.[10] At its next meeting the committee dumped founder Urabe in favor of Ii Yashirō. Urabe took his deposition with good grace. No one else much cared. The reorganized committee's first move, two weeks later in mid-December, was to present the Chief Cabinet Secretary with revised wage demands, more than doubling the original claim: 1,500 yen a month average instead of 700. That would automatically make the average year-end bonus 3,000, and this was wanted immediately. If not, a million government workers would strike.

As the year's end approached, I advised General MacArthur by memo of the possible joint walkout of government employees. Privately, I thought that even though public opinion favored a traditional year-end bonus, neither the workers nor the union leadership was ready for a New Year's strike. Despite tense moments and harsh words, the unions and government patched up an interim accord, a bonus was paid, and everyone went off for a week to celebrate the New Year, leaving 1946's problems behind without regret.

It was by no means a holiday for everyone. For Tokuda, a master strategic opportunist, had decided to launch his long-cherished general strike to overthrow the government. The revolutionary road to power led through a general strike by way of labor crises, as he told Hasegawa Kō, in late 1945. As early as April 20, 1946, Nozaka Sanzō, the number three Communist leader, had declared to a meeting of Communists, left Socialists, and "progressive" intellectuals of the Democratic Peoples League in Kyōritsu Hall in Tokyo, that the organization of a general strike in the near future was essential.[11] Statements of that kind by top party leaders at public meetings represented party policy, not personal opinion. In the months that followed, the general strike became the lodestar of party organization and tactics. Only the exact timing remained. Now, during the holidays, Tokuda made his move. He called a secret "national representational conference" in Tokyo for the end of the first week in January 1947. To the hundred Communist activist leaders who secretly attended, he urged that now was the time for the general strike.

After the arduous labor of 1946, conditions could not have seemed more favorable. Consider:

• With the onset of winter, economic distress was at its worst.

• A general strike, unlike an ordinary strike, would require of most workers the easiest thing in the world—to stay home and do nothing. With rail transport paralyzed they couldn't do otherwise anyway.

• Communist party membership had reached 60,000.[12] (In April 1917, just before their revolution, the Bolshevik party in Tsarist Russia had only 49,000 card-holders in a population double the size.)[13]

• Disciplined Communist Party fractions and secret Communists in high positions strongly influenced or controlled unions with well over a million members.

• The *Sanbetsu* unions, their "voice of the working class," had grown to more than 1.6 million members, double that of the rival *Sōdōmei*, and had had valuable experience in coordinating members unions in joint strike actions.

• The Youth Action Corps now comprised more than 10,000 fighters in a score of unions, all reporting directly to the Communist Party Politburo.[14] Often spoiling for action, the YAC men were of military age, including many demobilized junior officers, tough sergeants, and ex-kamikaze flyers who gloried in military discipline. "Many of them believe," one critic wrote later, "that they had been betrayed by their fatherland. The hostility they felt towards the enemy during the war was now directed against the capitalists. Trained during the war to obey orders from their officers, they were now ready to follow the orders of the union struggle committees. The hands that once held guns now waved the red flag."[15]

• The Yoshida government had almost completely alienated the labor unions in the last months of 1946.

• The Socialists, on the other hand, had finally consented to work with the Communists, if only for the overriding purpose of compelling Yoshida to resign.

• Whether by chance or design, the fall strikes had anesthetized the public to the basic difference between industrywide economic strrikes and a fundamentally political general strike. Ever since September the *Sanbetsu* unions had used the word *"zenesuto"*—short for *"zeneraru sutoraiki"* (*"*general strike*"*)—over and over again for any strike that extended beyond one factory. By January the distinction between a limited *"zenesuto"* and a general *"zenesuto"* had been all but obliterated, and with it public apprehension of the latter.

• And now Tokuda had found his ideal general strike instrument in Urabe's reorganized and renamed Joint Struggle Committee. With no history, hence no enemies, and no constitution, hence no limitations on the power of its officers, the committee was infinitely malleable. Its Communist control was permanent once the allocation of union representation on the committee was made in December, as even the adherence of unions with a million more members in the succeeding weeks did not alter the original representation.[16] Those unions had no representation in the strike decisions at any time. And finally, the Joint Struggle Committee was already in dispute with the authorities; there was no need to pick a new quarrel, just exacerbate the old one. It was a perfect setup.

It is typical of the long chain of the Communists' deceptions in their general-strike drive that the critical "national representational conference" called by Tokuda in the first days of 1947 became an historical nonfact. Communists never divulged its occurrence even many years afterward, and such Socialists as Katō Kanjū (in June 1973) were shocked and disbelieving when I told them that it had taken place. Nevertheless, there is no doubt as to what happened at the meeting. The conference agreed to turn the existing wage negotiations of the government workers into a general strike aimed at overthrowing the government.[17]

Events thereafter moved rapidly. On January 7, 1947, the Government Workers' Joint Struggle Committee formally decided that in the absence of a reply to its doubled demands, it would launch a general strike some time between January 27 and February 1. Emissaries fanned out from committee headquarters in the Railway Union offices in the Transportation Ministry Building. On January 9 they visited the Socialist Party, soliciting support. The Communist Party needed no invitation; it issued a fervent endorsement before the Struggle Committee people could reach them. On January 11, the leaders of a giant rally of more than 400,000 on the Imperial Palace Plaza, called originally by the government workers to reinforce their wage demands, converted the assemblage on the spot into a "grand meeting on the establishment of the strike setup," which noisily adopted a resolution for a general strike sometime between

January 27 and February 1.[18] (Actually, in view of the large numbers and inadequate amplification system, it is questionable whether most of those in attendance even heard the resolution.) The Communist machine had gone into operation less than five days after the "representational conference."

TOWARD THE SIX-MILLION-MAN STRIKE

Rallies and demonstrations followed regularly every few days on the Imperial Palace Plaza or, as the Communists now called it, the "People's Plaza." Marchers advanced on the Prime Minister's Official Residence (at which Prime Minister Yoshida never resided). At the same time, almost as an afterthought, Ii, as chairman of the Government Workers' Joint Struggle Committee, officially notified the government of the impending strike. Simultaneously he raised the ante again, now to an 1,800-yen average monthly wage plus higher dependency allowances.

The new demands would provide the government workers with enough pay to buy the entire 1946–47 rice crop collection six times over at the official consumer price,[19] thereby exploding the consumer price structure and with it all the collective bargaining gains of the preceding fall. It also would raise the government's wage bill by 260 percent instead of the original 40, and far surpass 1946–47 total government revenues.[20] The Communists were deliberately making it impossible for the government to agree or for Dr. Suehiro and his Central Labor Relations Committee to mediate.[21] For Ii and his comrades, talking was only a method of fighting. A new government, not a higher wage, was the objective.

We in the Labor Division knew nothing of the crucial Communist "national representational conference," nor were we aware that the Government Workers Joint Struggle Committee had been captured by the Communists. But the sudden and repeated calls for a general strike, the increased tempo of the demonstrations, and Ii's escalating demands convinced us that something serious was afoot. On January 15, I advised General Marquat that a strike of some 2 million government workers was now a probability. Since serious doubts as to the SCAP's course had been raised by the Communists,[22] I recommended that SCAP publicly advise the Ministries of Transportation and Communications and the Central Liaison Office that stoppages in transportation, communications, and other services required by the Occupation would be directly prejudicial to the Occupation's objectives and needs and that the Imperial Japanese Government be directed to take the necessary measures to avert such stoppages after consulting with the appropriate SCAP sections.[23]

Marquat took my recommendations up to MacArthur that evening, and then the next day, to conform with channels, sent his own memo to the Chief of

Staff. It was almost an exact copy of mine, except that he recommended that the communication with the Japanese Government be informal, thus not public.[24] In this he was almost certainly reflecting the "Old Man's" view of the night before. The difference was important, for without a SCAP public announcement in some form, the unions would still not be sure of where General MacArthur stood.

In any event, our memos were out of date almost as soon as they were written. On January 15, an All-Joint Struggle Committee, including not only government unions but some twenty-five large unions in private industry, was inaugurated. All the private unions included currently were in negotiations with management.[25] Seven additional unions, totaling more than 600,000 members, officially joined the movement.[26] In no case did the workers themselves get a chance to vote on the issue. In almost every case, the unions belonged to *Sanbetsu,* and in most of them the union leaders were Communists. Within a few days the prospective strike ranks had reached close to 4 million.

Once again I approached General Marquat. If SCAP did not clarify his position soon, the strike would expand even further, making it all the harder to call off without unfortunate incidents. Private notification to the government would not work. The Occupation authorities had to tell the unions directly that a general strike would not be tolerated. Once again General MacArthur refused to intervene personally. Let Ted Cohen tell the unions, he told Marquat.

My office was full the next few days with invited labor groups as I passed the word. Over and over I repeated that General MacArthur simply would not tolerate a general strike, and if the labor unions defied him they were putting themselves in jeopardy. I could not, of course, tell them that if military forces were used and control of the action passed from the SCAP Headquarters to the Army, the unions would be dealing with far less sympathetic Americans. I dreaded the prospect of the Chief of Staff's intruding into the deep waters of labor politics in a foreign country like Japan with General Willoughby as his political guide. American soldiers fighting Japanese workers would not make an edifying spectacle for the world, even if pleasing to the Communists. But unable to name American names, my warnings of danger carried little impact. Perhaps some of the labor leaders remembered when I had also warned that SCAP would not permit a national railway strike and, in the event, MacArthur had not moved at all.

Ii Yashirō, the strike generalissimo, was my most frequent and argumentative visitor, coming each time with a different group. I argued with him in Leninist terms. If the American state, I said, was the "committee of the capitalist ruling class" and General MacArthur was only its tool, and if a general strike, according to Lenin, was in essence a revolutionary situation, how could he expect anything but the sternest action by the Occupation Forces to suppress it?

Is that what he wanted? Was he willing to face the consequences, for both himself and the entire labor movement?[27] Ii politely ignored my theoretical foray. His strong point was agitation and action, and besides he would accept his Leninist theory only from Yoyogi Headquarters, not from our Forestry Building.

Meanwhile the Communists vigorously pressed *Sōdōmei's* Socialist unions to join them. The conservative Socialists, like Nishio, were opposed,[28] but Takano Minoru, the *Sōdōmei* vice president, persisted in pushing for Socialist–Communist unity. The Socialists must participate, he insisted, or be discredited with the workers. At a climactic meeting in his house on the night of January 20 to prepare the official strike proclamation, the Communists Tokuda, Shiga, and Nozaka finally agreed to change their demand for a "people's cabinet" into one for a "coalition party cabinet." Takano heaved a sigh of relief. To him it meant the Communists were recognizing the principle of parliamentary supremacy, and besides with ninety-three seats in the Diet's lower house to the Communists' five, the distribution of Cabinet posts would be all in the Socialists' favor.[29] Despite some misgivings, Takano's arguments sounded persuasive. By the early morning hours, when the meeting broke up, the Socialists and *Sōdōmei* were leaning toward participation.

In the morning their doubts were rudely cleared away. When one of the meeting's participants, the intense Kikunami Katsumi, head of *Sanbetsu,* returned to his home at 4 A.M., two young shabbily dressed nationalist thugs were waiting for him there. They invited themselves in, sat with him in his parlor, politely requested him to stop the general strike, and, when he refused, stabbed him repeatedly with long knives. They departed, leaving him bleeding profusely on the tatami mats and apparently dying. He survived, but on January 21, radio broadcasts and newspaper extras were filled with bulletins about the assassination attempt. The public was shocked and horrified. "We must close ranks in the face of reviving prewar terrorism and murder!" the Communists trumpeted. The Socialists felt the same way. Now was no time for dissension. On January 21 most of the reluctant moderates fell into line. Six million workers had become entangled in the general strike. The avalanche had begun to roll.

THE MACARTHUR STATEMENT

Uninformed of the details of the tense and complex negotiations between Socialists and Communist unions, I could nevertheless see the strike movement growing despite my efforts. Reluctantly, I reported to General Marquat, on the same day the Socialist fell into line, that informal SCAP communications were of no use. We had only ten days left. Only a public and authoritative statement, preferably by General MacArthur, could now stop the strike. But that evening

General MacArthur demurred once more at intervening personally. Instead, General Marquat, who was recognized as one of his representatives,[30] would read a statement to the union leaders.

Coming down from the SCAP's office that evening, Marquat sat down at his green-ribboned typewriter and, with me at his side, pecked out a draft statement, newspaperman-style. The statement was 80 percent Marquat, 20 percent me,[31] and 100 percent MacArthur, down to the last oratorical flourish. Next morning, Marquat went back up to the sixth floor of the Daiichi Building for MacArthur's final approval, while I got busy summoning the strike leaders to Marquat's second floor office in the Forestry Building at two o'clock that afternoon.

It was perhaps the most critical, dramatic, and yet exasperating meeting I remember in that office. The union leaders, some fifteen of them, tense but impassive and bundled heavily against the cold damp of unheated Japanese factories and offices, perspired profusely in the warm, richly furnished, curtained, and carpeted room. To them the American major general with his carefully trimmed moustache and elegant personal grooming must have seemed a bit of a dandy. None of them knew of his humble background and laborious ascent through the ranks or of his natural kindliness and compassion.

The general opened the meeting in a friendly fashion and immediately reported that the government had consented to a general wage increase to be made public in the course of the day. (This was a concession he himself had pressed upon the government, through his Finance Division, earlier in the day.)[32] It should be, he thought, an acceptable stopgap until the Wages Commission, which would begin work in two days, reached its conclusions. Then, after stressing that he spoke as General MacArthur's representative and that his words should be regarded as coming from General MacArthur himself, he read them the prepared statement he had worked out with me at his side. Labor's rights in Japan were fully recognized and, in fact, had been established with SCAP's approval. But such rights had limits. A general strike or "coordinated work stoppage" that endangered Occupation objectives[33] would be dealt with summarily by the Occupying Powers. Moreover, American aid was conditional on the American people's expectation of a maximum Japanese effort to rebuild their country. A general strike demonstrating the contrary, he warned, could jeopardize American aid. The government had agreed to take "certain ameliorative actions," and SCAP expected organized labor, too, to take action without delay. "He [the Supreme Commander] will not permit a coordinated action by organized labor to provoke a national calamity by a general work stoppage," was his concluding point. He requested a reply to "these instructions" by January 23, the following day.

The ESS Chief waited until his interpreter had finished. There was dead silence in the room for a moment. Then he added, "You are not authorized to make this statement public."

I had already protested this last condition, before the meeting. How could a handful of leaders redirect the course of 6 million workers if they could not tell them why? Labor unions didn't work that way. Marquat replied that the "Old Man" wanted it that way. But when the union leaders asked for clarification of the statement's confidentiality,[34] the general had already seen the point of my objection. They could communicate the gist of the statement within the union for discussion purposes, he said, and they could take notes on his statement, but they could not divulge it to the press. MacArthur had once again refused to issue an unambiguous public order. It now could be taken only as a warning.

Indeed, the strike leaders seated around the room interpreted it variously. The two Socialist leaders who spoke, Hara Hyō, vice president of *Sōdōmei,* and Urabe Hideo of the Public Workers, were both conciliatory, thanking the general for SCAP's sponsorship of labor rights. But the Communist Nakahara Junkichi of the Electric Power Workers probed for the limits of legality: Were "sabotage," working to rule, simultaneous vacations, or individual strikes permitted? No, Marquat said.

It was all the government's fault, said Ii. When the workers wanted to negotiate, the government ran away. The Yoshida government oppressed the workers but blamed its economic measures on SCAP. When I described the government's concessions of that day, raising the average wage 42 percent, Ii replied that that would still leave his people far below private industry. If the workers did not like the government, I offered, why could they not vote them out of office at the next election instead of striking?[35] Moreover, the eighteen-member management–labor–public Wage Commission was due to start work in two days. Judging from the course taken by the public members of the CLRC in the electric power mediation, the commission should be quite responsive to labor's viewpoint. So why the strike? Ii replied abrasively and doggedly, as though MacArthur's statement had not existed, that if there were no settlement by January 31, the general strike would automatically begin. He quoted the Far Eastern Commission's Sixteen Principles at us, then added slyly that he did not know how American labor unions were run, but in Japan they were democratic. He would have to go back to the membership for an answer.

Iwama was more flamboyant. He spoke bitterly of the distress of his teachers and then presented Marquat with a petition signed (that is, "chopped" with personal seals) in blood by fifty of his union members. The blood, of course, was intended to show their sincerity. But as it was the very day after the ultra-nationalist knifing of Kikunami, I was shocked. Before the general had a chance to comment, I jumped up and emotionally accused Iwama of following the same pattern of intimidation as the prewar nationalist assassins, who had also signed petitions in blood that ultimately brought so much woe to the workers and peasants of Japan, and of China too. Personally, I declared, as a labor supporter, I was ashamed to see a labor leader in Japan using such cheap, theatrical Fascist tricks. It was an insult to the memory of the millions who had died in the war. Taken aback by the unexpected onslaught, Iwama silently withdrew his petition.[36]

That evening, when Marquat reported the meeting in detail to General MacArthur, the Supreme Commander greatly relished my exchange with Iwama. The professed democrat had been caught in one of the most notoriously repugnant militarist acts of the past. He had given himself away.[37]

Judging from their reactions at the meeting, the Socialist *Sōdōmei* seemed sure to pull out of the general strike, and the following day it did. But the reaction of the others present was puzzling. Ii changed the subject without acknowledging Marquat's statement as MacArthur's order. Two-thirds of the strike leaders at the meeting also behaved as though nothing important had changed; except for Nakahara of the Electric Power Workers, no one even admitted the existence of an order. I could understand defiance or compliance, or even something in between. I could not comprehend their deliberately acting like zombies, unseeing and unhearing. Then it dawned on me—they could not respond because they were under Communist discipline and had not yet gotten the party line. After that response, or lack of it, we could no longer doubt that the general strike was under Communist control.

When the meeting was over, I suggested to General Marquat that in some unions the leaders might not be able to hold the fired-up membership in check. "The Old Man will never believe that," he retorted. In MacArthur's American experience, union leaders controlled the rank and file, not the other way round. Advocate of labor unions as democratic institutions that he was, he was still too worldly-wise to believe that in real life critical decisions were made just by majority vote. In the general strike situation he was proved correct.

The *Sōdōmei* leaders did not need the three-day grace period allowed by Marquat. The very next day, their representatives advised us formally, and with manifest relief, I thought, of the withdrawal of their *Sōdōmei* federation and its major principal constituent unions from the strike.

THE COMMUNIST WAR OF NERVES

The Communist union leaders, however, used the three days to show that no real MacArthur order existed and that they had friends in GHQ who presumably would protect them. They were not anxious to spread the actual text of Marquat's statement. Only three union men visited our office to take notes.[38] The *Sanbetsu* notes, published eight years later in Japanese,[39] were reasonably accurate. There had been no misunderstanding as between what Marquat said and what the *Sanbetsu* Communist leaders thought he said.

On the other hand, the Communist Party Headquarters fraction issued a handbill[40] the following day, January 24, that denied the "rumor" that "'if a general strike were declared, GHQ would prohibit it by military administrative action.' . . . General Marquat on the 22nd," it continued, "was not General MacArthur's representative but a private individual."[41] The Communists were not going to give up the general strike so easily. As Lenin had said, "conceal the truth" and "employ illegitimate methods."

If MacArthur had once again avoided an unambiguous public strike ban, the Communists had evaded an unambiguous public reply. The General undoubtedly had good reasons for his reluctance to act early. In the United States such an action might be construed as strikebreaking or, at the least, a tacit admission that his democracy in Japan was not working altogether smoothly. A high-powered newspaper publishers' and editors' group, including Roy Howard, owner of the Scripps-Howard chain of some twenty-six dailies and head of the United Press; Erwin Canham, editor of the *Christian Science Monitor;* Carroll Binder, editor of the Minneapolis *Tribune;* and Wayne Coy, assistant publisher of the Washington *Post,*[42] was due to arrive in Tokyo on January 26. It would be better to handle the affair without a public prohibition.

From the internal viewpoint in Japan, the case was even stronger. The Supreme Commander, to conserve his uniquely unchallengeable authority, had to stay above the battle, descending only to rescue order from impending chaos. Moreover, for maximum effect, a formal ban had to come just before its actual application so that its impact would not wear off and the Communists would not have time to devise ways of evading it. Quite probably, however, both MacArthur and Marquat misjudged the effect on the Communist strike leaders. Japanese Government officials would go to great lengths to forestall formal SCAP orders, because that would reveal that they were not actually running the country as they pretended. But the strike leaders' prestige derived from their daring to challenge authority. The higher the authority, the more they gained in stature. They had no incentive to cave in to a mere warning.

Tokuda, Ii, and the other Communists embarked instead on a war of nerves on three fronts: labor, government, and GHQ. On the first, they had to hold the unions together and conserve their hegemony; on the second, to browbeat the cabinet into concessions, surrender, or breakup; and on the third, to delay Occupation action and if possible work out conditions for some kind of a "general strike."

The lying leaflet was one tactic in the battle of the first front. Indeed, the whole Communist strike machine, built up so carefully in the preceding months—union Communist fractions, *Sanbetsu,* Youth Action Corps, Joint Struggle Committees—were all thrown into the effort. *Sōdōmei*'s defection was a blow, but except for its Municipal Transport Workers Union, which could stop the street cars, buses, and subways in Tokyo, no *Sōdōmei* union was strategically placed. The same applied to the National Council of Trade Unions, a minor grouping, which also quit the strike. The Communist machine held the key unions firmly—railways, communications, and government administrative workers.[43]

Through it all the Youth Action Corps activists worked tirelessly. They visited and threatened all the doubtful unions and labor organizations, harassed the Socialist Party headquarters three to ten times daily,[44] and intimidated workers on the factory floor. Meanwhile, the Communists radiated supreme self-confidence.[45]

With the withdrawal of *Sōdōmei*, the Communist grip tightened on both Joint Struggle Committees. In the All-Joint Struggle Committee, the Communists had not been able to load the representation as successfully as in the Government Employees JSC. Only a bit more than one-third of the thirty-six-man All-JSC—consisting of the president and secretary of each of eighteen unions—was under Communist Party discipline and subject to the Politburo's orders passed on by Hasegawa Kō. But all the Communists needed to do, Hasegawa told me later, was convince five out of the remaining twenty-three Committeemen. They were able to do so up until the final hours.

On their second front, the Communists launched a direct assault on the cabinet. Within hours of Marquat's mention of it, the Joint Struggle Committee turned down the government's 42 percent wage increase offer. Thereafter, the scene shifted to the Central Labor Relations Committee, where the Joint Struggle Committee turned the sessions into a propaganda circus and a device for prolonging the dispute till the first of February. At a meeting at the Prime Minister's residence, the Communists seized upon the quiet departure of Deputy Prime Minister Shidehara and State Minister Uehara Etsujirō from the meeting to declare immediately that the government was sabotaging the negotiations and to demand that the meeting be terminated.[46]

At the following meeting, Dr. Suehiro and Nakayama Ichirō,[47] the new Chairman of the Central Labor Relations Committee, came up with a compromise 1,200-yen monthly wage, which would more than double existing levels. Nishio Suehiro, Socialist Party secretary general and labor representative, called the plan excessive, inflationary, and irresponsible. Tokuda and Ii, both also labor representatives on the CLRC, fell savagely on Nishio as a "traitor to the working class." The meeting nearly broke up right there. With the labor representatives, both Socialist and Communist,[48] against it, although for opposite reasons, and the government, too, the proposal was voted down in a flurry of declamations.

Finally, on January 29, Finance Minister Ishibashi, pushed by Suehiro, agreed to raise the wage level to 1,130 yen a month, roughly on a par with private industry and consequently awkward for Ii, Dobashi, and Iwama (of the

Teachers) to reject out of hand. But the resourceful Ii suddenly raised the question of income taxes on the wage increase. Ishibashi, he declared, was using a subterfuge to give the workers a raise with one hand and take it back with the other.[49] Ishibashi took the charge as a personal insult. "Go ahead and strike then," he snapped. The negotiations broke down. The next day each of the parties, Ishibashi, Ii, and Suehiro, went on government radio to defend his position, but it was too late. Time had just about run out.

To those tactics the nation's press responded with disfavor. The principal national dailies[50] denounced the strike in editorials and remained highly critical. The *Tokyo Shinbun* declared on January 27 that "if the government workers actually carry out their strike, this alone would be sufficient to bring certain ruin to Japan." A nation with an abiding faith in mediation and consensus had condemned the cabinet only two months before for rejecting a Central Labor Relations Committee mediation proposal in the electric power wages dispute. Now it condemned the union's recourse to force in the face of ongoing mediation.

The sixty-nine-year-old Prime Minister, Yoshida Shigeru, would not budge. He was no Satō Eisaku, eager to avoid trouble; quite the contrary.[51] If Tokuda were to overthrow the Cabinet, the Communists would actually have to pull off the strike. But SCAP was in the way. The third front had become, as it was bound to from the beginning, the most crucial.

Ii and the Labor Division

One thing the Communist strike leaders could not understand was Mac-Arthur's reluctance to issue an open directive. Many of them convinced themselves that there was a hidden weakness somewhere, that either a U.S. or a Far Eastern Commission directive forbade him to ban the general strike. Led by Ii, they descended on the Labor Division to probe for the soft spot and at the same time to try to trap us into publicly quotable statements supporting their position. In the week of January 22 to 28, Ii must have visited me at least once daily with different groups—well over a hundred persons in all—to prove to them that SCAP had not absolutely prohibited the strike.

After we discovered their lying handbill on January 25, it was pointless to try to convince Ii of the truth. I told Costantino that we had to shift our focus to the responsibility of the strike leaders for what might ensue. Every Japanese I had spoken with about the Pacific war since my arrival in the country had been bitter about General Tojo's irresponsibility—"insincerity," they called it—in dragging Japan into a war that he knew he could not win and thereby visiting enormous destruction on a hapless people. Now, if the Japanese labor movement faced a similar fate by triggering an American military response, I wanted the labor people to blame the Communists, not GHQ, General MacArthur, or the United States. Both Costantino and I spoke in that vein to the labor leaders who thronged my office. Ii and we were, of course, talking at cross purposes.[52]

Typically, I would start the meeting off asking whether the unions' replies to Marquat's warning of January 22 had been received, and Ii would reply, not yet. Then Ii would launch into a diatribe against the Japanese Government. Costantino and I refused to discuss the issues of the dispute; those were under mediation, we said. But when Ii accused the Yoshida government of not acting democratically, I charged him with acting like a fascist himself. He had repeatedly told us he needed to consult with his membership about Marquat's warning, and that was taking several days. Yet the Joint Struggle Committee had taken less than twenty-four hours to reject the government's 42 percent wage raise offer. Obviously, the committee had not consulted with its membership about that. Why was it afraid to ask its union members? Was it because its interests and those of the members differed? Did the leaders have an ulterior motive in pressing for the strike? It would all become known in the end, I warned. Were they not just sacrificing the workers? Was that the proper thing for labor leaders to do?

Ii denied it all. On the contrary, he declared, the strike leaders had nothing but the workers' welfare in mind. And they of all people understood the thinking and feeling of the masses best, for they themselves were of the masses, he said.

Ii never allowed the exchanges to become too heated, for he was determined to avoid a break with Labor Division—and with GHQ, for that matter. After all, whatever happened, General MacArthur and his Headquarters would still be in control of Japan afterward. And so he remained calm in face of my most scathing denunciations of his sincerity. He would pause to allow things to cool off, quietly assure me of his personal respect, hope that we would continue to help him in the future, thank Costantino for his efforts, and express his admiration for General MacArthur and his gratitude for food relief. When I accused him of acting like an enemy of the workers, he responded that it was a misunderstanding he could explain if I gave him the time. I said no explanation was needed; the facts spoke for themselves. He could see I was in a bad mood, he answered soothingly, and would come back later when my mood was better. I snapped back that I was always in a bad mood when workers were being sacrificed, and besides the issue was not my mood but his recklessness in exposing trade unions to the uncertainties of military action. Still, Ii retained his self-control.

Neither of us, obviously, would convince the other. But some of those who came with him may have been affected. After the affair was over, the Communists were met everywhere with charges of recklessness, and some of those who were most critical had been among the visitors to my office during that week. In any case, I became the first casualty of the strike with a severe and painful ear infection, contracted no doubt from the winter coughs, sneezes, and sniffles of my stream of union visitors that week. From January 29 till after February 1, I was in the hospital, on the sidelines.

THE STRIKE BAN

Of course, it really made no difference. The impasse was not a matter of personalities. By January 30, with the scheduled strike less than two days away, Marquat had still not received the All-Joint Struggle Committees' reply to his warning. He had the Labor Division summon the committee once again to his office. In the absence of General Marquat, who was late, and on his orders, the inexperienced Driggs Collett, Chief of the Labor Division Manpower Branch, presided at the start. Costantino, alert and silent, attended.[53] Collett began by reading Marquat's announcement that all the union leaders assembled were ordered immediately to send out messages to call off the strike, to use all available communications means to do so, and to bring GHQ the confirmations in six hours. He was soon, however, drawn into an argument when Ii asked him whether staggered strikes would be permitted instead of a simultaneous strike. Ii cited the Far Eastern Commission's "principles" and insisted that the strike was in furtherance of the Potsdam Declaration to remove obstacles to democratic tendencies. Collett was floundering when Marquat walked in. The discussion immediately ceased.

Marquat was blunt and brief. He represented MacArthur. His words expressed MacArthur's ideas. SCAP was taking no position on the wage issue. Marquat's statement of January 22, although oral, had nonetheless been official, and now it could be quoted. He was now again notifying the unions that they could not strike, that they had to call off the strike, and that they must bring GHQ copies of both their cancellation orders and confirmatory replies in six hours. (By then it was eight o'clock in the evening.) Union representatives would be held responsible for noncompliance. The leaders of unions that engaged in forcible strike actions would be arrested by the Occupation and tried in Occupation provost courts. (At this, Collett told me later, the strike leaders looked at each other uneasily.) Copies of dispatched strike cancellation orders and replies, however, would be considered in mitigation in sentencing if deposited in GHQ within six hours.

General Marquat brushed aside all attempts to discuss the issues further. When asked about staggered strikes, he replied the question was irrelevant. When asked by Ii what he meant by a forcible strike action, he said any strike action. When Ii said the strike ban was one-sided, Marquat asked why the strike cancellation orders had not been dispatched on January 22. His only palliative was a reassurance that the Supreme Commander still respected all of labor's rights, including those delineated by the Far Eastern Commission. When he asked the labor representatives which of them had sent out messages canceling the strike, the *Sōdōmei* leaders replied that they had. The *Sanbetsu* representatives, however, declared they had no authority to do so, for *Sanbetsu* was only a federation, and the Joint Struggle Committee was only a committee. Marquat snapped that if they had authority to call a strike, they had authority to cancel it. Then he got up and left.

Costantino, who had been quietly listening all the while, then summarized the situation. The six-hour deadline would expire at 2 A.M. They were losing time. When Ii, trying to maintain his relations with GHQ, said he trusted and believed Costantino and hoped he could call on him in the future, however, Costantino lost his calm. In all his years with labor, he retorted emotionally, he had never deceived the workers, but those who were now defying the strike ban were doing so, secretly stabbing the Japanese workers in the back. The meeting was over.[54]

No new union instructions to call off the strike went out. The Joint Struggle Committee returned to a strike headquarters buzzing with wild rumors about the composition of the coming "people's government."[55]

Instead of complying with Marquat's demands, the Joint Struggle Committee scurried about on other errands. After an abortive visit to GHQ late that night,[56] Ii received word of a summons to go to a Central Labor Relations Committee bargaining session with Prime Minister Yoshida at Yoshida's official residence. But when he and the others rushed over there on foot from GHQ, they found Dr. Suehiro and some CLRC members but no one on the government side except for some Diet guards. Frustrated but fired up with excitement and vitamin shots,[57] Ii and a few hundred supporters marched in front of the deserted Diet Building in the early morning "ghost" hours, defiantly singing "The Internationale" to the cold, dark, and empty streets. It was a strange prelude to a revolution, or even to a general strike.

Daybreak of January 31 came without even one additional strike cancellation delivered to GHQ. The result was not entirely unexpected. Military contingency planning was under way in the Far East Command part of GHQ. In ESS, Colonel Ryder, the Section Executive Officer, hurriedly put together a memo on the economic consequences of a general strike and what to do about it.[58] The memo was sketchy and not altogether accurate,[59] but even after discounting the occasional errors, the picture was grim. The Japanese economy did not have the margin of strength to absorb a general strike. When Marquat went up to see General MacArthur that morning of January 31, he brought with him the report and the inescapable conclusion that there was no time to lose.

Immediately after MacArthur's usual 10:30 A.M. arrival at his office, Marquat was there to brief him. MacArthur then got busy on a public statement. At 2:30 that afternoon his Press Relations Office issued it to the newspapers and the radio. At last it was open and official. "Under the authority vested in me as the Supreme Commander for the Allied Powers, I have informed the labor leaders whose unions have federated for the purpose of conducting a general strike that I will not permit the use of so deadly a social weapon in the present impoverished and emaciated condition of Japan and have accordingly directed them to desist from the furtherance of such action.''

To a tense and frightened general public, MacArthur's statement brought electrifying relief. Swarms of newsboys with their clanging bells ran through the streets hawking the extras, and the radio blared forth the tidings. It seemed to the people everywhere that the Supreme Commander, after giving the Japanese every chance to settle their own affairs, had intervened at the last moment to save them from themselves. It was brilliant political theater, if not exactly true, for MacArthur had actually been trying to stop the strike for two weeks. The order, however, came only at the last possible moment, nine and one-half hours before the scheduled strike start. Would there be enough time? Could a frontal clash be averted? It seemed at the least that unpleasant American–Japanese incidents could not be wholly prevented. Someone, somewhere, probably would not get the word.

Within half an hour, the statement reached the Joint Struggle Committee headquarters in the Central Labor College Building in Shiba Park. Despite nine days of the clearest warnings, it arrived with the impact of a bomb.[60] Several people urged Tokuda to flee, for according to reports two truckloads of MPs were coming to arrest the strike leaders. Tokuda's reaction, according to Ii, was a nervous ''Is that so?'' Suzuki hurriedly got up and left. The weary and excited Ii had just completed, together with his staff, his strike dispositions, and especially those of the Youth Action Corps. One YAC detachment, assigned to headquarters, had only that morning repulsed an ''attack,'' that is, an antistrike demonstration, by some out-of-town workers. News correspondents wandered throughout the strike offices, urgently questioning everyone they could catch for the latest story. The atmosphere was hectic.

Tokuda did more than say, ''Is that so?'' He immediately instructed Hasegawa Kō[61] to contact all the Communist members of the All-Joint Struggle Committee for their best estimate as to whether they could hold the membership in line for a strike in defiance of MacArthur. Two hours later, hours filled with frantic telephone calls and rushing messengers, Hasegawa reported back to the boss: They could not. Without hesitation, Tokuda instructed Hasegawa to tell Ii the strike was off.

WINDING DOWN

At just about the same time, several uniformed Nisei from Japanese Liaison of G-2 appeared at the Joint Struggle Committee headquarters with a list of committee members wanted at General Marquat's office. Ii's name was on the list, but he tarried, arguing with Tokuda privately and vehemently. Ii insisted that the strike go ahead even if he and others were arrested. Other Communists joined in, Suzuki Katsuo of the Engine Drivers on Ii's side and Hasegawa Kō on Tokuda's. But Tokuda drew Ii downstairs, Ii expostulating and Hasegawa behind them listening, to the old black party car. Both Tokuda and Ii entered the vehicle for the trip to GHQ, Ii still objecting. By the time they arrived some five minutes later Ii had accepted Tokuda's order. Tokuda, Hasegawa said later, had put it as a matter of "party discipline," and Ii had to comply.[62] He could defy the Supreme Commander for the Allied Powers, but not the Communist Party.

Always more realistic than his wrought-up followers, Tokuda was quite prepared to draw back from the brink at the last moment. (Had he not sought a last-minute settlement with Satō rather than go ahead with a national railway strike?) All the party's gains and the complex organization it had constructed since the war could be destroyed in short order if the Occupation Army crushed the strike and put the Communist Party leaders back in jail. But Ii was completely committed emotionally. His revered mentor had told him to reverse course, to exchange audacity for prudence, but the change was too drastic, leaving the strike commander frustrated and despondent.

The confrontation between Marquat and the dozen or so strike leaders who had been summoned to his office is clear in its main outlines.[63] The general, impatient and ready for drastic action if necessary, interviewed the leaders individually in different rooms. From them he secured pledges of compliance and had three of the top leaders write out drafts of radio broadcasts canceling the strike. The radio was the fastest and probably the only way of reaching the millions poised to strike. The statements were translated into English, typed, and submitted for Marquat's approval, after which the selected leaders were transported to Radio Tokyo seven blocks away by jeep and put on the air to read their statements. Then they were free to leave. Marquat could then report to MacArthur that the job had been accomplished.

The three leaders' statements were made on Japanese radio like clockwork, Ii at 9:21 P.M., Dobashi of the Communications Workers at four minutes after ten, and Suzuki of the Railway Workers at 10:33. In his broadcast, Ii said MacArthur's order was one-sided and that he did not understand it. Suzuki simply regretted it. All three bitterly criticized the Japanese Government, with Suzuki pledging to continue to try to overthrow it. Ii thanked the "Allied Powers," presumably including Russia, for their food aid. He ended with the slogan "One step backward, two steps forward!" used by Lenin (also, incidentally, by the Japanese military high command in reporting defeats in the last war) and with a "Banzai!" for the workers and farmers of Japan. But none of that mattered as far as Marquat was concerned. Each statement had included an unequivocal order to abandon the strike, and that was enough. The general strike was over before it had begun.

Ii immediately went over to strike headquarters to report to the Joint Struggle Committee, its staff swollen by hundreds of last-minute strike workers, but the meeting was an anticlimax. His dejected audience had already heard the news over the radio. Ii could not conceal his tears.[64] GHQ had "said to us," he told the disconsolate crowd, "'If you fellows don't stop, the labor movement will be destroyed. The unions will die!'" Marquat had warned, he added, that GHQ repression of the strike would leave the Japanese with only puppet unions. Once again he concluded: "One step backward, two steps forward!"

The Aftermath

It did not quite work out that way, at least for the Communists. To everyone's relief, the leaders snuffed out their 6-million-worker strike as though it were a candle, with no sparks and no untoward incidents, a witness to the efficiency of their control organization. Otherwise Communist prestige plummeted. The government workers' wage dispute was settled quietly three weeks later at a 1,200-yen average monthly wage, exactly what mediators Suehiro and Nakayama had proposed on January 29 and what Finance Minister Ishibashi had come so close to accepting when Tokuda and Ii torpedoed the plan. Driving the country to the brink of disaster in the succeeding days, the Communists had gained the workers nothing.

A storm of public criticism broke around their ears. One typical comment bitterly accused the JCP leaders of being "megalomaniacs" who "believed in strike for strike's sake."[65] Some newspapers and public figures apologized to General MacArthur in terms reminiscent of those used until then only for the Emperor. "We regret very much," the *Mainichi* of February 1, 1947, wrote "that we have had to trouble the Supreme Commander to avert the grave disaster that was sure to follow." MacArthur emerged the hero, as the Communists came out of the affair the villains.

The April 1947 Diet elections, less than three months later, provide one measure. With a tenfold increase in party membership since the April 1946 elections, the Communists had looked forward confidently to at least twenty seats in the House of Representatives. They ended up with only four, a loss of one. Their share of the popular vote remained slightly below 4 percent. All of the tumult of the past year had brought them no electoral progress whatever. Their proletarian rivals, the Socialists, in contrast, increased their vote share from 18 to 26 percent, and their Diet representation from 93 to 143, becoming the largest political party in the nation[66] and winning the Prime Minister's post as well. But then, in the end, they had disassociated themselves from the general strike.

In the trade unions, too, the Communists lost ground. A week after the general strike fizzle, when *Sanbetsu* confidently proposed a merger with *Sōdōmei''* to fight the coming capitalist onslaught,'' *Sōdōmei* angrily demanded an investigation of the Communists' irresponsible conduct in fomenting the general strike. Criticism welled up from white-collar employees and union intellectuals as to the Communists' dictatorial methods, particularly those of the Youth Action Corps. After the devastating April election, the *Sanbetsu* called for a series of ''self-criticism'' meetings. It was their clearest admission that something had gone wrong.

Held for five days in May, the meetings were a whitewash.[67] It was no wonder that *Sanbetsu* started sliding down hill; its leaders were seriously out of touch with their erstwhile followers. A substantial number of local unions[68] withdrew from the federation. Dissident railway workers founded an anti-Communist Democratization League, which rapidly spread to Dobashi's Communications Union and even to *Sanbetsu* headquarters. Hosoya Matsuta, the leader of the ''October Offensive,'' defected from the Communist Party and aligned himself with the new league. In time the league, by then augmented by large sections of former Communist bastions like the Teachers and Electric Power Workers, left the *Sanbetsu* and organized a New *Sanbetsu*. As it turned out, neither the old nor the new had much future.

The leaders of the general strike drive fared poorly, too. The Communists were badly defeated in the December 1947 Government Railway Workers' Federation elections, and Ii became a party functionary. Hasegawa split with a ''Tokuda-less'' party in the early 1960s because it had become too bureaucratic and deskbound. Tokuda and Itō Ritsu, who had commanded the YAC during January 1947, were both purged by General MacArthur in May 1950. When the Korean War broke out in June, both went underground, eventually fleeing, although SCAP was not chasing them, to Communist China. Itō did not return until September 3, 1980, a sick man. He had spent ten of his thirty years in China in prison. Tokuda, Japan's greatest modern revolutionary, never came back at all. He died in China in the mid-1950s, a stranger in a strange land.

There were changes in GHQ as well. Americans at home were surprised at the sudden disclosure of trouble in General MacArthur's domain, but no one called him a strikebreaker. The newspaper publishers and editors who happened to be in Japan at the time were confronted with a totally unexpected and dangerous national crisis in a country that they had understood to be tranquil. Roy Howard, the most eminent, turned for an explanation to his bureau chief, Miles Vaughn, an ''old Japan hand'' from before the war with excellent contacts among disaffected Japanese big business and the old guard. Those elements, many of whom were in the process of being purged, unsurprisingly blamed the radicals in SCAP, among whom they included prominently Costantino and me. Vaughn had never once in his tour in Japan visited the Labor Division or sought to interview me. When Howard, who fancied himself a Republican kingmaker, went up to see General MacArthur, he pressed the General on "radicals" in key positions. Dramatically he told MacArthur that as long as radicals like me remained in our posts, the General could not hope to get the support of the Scripps-Howard newspapers for the presidency. MacArthur according to General Marquat,[69] dug in his heels. He refused to accept pressure about his aides. He regarded mutual loyalty as one of the cardinal virtues. Moreover, knowing the facts, he could not fathom what was behind the attack. He was to say, when I finally said my farewells to him three and a half years later, "Who's been out to get you, Ted?"

In any event, MacArthur's solution was to wait a few months, then transfer Costantino to a post in the Army's Judge Advocate's Office, where he could use his legal training, and to promote me to the post of Economic Adviser and Special Assistant to General Marquat. As my successor he chose James Killen, whom I had just recently secured as my trade union adviser. Killen was a union man, a vice president of the Paper, Pulp, and Sulfite Workers Union who had been sent to Japan by the AFL with President William Green's personal approval.

That solution was eminently satisfactory to me. I had always expected that in such a hot spot as Chief of the Labor Division, with the duty of encouraging labor unions and permitting strikes, I was bound to engender plenty of hostility. The fact that I was young, a civilian without a power base, and a New York Jew, hence presumed to be a radical by many of the Regular Army brass whose origin was small-town and Southern, could not help. One summer night in 1946, working late, I confided to Costantino that in the circumstances I had the choice of being ultra-cautious and keeping my job or, if I really tried to do the job right, eventually getting fired. Unmarried and with no responsibilities, I tried to do the job right. I gave myself twelve months then, and I lasted sixteen. I was succeeded by a man I was sure would maintain the integrity of the labor policies I had so far followed. In my sixteen months I had seen the firm establishment of labor rights and the growth of a multimillion-member democratic labor movement. I was in complete agreement with MacArthur's judgment that I was by then a political liability in my labor job, and I was anxious to get on to something wider and more varied.

The general strike that never took place was nevertheless a watershed in the Occupation, particularly in Japan's developing response to the democratization pressures applied by America. It was the high-water mark of extremism. Until then almost anything, no matter how helter-skelter, that promised to "democratize" the country was welcomed. But the traumatic experience of being hustled helplessly to the precipice in the name of the workers and the dramatic last-minute rescue by General MacArthur completely transformed the national mood. Suddenly, the Japanese people again became conscious of the need for limits.

Part V

THE LIMITS OF

DEMOCRATIZATION

ON RETURNING to Tokyo from Shanghai after a brief visit early in 1949, I was struck by the slow gait of the Japanese pedestrians in the city streets. It was something I had never noticed before. The Japanese had always seemed to be walking fast enough. But in comparison with the frenetic pace of the Chinese I had just left, rushing about constantly to keep up with a runaway inflation of 10 percent daily while nervously watching for the imminent entry of the approaching Communist armies, the Japanese seemed settled, even stolid. And then it hit me. Life in Japan had become normal.

Normality, of course, is relative. As Mort Sahl's bank teller replied to the holdup man who told him to turn over the money and act normally, "Please define your terms." I define normality in this context as a national return to day-to-day living with the assurance that life would go on pretty much as the day before, that the rules governing people's conduct and activities would not suddenly be changed from outside. Beginning with mid-1947, Japan entered a period of such social stability, permitting and even expecting change, but not turmoil, upheaval, or convulsions.

After two years, the long series of democratization shocks was close to its end; democratization was reaching its limits. "The pattern has been etched, the path laid," General MacArthur declared in a New Year's message to the Japanese people. "The development now lies in your hands."[1] The second phase of the Occupation had begun, and with it a new latitude for the Japanese people in defining the third turn in their history.

301

16

A Kind of Normality

SCAP CONSOLIDATES HIS REFORMS

WITH THE COLLAPSE OF the general strike, followed by the April 1947 Diet elections, an unexpected calm fell upon Japan. Ever since the end of the war, the people had been living in the midst of uncertainties, both personal and national. Their apprehensions had climaxed in what appeared to be a mass attack on the foundations of civilized life. But when the assault crumbled public tensions relaxed, and the country heaved a huge sigh of relief. Things after all were not so bad. Mass starvation no longer threatened, and industry had begun to revive. Also spring had come. It was time to take a longer and more reflective view. Like the Chūō line train traveling from the Niigata snow country to the mild Kantō plain, once the mountain tunnels were passed, the storms were left behind.

That is not to say that living problems, and serious ones too, did not remain. The letters to the editor column in the leading newspapers and magazines told of constant frustrations and anxieties. One letter to *Fujin* (*Women*) in August of 1947 told of such a shortage of firewood for cooking that a mother instructed her first-grade son to follow the wood-burning buses on his way home from school and pick up the chips that fell from the burner woodboxes. Another letter from a housewife[1] recounted how she was arising at four thirty in the morning to do the washing and prepare her husband's breakfast of *o-kaiyu* (rice gruel)—*go-han* (steamed rice) was just too scarce to be served straight—but her husband was getting thinner every day. A third, also sent to *Fujin*, lamented, "We by no means seek luxury and easy living, but we cannot stand the life of lower animals which is ours at present. We are clad in rags and from morning to night we must hunt for our food. We want at least time and ease of mind to watch our children grow." In a school composition, one little girl whose family was homeless envied the snail "because he carries his house with him."[2]

303

AFTER TWO YEARS

Indeed, the crying need was for even the smallest dwelling where a family could live independently. Two years after the last air raid, a prime qualification in a marriage partner, according to the *nakōdo* marriage brokers, was having a room the couple could share. Simple frame dwellings were springing up on burnt-out lots at the rate of 200,000 a year officially[3] and many more unofficially, but well over 2 million had been destroyed in the war.[4] And then there were the 7 million repatriates, many of whom no longer had homes, or burnt-out lots, or even relatives with whom to take refuge.

The passageways in Ueno Station had lost almost all their nightly residents, but packing crates in the devastated areas around Ikebukuro Station were still serving as home for thousands. One repatriate family living there comprised eight brothers and sisters and an ailing mother—the father was a prisoner of the Russians—and the twenty-three-year-old eldest sister, formerly concertmaster and first violinist of the Manchuria Philharmonic Orchestra, supported them all by playing dinner music for the officers billeted in the Imperial Hotel where I lived. Most of the repatriates' lives were tragic, but the unrepatriated caused their families even more pain.

The most pervasive sorrow, in fact, was that of the Japanese whose husbands, fathers, or sons, 400,000 in all, were missing in Siberia, presumably being held as prisoners two years after a war had that lasted barely a week. (By way of comparison, 510,000 Japanese fell in the entire eight years of the Greater East Asia War.)[5] Popular music reflected their longing. The Slavic-sounding "Khabarovsk" and the nostalgic melody of "Hills of a Strange Country" ("the day I come home, then only will spring come") were at the top of "the charts." Not until 1949 did the 90,000 who actually did return finally make it.

The face of the cities seemed to reflect the new mood, discarding that bombed-out look. In the second spring of occupation almost all the marks of wartime destruction in the cities were covered by kindly foliage. Government officials talked grandly of taking advantage of the devastation this time—unlike the haphazard rebuilding of Tokyo after the Great Earthquake in 1923—to plan rational cities with broad boulevards, squares, and circles. Unfortunately, there were no funds, and individual families, unable to wait for shelter, simply built their own structures out of whatever lumber they could find in the same haphazard manner as before.

In the Asakusa amusement-cum-shopping area (where some 75,000 people had perished in a single air raid in 1945), dozens of temporary stalls selling used clothing and military attire were set up every morning and dismantled every evening near the provisional temple of Kannon, Goddess of Mercy and patron saint of travelers. Every week there seemed to be a few more of them. Amputee veterans in their white cotton kimonos and khaki army caps still appeared quietly awaiting handouts on the shopping walk leading to the temple. But one also saw small bands of ambitious young musicians and singers gradually appearing in the open spaces before the temple, rendering the latest tunes of the day with verve and the assistance of electronic amplifiers. They were looking forward, not back, to normality.

Even personal conveyances reappeared on the city streets. There were still no private autos, of course, but in place of the "one-yen taxi," which had disappeared, and whose price at least was never to return, a new hybrid vehicle—a union of bicycle and rikisha—became available. Early in January 1947, Ōzu Kinnosuke, the notorious gangster boss of Tokyo's Shinjuku *tekiya* street stall keepers—he had endeared himself to me by wearing a stiff formal collar and tie with no shirt over his long underwear—inaugurated the operation of a fleet of those "pedicabs." The cyclists, Ōzu told the newspapers, were repatriates, recruited as part of his plan to relieve unemployment. His emulators were legion, and the pedicab became the characteristic form of personal public transport in Japanese cities from 1947 to 1950. But the way of the innovator is sometimes hard. Before the year was out, Ōzu was languishing in jail, his rackets smashed, and his gang in disarray. Police hounding of gangsters is also part of normality.

As the Japanese tried to pick up the threads of their private lives once more, a certain degree of tranquility descended on their political life as well. Overt strike and strident confrontation subsided after the Socialists replaced the Liberals at the helm of government in April 1947.[6] More reasonable and less pugnacious than their Communist rivals, who had been discredited by their general strike and election failures, the Socialists now represented the economically dissatisfied. The new prime minister, Katayama Tetsu, was a mild, conciliatory gentleman, unlike his feisty predecessor. He was, moreover, a Christian, a Presbyterian to be exact, a fact that moved General MacArthur to remark on the new Christian era in the Far East, which now featured three Christian heads of government: Katayama, China's Methodist Chiang Kai-shek, and the Philippines' Catholic Manuel Roxas.[7]

The new prime minister could respond, as though on cue, by informing his people that "government in the future must be guided by a Christian spirit of morality" and "permeated by a spirit of Christian love and humanism."[8] Still, it was questionable how Christianity's new Oriental blossom could seriously affect a nation of Shintō-Buddhists, for Japan had at most a million or so Christians and only 300,000 church members.[9] In fact, Japan was guided by the preachments of a more temporal ruler. In the spring of 1947 General MacArthur, deeply affected by the experience of the general strike turmoil, decided it was time to consolidate the momentous democratic reforms he and his men had wrought so far.

The near-catastrophe of the "two-one" general strike had impressed on him as perhaps nothing else could the urgency of ameliorating the workers' distress that had given extremists the lever they needed to upset the social order.

The Occupation, having provided the democratization circuses, now had to provide bread or risk imperiling public peace and disillusioning the Japanese people. One could not build a free, democratic order on a foundation of destitution.

Just one week after he forbade the general strike, MacArthur had written Prime Minister Yoshida that the time had come for new elections. "Momentous changes" had occurred since the last general election, he said,[10] and also, although he did not say so openly, events had thrown the popular mandate of the conservative cabinet into doubt. A month and a half later, he overruled the conservatives' resistance to direct economic controls as well. On March 22, 1947, he signed an ESS-prepared letter directing the prime minister to institute integrated controls across the board over the economy.[11] "So long as your needs continue to be greater than your productive capacity," MacArthur told the Japanese people in justification of his action, "controls upon your internal economy will be essential lest the weaker elements of your population perish."[12] From March on, control and management of the Japanese economy joined democratization as the top priority of the Occupation.

Indeed, as time passed, economic control exceeded democratization in importance. The democratization drive continued, but its momentum fell off, as though the democratization mainspring, tightly wound in Washington and released by MacArthur on his arrival in Japan, was now winding down. True, in July SCAP ordered the dissolution of the Mitsui and Mitsubishi trading companies[13] and in September the decentralization of the police force to strengthen popular local government.[14] But then our Antitrust Division had taken no important initiatives in the six months from October 1946 through March 1947, when it had no regular chief, and police decentralization had been recommended as early as June 7, 1946, by SCAP adviser Lewis J. Valentine, former New York City Police Commissioner. Only General Willoughby's determined opposition had stalled the police reform for so long, until finally General Whitney, egged on by a persistent Colonel Kades, appealed to General MacArthur to let Government Section handle it instead.

CHANGE IN OCCUPATION POLICY

In general, brand new SCAP-sponsored democratization initiatives were few. Of the five principal new reform efforts that followed General MacArthur's March 22 letter, GHQ initiated only two, the "de-feudalization" of the Japanese bureaucracy and the deconcentration of big business. The first was the product of an advisory commission that reached the shores of Japan in the fall of 1946, while the second emanated from another advisory commission that arrived even earlier, in January 1946. Rightly speaking, the thrust of both derived from an earlier era. The attempts to nationalize the coal mines, socialize distribution channels, and recover the vast government-owned military stores left over from the war from the private, usually big-business, hands into which they had fallen were all initiated by the Japanese. By the middle of 1947, SCAP, still fiercely protective of democracy, was sated with democratization.

That did not in the slightest, however, mean abandoning any of the democratic achievements of which MacArthur was so proud, or even relaxing the progressive implementation of democratic reforms already set in motion. It was not until December 1947 that the Diet finally enacted the revised Criminal Code, which, incidentally, abolished the crime of adultery, legally applicable only to women before the war, because it was sexually one-sided. The final application of the revised Code of Criminal Procedure with its provision for the right of *habeas corpus* had to wait until July 1948, almost three years after the war's end. The village land committees began their redistribution of farm plots in the latter part of 1947 and continued well into 1949.

And so it was with a number of other reform programs. The only diminution of democracy was the 1948 cancellation of government workers' collective bargaining rights. In spite of the controversy about the economic deconcentration program, no SCAP measure, once actually effected—for example, the dissolution of the Mitsui and Mitsubishi trading companies—was ever rescinded during the life of the Occupation.

Later on, in 1949 and 1950, Washington forgot about democratic reform in its effort to rebuild Japan along standard Marshall Plan lines, but that was not true of 1947 and 1948, and it was never true of MacArthur. Still, it is not surprising that Japanese who followed Occupation activities from the outside telescoped the second Occupation phase, that of 1947–48, and the third of 1949–50 into one and mistakenly concluded that SCAP had "reversed his course" in 1947.

Indeed, in later years some Japanese academics, contemplating the "big picture" in hindsight, would attribute the "reversal" to the intensifying "cold war" and new American strategic interests. They propounded a highly plausible scenario for the years 1947 and 1948 in which the United States, having purposely weakened Japan as a future rival by means of a sweeping democratization in 1945 and 1946, then had to reverse its course and build up Japan economically as an ally against the Soviets and world communism. That view reduced American motives to the most narrowly selfish and hence the most readily understandable to the public at large. The proposition was particularly believable because so much about it was true, even if its central conclusion was not. The "cold war" did intensify; SCAP-sponsored democratization did peter out; and the United States did support the revival of the Japanese economy. Insofar as Washington was concerned, the analysis may have fairly summed up what happened. But in 1947 and almost all of 1948, the Washington agencies did not control Japan.

MacArthur and his staff did. And to those of us on the ground in GHQ, that was not what happened at all. The scenario was just too cynical, and too simple besides.

First, the chronology, and hence the sequence of cause and effect, was all wrong. MacArthur was fighting his sector of the cold war as early as spring 1946 in the Allied Council for Japan when the SCAP reform wave was at its height. Second, he never accepted the argument that his democratic reforms weakened the country. Most such allegations he put down to special pleading by those whose personal interests were adversely affected by one or another democratization measure. Third, when it came to fighting communism and the Soviets, MacArthur felt that democracy was an essential element of Western strength, a weapon in the battle, not an encumbrance. Finally, with the one exception noted, MacArthur never reversed his democratization accomplishments.

Perhaps the best example of how democracy fitted into the cold war in MacArthur's conception was the Allied Council session of July 10, 1946, when General Derevyanko, the Soviet member, challenged the Occupation labor program. As GHQ Labor Chief, I was called upon to help refute the charges, but instead of a factual report, the American chairman, George Atcheson, launched a blistering attack on Soviet labor practices at home. Were industrial strikes permitted in the U.S.S.R.? Was full freedom of labor unions guaranteed there? Were daily working hours set at eight? I was not surprised. Before breakfast that morning Atcheson and I had gone over the strategy for the coming session as MacArthur had dictated it to him the night before. Derevyanko was nonplused, unaccustomed to being interrogated publicly on Soviet domestic shortcomings, which surely were outside the ACJ's jurisdiction, and could only manage an invitation to Atcheson to visit the Soviet Union and see for himself.

Back home, the State Department's Hugh Borton, Chief of the Japan Division; Llewellyn ("Tommy") Thompson, Chief of the East European Division; and Brigadier General Frank McCoy, Chairman of the Far Eastern Commission, looking at MacArthur's action from a different vantage point, shuddered. "The world [has] been treated to a series of public demonstrations of name-calling ill-befitting an international body," Borton complained in a secret memo to his boss, John Carter Vincent.[15] In Tokyo, however, MacArthur had made his point: Who were the Soviets, with their sorry labor record, to question a democratic labor program? And those were the headlines he got the next day. Democracy was a weapon, and he would not allow the U.S.S.R. hypocritically to appropriate it. Abandoning democracy to fight a cold war "better" was incomprehensible to the General.

Indeed, it was not that the Occupation had reversed its course, but rather that the original democratic impulse, JCS 1380/15, the overall directive to MacArthur, was close to exhaustion. That was inevitable. Long as its list of mandated reforms was, it was not infinite. MacArthur, moreover, had a dread of long occupations. "History points out the unmistakable lesson that military occupations serve their purpose at best for only a limited time, after which a deterioration rapidly sets in," he once told Congress,[16] and accordingly he set about headlong to accomplish the directed reforms as soon as possible. (Perhaps he also wanted to be free to return to the States before the 1948 presidential campaign.) By mid-1947 most of the democratization projects had been accomplished insofar as SCAP was concerned, and all had at least been started. No one in GHQ visualized democratization as an endless process. Least of all did anyone there assume, as the Japanese "progressive elements" thought, that socialism was the next logical step. It was time for the Occupation to consolidate its achievements prior to an early exit.

DOMESTIC POLITICAL CHANGE IN THE UNITED STATES

Binding as Washington's JCS 1380/15 directive was, and overwhelming as MacArthur himself was, they were not the only democratization impulses in GHQ. In 1945 and 1946 a strong complementary impulse had developed among those dedicated staff officers in the theater who sought always to improve the implementation of their reform missions and who produced even more detailed directives and guidance for the Japanese. Now that impulse, too, was declining, not because of the cold war. It was rather the natural result of a drastically changed political climate back home, particularly with the November 1946 U.S. congressional elections.

The foreign policy of any nation is largely a function of its domestic politics, and foreigners have found it notoriously difficult to comprehend the impact of domestic developments in the United States on themselves and their countries. In a military occupation with controlled communications channels, it was even harder. The Japanese people, consequently, never became aware that the 1946 elections constituted a psychological watershed. For the first time since 1932, the Republicans and their Southern Democratic political allies decisively defeated the New Dealers. Labor was rejected. Business was in the saddle. The Occupation authorities now had to defend their requests for funds for Japan before a Republican Ways and Means Committee in the House and the equally conservative Appropriations Committee in the Senate, and neither of those groups was partial to reform crusades in the United States or elsewhere.

More fundamentally, the election returns shook the certainties of JCS 1380/15. Conservative visitors to General MacArthur, like the publishers Roy Howard in February 1947 and Colonel Robert McCormick of the *Chicago Tribune* in November, wanted to know what we were doing pursuing New Dealish policies in Japan when the American people had decisively rejected them at home. Even nonpolitical officers who had lived outside their country for years because of the war and the Occupation—MacArthur himself had not been back in the States for almost ten years—still liked to know which way the wind was blowing, and the 1946 election returns told them. Those who were not so nonpolitical whooped with joy.

The conservative climate intensified as the 1948 elections drew nearer. Several months before that event, one former Navy commander, now a civilian industrial coordinator, was regularly intoning that "on the first Tuesday after the first Monday in November everything is going to be changed," after which he glared significantly at his intimidated audience. Reforms and reformers lost prestige and even respectability, while many of the Headquarters brass cozied up to GHQ civilians with big business connections.

As it was, the changing nature of SCAP interests and responsibilities—the efficient management of an economy was different from instituting a radical reform and called for different temperaments—had brought conservative elements to the fore anyway. Officers implementing social reforms had thought in terms of ideals; those now in demand thought in terms of practicalities. GHQ's friends and collaborators among the Japanese changed too. At the beginning the Americans felt kindly toward the suppressed victims of the militarist regime—workers, peasants, liberals, silenced intellectuals, and imprisoned radicals—but did not extend their tolerance and understanding to Japanese businessmen, who were presumed to have been willing cogs in the war machine. After mid-1947, however, SCAP officials began to see their many practical problems through the eyes of Japanese industrialists and bankers. Increasingly, General Marquat, the ESS Chief, found himself talking about letters of credit, not reform projects, with businessmen in his section, some intending to return to private business and some on leave from big corporations. Business terminology flourished. ESS officials talked of doing something "by the close of business Thursday," as though GHQ were really in business, and words like "bankable" and "prudent" gained in favor at the expense of "democratic." It may have been a kind of exhibitionism, too. But the change in GHQ vocabulary was also a sign of GHQ's changed mood.

Finally, with the 1948 elections coming up, American domestic politics reached out to Japan. MacArthur came under much closer scrutiny from the would-be kingmakers in the Republican party. Following attacks on the "New Dealers" in GHQ in the American press and on the Senate floor, a troubled Henry Luce sent a series of urgent cables at the end of 1947 to his man on the spot, the *Time–Life* correspondent Carl Mydans, asking him for rundowns on reputed SCAP radicals. An apologetic Mydans dutifully interviewed them in confidence and sent back reassuring cables about most of the "accused," including me. Inevitably word of his inquiries got around and intensified the new GHQ suspicion of reformers. Which of them were really hidden radicals? In the summer of 1948, when Thomas E. Dewey seemed a shoo-in, his staff compiled a hit list of SCAP "New Dealers" to be fired when their man was elected. As I later found out, I was on the list. Their inquiries, although perhaps not their purpose, could not be kept secret. The resultant pall of uncertainty could not but dispirit the GHQ reformers.

Meanwhile, the Japanese moved in the opposite direction. In one of history's small ironies, just as SCAP democratization impulses dwindled, the first leftist-led government in the annals of Japan took office. The relative positions of the two parties were now reversed. Where SCAP had had continually to push the government into sometimes unwelcome reforms, now the Socialists were eager to "democratize" in their fashion, and SCAP was the reluctant party.

THE SOCIALISTS AND GHQ

One could very well have expected conflict or at best strained relations between a Headquarters sated with democratization and steadily being pushed from the outside into more conservative positions and a government whose prime minister cheerfully announced he was going to nationalize basic industry.[17] The reality, surprisingly, turned out to be the opposite. To begin with, General MacArthur was determined to cooperate with whatever cabinet emerged from the April elections as his seal of faith in Japanese parliamentary democracy. For their part, the Socialists, new to the corridors of power and the machinery of office, were eager to get any help they could from their friends, and fundamentally they still viewed the Occupation as friends.

It had been different with their predecessors. As General Whitney later put it, the Japanese conservative leaders, "accustomed as they had been all their lives to ordering the affairs of their country pretty much their own way, found it extremely difficult to be elastic" in their dealings with SCAP's staff.[18] In our own section, the Economic and Scientific, we had had to deal with the headstrong stubbornness of ministers like Ishibashi Tanzan and Zen Keinosuke.[19] The new Socialist officials were exactly the reverse. They came to GHQ brimming with amiability and good will.

There was a personal element too, for many of the new Socialist government leaders were undeniably attractive personalities. Tsuru Shigeto, the Deputy to the Director General of the Economic Stabilization Board and a brilliant economist, had graduated from Harvard in 1935 and then lectured there. He and Sherwood Fine, General Marquat's economic adviser and a Columbia University Ph.D. in economics, spoke the same language. Other Socialists were clearly men of principle and strong character. Among the leaders who had been jailed for their convictions were Katō Kanjū, in and out of prison since 1937 for his antimilitarist activities; Education Minister Morito Tatsuo, incarcerated for a magazine article on the anarchist Prince Kropotkin; Wada Hiroo, the ESB Director-General, a member of General Suzuki Teiichi's Wartime Planning Board from 1944, but who had spent the preceding three years, from 1941 to 1944, in solitary confinement as a suspected radical; and Mizutani Chōsaburō, the new Commerce and Industry Minister, who had long been the most notable civil liberties lawyer in the country, bravely defending a long list of student, labor, and intellectual dissidents. One had to respect such people, even if one did not agree with their ideology.

But the most compelling reason the two groups, the American military and the Japanese Socialists, got along so famously was that, whatever their outlook or ultimate goals, they agreed on what had to be done immediately: first, use Japan's meager resources more effectively and, second, redress the current inequality of postwar sacrifice among the people. And both insisted that direct government controls be used. Their consequent partnership was, in large part, a marriage of convenience.

To MacArthur and his men, there was no question but that such measures were imperative to consolidate his historic democratic reform structure. Moreover, the new measures should help convince the economy-minded Eightieth Congress that the Japanese were worthy of American aid. More efficient use of Japanese food and production and more equitable distribution would attest to the depth of the Japanese commitment.

Meanwhile the GHQ monetarists who favored reducing the money supply were swamped by events. The government workers' February wage settlement, which followed the aborted general strike, suddenly added more than 20 billion yen annually to expenditures. (The 1946–47 general account, that is, all government expenditures other than the government enterprises, had amounted to only 119 billion yen in all.) The costs of the Occupation Forces in the new budgetary year rose by 25 billion yen (from 46 to 71 billion). There was now no hope of damming the flood of new money. The 1947–48 budget dropped even further out of balance—only 58 percent of the expenditures were matched by revenues[20]— and the Bank of Japan note issue soared by 134 percent during 1947.[21]

All that was left was direct control of basic commodities. The MacArthur letter of March 22, drafted by ESS, dutifully talked of ''sound public finance'' along with all the other measures needed to rein in inflation. But it was the Economic Stabilization Board alone—not the Finance Ministry or even Finance and ESB together—that the Supreme Commander designated to develop and carry out ''the integrated series of economic and financial controls which the current situation demands.'' After more than a year of internal disagreement in ESS, SCAP for the time being had come down on the side of the direct controllers. The Socialists, whose idea of a good economy was a controlled economy anyway, couldn't have agreed more wholeheartedly.

There was more on their part than ideology. True, they wanted to start the socialization process as quickly as possible, but that was only one-third of their

1947 program. Their constituents, the distressed workers, urgently demanded a better deal, and for them the more efficient use of resources and greater equality of distribution—the other two-thirds of the party program—were the only ways open to improve matters in a short time. Ever since the end of the war, a bitter struggle had raged under cover, camouflaged by dozens of related issues: Who was going to get what from Japan's very limited means?

The business and financial interests, represented by Yoshida's Liberal Party, gave first priority to recapitalizing the enterprises, mostly private, that had been devastated by the war, even if the workers had to endure their painful sacrifices indefinitely. The trade unions and the Socialists demanded that the limited resources be applied to raising the abysmally low living level of the urban and working population. Later Washington, at the third corner of the triangle, insisted that Japan's resources be utilized increasingly to promote exports and relieve the financial burden of American aid to Japan. Later still, the U.S. Administration would come down on the side of greater industrial investment as opposed to improved living standards.

In 1947 and 1948, however, SCAP scrupulously refused to take sides in this issue, considering it an internal matter. By supporting the enforcement of direct controls, however, GHQ policy inevitably served to increase the workers' share of the national wealth, placing more goods in legal and basically egalitarian rationing channels and less in the free or black market, where goods went to the highest bidder. When the new Socialist-led government took office, SCAP officials and Japanese Socialists found themselves aligned in a common effort.

The cooperation worked. Throwing themselves into a black market eradication campaign with an enthusiasm that their predecessors had never been able to muster, the new government's leaders assigned agents to search train passengers at stations and truck riders at checkpoints, to investigate warehouses and factories, and to conduct sweeps of the main shopping areas. The "Chinatowns" in the big Japanese cities were particular targets. For one year in 1947–48, difficult as it is to believe today (1982) when Tokyo alone has more than 70,000 eating and drinking establishments, all restaurants were closed down throughout the country. In 1947–48 some 60,000 economic violations were being uncovered on the average per month![22] How many inspectors, a veritable army, and how many inspections, a veritable war, that must have entailed! Seldom, if ever, has such an effort been launched in a democratic country in peacetime.

In the end, the gigantic effort, assisted by improved supplies and backed by massive American military support—at one time Eighth Army Military Government teams in the field were deployed all over the country to check the price of fresh fish—succeeded. Coal, some 50 percent of which was moving from mine to black market in the last months of 1946[23] under the Yoshida Cabinet, was almost all in official channels by 1948. Consumers who had bought 20 to 40 percent of their rice in the black market, depending on the month, in 1946–47[24] resorted to the black market for only 8 percent of their needs in 1948–49.[25] By the end of 1948, the government had largely extirpated the black market in essential commodities. The unemployed and the low-paid, the impoverished and the destitute, had their safety net. Both SCAP and the Socialists substantially attained their goal of greater equity in consumer goods distribution.

True, the consumer price index rose 167 percent in 1947, but only 55 percent in 1948.[26] Meanwhile wages also zoomed. In May of 1947, when the Socialist–Democratic coalition took office, the average factory worker in large establishments was earning 1,373 yen monthly. In October 1948, the month the coalition fell, his wages were 6,423 yen, nearly five times as much. Over the same period, the consumer price index rose to less than two and a half times as much.[27] From October 1947 to October 1948, wages rose three times as fast as consumer prices.[28] The government's deliberate pro-labor–consumer policies, supported by increased production and more abundant U.S. relief food, succeeded in what they were supposed to do.

Afterward the U.S. Treasury Department and the Federal Reserve Board, would attack the management of Japan's economy in 1947 and 1948 for not halting the inflation. But that was not the point then. For while such an objective was primary in Washington, it did not have first priority in Tokyo. Blaming Tokyo for not attaining Washington's objectives was like blaming a dog for not being a cat. In reality, the alliance between SCAP and the Socialists was surprisingly fruitful.

None of that cooperation, however, applied to the socialization of key sectors of the economy. The new Socialist leaders of the nation eagerly wanted some nationalization as a "logical" extension of SCAP's democratization so far. SCAP, of course, did not concede that to be a logical extension at all. In seeking, then, to turn postwar Japan onto a socialist track, like so many other nations right after the war, the Socialists would have to go it alone.

17

Coal Mines and *Kōdan*

NATIONALIZING IN THE LIGHT AND IN THE DARK

WHAT DOES A Socialist party do when it finally wins power and attains office, if it is to remain true to its faith? What else but begin to institute socialism? And what does an occupation commander, himself a believer in free enterprise and representative of a fervently capitalist country, which, moreover, is supporting the occupied land financially, do in response? When the Occupation laid down the reform baton in the summer of 1947, the Japanese Socialists snatched it up—and ran off in a different direction, leaving General MacArthur and his staff wondering what to do about it.

Both the Socialists and SCAP, however, had serious parliamentary obstacles in the way of what they wanted to do. The Socialists headed a cabinet coalition that included parties opposed to socialism. The Supreme Commander, having championed the new democracy and ratified the first election under his new constitution—"no one can justly criticize their choice," he said of the results[1]—would be denying that choice if he prevented the resultant government from carrying out its election platform. The Socialists euphorically disregarded the Diet arithmetic that gave them only 143 seats (178, counting Communists and Cooperative Democrats) out of 466 in the lower house and decided to try nevertheless. Prime Minister Katayama asserted that the election had mandated a government "which will make for a change in the basis of our national structure from capitalism to socialism"[2] and told Russell Brines of the Associated Press that his new government wanted "gradual socialization of key industries," specifically fertilizers, coal, and banks to start with, and going on from there to buying out the owners of other private industries as well.[3] The SCAP staff wondered, with government income only 60 percent of expenditures, what he would use for money. MacArthur said nothing.

But the Socialists for the moment were beyond such practicalities. Only two years before, their leaders—agitators, lawyers, journalists, scholars, trade union organizers—whether in prison or out, had been in political oblivion. Now they found themselves vaulted suddenly to the helm of state. Socialism was, in their view, a logical extension of democracy.

There were, of course, dissenters, both in the new coalition cabinet and in the heterogeneous Socialist party. The Democrats, led by Ashida Hitoshi, could not forget that the Socialists, with the largest Diet delegation, had still won only 26.2 percent of the popular vote, while they themselves had collected 25.9. They joined the cabinet, Ashida said, to act as a "check on the socialist planners" in the prime minister's party.[4] That hardly needed saying. From the very beginning of the new cabinet formation process, the left-wing Socialists had refused to participate in a partnership with the Democrats (who had been partners of Yoshida in the cabinet just past), arguing that it was futile to expect capitalist representatives to cooperate in dismantling capitalism. (The Democrats didn't want the left Socialists either; they considered them a "security risk.") The discord was to divide the party permanently in two, between reformers and revolutionaries. Eventually the party would split formally.[5] Meanwhile, a few of us in SCAP awaited the first socialization move and wondered how the socializers in the cabinet thought they could pull it off. And besides, what would the "Old Man" say?

Indeed, for SCAP it was an entirely new problem. The JCS 1380/15 planners had hardly envisaged that in less than two years of occupation, a Japanese government might want to socialize the country. The directive, consequently, had nothing to say about it. After the 1946 elections, moreover, it would have seemed incredible to the American public that any socialization could proceed anywhere in the world under the American flag. In Washington, the new conservative congressional leadership reacted with anger and dismay at the possibility that the new British Labour government would push for socialism in their West German Occupation Zone. Navy Secretary Forrestal declared in one cabinet meeting that "the government should make it clear that we do not propose to endorse socialization in Germany under any circumstances." The United States was aiding England financially and, Forrestal added in his diary, "we did not propose to have our money used to implement a German system contrary to our own."[6] As for MacArthur, why everyone knew what he thought about socialism. The prospects looked bleak.

Talks with Socialists

To the Japanese Socialist leaders, however, the prospect looked different. One day in May 1947, shortly after the election, I was visited by the Katōs, Kanjū, the leading left-wing Socialist, and his wife, Shizue. A year before Mr. Katō had asked me whether I thought the Socialist party should join a Liberal coalition, and my contrary opinion had, unbeknownst to me, swayed the Socialist Central Executive Committee into rejecting the idea. Now, Katō wanted my advice on whether he should accept a ministerial post in the forthcoming Socialist–Democratic coalition cabinet. Again, speaking strictly in a personal capacity, I counseled him against it on the grounds that he, as a convinced Socialist, would want to begin instituting socialism, whereas under the conditions of an American military occupation that was hardly likely to be allowed, and he would wind up frustrated and, what is worse, discredited among his followers. Why not wait until after the Occupation? I asked.

Katō was surprised at my assessment. Like many other Japanese Socialists he had grown to identify labor union causes with socialism. The Occupation had defended labor against the capitalists; why would we be so insistent on maintaining capitalism? Besides, the American capitalists needed the Japanese Socialists as their only reliable bulwark against a revival of militarism and *zaibatsu* big business imperialism. Hence logically, they should not object to the institution of socialism in Japan. American capitalists supporting Japanese Socialists to protect their profits against Japanese capitalists allied with militarists? I had to assure Katō that people just did not think that way in the United States. I cannot say I convinced him, but he did pass up the cabinet.

A few weeks later, the first government move came when the new Commerce and Industry Minister, Socialist Mizutani Chōsaburō, came to pay his respects to General Marquat at the beginning of June and to meet the general's few close advisers, of which I was now one. On his way out of the room after the meeting, Mizutani took me by the arm and asked to speak with me privately. Then, safely in my adjacent office, he asked me if I would help the Socialists to carry out their platform plank of nationalizing the coal mines. The election and postelection rhetoric had now come down to cases. Coal it would be.

Coal was a natural choice. International socialist thought had long called for the nationalization of basic industries, and what could be more basic to an industrial economy? Rail trunk lines, telecommunications, and electric power were already national enterprises in Japan, while heavy industry was subject to reparations removals. What was left? But when I asked Mizutani why coal, he gave a different reason. The Japan Socialist party, he said, was a mixture, consisting of Fabians, Christian Socialists, Marxists, non-Marxists, revisionists, and just plain social reformers. But one thing they all had in common was an admiration for the recently victorious British Labour party, and the latter had started its nationalization program with coal. No one in the Japanese Socialist party, therefore, could object to nationalizing coal. It was a political, if not ideological, natural.

If coal was an obvious choice, Mizutani as chief nationalizer was anything but. Although his family had been innkeepers for sixteen generations in Fushimi near Kyoto, often acting as hosts in Tokugawa times to the great feudal lords and their retinues, until, finally, under his elder brother the family business went bankrupt, Mizutani himself had never had any business experience. He was no economist or engineer, nor did he know much about industry or finance. He was in fact a practicing lawyer. A short, chubby, smiling idealist with thick horn-rimmed glasses, Mizutani polled the highest in his electoral district, the Kyoto Second, in 1947 and was elected five more times from then to 1958. His popularity was partly because of his prewar civil liberties record and partly because he put on no airs. At one point, he did not disdain to go on an underground coal mine inspection tour clad only in loin cloth and *jikatabi* (split-toe sandals) and carrying a safety lamp just like an ordinary miner. (His photograph, the semi-nude minister, hit the front pages the next day.)

When he entered my office that day, Mizutani did not know me personally. His Socialist comrades who did had vouched for me as a protagonist of labor unions, and they had no other "friend" near General Marquat. I told Mizutani candidly that neither the U.S. Government nor General MacArthur personally looked with favor on socialism. On the contrary, the U.S. Government was a strong supporter of private enterprise, particularly after the Republican congressional election victory the preceding November. Therefore, no one in GHQ would help him to nationalize coal mining. But, I added, MacArthur was also dedicated, perhaps more than the minister realized, to a true parliamentary democracy in Japan, and he might be loath to veto a Socialist effort to carry out election promises. What GHQ was principally interested in, however, was more coal. The minister had better have constructive suggestions along that line.

Mizutani, a responsible man, quickly discovered that coal mining was also a very special industry. Considered by almost everyone to be the key to Japanese industrial recovery, it was also a sick industry. It was, in addition, the most emotion-provoking, a semifeudal operation where the miners detested the operators as feudal overlords and the operators looked down upon the workers as in no other industry. It was also the only Japanese industry during the war to use large-scale foreign slave labor in the homeland, Nazi-style. Coal was, in short, a subject that hardly any Japanese could approach dispassionately. In proposing to nationalize coal, the Socialists were stirring up a hornet's nest.

The production decline in coal had been catastrophic. From an average of 4.5 million metric tons mined monthly in 1940–43[7] (plus imports of three-quarters of a million tons a month)[8] coal output had nosedived as the 140,000 impressed Korean and Chinese miners (out of a total mine work force of 240,000) joyfully liberated themselves at the end of the war and went home.[9] In November 1945, the mines produced only half a million tons, not even enough to operate the national railways,[10] and there were no imports. By May 1947, eighteen months later, monthly production tonnage had recovered only to some 2 million, and there were still no imports. Japan urgently needed at least 3 million tons a month, the Coal Board said; 4 million, said our Industry Division.

Even after Japanese recruits replaced the departed Koreans and Chinese— a Labor Division program featuring double food rations had recruited 150,000 new miners by March 1946[11]—production lagged badly. The mines had been "decapitalized," during the war, worked to exhaustion with little maintenance.[12] Accidents and breakdowns had resulted. In one typical mine, breakdowns in 1944 were almost seven times as numerous as in 1940.[13] Productivity sagged from more than 20 tons per underground miner per month in 1941[14] to only 7 tons in July 1945, just before the surrender.[15] The first priority, obviously, was to rebuild the mines' capital structure.

But on the question of how to do so there was violent disagreement. Among large Japanese industries coal mining was unique in the degree to which the owners were individual and individualistic entrepreneurs. Big business *zaibatsu*-affiliated companies mined 60 percent of the coal, but 40 percent was produced in a much larger number of family-owned feudal baronies dating from the turn of the century,[16] and arrogance toward employees was very common among the small operators.

The big business mines were run by university-educated consensus-type businessmen who kept a low profile. But the family mine operators were often likely to be boorish and crude provincials, to whom the mine workers were little better than draft animals and who spent large sums of money on *geisha* and gambling while crying poverty because of the controlled price of coal. One of them, a Baron Horikawa, a friend of mine, lived in comfort all through the postwar years on the proceeds of his one relatively small mine in West Kyūshū without ever having to attend to business. His workers, of course, did. To the miners who were being constantly exhorted to work harder as a patriotic act, such coal barons were a constant focus of outrage.

The big business coal operators and some of the bigger private coal owners were tarnished with an even dirtier brush, the use of slave labor. Perhaps no group of industrialists was closer to the Japanese military imperialists. When the Army needed more coal for war industry and the operators more manpower to provide it, their common solution was to transfer Japanese miners to manufacturing and to import unskilled and enslaved—they called it "contract labor"— Koreans and Chinese for the Japanese mines. Many of them were captured, in what Japanese involved called "rabbit hunts," by raiding parties akin to eighteenth-century English press gangs, supported by the Kwangtung Army. In the mines abuses were inevitable, from top management down to foremen holding quasi-military ranks in the wartime *Sanpō* labor front, and the mistreatment was not restricted just to the Koreans and the Chinese. GHQ Labor Division investigators in 1946[17] repeatedly heard bitter accounts of the *kangoku-beya* or prison-cell system, where "free" miners as well as the conscripts were regularly required to sleep in the pits to save travel time between portal and mine face and thereby increase production. They hardly saw the sun, or the moon either.

The Japanese miners who remained in the pits after the war did not forget, and the newcomers recruited by higher food rations had new and equally bitter complaints. When they arrived in the mining towns, the only housing available to them and their families was usually the recently vacated conscript barracks. Barely adequate for single men, the ramshackle buildings forced miners and their families, averaging eight people, to squeeze into six-mat rooms of 108 square feet, say 9 by 12, according to coal mine union leaders. They lived there for months on end "temporarily" while miners' housing construction lagged badly.[18] The miners were sure government housing funds were being diverted to cover operational losses or for shadier purposes.

Supplementary rations, moreover, were usually late, which meant either that the miners' children would go hungry—regular rations were weeks behind—or the miners could not eat enough to work hard. (On one occasion output rose 30 percent when the ration was fully met for several weeks.) In the rainy season, the coal town streets turned into muddy quagmires, despite repeated company pledges to pave them. Even distribution of surplus Army uniforms was unsatisfactory.

The Battle of the Coal Miners

It is not surprising that to the miners the operators appeared as the principal cause of their misfortunes. Before, after, or during the war, they were still the same, unreformed and unreformable. The best example was the head of the Coal Association himself, the sixty-seven-year-old Kajima Taichi, who in his own person was both a *zaibatsu* type and a private coal baron and an intimate of the Army clique as well. Having worked for Mitsui Trading Company for three years in his younger days, he then inherited the family business, the Kajima Coal Company, meanwhile marrying the sister of Aikawa Gisuke, head of the Army-backed Hitachi–Nissan–Manchuria Heavy Industry combine, economic overlords of Manchuria. His mines had used slaves too. The mine operators were not just ordinary employers; to the miners they were their worst enemies.

When the operators, throughout 1946 and early 1947, proposed the "obvious" solution for recapitalizing the mines, namely raising the coal price ceiling so that they could make profits that they could reinvest in the mines, the miners reacted with fury. With the blood and sweat they had put into the mines, they resented rewarding the operators with higher prices and fabulous profits arising from the shortages that the operators had themselves created by refusing to invest in the past.

The operators, however, contended that after October 1946 wages alone amounted to 80 percent of the official sales price, leaving only 20 percent for mine timbers, rails, all other materials, and wage supplements. Before the war those other expenses had taken 86 percent of the sales price.[19] There was nothing to invest, they protested. The Mitsui Coal Mining Company, for example, reported its per ton cost in March 1947 as more than 943 yen, triple the selling price, and its losses in the five months November 1946–March 1947 as 435 million yen. Even huge government subsidies for investment, running at the rate of almost a billion yen a year for the entire industry, could not stanch the continued hemorrhaging of the coal industry on that scale.[20]

"Accounting methods!" the left-wing critics retorted. Productivity varied greatly by mine; some could make money while others were losing, but the operators wanted the coal price set at a level at which all could make a profit, and some a scandalous one. In fact, many operators, they charged, were already making scandalous profits by selling to the black market or at black market prices. Official prices were mostly for the company books, the would-be socializers contended. SCAP sources were their proof. At one well-attended press conference on February 12, 1947, Industry Chief Reday complained that almost half the product of the Kyūshū coal mines had moved into the Osaka Kansai black market "in the last few months."[21] Where Reday got his figures I don't know, but few disputed them. Far from subsidizing losses, it seemed, the government was rewarding profiteering.

But if the government took over the mines, the left-wingers said, then any help to the industry would go to production and recapitalization, not to the owners' pockets. In the first Socialist electoral plurality in history the Coal Miners' Union saw a way for them to better their lives at last. "By the state control of coal mines," a Union resolution brought to me in the summer of 1947 proclaimed, "we workers shall be liberated from the yoke of capital and be given access to livelihood security."[22] Coal nationalization was, to them, a crusade. But to the Socialist party leaders and economists, it was also the best way to revive the industry.

I do not know how much Mizutani could have absorbed about coal mining in the next two weeks before his first working visit with Marquat, but it was still primarily a political and ideological problem to him. After an exchange of courtesies, he plunged in. His party, he advised the general, had run on a platform of nationalizing coal, and the cabinet was now preparing to propose state control over coal mines as a first step in that direction. He hoped GHQ would help him to put the measure into effect. The general heard him out and then, in a *non-sequitur* typical of Marquat when he didn't want to give a direct answer, launched into an emphatic discourse on the need to mine more coal. He made no reference to nationalization, state control, or Mizutani's proposal. Mizutani was completely nonplused, but he quickly recovered. "That's exactly what I was talking about," he rejoined and pledged his best efforts to fulfill the 1947 target of 30 million tons. In fact, that was the whole purpose of state control, he assured the general.

After the meeting, Marquat asked me what I thought of state control. I was sure, I said, that Washington would not like the idea, that many of those in GHQ might be horrified, and that the Supreme Commander might not be too happy about the proposal either. Still, the Japanese had made the proposal, and there was nothing in our Washington JSC directive that prohibited nationalization of any industry *per se*. On what grounds, then, could SCAP object to state control? Second, Japan was no stranger to public ownership of national enterprises, rare as it was in the States. Trunk railways, telecommunications, tobacco, salt, camphor, radio broadcasting, and even, in a way, electric power were all state industries.[23] Moreover, coal mine nationalization had been an openly proclaimed plank of the Socialist party in a democratic election, as a result of which the current cabinet was in office. The Command could be criticized if, having allowed the Socialists to campaign on such a plank, it now prohibited them from implementing their pledge once they won. The election could be denounced as phony. Finally, I said, I did not see how the Socialists could get their plan through the Diet anyway, when the conservative parties held such a big majority.

Marquat listened to me without comment. Undoubtedly he asked others their opinion too. At any rate, two days later he called me into his office to tell me that he had taken the matter up with the Supreme Commander, and General MacArthur would not object to any way the Japanese reorganized their coal industry so long as it did not conflict with the Occupation interest, that is, to mine more coal. (Three months later, when the Japanese government submitted its draft of the bill on the State Control of Coal Mines, MacArthur put that decision in writing in a letter to the prime minister.)[24]

It was an extraordinary decision, if only for what it revealed about MacArthur that was contrary to common perception in America, where he was supposed to have a phobia about socialism. True, MacArthur disapproved of socialism. He much preferred free and competitive private enterprise, which, he said, "it is my firm purpose to see entrenched in the Japanese system before the Occupation withdraws." But, he added, "it does not suffice merely to issue an edict that there shall be no socialism."[25] On the contrary, he had hailed the selection of a Socialist prime minister as "expos[ing] the complete falsity of propaganda . . . deprecating the recent Japanese elections as designed to strengthen reactionary forces opposed to democratic growth."[26] He would not stand in the way of this democratic process, nor would he ask anyone in Washington what to do. Coal mine nationalization remained a theater affair. From then on it was up to the Japanese. But, perhaps at Marquat's urging, he did insist that they mine more coal.

Mizutani, his lesson learned, never mentioned political ideals to Marquat again, only coal production. And that became his public strategy as well. The Socialists had abandoned nationalization for the time being under the three-party coalition agreement, but the other parties had agreed in return to support "state control," whatever that meant. Mizutani explained to the Japanese reporters that state ownership or even state management was not politically possible at present, but state control was. Indeed, he said, it was the only real way to foster production.

The key question, of course, was how effective a state control was meant. If the Democrats could be held to their agreement to set up a state control organization, then at a later time the organization set up for that purpose would be available to take over the mines. Mizutani must have thought he was being both realistic and shrewd. But he badly underestimated the passion and vehemence on both sides. Probably he also undercounted the number of Democratic Diet members who were themselves coal mine owners or subservient to them and, being himself an honorable man, miscalculated the lengths to which they would go to sabotage his plans.

The coal operators saw the matter quite differently from the unions. The plight of the miners, they argued, was no different from that of all Japanese after the war. It was not the mine owners' fault. Once the enterprises and the country were on their feet, it would all improve. Meanwhile they saw no reason to lose their ancestral properties. The big business coal companies may have been concerned about large public policy issues, but the "medium and small coal mine operators," as Yamakawa Ryōkichi, President of Mitsui Mining Company, would testify, "were frantic."[27] Deciding "in their hearts that the large operators were not worth relying on,"[28] the smaller ones resuscitated their old Kyūshū mutual aid association (the Gojo-kai) to fight the measure any way they could. For them it was a crusade, too.

For three months the battles over the program were fought quietly within ministerial walls. Mizutani's Commerce and Industry aides drew up a bill, then sent it over to the Economic Stabilization Board and the Finance Ministry for agreement. The ideas of the three agencies were far apart. At the middle-of-the-road MCI, the officials planned to designate only the large mines and then only for a year. They proposed to establish two new public corporations or *kōdan*, one to operate the designated mines, the other to procure all the necessary mine supplies. They also wanted to set up a tripartite advisory council, representing owners, labor union, and public, to counsel the operating *kōdan*.[29]

When that proposal reached the Socialists in the ESB, however, they objected violently. They drastically modified the plan to extend state control to three years, replaced the public corporations with ministerially appointed controllers from the civil service, provided for annual and quarterly production plans down to the individual mines, and set up three cumbersome levels of supervision—national, regional, and local—to ensure the plans were being implemented. In their tripartite councils they eliminated the owners' representatives altogether in favor of representatives from among the engineers, mine controllers, and even nondesignated coal mine owners! "The only remaining prerogatives of ownership," I advised Marquat, who had designated me to coordinate everything relative to state control in ESS, "are to be receipt of dividends when ordered by the Minister of Commerce and Industry and, subject to government approval, transfer of assets."[30] Even that was not enough for the Socialist Party Coal Production Committee, which talked of state control applied to all mines and forever.[31]

But when the plan arrived at the conservative Finance Ministry, whose minister was a Democrat, it hit a stone wall. Once more the bill was revised, this time in the opposite direction. Now the controllers were to be appointed by the owners, the quarterly production plans were to be drawn up by the owners subject to later ministerial veto, and the advisory councils were turned into bipartite groups, just labor and management.[32] It came out looking more like a plan for self-control.

Even so, fireworks erupted. The small and medium operators wanted no control of any kind at all, and they had put together a war chest to ensure against it. Lobbying hit a new high, or low, depending on the viewpoint. Outside the Diet the high-class *geisha* restaurants did a great business. According to the Socialists' party newspaper, *Shakai Shinbun,* the manager of the Ryūmei-kan restaurant near the landmark Greek Orthodox Saint Nikolai Church in Kanda, Tokyo, divulged that in the July–October 1947 period the coal operators had given lavish parties every single night for Diet members, perhaps a hundred in all. Takeuchi Reizō, Coal Association President Kajima's most effective lieutenant, who had come from Kyūshū for the purpose, seemed to be in charge. Mahjongg, gambling, stay-over women, and private cars—with plenty of food, although restaurants were supposed to be closed—were *de rigueur.* In September, the manager testified, three Democratic cabinet ministers attended a big banquet and led the guests in toasts to the defeat of the state control bill, which they officially supported. In the same month some of the legislator guests at a smaller gathering that ended riotously were arrested for gambling in a public place by police who had come to investigate the noise. They were taken to a police station until they sobered up and were released.[33]

How much of this was true and how much exaggerated in a partisan newspaper is hard to say. But the Ryūmei-kan was not the only restaurant that figured in reports of similar lobbying tactics in other newspapers—the guest lists of five other restaurants were subpoenaed by the Diet Committee on Illegal

Transactions in August of the following year[34]—and for every report printed, twenty rumors circulated, while few tried to deny them.

As early as August the Coal Miners Union had protested those "disgraceful activities in which a vast amount of money is lavished," complaining "that the capitalists and operators have still no concern for the future of our country if only their selfish interest be secured." They charged that a secret slush fund of ten yen per ton on all coal being mined was being raised by the Kyūshū Coal Operators for lobbying purposes.[35] What particularly outraged the miners was that every ton they dug so patriotically meant a bigger slush fund. (They were not wrong. A year later a trustee of the Kyūshū Coal Operators Association, Kiso Shigeyoshi, testifying before the House of Representatives Committee on Illegal Property Transactions, confirmed that the sum had reached 10 million yen.)[36] Others alleged the sum was much larger, perhaps twenty times as much, and that much of the money came from the government by way of loans from the Reconstruction Finance Bank.[37]

With that kind of anti–state control money around, it is not surprising that at every step the Socialists ran into obstacles. The three-party coalition negotiations to approve the government bill took three months, and by that time thirty-seven of the bill's sixty-eight articles had been completely rewritten and the bill emasculated.[38] Meanwhile, the scenes of the debate on the Diet floor reached extremes of boisterousness not seen since the 1920s. "No words can express the acts of violence done in the Diet by the honorable Members of Parliament," a company clerk lamented in a letter to the *Minpō*. "Striking each other with fists, attacking the guards and climbing upon the stenographers' desks, etc.—what a scene!"[39]

The final indignity was the attempt of some Democrats to eliminate an effective date from the bill so that the law would never be applied at all, but the Socialists did manage to get the legislation enacted on December 8, 1947, to go into force in four months. It had no real effect in any case. I do not remember any mine's being designated under its provisions, although some must have been.

When the Socialist–Democratic coalition cabinet was replaced by a Democrat–Socialist coalition cabinet in March 1948, Mizutani once again became Minister of Commerce and Industry. Neither in his accession statement nor in his subsequent press conference did he even mention state control of coal mines. Instead, he pledged fervently once more, as he had in Marquat's office the previous June, to increase coal production. Indeed, during his two terms, from June 1947 to October 1948, coal extraction increased by 42 percent.[40] Miners' real wages during that same period rose 71 percent as well. But neither followed from applying the Socialists' remedy of coal mine nationalization or even state control. MacArthur, for his part, had got the best of all possible worlds: respect for democratic election returns, preservation of private enterprise, and more coal, too.

THE KŌDAN

But while the Supreme Commander was reluctantly permitting the Socialists to try to nationalize coal in the glare of the public spotlight, unknown to him, a group of GHQ officials at midlevel was unwittingly pushing in administrative obscurity toward socialization in a new field: the channels of wholesale distribution. The Americans were almost certainly not aware of the significance of their actions, but the new coterie of Socialist economists and technocrats who had swept into the governmental economic control offices after the elections, especially into the Economic Stabilization Board, quickly caught on to the possibilities. It was a marvelous target of opportunity, and its potential was even farther-reaching than that of coal. If the government came to *own* those distribution channels as monopolies and could dictate what they would buy and sell, then all industry, on the one hand, and all retailers and consumers, on the other, would fall into line. The Socialist newcomers leaped at the opening, and with GHQ's blessing they almost succeeded.

The first official mention of such a program appeared on June 11, 1947, when the prime minister issued a White Paper on the economic crisis.[41] Tsuru Shigeto, the ESB Deputy Director General, was its principal architect. Part II, paragraph 1, pledged to assure the distribution of essential materials, such as "basic production materials, major consumers' goods, important foodstuffs, etc."—what was left out?—by means of a *"kōdan* system." The word *"kōdan"* had never been mentioned in the election campaign. And what on earth was a *"kōdan* system"?

The *kōdan,* or public corporations, were a brand-new postwar device, less than six months old. At the time the Socialists acceded to office there were ten of them in existence,[42] all established in the last Diet sessions by the outgoing conservative government. The new Socialist administrators knew of them, of course, but only as technical administrative agencies, nothing very important. In their initial conversations with SCAP officials, however, the Socialists discovered to their surprise that the *kōdan* were a major SCAP project and that GHQ wanted more of them. The SCAP officials were determined to set *kōdan* in place of the old wartime industry control associations that had regulated, and still were regulating, the allocation of scarce materials, which is to say almost all materials. But if enough public corporations were created and enough commodities covered, distribution would automatically be nationalized. It would be a highly unorthodox procedure by traditional socialist theory, to be sure, but effective nevertheless. No need to mobilize the party faithful, as in the case of coal nationalization, no call to the labor unions or appeals to the "masses"—in sum, no sweat. The new Socialist officials merely had to help the Occupation along.

As usual, the Americans were just carrying out their Washington directive. "You will dissolve the Control Associations. . . . Any necessary public function previously performed by these associations should be transferred to public agencies, approved and supervised by you.''[43] The *kōdan* were precisely those new public agencies.

Now the control associations, privately organized, owned, and staffed, had been the most visible part of an unholy alliance between the Japanese Army and big business to organize the economy in support of the war. In the early 1930s, Japanese big business may briefly have opposed the militarists, but by the end of the decade, cowed or convinced, they were full partners in industrial war mobilization. Moreover, they participated on their own terms, that is, that business be allowed to manage the economic mobilization effort. The military, true, set the end product requirements. General Suzuki Teiichi's Cabinet Planning Board (made up mostly of civilians, many of whom turned out later to be antimilitarist by conviction and were arrested for it) translated them into industrial targets and allocated raw and semifinished materials by industry. But private business itself, in the form of associations authorized by law,[44] actually decided how much each individual user was to get of everything.

By the end of the war a network of some nineteen national "control associations" (*tōsei-kai*),[45] hundreds of "control unions' (*tōsei-kumiai*, for smaller enterprises or prefectural rather than national in scope), and a significant number of *eidan* (literally, "business units," wholly government-owned and government-managed corporations), and "control companies" (*tōsei-kaisha*), which bought and sold or otherwise operated for their own account, smothered wholesale distribution. Not a kilogram of any industrial material could move legally, nor could factories be expanded or consolidated, without the intervention or approval of some private, yet official, body.

How well the private associations ran the economy might have been open to doubt, but that they ran it in accordance with the interests of their biggest and most influential members, that is, the giant financial and industrial combines, was not. From the beginning the representatives of the *zaibatsu* financial combine companies (in the control associations) and of their subsidiaries or suppliers (in the control unions) sat on the boards of directors and furnished officers, staff, and most of their financing. In control companies, the *zaibatsu* were the principal shareholders. For example, the monopoly Nippon Warehouse Company, formed for most efficient utilization of space or materials handling facilities, was owned almost exclusively by the Mitsui, Mitsubishi, and Sumitomo warehousing companies.[46] The near-monopoly Japan Lumber Company was effectively the joint property of Mitsui Honsha, Mitsubishi Honsha, Sumitomo Honsha, Kawasaki Heavy Industry, Oji Paper (a Mitsui company), Nissan, and the Imperial Household.[47] And so on.

There was nothing new or startling about this. The control machinery accurately reflected the existing economic oligarchy in the nation at large. But in an occupation dedicated to economic democratization, its continuance was intolerable. Regardless of a model constitution or the best devised of political processes, MacArthur's democratization would be a farce if all businesses remained at the mercy of the big companies through their postwar control of scarce materials. Still, in the midst of extreme shortages of all kinds, no one in SCAP was going to endanger individual factories or the economy in general by abolishing distribution controls and relying on an unpredictable free market. Government controls over scarce materials, the responsible SCAP officials felt, had to be continued and improved—JSC 1380/15 even told them so—but not through the control associations and their related organizations.

DISSOLUTION OF THE CONTROL ASSOCIATIONS

The Japanese public was not particularly interested. Who can get excited about wholesale distribution channels? But within GHQ, particularly in ESS, there was passionate concern. Not only did GHQ have to dismantle the system that had mobilized Japan's industrial might for war, but the missions of most ESS divisions were affected: Finance Division regarding subsidies and budget, Industry to ensure the supply of industrial materials for production, Price Control to reinforce official prices, Foreign Trade needing adequate government-to-government trade agencies, and, finally, Antitrust to break up the grip of the *zaibatsu*. Indeed, so many ESS agencies got involved, often working at cross purposes, that General Marquat had to establish a Controls Coordinating Committee. Fully half of ESS was involved.

The Japanese concerned, however, were singularly uncooperative, even obstructionist. The Americans wrestled all through 1946 to dismantle the wartime control structure while tightening controls, but Japanese industry and government officials, and the control association functionaries too, dragged their feet. They carefully explained to GHQ that detailed economic controls had never been a government function—any more than the printing of government forms had been; one had to go to the bookstores to get them—and government had no trained personnel for the purpose. If government added new officials with civil service rank, what could be done with them after the emergency was over? The political parties, both conservatives and Socialists, simply denied the problem, the former because economic democracy did not interest them, the latter because the solution to a grasping oligarchy was nationalization, they thought, not adversary regulation by government. SCAP officials were fighting a constant uphill battle without the Japanese allies that so many other SCAP democratization causes had attracted.

The whole process was frustrating, and progress was painfully slow. Almost a year after the war's end only a handful of the wartime distribution control bodies were out of business,[48] and SCAP officials, recognizing that informal negotiation was simply not getting results, had to issue a formal directive on August 6, 1946, dissolving all the rest. That did not mean immediate compliance either. It was not until the end of September 1946 that the infamous National General Mobilization Law of 1938—whose labor provisions conscripting industrial workers, banning strikes, and dissolving labor unions had been annulled twelve months before—finally went out of force with respect to materials. It was too badly needed, Japanese government emissaries had argued, to rebuild postwar Japan. Even then, when GHQ insisted on its repeal and replacement by the Temporary Supply and Demand Act, the Ministry of Commerce and Industry proposed forty implementing ordinances for the new law, which, disgusted SCAP officials found, would have restored the old system once more.[49]

Once again, the SCAP officials appealed for a formal directive. The ESS Chief, General Marquat, was reluctant. After George Atcheson's statement in the Allied Council for Japan that American and Japanese aims were identical (the antitrust people thought they must be dreaming when they heard that), the Supreme Commander was reluctant to issue formal directives. Still, there was no other way. On December 11 SCAP once again instructed the Japanese Government to "withdraw from industry the powers of distribution control"[50] and further "to submit plans for carrying on distribution functions through a government distribution corporation." What was to become the *kōdan* was now officially the GHQ great white hope.

When the Socialists on June 11, 1947, announced their policy of establishing a *"kōdan* system" then, the SCAP people did not look too closely at the exact wording but welcomed the pledge. They were thoroughly fed up with the old-line economic control functionaries and with everything about the old control system. Universally, they agreed, the control associations were corrupt. In one internal memo, Industry Division Chief Reday wrote that "the present Industrial Equipment Corporation [an *eidan*] has an extremely unsavory reputation for inefficiency and graft." The Antitrust Division Executive Officer, Colonel Kupferer, found that "the Petroleum Distribution Control Company has been wasteful and corrupt . . . a considerable amount of gasoline has found its way into the black market."[51] And Antitrust Division Chief Henderson generalized that "the organizations were so corrupt from a managerial point of view that industry was refusing to comply with the orders of the Associations."[52] What they said orally in GHQ offices was a lot stronger. In contrast, the unborn *kōdan* were as yet pure. And no one noticed the difference between *kōdan* as such and a *"kōdan* system."

The ESS officials had as their model the American temporary wartime government corporations dealing with imported petroleum and rubber or the U.S. Government's trading arm, the U.S. Commercial Company. To Antitrust, that kind of a government entity in corporate form, combining operational independence, regular commercial legal liability, and official status, was best suited to avoid conflicts of interest. The *kōdan* was attractive to Finance because it was self-supporting. To Industry and to Price Control, a monopoly *kōdan* offered the tightest form of distribution control, for if every producer had to sell only to the *kōdan* and every user or retailer had to buy only from the *kōdan,* black market diversion would be minimal. With everyone engrossed in his own mission, it occurred to none of them that the *kōdan* were also an excellent way to socialize the Japanese economy. It had, of course, occurred to the Japanese Socialists in the Economic Stabilization Board.

One day in mid-June a troubled stateless "foreign national" employed by SCAP in the Industry Division, Hans Ries by name, came up to see me in my new capacity as Economic Adviser. A prewar businessman from Germany with experience in the Far East, particularly in Japan, where he had sat out the war, part of the time in prison as a suspected spy, Ries had had plenty of contact with the Japanese trade bureaucracy. He asked me if I knew anything about the *kōdan.* Yes, what about them? As far as he could see, they were proliferating out of control. The Japanese were building up a bureaucratic machine as bad as anything in wartime, but no one in Industry Division seemed to be concerned about it. Was I?

Now, Ries was an enthusiastic worrier by nature and scathingly critical about Japanese economic administration at any time, but a quick though careful look bore him out. *Kōdan* seemed to be breeding like rabbits. Of the ten *kōdan* established by the old conservative Diet, only two—petroleum and solid fuels— had dealt with internal distribution, and the conservatives' distaste for formal public intervention in business had kept the concept within very limited bounds. Now, however, the ESB Socialists were talking of perhaps a dozen more *kōdan,* all of them, aside from the two *kōdan* intended to supply and operate the coal mines under state control, aimed at monopolizing internal distribution. ESB had informally proposed legislation to SCAP to set up three more to take over the wholesale distribution of iron and steel, fertilizers, and "daily necessities," respectively. In addition, they had several others in the planning stage, they confided to our people. The Agriculture and Forestry Ministry also had four new *kōdan* on the drawing board. The SCAP officials had welcomed them all.

With those new proposals, the full force of the phrase "*kōdan* system" struck me for the first time. If all "basic production materials, major consumer goods and important foodstuffs, etc." were placed in *kōdan* hands, what would be left for private wholesalers, and what would become of the free market? Manufacturers would naturally produce what their customers, the *kōdan,* ordered in accordance with government production plans, and consumers could get only what the *kōdan* had. The market economy would be out. Relations between makers and users would be severed at the wholesale level. It sounded very much like the Soviet system. Furthermore, what was becoming of our JCS 1380/15 order to effect a "wider distribution of the means of . . . trade"? We seemed to be going in the opposite direction. I wondered if the *kōdan* partisans in ESS, almost every one of them a dedicated free enterpriser, realized what they were doing.

Especially pernicious to me was the proposed "daily necessities" *kōdan*. Not only was its scope almost infinitely extensible, but it would have dealt in small, easy-to-conceal articles—electric light bulbs, pencils, toilet paper, notebooks—and the *kōdan*'s monopoly could therefore be enforced only by searches in a much greater range of premises, particularly in private homes. In Japan, much light manufacturing, especially in "daily necessities," took place in cottage industries, with living quarters on the premises. Retail stores also normally had *tatami* rooms in the back. They would be prime places of suspicion. But looking for electric bulbs under *tatami* floors, in *futon* bed rolls, or above ceiling boards would involve massive invasions of privacy, quite different from searching for steel bars or oil drums in factories, storage yards, or warehouses.

I doubted very much that the police, with their history of arrogance toward private individuals, could be trusted to exercise self-restraint or even to obtain search warrants as required by chapter III, article 35 of the new Constitution. Already they were coming fairly close to violating that charter by body searches for concealed staple foods of passengers at train stations and truck riders at check points. Our own MPs, often working in tandem with the Japanese police, were not a good influence either. At that very time, the Army's G-1 and Judge Advocate had them searching without warrants in homes for PX goods and commissary supplies. I myself knew of cases of vicious gossip, informing, and even blackmail by neighbors. Was that ugly situation now going to apply to "black-market" goods as well? To disregard basic civil liberties in order to distribute electric bulbs or toilet paper more equitably would certainly be indefensible.

Over the next several days I voiced my doubts to the various ESS officials involved. Suppose we had a "public corporation system" covering all major commodities in the States, I said; what would happen to private businesses? Sure, the *kōdan* were supposed to be temporary, set up for a year, but they were also infinitely renewable, and no one expected the life of any *kōdan* to end at a year. Almost to a man the Americans were shocked at the possible implications of what they had been fostering, thinking only of their own missions, not socialization, the shape of the overall economy, or civil liberties. It did not take much to convince General Marquat and Sherwood Fine, his economic adviser, to take another look. In the latter part of June, while Tsuru and his group were working feverishly at the ESB to establish the *kōdan* system, the general presided at a special meeting in his office of some fifteen ESS control specialists to reassess that program.

It was found wanting in short order. Although the meeting's results were just what I wanted, I cannot credit my eloquence with achieving them. Once the specialists realized they were collaborating in fashioning a straitjacket for private business, the ESS officials shrank from the whole idea with horror. No one rose to defend the *kōdan*. It took less than an hour for the ESS men to express themselves and for the general to rule that while individual *kōdan* proposals would be considered on their merits, a "*kōdan* system" would not be approved by SCAP. The ESB was informed the next day.

Faced for the first time with opposition, the *kōdan* system project that had sprouted so rapidly in bureaucratic obscurity shriveled like a mushroom exposed to the morning sun. Unlike coal mine nationalization, a *kōdan* system was an elitist project of the Socialist technocrats, without popular support or even knowledge. No Japanese minister could protest that it had to be carried out in fulfilment of the election platform. The iron and steel, fertilizer, and "daily necessities" *kōdan* were quickly dropped. In time the two coal *kōdan* were rendered unnecessary by the defeat of effective state control of coal mines. The four new *kōdan* bills introduced into the Diet—animal feed, oilstuffs, liquor, and nonstaple groceries—were all Ministry of Agriculture and Forestry projects and minor at that. The industrial economy was not affected. When a middle-rank Finance Division official announced SCAP's policy *en passant* at a news conference on August 12—SCAP would allow new *kōdan* only when absolutely necessary, he said[53]—it came as an anticlimax.

And yet two months before, it was anything but. On the contrary, without the SCAP opposition that so suddenly and belatedly arose, ESB could easily have succeeded in creating a dozen more *kōdan,* and with them a "*kōdan* system." There was no public support, but there was no opposition from a public that favored stringent anti–black market measures. Wartime distribution controls had dulled the public's perception of a free, but not black, market. Some big private wholesalers had more pressing problems—Mitsui and Mitsubishi trading companies had been ordered by SCAP to dissolve—while others, like the rice dealers, had ceased to exist. The politicans were simply not interested in administrative complexities. No one from the Japanese side would have stopped a *kōdan* system and socialized wholesaling.

In the March 1948 cabinet shakeup, the ESB Director General's post went to a Democrat, and the Socialist Tsuru and his friends were out of that agency. Then, as supplies generally improved, the successor agencies to the wartime control structure withered away, solving the problem of the control associations. At the end of 1948, the conservative Second Yoshida Cabinet took office, dooming any remaining Socialist dreams.

Like coal mine nationalization, the nationalization of distribution channels turned out to be a nonevent. Unlike coal, however, hardly anyone ever knew that the transformation was actually already in the making. Close was not enough. The Socialists missed their target of opportunity as they missed their target of tradition.

They would still have one more target of opportunity, another chance to alter the balance of postwar economic forces in Japan significantly by utilizing the immense Japanese government-owned military stores left after the war for Socialist objectives. It would be their last chance during the Occupation period.

18

The Normality of Scandal

THE JAPANESE ARMY'S MISSING SUPPLIES

ONE SHOULD NEVER FORGET THAT the apparently trivial may turn out to be the balance wheel of human affairs. Despite all the great issues confronting the nation, ordinary Japanese in 1947 and 1948 were weary of the cosmic and the crucial. They were turning away from them and back to matters on a human scale. Conversations on public affairs shifted from political philosophy to gossip. Increasingly, the public became absorbed in the foibles and weaknesses of individuals and their scandals. The variety of human interest distractions multiplied, while political leaders contended for the nation's steadily waning attention.

Improving supplies of paper and additional movie houses helped. The number of magazines *not* dealing with the weighty subjects of politics, economics, international relations, and national reconstruction grew prodigiously. The Publishers' Association in the summer of 1947 listed among applicants for paper allocations 165 literary reviews, 85 women's and children's magazines, 132 science magazines, and 168 periodicals in amusement, art, and "life."[1]

American movies, rented for yen by the Motion Picture Export Association, an export consortium of American distributors, started to come into the country in quantity. In August and September 1947, for example, *Kitty Foyle* with Ginger Rogers, *One Foot in Heaven* with Frederick March, *Gentleman Jim* with Errol Flynn, *The Shop Around the Corner* with James Stewart, *The Human Comedy* with Mickey Rooney, *Appointment for Love* with Charles Boyer, and

Jane Eyre with Joan Fontaine (an alumna of the American School in Japan) opened in Japan. They exposed the Japanese to the postwar world outside, with unpredictable results.

THE RETURN OF SCANDAL

A searching reexamination of traditional mores was one consequence. A survey of 542 female employees of the Agriculture and Forestry Ministry made by the women's section of the Ministry labor union revealed that 85 percent believed in ''recognizing'' office love affairs, and 79 percent preferred a love marriage as opposed to the traditional arranged marriage favored by only 21 percent.[2] Others, however, were not so sure that greater romantic freedom was so desirable. A census of eleven mental hospitals in Metropolitan Tokyo put the number of women inmates at 2,131 about equal to the number of men. That was a far greater proportion of women than before the war. The authorities ascribed the increasing percentage of female inmates to the greater number of unsupervised love affairs postwar and also to the ability of women to endure the poor food at those hospitals better than the men, who either ran away or died.[3]

The educational authorities of Tokyo attacked the subject from still another angle. A survey of 8,580 girl students disclosed that 734 had at one time or another been winked at by men in trains or street cars and 413 had been followed by them after they got off, but only 44 had received love letters (thereby proving that it is easier to wink than to write a letter). The authorities solemnly advised the parents of girl students to instruct them not to look back when winked at or followed, for temptation might ensue.[4]

Novel postwar conditions incited surprising twists in public behavior, unthinkable before the war. Take the Emperor system. The Socialist Matsumoto Jiichirō, long-term leader of the ''untouchable'' *burakumin* class and newly chosen Speaker of the House of Councillors, not only declined to wear a necktie when presiding over the House, but refused flatly to be received in audience by the Emperor on the occasion of the Diet's opening in 1948. He was absolutely opposed, Matsumoto declared, to ''a human being worshiping another human being.'' (This was the same Matsumoto the Communists had boomed for prime minister on the eve of the general strike.)[5]

That was just among human beings. On the level of deities, the forty-five-year-old self-styled Sun Goddess Jiko-sama, who by her own account outranked the Emperor because he was only a *descendant* of the Sun Goddess, decided to show her displeasure by moving to Gotemba in Shizuoka Prefecture. There she and her sixteen ''ministers,'' including the brilliant Chinese *go* master Wu Ching-yuan, settled down to await the destruction of the world.[6] Meanwhile, the youth section of the Government Railway Labor Federation protested the special treatment accorded the Imperial trains. It was undemocratic and furthermore caused them too much work.[7] Investigating the Emperor's personal assets as befitted a democracy, the Kōjimachi tax office reported that he owned only sixty major articles of clothing, including twenty-three foreign-style suits, sixteen overcoats, and thirteen hats. The Empress naturally had more, ninety-seven in all.[8] In 1945 and 1946, the public had seriously debated the retention of the Emperor system. By 1947, the serious issue was settled. Only the odd trivia were news now.

The newspapers also beguiled the public with the spectacle of the new proletarian Socialist ministers living in an unaccustomed patrician style. Commerce and Industry Minister Mizutani shared the residence of Prince Takeda with the Takeda family. The Takedas had nowhere else to go. To Matsuoka Komakichi, former steel worker and now Speaker of the House of Representatives, was assigned the official residence of Prince Kita-Shirakawa, with sixteen large rooms and gold chrysanthemum crests all over. They made his wife uncomfortable, a reporter wrote. The public surely sympathized.[9]

Instead of the serious soul-searching of the year before about Japan's identity in a new kind of world, a search was made for a national bird to set beside the American eagle. The recommended choice was the pheasant, which, experts said, in addition to being indigenous, is "strong like a man and full of maternal love." The crane was a close second.[10]

The International War Crimes Tribunal droned on through all of 1947 and much of 1948. It was not until November 1948 that the verdicts were handed down. Meanwhile there was no shortage of local crime. A mild-looking watercolor artist, Hirasawa Sadamichi, strolled into the Shiina-machi, Tokyo, branch of the Teikoku Bank on the afternoon of January 26, 1948, and "on behalf of the local health authorities" instructed the bank employees to drink a preventive against dysentery. It turned out to be potassium cyanide. Twelve of them died, and he successfully robbed the bank. News like that was strong competition for democratization politics. Gangster doings, particularly those of the Shinjuku street stall boss, Ōzu Kinnosuke, were splashed across the front pages. An *Asahi* poll in Tokyo, Osaka, and North Kyūshū revealed that 96 percent of those asked had heard of the gangster boss system, a greater percentage, undoubtedly, than those who had heard of the *kōdan* system, the proposed system for state control of coal mines, or even the capitalist or socialist systems.[11]

From the sublime down to the ridiculous, the public was titillated. A people with a remarkably high level of personal honesty nevertheless read with relish of a wide range of peccadillos. Thus larceny: Out of the 1,200 electric bulbs installed in five gaily decorated Tokyo trolley cars to celebrate the new Constitution, 400 had disappeared after the first day.[12] Then fraud: A new brand of black market cigarettes, produced "somewhere in Gifu Prefecture" and being sold for two yen per piece as "specially cut and mixed," turned out to be mixed all right, but with dried horse manure. One official of the Tokyo Tobacco Monopoly Bureau, after trying several, in itself a kind of compliment, concluded that "they don't smell as bad as one would think. They're just unsanitary, that's all."[13] Or public morals: At Gotanda in Tokyo, six sets of Japanese saké cups with cunningly concealed pornographic pictures were confiscated by the police—because the price was too high. Everyone had to join in fighting inflation, after all.[14]

The various branches of intimate entertainment could not but provide morsels of food for thought, or risibility. The 3,400 dancers of Tokyo's dance halls kicked up a storm, objecting violently to obligatory police venereal disease checks. They were not prostitutes, they protested.[15] As proof, the Taxi Dancers Union pointed to the results of recent examinations of their members in Tokyo, which showed that 80 percent were virgins.[16]

On the more traditional side, nine *geisha* visited Prime Minister Katayama to ask that the *machiai* restaurants just ordered closed be reopened, even without food or drink, to avoid throwing the members of the Geisha Labor Union out of work.[17] The prime minister gallantly acceded, and the government allowed restaurant *geisha* parties where only tea was served.[18] It was those same restaurants, serving something stronger than tea, that helped sink his Coal Mine State Control Bill.

Toward the end of the year, *geisha* Okada-san, famous in the 1930s for having cut off her lover's penis because of his unfaithfulness and carrying it around in a *furoshiki* scarf, announced that she was considering appearing on the stage to reenact the high point of her life for 50,000 yen a day.[19] In the end, she accepted a mere 30,000 yen daily and proved a great disappointment.[20] But even 30,000 yen was more than the prime minister himself received in a month. Things were returning to normal.

Even the political news was unusually lively, what with the riotous parties being held in the Kanda neighborhood by lobbyists against the Coal Mine State Control Bill and the spread of their spirit to the Diet. Restaurants were closed, but liquor was available on the Diet premises. During one of the debates, a Democratic member named Ubukata Kaikichi appeared on the Diet floor in a state of intoxication and began urinating there. Later, when sober and hailed before the disciplinary committee, he resigned, apologizing for any disturbance he may have caused and hoping that his resignation would help clean up Diet politics.[21] No doubt. On the other hand, when three Liberal anti–coal mine control members were cited for unbecoming behavior during one of the turbulent sessions on that issue, the disciplinary committee was unable to secure a quorum to deal with their case.[22] There must have been a moral in there somewhere.

The Mystery of the Japanese Military Supplies

With the human comedy in such full swing, it was perhaps inevitable that when some really important scandals came along, they would just merge with all the others, deplorable, to be sure, yet entertaining food for gossip. No one would look for any deeper significance. And that was what happened with the disappearance of the Japanese military supplies.

Almost from the beginning of the Occupation, rumors had repeatedly cropped up about hidden Japanese Army treasure, from gold bars sunk in Tokyo Bay to bullion burried in hillside caves. Then the "treasure" turned into copper ingots, aluminum, wire, chemicals, and even Army uniforms. In the summer of 1946 a European resident was found dead in the subbasement of the Osaka Kaisha Building,[23] just two buildings away from the main officers' billet of the Osaka military command. It was whispered about that he had been murdered in a quarrel over Army stores from the Osaka arsenal.

Lieutenant Colonel William E. Homan, when he first assumed command of the 441st Counter Intelligence Corps in the autumn of 1946, dropped into our Labor Division office to see an old combat comrade, Major Antony Costantino, then my Labor Relations Branch Chief. Homan told us that he had been astonished, on his assumption of command, to be informed of several cases involving caches of illegal goods with merchandise in the million of dollars. A newspaperman in civilian life, he unfolded yarns fit for the Sunday supplements. In one, a CIC agent was supposed to meet a Japanese informer at midnight on a deserted road near Odawara, south of Tokyo, to receive specific directions to a hoard of Army goods. His informant never showed up. Homan was sure he had been murdered by Japanese gangsters, and the goods had been hijacked. Other tales were equally lurid. With no one looking for them, clues kept turning up all over the landscape.

For almost two years, nevertheless, no secret treasure materialized. Aside from one minor seizure of a quarter-million dollars' worth of gold and silver reported by our Public Safety Division,[24] the bullion in SCAP custody held very steady month after month at 183 million grams of gold and some 2 billion grams of silver (worth $250 million and $46 million respectively). All of it had been transferred from Japanese government custody at war's end, none from buried treasure.[25] Seizures of other goods were on a small scale, the usual inventories of black market operators. That was all.

But just about the time that the Socialists took office, a strange tale began to unfold. In May 1947 a maverick Liberal party politician, Sekō Kōichi by name (from Wakayama Second electoral district), began to charge in a series of speeches to Liberal Party clubs and then to the procurators that at least 100 billion yen worth of Army stocks desperately needed by the economy was being hoarded secretly. Now those were figures worth looking into. Seko himself had been appointed Parliamentary Vice Minister of Home Affairs the preceding year. Parliamentary vice ministers in Japan, however, were not supposed to do anything. Apparently not understanding that, he had appointed himself investigator of "hoarded goods." As vice chairman from February to April 1947 of the Hoarded Goods Committee set up by the prime minister at Sekō's insistence, and over the objections of the Economic Stabilization Board's Director General Zen, he not only continued his investigations but seized "illegal" stocks that he uncovered on his committee's—that is, his own—authority. His confiscation orders, called "Sekō letters," 140 of them in all, were themselves probably illegal, but no one wanted to defend the hoarders who were obviously guilty of something or other, no one was sure exactly what.

Now, Sekō's charges were usually combinations of concrete data, such as his own discoveries (like the 6,000 reams of paper and 1 million pounds of millet jelly he had found in a Tokyo warehouse), and common sense. But they also included flights of "logical" fancy, for example, his calculation of the amount of gold that must be hidden somewhere on the basis of the wartime Tōjō Cabinet's budget to buy up gold ornaments from the people.[26] He came up with a figure that no one else was able to approach. No one knew how seriously to take him.

In the course of his charges, however, Sekō declared that two or three of the new Katayama cabinet ministers were personally involved in hoarding goods illegally. *That* not only earned him an interrogation by the Procurator General and a lawsuit by one of the accused, the right Socialist State Minister Nishio Suehiro (Sekō was unable to substantiate that particular charge), but also caused the Diet on July 25, 1947, to set up an investigation committee, headed by the left Socialist Katō Kanjū, to probe the entire matter of hoarded and concealed goods. Colonels Kades and Frank Hayes in the Government Section abetted the move as an excellent means of promoting the Diet's power under the new constitution. That blew the lid off the affair.

For at bottom, Sekō was not wrong. The Japanese Army had prepared for a two- or three-year battle for the final defense of the home islands and had never fought the battle. In contrast to the Imperial Navy, which had been sunk, and the air arms of both services, which had been shot out of the skies, the Army had fought only minor skirmishes on the ground in China and peripheral engagements, bloody but small in scale, in the South Pacific. Its supplies were largely intact. So also were the reserve stocks of uniforms, provisions, and equipment that had been put aside for a ghost army of some 4 million men who had never been mobilized.[27] However much the fire bombings had devasted the wooden dwellings in the cities, moreover, they could not have destroyed the raw and semifinished materials in the war production pipeline, particularly metals and metal products, or, for that matter, underground fuel stores. What had happened to them?

The truth, laboriously pieced together from SCAP sources and Japanese documents uncovered by Katō's committee, gradually emerged: The vast bulk of the military supplies left at the end of the war had simply been stolen. In possibly the greatest raids ever made on the resources of a state in modern time by its own citizens, aided by patriotic Japanese officers determined to save the substance of their country from pillaging by an occupation force, tens of thousands of Japanese, if not more, had pillaged it first. Since then they had been concealing their booty.

When the war suddenly ended in mid-August 1945, the back doors of the arsenals and military warehouses were opened, and vast mountains of supplies moved out. On August 14, 1945, the day when the Japanese accepted the Potsdam Declaration, the cabinet decided to deprive the incoming Americans of its military stores by "civilianizing" them, that is, distributing them to "government organs, public organizations, private factories, and to private persons."[28]

The decision of course, was in violation of the basic concept of "unconditional surrender" in article 13 of the Potsdam Declaration. Speed and secrecy were therefore imperative to complete the operation before the Americans arrived and to preserve its results afterward. By secret order #363, on the very next day, the day the Emperor read his surrender rescript by transcription over the radio, the Minister of War authorized the disposal of everything except arms and armaments free of charge to prefectural governments and public bodies. Such gifts were to be supplemented by sales to private corporations at low prices and with deferred payments.[29]

Another order of August 16 instructed each unit to burn or otherwise destroy all military documents except financial papers and contracts. On August 17 and 18 conflagrations in military offices broke out all over the country.[30] In Tokyo huge fires erupted at the Army and Navy ministries and at the Imperial General Staff Building, across from the Imperial Palace grounds. (The Americans, on their arrival shortly thereafter, marveled at the accuracy of their precision bombing, for the civilian ministries across the street from the Army and Navy ministries were untouched.) Financial records and contracts, too, went up in flames, for there was no time to segregate them. Nothing was allowed to stand in the way of the operation. To avoid delays normally involved in securing higher-echelon approval, the high command allowed military units to dispose of stocks on their own.[31]

On August 20 in Manila, the Americans made it very clear to the presurrender mission led by Lieutenant General Kawabe Torashiro that *all* military property, not just arms and armaments, was covered by the August 14 surrender,[32] but the Japanese did not halt the dispersion rush. Secret order #363 was not canceled until August 28, eight days later. The original order had taken one day to issue, but it took eight days to cancel. A companion order on August 28 to retrieve the already distributed material was only partly effective. From

August 14 to September 2, 1945, a period when Japan was neither under American attack nor under American control, an estimated 70 percent of the stores held in arsenals, munitions factories, and military warehouses throughout the country was illegally disposed of.[33] Perhaps 30 to 60 percent of that 70 percent was actually retrieved.[34] The rest, amounting to a third or a half of the original, disappeared without documentation or records.

The Japanese officers who had thought they had been performing a patriotic act by violating the surrender terms must have been taken aback when, having been obliged to turn over the remaining stores to the Americans, they saw the Americans give them back, except for actual armaments, to the Japanese Home Ministry. The only condition was that they be used to succor the stricken economy.[35]

The Home Ministry resumed distribution of those goods, later to be termed "special goods" by the Sekō Committee—as distinct from the "concealed goods," those that had disappeared illegally—in accordance with the old principles: gratis to prefectural and public bodies, and at very low prices and deferred payment to private enterprises, except in emergency. One such emergency gave license to a further spasm of looting when, shortly after the New Year, SCAP designated the Osaka arsenal, biggest in Japan, as a possible reparations facility.[36] The Osaka Railway Bureau, designated by the Home Ministry as supervisor of the arsenal, hurriedly notified all its suppliers to come and pick up whatever materials they chose free of charge during a five-day period ending February 15 as "an emergency release." The suppliers, and undoubtedly their friends too, mobilized everything that could move—trucks, oxcarts, bicycles with "rear cars," barges, and even small steamers—to loot the installation for a second time; the first had been in August 1945 under the very noses of the U.S. 25th "Tropic Lightning" Division.[37] Records of "special goods" distribution were supposed to be kept, but in practice none were. Finance Minister Ishibashi was to complain that in 1946 he could secure documentation for only 2 or 3 percent of the releases.[38]

In special circumstances "extraordinary" channels of distribution were set up. Most notable was the Arms Disposal Committee (ADC), assigned to distribute metals and primary metal products, which the prefectural governments presumably could not handle. The committee members were among the biggest heavy industry firms in the country.[39] Its chairman was the engaging Americanophile Komatsu Takeshi, vice president of Nippon Steel Tube and M.A. Harvard, 1911. The committee's authority came straight from the Home Ministry and the Commerce and Industry Ministry.

The arrangements between the ADC and the government were exceptionally cozy. The ADC articles of association were dated the same day, October 31, 1945, that the joint ministerial ordinance instructed the companies to form the committee. That was fast action, indeed. A slight slip in timing, and the companies would have complied with the order *before* it was issued. In fact, although a draft contract under which the ADC would sell all its arms-production materials to the Home Ministry at prices unspecified had been negotiated in November 1945, the parties had neglected to sign it. And so on May 16, 1946, a formal contract was signed, with an added provision retroactively authorizing everything that the ADC had done since November 1 of the preceding year.[40]

Finally, there were the goods in the war industrial pipeline, neither "special" nor "concealed" that just sat where they were and became "private" property by default. Factories, for example, to which had been sent Army-owned material for processing, whether fabric for clothing, leather for shoes, or primary metal products for further fabrication, simply "forgot" that the Army owned it once the Army records were destroyed. (If such primary contractors had sent the material on to subcontractors, however, they did not forget, we may be sure.) Where factories had financed their own materials by bank loans against Army contracts, the inflation quickly depreciated their obligation, while the materials remained, ever rising in value.

The opportunities for quick and enormous profit in dealing with any of those goods were almost endless, and so were the possibilities of graft. In the most important cases, where the prefectural governments, having received goods free, had to sell them at no more than the official prices when the black market was several times higher, the discrepancy between the two was enough to tempt Diogenes himself. One Home Ministry accounting received later in 1947, when I was coordinating the ESS effort regarding hoarded goods, showed official sales by the prefectures in 1946 of Army tunics at fifteen yen each, trousers at the same price, *tabi* socks at one yen per pair, and fur hats at eight yen apiece. (At the 1946 fifty-to-one military conversion rate, those were equal to thirty cents, thirty cents, two cents, and sixteen cents, respectively in U.S. currency.

Nor were "extraordinary" channels like the Arms Disposal Committee less generous. Their records would show, in August 1947, that the committee had bought some 1.3 million tons of metals at an average price of 1,000 yen a ton and had sold them to private corporations over a period of several months for an average price of 698 yen a ton, an out-of-pocket loss of 30 percent. Meanwhile domestic prices were soaring, and the yen was depreciating. The merchandise was worth, by conservative estimate, at least $100 per metric ton[41] or $130 million. The ADC's total receipt of 900 million yen from the sales were worth, in March 1947, only about $9 million. The balance was a subsidy to the metals manufacturers. Then the Arms Disposal Committee approached the government to make up their losses!

Missing the Forest for the Trees

Sekō had declared that the motive of his investigations was to avert an economic crisis caused by shortages of critical goods. Katō's report had proclaimed its purpose as "suggesting an immediate method by which Japanese industrial production can be increased . . . inflation can be retarded . . . export revenues released."[42] But as name after famous name became involved in scandal—all the way up to Prime Minister Ashida himself,[43] to say nothing of the hundred or so ordinary Diet members who received scandal-related political donations—it became harder to keep the original objectives in mind. Fewer of the culprits or accused persons had any connection with Army stocks,[44] but the investigations went on and even expanded.

In August 1947, General Whitney, Chief of the Government Section, had become personally interested. In the succeeding months he, his deputy, Colonel Kades, and their assistants met repeatedly with the Justice Minister and Procurator General and agreed to help in the investigations. More than 1,500 new prosecutors were added to the Procurator General's staff, and special headquarters were set up regionally. The Katō Committee on Hoarded Goods was reorganized under Katō's successor, Mutō Unjirō, another Socialist, as the Committee on Illegal Transactions, that is, dealings of any kind, not just in hoarded goods. Kades redefined the issue to the national conference of prosecutors in February 1948 as one of equality under law. "The world is watching to see," he said grandiloquently, "whether it is true under the new Constitution, as it was under the Meiji Constitution and as it was actually enforced by the Tokugawa Shogunate, that courtesy should not be extended to the 'commoner' and punishment should not be administered to the 'gentleman.' "[45]

With the line drawn so clearly between the white hats (prosecutors and Diet investigators) and the black hats (corrupt politicians), the government went off on a national chase after the black hats. No one was more enthusiastic than the Socialists, for the targets were almost all either conservative politicians connected with the preceding cabinet or businessmen, often big businessmen. The one awkward exception was Chief Cabinet Secretary Nishio, but he was a leader of the party's right wing. Indeed, the Socialists treated the chase like a morality play. Committee Chairman Katō Kanjū could start his report with a statement of high economic purpose—to increase production, retard inflation, and develop export revenue—but his conclusions and recommendations had little to do with economics and everything to do with investigating fraud and apprehending the guilty. What made the morality play even more instructive to the public was that the victims were often peasants or workers.

In the very first big hoarded goods case, a Liberal party politician named Nakasone Ikutarō[46] had collected 20 million yen from some farmers' and workers' organizations to buy 600,000 Army uniforms but had used part of the money to run for election to the Diet, meanwhile passing on a good share to Japan Liberal Party power broker, Tsuji Karoku. Tsuji, in turn, had donated money to twenty-six conservative election candidates, had built a house for party president Hatoyama, and had bought a restaurant for party meetings. The uniforms were never delivered; the farmers and workers lost their money,[47] and Nakasone lost the election. Meanwhile big companies were displaying extraordinary ingenuity in concealment: stashing a million dollars worth of machine tools and rubber at the bottom of Lake Inawashiro, near a hydro-electric plant;[48] building workshops over a store of 80 tons of aluminum, tin, copper wire and sheeting, and scrap iron, in Okayama City;[49] and so forth. What object lessons for the masses!

In the excitement and glow of self-righteousness, however, the Socialists lost their ideological sense of direction. With a little imagination it would have been easy to devise schemes for harnessing the Army stocks to socialization, for example, using the proceeds of their sale to compensate the owners of industries to be nationalized, accepting corporate stock in return for the Army materials left behind in factories, and so on. But nothing of that kind emanated from either Socialist leaders or Socialist theoreticians. It was as though the military stockpiles existed in another universe of discourse. How was that possible?

The fact was that the Socialists, and not they alone, never appreciated the immensity of the stocks involved. As Sekō had said, the Army had had supplies for two and a half years of fighting, perhaps even more. But that just began to tell the story, obliterated as it was by the wholesale destruction of records and the decentralized manner of distribution. From fiscal 1942 to fiscal 1945, the budgeted special war expenditures account rose from 40 to 62 percent of the *total* national income![50] Over the four-year span of the Pacific war, about *half of everything Japan produced* went for war purposes. In terms of March 1945 yen, total budgeted war expenditures for four years reached about 280 billion yen, or somewhat more than $20 billion U.S.[51] And a good part of the production procured was stocked and remained intact at the end of hostilities.

In this light, the figures tossed about afterward, like Sekō's August 1947 estimate of war-end stocks at 240 billion yen at May 1947 official prices, that is, roughly 14 billion,[52] seem not at all unreasonable. Former Finance Minister Ishibashi recalled before the Katō Committee that in November 1946 he had received from the Allied authorities, presumably G-4, a list of goods surrendered by Japan and turned back by the Occupation, that is, the so-called special goods. Those were valued at 100 billion yen, he said. He did not say how they were valued and when. If valued in September 1945, at the prevailing military exchange rate of 15 yen to the dollar, they would have been worth over $6 billion U.S. If valued in the fall of 1946 at official prices, they would have been worth (at, say, 64 yen to the dollar) only $1.5 billion, but the free market value would have been far higher, perhaps double.[53]

Those figures applied, of course, only to the ''special goods.'' They did not include the concealed goods (that is, looted but unrecovered), which amounted to between half and the full value of the special goods. Nor did they include the Army materials left in the factories quite legitimately for processing. Probably no one can now ascertain the value of all the military stocks in existence at war's end with any exactitude; only a rough order of magnitude can be expected. But viewed from any angle, that they ran into several billions of U.S. dollars at the least seems undeniable. Liquidating a gigantic military establishment does not come cheap.

No one at the time recognized the true dimensions of the liquidations, not the politicians, the Japanese government economists, the SCAP officials, nor the press. The significance of the G-4, Sekō, and Ishibashi figures was never really absorbed. Money figures, anyway, were hard to comprehend in the middle of a rampant inflation. Suffice it to say that all Japan's factories and mines producing at the 1947 rate would have taken at least two years to produce the value of that part of the military stockpile that went into hiding at the end of the war.[54] And that was only *net* production. In reality, much more would have to be produced in materials and fuels to be used in the productive process, to say nothing of all the goods needed by the workers to stay alive while they produced them. By any measure, the economic importance of the military stores far dwarfed the coal mining industry over which such a furor had erupted in the Diet, which was producing only some $50 million of product in 1947,[55] only 1 or 2 percent of the military stores. The military stores also far overshadowed the American industrial recovery aid program for Japan, for which $75 million and $165 million were budgeted for 1948–49 and 1949–50. They even substantially exceeded the total of all American aid ($2.2 billion) during the seven years of occupation.[56]

At the time no one perceived their overwhelming importance. Just as we all in those days saw individual Japanese civilians wearing articles of military uniform—tunics, caps, pants—without visualizing the Army of 4 million for whom they had been prepared, so the Japanese public and the government, and SCAP as well, read the Katō and Mutō committee reports and savored the scandals without realizing the magnitude of the goods involved and their consequent transcendent importance to their country's recovery. Nor, to my knowledge, has anyone realized it since.

American-financed industrial imports were crucial, to be sure, for they filled critical gaps in Japan's availabilities. But the leftover military stores constituted the indispensable base upon which Japanese recovery proceeded. They were the precious profit of Japan's decision to surrender before being invaded. Had Japan fought on, and had those supplies been consumed, dispersed, or destroyed, who can tell how much Japan's postwar economic recovery would have been delayed? In large part the supplies left over from the war were the key to Japan's ultimate economic rehabilitation.

WINDFALL FOR THE OLD GUARD

Even allowing for the Socialists' inability to comprehend the magnitude of the military stores, they could not have been blind to the impact their manner of distribution was having on the balance of forces in Japanese society. From the beginning, a harassed Japanese military under pressure had disposed of whatever it could as fast as it could through available channels. Those channels were dominated by the prewar powers in society. Inevitably, the distribution of the Army stocks served to reinforce the old regime.

I do not charge that the military intended or conspired to achieve that result. But it could not have been otherwise. When the arsenals gave away their goods, they needed recipients who could handle, transport, and store large volumes on short notice, especially since 80 percent—according to the prosecutors recovering them later—was in heavy and bulky items, like iron and steel, metals, and their manufactures.[57] Naturally, they notified all their suppliers, those who had been collaborating in military orders and profiting from war production for years. Similarly, when "public bodies" were called on to help, they were usually control companies (*tōsei kaisha*) or control operating bodies (*eidan*) dominated by the giant *zaibatsu* financial combines. Labor unions were not yet in existence at the end of the war, and factory mutual credit societies were ordinarily under management's thumb. When prefectural governments were given charge of consumer goods their first customers were local notables—entrepreneurs, manufacturers, money lenders, *rentier* landlords, and politicians— the backbone of the postwar Liberal and Democratic party local machines. Even repatriates and welfare associations were dominated by the old guard when the distributions were made.

Most favored, perhaps, were the manufacturers who simply took over the materials they were processing for the Army while the Army benevolently looked the other way. By their very nature—that is, the simple assumption of ownership without physical movement of goods—such appropriations were invisible. In the biggest case uncovered by the prosecutors, Nakajima Aircraft Company, makers of the famous Zero fighter, inherited, together with its subsidiaries, a vast quantity of aircraft components and parts, iron and steel materials, textiles, rubber, electric wire, and so on. The hidden goods were worth, prosecutors said in February 1948 9 billion yen, or $40 million.[58] Three years after the war, hardly any of the military-owned material had yet left the numerous wartime premises of the firm (now renamed Fuji Industrial Company) and its associated subsidiaries and subcontractors. But the stores had been effectively "stolen" just the same. In general, industry got windfalls across the board. Workers and farmers got relatively little.

The result was that large segments of the propertied classes, on the verge of being suffocated economically by the military defeat, were resuscitated by the distribution of the military stores. Numerous locally prominent *rentiers*, losing their agricultural investments to the SCAP-sponsored land reform, still retained some liquidity and the personal connections to enable them to recoup by dabbling in military goods. So did those with liquid funds received from government war-damage insurance benefits when their factories were bombed and burned out or from war contract cancellation fees. Investing in Army stocks turned out for many of them to be a bridge back to their prewar economic status. The property of the nation as a whole was skewed, in effect, to restore the old regime.

To the conservatives, that must have seemed fitting and proper. But the Socialists, whose entire ideology was aimed the other way, did not seem to notice it. They were prepared to seize *private* property, like coal mines. Somehow it never occurred to them to reseize *government* or *national* property on a scale that would have given them control of the economic restoration. After a series of sensational investigations and scandals, no more than some 15 billion yen worth (about $60 million in June 1948) was retrieved in all, only a small percentage, at most, of the total. Even in the open-and-shut case of the Arms Disposal Committee, the chairman, Komatsu, went to jail for a short while,[59] but the goods were gone. The Socialists never saw the Army goods distributions in institutional rather than personal terms. It was, after all, an age of scandal.

Indeed it was left to GHQ to make the only serious effort to recover the military goods on a broad scale, and the reasons had nothing to do with socialism or the Socialists. In October 1947, I approached General Marquat with the latest reports on the burgeoning Sekō affair and the work of the Katō Committee. We were all aware in ESS that very substantial quantities of industrial raw materials were being hoarded, I explained, and their unavailability to the productive economy was a drag on recovery. It was obviously a serious problem, and it came under the ESS's purview.

As it happened, someone in our Industry Division had given me an informal list of materials known to have been in the Osaka arsenal when the Occupation began and that could not longer be located. I told Marquat of the list, which had apparently been compiled from reports given to G-4 by the Home Ministry in the fall of 1945. Its implications were staggering. In only the one arsenal, which although the biggest was still only one of seventy in the country, the Japanese Army had had in stock from three to ten months of current (1947) national production of copper ingots, zinc, brass, lead, mercury, and pig iron. In addition the arsenal had possessed very substantial quantities of cobalt, tin, antimony, aluminum, leather, cooking coal, timber, paint, copper wire, hemp, lubricating oil, and grease,[60] and now none of it could be found. And what had become of the twenty-six gold bars, the 20 tons of silver, and the 600 carats of diamonds? Where had those disappeared to?

Up until that time, SCAP had only asked the American Congress to finance the importation of food relief, emergency petroleum products, and medical supplies. ESS had also arranged a $130 million revolving foreign bank credit, secured by the gold and silver bullion in the vaults of the Bank of Japan, to finance the importation of raw cotton for export processing. But now we were preparing a $75 million appropriation request to cover the import of industrial raw materials. Five of the items we planned to import were on the Osaka Arsenal list of vanished inventories. How could we justify such a request if they were still in Japan and we made no effort to find them? It would be particularly embarrassing to the Supreme Commander if someone discovered caches of any industrial materials after we had bought them elsewhere with U.S. tax money. The individual investigations that Government Section was so actively pushing through the procurators were aimed at indictments and convictions. They required voluminous evidence for the purpose, and that took a great deal of manpower. The procurators were looking for malefactors; we were looking for goods. We needed a much broader approach, and also a shortcut in time. Marquat asked me for a recommendation.

The Frustrated GHQ Plan

A few days later, after checking with our ESS specialists, I proposed that SCAP require all factories, warehouses, storage yards, and owners to report all critical materials in their possession. Those who reported them would be presumed to be the legal owners, at least vis-à-vis the government. Materials unreported and subsequently discovered would be subject to confiscation. True, two earlier inventories had been tried unsuccessfully by the Japanese Government, but I was sure they had been sabotaged along the way. With SCAP's resources and power mobilized for the purpose, I was confident that we could uncover far more than enough to justify the effort. Marquat thought it worth the try; not to do it could expose the Command to charges of laxity with U.S.-appropriated funds. The ESS staff worked out the action, Government Section and G-3 (Operations) concurred, and on February 21, 1948, the Supreme Commander formally ordered the Japanese Government to require such inventories as rapidly as possible.[61]

The whole affair turned out to be a lesson in the art of the possible. The key Japanese agency involved, the Economic Stabilization Board, killed the project with kindness. Against ESS advice it prepared an inventory questionnaire so detailed—they were going to do it right, the board members told us—that the respondents found it hard to answer and easy to explain why they hadn't. Also, it took the ESB two months to compile the questionnaire, another month to mail it out, and a fourth month to wait for the replies. Meanwhile the follow-up investigators had nothing to work with. It was hard to believe that the ESB personnel were not impeding the operation on purpose.

Even the lateness and paucity of replies—only 40,000 where we had expected 400,000—would not have doomed the enterprise. That would just have subjected a great many more hoarders to confiscation when the investigators found them. Alas, our investigation broke down, too. For the enterprise depended heavily on full mobilization of SCAP resources, particularly the Counter Intelligence Corps teams, which under Bridgadier General Elliott Thorpe had been so active early in the Occupation in ferreting out precious metals hoards.[62] We even had arranged for tactical troop manpower to help the CIC teams. General Willoughby, Thorpe's successor, however, did not see the CIC mission that way. He had been watching the Government Section campaign against the military stores hoarders with distaste and misgiving. Openly partisan in Japanese politics—he was the only such officer of high rank in GHQ—he trusted only the most conservative Japanese elements, and even better the former top military officers, the important career bureaucrats, and the old-line Liberal party politicians to be reliable opponents of communism. But those were the very people most likely to be inculpated in wrongdoing with Army stocks, as the developing Katō investigation was just then demonstrating. Willoughby could do nothing to stop Whitney from weakening his anti-Communists, but his section was not going to participate in making the situation any worse.

I had figured that, even so, Willoughby could not afford to reject a formal request to help protect U.S.-appropriated funds. That was commandment number one to a high-ranking officer. But I was wrong. In early February 1948, when I sent over a checknote signed by Marquat inviting CIC participation in enforcing the national inventory,[63] Willoughby held it for ten days and then had his deputy reply that the CIC was only "observing and reporting," adding that "CIC will help other sections if practicable." He did not respond at all to our request for a meeting.[64] In other words, "no." We had thereafter to rely on the military government teams instead. But they had no undercover investigatory capacity—no training, no informers or reward money, no undercover investigators, and no close liaison with the Japanese police. They tried manfully under Brigadier General Beasely but came up with nothing.

The continued noncooperation of the ESB officials, working directly under such active and avid Socialists as Director General Wada Hiroo and his deputy, Tsuru Shigeto, was far more surprising. If only for the reasons that had impelled Willoughby to disfavor the drive against hoarded goods, the ESB should have been for it. From the beginning, however, the Director of the Enforcement Bureau was apathetic, constantly denigrating Sekō's charges as exaggerated and Sekō's results as inferior to his own.[65] Meanwhile, the ESB disregarded 65 percent of the tips on hoarded goods from April through November 1947, retrieving only 95 million yen worth (less than a million dollars) in those eight months.[66] In contrast, from November through February 1948, in half the time, the prosecutors found over 11.3 billion yen worth.[67] One had to wonder where the ESB sleuths had been looking. Indeed, the Deputy Director of the Enforcement Bureau was so dilatory and diversive in implementing the inventory directive that the SCAP officials dealing with him asked me to ask Government Section to order him removed from his position.[68] His was the only formal removal ESS requested in the whole course of the Occupation. But it was too late.

In a project such as the SCAP-directed inventory, time was of the essence—it was too easy to cover up, given the opportunity—and in the changed atmosphere of 1948, when SCAP officials could only advise, no longer order, they could not overcome the roadblocks of the ESB officials. Undoubtedly the whole inventory project, seen in retrospect, was too ambitious. After all, who could have screened 400,000 returns or even a significant part of them? But certainly without the wholehearted administrative support of the Japanese Government and CIC investigative follow-up, the project was hopeless. It was bound to fail, and it did.

Afterward it seemed to me that the Japanese Government and people were not really that indignant or dedicated to the idea of a thorough uprooting of the illegal and irregular Army goods distributions that had taken place. By 1947 and 1948, too many people, their relatives, or their friends were involved in some little piece of the action. Even workers or farmers who bought part of an Army uniform cheap from a dealer who was not supposed to have the goods may have thought themselves deserving beneficiaries of the arrangement. How bad could it be? It was all very human to derive satisfaction from the fall of the mighty or the punishment of some "greedy politicians" who went too far. But I doubt that many people really thought that playing fast and loose with military stores when there no longer was a military was truly wrong.

That is the only way to explain the obstructive actions of the top ESB officials and the fact that there was no public demand to reverse the end-of-war distributions of the Army stocks. Everyone was in it. In a time of scandal, it was just another scandal.

Whatever the explanations, however, two facts do stand out. First, beginning with late 1947 the hoarded goods did start to come out of hiding, fueling an impressive industrial advance—production rose 60 percent during 1948[69] *before* the arrival of any American-financed industrial materials. Second, the Socialists never took advantage of those assets to promote their cause. On the contrary, they stood by, unaware or indifferent, as the *distribution system proceeded* to restore the old social order. Although the Socialists were only peripherally involved in the hoarded goods abuses, the scandals still helped topple them from office. After all, they were the "ins," and a public expecting a higher morality of them because they were Socialists felt correspondingly let down. With the scandals and their ousters, the socialist-type democratizers had reached their limits. Japan's third turn was destined to be capitalistic.

Part VI

THE LAST TARGETS:

OLIGARCHS AND

BUREAUCRATS

A YEAR AND A HALF after his occupation began, in his first and only press conference with ordinary American working reporters in Japan, General Douglas MacArthur announced that the Occupation had no further major democratic reforms to propose. "The process of democratization is one of continuing flux," he said. "It takes years." But "insofar as you can lay down the framework, it has already been accomplished. There is little more except to watch, control and guide."[1]

The place was the International Foreign Correspondents Club in downtown Tokyo, the time March, 19, 1947. But the General was being excessively optimistic. Within months his Headquarters, and Japan too, were embroiled in two of the most bitter controversies of the Occupation, and both were precipitated by new SCAP "reform" orders aimed at the Japanese Government. Their targets: the financial oligarchs and the government bureaucrats.

Before the war Japanese were wont to say that of all the innumerable *batsu*—that is clans, cults, cliques, and other groupings of Japanese society—the most powerful were the *gunbatsu* (the military), the *zaibatsu* (the financial combines) and the *kanbatsu* (the bureaucratic elite). With roots deep in Japanese history, for good or for ill, they had made the country what it was. After the war the discredited *gunbatsu* were dissolved at SCAP's first stroke, never to return.

351

But both the *zaibatsu,* dating their rise from the great Osaka merchants and the seventeenth-century House of Mitsui, and the *kanbatsu,* going back to the shogunate and clan bureaucrats of feudal times and reinforced by the *samurai* nobility, who flocked to staff the new imperial government of Meiji, remained as solidly entrenched as almost any Japanese institution could be. It would take a lot to remove them. Why was SCAP starting so late in the day.

The trouble was not that SCAP was starting late but that the original American approach had changed late in the day. The battle against the *zaibatsu* had started out as a program to dissolve the existing giant business combines. The American goal then shifted to ensuring free competition. Then it changed again, to breaking up any "excessively" large concentrations of economic power. The campaign against the "feudalistic" bureaucracy, on the other hand, began as an inchoate suspicious, hostile attitude. But as time went on, that too was given a new focus: a reform of the Japanese administrative apparatus into a civil service system along U.S. federal lines. In mid-1947, accordingly, two entirely new programs emerged.

The two new reforms, so different from each other in subject, outlook, and methods, did have two characteristics in common, and those made them both controversial. First, they tried to impose uniquely American solutions on Japanese problems. Second, the two men charged with shaping and implementing the second-generation democratic reforms were both strong-willed yet narrowly focused persons with an overweening sense of mission. Edward C. Welsh, who took on the *zaibatsu,* and Blaine Hoover, champion of the civil service system, were both crusaders.

Welsh was wiry, quick, intelligent, articulate, and contentious, Hoover was ultra-conventional, bulky and plodding, even stodgy. But they had in common a stubbornness and an inflexibility that made them poor staff men and encumbrances to MacArthur in the finely balanced three-way relationship among Washington, SCAP, and the Japanese. In the end, the General more or less bought the arguments of one and rejected the methods of the other. In both cases, the outcome damaged the Occupation. Welsh ended up by exacerbating the distrust of the Command in Washington. Hoover poisoned the relations between the U.S. Government and the Japanese labor movement. In neither case did the reformers succeed in their professed aims. The oligarchs were not pulverized, and the Japanese bureaucracy remained happily elite and disproportionately powerful, as before, but the side effects lingered for a long time.

In an occupation whose reform framework had already been laid down and was dominated by such a strong-minded commander, how could such a contretemps have come about, anyway?

19

The Assault on the
Zaibatsu

There's something rather fishy
About the Mitsubishi
And the rest of the zaibatsu
Are also not so hot-su.[1]

SO SANG THE CHEERFUL QUATRAIN posted one morning on the bulletin board of the Daiichi field-grade officers' billet in Tokyo in the spring of 1946. The verse drew a few growls from grizzled Army types, who thought such doggerel had no place on an official bulletin board, but it drew lots of chuckles too. It reflected the prevailing opinion in the U.S. Government of the monster Japanese business combinations that had dominated the national economy and invaded the Asian mainland. George Atcheson, MacArthur's State Department adviser, wrote President Truman in November 1945—Truman called it "very illuminating"—that "there are men here who have merely (as the Japanese put it) re-painted their signs. . . . The big business people are the most obvious sign re-painters. They are fundamentally conservative and reactionary; since the days of the Meiji Restoration they and the military have been mutually dependent."[2] Reparations Commissioner Pauley recommended in December 1945 that the plant-removal program be used to destroy the wealth of the *zaibatsu*.

THE DISSOLUTION PROGRAM BOGGED DOWN

Atcheson and Pauley were not alone. Not only could no one visualize a real democracy flourishing in a country where a few giants maintained a tight economic grip, but the *zaibatsu* in themselves were odious objects to Americans. Had they not been willing participants, to their own profit, in aggressive imperialism? Had they not turned out the tanks, planes, and ships that killed countless Americans and Asians, engaged in military-industrial espionage abroad, helped to exploit and subdue the newly conquered territories by all means at hand, and pressured American and European firms out of the Greater East Asia Co-Pros-

353

perity Sphere? As General MacArthur put it later, "The record is thus one of economic oppression and exploitation at home, aggression and spoliation abroad."[3] Few Americans immediately after the war would disagree with MacArthur's assessment or that of the bulletin-board bard. From whatever viewpoint, they were almost all against the *zaibatsu*.

And yet an attitude, no matter how unanimous, is only half a policy and cannot fly any more than a one-winged bird. When Colonel Kramer, first Chief of ESS, was asked by reporters in October 1945 why the Occupation was breaking up the *zaibatsu,* he replied that, first, it was necessary to show those companies that war did not pay and, second, the *zaibatsu* organization lent itself readily to a totalitarian order.[4] That did not sound very convincing, but it was not Kramer's fault. The United States had no comprehensive policy on the subject. Aside from general principles, the planners had produced nothing.

True, there were good reasons for the unreadiness: the sudden end of the war, the prior reluctance of State Department's moderates—"the Occupation authorities should not attempt long-range reforms or reorganization of the economy," they had said—the short time available after the summer of 1945 triumph of the "radical reformers" in State, and finally the complexity of the subject. There never was a Civil Affairs Guide produced or a SWNCC paper assigned on the subject. Indeed, the only government work on the *zaibatsu* that I know of prior to the end of the war was research for a Civil Affairs Guide and later for a policy paper prepared in the OSS by a young research analyst, Eleanor Hadley, and it never went beyond research. The result was a peculiar and largely unworkable paragraph (25b) in the JCS 1380/15 directive:

> You will require the Japanese to establish a public agency responsible for reorganizing Japanese business in accordance with the military and economic objectives of your [command]. You will require this agency to submit, for approval by you, plans for dissolving large Japanese industrial and banking combines or other large concentrations of business control.

The paragraph effectively left the initiative to the Japanese "public agency" to determine how large was "large" and whether "concentrations of business control" applied to industrial operating companies, or to combines only. It also offered no criteria governing SCAP's "approval." It said nothing about what to do with the assets of the dissolved companies. It was a strangely casual way to handle one of the most complicated areas of Japan policy.

When Kramer, battling gamely to apply the directive, nevertheless managed to get the four biggest *zaibatsu* holding companies—Mitsui, Mitsubishi, Sumitomo, and Yasuda—to submit plans for self-dissolution, checked them, and sent them back to Washington for approval, Assistant Secretary of State Will Clayton suddenly called a halt. Clayton, himself a big businessman, was aware of some of the complications and pitfalls of a program that size. His top adviser on Japanese affairs, Edwin Martin, the New Dealer who had participated in drafting the paragraph, turned over the *zaibatsu* self-dissolution plans to the "experts" in the Antitrust Division of the Department of Justice. Both sets of experts, in State and in Antitrust, agreed they were inadequate. (Kramer had thought the same, for on December 6 he approved the *zaibatsu* plans as "a preliminary step" only.)[6] Washington guidance was essential, and Clayton formally proposed to Assistant Attorney General Wendell Berge, his opposite number in the Department of Justice, that a joint expert mission of the two agencies be sent out to Japan for a few months "to prepare criteria to guide us in deciding when our objective of destroying their [that is, the *zaibatsu*] influence over Japanese political and economic life has been met."[7] Berge swiftly concurred, and the two agreed on the appointment of Professor Corwin Edwards of Northwestern University, then a consultant to State Department, to head the mission.

That selection was the single most important decision in the setting of *zaibatsu* policy. Several different ways of handling the *zaibatsu* had come under discussion within the U.S. Government: nationalization of the *zaibatsu* enterprises, giving away their most prized assets as foreign reparations (Pauley), selling their industrial plants to independents to equalize industrial size, and building up cooperatives and trade unions as countervailing forces, both economic and political. And then there was the classic American solution: busting the trusts and ensuring free competition ever afterward. Edwards's convictions would decide in large part which course to favor.

Clayton, leaning toward the last solution, suggested in his letter to Berge that perhaps people charged with the enforcement of the Public Utilities Holding Company Act of 1935 would be suitable recruits for the mission. Berge's own experience was in U.S. trust-busting. Neither knew much about Japan or about the *zaibatsu*'s historical role in developing Japanese industry, but they knew an expert when they saw one. Without deciding a policy, they chose a man. In so doing they decided the policy of the U.S. Government just as surely: trust-busting plus free competition. The rest was detail.

Corwin Edwards, a large, sandy-haired, soft-spoken bear of a man, was devoutly convinced of the necessity of free competition as a universal ethical good. To him, democracy meant freedom of choice, whether of goods, policies, or people. He saw the world as a kind of market place. Competition kept everyone running scared and responsive to the public will, while monopoly tended toward despotism. I remember him expounding his philosophy of government one day while we were both standing outside the Daiichi Hotel waiting for an Army bus to GHQ. The problem with governments, he said, was that they were monopolies. If he had his way, he told me, he would like to establish a hypothetical republic of the North Pole, with no structure, no functions, and no cost, therefore no taxes. He would then give everyone in the world the choice of becoming a North Pole citizen or remaining with his own country. The governments of the world would then have to compete for their citizens' allegiance at least against zero. If the disadvantages of remaining a citizen outweighed the advantages, the people would flock to North Pole citizenship. To hold them, governments would have to do more for their people at less cost. A fantasy, of course, but revealing. To Edwards, competition was the soul of democracy.

The composition of the rest of the mission, and I am sure Edwards had a lot to do with it, reinforced the decision to attack the *zaibatsu* problem along American lines: two special assistants to the U.S. Attorney General, the head of the West Coast offices of the Antitrust Division of the Justice Department, and one man each from the Federal Trade Commission, the Securities and Exchange Commission, the Tariff Commission, and the Federal Communications Commission.[8] It was an array of offices and people that had had nothing much to do with Japan. It was not surprising that even the most imaginative and sensitive among them, J. MacI. Henderson, the West Coast Chief of the Antitrust Division, and Raymond Vernon, Assistant Director of the SEC, considered their assignment to be not *whether* to break up the *zaibatsu* and institute free competition, American-style, but *how* best to do so, that is, to draw up the most thorough and foolproof blueprint that lawyers, accountants, and technical experts could devise. In essence they assumed their basic conclusion. They arrived in Japan on January 7, 1946.

THE JAPANESE-STYLE CORPORATION

The Japanese people, however, and not only Japanese big business, did not agree with those basic conclusions. Their history was too different from the American. Where the Americans saw free competition as the essence of democracy, the Japanese saw unbridled competition as a danger. People had to cooperate with others, not fight them. No one was foolish enough, the Japanese thought, to believe he could conquer a hostile world by his own efforts. (American tradition, of course, made exactly that a national fetish.) American populists, imbued with the legend of family pioneering that conquered a continent, were confident of their ability to handle nature but afraid of malevolent human combinations in restraint of trade, which swindled them. The Japanese, facing typhoons, earthquakes, fires, and inadequate land resources, sought salvation in benevolent human cooperation. Thus it was that one of the Edwards mission members came back to the Daiichi Hotel, after a long day's discussion with Japanese business leaders, marveling at their businessmen's concept of competition. "They're all in favor of free competition," he told me as we sat down to drink in the lobby bar, "and they want us to help them draw up regulations to control it properly! Wow!"

The Edwards mission indictment of the *zaibatsu* injustices was easy to formulate. Henderson, for example, was particularly critical to me one day about the banking structure. Under the old regime small businesses and individuals deposited money in the banks; big business disproportionately got the loans. Money was shifted from country to city the same way. The percentage of bank loans to the six urban prefectures far exceeded the percentage of their deposits; for the forty-one other prefectures it was the other way around. The banks soaked up funds from agriculture and small business, then delivered them to industry and big business. The tax laws applied higher effective rates to workers and farmers; meanwhile big new industries received government subsidies. It was all unfair. Ordinary Japanese were the victims.

What Henderson was attacking, however, was the system of capital mobilization that had enabled Japan to industrialize in half the time it took Europe and had thereby protected the nation's integrity from foreign incursions, while their Chinese and other neighbors were victimized by European imperialism. The Japanese deeply appreciated that fact in a way foreigners could not and were a lot slower to criticize its defects. Radical labor demonstrations during and after the Occupation denounced the *"shihon-ka,"* or capitalists, in the abstract but rarely named names, except that of the demonstrators' own employer. The big dailies like *Asahi,* darling of the radical intellectuals, might attack politicians, capitalists in general, capitalist imperialism, and the like, but never printed a word criticizing Mitsui, Mitsubishi, or any of the other big-name corporations. It was not to avoid offending *zaibatsu* advertisers, of which there were then few. It was rather that, just or unjust, the Japanese could see no workable substitute for the *zaibatsu* in rebuilding industry and particularly in expanding exports on the scale needed to regain Japanese economic independence in a harsh world. The *zaibatsu* organizations were national assets. The Edwards people did not think in such nationalistic Japanese terms; they focused on the manifest social injustice of the system and missed the point the Japanese were more concerned about.

Furthermore, the mere fact that small and medium businessmen logically should have been resentful of *zaibatsu* domination did not necessarily mean that they were. In the United States the Western farmers and the small and medium businessmen who felt themselves pushed around by the trusts constituted the heart of the antitrust movement, and it was natural for the Edwards mission to assume similar anti–big business feelings in Japan. But the government railways never discriminated against the Japanese peasants in the American style, nor were the rice dealers and local moneylenders *zaibatsu* firms. The circumstances were quite different.

Indeed, the small firms rarely were *zaibatsu* competitors; they were more typically subcontractors, suppliers, processors, and agents. To them the *zaibatsu* company was their lifeline—customer, financier, and supplier of materials. Without the large firm, the small ones could not exist. From time to time, to be sure, *zaibatsu* personnel acted in domineering fashion, sometimes forcing smaller companies to swallow losses. In such cases, the small men would bemoan their bad luck, but they would not reject the system. It was hard for outsiders, especially lawyers and academics, to understand. One had to be involved and experience it personally. Many years later I had such an experience. A medium-size garment maker, who had been producing ladies' blouses on my orders to Mitsubishi Trading Company and who had received defective fabric because of the negligence of a Mitsubishi staff man, urged me to take a strong line with Mitsubishi and reject the goods. When I asked why he didn't do it himself, since he stood to lose a substantial sum by Mitsubishi's error, he replied, "Oh, I can't. I need them too much. But *you* can." I did as he had urged and was blackballed by Mitsubishi. He accepted the blame and made lots of money with them for years afterward.

In characteristically feudal fashion, tens of thousands of satellite businesses acknowledged the protection of *zaibatsu* seigneurs and remained loyal through thick and thin. To them the American attack on the *zaibatsu* was not a democratic benefit but a dangerous threat to their own survival. Anti-*zaibatsu* public opinion, on which the Edwards mission relied for the long-term enforcement of their program, just would not arise in small and medium business circles.

Finally, Edwards and his men could never fathom the interpersonal relations within the Japanese *zaibatsu* structure. No doubt holding companies, interlocking directorates and shareholdings, reciprocal loan arrangements, shared banks, and the whole maze of financial arrangements were powerful binding agents, which could be dissolved by reform measures. But the typically Japanese *oyabun–kobun* (patron–client) relationships within and at every level of the companies formed a network of personal obligations, and those could not be dissolved. The higher-ranking company officers owed personal protection to their subordinates, who owed them personal loyalty in return, all the way up and down the company ladder. Even breaking up a company could not change that. When SCAP broke up the Mitsui and Mitsubishi trading companies into hundreds of fragments—213 successor companies in all—six months after the order, the employees loyally rallied round the new fragments formed by their old section or subsection chiefs (*kachō* and *kakari-chō*), who in turn adhered to the companies organized by their old division chiefs (*buchō*) and directors, and all of them recombined as soon as they could. Within five years, like droplets of mercury coalescing into ever bigger drops on contact with each other, both the Mitsubishi and the Mitsui trading companies were substantially reconstituted as before. Two hundred thirteen became two again. Their staffs had been held together by personal relations in the meantime.

I do not claim that I understood all this at the time. Much of it I learned later doing business in Japan, especially as an adviser to Daiichi Bussan, the biggest of the drops that shortly became Mitsui Bussan trading company again. Nor did anyone else in GHQ understand it then, not even the "old Japan hands" among us. Perhaps some of the Edwards group glimpsed the complexity and subtlety of the *zaibatsu* internal arrangements, but there was nothing they could do about them. Their mission was dedicated to breaking up the system with the weapons they knew about and had at their disposal: the laws, regulations, and devices of American trust-busting, to be exercised by a Supreme Commander and a subordinate Japanese government. The more their study revealed the strength of the *zaibatsu* and how deeply they were embedded in Japanese society and the Japanese economy, the more firmly Edwards and his men concluded that extreme measures were necessary. The result was what was later to become FEC 230.

FEC 230

When Edwards's people went back home, they wrote up a report that admitted no doubt as to what should be done and submitted it to the State Department. Then they disbanded, leaving Vernon, now transferred to State Department, and Henderson, now chief of the SCAP Antitrust Division, to carry on. It was getting late. A year after the end of the war, the United States still had only recommendations for a policy on the *zaibatsu*. Not until October 27, 1946, did Vernon announce that the Edwards mission report was being transmitted to the eleven-nation Far Eastern Commission. Not until May 12, 1947, did the State Department actually do so, and then as a "confidential" paper under the rubric FEC 230. Its measures went beyond dissolving the *zaibatsu* combines, and also beyond ensuring free competition in the market place, to the third and overriding objective: to "destroy" any and all "excessive concentrations of economic power" and "to prevent the future creation of new concentrations."

Now, that was a daunting task: to control the future from the base of a short-term military occupation. Every single future contingency had to be taken into account and provided for now. The experience and imagination of every one of the eight mission members had been mined and every possible antagonist's move anticipated and countered in advance, as in a gigantic chess game. FEC 230 was not a simple set of principles and rules but a manual for trust-busters in Japan, always leaning in the direction of greatest stringency.

Ingenuously, the State Department letter transmitting FEC 230 called it a "statement of broad policy." In actuality, its recommendations—I counted more than 250 of them—covered eighteen single-spaced, legal-size pages, supported by 300 pages of factual data. They dealt with everything from the dissolution of holding companies to public education in trust-busting. Almost no measure that had been found useful in the United States to foster free competition was omitted. And a few new ones were added.[9]

But the prime innovation of FEC 230, in which it went beyond American law and practice, was to rule that *all* "excessive" concentrations had to go. The U.S. trust-busters back home had never argued legally that "big is bad." But FEC 230 declared that "absolute size . . . is to be considered grounds for defining a specified concentration as excessive."[10] "Excessive" and "large" are relative, but the drafters spelled out their intentions unmistakably. "It is intended that the ownership of the *bulk of Japanese large-scale industry* should be affected by the policies set forth in this paper," it said.[11] Even more specifically, the document added that "SCAP's Schedule of Restricted Concerns . . . comprehends the Japanese enterprises considered to be excessive concentrations within the meaning of this paper." Now the SCAP Schedule of Restricted Concerns (companies that needed GHQ approval to dispose of or acquire assets) comprised 1,137 firms with 1,621 subsidiaries and 907 affiliates.[12] What was left? Japan was to be converted into a country of small and medium businesses.

The treatment of Matsushita Electric Company, now known in the United States under the Panasonic or National brand name, was a striking illustration of the change from the anti-*zaibatsu* policy of JCS 1380/15 to the deconcentration program of FEC 230. SCAP Antitrust officials in March 1946 had called it "the only company of the top nine which is not linked in some way with the *zaibatsu*".[13] No one ever accused it of having a monopoly in its field of electronics or electrical appliances; it competed fiercely with at least Hitachi, Mitsubishi, and Tōshiba. And two-thirds of its 1,200 shareholders were employees of the company. And yet Antitrust put it on the schedule of restricted concerns. Under FEC 230 it was designated, when the time came, for consideration as an excessive economic concentration.

While FEC 230 gestated, the world of the U.S. Government had changed drastically. By the time the report emerged into the Far Eastern Commission, the war had been over for twenty-one months, the top executive echelon in Washington's military–foreign relations establishment was much more conservative, the new Eightieth Congress was pro–big business and anti–New Deal, the Cold War was at its height, punitive feelings toward Japan had receded, and General MacArthur had announced that the SCAP-mandated reform phase of the Occupation was over. American corporations with prewar ties in Japan were beginning to resume them. Still, the Edwards report had changed hardly at all. Its viewpoint was still essentially that expressed by Corwin Edwards in January 1946, when the New Dealers were still strong. The Washington trust-busters still felt they had to make the effort. To have a fighting chance, they needed an exceptionally fast, able, convinced, and aggressive executive on the spot. In April 1947, State and Justice recommended, and War accepted, Edward Christy Welsh to make the attempt, and he was just that kind of executive.

THE GO-GO ED WELSH

When Welsh, just turned thirty-eight, arrived in Tokyo to take over the leaderless SCAP Antitrust and Cartels (AC) Division—its previous chief, Henderson, had departed for the Philippines six months before—he carried an advance copy of FEC 230 with him. He also brought a passionate and almost complete agreement with its provisions—I say "almost" because he was less tolerant of cooperatives and labor unions than FEC 230—plus a determination to put it into effect in the shortest possible time. To others, the SCAP antitrust record may have appeared creditable. The forty-five biggest Japanese holding companies had been designated for dissolution, freeing 250 operating companies from their control.[14] The *zaibatsu*-dominated control associations had been ordered dissolved. And on March 31, 1947, the Diet passed an antimonopoly law prohibiting collusion in price-fixing and limiting production, restricting patent licensing, and banning a number of other practices inhibiting competition. Any trust-buster worth his salt, however, knew that all those actions were reversible. The only way to prevent reversals was to break the combinations down so fine that they could not easily recombine. That included not just trading companies but the large operating companies as well. With FEC 230 in hand, Welsh leaped to the attack.

His first move was to get General Marquat's approval of a directive to dissolve, indeed to pulverize, the Mitsui and Mitsubishi trading companies, which before the war had handled some 70 percent of Japan's foreign trade. Speed was urgent, Welsh insisted, because private foreign traders were scheduled to come to Japan beginning in August, and they could not be allowed to deal with companies that would be shot down after they placed their orders.[15] Of course, if the companies were not to be shot down, speed was not essential, but Welsh didn't mention that. Nor did he get a concurrence from the other SCAP agency most deeply involved, the Foreign Trade Division. Nevertheless, with his prestige as the nominee of three Washington departments and the concurrences only of Sherwood Fine, Marquat's overall economic adviser, and the U.S. Commercial Company representative (who had never been asked to concur on any policy matter before), Marquat signed and MacArthur approved. Full speed ahead!

When it came to the industrial operating companies, however, such fast individual SCAP treatment was just not practical. They were too numerous. Welsh needed a Japanese agency under his control with sufficient legal authority; otherwise the Antitrust Division would be issuing directives ad infinitum. Colonel Kades, the Deputy Chief of Government Section, who was just then engaged in finishing off the economic purge, which covered many of the *zaibatsu* executives, came to Welsh's assistance. Why not use the Holding Companies Liquidation Commission? That body had been set up by Imperial Ordinance in November 1946 to handle and dispose of the shares in operating companies surrendered by the four *zaibatsu* holding companies—Mitsui, Mitsubishi, Sumitomo, and Yasuda—that Colonel Kramer had persuaded to dissolve themselves. From a quiet custodial organization, the HCLC could be made into a powerhouse executive to break up Japanese economic concentrations.[16]

Welsh agreed and set to work drafting an appropriate bill with the intention of introducing it at the Diet session scheduled to begin on August 10. With luck he might have most of the job done by the end of the year. That same bill four months later created such a commotion in the Diet that the SCAP representative there ordered the Diet clock stopped to obtain the necessary time to put it through. After all, American legislative tricks were also part of democratic training.

No one in GHQ particularly objected to the idea. But to give the HCLC authority constitutionally, deconcentration standards had to be included in the law, and those Welsh borrowed almost verbatim from one part of FEC 230 or another. Then he asked the various ESS divisions concerned, and most were, to concur, not with the idea but only with his standards. If the divisions objected to the substance of a criterion, Welsh simply replied that *that* had already been decided in Washington, citing the relevant provisos of FEC 230. Permissible disagreements thus came down to phraseology only. Logically, Welsh seemed correct, and yet the divisions felt that they had been flummoxed somehow.

Then Welsh turned to meetings with the Japanese agencies involved, including the days' old Fair Trade Commission just established by the antimonopoly law. They were "quite well convinced," according to Welsh, "that the measure prepared by the AC Division was the most effective method of eliminating concentrations of power."[17] Now that was not the same as saying they agreed with the measure. Nor did the agencies consulted amount to more than a small part of the Japanese Government. The Minister of Commerce and Industry, whom Welsh did not contact, wanted just the reverse; he was working on nationalization, not breakups. The Economic Stabilization Board objected passionately. I remember when the Director General's deputy, Tsuru Shigeto, came to Sherwood Fine's office, despondent and distraught after a meeting with Welsh. Somehow, he complained, he could not make Welsh understand that the newly elected Socialist-led cabinet was totally opposed on ideological grounds to industrial deconcentration and also that the Japanese people as a whole would consider it a violation of their tradition. Happily reporting agreement from everyone, nevertheless, Welsh sent the bill up to General Marquat for approval. The road seemed clear.

But Marquat was in no hurry to act. The whole thing sounded wrong to him. It made no sense to break up operating industrial companies when ESS was striving strenuously to increase production, especially when the Occupation was asking Congress for hundreds of millions of dollars of economic aid a year. His deputy chief, Colonel Ryder, had checked Welsh's proposals with "policy," that is, with FEC 230, and had reported no conflict. The division concurrences seemed to be there. His economic adviser, Sherwood Fine, also agreed. For each of Marquat's doubts, Welsh had a ready answer. Would not deconcentration damage industrial efficiency? Free competition was more efficient, Welsh asserted. Besides, the reorganization would be limited to ownership and financial structure, not physical facilities. The factories could keep right on working. Would not the uncertainties of reorganization hamper future development and planning? Certainly. That was why deconcentration had to be completed as rapidly as possible. Did not the standards apply too broadly? Why, no, at least 95 percent of Japanese corporations would never be designated. And so on. Each reply somehow left a residue of unanswered query.

It was a little too glib. In his four months on the ESS staff, Welsh had increasingly come to be known to General Marquat as a clever advocate, but not as the judicious, unbiased adviser he badly needed. In the absence of checks and balances in a military command, an all-out advocate was a dangerous staff man. In a technical field with an untechnical commander, he could be even more dangerous. Marquat hesitated.

At that point, as a special assistant and new adviser to Marquat, I received a copy of Welsh's proposed new deconcentration standards[18] for comment. I had expected them to be tough and unsympathetic to the peculiar characteristics of Japan's forced-draft industrialization experience. I had not expected them to be so vague and arbitrary. They defined as an excessive concentration any company, whether manufacturing, banking, or distributive (wholesaling, trading, retailing) if its removal from the market would cause a substantial price increase in the goods or services it supplied. Such a definition assumed a free market, which did not exist in Japan, where everything was under strict allocation, price control, or credit control, and it also presumed an oversupply margin bigger than the company involved, when in fact Japan was critically short of almost everything. Moreover, the standards expected the HCLC, which would have the power to designate excessive concentrations, to be able to predict market movements in the future, including the effectiveness of price controls. The whole concept was unreal. Under existing conditions an excessive concentration would be what the HCLC said it was, and that in turn could be what Welsh thought it was. If the HCLC needed standards in which to clothe its actions constitutionality, I thought, those proposed by Antitrust amounted to no more than a fig leaf. If Welsh were an extremist, Japan's industry would be in for rough times. Tsuru was right to be shaken.

COURSE ADJUSTMENT

Thus it was that I approached General Marquat some time after the Tsuru meeting to express my concern at the mad rush to break up the *zaibatsu* operating companies. Marquat perked up his ears. It was the first criticism of the *zaibatsu* break-up from the "liberal" side. He asked me for a staff study on the subject. Meanwhile I was to meet with Welsh and Fine to try to work out an agreed position. The meeting of the three of us in Fine's office on August 1, 1947, went nowhere. Welsh did not believe I had anything to tell him. I was an intruder, and ignorant of the subject at that, while he had collaborated in a book on it.[19] If he had the time, he could set me right patiently, like a teacher with a dull student, but he had no time. He was driving hard to carry out a U.S. policy. It was intolerable that I, whom he knew as just a "labor man," should hold him up.

The fact was that Welsh was always driving hard and was always intolerant of being held up. A few months later, during a billiard game at the Imperial Hotel with me and Ryder, he gave us some clue as to what drove him. As a boy he had not been accepted by his peers in the Midwestern city where he grew up, he said, because he was "the rich kid from the big house on the hill" who obviously could not play marbles well because he had to keep his pants clean. Welsh responded by beating the others at their own game and thereafter excelling in everything he tried in order to prove himself. He was still doing it. He found it hard to compromise with lesser mortals, especially with the stakes so high and his opinion of me so low.

Meanwhile, in the course of my working up the staff study Marquat had asked for, two surprising facts turned up. The first was that Welsh's proposals really were in line with FEC 230—he had not been exaggerating them—and the second was that FEC 230's status was ambiguous. The Joint Chiefs of Staff had never formally dispatched it to MacArthur, either as a directive or for guidance as a State–War–Navy Coordinating Committee (SWNCC) policy. It had been sent only to the Far Eastern Commission.

It also became clear from my study that Welsh had been cutting corners internally, exaggerating the concurrences of other SCAP agencies, neglecting to consult interested divisions or consulting them on only pieces of his actions, and generally papering over differences within GHQ. GS, Welsh advised Marquat, concurred with his action. Perhaps with part of it, but Welsh neglected to mention that General Whitney, the GS Chief, thought the HCLC Bill unconstitutional as written. The Japanese who he said agreed with him agreed only that his action would be effective. Those who disagreed were not mentioned at all.

As long as a bill was before the Diet, it was subject to public scrutiny. As long as a deconcentration measure was under discussion within GHQ, other officials might raise questions. But once the law was passed, the standards established, and the procedure set up, all follow-up would be the exclusive province of the Antitrust Division and its Japanese satellite. The HCLC would designate companies as subject to deconcentration and tell them why, the companies would have to prepare corrective reorganization plans—going so far as to split into several units—the HCLC would accept, reject, or modify the plans and then issue the reorganization orders. Appeals could be made only to the HCLC and the prime minister, and then only on matters of fact. There was no place in the procedure for any GHQ division to protest any individual deconcentration order. Indeed, no one else in the SCAP GHQ would even know what was being considered until it was all over. Given Welsh's penchant for sliding around obstacles, it seemed a very risky proposition to me.

Now, in a military headquarters one does not voice his personal mistrust of a brother officer and gentleman. My staff study therefore emphasized the uncontrolled authority of the HCLC, not the Antitrust division. (Welsh, in his comment on the staff study and on several other occasions, however, could never understand why I was so worried about the HCLC's broad legal powers. He had them under his close control, he assured me. That, of course, was precisely the problem.) Furthermore, with so much at stake for each company and temptation inevitable, who was going to check HCLC wrongdoing if the only control was the Antitrust Division, not one member of which knew the Japanese language? For example, the labor union of the Taishō Fire and Marine Insurance Company had charged bribery of an HCLC section chief in a memo sent to General MacArthur, with copies to Whitney, Welsh, and me.[20] Welsh never mentioned it, but SCAP could easily have been tainted with scandal.

FEC 230 was an extreme document, written as tightly as possible to prevent neglect or evasion by a lackadaisical or unsympathetic future administrator. But the administrator had turned out to be a hard-driving trust-buster, as committed as the Edwards group ever was and in some ways even more extreme. For example, Welsh refused to implement FEC 230's recommendation to sell divested securities on a preferential basis to trade unions and cooperatives on the grounds that it was "not desirable for trade unions to own securities" and that cooperatives' functions had to be limited "until there is evidence and experience" that there would exist "no undue risk in the development of democracy in Japan," a matter presumably of many years.[21] Antitrust's view, Deputy Chief Irving Bush explained to an intersection GHQ meeting, was derived from U.S. experience with the Wisconsin dairy cooperatives, which given antitrust exemption, became monopoly agro-businesses. The Wisconsin experience meant more to Welsh and his men than the realities of Japan, with its depressed peasants. An extreme document to begin with, FEC 230 was being interpreted even more extremely.

Although my private report to Marquat was rather moderate (while urging controls on the HCLC, it supported a measure of deconcentration and warned against damaging Welsh's "face" in public),[22] when Welsh somehow got hold of it, he exploded. Within hours I was in receipt of a lengthy and scathing reply—he was not known as "a man of a few thousand Welsh-chosen words" for nothing—but it boomeranged. Word of our exchange got out within ESS and set off a sometimes acrimonious debate within the section. Those who had suppressed their doubts now raised them, and those who had accepted FEC 230 as inevitable now began to pick holes in it. The bitterness grew to the point where William Turnage, the Chief of the Research and Programs Division, advised

Marquat that "the conflict within ESS is a conflict of ideologies" and lambasted those who, like me I suppose, opposed Welsh for not applying U.S. policy properly when they really meant they were opposed to the policy in the first place.[23]

POLICY IN WASHINGTON

But the real controversy erupted outside the section. From the beginning, it had been only a matter of time until the current Washington defense–foreign policy establishment leaders found out what FEC 230 provided and what Welsh was doing to enforce it. On the surface, the document had gone through proper channels and been approved by the secretaries of State, War, and Navy. In reality, it seemed highly unlikely to me that such busy men as Marshall, Patterson, and Forrestal in the cold war crisis year of 1946–47 had studied its detailed provisions, and even more unlikely that the latter two, a Wall Street lawyer and a leading investment banker, agreed. Nor did I believe that assistant secretaries of State like Clayton or Hilldring had examined the document and knew its contents solidly; it was too detailed. I knew for a fact that neither MacArthur nor Marquat had. True, State had sent MacArthur a preliminary copy of FEC 230,[24] and MacArthur had radioed in return that he had no substantive objections. But in actuality, each radio had been drafted by the respective responsible official in Washington and Tokyo, namely Vernon in State and Henderson, then our Antitrust Chief, in GHQ. Both, of course, were former members of the Edwards mission, and both were patting each other on the back for their good work, so to speak, over their superiors' signatures.

That kind of top-level inattention could not last. In July 1947, the Civil Affairs Division in the Pentagon sent MacArthur a radio asking when the implementation of FEC 230 would be completed.[25] Completed? Why, it was only two months since its submission to the Far Eastern Commission! Any deconcentration effort that had to be so rushed could hardly deconcentrate very much. The counterpressure had begun. In September, when Under Secretary of the Army Draper visited Japan on his first orientation trip, he invited General Marquat to tell him of any Washington directives that were impeding Japanese economic recovery. Marquat was tempted to recommend some modifications in FEC 230, and at his request I even drew up such a memo,[26] but after he saw MacArthur, he dropped the idea. The "Old Man" had no desire to get embroiled to no purpose in someone else's battle at a distance of 10,000 miles.[27]

Then a clever, effective, and not overly scrupulous lawyer, James Lee Kauffman, retained by Libby-Owens-Ford, a leading U.S. glass manufacturer and subsidiary of Ford Motor Company, lit a fire under the stew. Kauffman, a prewar practicing attorney in Tokyo of some eminence—he was later awarded the Order of the Sacred Treasure—had been to see Welsh in the summer of 1947 to try to prevent the breakup of Nippon Sheet Glass, in which his client had a substantial interest.[28] Welsh brushed him off. After returning home, Kauffman issued a blistering report on the Occupation's entire democratization program, criticizing not only deconcentration but also the poor quality of Occupation personnel; their excessive salaries and luxurious mode of living; the pampered Japanese workers, who he said were behaving like American Indians who had just discovered oil on their property; and also several SCAP officials, including Welsh, Fine, and me. His inaccuracies were legion,[29] but his report was plausible and certainly sensational. It was widely circulated in Wall Street and at the highest levels in the U.S. Government, reportedly reaching, through Forrestal, a cabinet meeting presided over by the President.[30]

In Washington George Kennan, recently appointed head of Secretary of State Marshall's Planning Staff, repeated some of its accusations over lunch on October 16 to Forrestal, including the allegation that "another . . . vicious feature [of the de-*zaibatsuing* process—Forrestal's words] is a provision by which labor unions are to elect the boards of directors and control management." (In fact, Welsh objected to allowing trade unions even to own corporate shares.) Kennan feared, according to Forrestal, who reported the conversation in his diary, that "the socialization of Japan had proceeded to such a point that if a treaty of peace were written and the country turned back to the Japanese it would not be possible for the Japanese to support themselves . . . resulting possibly in near anarchy, which would be precisely what the communists would want. The social policy had been carried out by a man named Welsh, formerly of the O.P.A."[31]

Kennan, State's most prestigious authority on the Soviet Union, was readily believed when he made such statements as this: "The ideological concepts on which these anti-*zaibatsu* measures rested bore so close a resemblance to Soviet views about the evils of 'capitalist monopolies' that the measures could only have been eminently agreeable to anyone interested in the future communization of Japan."[32] Forrestal must have been deeply impressed by Kennan's fears, for almost two months later, on December 13, he wrote R. T. Stevens: "I have just recently discovered that some ex-O.P.A. boys have been writing up laws for Japan which in certain respects impose state socialism on the country."[33] In fact, both Forrestal and Kennan were 180 degrees off course. Welsh's measures aimed at free competitive capitalist enterprise, not socialism, and they both should have known it. But then, if Forrestal had read FEC 230 before he or his Navy Department deputy on SWNCC approved it for transmission to the FEC, perhaps Welsh would not then have been trying to carry it out.

The point man in the Washington drive to stop Welsh's deconcentration, however, was Army Under Secretary William Draper. (Draper, vice president of Dillon Read when Forrestal was its president, presumably was thinking on Forrestal's wavelength.) On his return from the Far East in late September, Draper launched a State–Army study on the disposition of *zaibatsu* securities. Then he dispatched the Kauffman report to MacArthur for comment. On October 21 a secret Washington Civil Affairs Division radio, undoubtedly inspired by Draper, raised the question of providing judicial review of HCLC orders, proposed other limitations on the HCLC's powers, and proposed that no new excessive concentration list be issued. The radio also advised that "State and Army are now reviewing U.S. position taken in SWNCC 302/2n [that is, FEC 230]" and asked SCAP to delay the enactment of the deconcentration legislation.[34] State, with Robert Lovett as Acting Secretary, finally seemed to be reconsidering its pro-FEC 230 attitude too. November 25 the American member in the FEC asked the commission for a delay pending "minor and technical corrections." To anyone who could read the signs, FEC 230 and the Welsh deconcentration program were in deep trouble.

THE DECONCENTRATION LEGISLATION

Welsh was ever the optimist. Washington misunderstood the pending action, he said. Once it had been taken, it would all be clear. Marquat's inclination through the fall of 1947, and I am sure he reflected MacArthur's, was to go ahead with the program—MacArthur would never reverse his course or admit he was wrong, nor would he disown a subordinate—but to implement it with moderation. Welsh repeatedly assured Marquat that he *was* acting moderately, that only a small minority of Japanese corporations, a handful, would be subject to deconcentration. In answer to a query from Marquat, he had agreed that "*zaibatsu* control *per se* has been abolished," and Marquat included that judgment in a radio to Washington on October 17.[35] Maybe to Welsh that meant only the *zaibatsu* holding companies had been dissolved—the "*per se*" was tricky—but to Marquat and the Supreme Commander the statement meant the anti-*zaibatsu* program was almost over. Then why the HCLC law? To apply to the few ultra-large operating companies not covered as holding companies. Why a new list of companies to be designated as possible excessive concentrations? Why not just use the restricted list? Because the new list would be smaller, thereby relieving many more companies of anxiety and uncertainty. Why not shorten the restricted list then? We might still need to restrict a company for other reasons. As usual, every question had an answer. Just trust Ed Welsh.

But could Marquat afford to do so? One day late in 1947, I happened to be in his office when the general walked in muttering in disgusted tones about that "damned FEC 230." I asked him why we were bound to carry out FEC 230. "Because it's U.S. and FEC policy," he replied in some surprise.

"Well, I don't know if it's U.S. policy, but it certainly has never been approved by the FEC," I retorted.

"But Welsh says it's the U.S. position.

"I'm not even sure that's true," I answered. "It's the U.S. position to present FEC 230 to the FEC and ask for their approval. Maybe it's only a way to 'deep-freeze' it for a while. Anyway, we've never gotten a JCS directive on it; so strictly speaking, we're under no obligation to do anything. In fact, other countries on the FEC could object if we carry out unilaterally before they've had a chance to study and comment on it."

"But I was sure it was FEC policy," he repeated dubiously. I urged him to read the State Department's transmitting letter carefully and decide for himself.

Marquat did take another look and decided that once again Welsh had not been completely candid. Earlier the Supreme Commander could have decided to wait for the FEC judgment, meanwhile questioning what seemed extreme. But Welsh had given him the impression that the FEC had already decided. After several of Draper's cables, Marquat had begun feeling strongly that MacArthur was being made the "fall guy," that is, first being given a policy by State and then being attacked by the Defense Department for carrying it out. At the very beginning of the Occupation, to prevent just such a situation, MacArthur had stubbornly refused to take orders from anyone but the Joint Chiefs of Staff, and the Army Chief of Staff, General Eisenhower, had backed him up.[36] But now MacArthur had been finessed into breaking that rule for the first time by a member of his own staff, when all the time he had had a way out.

Others outside the Command were even less trusting. Senator William Knowland was one of them. In early December 1947, just as the Japanese Diet was passing Public Law 207, the Elimination of Excessive Concentrations of Economic Power, in disregard of Washington's request for a delay, the junior senator from California rose on the floor of the U.S. Senate, waved a copy of FEC 230 aloft in disregard of its "confidential" classification, and denounced it heatedly as the work of irresponsible New Deal radicals still in the U.S. Government. That earned him his photograph, together with that of the title page of FEC 230, on the cover of *Newsweek* magazine. Knowland also got wide coverage in the national press as a defender of free enterprise. Suddenly what had been a technical operation, so technical that assistant secretaries could not spare the time to read the particulars, had become a national controversy.

Welsh had neglected to mention to Marquat a subsidiary piece of legislation he had in the works, the Law to Terminate *Zaibatsu* Family Control—why bother the general with unnecessary complications?—and so Marquat was astonished to receive on January 8, 1948, two radiograms from Draper addressed to MacArthur personally complaining about this new Welsh coup. The first[37] passed on the complaint of William E. Knox, president of Westinghouse International Electric Company, that the new law would compel the discharge of three key Mitsubishi Electric officials[38] and make it "virtually impossible" for the company to participate in Japan's reconstruction and rehabilitation. The second[39] wanted to know if SCAP had started a new purge of businessmen beyond the 2,000 that General Whitney had set as the maximum to be affected by the economic purge. Was the economic purge in an "initial rather than terminal stage"?

On the same day that Draper dispatched his radios, Kenneth Royall, Secretary of the Army and Draper's immediate superior, told the Commonwealth Club in San Francisco that "extreme deconcentration . . . may impair manufacturing efficiency, reduce overall production and exportable surplus, and may postpone the day when Japan can be self-supporting."[40] Now the big three of the Defense Department on matters relating to Japan—Forrestal, Royall, and Draper—were all lined up with State's Lovett against the deconcentration program as it stood. The liberal regular civil service officials—Vernon, Martin, and the rest—were clearly outgunned. Corwin Edwards's star was no longer ascendant.

Apparently that had no effect on Welsh, as he rushed to complete his action before anyone could stop him. His bombshell dropped on February 8, 1948. On that day the HCLC designated 257 manufacturing companies as subject to deconcentration procedures, and a few days later it added sixty-eight distributive firms. In numbers the designees constituted only one-third of 1 percent of all the corporations in the country—that was Welsh's promised handful—but they accounted for "80 percent of all Japan's industrial, financial, and commercial enterprise."[41] Far from the tapering off that Draper had been led to expect, it looked like big business was under renewed assault.

The effect on the Japanese public was mainly puzzlement. Newspaper editorials dutifully praised the announcement, but in a *Jiji* public opinion poll taken right after the passage of the deconcentration law, only 9 percent favored the new law, 11 percent were opposed, 10 percent had various other opinions, and a whopping 70 percent didn't know.[42] Deconcentration was over their heads.

THE SCAP RESPONSE

Marquat could not hide his feeling that he had been betrayed. Eighty percent was the "small minority" Welsh had promised him? True, Welsh was quick to explain that designation did not mean deconcentration, and most designees would not be deconcentrated. Marquat no longer believed him. He had assured Draper and the others in Washington that any further deconcentration action would be restrained. He, and MacArthur too, seemed unable to control Welsh.

Like others before him, Welsh had overrated the Supreme Commander's support and misinterpretated Marquat's friendliness. MacArthur always supported his people to the outside world, and Marquat always accorded diplomatic treatment to those who might have influential connections back in Washington. Welsh had thus been emboldened to try to outrun the Washington whirlwind. Meanwhile, MacArthur would protect him. But Welsh had been too sanguine about just what the General believed.

In relying on MacArthur's detestation of the *zaibatsu,* Welsh had made no mistake. The Supreme Commander had encouraged Colonel Kramer, his first ESS Chief, to dissolve the big four combines, had defended Whitney's economic purge, a good part of which was aimed at *zaibatsu* people, and had approved of the objectives of Corwin Edwards's program. MacArthur had a populist's distrust of big finance. He could tolerate bigness in industry, for he could see the material results, and he was proud of American big business productivity, but financial institutions were too prone to exploit the little man. Besides, there were no physical limits, as in manufacturing, to their expansion. In Japan, where they were much larger relative to the total economy than America, they had gotten far out of hand.

So at first MacArthur personally answered the deconcentration critics blast for blast. In three statements made early in 1948, the General sought to answer Knowland's December speech and put the whole issue in the perspective of democracy. In his New Year's Day message to the Japanese people, he forcefully denounced "that system which in the past has permitted the major part of the commerce and industry and natural resources of [this] country to be owned and controlled by a minority of feudal families and exploited for their exclusive benefit. The world has probably never seen a counterpart to so abnormal an economic system. It permitted exploitation of the many for the sole benefit of the few . . . and set the course which ultimately led to war and destruction."[43]

Two weeks later, in a statement intended for the House and Senate Appropriations Committees, MacArthur enlarged on the theme, adding that the "Japanese are rapidly freeing themselves of these [oligarchic] structures to clear the road for the establishment here of a more healthy economy patterned after our own concepts of free private competitive enterprise."[44]

When no one paid as much attention as he thought they should, MacArthur predicted to Senator Brien MacMahon that the alternative to deconcentration was bloody revolution. "The Japanese people, you may be sure, fully understand the nature of the forces . . . which have ruthlessly exploited them in the past," he declared. ". . . if the concentration of economic power is not torn down and redistributed peacefully and in order under the Occupation, there is not the slightest doubt that its cleansing will eventually occur through a bloodbath of revolutionary violence."[45]

In a letter to a private citizen who had notified him of charges by the "Committee for Constitutional Government" in New York that the Occupation was fostering socialism in Japan, he declared that, on the contrary, "if business were allowed to continue with its concentration of economic power, it would lead to concentration of power in government" and therefore the death of democracy. That, he emphasized, would certainly lead to "socialism of one form or another."[46]

But MacArthur's central populist perception that big business *per se* was a threat to political democracy did not mean he accepted Welsh's mechanical criteria for dismantling excessive concentrations. That was antitrust theory, and MacArthur would not go much beyond American antitrust practice. To him according to Marquat in an aside to me one day, the designation 325 companies after two and a half years of SCAP anti-*zaibatsu* actions sounded crazy.

Welsh, moreover, would not divulge what HCLC intended to do with the designated companies. The Japanese press, with inside sources in HCLC, was reporting in February that Nippon Iron and Steel Manufacturing Company was preparing plans to reorganize into five companies, Nissan Chemical into eight, Nippon Steel Tube into three, Mitsubishi Heavy Industry into twenty-three, Hitachi into eight, Mitsubishi Mining into five, Fuso Metals and Mitsui Mining into four each, and so on.[47] I showed the news reports to General Marquat, but the Antitrust Division insisted the press had no advance information. Maybe so, but Marquat decided he was not going to be taken unawares again.

After a three-week delay occasioned by the visit of a high-powered Washington economic mission, Marquat made his move. One Sunday morning early in April 1948, after the visitors had left, I dropped into Marquat's office to see if I could help him in any way. A few minutes later in came the general, straight from a meeting with General MacArthur. He had just proposed to the "Old Man" that SCAP establish a board of independent outside American businessmen to review HCLC orders and corporate reorganization plans under the new law. MacArthur had agreed to the idea, provided only that the board operate under him, not Washington. Now Marquat had to draft a radiogram to Draper explaining the proposal and asking the Army Department to recruit the board members. He asked me to help him work it out.[48]

My only substantive suggestion was to change the composition of the new Deconcentration Review Board from five businessmen to two businessmen, two government officials—I suggested the Antitrust Division of the Justice Department and the Securities and Exchange Commission—and a chairman. Welsh was not consulted at all. When Draper accepted the proposal and recruited the members, he chose a businessman, Roy Campbell, president of the New York Shipbuilding Corporation, as the chairman. With this veto power over him, Welsh's ride was over. On April 7, Draper announced in Washington that the U.S. Government was abandoning most of FEC 230.

From then on deconcentration wound down. Whether or not Welsh had planned it that way from the beginning, the HCLC removed 194 firms from designation at the beginning of May. In two more months the HCLC dropped thirty-one more, then announced all the banks were being dropped as well. By the time the new Deconcentration Review Board arrived in Tokyo and took its first action on September 11, 1948, there were not that many cases left to review. The board promptly announced it would not approve any deconcentration orders without a *prima facie* showing that a company was in fact restricting competition. That sloughed off Antitrust's theoretical standards, now written into law. Just engaging in two unrelated lines of enterprise, the board ruled, was insufficient reason for deconcentration. That made conglomerates legal again. HCLC's actions had to be directly related to the specific characteristics that made an organization an excessive concentration. There would be no sweeping reorganization order without due cause. Finally, all doubts as to excessiveness were to be resolved in favor of the company. That directly reversed FEC 230.

Surprisingly, some companies were deconcentrated. Among the most important were Nippon Iron and Steel, split into Yawata and Fuji; Oji Paper, divided into five companies; and Mitsubishi Heavy Industry, split into three: West Japan, Central Japan, and East Japan Heavy Industry. The deconcentrations did not last; the divided companies recombined after varying periods of time. Even Welsh's early breakup of the Mitsui and Mitsubishi trading companies failed. By 1952 the most important Mitsui successor, Daiichi Bussan, was prestigious enough to employ the former chief cabinet secretary as a secret adviser. His name was Satō Eisaku, the later prime minister.[49] (I know because I, too, was also a Daiichi Bussan adviser at the time, and we both once worked on the same problem, although from different angles.)

THE CORNERSTONE OF ECONOMIC GROWTH

Deconcentration, then, failed to deconcentrate, at least on the scale envisaged by Edwards and Welsh, and Japan did not become a country of only medium and small businesses. But deconcentration was a relatively late Occupation goal. The earlier business democratization objectives, breaking up the combines and enlarging the area of free competition, were achieved in surprising degree and, together with the fallout from the deconcentration battle, did much to transform the business face of Japan.

True, the operating companies in *zaibatsu* combines did seek to recombine, or at least to work together informally. Several Mitsui companies jointly financed a brand-new Sony Corporation, capitalized a new petrochemical company, and established a group computer center. Mitsubishi Trading Company automatically went back to representing the old Mitsubishi industrial companies as sales and procurement agent. But the new combines were far looser than before, and collegiality replaced dictation from combine *honsha* offices. The *zaibatsu* banks and trading companies were free to finance and represent others as well, and the manufacturing companies were free to make other arrangements too. Mitsui companies were no longer tied to Mitsui, Yasuda to Yasuda, Nippon Kōkan to Asano, or Hitachi to Nissan. The Tuesday or Thursday lunch clubs where the heads of former combine companies discussed policy and arrangements did not reconstitute the old combine chains, but rather preserved the old school tie.

The Anti-Monopoly Law fell far short of American concepts. Industry price-fixing, production limitations, and export quota assignments, banned in theory, were legitimized with the holy water of Ministry of International Trade and Industry (MITI) sponsorship. The Fair Trade Commission to the contrary notwithstanding, there was a way around every antimonopoly restriction, provided it was important enough to the national interest. Government guidance replaced Antitrust's prohibitions. The adversary attitude of government toward business, the soul of trust-busting, never came to Japan. A people devoutly convinced of their imperative need to cooperate to survive simply could not permit it.

And yet, despite the mass of MITI regulation, domestic competition flourished as never before, whether in automobiles, candy bars, English schools, home appliances, cosmetics, or supermarkets. Indeed, it was the honing of competitive skills at home that produced the up-to-the minute designs, fine quality, and low price that made the Japanese such formidable competitors abroad. No lazy monopolists could have done anywhere near as well.

In 1945, JCS 1380/15 had directed a ''wider distribution of the ownership of the means of production and trade,'' and that too came about. Where before the war shares in corporations were closely held and only a few score issues were publicly quoted, thirty years after the war millions of Japanese held stocks in 1,300 companies listed in the Tokyo *Kabutochō* and the regional exchanges. Only fifteen years after Welsh was squelched, 135 million shares were being traded daily[50] as compared with only 100,000 a day before the war,[51] and the numbers rose astronomically thereafter. It was a remarkable achievement, ''people's capitalism'' in a land with Japan's long oligarchic history.

Unquestionably, the SCAP anti-*zaibatsu* program gave the process its initial impetus. When the stock exchanges reopened in May 1949, a ready supply of ''blue-chip'' corporate stocks was available, 73 million out of the 166 million shares seized from the dissolved *zaibatsu* holding companies and held by the HCLC, to fuel the exchanges' growth, and 70 million more had already been sold publicly to non-*zaibatsu* investors at very low prices. The old exclusive ownership pattern had been broken for good.[52] And yet the general democratization and SCAP measures that were not aimed at the *zaibatsu* were equally or even more important. The land reform, for example, by abolishing *rentier* farm ownership diverted the 800,000 prewar *rentier* landlord investors into corporate shares. The labor reforms, too, by expanding worker income and savings, made possible for the first time in Japanese history mass worker purchase of stocks, many in their own companies.

In the same way, when the Occupation assaulted the large combines and put them on the defensive and under public scrutiny as never before, it opened up a window of opportunity through which independents climbed with unexpected alacrity. Credit became more equitably available to everyone, and superior engineering, ingenuity, and sales promotion counted for more than established status and connections. And so Honda outsold Mitsubishi in motorcycles, and both Subaru and Honda outsold Mitsubishi in automobiles. Lotte Chocolate, owned by a Korean resident of Japan, successfully challenged Morinaga and Meiji. Hundreds of independent export makers, in transistor radios and cameras, among other items, benefited from direct contact with buyers and even set up their own distribution abroad. The more open business structure outlasted the specific SCAP, HCLC, or Fair Trade Commission rulings that made it possible in the first place.

But the most important of all was Japan's postwar transformation into a consumer-oriented society, a change made possible only by SCAP's economic democratization. The disarmament of Japan and the American defense umbrella in the long run reduced tax requirements for armaments and left all classes with more money than they otherwise would have had. Still, the burgeoning consumer sector of the economy could not have burgeoned without more and increasingly prosperous consumers. The most numerous were the Japanese workers, both blue-collar and white-collar, and the economically liberated farm families. Catering to their ever increasing purchasing power—by the 1970s most Japanese were reporting themselves to poll-takers as members of the middle-class—became big business. For the first time in Japan's history a consumer mass market was born. And it corroded *zaibatsu* influence irreparably.

The strong point of the *zaibatsu* had been their unmatched ability to mobilize capital and resources for large-scale projects. That was fine in basic industry and especially advantageous in supplying centralized military procurement, but the *zaibatsu* were out of their element in a consumer market that demanded novelty, flexibility, sensitivity to consumer preferences, and attention to mercurial fads and fashions. The variety of consumer goods proliferated astonishingly, as in other mass consumer economies around the world, and the relatively small number of *zaibatsu* companies, large though each might be, could not keep up.

To take a recent example, in six hours of random Japanese television viewing in 1982, out of sixty national commercials, I counted forty-three advertised products and services that had not existed on the Japanese market before the war: such as supermarkets, tract houses, integral kitchen cabinets, credit cards, pizza pies, tampons, and aluminum window frames and sashes.[53] Only ten of those were sold by identifiably *zaibatsu* companies. The others were the products of the new wider dispersion of the ownership and management of the means of production and trade.

Still less suited to the *zaibatsu* capabilities were the multifarious service-oriented activities that emerged from consumerism: supermarkets, trading stamps, house-to-house selling (of cosmetics, pantyhouse, encyclopedias), resort hotels, recreational real estate, travel agencies and group tourism, taxis and car rentals, automobile insurance, and the whole range of the entertainment industry, from commercial radio and television to golf courses and driving ranges, amusement parks, movies, and entertainment publishing. All were more successfully handled with moderate capital and much entrepreneurial innovation than with heavy capital investment and routine operation.[54] The ex-*zaibatsu* old-line companies, with their heavy emphasis on manufacturing, shipping, and finance, grew, but specialized manufacturing and service enterprises grew more.

The rapid postwar growth of the more open economy, added on to the original SCAP business reforms, broke the *zaibatsu* near-monopoly on private capital supply. Alternative sources welled up. The nonagricultural land boom sparked by the search for suitable new industrial sites and suburban housing developments put money—available for industrial investment—into the hands of farmers, including many beneficiaries of the land reform, when they disposed of those holdings at astronomical prices twenty years later. Not only land reform land was affected. In one year, the highest personal income in Japan was reported by a farmer who was selling off forest land that had been held in his family for generations. Urban lot owners, too, realized handsome profits by disposing of their property at prices fifty or one hundred times higher than their original cost, even after adjusting for the inflation. Private savings of workers with high midsummer and year-end bonuses went into industrial stocks as well as bank deposits. My secretary, after fourteen years of service with me, owned shares in five companies and a small apartment that she rented out for income. She was not unusual. *Zaibatsu* money was just not that indispensable any more.

If all the other subsequent economic developments that contributed to the restructuring of Japanese business seem, in retrospect, to lessen the importance of the SCAP anti-*zaibatsu* drive, how much impact they could have had if the *zaibatsu* grip on the economy had held firm in 1945, that is, if the Supreme Commander had simply accepted the combines as natural when he entered Japan, is open to question. At the other extreme, one has to wonder what would have happened to Japan's subsequent unparalleled economic surge if FEC 230 had been applied in all its rigors.

That, of course, was the nightmare of Under Secretary of the Army Draper, and Welsh, who was determined to make it happen, was his chief bugaboo. For the better part of a year the two dueled, one superior in rank and position, but the other on the spot controlling the action. The Army Under Secretary applied pressure to MacArthur and Marquat, but Welsh seemed to go ahead on his predetermined course and on his own schedule regardless until the final dénouement. To the Washington conservative leadership, "New Dealers" and "radicals" appeared to be deceiving and misleading the economically unsophisticated generals in Tokyo with impunity. In point of fact, MacArthur detested the *zaibatsu* too, and he never really lost control. But in the short time it took to assert himself, the Washington distrust of the SCAP staff became set in concrete. That had much to do with the Washington decision before the end of 1948 to take the direction of economic affairs out of MacArthur's hands altogether. Welsh had no such intentions, but his SCAP career did have that effect. In return, he— the devout advocate of free-market capitalism—had to suffer the ultimate wrong, being called a "socialist" and having his program misunderstood as Marxist by even the most eminent historians.[55]

The new structure of business power that emerged from it all, neither socialist nor free competition nor *zaibatsu* machine, was a central part of the new Japan when it completed its third turn.

20

"Defeudalizing" the Civil Service

ITS FATHER WAS feudalism, its mother the general strike. The drive to reform the Japanese bureaucracy was generated by hostility toward the father and fear of the mother. The professional civil service reformers who mounted the campaign chose feudalism as their target. The Supreme Commander, General Douglas MacArthur was more concerned with preventing another attempt at revolution by government workers' strikes. The two goals, however, were unrelated: The new trade unions were in no sense feudal remnants to be eliminated, and the old-line "feudal" Japanese government bureaucrats were unlikely to lead any kind of strike. Still, the same model was presented for achieving both goals: a U.S. federal civil service system that was hardly related in its design to either. Unsurprisingly, the reformers never accomplished the defeudalization, and their pursuit of strike prevention brought consequences different from, and much graver than, what anyone had intended.

It is questionable that the civil service reformers really understood what they were up against when they aimed at "feudalism" in the Japanese bureaucracy. Blaine Hoover, the reformers' chief, wrote of his program in July 1948 that "it will break up one of the ruling cliques of presurrender Japan—the tightly-knit, exclusive and self-perpetuating bureaucracy which exercised the powers of government over the people in the feudal concept of divine right—and will substitute therefore a body of democratically selected officials who will administer the law in the concept of service to the people."[1]

It sounded fine to the American ear, but the noble phrases did not really stand up. The Japanese bureaucracy was so "exclusive" that it could accept as a probationary assistant procurator in the Justice Ministry an Okinawan both of

378

whose grandmothers were, he said, "prostitutes." (The charge, by Tokūda Kyūichi, the communist leader, was actually an exaggeration; they had worked as waitresses in teahouses.) Nor was the bureaucracy self-perpetuating—certainly it was not hereditary—any more than any system that depended on entrance examinations and a selection process devised, of course, by the incumbents.

Tightly-knit? Surely it was that. But in a society of cliques, where all had their own unions and associations and where employees wore their company badges in their lapels, that was to be expected. Subservience to superiors, arrogance to inferiors? That, too, was characteristic of Japanese society as a whole. What then was "defeudalization" really aiming at?

The Move Toward Civil Service Reform

A few weeks after my arrival in Tokyo at the beginning of 1946, Colonel Kades, then Chief of Government Section's Public Administration Division, introduced me to a young, bespectacled lieutenant in the Transportation Corps, Milton J. Esman. Esman's desk was an oasis of quiet in a tumult of bustling reform activities, for he was in charge of the civil service under Kades, and it seemed that no one else was interested in the subject. No paragraph in the Joint Chiefs' directive JCS 1380/15 even mentioned the bureaucracy. Esman really had no official mission.

The lieutenant nevertheless doggedly insisted that SCAP had to reform the civil service. When I asked him why, he replied that no matter how well conceived the Occupation democratization, it would have to be applied by government officials, and if they remained reactionary bureaucrats, they would sabotage the reforms as soon as the Occupation was over, if not before. His answer had a kind of logic to it. But how was Esman going to democratize the bureaucratic machine, I wondered, without replacing the people in it wholesale? Alternatively, how was he going to brainwash them into democratic beliefs? Surely mind-set was more important then organization, grades, titles, and all the other trappings. Still, the goal was desirable. I wished him good luck and forgot about it. Esman persevered, nevertheless. Kades, sympathizing with him and certainly with his objective, suggested that Esman prepare a memo for General Whitney, the Chief of Government Section.

Esman tried and was shot down twice. On January 30, 1946, he wrote Whitney that the Japanese bureaucracy was "incompetent to manage a modern democratic society," especially now that "the police were no longer available to perform the operating functions of government."[2] How a deskbound Esman felt competent to make such a sweeping judgment was baffling. In any event, his timing was wrong. Three days later General MacArthur instructed Whitney to draft a model constitution to be handed to the Japanese government. On the same day Whitney constituted the Government Section as a "committee of the whole" to prepare such a draft. No one, including Esman, had time for anything else for a month. When things were quieter Esman tried again, this time in May, with concurrences from five other staff sections. But in the absence of a Washington directive Whitney again turned him down. Esman's subject simply had too low a priority. The project seemed moribund.

It was revived by the curiosity of a Japanese aristocrat and the wily maneuverings of an American colonel. Viscount Shibusawa Keizō, the urbane finance minister, an ex-governor of the Bank of Japan, and head of the Shibusawa *zaibatsu*—his grandfather, one of the Meiji giants, had founded the Daiichi Bank and the NYK shipping line—had become involved with government employees' wages in the spring of 1946, when I twice vetoed his ministry's Allowance Bureau wage revisions as unpardonably regressive. Shibusawa found the complexities of the government wage system bewildering, as he later told me. There were allowances for seniority, dependents, cost of living, serving in Hokkaidō, working under water, and handling high voltages, to name a few, plus semiannual bonuses minus withholding taxes. Hearing from his aides who had been discussing the relatively simple U.S. federal wage structure with the Labor Advisory Mission members just then in Japan, Shibusawa, in the open-minded Meiji tradition of his grandfather, sent a letter to General Marquat, the ESS Chief, asking for an American expert to help him establish the "CAF" system" in Japan.[3]

Shibusawa did not quite understand the American system—CAF, that is, clerical-administrative-fiscal, covered only one of the three main categories—and he was a poor Japanese bureaucrat in the bargain, for he had violated protocol by going outside proper channels. He should have written Whitney, not Marquat. When all that was pointed out to him, he good-humoredly apologized, and the cabinet then confirmed the substance of his request. It agreed to ask GHQ for experts, not just one expert.[4] The new request was brought over to Government Section, with a covering memo to Kades.

For the colonel it was a heaven-sent opportunity, for now he no longer needed a Washington directive. SCAP could now democratize the Japanese bureaucracy at the Japanese government's request. With the cabinet letter in hand, Kades approached Whitney with the idea of a civil service advisory committee from Washington. Other problems had been assigned to advisory missions, why not this one? Whitney sold MacArthur. A few months later Esman went home sporting a newly awarded Army commendation ribbon. From then on bureaucratic reform was in the hands of blue-ribbon advisers from the States.

THE HOOVER MISSION

Shibusawa had wanted a model of a new wage classification system. Kades may have envisioned breaking the "reactionary" grip of the *kanbatsu*. What they both got was something else: a modified copy of the U.S. civil service system. As in the case of other advisory missions to SCAP—the Edwards *zaibatsu* mission, for example—the selection of their key personnel in Washington rather than the facts of life in the field determined the mission's eventual recommendations. The chairman of the new mission, chosen by the Army Department and cleared with Whitney and MacArthur, was Blaine Hoover, president of the prestigious Civil Service Assembly of the United States and Canada, an umbrella organization of civil service professional societies, not trade unions. Three technical experts would assist him.[5] A lifetime of personnel administration within the U.S. federal civil service system was the basis, if not the sum, of their expertise. They knew nothing of the bureaucratic "feudalism" they were appointed to break up. From then on, an essentially political problem, rooted deeply in Japan's history and society, was to be resolved on wholly technical grounds.

On its arrival in Japan in November 1946, the mission launched itself into a comprehensive series of familiarization briefings by the appropriate SCAP agencies. No agency in GHQ could complain on that score. Of course, visiting experts in principle came to Japan as teachers, not students, but some minds were more closed than others. When I briefed the Hoover group as SCAP Labor Chief, it seemed to me that members were screening what I said, absorbing factual data they thought usable but rejecting information that did not fit their preconceptions. When I tried to explain the Japanese employer–employee relationship as an exchange of protection for loyalty, not money for work, their eyes glazed over. When I talked of the network of patron–client (*oyabun–kobun*) relationships that pervaded all large Japanese organizations, including the government bureaucracy, it drew no follow-up questions. To me that was the central problem of "defeudalizing" the *kanbatsu* bureaucracy. Wasn't that what Kades and Esman had talked to me about? But the mission men were more interested in a comparison of governmental and private wage scales. They had no room in their mental baggage for the psychology and attitudes of the people for whom they had been called upon to prescribe their modern, scientific, nonfeudal administrative system.

Instead, they used purely American concepts of equal opportunity for promotions and fair play for civil service workers, or the noble idea of service to the public.

Because the Hoover Mission saw everything through American eyes, it ignored perhaps the most striking feature of the tightly knit Japanese bureaucracy, the "old school tie." Tokyo Imperial University graduates dominated the upper levels of government administration, and an official who was not from that university was from another in the small group of Imperial universities. Knowing each other's capabilities from school, or being vouched for by a schoolmate, the officials not only had background and views in common, but felt mutual confidence and trust. They would not let each other down. Hence they advanced each other more rapidly than "outsiders." That was not only a civil service phenomenon. The same universities provided the bulk of the management of big business and even political party leaders.

But the Hoover mission ignored the educational elitism in the government bureaucracy, which had inevitably created the "tightly knit clique" they were trying to break up. Unsurprisingly, ten years after the Hoover civil service reform, in 1958, 98 percent of the highest grade government officials, 82 percent of the second grade, and 57 percent of the third grade were still graduates of the seven national, formerly Imperial, universities.[6] Those subtleties of Japanese society and the *kanbatsu* may not have been amenable to any constructive tinkering by foreigners from the outside anyway. But to the Hoover mission they did not even exist.

Hoover's analysis was almost totally irrelevant. In September 1948, when Howard Handleman, head of the International News Service Tokyo Bureau, visited Hoover in his Daiichi Building Office, Hoover delivered an indictment of the seven deadly sins that had afflicted the Japanese administration system: overstaffing, inefficiency, poor discipline, poor training, ineffective employee evaluation and utilization, classification based on civil service rank rather than duties and employment, and examinations testing general rather than specialized knowledge.[7] Unsurprisingly, his prescription turned out to be in the main equally conventional, a compound of merit examinations, "scientific" job descriptions, wage classifications, efficiency ratings, plus an independent civil service authority. What had all this to do with feudalism? An American arrangement designed historically to eliminate the spoils system was to be applied to a country that had none. I sometimes thought that if the Mission had been sent to the Arctic Circle instead, it would have come up with the same prescription for the Eskimos, seals, and seagulls.

If Hoover's proposals had gone no further than to impose a strange and perhaps ill-fitting arrangement on the bureaucracy, few would have cared much. But one of the deadly sins alleged by Hoover was "poor discipline." In the U.S. federal civil service, discipline applied to *individual* behavior: arriving on time, staying sober in the office, carrying out assigned duties, and so on. Hoover, however, expanded the meaning to include behavior of groups, and that got him into labor relations. The longer the mission stayed in Japan, the more developments—the general strike campaign led by government unions in January 1947, the subsequent friction between government and government unions in wage negotiations, and the occasional new strike threat—convinced Hoover that the crux of his problem was discipline of government labor unions. His response was to apply American practice.

Now, when I as Labor Chief had briefed Hoover in December 1946, I emphasized the sweeping differences between Japan and the United States with regard to government labor. I had pointed out the high proportion of government workers in the Japanese labor movement, perhaps 30 percent, as well as the high percentage of unionization in government (almost 100). I had also stressed the large number, almost a million, employed by government in industrial enterprises, such as the rail trunk lines, telephones and telegraphs, tobacco, salt, and camphor, all of which were privately operated in the United States. The distinction between public and private that served roughly to separate government administration from industry in America did not apply in Japan.

That was why, I explained, the labor relations rules were different in Japan. They varied according to the work being done, not who the employer was. In government, everyone except firemen, policemen, and prison guards could join a union and bargain collectively. Only those actually engaged in government administration were forbidden to strike, for a work stoppage on their part could bring the government to a halt. Those who worked in immediately essential services, like the rail and telephone and telegraph workers, could strike only after compulsory mediation and cooling-off period, along the lines of the U.S. Railway Labor Act. The rest, like teachers and custodial workers, were unrestricted. Those rules, I told him, had been embodied in SCAP-sponsored labor legislation, particularly in the Labor Relations Adjustment Law, enacted only weeks before. Finally, I pointed to the bitter battle between Communist and anti-Communist labor leaders among the government workers and warned against doing anything that would compromise the pro-Occupation anti-Communists and thereby the Labor Division mission as well.

The differences I outlined between American and Japanese practices were in some respects extreme—for example, in those days teachers' strikes in the United States were considered not only unprofessional and unrespectable, but were often illegal—and I watched for Hoover's reaction as I talked. There was none. I could not tell if he was absorbing my information or outraged by it. One of his men simply wondered aloud if government employees should be treated like industrial labor.

The Ban on Collective Bargaining and Strikes

Five months later, when I came back from Washington in May 1947 to find I had been promoted out of the Labor Division, one of the division members told me that Hoover's completed plan prohibited collective bargaining and strikes for government workers. That was not a surprise, but the report that Kades and

Whitney were supporting Hoover's recommendation was. Kades had always been a stalwart supporter of the "radical reform" from his Washington days and had worked consistently and cleverly to help Labor Division in its mission. Of course, almost no outside advisory mission's report could be rejected out of hand—I know of only one that ever was, and it was promptly classified top secret—for in receiving and publicizing such a group as "experts," GHQ was automatically admitting its own relative lack of expertise. How could nonexperts contest the views of experts? In this case, particularly, Whitney had sold the idea to MacArthur, had vouched for Hoover's committee on its arrival, and had given the "Old Man" glowing progress reports. Still, one could accept a report without accepting all of its recommendations or could modify it in application. That is what I hoped for.

Late one afternoon, I ran into Kades with his newly arrived wife at the Daiichi Hotel bar, joined them for a drink, and asked him whether it was true Hoover was recommending the end of collective bargaining in government and, if so, what could be done about it. Yes, it was true, he said, and nothing should be done about it, because the recommendation was correct. When I asked how SCAP could withdraw rights already accorded the workers, he denied the Occupation had granted them. Technically that was true, but only technically. His wife was surprised. "But, Chuck", she protested, "this is exactly the opposite of what you've always stood for!" Kades brusquely told her to keep quiet. Clearly, everything had been settled within the Government Section. Whitney was backing Hoover 100 percent, and Kades was following the section line.

For the Japanese the Hoover report could have been useful if they could have selected what they needed and ignored what was inappropriate, as they used to do in the Meiji period when they sought out foreign models to follow. The collective bargaining ban, for example, was inappropriate, at least politically, if only because the new prime minister, Katayama Tetsu, was a Socialist as well as a longtime defender of labor rights. Even though the report was in response to a Japanese government request, however, the Japanese were not free to reject it if SCAP insisted. Katayama could only try to ignore the portions he didn't like. When Hoover presented his report to MacArthur and the prime minister and then went back to the United States to recruit for his projected new Civil Service Division,[8] Katayama's experts drew up a National Public Service Bill, which implemented all of Hoover's ideas on a central civil service structure, servicewide standards, and an independent national public service authority. The bill said nothing about abolishing collective bargaining or strikes. The Government Section, supposed to check the draft in Hoover's absence, let the omissions stand, and in October 1947 the lower house passed the bill in fifteen minutes.

Curiously, on his return to Japan Hoover did not discover the omissions for several weeks. When he did, he angrily decided he'd been deceived by the Japanese and demanded that the new law be revised to prohibit collective bargaining and strikes. Whitney, somewhat embarrassed by Government Section's "carelessness," supported him. By May 1948 the Socialist Katayama was no longer prime minister, and Hoover's new Civil Service Division, working with the officials of the new National Personnel Authority, had completed its drafts of the Public Service Law revisions banning collective bargaining and strikes and providing heavy penalties for infractions. It sent the draft around to the interested SCAP agencies for concurrences. When the draft reached the ESS Labor Division, with James Killen at its head, an aroused Killen absolutely refused to go along.

Labor Division's views on the subject were nothing new. They were derived from Washington directives and had been incorporated in the existing legislation. In the many succeeding months the Labor Division staff, working largely as technical consultants to the mission members, continually repeated those views. The frosty Hoover was almost always absent from those informal discussions, but his friendly subordinates seemed to be absorbing a good bit of what Labor Division said. The Labor Division people sensed a gap between Hoover's rather authoritarian views and those of his assistants.

They therefore found it hard to believe that their sensible mission friends really agreed with Hoover that government tobacco or camphor or even railway workers striking for higher wages would be engaging in revolution, or that because the Japanese people paid the taxes that supported government they were entitled to continuous service, no matter what. (Transposed to private industry, that meant no strikes as long as the employer met his payroll; besides, the government enterprises were supposed to support themselves by selling railway tickets, stamps, tobacco, salt, comphor, and cigarettes.) Even less could they imagine that the mission's parent Government Section—the spearhead of the democratization reforms really concurred with Hoover's simplistic historical blooper that "the government of Japan—and every job in it—was created by the people of Japan to serve the people of Japan".[9] Everyone knew that the Meiji builders hardly had the people of Japan in mind at all.

And so, eschewing philosophy, the Labor Division people had been talking cases to the Civil Service staff. Collective bargaining did exist in U.S. Government agencies, notably the Tennessee Valley Authority and the Inland Waterways Commission. There were precedents, too, on how to handle collective bargaining disputes in government, as witness the Whitley Councils in England. They were all reasonable men on both sides, and reasonable men could work out compromises. Bernarr Mazo of the Labor Division had long, enlightened conversations with the mission's DeAngelis, who liked Mazo so well he wanted him for the mission. But all the pleasant staff conversations foundered on three rocks: the principals, Hoover, Whitney, and Killen. There was little inclination to compromise among them.

Perhaps it was too much to expect Hoover, who had spent a good part of his life fighting the encroachment of civil service trade unions on his Civil Service Assembly in the United States, to keep an open mind on unions in Japan.

Perhaps he was exasperated by the ingratitude of the government unions for his efforts to raise their status, pay, and treatment. Probably he viewed their leaders as extreme radicals, too. Anyway, Hoover's legislation was more severe than anything in the United States. All his provisions were modeled on U.S. precedents, except penalties for infractions. Whereas the Hatch and Taft–Hartley acts provided a jail penalty for only one offense (extorting political contributions from subordinates),[10] Hoover's revisions called for prison sentences, in some cases up to three years, for twenty infractions.[11] This departure from American precedent was an indication of his implacability. He would not even talk to Killen about it.

Whitney, for his part, had begun by viewing Hoover's reform as a new SCAP achievement, one certain to bring widespread acclaim at least on the part of Hoover's powerful political lobby back home. But in the latter part of 1947 and in 1948 a new element entered the equation, for MacArthur had become increasingly disturbed by the massive Communist-led strikes, featuring especially government employees, against U.S. Marshall Plan aid in Italy and France. In his letter to the prime minister about collective bargaining for government workers,[12] MacArthur would later remind him that "only recently . . . the great Western democracies" had had to call out the Army to reinforce the civil police to maintain peace. In Japan, moreover, the general strike ban had settled nothing permanently, for that was not a Japanese law but an Occupation order.

Indeed, the government workers had resumed their agitation; in the course of their collective bargaining they frequently talked strike. In February 1948, Marquat had had to advise the All-Communications Union that any "coordinated work stoppage" would be covered by the general strike ruling. Unquestionably, with the Occupation's departure, if not before, government strikes would break out. How could they be controlled without contradicting the general Occupation labor emancipation policy and indeed MacArthur's own promise of January 31 1947, that "I do not intend otherwise to restrict the freedom of action heretofore given labor in the achievement of its legitimate objectives"? Hoover's bill proposed precisely to restrict that freedom. But what if government employees were not considered to be "labor" in the usual sense? Then there could be no collective bargaining, no disputes, and no possibilities of a government strike. Whitney came increasingly to the conviction that Hoover's new program was the answer.

KILLEN AND HOOVER

But James Killen, my successor as Labor Division chief, stood athwart the path. In the spring of 1948 Killen had held the post less than a year. A tall, handsome, youthful-looking "labor skate," he presented a direct physical contrast to a Hoover, who was twenty-five years his senior, with brushed-back gray hair, rimless glasses, and an often pedantic manner. Aggressive and articulate, Killen loved to pepper his talk with labor slang like "Let's pull the plug, Buckley," meaning negotiations were at an impasse, let's strike or, in GHQ, let's get the unpleasant business over with.

Killen had been a child of fortune in his own union, the Paper, Pulp, and Sulfite Workers, where the old president, John Burke, had adopted him as a protégé and had moved him rapidly up the union ladder to a vice presidency. On his arrival in Tokyo as my adviser while I was out of the country, MacArthur had asked to see him, partly as a courtesy to the American labor movement. He was impressed with Killen personally as a solution to his own domestic labor problem, namely, my unpopularity with American conservative political figures, and appointed Killen Chief of the Labor Division while promoting me upstairs.

In the next year, Killen had two or three personal meetings with the Supreme Commander, including one just prior to his departure to attend the 1947 AFL convention. That was highly unusual, for hardly any division chiefs ever saw the General at all. Killen was sure he had found favor with the "Old Man," and he was probably right. Of course, MacArthur was also keeping his lines open to the American labor movement. Bolstered by his belief in MacArthur's support and endowed with a natural combativeness,[13] Jim Killen was not one to retreat where his labor principles were involved.

On the contrary, as a union negotiator who had faced his share of tough nuts across a bargaining table, Killen almost always was prepared for a fight. As a lifetime labor organizer, he knew that unions existed to bargain collectively, and without that right a union had no purpose. As representative of the AFL in Japan, he would not lower the labor banner an inch. For a union leader such as he to lose labor rights that had previously been gained by a nonunion man, me, would be personally embarrassing. He was quite ready to take on Hoover and, perhaps rashly, Courtney Whitney, who had not lost a battle within GHQ yet, as well.

In any case, resolution of the deadlock could not be long delayed. The Diet was in session; it was time to present it with Hoover's revisions if the new rules were going to be put into effect soon. Various government workers' unions were talking strike. The All-Communications Workers even set a tentative date, August 4, if MacArthur would let them. Indeed, the union was ready to tailor the dispute action to whatever SCAP would allow. With Labor Division (ESS) and Civil Service Division (GS) at an impasse, only the Supreme Commander could make the decision. MacArthur called for a full-scale presentation in his office by both sides for July 21.

In the looming clash, Whitney's full backing of Hoover was assured, but Marquat, Killen's Chief in ESS, was in a quandary. Primarily interested in economic recovery, he prized labor peace, and government workers' unrest had a nasty habit of spreading to private industry. Privately Marquat thought little of Hoover, whom he considered a liability and a danger to MacArthur. He had a much higher regard for Killen, but for whom was Killen really working, the Command or the American Federation of Labor? A Hoover victory would reflect unfavorably on ESS, but was Killen's solution really in the best interests of Japan? It was a tangle of uncertainties. If Marquat opposed Killen, the division chief might bring the American labor movement down on the Supreme Commander's head, and MacArthur liked to pick his own fights. If he agreed with Killen, however, Killen might quote him in opposition to the "Old Man." If he did nothing, he would be surrendering the field to his archrival, Whitney. Above all, the bureaucratic infighting aside, Marquat really wanted to know the best course to pursue. He was a clever man, but he had no background in labor.

Marquat turned to me, his former labor chief. One afternoon, about a week before the scheduled showdown, he told me casually that the Supreme Commander had asked him the night before how I stood in the controversy. (MacArthur was evidently concerned that I might be siding with Killen in talking with American correspondents.) Marquat had immediately reassured the "Old Man" that I had been staying completely out of the affair and that I would remain loyal no matter what. I thanked him for his unhesitating support and told him that in fact what he had said happened to be true. I had promised Killen on his assumption of the post of labor chief that I would not interfere with him or undermine him in any way, and I had kept my word. Nevertheless, Marquat said now he needed independent advice from outside Killen's Labor Division. Would I advise him personally and independently on the issue?

Regardless of the details, I responded, the deprivation of established labor rights was a very serious affair that could boomerang on the Occupation. Details of existing law might be modified, but principles should not be abandoned in full public view, and MacArthur had pledged to protect labor rights only eighteen months ago. The unions had certainly not forgotten his promise. The GS plan would break that commitment. Hoover was unnecessarily extreme; he was proposing to tear down the house of collective bargaining to keep it from catching fire. Surely there was a more moderate solution, some more practical middle course. Further, I said, while Killen could probably best Hoover in a debate in front of the "Old Man," I doubted that he could lick Whitney. In such conditions, the best we, that is, ESS, could hope for was a compromise.

Granted, Marquat said, but what kind? Well, Hoover was against both collective bargaining and strike rights for government workers. Killen favored both but would accept some limitations on strikes,[14] although not on collective bargaining. The only possible compromise would be to forbid or limit collective bargaining for some of the government workers, but not most. In the United States the administrative workers could not bargain collectively, although the employees of the Tennessee Valley Authority and the Inland Waterways Commission could and did. I asked for time to work out a compromise that both Killen and Hoover might accept, if MacArthur indicated he wanted one.

A COMPROMISE PLAN

Two days later, on July 17, I presented my compromise to Marquat.[15] Essentially, it proposed that workers in the administrative agencies plus the post office would come under the civil service. Government enterprise workers— railways, salt, camphor, tobacco—plus telecommunications would not. Teachers would remain in their special category. Civil service workers could bargain collectively, but only on matters not set down in the laws, that is, only on wage levels, hours, and general working conditions. Everything else including the servicewide standards, classification system, indeed the whole Hoover civil service structure, would be excluded from collective bargaining and remain solely under the jurisdiction of the National Personnel Authority.

As to strikes, they would continue to be forbidden to administrative workers, including police, firemen, and prison guards. Further, the compulsory "cooling-off" period accompanied by compulsory mediation already in force for those engaged in designated "public welfare works"—railways, telecommunications, water, and health services were designated at the moment—could be extended by the prime minister from one to six months if he found a strike would seriously endanger national health or safety. The prime minister would also be empowered to designate additional "public welfare works" after consultation with the Central Labor Relations Committee. Where strikes were forbidden and mediation failed, compulsory arbitration would be invoked. Penalties for violations would be limited to discharges with or without separation allowances and deprivation of special benefits like supplementary food rations. My proposal said nothing about political rights. That was not an economic section's business.

Marquat went over the proposal with me in detail. He agreed that if the Supreme Commander were really looking for a compromise after hearing Hoover and Killen out, this could well serve as a basis. Marquat was not going to interfere with Killen's presentation, nor would he even propose my compromise to the "Old Man" if Killen objected, for Marquat would not give the impression under any circumstances that he was undercutting Killen. But if MacArthur were anxious to avoid a break with American labor and Killen would concede that half a loaf was better than none, then the proposal might work. Marquat asked me to get Killen's assent to Marquat's submitting the compromise to the Supreme Commander if it looked like Hoover's plan would otherwise be approved.

My mission was doomed from the first. Killen, holed up in his office behind the Daiichi Hotel like a brooding, wary bear, had already decided to stick to his principles to the end. He credited me with the best intentions in the world, thanked me for not undercutting him as Labor Division chief, and appreciated Marquat's pledge not to introduce any plan without his say-so. But he still would not play. A compromise would be better than a total defeat, he conceded, but he would not yield. "You are a career bureaucrat," he told me tiredly, "and for you it is right to compromise to save whatever you can. If I were in your place, I would probably do the same. But I'm not a career bureaucrat. I'm a labor union man and I'm eventually going back to the labor movement. I can't agree to compromise my movement's principles."

No amount of talk could persuade Killen. He was confident that he could convince MacArthur of the peril of Blaine Hoover's course and intended to stake everything on principle and his own persuasiveness. With respect to our relative careers, his crystal ball turned out to have been cloudy. Some two years later I left the government service, my nine-year bureaucratic life over, while Killen, after a brief interruption, remained on the government payroll until his death some twenty years later.

THE SHOWDOWN

The six-hour "showdown" between Hoover and Killen on July 21, 1948, was unique in the Occupation Headquarters. Killen argued singlehandedly as Marquat kept silent, while for Government Section, Hoover and Frank Rizzo, acting Government Section Deputy Chief, took turns. Whitney also interceded. For two sessions the protagonists stated their case and answered the "Old Man's" questions. According to Killen's account[16] he argued forcefully and rather successfully in the afternoon session. He stumped Hoover with such questions as: If the government owned the coal mines, should the miners be recruited by civil service examination? In fact, according to Killen, MacArthur several times agreed with the principle that teachers and employees in other nonessential government activities should retain the right to bargain collectively. But during the break that followed Whitney got to MacArthur privately—"upon entering SCAP's office for the evening session, the conferees found General Whitney already there," Killen wrote significantly in his statement—and Whitney had meanwhile changed the Supreme Commander's mind. Thereafter MacArthur was a Government Section convert.

Now the focus of the discussion changed. The Supreme Commander, Killen recalled, repeatedly called attention to past and currently threatened government strikes. MacArthur cited with strong approval the Hoover principle that the authority of the state must be supreme, above challenge, and certainly not "on an equal footing in any respect with that of a minority group." Killen apparently did not disagree. But he did protest, vainly as it turned out, against the notion that collective bargaining necessarily implied strikes. In England, he pointed out, the Whitley Councils were just then settling government workers' collective bargaining disputes by compulsory arbitration.

MacArthur was unimpressed with experimental English methods. On the basis of his own observation, the bargaining power of a union was inseparable from "its inherent power of compulsion," he said.[17] A government union left free to bargain would use that power, legally or illegally. A dispute over even limited issues could turn into a strike and then into a "mass uprising." Such a state of affairs, MacArthur reminded Killen, could not be tolerated in a Japan that had renounced war and an Army establishment and was therefore a "powerless state." Killen's reassurances did not reassure MacArthur, and Killen would go no further except to warn of a "trail of labor resentment" if Hoover's plan were adopted. MacArthur himself made no move to explore a compromise. And Marquat, with my compromise proposal in his pocket, would not volunteer it on his own.

The Supreme Commander told the weary but keyed-up participants at 9:00 P.M. that he would let them know his decision in the morning, but he had in fact already made up his mind. Shortly after eight the next morning, July 22, Whitney passed the word to his Government Section people that MacArthur had decided in their favor. Later that day, MacArthur sent the prime minister a letter embodying that decision. Killen got his notification later in the morning from the American news correspondents asking him for comment. So recently MacArthur's "fair-haired boy," Killen was now humiliated at being publicly bypassed, and right after MacArthur had promised he would not make any decision public without seeing him once more. At least, that was what Killen told his Labor Division staff.[18]

After several days' further pondering, during which he persuaded Katō Kanjū, the Labor Minister, not to resign but to try to ameliorate the application of SCAP's letter, Killen gave up. He submitted his own resignation, effective in sixty days or at the convenience of the Command; MacArthur accepted it effective the next day. In less than two weeks Killen was on a ship bound for America with his family. MacArthur's only concession to Killen's status was to allow government payment of his and his family's passage home. (Paul Stanchfield,[19] Killen's deputy chief, who also resigned in order to impress everyone that the issue was principle, not personality, was not so lucky. He had to pay his own fare, besides which hardly anyone noticed his resignation.)

Killen may have taken the decision as a complete defeat, but Frank Rizzo, one of the Government Section representatives at the confrontation, reminisced many years later that "we looked on it as a seventy–thirty decision,"[20] because MacArthur in his letter to Prime Minister Ashida advised the Japanese Government to split off the government railways and monopoly enterprises as separate government corporations and let their employees bargain collectively, although not strike. Instead, mediation and arbitration procedures were to be set up. That recognized a reality that Hoover had defied. But the remaining three-quarters of the government employees, including 700,000 communications workers and teachers, could now no longer bargain collectively, depriving them of a right they had had *de facto* for three years and *de jure* for two.[21] MacArthur also advised the prime minister to separate telecommunications from the postal service for reasons of "efficiency," a somewhat strange and incongruous piece of advice in the circumstances.

Although addressed to Prime Minister Ashida, MacArthur's letter seemed almost more concerned with American labor reaction than Japanese, for it quoted Franklin D. Roosevelt, surely not one of MacArthur's favorites, but still an idol among American unionists (the Japanese workers hardly knew of him at all) at great length in support of his decision. (In point of fact, Roosevelt's stand against government strikes was not a true parallel, for the late president had been talking only of public employees who "have to do with the functioning of government." On collective bargaining, Roosevelt had pointed out that no administrative official could bind Congress to make the necessary appropriations. MacArthur never raised the question.) In any event, MacArthur need not have worried. When Killen, back in the United States, charged at the AFL convention in November that the Supreme Commander had been working against labor and inadvertently helping Japan's Communists, he got only scattered applause. MacArthur was still an untouchable hero to the American "working stiff." Killen was unknown. Hardly any of the convention delegates present cared much about Japan.

The Reaction

The Supreme Commander really should have worried more about the Japanese reaction. At first, they were deceptively docile. All three major political parties deferred to his authoritative advice. On July 31 the Democrat-Socialist coalition cabinet issued an emergency Postdam Ordinance (Number 201) suspending all government collective bargaining in progress. Of the coalition ministers, only Katō Kanjū, unluckily labor minister just then, showed any fight. He tried to argue with General Whitney, but the general just showed him a mountain of telegrams from American civil service organizations supporting Hoover to prove the Hoover legislation could not possibly be harmful to civil servants.[22] The other Socialist officials did nothing.

A few months later the Liberals, having in the meantime succeeded to office, accepted the burden of pushing Hoover's legislation through the Diet, though without enthusiasm. In the Diet debate, Deputy Prime Minister Hayashi Jōji, when challenged as to the constitutionality of the bill, first referred briefly to MacArthur and then innocently commented that, well, the preceding cabinet (the Socialists and Democrats) had already decided it was constitutional. Labor Minister Masuda Kaneshichi, upset by the severe punishments provided in the bill, denied that the government would enforce the penalties as written except for unusual cases.[23] Prime Minister Yoshida and other ministers contented themselves with brief, noncommital replies on interpellation. No one wanted any part of an unpopular act imposed without any real Japanese consultation.

But the labor unions and non-cabinet Socialists were not so inhibited. The newspapers trod cautiously, but Occupation intelligence revealed that dissent was boiling beneath the surface. MacArthur was shocked. At first he blamed the discontent on the Communists. In a curious confidential radiogram to Under Secretary Draper, drafted by Whitney and dispatched two months after the Hoover–Killen showdown, he complained that "following the Soviet attack on the principles enunciated in my letter to the Prime Minister of 22 July, the situation here has become increasingly ideological with manifest encouragement to local Communists and any public lack of support by the American Government would gravely weaken our position in Japan and throughout the Far East, and render that of the Supreme Commander extremely difficult if not untenable."[24] That was pretty powerful stuff—the whole U.S. position in the Far East threatened by a civil service reform law. One has to wonder whether a responsible leader should have deliberately risked such a consequence if he had anticipated such a reaction. Killen had warned him. But of course, neither he nor Whitney believed it. When the law was passed at the end of November, MacArthur remained baffled. It was, he said, "a strange political and social phenomenon . . . that many of the very employees who will be protected under the National Public Service Law continue to remain under the spell of a thoroughly discredited leadership."[25]

Discredited? With whom? In truth, MacArthur had lost touch with the government workers. For all his powers of empathy and imagination, he was unable to put himself in their place. To him, perhaps, they were civil servants, but the vast majority thought of themselves as workers—why else had they joined labor unions in droves?—no matter what terminology the new law used. They could not forget that in the fall of 1946, dreading the coming winter, they had sent their leaders from door to door and minister to minister and had been turned away as unwelcome beggars . . . until they threatened to strike. Since then high-ranking government officials had had to recognize and negotiate with them. When MacArthur canceled their right to bargain further on July 22, he was, in the workers' eyes, once again turning them into mendicants and wards of the *kanbatsu* elite in the National Personnel Authority, no matter how well-meaning the latter might have been. Not only their economic well-being but their self-esteem was involved.

Indeed, to the Japanese workers generally MacArthur seemed a different man from the Supreme Commander who had ordered the prime minister to encourage labor unionization, had protected collective bargaining, and had intervened in only one strike, *in extremis,* and with the greatest reluctance. Now he had abandoned them, and they, in turn, abandoned those who had collaborated most faithfully with him. In the January 1949 elections the following month, former Prime Minister Katayama Tetsu, Deputy Prime Minister Nishio Suehiro, and Labor Minister Katō Kanjū, all Socialists but pro-American and anti-Communist, were resoundingly defeated. Katō, the investigative hero of the hoarded-goods scandals, was beaten so badly that he had to change his electoral constituency from then on.[26] The election results showed a massive shift in labor allegiance away from the Socialists. The beneficiary: the Communist party of Japan.

The 1949 lower house elections have gone down in Japanese history as the postwar political turning point. The conservative Liberal party captured 264 out of the 466 Diet seats and inaugurated the era of conservative majorities that has lasted ever since. But an almost equally decisive change took place among the parties of the left. Three million voters deserted the moderate pro-American Socialist ranks, and of those 2.6 million went over the the Communist party and the extreme anti-American Farmer-Labor Party. The Socialist 1947 total of 7.2 million popular votes fell to 4.1 million; the Communist rose from 1 million to 3 million, and the Farmer-Labor Party, which had not existed in 1947, garnered 600,000. MacArthur declared after the election that the results were a "clear and decisive mandate for the conservative philosophy of government."[27] U.S. Assistant Secretary of State Saltzman was perhaps more perceptive when he called attention to the "polarization of politics in Japan."

With the sweeping electoral defeat of the moderate Socialists, the leftist faction, those who had warned against excessive reliance on America, took over the party. Suzuki Mōsaburō, he who had come running white-faced to warn the Communist Tokuda that MacArthur had banned a general strike, was elected secretary general by 390 to 262, and the left-wingers also captured the Central Executive Committee, 21 to 17. The margin was provided by five ostensibly neutral labor union representatives who switched *en bloc* to the left.

Suzuki was no Communist—in 1947 he had joined with Katō in a memorable denunciation of the Communists—but he had always been wary of capitalist America's intentions. MacArthur's letter withdrawing labor rights already granted vindicated, he felt, his longtime suspicions. Neither Soviet Russia nor the United States could be trusted to defend the Japanese working classes. The only safe course for Japan was to be independent and neutral.

Probably the best example of his thinking was a dialogue between Suzuki and Norman Thomas, the longtime American Socialist leader, to whom I introduced him in April 1952 in the quiet lobby of the then recently opened Nikkatsu Hotel in Tokyo. In response to Thomas's question, the mild-mannered Suzuki declared that Japan's defense needs were best met by a United Nations military force. Thomas asked him against whom Japan expected to need defense. "The Russians," Suzuki replied. And would the U.N. force include Russian soldiers?

"Yes," answered Suzuki.

"But how," I interjected, "can you expect Russian soldiers on a U.N. force to resist Soviet invaders?"

"Hah!" Suzuki snorted, "You Americans aren't always logical either."

Suzuki and his fellows had been burned by trusting the United States, and they weren't going to make the same mistake twice. That attitude lasted for the entire seventeen years Suzuki remained head of the Japanese Socialists, and well beyond.

The Communists took even greater advantage of the government workers issue than the left Socialists. In the months following MacArthur's July 22 letter, the party circulated petitions opposing the civil service revisions and secured millions of signatures. The Communist Diet member Kimura Sakae claimed 5 million in all.[28] Even allowing for some exaggeration, it was the first time so many ordinary Japanese had put themselves on record as directly opposing the wishes of General MacArthur, an unthinkable development only a few months before.

In December 1948 and January 1949, the Communists launched campaigns in all the unions they dominated aimed at defeating everyone who had collaborated in any way with the law's revision. (Katō Kanjū, the militant who had spent months in Kempeitai military police prisons, suddenly became a traitor to the working class.) When the election returns were in, a jubilant Tokuda Kyūichi, the Communist boss, denied that anti-Americanism had anything to do with the results. That was disingenuous, but under an American military occupation it was not wise to be openly anti-American. Another Communist party "spokesman," however, was more candid. The antistrike, anti–collective bargaining legislation sponsored by General MacArthur, he said, was definitely one of the three main reasons for his party's gains. The other two were the sweeping military successes of the Communist armies in China and disillusionment with moderate policies.[29] Supporting that statement was the relatively high Communist vote in rural areas, where sixteen out of the party's thirty-five successful candidates were elected, and in electoral districts where government union workers like railwaymen, teachers, and telecommunications and postal employees predominated among organized labor.

In May 1947, General Whitney had gone out of his way repeatedly to deny SCAP's involvement in the elections. In 1949, willy-nilly, MacArthur had become a key though unspoken issue. And there he lost.

The Outcome

What did the reform accomplish in return? Government administrative efficiency improved over the years, but whether the Hoover reform or the recovery from wartime devastation and shortages—two huge new buildings were completed downtown for the Ministry of International Trade and the Foreign Office, for example—contributed more, I am not competent to say. Labor relations were "stabilized" in the short run. The communications workers had to call off their strike, and the following year the various government departments took advantage of the provisions of Hoover's new law to discharge 11,000 alleged Communists, most of them union activists, for neglect of duties, including 2,741 from the Communications Workers, 2,591 from the Railway Federation, and 1,750 from the Teachers.[30] A public corporations labor relations law was enacted to cover collective bargaining at the government enterprises. But unrest continued, as evidenced by ugly incidents like the murder of the Railway Corporation president,[31] the Mitaka "runaway train,"[32] and the Matsukawa case.[33] In the long run, Hoover's revisions did not abolish strikes or collective bargaining outside the corporations. In the 1950s and 1960s, year-end postal slowdowns and no-overtime campaigns disrupted the mail service almost every year until the government acceded to bonus and wage increases, pressed not by collective bargaining but by union petitions plus discussions. It was hard to tell the difference. After 1950 the government never tried to enforce the law in its full rigor and rarely applied its jail penalties. The three-year prison punishment was never, so far as I am aware, even sought.

Nor did the new structure visibly eradicate "feudalism" from Japanese officialdom. The *kanbatsu* were not weakened as a clique; on the contrary, with the removal of their prewar military rivals, the civil bureaucrats greatly strengthened their power and influence. More than ever they remained the elite, and their upper reaches became fertile breeding grounds for new political leaders. Six of them, Yoshida, Kishi, Ikeda, Satō, Fukuda, and Ōhira, occupied the prime minister's office for some fifteen of the thirty years that followed Hoover's crusade to break up the "tightly-knit, exclusive and self-perpetuating bureaucracy." And no wonder, for Hoover's "defeudalization" was simply unrelated to Japanese feudalism, in government or out.

There was one crucial long-lasting consequence, however: Killen's predicted "trail of labor resentment" against the United States. It fairly began on June 22, 1948, but it grew steadily thereafter. In West Germany an equally socialist and Marxist labor movement undergoing a similar but harsher American occupation remained steadfastly pro-West. In Japan, the labor unions simply trusted the United States no more. In 1961, West German crowds greeted President Kennedy with wild enthusiasm. In mid-June 1960, President Eisenhower could not even land in Japan.

How far the Japanese workers and intellectuals had progressed down the road of alienation from America was powerfully demonstrated by more than a million Socialists, Communists, trade unionists, and sympathetic intellectuals parading and protesting on the streets of downtown Tokyo on June 30, 1960, against the U.S.–Japan Security Treaty.

Climaxing days of steadily growing demonstrations, the crowds of that day took over the heart of the capital city. They paraded ten, twelve, and fourteen abreast, monopolizing the few wide streets and prescribing an erratic course around the Diet Building at a distance of a few hundred meters. Everyone within the course was locked in. In seemingly endless numbers the paraders marched, banners flying and placards bobbing, hour upon hour, all day and a good part of the night, shouting antitreaty slogans and thundering "Kishi-wo taose! Kishi-wo-taose!" ("Down with Prime Minister Kishi!") in unison. (I walked along-side, enthusiastically shouting "Khruschev-wo-taose!" into the din, and we waved at each other amiably.) At intervals, lines of demonstrators, wearing red warrior *hachimaki* headbands, snake-danced wildly over the streets. From the distance the shouts reverberated like the full-throated roar of a stadium football crowd. Regular traffic disappeared, and the occasional driver of a taxi, lim-ousine, or private vehicle had humbly to beg the parade marshals to let him through. Never had the Japanese police been so gentle toward the people. Truck-loads of them parked in the neighboring side streets but made no move. I saw one excited demonstrator spit in a policeman's eye, and the officer only wiped his face impassively. To all appearances, the government had abdicated. It was the nearest thing to a revolution I had ever witnessed. Late that night, around midnight, the demonstrators made a futile attempt to capture an empty Diet Building—the session had been adjourned *sine die* that afternoon—and the whole affair petered out like a morning mist as dawn draws near. But the outcome could have been very different with a Lenin or a Tokuda[34] on the scene.

I shall never forget looking westward earlier that evening from the eighth floor of the Toranomon Building in central Tokyo at the marching contingents. They approached along the broad avenue the American Army had labeled "Tenth Street" and the Japanese had renamed "Outer Moat Street" (*Sotobori-dōri*) and then passed us below to turn north toward the ministries and the Imperial Palace grounds. There were no street lights, and as dusk fell an inde-scribably beautiful and uniquely Japanese scene met the eye. The paraders had lit Japanese lanterns, and in the gloom the parade was transformed into a sea of bobbing lights, like swarms of regimented fireflies, advancing upon us from as far as the eye could see. Leave it to the Japanese, I thought. When they make a revolution, it will be the most esthetic ever.

History is the queen of ironists. Gazing transfixed at the spectacle, I recalled that twelve years before, MacArthur had warned of a "mass uprising" when he declared to Killen that Japan, "the powerless state," could not stand the strain of having government workers bargain collectively. Now the same Ja-panese workers looked very much as though they were launching just such a mass uprising, but in circumstances that had their inception in his decision that day.

Part VII

TO RESCUE THE
AMERICAN TAXPAYER

"Pray for General MacArthur's success in the presidential election," the front of a two-story wooden building in Tameike, Tokyo, exhorted. The time was early 1948, before the Wisconsin Republican primary. A large outdoor billboard in English nearby explained why. "No doubt, General MacArthur is the real and foster father and moreover, he is the benefactor of the newly born Japan. We are sure that happiness and improvement will be brought about in Japan if he is elected president because he understands Japan fully and he has humanity."

Passing Occupationnaires chuckled at the phrasing and pretensions of Oda Toshiyo, self-styled chairman of the Association for the Promotion of Eternal World Peace, who signed the appeal and ended it with the words, "May God give the glory to the believer who is always with God and his nation." Some kind of a religious nut, no doubt. In a few months, the signs had disappeared together with MacArthur's presidential hopes. The building contractor Oda was no longer heard from—at least, not publicly.

No one laughed, however, at Oda's sentiment that General MacArthur, who understood the Japanese and had "humanity," was their best American protector. On this there was almost universal accord among Japanese at all levels. But history has its little ironies. While the Japanese were thinking they needed MacArthur to protect them from less sympathetic Americans, top-level Washington officials were deciding that someone was needed in Japan to protect the U.S. Treasury from the Japanese and their endless requirements for aid. In the mood of the times, the result of the ensuing internal power struggle between Washington and Tokyo was foreordained. Within a year MacArthur had been superseded as supreme arbiter for Japan, at least in the all-important economic sphere. Chairman Oda would now have to put his trust in others.

21

William Draper and the Marshallization of American Aid

IN THE GATHERING GLOOM of September 18, 1947, enlisted men and junior officers working late at Haneda[1] air base were startled to see a shiny black 1942 Cadillac flying the flag of a five-star general, accompanied by two jeeploads of tall MP honor guards, sweep to a stop in front of the newly completed two-story terminal building, and General of the Army Douglas MacArthur and his wife, Jean, emerge onto the floodlit tarmac. In a rare sortie from behind his own bamboo curtain, the Supreme Commander was personally welcoming the new Under Secretary of the Army, William Henry Draper, Jr., to Japan. On that day and those to follow, no honor was too great for Draper. He returned home with the MacArthurs and stayed with them at the American Embassy. The day after he arrived a weary First Cavalry Division, exhausted by three days of continuous struggle against a disastrous typhoon-fed flood that had inundated parts of the capital city, turned out to give Draper a full military parade and review on the Imperial Palace Plaza. A week later, after a red-carpet visit to Korea and the principal military posts in the field, as well as intensive conferences at MacArthur's GHQ, the Under Secretary made his first significant pronouncement. Before a full complement of reporters assembled for the purpose, he declared that the new prime objective of the Occupation of Japan would be "to reduce the costs to the American taxpayer."[2]

Compared with the sweep and nobility of MacArthur's oft-proclaimed vision of a new Japan, Draper's words sounded narrow and niggardly. But Draper was speaking from another world, one burdened financially with all the world's problems and now demanding down-to-earth practicality in the Orient. Japan was down and out, and America was supporting it. For how long? "Tremendous costs have accrued to the victor," the Under Secretary explained. "Neither victor nor vanquished can long endure these conditions."[3] Indeed, it was a new kind of vision that Draper brought. Treated everywhere in the Command with the pomp of a high military potentate, he spoke the language of an accountant.

DRAPER AND THE MARSHALL PLAN

In an address a few weeks later, on October 10, to a gathering of New England bankers, stockholders in the Federal Reserve Bank of Boston, Draper amplified his Tokyo remarks: "Primarily, the objectives of our several military occupations should now be directed to bringing about the economic recovery of Germany and Japan," he asserted. "Japan and Germany [are] now demilitarized, de-Nazified and stripped of their war lords." Now they should be permitted a "reasonable recovery" so as to "become self-respecting, self-supporting members of the community of nations" and "end the cost of maintaining our occupation administrations and our cost of supporting the civilian population and bring the soldiers back home."[4]

At first hearing, Draper's statement seemed mostly an echo, not much more, of Secretary of State Marshall's historic Harvard commencement speech four months earlier. Marshall had pledged America's resources to the economic rehabilitation of postwar Europe and initiated the giant plan that thereafter bore his name. Draper, too, was proposing that the United States assist the recovery of foreign nations. But Marshall had referred to sovereign and friendly nations, whereas Draper was talking about enemies. Marshall spoke of fundamental goals for Europe, "to permit the emergence of political and social conditions in which free men can exist."[5] Draper was just saving his country money. While Marshall invited the Europeans to formulate their own recovery projects, Draper was going to *tell* the Japanese what to do. In both Europe and Japan, the recipients were duly thankful. But while the Marshall Plan in each of the West European countries became a truly national effort, in Japan it was to become a source of bitter dissension.

The Under Secretary was a solid success with the Supreme Commander as well as with his economic chief, General Marquat. Of course, anyone with the purse strings in his hands is not likely to be a wallflower, and Draper controlled the Occupation budget. More than that, Draper, a banker in civil life, was the first high-ranking Washington official to be personally interested in the details of the budget for Japan.[6] But most of all, Draper had come with a proposition to go beyond mere relief. He wanted to revive the Japanese economy.

To MacArthur, who had bitterly resented being "starved" during the war for the benefit of other theaters and who had been saddled by an occupation directive not to accept responsibility for Japanese economic rehabilitation—knowing all the while that history would nevertheless judge his occupation by the shape in which he left Japan's economy—Draper's visit was a happy opportunity. Congressional funds to finance industrial rehabilitation and self-support could well crown MacArthur's occupation with final success. To MacArthur and Marquat, Draper was potentially the Occupation's most valuable ally in Washington.

Marquat's people in ESS were equally encouraged. Within weeks of the Under Secretary's first visit, Sherwood Fine, the general's "big picture" economic adviser, and a group of section economists put together a "Green Book"—its formal title was "Possibility of a Balanced Japanese Economy"—spelling out how self-support could be reached some time between 1951 and 1953 with the help of Congressional appropriations.[7] With Draper's support in Washington, the chances of putting the program on the rails were bright. As Fine put it in one optimistic moment, "Everything great in '48!" When I countered with "Everything fine in '49!" he went on to "Everything nifty by '50!" "Done by '51!" and "Through by '52!" By 1952, in fact, the program *was* through. Japan had become self-supporting.

On its own terms, the Draper drive to rescue the American taxpayer appeared to succeed brilliantly. Within a short span of years, the Japanese economy did recover to the point of achieving self-support and ending American aid. The Japanese then went on to achieve a prodigious growth rate and become one of the world's mightiest economic powers and an ally of the United States for decades. Draper, for all his narrow and niggardly approach, was clearly vindicated.

Or was he? In retrospect, it is not at all clear that Japan's remarkable economic rebirth, although it followed the implementation of Draper's program, was in fact caused by it. Indeed, it is more likely that the massive economic revival had started many months before. And when the Occupation came to an end, one-third of the Japanese people—the trade unions, socialists, and most of the intellectuals, all of them prominent among the very elements the American planners at the end of the war had counted on to keep Japan peaceful and democratic in the future—turned out to be vigorously opposed to U.S. world leadership and unsympathetic, if not hostile, to the United States itself.

It was a high price to pay, a price not exacted by any of the other postwar recovery programs sponsored or assisted by the United States throughout the world, not even in West Germany, whose case was so similar. Was the high-pressure—as it turned out—American effort really worthwhile then? Or would not a slower, more measured approach, one that would take into account the sensibilities of the whole Japanese nation, not just part of it, have achieved the same economic results, perhaps a year or two or three later, but without the political cost?

On May 1, 1952, only three days after the Occupation formally ended, the Communists and their allies staged the biggest and most violent anti-American riot in history on the Imperial Palace Plaza. After that, anti-American demonstrations became endemic, and not just by the Communists. The American recovery investment in Japan had brought a disappointing return in that very sector of the Japanese working class and its allies whom the Occupation had freed, favored, and fed. Of course, in international relations one cannot bank gratitude. All the same, policies are successful only when they bring desired results, and the results here were certainly not desired. How did they come about? The answer lies in a complex tale, principally of Americans, in two cities, Washington and Tokyo.

TWO BANKERS

Central to the whole affair were two bankers, William Draper of Scarsdale, New York, and Joseph Merrill Dodge of Grosse Pointe, Michigan. Draper, the investment banker, quondam vice president of Dillon Read & Company, initiated the project of ending reliance on U.S. funds as though the attainment of Japanese self-support were one of his firm's deals, so much to be invested by the U.S. government for so much anticipated return. Dodge, the commercial banker, president of the Detroit Bank, put the investee's house in order so it could maximize the effectiveness of the investment. Neither was concerned with the original vision of democratization and social reform as indispensable for the removal of the root causes of militarism and war. Draper and Dodge were not lawyers, professors, bureaucrats, philosophers, or politicians. They were practical men of affairs who dealt not in intangible hopes, concerns, and aspirations but in money and the material things it stood for. An occupation devoted to their goals would be very different from the one that had existed so far.

With respect to expertise and ability, two better men could hardly have been chosen. Both were highly experienced practical economists, incisive and clear-thinking. But almost two years separated their entrances on the Japanese scene. Let us, therefore, start with the man who began it all.

WILLIAM DRAPER

Draper had been a banker almost all his life. When he was demobilized as an infantry major after World War I, he joined National City Bank in New York, switched to Bankers Trust, and in 1927 entered the prestigious Wall Street investment house of Dillon Read. In ten years he had become vice president under its new president (and future Secretary of Defense), James Forrestal. During World War II Draper served two years as a regimental commander under—far under, to be sure—General MacArthur. In Washington when the European war ended, he was appointed Chief of the Economic Section of the Allied Control Council in Germany and Economic Adviser to the new Occupation commander, General Lucius Clay. With the establishment in 1947 of the Department of Defense and the unification of the armed forces, Draper, fifty three years old and a major general returning to civil life, seemed the ideal man to take over the supervision of both the German and Japanese occupations in the Army Department. On August 29 President Truman appointed him Under Secretary of the Army.

On his arrival in Japan, only three weeks later, he made a universally favorable impression on the senior GHQ staff, instantly knowledgeable of our economic problems, unlike some of the previous Washington emissaries. Courteous and soft-spoken, the slender, elegant Draper, his dark mustache neatly trimmed on a long face, and almost always clad in banker's pin-striped navy blue, seemed the impeccable product of an Ivy League school, not the more pedestrian New York University, which he had actually attended. In some ways, Draper had unsuspected dimensions: He was an enthusiastic amateur magician and had been part-time police chief of Scarsdale, New York. In later life, he was also to become active in Polish-American circles, for his second wife was of Polish extraction. But in other ways his dimensions were more limited than one would have supposed. Coming to the most remarkable reform occupation in history as its supervisor, Draper, in eighteen months as under secretary, never showed any curiosity so far as I know about any of its historic reforms. He was not opposed to democratization exactly, but that was the business of others. Draper the banker could not understand MacArthur the populist reformer.

THE "EASTERN ESTABLISHMENT"

Today, it is difficult to comprehend how one man on a subcabinet level could make such a drastic change, especially when both chief executives involved, General MacArthur, with his sweeping democratization in Japan, and President Harry Truman, with his Fair Deal reforms in Washington, differed so markedly from him in outlook. We tend to forget how extensively, in the critical years from 1945 to 1950, executive powers were delegated in the far-flung reaches of the new *ad hoc* American imperium. Truman and Secretaries Marshall and Forrestal faced continual international and domestic crises and had the overhanging threat of World War III to worry about. Truman and Marshall, at least, were happy to leave well enough alone in Japan, where things seemed to be going smoothly. I cannot remember in five years in GHQ ever hearing Marquat, Whitney, or anyone on that level saying, "The President wants . . ." In Washington, Japan Occupation policies were subordinate, left to the next level of government or even the one below that: secretaries, under secretaries, assistant secretaries, and their principal advisers. If Draper could operate successfully at his level, while getting the necessary funds out of Congress, keeping the peace with MacArthur, and following the general line of the Marshall Plan, hardly anyone in Washington would worry about the deeper implications of just what he was doing in Japan or how. It was precisely at this level that Draper operated best.

Draper, moreover, was a force to be reckoned with because he accurately represented the remarkably uniform views of the American defense–foreign policy establishment in 1947 through 1949. Typically from big business, big finance, and big law circles in the Northeast, the Administration leaders in State and Defense were exceptional in their internationalism at a time when isolationism still had a strong following, but they were economically orthodox, with a firm faith in free enterprise as the bedrock of political democracy and an aversion to populist causes. In the Truman cabinet, they were likely to be bankers.[8] Draper was at one with the establishment in beliefs. He had worked for ten years as Forrestal's junior in Dillon Read. No one needed to look over his shoulder. Almost automatically he was assured of unquestioning establishment support in the actions he took toward Japan.

It would have been otherwise a year or so earlier. Then the immediate postwar leadership of the U.S. Government, at least with respect to Japan,[9] had all been great believers in the "politics of attraction," the power of democratic ideas to enlist the masses of the world in resistance to the spread of Communism. W. Averell Harriman had chortled from Moscow that the Occupation policy of "housecleaning and encouraging liberal tendencies in Japan" had "the effect of stealing Communist thunder and thus irritates USSR because fundamentally USSR prefers crusading against reaction to competing with liberalism."[10] John Carter Vincent had gone on network radio in America to declare that violence in occupied Japan would be tolerated by the Occupation authorities if aimed at feudal remnants.[11]

But now Acheson, McCloy, Harriman, and Vincent were gone, and with them the democratization-first atmosphere. The new bankers, aided and abetted by a North Carolina–New York lawyer, Kenneth Royall, as Secretary of the Army, and George Kennan, as chief of Secretary Marshall's new State Department Planning Staff, had entirely different ideas. Forrestal, the intellectual spokesman of the new group in the cabinet, could not see any hope for the survival of representative governments in the midst of economic despair, and to him the solution was not more reform but more business. "We would have to turn to business," Forrestal said to the cabinet meeting of March 7, 1947, "if what we are talking about is in reality holding out the hope to people in stricken countries that they may again make a living, and the way to provide a living for them will have to be opened by business."[12] Royall, for his part, proposed to SWNCC in August that the way to solve the coal production problem in the Ruhr was to send American businessmen to take over management of the mines.[13] Draper sent a steady stream of high-level American business executives to probe, diagnose, and recommend what to do about the Japanese economy.

Nowhere, perhaps was there a greater unanimity of view in the defense– foreign policy establishment than in its fear of too heavy a financial strain on the U.S. economy. The President himself was "a hard money man if I ever saw one," Forrestal said, "believing as I do that we can't afford to wreck our economy in the process of fighting the 'cold war'."[14] The other bankers in government all agreed with him that the American taxpayer would not stand for an excessive foreign aid program. At one luncheon in June 1947, Lovett (Brown Brothers Harriman) expressed his alarm to Forrestal (Dillon Read) and John Snyder (First National Bank of St. Louis) at the way Marshall's Harvard commencement speech was stimulating the free-spending inclinations of certain government officials. In a Los Angeles talk, the counselor to the Secretary of State, Benjamin V. Cohen, a lawyer and a Roosevelt favorite, had just set forth a European aid figure of $5 billion annually for several years. (To Forrestal, who had been battling in vain for a few hundred million dollars more to keep the fleet in battle readiness, the sum must have looked mountainous.) With Snyder in accord, Lovett ridiculed the figure as utterly unrealistic, the product of New Deal economists in State. The experts at *his* bank, he declared, had concluded that a loan of $1.5 billion to $2 billion would be quite adequate.[15]

As it happened, Cohen turned out to be right and the bankers wrong. The banker-statesmen also misjudged the ordinary American taxpayer, who, having sacrificed so much to win the war, was easily reconciled to a little more sacrifice to win the peace. Draper constantly worried that the "American taxpayer" would turn him down. As it happened, however, the ordinary American worried least of all about aid for Japan. It was only the tail of an international American assistance kite that flew in the world's skies for years thereafter. And the American economy did not collapse.

An Authoritarian Aid Program

Seen in this light, Draper's Tokyo bugle call and the subsequent reaction in GHQ had a faintly ludicrous air about them. In any one year, Japanese aid never took much more than 1 percent of total American federal expenditures, or $3.40 per American, and by far the largest of that consisted of surplus grain that the U.S. Government had already bought anyway to support domestic farm prices. Whatever was done in Japan would hardly make or break the American taxpayer, and everyone in ESS, and elsewhere in GHQ, knew it.

The limit of our real, as contrasted with our expressed, concern for the poor American taxpayer was forcefully brought home to me at an ESS division chiefs' meeting in the spring of 1949. Our comptroller had advised that because world commodity prices had turned downward, our imports were costing less than anticipated and we would have an unexpended balance of some $20 million in Congressionally appropriated funds on June 30, 1949, after which they could no longer be used. General Marquat, who had been advised previously, had asked the chiefs if they could not advance any of the 1949–50 fiscal year programs to take advantage of the windfall, but the time was short. In the meeting no one came up with any feasible proposals, and several clearly frivolous projects were suggested. I thereupon naively proposed that we turn the surplus back to the U.S. Treasury, on the theory that this would certainly burnish General MacArthur's reputation as a defender of the long-suffering American taxpayer. I was met with shocked silence. General Marquat gently set me right. "Evidently you haven't had much experience in trying to get money out of Congress, Ted," said this man who had remained a Regular Army captain for seventeen long years because of Congressional parsimony between wars, "or you'd know that once you've gotten money out of them, you never, *never* give it back."

Nevertheless, Draper had sounded the note, and everyone in GHQ sang the song. In meeting after meeting with Japanese officials, Marquat and lesser lights in ESS conscientiously lectured them on the subject of relieving the American taxpayer, as though Representatives John Taber and Otto Passman were somehow secretly listening in.[16] (When Passman finally came to Japan and met with a small group of us in Marquat's office, he turned out to be against all foreign aid, no matter how economical, and not at all interested in our figures.) The first time Yoshida heard our new party line after resuming the premiership in October 1948—no one had talked about the U.S. taxpayer in his first term, 1946–47—he looked puzzled, declared it a technical matter in which he was unversed, and passed it down the table to his then Finance Minister, Izumiyama Sanroku.

I suppose no damage was done by reminding the finance ministers that GHQ was serious about not wasting U.S. aid. The harm arose rather from the implicit revision of U.S. priorities, the preoccupation of the American government with economizing on aid funds rather than achieving the great objectives worthy of the wartime sacrifices. American policy was trivialized, when what was after all only minor American tax relief was held up as the new ultimate SCAP goal. No one in GHQ talked any more about a "new society." The Occupation as a source of inspiration for a better Japan, a cause that had brought such a sense of liberation to millions of ordinary Japanese in earlier years, just dried up. Their dreams were unsaddled, unbridled, and left for other riders.

Such considerations went over Draper's head. It was not only a lack of empathy with the ordinary Japanese—I rather doubt that he had much empathy for working-class Americans either—but nothing he or the Washington economists did ever betrayed a sense of Japan as a *different* country. His was a curiously denationalized application of a universal international aid formula. In

Europe, where Americans sensed their limitations, Marshall had wisely and modestly declared that "it would be neither fitting nor efficacious for this Government to undertake to draw up unilaterally a program designed to place Europe on its feet economically. This is the business of the Europeans."[17] The Americans knew enough about conflicting economic interests within and among the European countries to realize that the United States could not set itself up as a referee without antagonizing at least some of them. Let the Europeans themselves decide the shape of the recovery program with all its difficult collateral questions: incidence of taxation, subsidies, price controls, duties, investment, nationalization of enterprises, and so forth. But in Japan, of which Washington knew far less, Draper saw nothing wrong with imposing the principal decisions from outside. It would have been a miracle if the United States had emerged from the exercise without some damage to its prestige, despite its aid program.

Draper, however, was a banker-economist, not a statesman. To him, the economics of U.S. aid to both Japan and Europe was basically the same: wartorn countries subsisting on American relief handouts, but with the talent, labor and productive facilities despite the war's devastation to support themselves by exports, provided the economic machinery was put to use and the flow of imported raw materials resumed. Draper proposed to apply the same pump-priming Marshall Plan approach, together with the associated economic techniques developed for Europe, to Japan. He did not concern himself with political techniques developed for Europe, for he was imposing, not persuading or negotiating, in Japan. Anyway, compared with their fundamental economic similarity, the political and social differences between Japan and Europe, as Draper saw them, were minor and could be disregarded.

Methodically, the Under Secretary went to work. First, he needed a concrete program: so much in appropriated funds to attain such-and-such levels of self-supporting trade in so many years. Second, he had to clear away any SCAP-made obstacles to economic recovery. Third, he had to get basic U.S. policy toward Japan changed to accept the recovery program. And fourth, the domestic economy in Japan had to be managed by the United States as occupying power in such a way as to maximize the effectiveness of the aid funds. With all those goals achieved, he could be confident of continuing Congressional funds and the success of his project. The Under Secretary was going to stay in the government only eighteen months. His reorganization of U.S. aid to Japan had to have top priority.

The SCAP staff met Draper's first need as promptly as the Under Secretary could have hoped. Within weeks of his first visit, SCAP's Green Book was on Draper's desk in Washington. The SCAP projections were a "bargain," although in somewhat the same way as a housewife's heavy spending at a sale. The Green Book asked for initially higher government appropriations but predicted that Japanese requirements would fall off sharply in the succeeding years. If

America would invest a total of $950 million to $1.2 billion over the next five years—an average of $190 million to $240 million a year—Japan would attain economic independence at the end of that period or before. Then, according to MacArthur's past messages to Congress—which were never revealed to the Japanese public—the Japanese could start repaying the advance.[18] In contrast, continuing relief was currently costing the United States $250 million annually with no end in sight.[19]

Draper now had his program. By the spring of 1948 he had secured the endorsement of the GHQ projections by all the principal interested Washington agencies. Insofar as the goals or even the main outlines of the trade plan were concerned, Draper, the Washington agency economists, and MacArthur's headquarters were in close agreement.

The Washington Approach

Next came clearing away what Draper considered the gratuitous obstacles to economic recovery in SCAP's "excessive" democratization. Convinced that only business, by which he meant large-scale business, could bring about economic rehabilitation, Draper's first target was the anti-*zaibatsu* program. Even before his formal appointment, he wanted to know when the FEC 230 deconcentration program, only recently submitted to the Far Eastern Commission, was going to be finished. On his September 1947 orientation visit to Japan, he pressed General Whitney to terminate the economic purge and General Marquat to end the business breakup. He even delicately invited Marquat to request Washington to soften the anti-*zaibatsu* policy in the interest of economic recovery, but General MacArthur would not let Marquat bite. It was Draper who forwarded Kauffman's savage criticisms of Welsh and peppered Tokyo with radio messages questioning the actions of our "runaway" Antitrust chief. By April 1948, however, Marquat had established a Deconcentration Review Board, and the business uncertainties that Draper had blamed on SCAP trust-busting evaporated.

Nor was there any SCAP disagreement with Draper's third objective, to persuade Congress and the American public that Japan's recovery was now as much in the U.S. national interest as that of the Marshall Plan countries. MacArthur had already asserted to Congress that a future Japan could be "a strong bulwark in the Western Pacific . . . against the reappearance and spread of those same causes which are calculated to plunge the world into future war,"[20] while assuring everyone that "even without external controls, Japan could not rearm for modern war within a century."[21] Still, some Americans did not forget so easily. Besides, the international situation was awkward.

In July 1947, the month before the President appointed Draper Army Secretary, the Far Eastern Commission had formally announced its adoption of the substance of State's original policy for Japan, SWNCC 150/4, featuring disarmament, demilitarization, democratization, and reparations. Then Mac-Arthur himself had praised the document as "one of the great state papers of modern history."[22] For the United States now to propose to reverse that policy was out of the question. Even a quiet reversal within the U.S. Government through the new National Security Council might raise hackles unnecessarily while the Soviets would be bound to raise a furor. In the circumstances, the Under Secretary might end up with a public controversy instead of a policy change.

But Draper was equal to the situation. On March 11, 1948, a blue-ribbon mission, selected and accompanied by a smiling Draper, arrived on our doorstep in Tokyo.[23] It was there to review U.S. economic policy toward Japan.

It was doubtful whether any of those men, except Herbert Feis, had given much detailed thought to Occupation facts or policies, and the group had been so casually thrown together that it had no chairman. It took three days before the members persuaded the elderly Percy Johnston to take the job. We advisers and relevant division chiefs were lined up to greet the visitors, and each commissioner had a top ESS official assigned to serve him. (I drew the ebullient and delightful Paul Hoffman, who was shortly thereafter named first Marshall Plan Administrator.) In all, the Johnston group stayed only two and a half weeks and got all its information from GHQ briefings. It must have been enough, for the committee's report, written in Washington after its return, went down the line 100 percent for the Draper policy, as though it had been prepared in Draper's office (and maybe it was). The committee concluded that the economic recovery of Japan should be a "primary objective" of the United States and endorsed the Green Book recommendations even to the very amount of the Congressional appropriations Draper was preparing to ask. The conservative Eightieth Congress, which greatly admired American business, was reassured.

In short order the executive branch announced it was accepting the Johnston committee's recommendations, and from then on they became the basis of GHQ policy. In theory, and according to the law, foreign policy changes had to go through the affected departments, the National Security Council, and the President.[24] But in this case normal procedure was shunted aside by a kind of tacit understanding, and any contrary parts of JCS directives and Far Eastern Commission official statements were deftly and casually bypassed. One had to admire Draper's finesse.

But if SCAP and Draper got along on the first three parts of the Under Secretary's master plan, cooperating particularly close in putting the arm on Congress for money, they disagreed increasingly on his fourth part: the management of Japan's internal economy and to what lengths to go to revitalize it. To Draper, the purpose of such management was primarily to ensure that U.S. aid funds would be used to prime Japanese production and exports. What was he then to think when, scanning the statistics provided by the SCAP staff, he saw consumption, that is worker's purchasing power as measured by real wages, rising 36 percent between July 1947 and January 1948, but industrial production flat, and industrial activity falling 10 percent in the same period? Clearly, if with commercial imports and exports balanced or nearly so, consumption increased more than production, the only reasonable deduction was that American aid—what else?—was supplying the difference.[25] SCAP was obviously lax. American aid was being diverted to temporary consumer amelioration. Hundreds of millions of dollars were being wasted to no purpose.

The SCAP staff never did agree with that kind of analysis. We attributed the continued and marked rise in real wages not to food shipments, which remained rather constant from 1947 to 1949, but rather to a series of local improvements, like vastly increased domestic food production, a far more efficient rationing system, and even the reduced bite the Occupation forces were taking out of Japanese resources (from 39 percent of the national budget in 1946–47 to 34 percent in 1947–48.)[26] For all of those we were cheerfully prepared for SCAP to take the credit, but none of them was at the expense of U.S. aid. Then there was the powerful impact of the hoarded Japanese military supplies returning to the civilian market, which we underestimated, to be sure, but which Washington neglected entirely. While we would loyally support the Under Secretary's counterinflation efforts—no one in GHQ thought the inflation was a good thing—to us Draper's alarm came from a phantom statistical radar blip, not from reality. Besides, with memories still fresh of the labor unrest of 1946 and January 1947, MacArthur and his staff welcomed higher real wages and higher workers' living standards as indispensable to consolidating the Occupation's democratic reforms and keeping the peace. We did not fear them at all.

Draper, however, never really asked us. From where he sat, far away, the overall failure to restart the economic machine was more important than local improvement, and the peculiarities of postwar Japan could not invalidate what he saw as a classic case of a monetary inflation suffocating a country. To him and the Washington economists and officials involved in European recovery, it was axiomatic that a sharp rise in the money supply had to create extra domestic demand, which in turn drained off a country's resources that could otherwise be used for exports and rebuilding the national industrial base.

And in fact all important statistical signs seemed to Washington to be there in Japan. The budget was wildly unbalanced; the money supply was expanding by 4 to 6 percent monthly through the first part of 1948; consumer prices rose 41 percent in the latter half of 1947 and 24 percent more in the first six months of 1948; and 1947 real wages were outstripping production. Draper could hear the alarm bells ringing. Japan appeared to be headed for economic disaster, like Chiang Kai-shek's China, and American aid funds were headed down a rat hole. For Draper and Washington, Japan in 1947–48 took on the makings of a crisis, the last chance for the United States to do something before it was too late.

Before the statistical peril, everything else receded in importance. As seen from the American capital, inflation took over not only the center but almost the entire Japanese stage. In the end, what started out to be the application in Japan of the sweeping concepts of the Marshall Plan in Europe, what Churchill had called "the most unsordid act" in human history, turned into just an anti-inflation program with no soul. And then its focus narrowed even further into a high-pressure crusade to reduce the money supply. MacArthur and his staff, concerned with other and to them equally or more important objectives, did not share Draper's sense of urgency or his apocalyptic analysis. The Under Secretary set out to impose his fearful views and stringent monetary remedies on Tokyo.

22

Washington Versus Tokyo

MacARTHUR LOSES CONTROL OVER HIS OCCUPATION

ON THE FIRST OF January, 1948, General MacArthur was the undisputed master of the Occupation of Japan. A little more than a year later he had lost control of the greater part of the Occupation mission that still remained: the direction of the Japanese economy. That had passed to Washington. It was a stunning reversal, unnoticed by the American public at that time, with profound implications for the future of the Japanese—and of the Americans, too. Thereafter, Army Under Secretary Draper's concern for the American taxpayer would have priority over MacArthur's concern with the democratic soul of Japan, and one-third of that nation would become increasingly alienated from America in consequence. The proximate cause? A subcabinet Under Secretary and four Washington economists.

LIBERALS AND CONSERVATIVES

It was not planned that way at all. When Draper embarked on his campaign to accelerate economic recovery in Japan, there was no indication that he expected any difficulty getting the Supreme Commander's cooperation. MacArthur had repeatedly demonstrated his appreciation of the urgency of recovery. Draper, for his part, had served under the General and highly esteemed his talents and

414

leadership qualities. MacArthur, he felt, was a unique and invaluable asset to America in Japan. Draper, facing the formidable challenge of bringing both Germany and Japan quickly to economic self-support, needed every asset he could get.

True, not everyone in Washington agreed that MacArthur was such an unalloyed asset. From the beginning many people, both liberal and conservative, doubted that the war hero, assigned to receive the surrender of the Japanese armed forces, had the necessary expertise in civil government or economics. Nor were they completely reassured by his brilliant early Occupation successes. The "liberals" in the capital wanted the responsibility for civil administration in Japan split off from the military Occupation Commander and turned over to a civilian under State Department control. That is what happened in the later stages of the Okinawa Occupation. The "conservatives" were cheerfully content to leave civil administration to the Army, provided a top-flight American businessman was put in charge of the economy. When General Hilldring became Assistant Secretary of State in 1946, it looked as though the liberals would have their way, because he favored their plan. As late as February 1949, however, when the Associated Press reported it as "under active consideration," the scheme was still hanging fire,[1] and the new U.S. Army Chief of Staff, General Omar Bradley, would propose the idea to the SCAP five months later than that.[2]

As for the "conservative" concept, as early as September 1946, Secretary of War Patterson had dispatched Frederick L. Devereux, a former vice president of American Telephone & Telegraph, to sound out MacArthur on the acceptability of a big business deputy. Though Devereux was embarrassingly effusive in his praise of the General—his remarks to us staff members on MacArthur sounded like divine services—MacArthur preferred his own loyal anti-aircraft officer to a tycoon with ties elsewhere. He would go no further than cosmetics when he accepted the vice president of Armco Steel, William Verity, as his civilian economic deputy. Verity was surprised to discover that the appointment put him under Marquat, the Economic Section Chief, who soothingly explained that in a military headquarters military forms had to be observed. The Armco executive was provided with a big office, the attached perquisites, and all the authority of a vice president of the United States. Marquat consulted him frequently and ostentatiously, but Verity had little to contribute. That was as far as MacArthur would go, and his popularity in the United States precluded anyone's ordering him to go any further.

So far as I know, Draper himself had little to do with any of those reorganization plans. He liked MacArthur where he was. He was not so certain, however, about the SCAP civilian staff. They were mostly unknown to Washington and particularly to the banking fraternity, which had begun to dominate the policy levels of the defense–foreign affairs establishment in the nation's capital in 1947. Some of the SCAP people, it developed, had served in New Deal agencies like Morgenthau's Treasury, the Office of Price Administration, or the Tennessee Valley Authority, which alone made them immediately suspect. Consequently, when the 1947 generation of conservatives entered high office and were genuinely dismayed by the extent of the Japanese radical reform that they discovered, they leaped to the conclusion that it was the fault of the SCAP staff rather than of the 1945 directives that the latter had been given to carry out. In the circumstances, James Lee Kauffman's report of September 1947 had a certain surface believability when he ascribed rampant "socialization" in Japan to GHQ New Dealers and radicals like Edward Welsh, our Antitrust Chief; Sherwood Fine, General Marquat's economic adviser; and me. Ultra-conservative American correspondents in Tokyo, Walter Simmons of the *Chicago Tribune,* Miles Vaughn of the United Press, and Burton Crane of the *New York Times,* echoed the general tenor of Kauffman's charges. And then came George Kennan, one of the most prestigious of the government's foreign policy experts, to sound the alarm.

Kennan, at that time the head of Secretary of State Marshall's brand-new policy planning staff, was the department's leading Soviet expert and hence presumably an expert likewise on international communism. At a lunch with Defense Secretary James Forrestal on October 21, 1947, five months before his first visit to occupied Japan, Kennan confided his fears that as a result of the actions of the SCAP staff "the socialization of Japan had proceeded to such a point that if a treaty of peace were written and the country turned back to the Japanese it would not be possible, under the present economic machinery, for the country to support itself. This would mean it would go through a period of economic disaster, inflation, umbalanced budgets, resulting possibly in near anarchy, which would be precisely what the Communists would want."[3]

As it happened, Kennan's vision was faulty. Nothing had been "socialized" under the Occupation, and industrial production jumped 58 percent in the next twelve months. That did not prevent Kennan, when he actually did visit Japan in February of the following year, from widening his suspicions. "One often heard it suggested at the time," he later wrote in his memoirs, "that this curious pattern of achievement on the part of SCAP was in part the result of Communist infiltration into the headquarters."[4] Perhaps one of those who made the suggestion was General Charles Willoughby, MacArthur's ultra-conservative intelligence chief, with whom Kennan spent an evening and who, it will be recalled, had devoted so much time and effort to a staff study on that very subject. MacArthur, Kennan related, only laughed when Kennan mentioned it. The General admitted there might be some Communist party members in GHQ but added that State probably had some too and dismissed the matter as not meaning much. Kennan was not reassured, and one can hardly doubt that he voiced his fears on his return. Draper, a close subordinate of Forrestal from their business days and at the very level in government to which Kennan would give briefings, must have been acutely aware of the suspicions then going the rounds.

Even though it was Draper who had sent MacArthur the Kauffman report, the impression I took away from personal conversations with the Under Secretary was that he did not buy everything that Kauffman said or, for that matter, Kennan's communist fears either. But the situation in SCAP must have worried him. Who *did* control SCAP decisions on the detailed, concrete issues that really mattered, the generals or the civilian "insiders"? True, MacArthur was no Ulysses Grant, but Draper's own frustrating experiences with Welsh made him wonder. If it had taken General MacArthur and General Marquat several months to rein Welsh in, who else might there be out of control that Draper didn't know about?

In early 1948 Draper had only a year of his intended government service to go. He could not issue direct orders to the theater, since the official chain of command—the President to the Joint Chiefs of Staff to MacArthur—went around, not through him. The Under Secretary was convinced that ESS on its own was too soft on the Japanese for whatever reasons and so disdained GHQ's own anti-inflation program. Quite clearly, he ignored our "Essentials of the ESS Economic Stabilization Program," which I had coordinated in May 1947 on General Marquat's instructions, and perhaps that was just as well, for the next six months witnessed the worst price and money supply inflation of the entire Occupation period. But Draper had no reliable regular channel for compelling the SCAP staff to be any tougher than it was. Pep talks when he visited Tokyo or when Tokyo's men visited him, pointed radio queries to the Headquarters, and passing along critical outside reports to MacArthur were clearly not enough. It would take MacArthur's commitment to a detailed list of no-nonsense financial measures to put out the raging Japanese inflation fires and an outside staff other than SCAP's to draw them up. Very well, then, he would go out of regular channels.

At first Draper thought of using the prestigious Johnston mission, whose primary purpose, we may remember, was to sell the idea of Japanese economic aid to Congress, in his internal management problem as well. The big businessmen of that group did indeed come up with the right kind of orthodox program: balance the budget, reduce subsidies, fire excess government workers like railwaymen, cut government expenditures in general, and so forth. They also recommended strengthening price controls and instituting wage controls. Except for the last, the SCAP staff readily agreed. MacArthur praised the Johnston people highly in public and accepted their report in general, but Draper could not be sure whether SCAP accepted their recommendations as immediate measures or as distant goals. And who would monitor the implementation after the mission dispersed?

As it happened, just as Draper was orchestrating the Johnston mission and its report, he ran into an unexpected roadblock that sent him up another street. The U.S. Treasury Department and the Federal Reserve Board suddenly refused to go along with his Japan appropriation request for 1948–49. Treasury? Federal

Reserve? What on earth were they doing vetoing aid to Japan? Since Roosevelt's death and Secretary Morgenthau's departure from government, Treasury had been keeping a low profile in foreign policy and the "Fed" was a strictly domestic agency, wasn't it? No one had given either of them a thought in connection with earlier aid requests. But now the rules had changed. For with the institutionalization of the Marshall Plan, all foreign aid budget requests were required to go through a new National Advisory Council (NAC), and on that council not only State and Army, but also Commerce, Treasury, and the Federal Reserve had been given representation.

Now the latter two agencies were threatening to veto Draper's proposals to Congress and particularly his request for economic rehabilitation funds in addition to food, petroleum, and medical relief. It was not hard to spot a China phobia in Treasury's attitude. The lesson was that a country could not use foreign aid effectively while it had roaring inflation, Treasury said, and Japan certainly had it. The Federal Reserve agreed. Unless Japan took drastic steps to contain the inflation, they would object to sending any American money Japan's way. Draper's drive was threatened with breakdown before it got started.

THE YOUNG MISSION

Now, Draper, if anything, was a resourceful man. On the surface, the new NAC setup had provided him with three more problems, three more agencies to convince or pacify. In reality, he now had two new allies in his campaign to get SCAP to do things right. Indeed, he could even let them carry the brunt of that fight. It was too late, he soothed the recalcitrant agencies, to do anything about Japanese counterinflation in time for the new fiscal year, which would begin July 1, 1948, and besides the brand-new economic rehabilitation request was not so big—only $75 million. If the agencies went along for now, Draper would agree to send their representatives to Japan to make their own survey and recommendations. The agencies agreed, and thus was born the Young mission. Unheralded before and unsung afterward, that group of government research economists headed by Ralph Young, Associate Director of the Research Division of the Federal Reserve Board, was to turn Washington–Tokyo relations upside down.

The SCAP Headquarters in Tokyo, isolated to an altogether improbable extent from Washington infighting by MacArthur's insistence on autonomy, heard only echoes of the scuffling. The advent of the Young mission mystified us. When I asked General Marquat why we needed another economic mission so soon after the last one—Young was in Tokyo only five days after the Johnston report was released in Washington—he simply pointed to the wording of the advisory radio message: They were to make recommendations on the technical steps leading to the establishment of a single commercial yen–dollar exchange rate. It was certainly a worthy objective, for at that time a dozen exchange rates were in place for different groups of export and import commodities, and indeed we had an ESS exchange rate committee making studies aimed at the same goal. Still, it sounded highly technical; the members did not appear to be on the policymaking level; and I excused myself from the specialists' discussions when they arrived.

That was a mistake, for although the Young group talked technicalities, its intentions were fundamental. True, the members recommended a single exchange rate of 300 yen to the dollar (plus or minus 10 percent) to be established promptly, and in order to dampen the continuing price rises they proposed a number of "technical" measures dealing with, among other things, bank reserves, credit controls, and income and property taxes. But when the impacts of all the recommendations were added up, they amounted to a sharp cut in the nation's current consumption, and specifically to a reduction in workers' real wages. Up to then SCAP had been trying to *raise* real wages. The report recommended a complete reversal of policy. The full implications did not emerge until late in the Young group's visit, and by that time its report was in final preparation and further discussion useless.

Perhaps the SCAP staff's discussions with the Young mission were too late from the start. Orville MacDiarmid, the State Department representative in the group, conceded many years later that "most of the members of the Young Mission had worked on Japan and knew in advance about where they wanted to come out."[5] Their evidently closed minds did not endear them to the SCAP economists. Not that the Young members were personally discourteous. MacDiarmid called some of them "disagreeable characters," but, perhaps because I knew three of them from before, I did not find them so. Unlike the big businessmen who preceded them, however, they were economists on the same level as the SCAP people, or so we thought, and still the Washington group refused the normal give-and-take of fellow professionals. Bureaucratically, their attitude was sound, for having discussed the situation at length with Under Secretary Draper in Washington, they saw no reason to start off all over again with his "subordinates" in Tokyo.

The mission stayed only eighteen days in all, a good part of which was given over to organizing, writing, editing their report, having it typed, and presenting it to the Supreme Commander. With that kind of rush schedule, the members had no time to get a feel for the country, to check their Washington preconceptions against reality, or to absorb the newest and latest data the SCAP staff gave them. Certainly the mission members had no time, even if they had wanted to, to persuade dubious or dissenting SCAP economists.

The rush episode left almost universal unhappiness, if not antagonism, among the SCAP staff. Many of our economists were fundamentally in agreement with the Young mission's central contention that only drastic budget cuts, no matter how painful, could seriously decelerate the inflation. Indeed, they had been fighting that battle within GHQ for two years. But even they found themselves protesting the mission's thinking on other grounds. Was this the right time to establish a single exchange rate, when prices had jumped 20 percent in the last four months? Even if 300 yen to the dollar had been calculated to keep 80 percent of current exports moving, wasn't it premature and short-sighted to abandon the other 20 percent to "sink or swim," especially when private export trade was only eight months old? Why sacrifice on the altar of stabilization such items as raw silk and ships currently being exported at 450 and 600 to theoretical future prospects? On the contrary, wasn't the object of stabilization to increase exports?

Our trade officials, themselves mostly businessmen in civil life, had never turned down any sale if they could help it. They could not understand Washington academics who thought selling was so easy that 20 percent of sales could be written off. Our price officials, for their part, shuddered at the prospect of tripling relief food prices. Our budget officers were aghast at the proposal to slash budget expenditures 20 percent across the board. How did those experts get such a nice round figure, and did they really comprehend the complex actualities of each account? Did they really want to fire one-fifth of all the police and close one-fifth of the schools, or did they wish simply to cut down all the government workers' wages? Or was the recommendation just pressure of a particularly irresponsible variety? No doubt the mission had answers, and good ones, to the questions, but for the most part the SCAP staff was left objecting to the empty air.

That was on the technical level. Wider questions, even some of potentially critical importance, were not raised at all. A deliberate depression of the living standards of still distressed workers, for example, especially now that labor was banded together in free trade unions, could well provoke waves of strikes, but no one thought to consult the SCAP Labor Division. "With the benefit of hindsight, I can see that we overstated the need to reduce consumption which was still only 65 percent of the 1934–36 base," MacDiarmid admitted much later.[6] But even that candid admission by perhaps the most thoughtful member of the Young mission betrayed a thought process tied to economic arithmetic rather than a sensitivity to the possible real effects of such a dangerous policy—massive parades, huge demonstrations, industrial conflict, and even, conceivably, violence. The Labor Division could have told the Young group of the threatened general strike of only a little more than a year before that almost overturned the government, could have warned of the weakness of the police in industrial labor confrontations under the new laws, and could have pointed out the consequent likelihood of dragging in the Occupation forces to maintain public order. But no one asked them. Similarly, the mission's painful package would have strained the political capacity of even a strong cabinet, and the incumbent coalition cabinet of Democrats and Socialists was inherently fragile. Could this government carry out the Young program without toppling itself? That, too, was outside the purview of the professional economists. They dealt only with economics; the rest was the responsibility of the Supreme Commander.

From the beginning, the man on whose shoulders that responsibility rested doubted the realism of the Young mission as General Marquat passed on to him, almost daily, reports of the economists' discussions with the SCAP staff. Then the chief of the mission, Ralph Young, visited General MacArthur in person to present his report, and that settled it.

Ushered into the General's sixth-floor office, the tall, spare, faintly condescending Young, looking like a red-headed stork, blandly informed MacArthur that, among other things, his document called for a directive to the SCAP to establish a single exchange rate before the end of October. MacArthur was not amused. Undoubtedly Young meant no offense, but under military protocol, even a high-ranking civilian, which in MacArthur's view Young was not, does not presume to issue operational orders to a theater commander, especially with dates attached. During his entire career the General had insisted on *lots* of leeway, for he refused to become some one else's captive scapegoat. Now Young wanted to impose a mindless timetable on him, as if he could not be trusted. Finally, Young appeared not to understand that Japan had other problems too: a civil service labor reform crisis involving a possible row with the American labor movement, mounting political scandals engulfing the first generation of Japanese leaders elected under the new Constitution, reparations claimants who had to be outmaneuvered, and, above all, a rapidly weakening Japanese government, the second in months, whose fall, expected at any moment, would adversely affect the political stability of the new Japanese democracy. To the Supreme Commander the humorless Young seemed pedantic and out of tune with the real world. The day after the interview, Marquat told a few of us that the Supreme Commander was "not impressed" with Dr. Young. "I told him," the irrepressible Marquat cracked, "that neither were we." The Young mission returned to Washington immediately, taking its report with it. "We were not urged to stay while they read it," MacDiarmid recalled.[7] And no wonder.

SCAP TACTICS

It did not take long for a radio message in MacArthur's unmistakable declamatory style to arrive in Washington, rejecting the Young report *in toto* as dangerous to social stability and jeopardizing the cooperation so far freely proffered by the Japanese people. Then GHQ classified the report "top secret," ostensibly because of the proposed exchange rate figure. That stopped all further distribution both within GHQ and in the United States. That was the only time in the whole Occupation that General MacArthur turned down the report of an outside advisory mission in its entirety.

The members of the Young mission, dispersed to their agencies, were surprised and for long afterward professed to be mystified by MacArthur's action. Thirty years later MacDiarmid, who had himself served in our Finance Division in 1946 and was familiar with MacArthur's style, could still complain somewhat resentfully that he remained "puzzled by the negative, almost vitriolic reaction from the SCAP staff. . . . Considering that the deflationary measures proposed by the Young Mission were considerably weaker than those proposed by the Dodge Mission a year later one finds it difficult to sympathize with the flood of condemnatory purple prose that SCAP cabled to the Pentagon."[8] The Tokyo economists, on the other hand, were relieved and gratified. They had been nervously wondering how far MacArthur would support them. Now, with the Supreme Commander on record, and given his batting average with high-level Washington and Congress, they felt that they had nothing to fear.

Indeed, in the months that followed the evidence of economic progress everywhere seemed to vindicate the SCAP policy. One had only to look out the window to see new construction or walk in the streets to see the improved clothing of the people. Statistics bore out the visual impressions. From industrial production to the rice harvest and even exports, everything was up.[9]

No recognition of those improvements came from Washington. Instead came a series of newspaper and magazine articles, usually datelined Washington, that unfavorably compared economic progress in occupied Japan with occupied Germany.[10] MacArthur, the writers commented, was a political success but an economic failure. In Tokyo we were sure that the reporters had obtained their data, and possibly their conclusions too, from the Washington economic agencies involved with Japan. Where else? MacArthur's political intuition had warned him that some such comparison was coming. Even before the Young mission, he had constantly quizzed Marquat on how Japan compared with Germany on this or that economic particular. We subordinates of Marquat had assured him that no such comparison was meaningful; that Japan had lost a prewar empire whereas Germany had had none to lose; that while both countries had lost their merchant marine, the impact was far more serious for an insular economy; that the ongoing civil war in China was depriving Japan of one of its best prewar customers; and that two of Japan's star prewar foreign exchange earners, silk and cotton textiles, had been lost, the first to technological displacement by nylon, the second by scrapping almost all cotton spindles in wartime to make armaments. Germany had its own special difficulties, to be sure, but how could the relative impact of each country's handicaps be compared in figures? The news stories, of course, carried no explanatory footnotes. Our assurances went for nought. MacArthur would later join the public relations game by contending that per capita U.S. economic aid to Japan was only one-fourth that afforded West Germany[11] but that did not help dispel the widespread public impression in the United States, in 1948 that Japanese economic recovery was faltering badly.

To us in Tokyo, it was a baffling business, this unwillingness of the Washington economists, conscientious and honorable men all, to concede the progress demonstrated by hard statistics. But, of course, to a large extent we were looking at different statistics. For the normal time lag of some two months in the publication and transmission of the economic data was bound to create misunderstanding in a year, 1948, when things were changing so rapidly. For example, the basic SCAP compendium of economic figures, *Japanese Economic Statistics,* for, say, September 1948, contained the statistics for August, but the booklet was not actually printed in the Far East Command printing plant until early November and did not reach Washington by air until late that month. By that time, the SCAP economists were already working with the October figures and even later preliminary data. In those two months industrial production climbed 10 percent, a rate typical of most of 1948, while urban consumer prices dropped 4 percent.[12] What appeared in Tokyo as a confirmed three-month favorable trend could easily be dismissed in Washington as one-month aberration. The doctors at a distance were prescribing for a convalescent patient under the impression that he was deathly ill. No wonder the prescriptions in Washington and Tokyo differed.

It was not only a statistical misperception. The Washington agencies, already convinced that SCAP was soft on the Japanese, did not believe that ESS was doing much of anything at all. The facts were otherwise. Marquat and his men were deeply deeply aware of the danger of provoking the collapse of a weak government, followed by an election in which MacArthur himself might be the main issue. If another weak cabinet were to emerge, SCAP might then be compelled to govern the economy openly, with all the blame for anything that might go wrong—the worst of all possible worlds. ESS was therefore treading very gingerly. Nothing could be done that would cause a minister to lose face publicly or to resign rather than offend a large part of his constituency and thus commit political hara-kiri. Especially, SCAP had to avoid directives, even indirect ones, to the Japanese to do something concrete and positive. The resultant meetings between General Marquat and the Japanese ministers could be almost comical, like a horse dancing, but they often achieved the desired results. Unfortunately, those were not visible in Washington.

I remember a typical meeting that illustrated Marquat's tactics perfectly. The general and his advisers met with four Japanese economic ministers in late June 1948, a few weeks after Young's departure. The issue was electric power workers' wages. The first of the ministers sitting around Marquat's huge table to speak was the Socialist Labor Minister, Katō Kanjū, arguing for a wage raise because of higher living costs. Killen, our Labor Division Chief, confirmed

Katō's data. Marquat, presiding, said that indeed the workers deserved a wage raise, but how would the government pay for it? Finance Minister Kitamura, a Democrat, suggested raising electricity rates. Oh no, Marquat replied, that would be contrary to the Johnston line of holding prices down, for nothing would have a wider impact on manufacturing costs than higher electric rates. Let's borrow from the Reconstruction Finance Bank, Mizutani, the Socialist Commerce and Industry Minister, ventured. Impossible, Marquat countered, because that's deficit financing, and Johnston is dead set against it. Well then, said the Democrat Kurusu, the Economic Stabilization Board Director General, we'll have to appropriate a special subsidy. But what other subsidy will you reduce? Marquat asked. Remember, Johnston bars any increase in subsidies.

Or, he added reflectively, maybe you could raise taxes. The ministers looked unhappily at each other. A tax increase was the last thing they could take politically. But the workers really need help, Katō insisted. And we are not objecting, Marquat asserted, provided the electric company can find the money. Once more the discussion went round the table, again to no avail. "It's okay to build the house," I whispered to Killen, "provided you don't use any building materials." The meeting broke up shortly thereafter to allow the ministers time for further internal discussions, which took weeks. The process was sloppy, disorderly, and unreportable. But in the meantime, the government spent no more money, which was the point, after all, and SCAP was blamed for nothing. That is, except in Washington, where SCAP was blamed for inactivity in a time of crisis.

In such obscure circumstances, trust between the American officials on both sides of the Pacific was imperative. But that was precisely what was lacking. Each side knew the other's priorities were different, and each put its margins for error in different places. The Supreme Commander duly supported economic stabilization as long as it did not impinge on the consolidation of his democratic reforms. Washington was all in favor of democratization, so long as it did not obstruct economic stabilization.

With their resentment at their abrupt rejection by MacArthur still strong, moreover, the Washington agencies did not put it past the SCAP economists even to "doctor" the statistics. Once in late fall Marquat came into my office with a radio message from Washington that "blasted" some ordinary routine SCAP economic statistics showing a decline in the food price index for the second consecutive month. No one in Tokyo had made much of the drop, because for every year prices fell when the harvest came in; indeed, the SCAP radio containing the data had been sent as a routine report to the Department of the Army for information, without the knowledge of General Marquat or any of his advisers. The Washington reply, however, severely questioned the reliability of our information, which in military protocol amounted to one headquarters calling another a liar. Apparently, strong emotions were boiling in Washington, and we were not aware of them.

THE NSC DIRECTIVE

The spurned Washinton economists, in fact, had not taken MacArthur's June rejection passively. In MacDiarmid's words, "warfare among the agencies" broke out when they received the SCAP radio rejecting the Young report. The Federal Reserve (Young and Arthur Hersey) and Treasury (Arthur Stuart) flatly refused to approve Draper's new 1949–50 appropriations request. In the State Department, the international consequences of refusing Japan further economic aid and the domestic political consequences of slapping MacArthur down publicly were better appreciated. Draper, who might have agreed on economic grounds with the hard liners, could not go against his own department. Further, he might well have been sympathetic, as a military officer himself, to MacArthur's reaction to Young's *faux pas*. The ranks of the NAC were split. Once again Draper came up with a compromise. No one could compel MacArthur to accept a mission advisory report, but the Supreme Commander could hardly reject a Joint Chiefs of Staff directive. Draper could also arrange to send MacArthur a high-level adviser to supervise implementation of the directive. Treasury and the Federal Reserve had to agree. It is hard to escape the impression that Draper had the whole maneuver planned in advance. Now he had a license to draw up the order he had always lacked, and this time within channels.

The Under Secretary immediately went to work with Paul Nitze in State to prepare a directive for the approval of the National Security Council,[13] which had replaced SWNCC. Draper secured Resources Board, Air Force, and also Labor, which was greatly reconcurrences from everyone involved and even some not so involved—Defense, Army, Navy, State, Treasury, Commerce, National Security Resources Board, Air Force, and also Labor which was greatly relieved at the absence of a wage control plan à la Johnston. The Federal Reserve, one of the chief instigators, had no standing in foreign policy before the NSC and was not asked to concur. One has to wonder what would have happened if the Fed had had no foreign policy standing before the NAC either. In any event, with such a lineup the approval of the President and the Joint Chiefs of Staff in early December was almost automatic.

The directive hit GHQ with the impact of a bomb on December 12. There was no customary advance warning. On the contrary, Sherwood Fine, Marquat's economic adviser, who was just then in Washington working on the 1949–50 budget presentation, had been kept completely in the dark, as though the Washington agencies feared MacArthur might mobilize his political supporters against them if warned in advance. Immediately on receipt of the advisory radio,[14] General MacArthur, who had never telephoned anyone since his arrival in Japan, phoned Marquat during the latter's lunch break at home to inform him of the radiogram and to summon him for that evening. Marquat asked me and Colonel Ryder, his Deputy Chief at the time, for comment. I must say I did not get the political significance at all. The nine-point, one-page radio, I told Marquat, repeated almost exactly the policies we were already following and even the old "Essentials of the ESS Economic Stabilization Program" of May 1947. In only one point was there a significant difference. The NSC directive called for a true balance in the consolidated budget "at the earliest possible date," as against merely significant progress toward a balanced budget. Finally, in a substantial improvement over Young, the radio set a target date, not a deadline, for a single exchange rate: three months after the initiation of the stabilization program. We seemed to be covered, I advised Marquat. But I had missed the point. MacArthur and Marquat, however, had not.

The very fact that the two programs were so similar was an indication that the target of the directive was not policy but performance, and this MacArthur grasped instantly. It was a massive vote of distrust in his economic stewardship, confirmed by the President. From here on Washington intended to call the shots. Moreover, the disagreement over priority of goals, democratization versus stabilization, was settled. The later directive from the NSC had to be conceded priority over the earlier, JCS 1380/15. Where they conflicted, economic stabilization and recovery had to prevail.

The Supreme Commander could not see the full consequences of the change in priorities, but the drastic limitations on his authority were immediately plain. Indeed, the Washington agencies hastened to make them so. Although the original JCS 1380/15 directive, including its ban on MacArthur's assuming responsibility for the operation of the Japanese economy, had been kept secret for more than three years and indeed was still secret, the Army and State Departments made the new directive public in an explanatory press release, issued in both Tokyo and Washington, only five days later. The release clearly delineated MacArthur's responsibility in the new program, that is, to direct the Japanese government to carry out a stabilization plan decided by Washington and not much more. The General was to be a transmission belt. Further, the use in the release of the phrase "responsible officials in Washington" coupled with a warning that Japanese performance of the program would "be weighed in connection with future aid requests" left no doubt as to who was in charge. After all, the document added, the U.S. Government was asking the same of the Marshall Plan countries as a condition of aid. Why not Japan?

But why Japan at this time? Because, the release declared, the Japanese inflation was continuing, which the "responsible authorities" asserted in a statement of economic faith that seemingly required no proof jeopardized the gains so far and future recovery as well. They and General MacArthur were gratified, they conceded, that industrial production had increased "47 percent" (actually 58 percent) from November 1947 to November 1948 and exports 48 percent. But, they complained, the price level and the Bank of Japan note issue had both risen 60 percent in the same time. What the release failed to mention was that most of the price inflation had occurred early in the twelve-month period and that the rate of increase since had fallen markedly.[15] As for the note issue, how could anyone expect Japan to conduct half again more business without a corresponding increase in the money needed to do it with? If the note issue had risen only 60 percent to accommodate a ''47'' (actually 58) percent increase in industrial production, that was a phenomenal improvement over the preceding twelve months, when the note issue had soared 138 percent while industrial production remained flat.[16] If the figures showed anything, it was that the inflation ''crisis'' was largely over.

MacArthur, however, did not waste his time disputing the directive or its justification. In a characteristic move, he leaped to put himself at the head of the new stabilization crusade. In a public letter to Prime Minister Yoshida on the very next day, he called on the Japanese people for sacrifice, increased austerity, and a ''temporary surrender [of] some of the privileges and immunities inherent in a free society.'' Especially would there be ''no place for interference by management or labor with the acceleration of production,'' ''political conflicts over the objectives to be sought,'' or ''ideological opposition.'' For ''the fundamental objective of this action,'' he declared, asserting its continuity with the sweeping democratization thus far, ''is the prompt achievement of that degree of economic self-sufficiency which alone can justify and insure political freedom. For there can be no political freedom as long as a people's livelihood is dependent on the largesse of others.''[17] Then he ordered his staff to draw up, point by point, a SCAP program to carry out the nine-point NSC directive. If, three years earlier, the Supreme Commander had been able to preempt the overall direction of Japan from an order to receive the surrender of its armed forces, why could not an order to transmit a stabilization program be enlarged to supervision of the program itself, provided he moved rapidly and energetically enough?

It soon became evident that such a move was not going to be easy. When Washington reacted so violently to our routine report on food prices, we in ESS were mystified. ''Apparently they won't believe anything we say,'' I commented to Marquat when he brought the radiogram responding into my office. ''The only way we can convince them is to do something irrefutable, like establishing an exchange rate.'' When he asked why, if that were true, we hadn't already done so, I told him that our section exchange rate study committee had been unable to agree on a figure, but I thought for political reasons we had to force an agreement on our experts if at all possible. Furthermore, with the rapid abatement in the inflation rate since the Young mission, we could now probably hold the rate. That would convince Washington once and for all. After reporting to the Supreme Commander, who approved the idea, and presiding over a meeting of some twenty of our economists and economic officials, Marquat asked me to coordinate an exchange rate proposal. We went to work with intense determination. The National Security Council wanted a single exchange rate three months after the initiation of the stabilization program? Well, we would beat them to it. If SCAP could come up with an exchange rate proposal immediately, how could the Washington agencies object? That was exactly what they had been pressing us for. MacArthur would once again preempt them and remain a major player in the game.

But Washington had other ideas. While we were revving up to do the job, MacArthur received a cable from Draper asking if he would accept an economic adviser, one Joseph Dodge, a Detroit banker, to oversee the implementation of the NSC directive. After some reflection, MacArthur replied that he would not object, provided the adviser would be acting under his (MacArthur's) authority. Draper agreed and informed the Supreme Commander that Dodge would come with the rank of minister and as personal representative of President Truman. MacArthur's "authority" would therefore be only nominal. As nearly as I could figure out the sequence of eents, our routine price cable had arrived just when Draper was trying to persuade Dodge to take on the job, and someone—Draper?—must have suspected that our radio report was a subtle move to sabotage the whole project by disproving the existence of the crisis that Dodge was supposed to handle.

If so, the suspecter greatly overestimated SCAP's knowledge of what was going on in the Washington corridors of power. But now there was no question that Washington was determined to prevent any MacArthur attempt at preemption. No one, not even the Supreme Commander, was going to shunt the President's personal representative aside. When our *ad hoc* committee made our exchange rate report, recommending 330 yen to the dollar, to Marquat, he brought it to the Supreme Commander, who could only tell him to hold it for Dodge's arrival.

General MacArthur had indeed lost the inflation battle, not *against* inflation but *over* the inflation, and with it he lost control of the major part of his Occupation's jurisdiction. There were to be no more letters to the prime minister on the subject, no more exhortations to the public. In theory Dodge, the new economic czar, was to stay only three months; in practice his "line" would last for the rest of the Occupation. Once Dodge landed in Japan, Draper could resign with peace of mind—and get married for the second time two weeks later. All the other objectives of the Occupation had now been subordinated to curbing the inflation and controlling the money supply. Draper's near tunnel vision of Japan's future had succeeded MacArthur's dream, at least in the eyes of the U.S. government.

On March 17, 1949, à propos of apparently nothing at all, MacArthur startled newspaper readers with a statement declaring, "I have no intention of seeking relief from my heavy responsibilities here. . . . I reiterate my intention to see this problem through to the signing of the peace treaty."[18] In fact, he had already been relieved of most of his responsibilities. A quarter of a century later, in 1973, the Japanese Government awarded Draper the Order of the Sacred Treasure First Class.

23

Imperial Accountant

DODGE AND DEFLATION

ALTHOUGH IT WAS EASY for the far-off government in Washington to overlook it, an occupation is at least equally the business of the occupied. In the year-long tug-of-war over Japan's recovery and inflation policies, the MacArthur Headquarters had pointed out the dangers to Japanese political stability if the Americans pressed too hard on the fragile cabinet coalition then governing the country. The National Security Council, egged on by the Washington domestic agencies, had disbelieved the warning. Now a tough Detroit banker was coming to town determined to press as hard as necessary, and he had the President's personal support. Would he not run smack into the situation we had been predicting? Would not the Japanese ministers balk, and would not the American instrument for governing Japan turn out to be too brittle? Unexpectedly, the answer turned out to be no because in the meantime the Japanese political picture had changed radically. The occupied took a hand, and Dodge was the beneficiary. Timing may not be everything, but it can often be the most important thing.

LUCKY JOE

In the two-month interval between the NSC directive and Dodge's arrival in Japan on February 1, 1949, two fortuitous events took place. Both were beyond economics and Dodge, too. First, a playboy finance minister was replaced by a hard-working and courageous individual dedicated to Dodge's brand of economics. Second, the first strong single-party cabinet of the postwar era, conservative like Dodge into the bargain, took office. Without lifting a finger, Joseph Dodge received ready-made the ideal instrument through which to work his will. Neither Dodge nor the Washington economists ever fully appreciated the difference those events made, but I always thought that if he had been a gambler instead of a sober banker, he would have been called "Lucky Joe" Dodge.

Politics in Japan, as elsewhere, contains a large element of farce. The day after a troubled MacArthur received the NSC stabilization directive in December 1948, the key Japanese figure in any stabilization program, Finance Minister Izumiyama Sanroku, was playing games in the Diet Building half a mile away. A charming, handsome fifty-one year-old with curly white hair and a dark moustache, Izumiyama had been private secretary to the revered Ikeda Seihin, prewar head of the Mitsui *zaibatsu*, governor of the Bank of Japan, and finance minister. On that December 13 he was celebrating the passage of his supplementary budget by the Diet and the impending end of the session. Wandering lightheartedly from party to farewell party in the numerous Diet rooms and matching saké toasts with his fellow legislators while debate droned on in the Diet chamber, Izumiyama became grandly lubricated. A woman legislator, Yamashita Harue, passed him in a Diet corridor, and Izumiyama tipsily reached out to embrace her. Unfortunately, she was a member of the opposition Democratic party.

Eluding his grasp, Yamashita hastened to the well of the House of Representatives and secured the rostrum on a point of personal privilege. She indignantly recounted the episode and denounced the salacious finance minister as not respectful of the improved status of women that General MacArthur had established. The House burst into a cheerful uproar. Izumiyama, completely unknowing and by this time feeling a little ill, wandered over to the Diet dispensary, where he fell fast asleep on an examining table with a wet towel over his face. A photograph of that edifying sight taken by an enterprising photographer through the dispensary transom appeared in the next morning's newspapers.[1] By the time Izumiyama awoke with a splitting headache, he was no longer finance minister, and his political career was in ruins.[2]

After the January 1948 election, Yoshida replaced Izumiyama with a gravel-voiced favorite of his, Ikeda Hayato, formerly head of the Tax Bureau. Ikeda thereupon fashioned a brilliant political career for himself, ending up as prime minister for the four and a quarter years between July 1960 and December 1964.[3] Meanwhile, he turned out to be almost indispensable for Dodge. Orville MacDiarmid, the former Young mission member, who attended most of the Dodge consultations with the Finance Ministry, said many years later that "it is to Mr. Ikeda . . . that I give most credit for the accomplishments of the Dodge Mission."[4]

The landslide election that Yoshida and his Liberals won on January 24, 1949, was even more important. With 264 seats captured out of 466, it would take many Liberal defections to endanger the cabinet. Those who disagreed with

Yoshida knew that if they quit their ministerial posts in protest, he would simply replace them without the slightest hesitation. And Yoshida, intent on forging strong ties with the United States, particularly its conservative elements, and trusting his finance minister on the economic aspects of government about which he himself was proud to know nothing, unhesitatingly enforced party discipline in support of the new Dodge stabilization program.

To Dodge, the government budget was the most powerful engine of control over a modern country and all its economic activities, far more effective than directives, laws, political controls, police force, or Army, and he set out immediately to establish his authority over it. When he first arived in GHQ and was installed by Marquat in a large nearby room with his small staff,[5] the first thing he did was to summon Finance Minister Ikeda and his principal assistant, Miyazawa Kiichi;[6] hand them copies of his ten principles for the Japanese budget, which he had composed before he had even set foot in Japan; and commandeer a vast amount of data on the budget in process. Only then did he meet the top ESS staff. To us he also handed copies of his ten budget principles. The first demanded a balanced consolidated budget, and the other points—I cannot remember them all—insisted that all deficits and subsidies be clearly shown, that old subsidies be eliminated or reduced and new ones forbidden, and so forth. Dodge did not want the SCAP people to brief him. Before he knew anything about Japan's problems at first hand, he was presenting us with his solution. (Marshall, it will be remembered had asked the Europeans for *their* solution.) Dodge would take care of the application of the principles for Japan himself through the Japanese government. He did not need us at all.

It was not that Dodge was hostile or condescending. He maintained friendly relations with Marquat and was affable with the small group around the general. In occasional lunches with us he was quite willing to listen as well as talk, especially after he returned to Japan later in the year without his entourage. At one lunch he confided to us the problems his Detroit Bank had had with bad loans in the Depression until he became president and solved them by depriving all the bank's officers, starting with himself, of loan authority. Another time he suddenly suggested to me that a taxi company would be a good business in Tokyo. The senior ESS staff, as well as his own group, often called the fifty-nine-year-old banker "Joe," sometimes even to his face. Even his standard banker's appearance—medium height, gray hair always combed straight back in place, rimless glasses, gray or pin-striped blue suits—was unpretentious and unintimidating. Only his distinctive self-confident bearing, that of the sober self-made pillar of the business community *par excellence,* marked him out from the crowd. After graduating from high school in 1908, Dodge went immediately to work in the Detroit Bank. His first college degree, an LL.D. from Wayne in 1948, was an honorary one. In addition to the Detroit Bank, he was also successively a director of the Packard and Chrysler auto companies, plus two insurance firms and a savings bank. He was quietly but obviously supremely competent.

However ordinary he looked, Dodge never left any doubt as to who was in charge. He had only three months to do the job, and he was going to be deterred by no one and waste no time on critics. On accepting the appointment from President Truman—he had insisted on the personal rank of minister—he warned the President that he expected to be attacked by special interests in Japan. He was rewarded by a typically combative Truman reaction, to the effect that Truman expected that and would support him all the way.[7]

THE BALANCED BUDGET

That was enough for Dodge. In Japan he refused to listen to criticisms of his deflationary (he preferred to call it "disinflationary") policy from any source, including the ruling Democratic-Liberal party. He once told a few of us that he had discounted all that in advance, so there was no point in hearing it. One can imagine the difficulties this kind of ruthless operation, without regard for Japanese views three and a half years and two democratic elections after the war, would have provoked if, lacking a strong and cooperative government and finance minister to cushion the shock, Dodge had had to impose his intentions by direct SCAP order.

Dodge's *modus operandi,* like the cultivation of the lawns of England, was fundamentally simple but not easy. It was painstaking accounting followed by painful surgery. He questioned every expenditure without revenue to match and brought every subsidy, no matter how indirect and well-hidden, to light. Day after day, Japanese Finance Ministry officials trooped to his Forestry Building office carrying masses of documents, only to go back, invariably, for more data. In a matter of two months, Dodge personally knew more about the details of each ministry's budget than the ministers and of every special account more than the specialists. More important, he understood the impact of each entry on the economy, as he demonstrated in two lucid discourses to an awed press corps. He maintained independent lines of communication to Washington, radioing reports of his findings, accomplishments, and recommendations every two or three days on the average. It was an awesome and strange job. Commissioners had been dispatched by imperialist nations to backward countries in the nineteenth century to safeguard the tax collections that secured foreign loans. But here was a foreign Lord High Imperial Accountant sitting in the capital of a large industrial power, tirelessly auditing every phase of its financial operations "for its own good." Dodge was demonstrating that control of the budget from one small office was more powerful than the 150,000-man Occupation army commanded by General MacArthur.

Ostensibly Dodge was only balancing the Japanese budget to curtail the money supply and halt the upward price spiral. But anyone who thought the Imperial Accountant would stop there did not know his man. Dodge had his own vision of Japan as an anchor of stability in the Far East, and that required a stable long-term economy, sufficiently well capitalized and efficient to make its way independently in a harsh world. A roaring inflation distorted price relationships, impeded efficient allocation of resources, created a climate of uncertainty, and discouraged private investment. Stopping it was, therefore, his first order of business.

But just as Dodge casually ignored eight of the nine stabilization principles of the NSC, he was not at all loath to expand enormously its first principle, balancing the budget. That was his authority for presuming to reorder the Japanese long-term economy his way. Meanwhile, being a commercial banker used to demanding $200 collateral for $100 loans, Dodge sought maximum safety margins in each of his deflationary actions.

His achievements along both lines—economic reorganization and inflation-fighting—were extraordinary. But the consequence of the former was to involve himself and the United States in the burning domestic issues of another country, and consistently on the conservative side. That inevitably alienated labor and the left, the one-third of the country that opposed the conservatives. The result of Dodge's extreme caution, moreover, was a super-deflation and an economic crisis that many Japanese asserted was worse than the one he came to cure.

Now, Dodge was no ideologue but a practical man of affairs. If he detested excessive government participation in commerce and industry—at one point he remarked with horror the fact that up to two-thirds of Japan's gross national product passed through the hands of the government—it was because he thought it inefficient and therefore a burdensome hidden tax on the economy, holding back its recovery. Government subsidies were particularly onerous. "Government investments and expenditures," he said, "are rarely as productive as private expenditures of the same amount."[8] Besides that, he added, the investment dollar was diminished by the expense of taxation and the cost of administering the subsidies. No one should be fooled. Governments only distributed other people's money. Before they could bestow benefits on someone, Dodge declared, they first had to collect them from someone else.

Many Japanese agreed. But to others the universal businessman's standards of efficiency and productivity were in themselves a kind of ideology. These others preferred instead to use government to protect small merchants and manufacturers, redress workers' grievances, and correct social injustices, all at the taxpayers' expense and regardless of loss in productivity and efficiency. They thought that in their own country such a choice was *their* business. Dodge, however, was sure it was *his* business. No one would challenge the propriety of insisting that the economy of an occupied country be managed in such a way as to reduce the financial burden on the occupier, of course, but Dodge went further. "The U.S. Government is rightly concerned," he said, "that lasting benefits to the Japanese economy must result from grants in aid or loans." What were lasting benefits was, naturally, to be judged by Joseph Dodge. But there was no doubt that "lasting" was meant to extend far beyond the brief remaining period of the Occupation.

Dodge, moreover, did not hesitate to jump feet first into the bruising conflict over priorities governing scarce Japanese resources, which underlay all Japanese postwar domestic politics. For the very reason that the controversy was political, MacArthur and the Occupation had stayed neutral as between the alliance of business and the conservatives, who wanted to recapitalize war-devastated industry first, and that of labor and the Socialists, who wanted to raise workers' depressed living standards first. That SCAP thought, was a decision for the Japanese to settle through their new democratic institutions; if not, what was a democracy for? Dodge decided the issue by himself. If the country was to be truly independent, he insisted, Japan had to accumulate capital by savings. Raising living standards could come about only by cutting government expenditures. Indeed, he said unsympathetically, the Japanese were living beyond their means. The crisis demanded that they cut back.

What crisis? Production and real wages were up, the rate of inflation and increase in money supply were way down. But if there was no crisis, what was Dodge doing there? The Detroit banker was experienced enough in the ways of government to know it was not enough to do well; one also had to look good. He simply denigrated the progress of 1948 as the temporary result of American aid, which, he said the Americans were determined to reduce. Then where would Japan be? "It is the height of folly," he said, "to point with pride at an increased production index which may actually represent only increased aid, increased subsidies, increased deficits." Try as I might I could not, when I heard that, make the connections. American aid in 1948 consisted almost entirely of food, and it *was* greater than in 1947. But how could that increase be responsible for a 60 percent rise in industrial production? Not by eliminating malnutrition as a drag on production, for that was long gone, or by releasing Japanese export proceeds to buy needed raw materials instead of food, for no export proceeds were being used for food in 1947 either. In fact, Dodge did not actually say that it was the food aid that caused the production rise. His words were too carefully chosen for that. But that there was a crisis he left no doubt. His Japanese listeners also did not doubt there was a crisis. But to many of them the crisis had been caused by the threat to curtail aid funds because Washington was dissatisfied with the management of their economy. In other words, it had been caused by the National Security Council and Joseph Dodge.

It didn't matter where the crisis came from. A crisis mentality swept over the GHQ. Of the 500 men and women who made up the Economic Section only a handful actually saw Dodge personally, and only a few more, given his method of operation, had anything to do with his program. But they all jumped in to fight the crisis. The Labor Division, which had bitterly opposed wage controls, for example, was now ready to embrace them if other wage stabilization efforts failed.[9] The others followed suit in their respective jurisdictions. Almost nothing was too extreme in the final struggle with the hated inflation.

THE DODGE LINE

Dodge, in his conservative way, was one of the most extreme. Certainly he was the most uncompromising. Take the imported food subsidy and the foreign trade account. At the very beginning of the Occupation, when starvation was an immediate threat and the urban population was too impoverished to pay more, aid food had been distributed through the ration system at the low ration price, disregarding actual dollar costs. Those yen proceeds were then used, when private exports started up again in August 1947, to pay the local exporters for their merchandise at cost plus a 10 percent profit, again disregarding the dollar export prices, which the ESS specialists sets at "world market" levels independently (sometimes deriving them from a handy Sears Roebuck catalog). Even though the resulting yen–dollar price ratios were gradually arranged into a series of exchange rate groups, the export rates remained significantly higher than the import rates. When the volume of aid imports was high and exports low, it did not matter that it took perhaps three dollars in aid imports to yield enough yen to pay for one dollar of exported fans, bicycles, toys, silk, and ships. But as exports grew, the foreign trade account fell into deficit and, it was clear, would soon be thunderously bankrupt.

SCAP officials had therefore set about gradually erasing the discrepancy between the yen and dollar prices of foods. In November 1948, even before the NSC directive, staple food prices were raised 42 percent[10] and more adjustments were on the way for the start of the next year's collections in November 1949. The subsidy could continue but was vastly reduced. Similarly, I and my *ad hoc* exchange rate committee had recommended in December 1948 that to ease the shock of a single exchange rate, ships and raw silk be subsidized temporarily. But recommending such subsidies even temporarily to Dodge was like trying to sell Calvin to the Pope. He just brushed our ideas aside.

In the same way Dodge remorselessly attacked the Reconstruction Finance Bank (RFB). Set up earlier in the Occupation to finance the rebuildng of war-ravaged industry because the commercial "city banks" lacked resources, the RFB had played a principal role in resuscitating coal production. But the bank's only resources were government-appropriated funds, in the form of RFB bond purchases, and that was enough to make it, in Dodge's eyes, an engine of inflation. Besides, he was sure that no government institution had enough incentive to be economical and efficient. The "city banks'" resources were still inadequate, but Dodge ruled that the RFB had to go.

I could only admire the ingenuity with which Dodge, at one stroke, combined the abolition of the three—food subsidy, trade account deficit, and RFB—with shifting the burden of capital accumulation onto the urban consumer. By establishing a single exchange rate with no exceptions, both food subsidies and the trade account deficit were wiped out. Indeed, as long as Japan's imports exceeded exports, the yen trade account showed a surplus. Then Dodge abolished the RFB and in its stead set up a U.S. Aid Counterpart Fund, a device borrowed from the Marshall Plan countries. Into that fund the yen proceeds of American aid imports were gathered for the prime purpose of making long-term industrial loans, like hydroelectric power projects, to aid the whole economy. Consumers, when they bought U.S. aid food, were now to pay for capital investment, while the government lowered its expenditures. Dodge had assured the Japanese that lowered government expenditures were the only way to raise urban living standards. In this case, at least, the lowered expenditures raised food prices and the cost of living instead.

When the Young mission had proposed reducing or abolishing the food subsidy, MacArthur had exploded. Such a move would jeopardize public tranquility, he complained. But April 1949 (Dodge's situation) was greatly different from June 1948 (Young's predicament). Once more it was a matter of timing. For meanwhile real wages had risen 44 percent, enhancing the worker's ability to absorb higher food costs, while the best postwar crop collection ever had permitted a 20 percent increase in the consumers' ration,[11] just about eliminating the need to buy on the black market. Finally, the existing food stocks in Japanese warehouses, which the Food Corporation had acquired at low yen prices, had almost doubled in quantity since Young (from 1.4 million tons to 3.2 million).[12] Averaging those with the new high-priced imports would automatically yield a much lower figure and cushion the latter's impact. None of those mitigating developments were achievements of Joe Dodge. One had to admire not only his ability but his luck in coming to Japan when he did.

By slashing, paring, and cutting in true crisis fashion and to a degree that no democratic government could undertake and survive, Dodge came up with an almost unbelievable budget. SCAP and the Japanese Government had raised the percentage of budget balance from 58 percent in 1946–47 to 88 percent in 1947–48 and then 92 percent in 1948–49. Before Dodge came, we had expected 1949–50 revenues to reach perhaps 96 percent of expenditures. By the time Dodge got through with it and the budget year ran its course, revenues were 108.7 percent of expenditures.[13] The surplus was almost a billion dollars, and that in a war-impoverished country, 20 percent of whose expenditures were earmarked for the costs of military occupation.

It was not all budget-cutting. Railway rates were raised sharply, and tax-collection efficiency was driven to the point of implacability. Every week, at our meetings with Finance Minister Ikeda, which continued parallel to Ikeda's sessions with Dodge, General Marquat would ask Finance Ministry Councilor Suzuki Gengo how many people had been arrested that week for tax evasion. No means for the government to sop up purchasing power was overlooked.

At the same time the government found it could not possibly invest the yen counterpart of aid food as fast as it could extract the money from the pockets of the consumer at the higher prices. Hydroelectric dams and stations, after all, take meticulous preparation and a long time for the design and manufacture of special equipment. Of the 129 billion yen the Counterpart Fund collected from the sales of U.S. aid goods, the Japanese Government was able to invest only 50 billion in capital projects that fiscal year. The rest, 79 billion, was simply withdrawn from circulation. The government used some of it to pay off RFB bonds and kept some immobilized in cash. The result was to demonetize fully one-quarter of the total note issue outstanding at the beginning of Dodge's exercise.

The effect was electrifying. The inflation stopped dead in its tracks. Consumer prices in urban Japan fell from an index of 142.8 in May to 131.4 in November. The Bank of Japan note issue declined in the same period as well, from 315 billion yen to 304 billion.[14] The fifteen-year-old inflation was over.

It seemed to be a miracle. Dodge himself was much impressed and elated. "It's a textbook example of how a budget can stop an inflation cold," he marveled to a few of us once at lunch after he had returned later in the year to check up on the progress of his program. Without question, he was absolutely right.

As the shape of Dodge's program began to emerge, however, local conservative and business elements angrily criticized it. These were the "special interests" Dodge had visualized in his Truman interview. When on February 23 Ikeda presented his first budget draft, Dodge promptly threw it out as violating his budget principles. Ikeda was personally relieved and grateful, because until then he had not been able to get the cabinet to credit his warnings that Dodge was really serious about balancing the budget. But elsewhere the adjustment was painful. The victorious Democratic-Liberal party's (DLP) campaign pledges had called for lower income tax rates, abolition of the sales tax, a limited rise in railway freight tariffs, and increased public works. Those would now have to be abandoned, even though they were only weeks old. The younger DLP Diet members, who had just finished making those election promises to their constituents, objected vociferously. But Ikeda, showing the streak of stubbornness that would characterize him as both finance minister and prime minister and that endeared him to an equally stubborn Yoshida, refused to budge an inch. He had hitched his wagon to Dodge's star and had declared that if he were prevented by party politics from carrying out the Dodge line, he would resign. Hirokawa Kōzen, the party secretary general, visited Dodge and Marquat in order to pacify the party members. Returning, he could only sigh that Dodge had put the party "in a difficult position".[15] Yoshida stood firm. The party revolt died.

Political pacification, however, did not allay the business distress that ensued from the enforcement of the budget Dodge finally approved on April 5. The statistics reflected it. All indicators were down.[16]

A black mood settled on small and medium businessmen. The big *zaibatsu* companies might still get assistance from their associated banks, but the RFB was gone, the commercial banks had less funds available for non-*zaibatsu* companies, and the tax collectors operated with unprecedented vigor and severity. At the end of July, after Dodge was "safely" out of the country, the finance minister, possibly to mollify his shaken cabinet colleagues, asked GHQ for a relaxation of the Dodge line in order to avoid a panic.[17] Marquat and his staff advisers, still under Dodge's orders and no longer with any independent authority—MacArthur was completely out of all this—quickly refused, and Ikeda withdrew his request.

Had not the commercial banks resorted to "overloans," that is, in excess of their assets, and had not the Bank of Japan supported them with a 60 percent increase in credit after Dodge left for the first time, the note issue would have dropped further by 30 billion yen, and Japanese business would have been left gasping like fish washed up on the beach.

For most of 1949 and early 1950, the Dodge line and its attendant hardships were the biggest continuing domestic story in the Japanese media. Now a string of small business bankruptcies captured the headlines. When asked by reporters for comment after one small businessman and his family committed suicide together and left a note blaming harsh government measures, Ikeda answered that under the circumstances "such incidents were to be expected." The nation was shocked. A short time later, when Ikeda visited us during the electioneering period before a House of Councilors election, Marquat in his jovial way asked him why he was not out campaigning. Ikeda looked rueful. "The prime minister thinks I can help the party more by not talking so much," he replied.

I seriously doubt that Dodge planned it quite that way. He had expected, he told us informally, a small surplus, which he would use to reduce the national debt. But the cumulative effect of his budget vetoes—he could not make an exception of one request without intensifying pressure behind the others—far exceeded his small surplus. Only six months after his budget went into effect, the Finance Ministry was already predicting a larger 3.3 percent surplus,[18] and six months later that surplus had tripled. "I do not think that any of us expected the Dodge program to be as deflationary as it turned out to be," an awed MacDiarmid commented thirty years later.[19] Presumably the "us" included Dodge as well.

In theory the Dodge "line" was intended to create a stable base from which the economy could take off again, this time on a sustainable course. In fact, for fifteen months afterward the economy showed little sign of recovery.

Industrial activity rose only sluggishly, and durable goods production, the key indicator of the new capital investment so avidly awaited by the Washington agencies to replace the alleged consumer binge, actually fell. Only exports, responding to the new exchange rate of 360 yen to the dollar, rose in early 1950, but the increase was smaller both in percentage and in absolute terms than the year before. It did little to dispel the general gloom. At mid-1950, the Japanese economy was at a stalemate.

All that gave no grounds for predicting that Dodge's name would go down in Japanese history with much luster or, for that matter, at all. Yet Dodge became an object of admiration in Japan for many years and was even quoted, like scripture, against Americans who proposed financial innovations the Japanese did not like. (Fifteen years later, when MacDiarmid returned to Tokyo as a representative of the World Bank and urged the vice minister of Finance to issue domestic bonds to finance much-needed public works, the latter replied, "But Mr. Dodge told us not to."[20] Still one more stroke of good luck was to befall "Lucky Joe" Dodge.

KOREAN WAR PROCUREMENT

On June 25, 1950, North Korea invaded South Korea, and in a matter of days the U.S. Army was turning to Japan to provide large quantities of all kinds of military support supplies, from galvanized iron sheets and cotton duck to prefabricated buildings and chemicals. Suddenly Japanese makers were besieged with orders for rush shipment, price secondary. Japan was the closest and fastest available supplier. Within only a month, the visible effect was startling. When I led a SCAP budget mission to the Civil Affairs Division in the Pentagon in July and August to submit our aid requirements for Japan for 1951–52, I was constantly reminded that "now with the war, Japan doesn't need aid any more." And no wonder. In the single month of August 1950, U.S. procurement officers signed contracts with Japanese suppliers for $60 million in goods and services.[21] Meanwhile our group, in Washington, was asking for only $150 million for the whole year. (Eventually Congress appropriated $100 million.) True, as we pointed out, some of the manufacturers for the U.S. Army required additional imported raw material input, while other manufactures were sold to the military in lieu of commercial exports. But those minor drawbacks were swept away in the flood of export orders. In the second half of 1950, receipts from "invisible exports"— which is where the proceeds of military procurement in Japan were listed— tripled, and during 1951 they reached almost $1 billion.[22] This was three-quarters as much as all other Japanese foreign exchange receipts for the year from the whole world.

From July to December 1950, for the first time since the end of World War II, Japan had a surplus in its international accounts. Industrial production zoomed at the same time, some 28 percent in the latter half of 1950. Japan was lifted to a higher plateau of economic activity, never thereafter to descend from it. Also, despite occasional subsequent dips into the red in its international payments, Japan had at long last essentially attained the elusive goal of economic self-support. No one can say what would have happened to the Japanese economy without the war, but in the actual event it took the Korean War to relieve Dodge's deflation.

The Japanese and Dodge

If imitation is the sincerest form of flattery, the Japanese soon stopped flattering Dodge sincerely. Just as soon as they safely could, the Ministry of International Trade and Industry set up a surreptitious export subsidy system for raw silk and ships, the very subsidies that Dodge had thrown out when our *ad hoc* exchange rate group had proposed it to him. Before the war, to save foreign exchange, the Japanese Government had "linked" the import of raw materials to export manufactures that needed such materials. Now the system was revived with an allowance for raw material wastage deliberately in excess of reality, allowing the makers to sell the excess import licenses to subsidize their exports. But for silk and ships, the government went further, allocating for their exports-linked import licenses for—raw sugar. Sugar a raw material in the manufacture of silk and ships? Well, perhaps not, but in a country with a war-starved sweet tooth, sugar import licenses went for unbelievable prices. And no subsidy appeared on the government's books that Dodge could see. Shipyards, further, were given special loan facilities at half the ordinary interest rates. It was a less than nimble company treasurer who could not use the credits for domestic financing as well. But then we had calculated that silk could move only if the exporters got 450 yen for each dollar, and ships only at 600. So ships and raw silk exports were saved by subsidies after all. Fifteen years later, Japan was building half the merchant ships in the world, and their export was Japan's biggest single foreign exchange earner.

More significant was the Japanese Government's more relaxed attitude toward a moderate long-term inflation, heresy by Dodge's standards. During the Korean War, it was true, the government could do little about stemming externally provoked price rises; American rush procurement was too pressing, and world commodity prices soared as a result of the war. But when the Japanese economic managers did have a genuine choice in the late 1950s and early 1960s, especially when Ikeda, Dodge's onetime ally, acceded to the prime minister's office in 1960, they opted instead for doubling the national income in ten years and a steady price inflation of some 6 percent annually. The Japanese economy grew rapidly, productivity soared, and real wages climbed. "Jimmu-irai"—not since Jimmu, the first Emperor—proclaimed the newspapers, had the Japanese had it so good. On the other side of the Pacific, meanwhile, the Eisenhower Administration, with Joseph Merrill Dodge as its first Director of the Budget, held inflation to very low levels, maintained economic stability, and saw the American economy grow much more slowly. Perversely, every year the yen waxed stronger vis-à-vis the dollar. Certainly the Japanese could claim that their policy was better than Dodge's.

Why then such high esteem for Dodge among Japanese financial officials and financial economists generally? In part, it was personal. Perhaps no other American figure was so accepted as one of them as was Dodge by the Japanese financial administrators. His lucidity, his logic, his monetarist convictions, and his resolution in rejecting political importunities impressed them. His defense of the prerogatives of the Finance Ministry gratified them. Under fire from the other ministries, which claimed that the Finance Ministry elitists had set themselves up as a superministry through their budgetary authority, and deprived of part of their turf by the SCAP-sponsored Economic Stabilization Board, the Finance Ministry officials now found their power restored by an economic czar who refused to deal with anyone else. (One American political scientist, thinking of the constant struggle of the other ministries to free themselves from traditional Finance Ministry domination, commented that Dodge set back democratization of the Japanese bureaucracy fifty years.) Dodge was more than a respected teacher; he became a protector, a kind of *oyabun* or patron, to the upper levels of the Finance Ministry. They owed him a great deal.

But most of all, Dodge proved that monetarism worked. After all, however one may qualify his achievement, he did stop a chronic inflation rapidly and solely by monetarist measures. It was a vindication of very great importance for the future, for ever since, the Japanese Government has been one of the most avid and successful practitioners of comprehensive monetary stimuli and depressants in the world. Whenever the managers of Japan's economy felt the economy was becoming "overheated," they applied Dodge's principles and methods in full confidence that they were in control of the situation. The rest of the government and the nation's business leaders, moreover, were able to share their confidence. In a country that was being constantly stimulated by a moderate inflationary policy, as well as by enormous capital investment, it was perhaps essential, if only psychologically, to know that the corrective was always close at hand.

There was one other vital contribution of Dodge, Detroit banker and international financial reformer. Dodge constituted the first postwar channel between the conservative Japanese big business elements and their bureaucratic and political allies in Japan and the top level of officials in the U.S. Government. From then on the Japanese conservatives were plugged into the top in the United States. Private American businessmen were always suspected of special pleading when they talked of Japanese needs to American decision-makers. Dodge, however, was irreproachable and prestigious, and he stayed three months and then came back again, long enough to form a close working relationship with Ikeda, the finance minister and future prime minister. Dodge himself became, three years later, Eisenhower's first Director of the Budget. In between, his connections within the U.S. Government and among the American financial community were the best. He was indefatigable in introducing conservative Japanese VIPs to their opposite numbers in the States, in testifying before Congress on Japan's behalf, and in declaring widely although privately that the Yoshida government was America's best asset in the Far East.[23]

Dodge, more than any other individual, engineered the historic tacit alliance between America and the Japanese conservative and business elements that endured for the decades that followed. Regardless of whether the Japanese conservatives accepted his economic philosophy in its entirety, they had good reason to honor Joseph Dodge from then on. Others, however, thought differently.

24

Labor's Disillusionment with America

THE WORLD LOOKS QUITE DIFFERENT to the worm and to the bird. The lofty view that Dodge, Ikeda, the Washington economists, and even GHQ took of Japan convinced them that in the end a successful stabilization effort would bring benefits everywhere, especially to the workers—for who suffers more cruelly from inflation than working men and women? The workers themselves were not so sure. From the worm's viewpoint, birds are more often predators than helpers. The Japanese trade unions and their members intuitively feared that the stabilization structure might be erected at their expense. The birds' warbling did not reassure the worms.

At the very inception of the new program, the State–Army press release of December 19, 1948, made it plain that any general improvement in Japanese living standards would have to await economic stabilization and, furthermore, would depend on the degree to which the Japanese supported the U.S. National Security Council directive. The Washington economists had meant to say only that the U.S. government would not spend money endlessly to no purpose in Japan. To Japanese labor the release sounded more like, "Do it our way or we'll cut American aid." General MacArthur, in his letter the very next day to the prime minister,[1] called for austerity and sacrifice. In Japan, however, sacrifice historically came at the expense of the lower orders. Having lost a good part of their confidence in him after he unilaterally abolished government workers' collective bargaining only four months before, the labor unions no longer believed the General so completely when he talked of equality of sacrifice. "There will be no place for interference by management or labor in the acceleration of production," MacArthur proclaimed. But the union leaders could not see why management would want to interfere with production anyway. The Supreme

Commander, it was clear, was talking about them, labor. "The Law in its majesty," Anatole France said, "forbids the rich as well as the poor to sleep under bridges." MacArthur meant to be impartial, but to Japanese labor his words sounded suspiciously like a ban on strikes.

Confirmation of their fears was not long in coming. Only two days later, Chester Hepler, the new SCAP Labor Division Chief, met in his office with the printing workers' representatives, and then with the electric power workers, and told both groups that strikes at just that time were "unpatriotic."[2] The word "unpatriotic" irritated the disquieted the union leaders. The odious Japanese military leaders had called labor unions "unpatriotic" for years and then had had them dissolved. The clearly implied strike ban upset them even more, especially at a time when both unions were in the process of negotiating wage increases. What bargaining power would they now have? The next day Hepler advised the *Zensekitan* coal miners' union not to strike either. The reaction was swift: Seventeen executives of the union publicly joined the Communist party three days later in protest.[3]

In the weeks that followed, Labor Division officials passed the word on to the coastal seamen and the private railwaymen too.[4] In March, the Labor Relations Branch Chief, Robert Amis, summoned leaders of the *Sanbetsu* Congress of Industrial Unions and warned them against "political" strikes. It was an "oral order," he said.[5] In April 1949 when the force of Hepler's earlier remarks had dissipated, Labor Division presented the coal miners with a carefully phrased letter signed by General Marquat, warning that a coal strike would be inconsistent with the new stabilization program.[6] And on June 9 Valery Burati, who had replaced Amis in Labor Relations while Amis replaced Hepler as division chief, privately counseled the government railway workers' union that it would do well to call off its selective strike immediately.[7] The union leaders seemed reluctant, and so on the following day an irate Amis formally directed them to "discontinue the strike by certain employees of certain electric railways in Tokyo," as the GHQ Public Information Office, the official SCAP voice, gingerly reported in a press release.[8]

It seemed that any time an important union threatened to go on strike, up jumped some GHQ official to tell it that it could not or should not. Whatever had become of American support for the Japanese worker? the Japanese union leaders wondered.

ECONOMIC STABILIZATION

The sudden American abandonment and even rejection of Japanese labor in late 1948 and 1949 seemed baffling. But the Americans involved did not think of themselves as abandoning labor. They were, they thought, protecting it. The Washington agencies were protecting labor against inflation. So was MacArthur, and from the loss of U.S. aid funds as well. Neither the Supreme Commander nor the Washington economists, however, personally understood the situation of Japanese workers. Wonderfully intuitive at times in judging the Japanese mind, MacArthur simply could not understand that the unions had lost confidence in him as protector. It took the election of the following month, with almost 2 million voters switching from Socialist to Communist,[9] to make the lesson plain. Even then, it was not at all clear that the Supreme Commander drew the appropriate conclusions.

But how could the Labor Division trio of Hepler, Amis, and Burati so misjudge the labor unions as to rush to prohibit strikes? The first two were federal civil servants long active in agencies devoted to the workers' interests, Hepler as Deputy Director of the U.S. Employment Service,[10] and Amis as head of the Birmingham office of the Wage-Hour Administration. Burati was a flaming labor advocate and ex-organizer for the CIO Textile Workers Union. He had even put himself at personal risk to testify for the Japanese labor defendant at a U.S. Navy Yokosuka provost court proceeding instigated by the base commandant himself, Captain Benton Decker, who in those days ran Yokosuka like a personal fief. When asked whether the accused, the head of the Yokosuka Base employees' union, had not by his actions provoked disrespect for the Occupation, Burati replied no, but that Captain Decker certainly had. (It did not help the defendant, who got six months in prison, but it did start a minor Army–Navy row when Decker complained to Tokyo that the Army was subverting him.)[11]

The answer was that the Labor Division trio were protecting labor too, but secretly, against Washington and MacArthur. For if the General and Washington perceived that the unions' actions might upset the stabilization applecart, they might formally crack down on labor activities and permanently weaken the new structure of democratic labor law. The trio's motives made little difference to the union leaders. From their vantage point everyone in GHQ, including their "friends," were preventing them from bargaining effectively.

But how could the GHQ officers do so legally? JCS 1380/15, still in force, allowed the Supreme Commander to "prohibit strikes and other work stoppages *only* when you consider that these would interfere with military operations or directly endanger the security of the Occupation Forces" (italics added). Printers interfering with military operations? Coastal seamen endangering the security of the Occupation forces? The NSC directive did not allude to strikes one way or the other. If it had, the Labor Department would not have concurred so quickly. So how could strikes be forbidden now by field officers?

When I alerted Marquat about Amis's actions, he asked him on what authority he had ordered the electric train stoppages ended—that was solely MacArthur's prerogative. A crestfallen Amis had to admit that he had only assumed it in the light of the NSC. Marquat was upset but did nothing to amend the release by the Public Information Officer, who had assumed the same.

The fact is that in practice the original directive had never gone far enough to be realistic. In 1946 the Supreme Commander had added one more ground for prohibiting work stoppages as inherent in his Commander's authority, that is, where strikes prejudiced Occupation objectives. As Labor Division Chief, I had repeatedly warned against a railway strike, against a postal workers' stoppage aimed at the SCAP-sponsored currency conversion, and the like. Now, the new NSC directive added nine more Occupation objectives, including the maximizing of production, and everyone in a position to do so jumped to get into the act. The Chief of Staff, who had managed to stay out of all civilian affairs since his arrival in Japan, now suddenly felt impelled to ring up Marquat when he heard the electric power workers were causing five- and ten-minute power outages. He was scandalized, he told our general, that the workers were violating the NSC directive. Marquat was not to be stampeded; he refused to concede any substantial damage. But the pressure from higher up passed on down the line.

Under pressure of concentrating on the new central objective of stabilization, almost everyone lost his peripheral vision. People no longer saw the equally or more important long-range objective of ensuring continued Japanese popular support after the Occupation departed. No wonder that support was inevitably undermined. In the decades that followed, American officials remembered the $2 billion of relief aid and the early American popularity, but never tried to understand the workers' feelings about an imposed no-strike stabilization program. Like Charlie Brown wistfully regarded his team's mountainous defeat on the scoreboard, they could only ask, "How could it happen when we were so sincere?"

Perhaps blindest of all to labor considerations was Joseph Dodge, whom the union leaders regarded, even more than MacArthur or the Labor Division, as the most accurate representative of America's real intentions. Because of the stabilization program, Dodge won a reputation in some labor circles as "anti-labor." It was undeserved, for Dodge had insufficient interest in the subject to earn him any kind of label relating to labor. At any number of meetings I attended with him in GHQ, and a few luncheons in the Imperial Hotel as well, I never heard him or any of his group mention labor, labor relations, or unions even once.

That did not prevent the unions, however, from being convinced that Dodge was against them. First, his apparently cozy relationship with Finance Minister Ikeda, while he steadfastly refused to see anyone else, bothered them. His consistent attacks on subsidies, some of which the workers regarded as the only thing keeping them afloat, were disturbing. But his most insensitive remark infuriated them: "Nothing," he told the press unsympathetically, "should have been expected [by the Japanese people] as a result of the war but a long term of hardship and self-denial." Now, the Japanese workers and city dwellers were all too cognizant of the penalties of having lost a war that no one had consulted them about in the first place. They had been paying heavily for three and a half years before Dodge arrived, with both the disruption of their lives and the burden of an occupation army. It therefore came with ill grace from a warmly clad and well-fed foreigner, staying in the best hotel in Japan to suggest—in wintertime, too—that they were insufficiently acquainted with hardship and self-denial. How could he know? That kind of sentiment was all too reminiscent of the Japanese aristocrats' historic indifference to the suffering of the "lower" classes.

In the months that followed, Dodge's so-called antilabor attitude seemed to be bearing fruit. Industrial leaders portrayed the Dodge line as one big *gōri-ka* (rationalization) drive. That struck a responsive chord with most GHQ officials, but the Japanese workers and their leaders remembered that ever since the 1930s, *gōri-ka* had been used as a euphemism for mass discharges and pay cuts. In the spring and summer of 1949, those bad old days seemed to be returning, this time under American auspices.

The tail end of the fateful civil service reform initiated the so-called Dodge squeeze. In April the National Personnel Authority announced the prospective elimination of 250,000 jobs in the central government and government-owned enterprises and another 250,000 in the local and prefectural administrations.[12]

As a warning to those who might object, the authorities declared that they would discharge the "undesirable and disloyal" elements first.[13] It was not an idle threat. Between July 1949 and October 1950 almost 11,000 government workers, more than half of them in the railways, communications, and teaching, were discharged for neglect of duty under the National Public Service Law.[14]

Industrialists, pressed by tight credit, followed the government lead. The financially troubled Oki Electric Company, one of the biggest maers of telephones, announced the discharge of 42 percent of its work force.[15] The equally distressed Tokyo Shibaura Electric Company developed plans to let 27,000 out of its 98,000 industrial workers go.[16] Other companies announced more modest but still threatening programs, and discharges followed. By the end of 1949, 330,000 industrial workers and 160,000 government employees, including enterprise workers, had been discharged.[17]

Wage cuts, unknown during a decade of inflation, were for that reason all the more demoralizing. The coal industry, unable to fire workers when production was so urgently needed, went all out to "rationalize" its pay scales. The Miike Colliery of the Mitsui Coal Mining Company, famous for its "Tankō Bushi" coal miners' song, which was featured at all geisha parties, announced wage reductions of 20 percent.[18] The miners, like the moon whose eyes smarted from the Mitsui smokestacks in the song, were deeply troubled by the company's actions. Cuts in the rest of the coal industry averaged 15 percent.[19] Cuts and proposed cuts proliferated.[20] They were all blamed on Dodge. As far as the unions were concerned, management had taken advantage of the stabilization program to launch an offensive against them, and the Americans tolerated, indeed even welcomed, the campaign.

In such a mood of suspicion and disillusionment, the unions quickly seized upon two other GHQ efforts, both entirely unrelated to the economic stabilization program—but one could never tell them that—as part of the overall American design to housebreak labor. The first was a SCAP drive to revise the current labor laws. The second was a campaign to eliminate Communists from key trade union positions in government and vital industries.

LABOR LAW REVISION

In normal circumstances, even during an occupation, there would no doubt have been good, if not urgent, reason for review and revision of the laws to reflect the experience of the first few years of operations. The Trade Union Law, particularly, had been enacted in a rush when there were few unions, not many more unionists, and no experience with democratic labor relations. But why should the initiative be SCAP's? The original idea, when I was in charge of the program in 1946 and 1947, had been to provide a framework for the Japanese themselves to work out their own democratic labor institutions and practices. SCAP agencies might be required to advise and assist if requested or might even be obliged to veto any proposed change compromising democratic principles, but initiatives for improvement were to be up to the Japanese. In most of 1948 that attitude prevailed. Both the Labor Ministry and the SCAP Labor Division worked along on revision ideas in an atmosphere of caution and deliberation.

With the arrival of the NSC directive, however, the circumstances immediately became abnormal. The Labor Division, like the other offices of ESS, had to be *seen* to be working feverishly to implement the new directive—all else was secondary—and inevitably the labor law revisions became part of the Labor Division's "stabilization effort." General Marquat had previously received a memorandum on the labor law revisions from Labor Division Chief Hepler in October 1948 and had hardly glanced at it, because it was highly technical.[21] Now, he suddenly tied Hepler's proposals to the new NSC directive. After all, if the new revisions promoted internal union democracy, he challenged Hepler, that would make it more difficult for outside agitators to capture unions and provoke strikes interfering with production, wouldn't it? Hepler, smiling at the general's oversimplification and naïveté in believing that the strikes were caused by "outside agitators," was afraid to disabuse Marquat, and possibly MacArthur too, for fear that they would then demand far more severe restrictions on labor activities. He thought he had to protect labor against the generals.

As far as Marquat was concerned, he needed no convincing; Hepler was pushing on an open door. From time to time at the staff section meetings in early 1949 the general would call on Hepler to enlighten the other division chiefs on the progress of his important "strike-curbing" legislation and Hepler would comply, never letting on that there was little connection between the revisions and strikes, or the NSC directive either. But as usual, Marquat was far ahead of Hepler. He knew the facts quite well, but he had to contend with William Verity of Armco Steel, Ormond Freile, and other arch-conservatives with potentially embarrassing connections in the States who, as section officials, were present at the staff meetings. Besides, Dodge's office was only a few doors down. No one was going to accuse Marquat of laxity with regard to work stoppages in the present "emergency." Just as Hepler thought he was preempting more severe measures from Marquat with unrelated labor law revisions drawn up long before, so Marquat was preempting potentially drastic antilabor demands from real antiunion elements by means of a little bit of harmless theater at section meetings. In the meantime, the revision bill became tactically imperative. GHQ had to push it.

If in GHQ it was so important to identify the labor law revisions with the economic stabilization program to give them legitimacy, one can hardly blame the Japanese labor leaders for doing the same. In their suspicious eyes the stabilization program looked increasingly like a grand design to restrain labor while industry rationalized. Why was GHQ, after a year of deliberate study, abruptly pressing to get the labor law revisions passed?

When the headstrong Robert Amis, now Labor Relations Branch Chief, repeatedly urged union leaders to withdraw their opposition to the revisions and then sharply warned the Labor Ministry's Labor Administration Bureau Chief, Kaite Saijiro, that strikes being organized by some unions on the issue would be "against Occupation policy," hence forbidden,[22] he confirmed the labor leaders' suspicions. Of course Amis's warning was unauthorized—a standing ban on strikes "against Occupation policy" was a figment of his imagination—but there was no way the unionists could know that. In 1946, the Labor Division and GHQ tolerated mass labor demonstrations and strikes against the far more important SCAP-sponsored Labor Relations Adjustment Bill, but now the Japanese labor unions were being silenced. Meanwhile a law that gave an unfriendly government the legal right to intervene in labor union internal affairs, as the unions understood it, was passing through the parliamentary process. It was not a situation to engender trust in the latter-day Labor Division.

THE RED PURGE

The "red purge" in private industry, in the course of which some 11,000 persons were discharged from July to October 1950[23] and more thereafter, likewise struck the unions as a cause for grave suspicions. In every one of its aspects, it seemed ambiguous, operating on two levels, one ostensible, the other real but concealed. Ostensibly, for instance, the firings took place independently in dozens of industries and hundreds of enterprises. Hardly anyone would have denied that they were, in fact coordinated. Although the reasons given for the discharges were uniformly for communist activity, the real reason is that those discharged were often the most energetic and effective union activists. In theory, being a Communist was not against the law—indeed, the Constitution guaranteed freedom of speech[24] and prohibited discrimination because of "creed"[25]— but a decision of the Fukuoka District Court in September 1950 denied those protections to Communists on the grounds that "the objective of the Japan Communist Party is the bondage of class dictatorial power" and "the guarantee of fundamental rights in the Constitution does not give the right—even in order to realize a certain ideal—to ignore the basic rights of others." Therefore, the court said "such action [the discharge of some Communists by the Asahi newspaper] was a necessary measure of protection against . . . the Communist Party—not a discrimination against the profession of a creed."[26] Finally, although the purge was apparently a completely Japanese initiative, everyone was certain, rightly or wrongly, that the Occupation was behind it all.[27]

From 1945 to 1950, the Supreme Commander and his men had wrestled with the vexing problem of Communists in labor unions as a part of the fundamental dilemma of how to protect a democracy from totalitarians while preserving its democratic character. From the very beginning, while denouncing communism, the Labor Division, with the tacit support of General MacArthur, had taken the position that union members were entitled to elect their own leaders regardless of political beliefs or affiliation. A union president might be a Communist, but as long as the members wanted him to be their president, he was their only legitimate representative. Outside dictation to remove him would clearly be contemptuous of the members' expressed desires, would destroy the legitimacy of the union, and would prove ineffective in the long run. Much more effective and enduring, we contended—pointing to the American experience of the AFL and CIO of "cleaning out" their unions of Communist infiltration—would be for the union members themselves to be convinced that the Communists were less concerned about their interests than with using the unions as a means to seize political power. Labor would then freely reject the Communists. That did happen in the case of the Yomiuri Newspaper Union in 1946 and in the aftermath of the general strike in 1947. Still, it was mostly theory and an exercise in faith, designed to work in the long run. Furthermore, it was a difficult and complex conception, hard for those unacquainted with the actual workings of labor unions—and that included almost all the high-ranking Army brass in GHQ—to understand, let alone feel confident about. And when a crisis erupted, very few would be willing or able to wait for the long run. In mid-1950, such a crisis did erupt. The North Koreans on June 25 invaded South Korea.

Even before that, the fragile arrangement promoted by the Labor Division was being threatened. On January 6, 1950, Moscow ordered the Japan Communist party to reverse its postwar policy of avoiding direct confrontation with the Occupation. On that day, the Cominform Central Committee, meeting in

Bucharest, denounced Nosaka Sanzō, the JCP's third-ranked leader, for being too predisposed to parliamentary activities and hence helping imperialism. After a short flurry of mutiny—the Central Executive Committee member Takenaka Tsunesaburō said the party would ignore the Bucharest criticism,[28] but he soon changed his mind—the JCP knuckled under. A series of incidents erupted in May on the Imperial Palace Plaza. In one, some Communists threw an Army _Stars and Stripes_ photographer into the moat. In another, a group of eight to ten Communists attacked American soldiers coming to the rescue of a Japanese policeman surrounded by a crowd of Communist demonstrators. Meanwhile _Akahata_ (Red Flag), uncensored like the other papers for some time, featured stories casting the _"akage"_ ("red-haired ones"), a code word for Americans, in a bad light.

MacArthur, never one to escalate gradually, reacted powerfully. On June 6 he abruptly purged, that is, banned from public activity, all the members of the Communist Party Central Executive Committee and followed that up the next day by purging seventeen editors of _Akahata_ as well. (Technically, he ordered the Japanese government to apply the provisions of his antinationalist purge directive of January 4, 1946, to the Communist leaders.) Communist Secretary General Tokuda and his comrades promptly went "underground,"[29] fearing more drastic Occupation action to follow. Perhaps the Communists had advance information of the war to come less than three weeks later.

In any event, with the hostilities, attitudes and assumptions changed drastically. The American drive for a self-supporting Japanese economy, which had so dominated Occupation thinking since the advent of William Draper, now quickly became moot, as special procurement orders poured into Japan. The safety of Japan, protected by four under-strength U.S. divisions in a state of combat unreadiness, had nevertheless been taken for granted; now it was put into question. MacArthur, who had seen to the demobilization of the Japanese military and the decentralization of the Japanese police, called for a 75,000-man constabulary to maintain public order. The Japanese, who only a few short years before had their own experience with American bombs, now watched with amusement from the sidewalks as the previously invulnerable Americans filed meekly out of the GHQ buildings in drills against possible air attacks. By whom—the North Koreans, the Russians? The Japanese did not take those possibilities seriously. Nor could they take the other American precautions seriously either.

But to the Americans they were a deadly serious matter. Communists in labor unions now became an immediate danger. Any number of factories producing for the U.N. army in Korea, most prominently Nissan Automobile in Yokohama, had Communist-controlled unions. No responsible security officer could overlook the potential for sabotage and espionage in such factories on the part of those who had just shown themselves to be disciplined tools of the Cominform and hence allies of the North Koreans and Communist Chinese.[30] And so, when Japanese employers, following MacArthur's "purge" lead as they saw it, began to purge, that is to discharge, Communists in key positions in their plants—as they had been doing on a small scale in 1949 and early 1950—the Labor Division not only did not object but encouraged them. It was a drastic change for a SCAP agency that up to then had confined itself to encouraging the anti-Communist Democratization Leagues within the unions and to propaganda and public preaching. Its impact on the mentality of the Japanese unionists as well as employers was great.

On top of the 11,000 government workers who had lost their jobs previously in what then had not yet been labeled a "red purge," the anti-Communist discharges reached a total of 22,000 in all, fifteen times the relatively small number the Occupation had purged from the higher levels of the economy in 1947 and 1948—to the acute distress of American conservatives. It was a large number to be fired, blacklisted, and deprived of their means of livelihood, often on vague and flimsy grounds. Certainly, many were Communists, but quite a few were not. As in all mass ideological purges, fine distinctions between Communists and non- or anti-Communists, or between key jobs requiring special security precautions and ordinary ones, were brushed aside as too time-consuming. Often management did not much care as long as the "troublemakers," that is, the most active union people, were removed. The number of "key" positions expanded beyond reason. In the Kantō Electric Distribution case, for instance, at an enterprise whose operations were almost completely routine, mostly billing customers and collecting the bills, 2,000 in "key jobs" were purged. It would have been hard to list twenty key jobs. And in all this, few of the labor leaders, like the sidewalk skeptics watching the GHQ air raid drills, really thought the exercise necessary. To them the ulterior purpose of the Draconian measure was clear: a big business attack on unions, using anti-Communism as camouflage, while the Occupation looked benignly on.

In the end, most of the unions' fears during the forced-draft stabilization drive and immediately thereafter turned out to be baseless or greatly exaggerated. The "red purge" was soon over. The labor law revisions were not used against the unions to any important extent. Democracy in labor relations survived. Moreover, except in government, where 160,000 workers lost their jobs, the discharges for stabilization reasons were never as bad as advertised, and new private employment took up the slack. By November 1949, six months after the Diet enacted Dodge's deflationary budget, paid industrial employment reached a record postwar high.[31] And even real wages, which Dodge and the stabilizers were at such pains to contain, rose 11 percent between May and October and 9 percent more during November.[32] But the anxiety and mistrust engendered by the Draper–Dodge stabilization program was never dispelled.

The Waning of the Labor Division

Little by little, meaningful communication between the Americans and the Japanese labor movement diminished. The two sides had less and less common ground. At the beginning of the Occupation, the SCAP Labor Division was ready and eager to talk about Japanese labor's concerns: unemployment, low wages, organizational problems, food scarcities. Now it wanted the Japanese unions to talk about the Occupation's concerns: stabilization, the Communists, and preventing strikes. The unions had, of course, quickly outgrown the initial rather elementary lessons in "how to run a union meeting" "how to write a collective bargaining agreement," "the function of shop stewards," grievance procedures, union constitutions, and so forth. (The Labor Education Branch had turned out pamphlets on all those subjects.) In some ways Japanese organizational techniques had since become more thorough and sophisticated than the American. But the Labor Division, its ranks depleted in 1948 by defections and resignations (the division's chief and deputy chief, and the chiefs of both the Labor Relations and Labor Education branches)[33] was more and more incapable of appreciating that fact.

Simplistic anti-Communist lectures, certain, whatever their other merits, to draw the plaudits of such highly placed GHQ officers as the Chief of Staff and G-2, became the order of the day. In one two-week spasm (from September 18 to October 2, 1948), the press reported five public anti-Communist speeches by the SCAP Labor Education Branch chief, including one address before 50,000 persons at Kōshien Stadium near Kobe. I could never find out how many others were not reported in the newspapers.

Similar discourses—sometimes harangues—were delivered to union officials visiting GHQ. But to the increasingly experienced and sophisticated executives of unions and federations, some of which numbered hundreds of thousands, anti-Communist lectures were thin fare. Even where the Japanese leaders agreed, they often left in despair at the ignorance of the newly appointed American labor officials as to the real complications and power struggles within the labor movement that made simple, pat solutions impossible. The SCAP people regularly talked down to the Japanese leaders, and those leaders were painfully aware of it. "I remember how humiliated I felt," Valery Burati recounted many years later,[34] "when Amis . . . shook his finger at Takano [Minoru] as to a child, and how Takano sat there calmly and kept his own counsel." Takano had had only twenty years of experience as a labor leader, Amis perhaps two months in labor relations. Thus it was that the steady stream of Japanese labor people, who had visited GHQ in the early days for assistance and encouragement, dwindled to a trickle. And when they came, the visit was usually an unpleasant chore for them.

As connections between the Labor Division and the unions became strained, the relations between the Labor Division and the leadership of ESS became distant, too. In 1947 physically, and perhaps symbolically, the Labor Division moved out of the ESS building into its own quarters almost half a mile away. The division got more space and the appearance of independence but lost the daily intimacy that alone could keep its officers aware of the nuances of changing GQP policy. As the reform fervor departed from GHQ, the Labor Division, whose sole reason for existence was reform, progressively lost the attention of its section chief. Hardly any of the Labor Division's actions in 1949 and 1950 received much attention from General Marquat or his advisers (including me, because, although an ex-Labor chief, I had promised my successors to stay out of labor affairs). We in the "front office" had no idea, for example, that Amis had "prohibited" a railway strike until we read about it in the newspapers.

Of all the SCAP officials, only Burati maintained regular personal contact with Japanese labor leaders like Takano and the Coal Miners' Union (Tanrō) chief, Mutō Takeo—he taught Mutō and his wife to play canasta—and he was, moreover, deeply committed to arranging the organization of the giant federation, Sōhyō, to unify Japanese labor. But when General Marquat heard of Burati's efforts and asked me what on earth Burati was doing, I had to tell him that SCAP had received no directive from Washington on the subject and that such an important project as national labor unification was Burati's own idea!

Even the tenuous Burati–Mutō–Takano connection soon broke down. Burati was sent home when his contract expired, after he protested vehemently against the Occupation–Japanese Government decision to deny the use of the Imperial Palace Plaza to the unions for the 1951 celebration of May Day. Mutō was defeated for reelection as Coal Miners' Union president. And the 4-million-member Sōhyō united federation that Burati had worked so hard to create broke away from its pro-American leadership to become internationally neutralist and opposed to U.S. military bases in Japan at its very first anniversary convention in March 1952.[36] Japanese labor had confirmed its disillusionment with America.

25

The Balance Sheet

STABILIZATION, ECONOMIC MIRACLE, BROKEN DIALOGUE

And so the bankers had their way. The American taxpayer was rescued, even though at his own expense and in a way he never expected. The foundations of Japanese recovery—stabilized prices, rational financing, and reemphasized private enterprise—were laid. In the mythology of the Occupation, and to a large extent in conventional Japanese wisdom as well, it was on this rock that the Japanese built their miracle economy. The American-backed recovery effort, supported by American financing, proved the key to a Japanese rebirth of dimensions that no one had even remotely foreseen.

THE ROOTS OF THE JAPANESE "MIRACLE"

In reality, it was by no means as simple as that. Without question, American aid—$2 billion over six years in food, fertilizer, petroleum products, and industrial raw materials—was indispensable. Without it there is no telling how long Japan's recovery might have been delayed and what social cataclysms might have been triggered by mass starvation and unrest. But whether the deflationary straitjacket into which the United States pushed Japan in 1949 in order to qualify for continuing aid had such momentous long-range benefits is open to question. The monetary push did indeed seem of overwhelming consequence in 1949 and 1950. But with the passage of the years and the improvement of perspective, its importance receded, and other features of the lengthening postwar economic terrain came to seem more important. They have far overshadowed the significance of the brief—only a year and a half—monetary squeeze that began and ended more than thirty years ago.

Foremost among those features, perhaps, was the inordinate Japanese passion for saving. The American bankers' insistence on ensuring adequate capital investment for the future by way of a super-balanced budget and counterpart fund was credited with laying the basis for Japan's subsequent rapid growth. But if ever anyone preached to the converted, it was the Americans telling the Japanese to set apart a greater part of their gross national product for long-range growth. How did anyone think the Japanese had industrialized their four small, poorly endowed islands in half the time it had taken Europe? The entire structure of prewar economic Japan, from discriminatory taxes, preferential interest and loans, industrial subsidies, and *zaibatsu* collaboration, up to suppressing labor unions and squeezing peasants—indeed the whole gamut of economic arrangements—was organized around the imperative of capital accumulation and industrial reinvestment.

The militarist decade and the war were an aberration in the use to which the capital thus raised was put, but the system of forced accumulation remained intact and, what is more, comfortably acceptable in principle to the Japanese people. It was not American lectures that caused the Japanese to resume the decades-long practice but rather an overwhelming national consensus that theirs was a poor country and everybody had to sacrifice to build it up. In a world more given to immediate gratification and satisfied with lower rates of growth, the saving of one-third of national income annually[1] was phenomenal, but it was not America's doing. The roots of that part of the 1980 Japanese national character lay in the 1880s, if not earlier, and certainly not in the sermonizing of the American bankers.

But even a massive national drive for capital accumulation could not have achieved anywhere near as much were it not for the American defense umbrella, which, beginning with the Occupation period, allowed Japan to invest the fruits of its savings in industry instead of an army and navy. In 1982, Japan spent less than 1 percent of its national income on defense. In 1936, the last year before the "China incident," it spent nine times as much on the Army and Navy openly and a good deal more in indirect support besides.[2] The release of funds released facilities and people, too. For example, the great naval shipyards at Kure in the early 1950s became a prime exporter to Daniel Ludwig's National Bulk Carriers, and Japan's brilliant career as shipbuilder to the world was launched. A brand-new Sony Corporation was staffed originally with demobilized electronics engineers from the Imperial Japanese Navy. Both Nikon and Canon were able to set aside the production of aerial bombsights for the design and development of one of Japan's first postwar export "stars," 35 mm. precision cameras.

Equally indispensable was the underlying beneficence of the Occupation toward the Japanese themselves. Without that basic attitude of helpfulness, reflected from the beginning in the sympathetic attitude of the great mass of officers, soldiers, and Occupation civilians, Japan's postwar handicaps might have proved too difficult to surmount. One has only to compare the American treatment of the Japanese with the Soviet pillaging and industrial plant removals in Eastern Europe, Korea, and Manchuria, to say nothing of the Russian enslavement of 600,000 Japanese prisoners of war. In contrast, the Occupation returned great amounts of surrendered Japanese military matériel to the civil economy and encouraged and allowed the return of much more that had been concealed or hoarded without confiscating any of it for U.S. purposes. In all, the quantities ran into billions of dollars in value, a tribute, of course, to the wisdom of Japan's early surrender, which preserved them from destruction, but a tribute also to the unselfishness of the American Occupation. Those stocks formed the unappreciated foundation of the initial postwar recovery.

Nor can one underrate the enormous contribution of the American Occupation Commander, General Douglas MacArthur, toward the rebirth of Japan. Playing one of the most improbable roles in modern history, foreign father figure to a conquered nation, the essentially populist General was able—in large part because so many thought he was ultra-conservative—to carry out a radical reform, inspired, although he did not know it, by New Deal ideas. The result was the transformation of a society based on mass sacrifice of the vast majority for the state to one based on democratic concepts of equity and justice. Converting a stern Occupation of control and restraint into one of reconciliation and cooperation, MacArthur protected Japan from reparations assaults, insisted on disproportionate food imports, and inspired the Japanese nation once more to believe in itself. The stability that followed was undeniable. It is highly problematical whether any other Occupation commander—certainly no other name on the list of high-ranking American military or naval officers of the time suggests itself— could have done nearly so well, and it is entirely conceivable that anyone else in such a unique and complex mission could have been disastrous for Japan, at least in the short run.

But by far the longest-lasting influence of Occupation policy on Japanese recovery was economic democratization, that portion of New Deal ideology that became official fiat only in the few weeks immediately after the surrender. The freeing of the farmers from their debts and rents and the unionization and collective bargaining of millions of white-collar and blue-collar workers created a domestic mass market for consumer goods for the first time in Japanese history. The passage of time makes it very difficult indeed to imagine now the abysmal poverty of the prewar Japanese peasant, who bought almost nothing above his very barest necessities from year to year. Nor were most workers much better off. To base a national economy on the purchasing power of those two classes, even though they constituted four out of every five Japanese, would have seemed suicidal. And yet, in less than a year the peasants were acquiring all kinds of secondhand goods with scarce rice, and in only another year or so, immediately after the land reform, they started expanding their houses, and with that, consumer goods purchases. (One peasant beneficiary[3] bought the grandfather clock he had been admiring in the village store window for years.) The workers' improvement was delayed until near the end of 1947, but real wages doubled in the following twelve months and then doubled again. Despite the monetary squeeze, by June 1950, just before the outbreak of the Korean War, real wages were already exceeding 1934–36 prewar levels by some 30 percent.[4] It was the very opposite of a policy of imposed sacrifice to make up Japan's wartime losses.

That the burgeoning purchasing power of those groups, plus that of the businessmen who served them, stimulated the whole productive apparatus is beyond denial, but that it also stimulated an enormous expansion of exports is unusually overlooked. It was long the axiom of the GHQ monetarists, and Washington too, that exports and domestic consumption were competitors for the national product. The opposite turned out to be true. It is an old businessman's aphorism that you can't sell goods from an empty shelf. Furthermore, as a rule, a maker with no experience can hardly make sophisticated goods to order. Manufacturers, whether big or little, can only modify and improve what they are already making. And that, of course, was the key to understanding Japan's postwar export achievement. Japanese industry had first to produce for domestic consumers—under highly protected conditions, to be sure—before they would be ready to stock their shelves with merchandise salable on the world market.

At first their motorcycles, with engines designed for three-wheelers, were too slow, their refrigerators were experimental, their televisions sets were too small, their automobiles rode like trucks and didn't look much better. But they could be sold domestically. With that market as a backup, and with the spur of domestic competition, Japanese makers were able to put great efforts into research, planning, the marshaling of capital, and physical plant expansion with consequent economies of scale. Nissan Motors was able to buy engine blueprints from Continental Engines for 1 percent of gross sales,[5] and YKK was able to invest in the latest zipper-making machinery imported from the United States. In time, the Japanese brought their consumer products up to and above world standards and captured world markets. But how could they have done so without enough local consumers in the first place?

Nowhere was this development more vividly demonstrated than in the hordes of electric appliance salesmen squatting in the village street across from the local food corporation office in the fall, when the farmers and their wives arrived in the 1950s and 1960s to collect their payments for the harvest. The electric juicers, rice cookers, vacuum cleaners, and "room coolers" that competed for the farm wife's eye, to say nothing of the small power cultivators the farmer bought, were all tried out on the Japanese first and then, suitably improved, sold overseas. A generation before, the same farmers or their parents had sold their daughters into mills and brothels to buy food, and only silk *habutae,* celluloid toys, and small electric bulbs could be offered to foreign buyers from what was then normal production for the Japanese market at home.

Thus did economic democratization unwittingly elevate Japan from a pre-war exporter of shoddy copies made to importers' orders at low prices to its present eminence as a premier maker and supplier of quality consumer goods to the world. Indeed, had the Occupation not launched its broad economic democratization, those new consumers could have come out of the immediate postwar period as impoverished and neglected as before. A Japanese industry concentrating only on exports and capital equipment—for that is where the purchasing power would have been—would have had a much harder row to hoe in developing world markets and building up the country. Increasing real wages, the Washington economists had thought, were a menace to the Japanese economy; instead they turned out to be its savior.

Indeed, an ingenious economic bureaucracy in the Ministries of Finance and International Trade and Industry put consumer purchasing power to work supporting exports very early. After all, who but the domestic consumer paid for high interest rates incorporated into high domestic prices to support low interest rates for exports? Who bought sugar high so that ships could be exported low, and who ultimately paid the exporters for their excess raw material import licenses, which they sold to producers for domestic needs at high prices? One wonders how that ingenious system could have worked without adequate farm and wage-earners' income to support it.

Compared to the Japanese passion for saving, the American defense umbrella, the fundamental beneficence of the occupiers, MacArthur's monumental role, and, above all, the epochal explosion of the domestic mass market consequent upon economic democratization, the contribution of the short-lived Washington forced-recovery-stabilization program of 1949 to the postwar economic miracle was, by any measure, relatively unimportant.

U.S.–Japanese Business Alliance

It was not unimportant at all, however, in Japan's subsequent relations with the United States. From the stabilization-recovery effort of 1948–50 emerged a long-lasting *de facto* alliance between the conservative and big business elements of both countries. Before the war there had been some close business connections—Westinghouse–Mitsubishi, General Electric–Tokyo Shibaura, Libby Owens Ford–Nippon Sheet Glass, Bache–Mitsui Bussan, B. F. Goodrich–Yokohama Rubber—but they were relatively few, and the Japanese had also been serious commercial rivals as well, especially on the Asian mainland. A weakened Japan now offered no such threat. Instead, the menace came from the Chinese Communist tide and a collapsing Nationalist government. American big business, sparked by Draper and Dodge, rallied round to prevent Japan, too, from falling prey to the Communists by way of a chronically depressed economy. The succession of American big businessmen who participated actively in the Japanese recovery program all passed the same message to the American business community: Help the Japanese economy, strengthen Japanese private business, and support the conservatives in Japan.

While American business went all out to save them, the Japanese conservatives were extremely helpful to the American Administration in return. In the difficult year of the Dodge deflation, that is, from the passage of his budget in May 1949 till the outbreak of the Korean War, the Yoshida regime assumed the burden of fronting for Dodge and absorbing a good bit of the enmity engendered by his policies. (True, it could always say when pressed too hard that it had no choice in the matter.) That was a small price for Yoshida to pay for the attainment of his central foreign policy goal: an alliance with the American conservative power, Japan's only sure ally in a chaotic, still hostile postwar world. And in that he succeeded. Japan had no more constant supporter in its efforts to join the United Nations, affiliate with the General Agreement on Trade and Tariffs, or ward off discrimination, in a word, to reenter the family of nations. And Yoshida entered the pantheon of master Japanese statesmen.

Mutually supportive policies were soon reflected in a growing network of personal relationships of conservative politicians and businessmen between both countries. Forged in the heat of the stabilization program, the Dodge–Ikeda relationship led all the rest. But other officials going abroad—Prime Minister Yoshida, Bank of Japan Governor Ichimanda, Ambassador Asakai (Yoshida's liaison man to ESS in his first cabinet), who played golf with President Eisenhower—cemented the connection. Visits of businessmen, however, were by far the most numerous. On the Japanese side, certainly, such visits were the easiest to get foreign exchange for. Soon the two-way flow of Japanese and American business executives across the Pacific dwarfed all other contacts.

A generation of Japanese businessmen who had been cut off from the West saw America first, while any number of business Americans made new ties in Japan or renewed their old ones. One visit, by Harold Bache to Tokyo in 1952, was replete with reunions, for he had worked briefly for Mitsui & Company in New York in 1921. The reunions culminated in the acquisition by the partners and associates of Bache & Company, then the second biggest American stockbroker and one of the largest commodity brokers in the world, of a quarter of the stock of Mitsui's successor, Daiichi Bussan. The doors that the alliance opened may be imagined. In the oil business, all the Japanese companies had American counterparts. Caltex held 51 percent of Kōa Oil, Tidewater 50 percent of Mitsubishi Oil, and Standard of New Jersey 55 percent of Toā Nenryō. Caltex built the Kawasaki refinery for Nippon Petroleum Refining. In comparison, parallel connections between other Japanese and American elements—educational, theatrical, labor, literary, scientific, musical, even religious—were primitive. After all, there was no economic benefit to Japan, and Japan was striving above all for its economic reconstruction.

It is no wonder that the American, especially the official American, view of Japan, refracted through the eyes of businessmen and business relations, became more and more aligned with the Japanese conservative view of things. By November 1953, the conservatives' tacit alliance between the two countries had grown so close that Vice President Richard Nixon could apologize before the Japan–America Society in Tokyo for the "excesses" of the Occupation. (The ex-occupationnaires still living in Tokyo were outraged.) Perhaps one of the "excesses" was the arrest by the prosecutors some five years before, on charges of theft of ex-Japanese Army goods, of the president of the society, who now sat beside Nixon on the dais and nodded approvingly at every word.

Conversely, official American ties to the Japanese trade unions, Socialists, and most intellectuals were shunned. Nixon's visit undoubtedly discouraged American Embassy officials from talking with the "left" in Japan. Samuel Berger, the labor attaché at the time (later Ambassador to Korea and Vietnam), had an argument over policy at the embassy with Nixon, who had insisted on meeting the senior staff. The Vice President recognized Berger as "one of Harriman's boys" in London, that is, a New Deal Democrat, and Berger soon found himself posted to New Zealand. But Nixon did not set the tone; he merely exemplified it. The American embassy staff was perhaps too intimidated by the current American "red purge" to want to be identified with "leftists," even Japanese leftists, in the line of duty. For example, the Fulbright Commission, set up to award American scholarships to young Japanese, had certified only conservative resident businessmen for its American nonofficial members. When a vacancy occurred in 1951, an influential friend in the Civil Information and Education Section in GHQ, still then in operation, recommended me, then a resident businessman in Tokyo, but one with numerous labor and Socialist connections, to give "balance" to the commission. The reply was that the commission needed no balance. The alliance with Japanese conservatives was enough.

The Japanese trade unionists and Socialists, and their intellectual allies, felt for their part that the Americans had encouraged them, misled them, even exposed them, and then cast them aside. The naïve enthusiasm of the early Occupation Socialist leaders that a "capitalistic" America would have to cooperate with them to make sure that those who had caused the war would not revive gave way to disillusion. The United States was a "capitalist" country, the new Socialist formulation ran, and so intrinsically warlike, while Red China and the U.S.S.R. were "socialist" countries and so inherently peace-loving. Every American move in the 1950s was viewed through a miasma of suspicion and contention. It was a bitter cup for Americans to drink after the devoted efforts of so many for the cause of the ordinary Japanese, the millions of tons of food shipped to them, and the huge sums of money expended on their behalf. Besides that, the new formulation was just plain silly. But neither side was listening to the other any more.

Eleven years after Dodge's departure from Japan, in the wake of riots and street demonstrations that had kept President Eisenhower from visiting and had overturned Prime Minister Kishi, an astute Harvard professor, Edwin O. Reischauer, in a memorable article entitled "Broken Dialogue with Japan," called attention to the fact that American and Japanese intellectuals were no longer in contact with one another.[6] The article caught the eye of President-elect Kennedy, who was impressed, invited Reischauer for a talk, and named him his Ambassador to Japan. Reischauer was one of the best of our American ambassadors, certainly the most popular, and he did succeed in reopening channels of communication. But the breakdown was not so simply repaired, for it was not a historical freak, an American oversight, or even the result of the anti-Communist paranoia of the early 1950s. Nor was it only an affair of Japanese intellectuals, who, by creating the climate of opinion in Japan within which the "real" political and economic powers worked, effectively limited those powers' freedom of action. For in Japan, the intellectuals were the natural allies of the left— the urban workers, the trade unions, and the Socialists—and those elements were not to be easily assuaged.

In the name of the American taxpayer, Forrestal, Draper, Dodge, and the U.S. Congress had pushed and financed Japan to a rapid attainment of self-support and an economic takeoff far beyond that, but on condition that Japan follow conservative "capitalist" lines. It is likely that the Japanese would have done so anyway. And quite probably they would have recovered almost as fast without the final American insistence on fiscal orthodoxy. But, because of the condition an opportunity was lost to America and years of work abandoned. For in the event, one-third of the nation saw those decisions as foreign dictation. The third turn in Japan's history, which has started in 1945–47 with an overwhelmingly pro-American national consensus, ended in an emotionally divided public and an incomplete alliance.

That could not, however, alter the third turn itself. By that time, the radical reform had already worked its way into the fabric of Japan's society. The last years of Occupation stewardship did not undo the labors of the first three and a half, nor were they intended to. Not for a moment did the monetarists and bankers dream of canceling the land reform, abolishing labor rights, or even recombining the *zaibatsu* trusts. True, not one Occupation democratizer in Washington, Tokyo, or anywhere else received the Order of the Sacred Treasure, any class. But democratization, confirmed by the Japanese people themselves once they became independent, had irretrievably transformed the social structure of Japan and in the course of doing so helped create a far more prosperous land than ever before.

Epilogue

ONE HOT, SUNNY August day in 1970, when I was still living in Japan, a roving television reporter approached several people in and around Tokyo, on the beach near Kamakura, on a Ginza street, at a noodle shop in Kanda, and on the train platform at Shibuya station and asked them if they knew the significance of the day. It was August 15, the twenty-fifth anniversary of the end of the Pacific war. His responses were mostly blank stares, some wild guesses, and a few shamefaced apologies, but only one or two correct answers. Later that evening, in a side street in the restaurant area near Tameike crossing, a street stall was set up, serving free to all passers-by samples of the cooked dishes that the hungry Japanese in 1946 and 1947 were substituting for unavailable rice: concoctions of sweet potatoes, cabbages, and U.S. Army surplus peas, all without soy sauce. The TV cameras recorded their sour faces at the taste and their surprise when they were told what it was. In 1981 a Japanese youngster happened upon his parents watching old postwar newsreel footage on television, joined them for a while, and then asked, "Okā-chan [Mama], what country is that?"

None of those reactions is particularly surprising, because Japan had been reborn in such a different guise, and if the children of the rebirth were not aware of the traumatic parturition, well, that was only natural. It has been otherwise with the older generations. To them, even today, almost four decades afterward, the short six or seven years of the military Occupation were of a momentousness without parallel. Their nation's headlong militarist course had just come to a shattering stop less than eighty years after abandoning feudal isolation, and where were they now to go? The Occupation told them, and the country was thereby changed. It was not just a matter of physical restoration and reconstruction, nor even the establishment of a political democracy, excised of its militarist demons and endowed with civil rights and political freedoms. It was the wholesale transformation of the economy and society. A once solidly stratified social structure turned mostly middle-class, an insulated land found its sons and

463

daughters—tourists and businessmen—poking into every nook and cranny of the civilized world and keeping up with the latest fads. Material affluence, in a land where impoverished farmers had sold their daughters to the mills and brothels, reached the levels of "my home," "my car," and all the other "mys." And Japan attained international respect and recognition as never before.

But how much of that was really attributable to a foreign occupation? The accomplishments of the Japanese for more than three decades have been their own, those of a highly gifted, innovative, capable, and industrious people. When the nation exhausted the possibilities of its previous course, the Japanese people would have had to change their direction anyway. Why could they not have pulled off the same kind of third turn without the Americans?

The fact is that they could not, and the older Japanese know it well. It was not only the massive food aid, the defense against foreign reparations claims, and American sponsorship of Japan in its return to the international community, nor was it yet the democratic political models like the Constitution, or even the American insistence on a radical economic democratization. There was also something more fundamental. In a recent television interview, Professor Takasaka Takashi of Kyoto University put his finger squarely on the reason. Of course, he said, no one likes a military occupation in his own country. But in Japan the Occupation was indispensable, for only a powerful force from outside could have broken the immensely tenacious traditional mold, and without breaking it Japan could not have made its postwar transformation. His words went to the root of the matter.

For it was not that Japan did not have the ability and imagination—most Occupation reforms indeed had Japanese advocates who were active before the war—but the old-line interests, and traditional habits of thought too, were too powerful and too well entrenched to be easily overcome. Even after a disastrous defeat, they were still in place. There is little question but that if the victorious Allies had stood aside and simply ordered the Japanese what to do—disarm, demilitarize, even democratize—the Japanese would have done so. But they would have done so in their own way. The old line would have remained intact, the old mold as constricting as ever. And that would have meant only a very partial transformation at best.

But that most extraordinary of occupations would not stand aside. It intruded brashly into every sphere of Japanese life. It allowed blind traditionalism no respite. Every institution, every privilege, every custom, every way of doing things, even the age-old insistence on the imperative of sacrifice of the individual, was questioned. The Japanese who themselves wanted to transform Japan were inspired and invigorated. The Occupation was their unexpected, invaluable, and, for a time, irreplaceable ally. American radical reform, applied by Douglas MacArthur, an inspirational leader without peer, did more than liberate Japan. It freed the dynamism of the Japanese people as well, and they went on from there.

A

Yen–Dollar Equivalency Table

To ASSIST in comprehension of the magnitudes of the various yen figures cited in the text in the absence of a unitary exchange rate for most of the Occupation, the following table of approximate yen equivalents of one U.S. dollar has been constructed on the basis of the monthly indexes for wholesale prices up to September 1946 and retail consumer price indexes thereafter in *JES*, with adjustments for the rising price levels in the United States. Since no exports or imports moved and no currency exchanges were made at these rates, they are merely a theoretical guide.

1934–36		3.4	1947	June	142
1945	August	13.6		September	190
	December	31		December	200
1946	March	40	1948	March	231
	June	55		June	248
	September	67		September	304
	December	71		December	324
1947	January	80	1949	March	355
	March	99		June	360 (official rate)

B

Abbreviations

1. In English

AC	Antitrust and Cartels Division, GHQ SCAP
ACJ	Allied Council for Japan
ACLU	American Civil Liberties Union
ADC	Arms Disposal Committee
AFL	American Federation of Labor
AFPAC	Army Forces Pacific
AFWESPAC	Army Forces Western Pacific
AJSC	All Joint Struggle Committee
AP	Associated Press
ATIS	Allied Translator and Interpreter Service, GEQ SCAP
BCOF	British Commonwealth Occupation Forces
BEW	Board of Economic Warfare, U.S.
CAC	Country and Area Committee, U.S. State Department
CAD	Civil Affairs Division, a special staff section of the C/S U.S. Army
CAF	Clerical-Administrative-Fiscal, a category of the U.S. Federal Civil Service
CASA	Civil Affairs Staging Area, in Monterey, Calif.
CCD	Civil Censorship Detachment, GHQ SCAP
CCS	Civil Communications Section, GHQ, SCAP
CG	Commanding General
CIC	Counter Intelligence Corps
CID	Criminal Investigation Division, Provost Marshal
CIE	Civil Information and Education Section, GHQ SCAP
C-in-C	Commander-in-Chief

CINCAFPAC	Commander-in-Chief Army Forces Pacific
CINCAFWESPAC	Commander-in-Chief, Army Forces Western Pacific
CIO	Congress of Industrial Organizations
CIS	Civil Intelligence Section, GHQ SCAP
CLO	Central Liaison Office, Japanese Government
CLRC	Central Labor Relations Committee, Japanese Government
C/N	Checknote
CO	Commanding Officer
COMNAVFE	Commander Naval Forces Far East
CPC	Civil Property Custodian, GHQ SCAP
CPS	Civil Personnel Section, GHQ FEC
C/S	Chief of Staff
CSCAD	See CAD
CTS	Civil Transportation Section, GHQ SCAP
DCA	Deputy Contraband Administrator
D C/S	Deputy Chief of Staff
DRB	Deconcentration Review Board, GHQ SCAP
EIS	Economic Institutions Staff, of FEA, U.S. Government
EROA	Economic Rehabilitation of Occupied Areas
ESB	Economic Stabilization Board, Japanese Government
ESS	Economic and Scientific Section, GHQ SCAP
ESS/LA	Labor Division of ESS
FEA	Foreign Economic Administration, U.S. Government
FEC	Far East Command
FEC	Far Eastern Commission
FEC-230	Policy on Excessive Concentrations of Economic Power in Japan, paper submitted to FEC
FSO	Foreign service officer
G-1	Assistant C/S or General Staff Section, Personnel
G-2	Assistant C/S or General Staff Section, Intelligence
G-3	Assistant C/S or General Staff Section, Operations
G-4	Assistant C/S or General Staff Section, Supply
G-5	Assistant C/S or General Staff Section, Military Government
GARIOA	Government and Relief in Occupied Areas
GHQ	General Headquarters
GS	Government Section, GHQ SCAP
HCLC	Holding Companies Liquidation Commission, Japanese Government
IMTFE	International Military Tribunal Far East
INS	International News Service
IP	Imperial Palace

IRAA	Imperial Rule Assistance Association
IRAPS	Imperial Rule Assistance Political Society
JAG	Judge Advocate General, GHQ FEC
JCAC	Joint Civil Affairs Committee of CAD and JCS
JCP	Japan Communist Party
JCS	Joint Chiefs of Staff
JCS 1067	JCS Directive to SHAEF, Supreme Headquarters Allied Expeditionary Force in Europe
JCS 1380 series	Basic Initial Post-Surrender Directive to SCAP for the Occupation and Control of Japan
JCS 1380/5	Part I, General and Political
JCS 1380/8	Part II, Economic and Financial
JCS 1380/15	Complete directive
JFGRWU	Japan Federation of Government Railway Workers Unions
JNR	Japan National Railways
JSC	Joint Struggle Committee
JWPC	Joint War Plans Committee of JCS
LRC	Labor Relations Committee
LS	Legal Section, GHQ SCAP
MCI	Ministry of Commerce and Industry, Japanese Government
MG	Military Government
MITI	Ministry of International Trade and Industry, Japanese Government
MP	Military Police
MPB	Metropolitan Police Board, Japanese Government
NCIU	National Congress of Industrial Unions (*Sanbetsu*)
NRS	Natural Resources Section, GHQ SCAP
NSC	National Security Council, U.S.
NSC 13/2	Recommendations with Respect to U.S. Policy Toward Japan
OAS	Occupied Areas Section, U.S. Navy
OCI	Overseas Consultants Incorporated
OEW	Office of Economic Warfare, U.S.
OIC	Officer in charge
OPA	Office of Price Administration, U.S.
OSS	Office of Strategic Services, U.S.
PHW	Public Health and Welfare Section, GHQ SCAP
PM	Provost Marshal
POLAD	Political Adviser, from State Department to SCAP
PWC	Postwar Committee of State Department
PWC-296	Japan: Economic Policies During the Military Occupation
RA	Research and Analysis Branch, OSS

RAA   Recreation and Amusement Association
RFB   Reconstruction Finance Bank
S-5   Planning Staff Section, Civil Affairs, in CASA
SCAJAP   Shipping Control Authority Japan
SCAP   Supreme Commander for the Allied Powers
SCAPIN   SCAP Instruction, that is, SCAP directive
SCAPIN 411   Directive on Rural Land Reform
SEC   Securities and Exchange Commission, U.S. Govt.
SHAEF   Supreme Headquarters, Allied Expeditionary Forces,
                      Europe
SFE   SWNCC Subcommittee on the Far East
SFE 182   Policy on Excessive Concentrations of Economic Power
                      (essentially same as FEC 230 and SWNCC 302/2)
SWNCC   State–War–Navy Coordinating Committee
SWNCC 70/5   National Composition of Forces
SWNCC 90/1   Control of Food and Agriculture
SWNCC 92/1   Treatment of Japanese Workers Organizations
SWNCC 150/1-4   Initial Post-Surrender Policy for Japan
TS   Territorial Studies Division, State Department
UP   United Press
VIP   Very Important Person
WAC   Women's Army Corps
WPB   War Production Board, U.S.
YAC   Youth Action Corps

2. In Japanese

Denkō   Electric Machinery Workers Union
Densan   Electric Power Workers Union
Kanrō   All-Japan Government Administrative Employees Union
Kōrō   All-Japan Government and Public Workers Union
NHK   Nihon Hōsōkyoku (Japan Broadcasting Corporation)
Nikkyōso   Japan Teachers Union
Rōhō   *Rōmu Hōkoku-kai*, Laborers Patriotic Association
Sanbetsu   Congress of Industrial Unions
Sanpō   *Sangyō Hōkoku-kai*, Industrial Patriotic Association (to-
                      gether with *Rōhō*, the wartime Labor Front)
Seinen Kōdō-tai   Youth Action Corps
Sōdōmei   Japan General Federation of Labor
Tanrō   Coal Miners Union
Yoyogi   Communist Party Headquarters at Yoyogi, in Tokyo
Zentei   All Communications Workers Union

C

Organization Charts

CHART 1. General Headquarters. Far East Command. September 10, 1947.

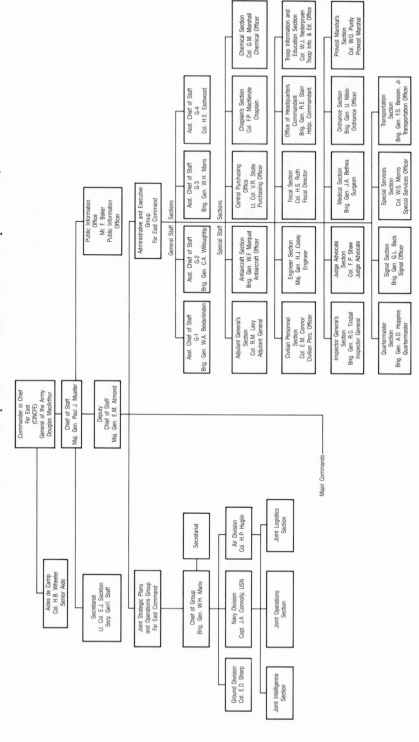

CHART 2. General Headquarters. Supreme Commander for the Allied Powers.
August 26, 1946.

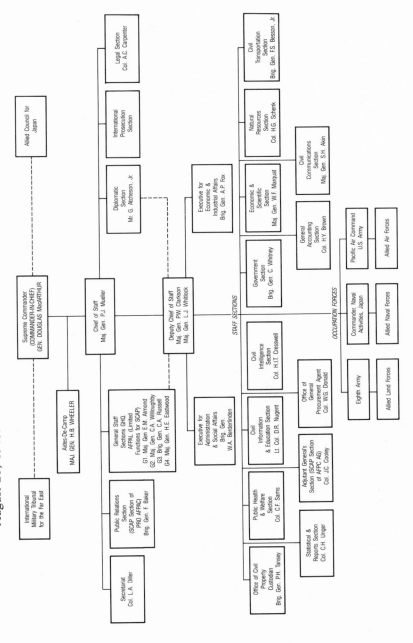

Notes

Sources Frequently Cited in Notes

Economic SCAPINS	*SCAPINS, SCAP Instructions to the Japanese Government issued by Economic and Scientific Section from 4 September 1945 to 8 March 1952,* Far East Command Printing and Publication Center
FRUS	*Foreign Relations of the U.S., Department of State,* Bureau of Public Affairs, Historical Office, annually
JES	*Japanese Economic Statistics,* GHQ SCAP, Economic and Scientific Section, Research and Statistics Division, monthly. Continued after the occupation by Economic Counsel Board, Japanese Government
JYB	*Japan Year Book,* Foreign Association of Japan, Tokyo, annually.
LDMR	*Labor Division Monthly Report,* Labor Division, ESS GHQ SCAP, mimeographed monthly. These are identical with the Labor chapters of the monthly SCAP Summations.
Mission and Accomplishments	*Mission and Accomplishments of the Supreme Commander for the Allied Powers in the Economic and Scientific Fields,* ESS GHQ SCAP, Tokyo, first edition September 26, 1949, second edition June 1950, printed by the Far East Command Printing Plant
NT	*Nippon Times*
OJEPR	*The Occupation of Japan Economic Policy and Reform,* Proceedings of a Symposium Sponsored by MacArthur Memorial, April 13–15, 1978, MacArthur Memorial, Norfolk, Virginia
PRJ	*Political Reorientation of Japan, September 1945 to September 1948,* report of the Government Section of SCAP, in two volumes, U.S. Government Printing Office
SCAP Monthly Summation	*Summation of Non-Military Activities,* GHQ SCAP, Tokyo
TCP	Theodore Cohen's papers, in the possession of the author's estate

Tōshiba Strike Materials	*Tōshiba Jūgatsu Tōsō Shiryō (Materials on the Tōshiba October Strike) 1946,* a collection of leaflets, mimeographed strike newspaper, and miscellaneous materials, bound and presented to the author by the Tōshiba labor union, in *TCP*
WP	*Willoughby Papers,* a collection of documents belonging to Major General Charles Willoughby, now in MacArthur Memorial, Norfolk, Virginia

A Personal Note

1. The Press Relations (later the Public Information) Office issued a continuous barrage of press releases, Government Section published its official history with hundreds of documents, the Economic and Scientific Section put out all its formal directives and economic statistics, various other sections produced dozens of special reports, and all sections joined in turning out a running account, the *SCAP Monthly Summation of Non-Military Activities,* amounting to a few hundred pages every thirty days through August 1948.

2. Alfred Oppler, *Legal Reform in Occupied Japan: A Participant Looks Back* (Princeton, N.J.: Princeton University Press, 1976).

3. William Woodard, *The Allied Occupation of Japan, 1945–52, and Japanese Religions* (Leyden: Brill, 1972).

4. Justin Williams, Sr., *Japan's Political Revolution Under MacArthur: A Participant's Account* (Tokyo, Tokyo University Press, 1979).

5. Elliott Thorpe, *East Wind, Rain* (Boston: Gambit Press, 1969).

6. Courtney Whitney, *MacArthur: His Rendezvous with History* (New York: Knopf, 1956).

7. Charles Willoughby, *MacArthur 1945–51* (New York: McGraw-Hill, 1954).

8. Mark Orr, who held an important position in the Education Division of the Civil Information and Education Section dealing with the education reforms, wrote about that phase of the Occupation in his doctoral dissertation: "Education Reform Policy in Occupied Japan," University of North Carolina, 1954–55.

   A few monographs have been written by individuals who were involved in the events but at some distance. Among those, Hans Baerwald, *The Purge of Japanese Leaders Under the Occupation* (Berkeley: University of California Press, 1959), and Eleanor Hadley, *Anti-Trust in Japan* (Princeton, N.J.: Princeton University Press, 1970), should be noted.

9. After the war, Fahs spent many years with the Rockefeller Foundation working on its Japan programs.

10. Daniel Seligman, "Luck and Careers," *Fortune,* November 16, 1981, p. 70. (Courtesy of *Fortune* Magazine; © 1981 Time Inc. All rights reserved.)

11. Today, the *Japan Times,* Japan's leading English-language newspaper.

Part I: The Plan and the New Deal

1. A kind of baggy work trousers, tight at the ankles, worn by women as a virtually mandatory uniform during the war.
2. *NT,* September 23, 1946, p. 3.

1. Unconditional Surrender

1. Japan's southernmost main island.
2. W. Averell Harriman, interviewed in the *National Observer,* December 13, 1975.
3. Message, U.S. Minister to New Zealand (Patton) to Secretary of State, September 20, 1945. *(FRUS,* 1945, VI: 179.)
4. Lassa F. L. Oppenheim, *International Law: A Treatise,* 8th ed. (New York: Longman's, 1960), II: 437.
5. JCS 1380/15, para. 3a, stated, "The ultimate objective of the United Nations with respect to Japan is to *foster the conditions* which will give the greatest possible assurances that Japan will never again be a menace to the peace and security of the world." Italics added.
6. *FRUS,* 1945, VI: 677.
7. SWNCCFE minutes of August 29, 1945, item 2, paras. 3, 7, 10.
8. SWNCCFE minutes of September 1, 1945, item 1, para. 3.
9. SWNCCFE Minutes of August 29, 1945, item 2, para. 5.
10. Statement by Captain L. S. Sabin, Navy representative at the meeting, SWNCCFE Minutes of September 1, 1945, item 1, para. 6.
11. Colonel Harold Miller.
12. Colonel William T. Ryder.
13. Letter from the Army's Civil Affairs Division (CAD) Director, Major General John Hilldring, and the Navy's Occupied Areas Seaction (OAS) Officer-in-Charge, Captain H. L. Pence, to the State Department's James Denn. *(FRUS,* 1944, V: 1191.)
14. According to Cyrus H. Peake (then in GS), April 1974.
15. Jim Bishop, Jr., *FDR's Last Year* (New York: William Morrow, 1974), p. 518.
16. *PRJ,* II: 774.

2. Threads in a Maze: Moderation Rejected

1. Conversation at Hugh Borton's home in Conway, Massachusetts, October 7, 1975. Borton was a professor at Columbia University and later became president of Haverford College. When I mentioned his remark to my cousin, the Harvard sociology professor Daniel Bell, his comment was: "Yes, but a likely accident, like an unwanted pregnancy in a brothel."

2. Established on March 1, 1943, in connection with the North African invasion.

3. John F. Hilldring, at a luncheon for the Trade Union Advisory Committee in Washington, April 1947.

4. Memorandum of conversation by Grew, May 28, 1945. *(FRUS, 1945, VI: 545.)*

5. CAC-222 (PWC 296b), "Japan: Economic Policies During Military Occupation," November 16, 1944, Part VII, in National Archives, Washington. Fearey later wrote a book, *The Occupation of Japan—Second Phase: 1948–50* (New York: Macmillan, 1950), with an introduction by Grew.

6. Years later, Hugh Borton remarked wonderingly to me on their "writer's block" when faced with the assignment to draft policy papers. They could not manage to put their policy down on paper. Cyrus Peake of Columbia University, then of the Foreign Economic Administration, reported a similar experience with a Japan FSO who had been his good friend in Japan before the war.

7. European Affairs, Middle Eastern Affairs, Latin American Affairs, and Far Eastern Affairs.

8. Hugh Borton, "Peasant Uprisings in the Tokugawa Period," *Transactions of the Asiatic Society of Japan,* Second Series 16, 1938.

9. Letter to General Whitney, February 15, 1946, *PRJ,* II: 624.

10. CAC-185b, "Japan: Abolition of Militarism and Strengthening Democratic Processes," May 9, 1944, *FRUS,* V: 1257–59. As it turned out, Kagawa had engaged in virulent anti-American foreign propaganda broadcasting in the months just before the war.

11. CAC-185b (PWC 152b), *FRUS,* 1944, V: 1259.

12. Senior Assistant Secretary Breckenridge Long, Assistant Secretary James Dunn, and Legal Adviser Green Hackworth, all of them members of the high-level Departmental Committee on Postwar Programs.

13. Hugh Byas, a former *New York Times* Tokyo correspondent, was against changing the political structure and abolishing the Imperial institution *(Government by Assassination* [New York: Knopf, 1942]). Anthropologist John Embree opposed destroying the democratic village institutions *(American Journal of Sociology,* November 1944). D. C. Holtom was against "redirecting and reconditioning the Japanese minds" except by Japanese liberals *(New Republic,* May 28, 1945). Kenneth Colegrove *(Amerasia,* October 25, 1942) and Wilfred Fleischer, *ex-editor* of the *Japan Advertiser,* also opposed abolishing the Imperial institution *(What to Do with Japan* [Garden City, N.Y.: Doubleday, 1945]). Professor Nathaniel Peffer of Columbia University thought the whole idea of an occupation fantastic ("Occupy Japan?" *[Harper's,* April 1944]).

14. Stimson had already decided on an "all points" rather than a "key points" occupation, according to Charles Kades, then Deputy Executive Officer of the CAD, in a conversation with me in New York on November 5, 1973. Yet on August 4, 1945, Stimson forwarded Grew a memo from outside the government recommending the Japanese be permitted to disarm and democratize themselves. *FRUS,* 1945, VI: 585–87.

15. Edward R. Stettinius, industrialist, was Secretary of State 1944–45.

16. Eugene Dooman, Joseph Ballantine, Earle Dickover, Frank Williams, Beppo Johanson, and Robert Fearey regularly attended the meetings, which normally had an attendance of eleven to eighteen. Grew, of course, was at a higher level.

17. *FRUS,* 1944, V: 1190–94.

18. CAC-111a (PWC 113), March 22, 1944, *FRUS,* V: 1220.

19. CAC-123 (PWC 114), March 22, 1944, *FRUS,* V: 1215.

20. Under Major General George V. Strong.

21. Jonathan Daniels, *White House Witness 1942–45* (New York: Doubleday, 1975), p. 91.

22. *Ibid.,* p. 86.

23. *Ibid.,* p. 83. Diary entry for November 17, 1942.

24. *Ibid.,* p. 86.

25. *Ibid.,* p. 87. Watson himself held the rank of major general.

26. Robert Bangs, Julius Shiskin, and J. J. Joseph, respectively.

27. State, War, Navy, the OSS, Lend-Lease, Relief and Rehabilitation, BEW, Treasury.

28. Rosenberg's erstwhile law partner, Nathaniel Witt, had been reported as early as 1942 by Whittaker Chambers to Assistant Secretary of State Berle to be part of the Soviet underground (*Witness* [New York: Random House, 1952], p. 457). George Wheeler, the head of the EIS Labor Division, would flee in 1945 with his family from his post as Deputy Director of the Manpower Division in the U.S. Military Government in Germany and settle permanently across the Iron Curtain in a job at the University of Prague. At least two others in EIS, plus the deputy Foreign Economic Administrator, were listed as Soviet informants by the highly respected David Dallin in his *Soviet Espionage* (New Haven: Yale University Press, 1955), p. 441.

29. The EIS numbered among its members several prestigious German refugees, including an ex-judge of the Prussian Supreme Court, Alfred Oppler, and a noted anti-Communist labor lawyer, Ernest Frankel.

30. The FEA had, in the meantime, swallowed the Board of Economic Warfare.

31. Letters from McCloy (War) to Donovan (OSS) on October 24 and from Hilldring to FEA Administrator Leo Crowley on September 15 ratified the agreements.

32. Andrew L. Wallace: "Formulation of the Initial Occupation Policy for Japan, 1942–45," unpublished Ph.D. dissertation, Claremont Graduate School, 1958.

33. *Washington Post,* September 21, 1944.

34. *The Forrestal Diaries* (New York: Viking, 1951), entry for August 5, 1944, p. 10.

35. David Rees, *Harry Dexter White* (New York: Coward, MacCann & Geoghegan 1973), pp. 239 ff., and Bradley F. Smith, *The Road to Nuremburg* (New York: Basic Books, 1981). The latter is essentially a reconstruction based on the documents contained in the *Morgenthau Diary* (Washington, 1967).

36. A photocopy of the original memorandum may be found in Henry Morgenthau, *Germany Is Our Problem* (New York: Harper's, 1945).

37. According to Kades, November 1973, in New York City.

38. David Gordon, representing James Perkins, special assistant to Leo Crowley. Perkins later became president of Cornell University, then president of the International Council for Educational Development.

39. Banning securities transfers without Occupation approval, safeguarding industrial plants for reparations purposes, registering nationals of neutral countries, and others.
40. For example, on May 1, 1945, the Navy Military Government Section sent a memo, drafted by Captain L. S. Sabin, to SWNCCFE, recommending the insertion into the U.S. Initial Post Surrender Policy for Japan a phrase to the effect that ''in the institution of economic controls, Japanese authorities will to the fullest extent practicable be ordered to proclaim and assume administration of such controls. . . . This provision from the German paper,'' Sabin explained, ''expresses a principle which is just as applicable to Japan as it is to Germany.'' On war criminals Sabin proposed to use exactly the same sentence as the language in the short German paper and in IPCOG-1, the post-defeat directive on Germany.'' (FRUS, 1945, VI: 538.)

3. Threads in a Maze: How the Radical Reform Took Shape

1. CAC-222 (PWC 296), ''Japan: Economic Policies During Military Occupation,'' July 4, 1944, revised as PWC 296b on November 16, 1944.
2. Formally, a proposal from Acting Secretary of State Stettinius on November 29 and a joint letter of agreement two days later by Stimson and Navy Secretary Forrestal. (*FRUS*, 1944, V: 1466–70.)
3. Edwin Martin later wrote a book entitled *Allied Occupation of Japan*. (Stanford, Calif.: Stanford University Press, 1948).
4. Dean Acheson, *Present at the Creation* (New York: Norton, 1969), pp. 302 ff., attests to Clayton's role.
5. Conversation on October 15, 1975, in Washington.
6. Later Under Secretary of State, then Ambassador to the United Nations.
7. The West Point hero of the Israeli war of independence three years later.
8. In conjunction with Harry Dexter White's Treasury staff.
9. PWC 290a, November 15, 1944.
10. *OJEPR*, p. 153.
11. SCAPIN 93.
12. Letters from Behrstock to authors dated August 13 and 27, 1975, in *TCP*.
13. SWNCC 100, ''Adjustments in Systems of Land Tenure.''
14. SWNCCFE minutes of November 15, 1945, para. 4c.
15. SWNCC 92/1, ''Treatment of Japanese Workers Organizations.''
16. Fowler later became President Lyndon Johnson's Secretary of the Treasury.
17. According to Brown, October 1975, in Washington.
18. In 1946 the AFL formally charged Wheeler with being a Communist, and the War Department dismissed him.
19. SWNCC 92/1.
20. Conversation with Martin, October 15, 1975, Washington.
21. SWNCCFE minutes of April 14, 1945, Para. II, 2.
22. *FRUS*, 1945, VI: 554.

23. *FRUS,* 1945, VI: 612.

24. Hugh Borton, *American Presurrender Planning for Postwar Japan* (New York: Columbia University, East Asian Institute, 1967), p. 23.

25. *New York Times,* January 2, 1944, sec. IV, p. 8.

26. *FRUS,* 1945, VI: 515.

27. Grew's memo of his meeting with President Truman and Judge Rosenman, May 28, 1945, *FRUS,* 1945, VI: 545–47.

28. Grew's memo of the meeting, dated May 29, 1945, *FRUS,* 1945, VI: 548.

29. Harry Truman, *Memoirs* (Garden City, N.Y.: Doubleday, 1955), I: 417.

30. Acheson, *Present at the Creation* (note 4 above), p. 162. Years later, Acheson conceded that Grew was right and he himself was wrong on the Emperor issue.

31. Truman, *Memoirs,* I: 22–23.

32. Except on civil unrest, where Dooman favored a moderate response, changes "to be permitted . . . so long as the unrest is not directed at the Occupation authorities and does not imperil their objectives," and the radicals favored the formulation that "the Supreme Commander should intervene only when necessary to ensure the security of his forces and the attainment of other objectives of the Occupation." Interpreted literally, this would require the Occupation to stand aside while revolution raged in the streets.

33. Lists of organizations to be dissolved and persons to be apprehended, follow-up actions like the seizure of the property of dissolved organizations, and the like.

34. In a conversation on October 15, 1975, in Washington.

35. SWNCCFE minutes of September 25, 1945.

36. Victor Lasky, *It Didn't Start with Watergate* (New York: Dell, 1978), p. 166.

37. Memo of May 1, 1945, *FRUS,* VI: 538.

38. Robert S. Ward, "Can Japan Win by Losing?" *Asia and the Americas,* May 1945.

Part II. MacArthur and His Men

1. Kase graduated from the Tokyo Imperial University, then went to the United States, where he graduated from Amherst College. After that he spent a year or so as a graduate student at Harvard.

2. *PRJ,* II: 736–37.

3. Truman, *Memoirs* (note 29, Chapter 3), I: 458–60.

4. United Press interview, November 16, 1947, *NT,* November 17, 1947, p. 1.

4. Douglas MacArthur and Japan

1. That night the editorial was censored. The Occupation, in the person of Major General Charles Willoughby, G-2 Intelligence, strode into the premises of the *Nippon Times* which was reproducing the editorial in English, declared it forbidden, halted

the press run, and dispatched scores of military policemen to all Occupation billets and to the Central Railway Station to retrieve the copies that had already gone out. "It was not in good taste," he said. Fortunately the episode was an aberration, not the rule.

2. The legendary first Emperor of Japan.

3. "Balance Sheet of the Occupation of Japan," from "Report on Civil Liberties in Japan," ACLU, June 1947, in *TCP*.

4. CAC-80 (PWC 111), "Japan: Occupation and Military Government: Composition of Forces to Occupy Japan," March 13, 1944. (*FRUS, 1944, V*: 1205.)

5. PWC 284a, "Terms of Surrender: Underlying Principles." November 13, 1944. (*FRUS, 1944, V*: 1278.)

6. Particularly, Admiral Ernest J. King, the Chief of Naval Operations. Jim Bishop, *FDR's Last Year*, p. 142.

7. *Ibid.*, p. 517.

8. Daniels, *White House Witness* (note 20, chapter 2), p. 110. The other was Huey Long.

9. *FRUS,* 1945, VI: 648. Italics added.

10. Truman, *Memoirs* (note 29, chapter 3) I: 432.

11. Memo to Ballantine, September 6, 1945. (*FRUS, 1945, VI*: 921.)

12. *FRUS,* 1945, VI: 668–69.

13. FRUS, 1945, VI: 664, 667. One of the Japanese motives, as revealed by Japanese Ambassador to Sweden, General Onodera, was to maintain links to the outside world and particularly neutral monarchies to protest any untoward action by the Americans toward the Imperial family. (*Ibid.*, p. 676.)

14. *FRUS,* 1945, VI: 671.

15. Truman, *Memoirs,* I: 456.

16. SWNCC 181/2, *FRUS,* 1945, VI, p. 712. Truman, *Memoirs,* I: 457.

17. Message, U.S. Ambassador to Court of St. James's Winant to Secretary of State Byrnes on September 22. (*FRUS, 1945, VI*: 720–21.)

18. Winant to Byrnes. (October 4, *FRUS, 1945, VI*: 735–36.)

19. Byrnes to Winant. (October 13, *FRUS, 1945, VI*: 751.)

20. Memo from Harriman to Byrnes. (August 11, *FRUS, 1945, VI*: 630.)

21. Stalin to Truman, August 16, 1945. (*FRUS, 1945, VI*: 667–68.)

22. Truman to Stalin, August 17. (*FRUS, 1945, VI*: 670.)

23. Stalin to Truman, August 18. (*FRUS, 1945, VI*: 687.)

24. Thorpe, *East Wind, Rain* (note 5, "Personal Note"), pp. 213–14.

25. Memos by Edward Page, First Secretary, American Embassy in Moscow, of conversations between Harriman and Stalin. (*FRUS, 1945, VI*: 787–93); also Harriman to Byrnes, October 26, 1945, *ibid.*, pp. 793–95.

26. Byrnes to Robertson, December 22, 1945. (*FRUS, 1945, VI*: 887.)

27. GHQ SCAP press release of December 30, 1945. (*PRJ,* II: 744.)

28. Statement to the ACJ, April 5, 1946, *ibid.*, p. 746.

29. JWPC 385/3 *et seq.*, in the National Archives, Washington, D.C. SWNCC 70/5 appears in *FRUS,* 1945, VI: 603–9.

30. Message of Australian Minister Eggleston to Byrnes, October 20, 1945. (*FRUS,* 1945, VI: 763–65.)

31. Memo of Assistant Secretary of War McCloy to Under Secretary of State Acheson, November 15, 1945. (*FRUS,* 1945, VI: 853–54.)

32. Memo by Edward Page, pp. 784–85.

33. Harriman made on last try. On November 12 he reported to Molotov that the British Commonwealth troops were on the point of sailing for Japan and reiterated the American desire to have Russian troops, too, but Molotov did nothing about it. Harrison to Byrnes, November 20, 1945. (*FRUS,* 1945, VI, pp. 861–62.)

34. As he eventually did with Remington-Rand after being removed by Truman in 1951.

35. *PRJ,* II: 739.

36. Quoted in *Time* magazine, December 20, 1941. White recalls the interview in *In Search of History* (New York: Harper & Row, 1978), p. 115.

37. General W. F. Marquat told me the story in October 1950. Marquat was Casey's fellow passenger. Casey later rose to major general and then became head of the New York subway system.

38. Letter of George Atcheson to Truman, November 5, 1945. (*FRUS,* 1945, VI: 825–27.)

39. D. C. James, *The Years of MacArthur* (Boston: Houghton-Mifflin, 1975), II: 795–96.

40. Colonel Sidney Huff and Colonel Laurence E. Bunker.

41. Cyrus Peake, then one of the senior GS officials, in a conversation in April 1974.

42. Thorpe, *East Wind, Rain* (n. 5, "Personal Note"), p. 166.

43. It is somewhat erroneously labeled his "second" library.

44. George Kenney, *General Kenney Reports* (New York, 1949), pp. 151–52.

45. More ominously, evocative of the pre-Mussolini factory seizures in Italy. But then MacArthur did not know about them.

46. *Time* magazine, December 29, 1941.

47. Message to the Red Army on the occasion of its twenty-fourth anniversary. Quoted in Robert Sherwood, *Roosevelt and Hopkins* (New York: Harper Brothers, 1948), p. 497.

48. Conversation with Kades in New York, November 5, 1973.

49. Memo from Martin to Gilcrist, March 28, 1946, *FRUS,* 1946, VIII, pp. 185–86.

50. Related to me on October 7, 1975, at Hugh Borton's home in Conway, Massachusetts.

51. Except to Sherwood Fine, his economic adviser. Fine told me about it after Marquat's death.

52. *FRUS,* 1945, VI: 842–43.

53. Statement of January 27, 1947, *PRJ,* II: 549.

54. Memo from Deputy Chief of Staff (Major General Almond) to Deputy Chief of Staff, SCAP, July 7, 1947, in *TCP.*

55. Cited in James, *The Years of MacArthur* (note 39 above), II: 50–51.

56. Cited in Whitney, *MacArthur: His Rendezvous with History* (note 6, "Personal Note") p. 33.

5. *The Corridors of Byzantium*

1. Conversation with Kades, November 5, 1973, New York.
2. Letter to Under Secretary Acheson. (*FRUS*, 1945, VI, p. 837.)
3. Formerly Commandant of Governor's Island and its polo field in New York Harbor.
4. Whitney, *MacArthur* (Note 6, "Personal Note"), pp. 90–91.
5. *Ibid.*, p. 225. The pen used to write the "Arthur" part of his signature was for MacArthur's son, Arthur.
6. Kades, interviewed in New York City, November 1973.
7. General Order #8, October 2, 1945.
8. In 1973, Kades said he did not remember those remarks but did not deny making them.
9. Again, told to me by Kades in the fall of 1946. In November 1973, he could not remember telling me this incident either.
10. Marquat recounted various incidents in his life to me during my five-year association with him, three and a half as his special assistant.
11. Interview with Elliott Thrope in Bangkok, where he was the military attaché, April 1949.
12. During one pre-Christmas season in Tokyo, Marquat found his car in a parade behind a float carrying a small but loud organ. The float unexpectedly backed up and hit his Packard. "We were following Handel's Messiah," he explained later, "when we got hit by the messiah's handle."
13. These figures are compiled from the GHQ telephone directories of April 25, 1946, and January 1, 1948, in *TCP,* plus the Weekly Civilian Strength Report as of January 17, 1947, forwarded by the Civilian Personnel Section to G-1 per CPS checknote of January 20, 1947, *WP.*
14. Dossier Summary A in "Leftist Infiltration into SCAP," CIS Report, in *WP.*
15. The visit earned the CIC a reprimand from the Chief of Staff, Major General Doyle Hickey, after I reported it to the Assistant Deputy Chief of Staff, Brigadier General George Kyser, for using an enemy agency—it was before the Peace Treaty—to spy on an American citizen.
16. Clay Blair, Jr., in his *MacArthur* (New York: Pocket Books, 1977, pp. 101, 112, 217; and James, *Years of MacArthur,* II: 156, 202, 240.
17. Thorpe: *East Wind, Rain* (note 5, "Personal Note"); (note 39, chapter 4), p. 95.
18. See James, *Years of MacArthur,* II: 292–93, re the departure of a large enemy convoy from Rabaul the first week of March 1943.
19. William J. Coughlin, *Conquered Press* (Palo Alto, Calif.: Pacific Books, 1952), p. 120.
20. Interview of Willoughby by Ian Mutsu, UP correspondent, in *NT,* February 13, 1949, p. 1.
21. Thorpe, *East Wind, Rain,* p. 96.
22. James, *Years of MacArthur,* II: 80.
23. Memo to the Chief of Staff and C-in-C; subject: Leftist Civilian Employees of GHQ, September 27, 1946, in *WP.*
24. Bratton, Duff, Wood, Jordan, Bethune, Myers, and Brown.

25. C. Nelson Spinks.

26. Memo for C-in-C, C/S, and General Whitney, June 7, 1947; subject: Leftist Infiltration into SCAP, in *WP*.

27. I do not mind using my own name, but for the others I have substituted the letters of their individual dossier summary tabs in the report.

28. *WP*.

29. *WP*. The note is undated, but the buck slip is dated August 17, 1946.

30. Secret memo to Colonels Wood *et al.;* subject: Leftist Classification of Civilian Employees of GHQ SCAP, September 18, 1946, para. 6, in *WP*.

31. Two who appeared to be working on the *zaibatsu* were in GS, which had no jurisdication.

32. Memo to Colonel Wood *et al.,* September 18, 1946, in *WP*.

33. Memo to Colonel Bratton and Dr. Spinks, April 23, 1947, in *WP*.

34. Richard Sorge, a German Communist, headed a spy ring in Tokyo that operated almost eight years. Detailed accounts may be found in Chalmers Johnson, *An Instance of Treason: Ozaki Hotsumi and the Sorge Spy Ring* (Stanford, Calif.: Stanford University Press, 1965), and in Gordon W. Prange, with Donald Goldstein and Katherine V. Dillon, *Target Tokyo: The Story of the Sorge Spy Ring* (New York: McGraw-Hill, 1984).

35. Undated memo from Willoughby to Spinks; subject: G-2 comments, in *WP*.

36. Undated memo from Willoughby to Spinks, in *WP*.

37. Cited by Willoughby in his memo of June 7, 1947.

38. Memo to Colonel Wood *et al.,* September 18, 1946, in *WP*.

39. Sebald's wife was the daughter of an equally famous Dutch legal scholar in Japan, Joseph de Becker, and a Japanese lady. Sebald's sister-in-law many years later married the newly divorced General Willoughby and on his death turned over his secret and somewhat incriminating papers to the MacArthur Memorial in Norfolk, Virginia.

40. Bunker, Fellers, and Diller.

6. The View at Mid-Level

1. In GHQ AFPAC/FEC, the Far East Naval or Far East Air Corps Headquarters, the custodial Headquarters and Service Group, or the local tactical units of Eighth Army, or part of a miscellany of foreign correspondents, businessmen (banks and insurance companies, airlines, Coca-Cola), Red Cross girls, and others.

2. Deducting in the peak year, 1948, the Allied Translator and Interpreter Service, the 441st Counter Intelligence Corps, the Statistics and Reports Section, the International Military Tribunal for the Far East, and Class B war crimes in Legal Section, some 1,835 remain in the operating SCAP sections; but half were administrative, secretarial, or clerical. Similar calculations apply to 1946 and 1950, with adjustments for the early use of enlisted men for jobs later held by civilians, the closing down of the war crimes trials, and so on. The Weekly Civilian Strength Report, January 17, 1947 (WP), lists 1,250 in the operating SCAP sections. Adding officers and deducting

administrative secretarial and clerical help leaves about 700 to 800 persons actually engaged in governing Japan.

3. The Ministry of Commerce and Industry was replaced by a new Ministry of International Trade and Industry in 1949, with the Third Yoshida Cabinet.

4. In the first Yoshida cabinet, May 1946 to May 1947.

5. From July 1946 to January 1947, in the first Yoshida cabinet.

6. One was a naval officer recalled to serve as Governor of Ponape Island in the Central Pacific. Others were assigned to Okinawa.

7. Daniels, *White House Witness* (note 2, chapter 2), p. 87.

8. There were 13 million worldwide.

9. Grade CAF-15, division chiefs, earned between $10,000 and $10,750; CAF-14, branch chiefs, earned $8,969. In 1946, U.S. senators, representatives, and under secretaries were paid $10,000, assistant secretaries, $9,000. A brigadier general earned $8,540, including rent, subsistence, and overseas pay. Washington salaries, however, went up, while Occupation pay, except for yearly increments, remained the same.

10. For a few it was altogether too much. One middle-aged man brought in as a tourism adviser spent his time making telephone calls in which he represented himself as the Chief of Staff, no less, and reserved rooms for his Red Cross girl acquaintances at the general officers' Imperial Hotel billet. He even requisitioned a four-engine C-54 for a trip to Korea with his friends and had it warming up on the tarmac early one morning when someone finally thought to check. The tourism adviser took a trip to the psychiatric ward of the 42d General Hospital instead of Seoul.

11. Industry, Finance, Antitrust, and so on.

12. A roly-poly doll that can be pushed over with a light touch and then will return to its original upright position. Named for the Buddhist Bodhidarma.

13. Very close to the city of Kyoto.

14. In Horikawa, Kawasaki City, between Tokyo and Yokohama.

15. Memo of May 18, 1950, in *TCP*.

16. Sometimes romanized as Dai-Iti. The word is, in fact, the same as the "Daiichi" in the name of the building in which General MacArthur's office was located. For convenience, I shall use Daiichi for the hotel as well.

17. By then promoted to brigadier general.

18. For example, Louis Budenz, *This Is My Story* (New York: Whittlesey House, McGraw-Hill, 1947).

19. Conversation at home of Takano Minoru in Totsuka, near Yokohama, April 19, 1973.

7. Men, Women, and Martinets

1. The story of the 1937 rape of Nanking was first published openly in the *Mainichi* of September 20, 1945.

2. Indeed, the Occupation forces once went so far as to order cars for women and children on the impossibly jammed Tokyo elevated loop line, an order greeted by at least half the population with great joy.

3. SWNCC 150/4, part 3, para. 3. Italics added.

4. JCS 1380/15, para. 4f.

5. Faubion Bowers, "The Late General MacArthur, Warts and All," *Esquire,* January 1967, p. 168.

6. Message to Congress, February 20, 1947, in *PRJ,* II: 762.

7. *NT,* February 25, 1946, p. 1.

8. JCS 1380/15, para. 4e.

9. Bowers, "Late General MacArthur," p. 168.

10. Case of Arden M. Gaddis, File JAGH-CM 324352, September 25, 1947.

11. Deputy Contraband Administrator Vesting Order GHQ #5, November 23, 1948, para. 7, lists one pair of baby shoes, two baby's overalls, two bottles of catsup, and a cheap Ingersoll clock. *NT,* June 3, 1949. Another part of the same vesting order lists a layette, some baby bottles, milk powder, baby shoes, a blanket, and some balls of pink knitting-wool.

12. According to a deposition by Thomas L. Blakemore, then in GS, made to the Provost Court on June 18, 1947, in *TCP.* He had given his friend ten old copies of American magazines, a used cake of soap, a tube of toothpaste, a box of Kleenex, a pack of playing cards, some water purification tablets, and a flashlight. All the items were used or partially consumed.

13. DCA Vesting Order Yokohama #9, November 5, 1948, para. (1), in *NT,* December 5, 1948.

14. The watches came from Ichikawa Koboru, Shōzō Ichisei, and Nakamura Matsunosuke, the lighter from Ozawa Sadao. DCA Vesting Order Kobe #11, October 11, 1948, paras. (6), (5), (4), and (3) respectively, in *NT,* December 5, 1948.

15. From Kimura Kiichi, DCA Vesting Order GHQ 5, November 23, 1948, para. (2). (*NT,* June 3, 1949.)

16. Shaw had already made one terrible blunder. He permitted a Stateside lawyer brought into Japan to defend a scapegrace lieutenant charged with black marketing stolen officers' club liquor to consolidate all the charges into one specifying only American liquor. Then the defense proved that it was all Japanese whisky, getting the defendant released.

17. DCA Vesting Order GHQ #2, August 14, 1948, para. g. (*NT,* September 19, 1948.)

18. Statement of August 28, 1946, in *PRJ,* II: 754.

19. Cited in the petition of the New Japan Women's Federation to General of the Army Douglas MacArthur, undated, in *TCP.*

20. Kyodo News Service, May 31, 1947.

21. David Carpenter in the Statistics and Reports Section and S. Driggs Collett in the Labor Division.

22. Incident recounted by Cyrus Peake in April 1974, one of the GS officials present.

Part III. A Question of Priorities

1. Institute of Public Opinion poll, Kamiyama Shigeru, survey director, cited in *NT,* September 11, 1946, p. 4.

2. *Ibid.*
3. JCS 1380/15, paras. 13, 13a, and 35a.
4. *Ibid.,* paras. 19 and 22.
5. "Comment on Far Eastern Commission Policy Decision," July 13, 1947, in *PRJ,* II: 774.

8. Defending Japan Against the Allies: the Twin Specters of Starvation and De-Industrialization

1. Shigeru Yoshida, *Japan's Decisive Century* (New York: Frederick A. Praeger, 1967), p. 51.
2. *NT,* April 8, 1946, p. 2.
3. Livelihood Section, Tokyo Metropolitan Government, in *NT,* July 10, 1946, p. 3.
4. *JES* #39, November 1949, pp. 44–52.
5. Truman, *Memoirs* (note 29, Chapter 3), I: 464 ff.
6. Lassa F. L. Oppenheim, *International Law* (note 4, Chapter 1), p. 437.
7. *Ibid.,* II: 455.
8. Truman, *Memoirs,* I: 468–69.
9. Represented by Eugene Dooman.
10. Represented by General George V. Strong.
11. Minutes of SWNCCFE meeting, April 18, 1945, para. II.
12. JCS 1380/15, para. 296.
13. Truman, *Memoirs,* I: 468–69.
14. Radio address, April 19, 1946, and *ibid.,* I: 473.
15. *Mission and Accomplishments,* 1949, sec. IV, para. 6b.
16. *Jiji Shimpo,* May 8, 1947.
17. *NT,* July 10, 1946, p. 3.
18. Yoshida, *Japan's Decisive Century,* p. 52.
19. *JES* #39, November 1949, p. 46.
20. *Ibid.,* p. 45.
21. Statement of May 5, 1946, in *PRJ,* II: 479.
22. *JES* #39, November 1949, p. 49.
23. *Ibid.,* p. 50.
24. *Ibid.,* p. 43.
25. Statement of February 20, 1947, furnished to the War Department for use in congressional Appropriations Committee hearings, in *PRJ,* II: 764.
26. Conversation at Sushi-Iwa restaurant in Tsukiji, Tokyo, June 26, 1973.
27. Conversation in Takano's apartment at Totsuka, April 19, 1973.
28. In a meeting of the Far Eastern Commission, the claimant nations overwhelmingly rejected using their own "absorptive capacity" as a criterion for reparations allowances. (*FRUS,* 1946, VIII, p. 518.)

29. James Byrnes, *Speaking Frankly* (New York: Harper Brothers, 1947), p. 225. Pauley calculated the value of the removed equipment at $858 million, but the loss to China at $2 billion, including deterioration of related equipment, cost of replacement, and so forth.

30. Boilers, turbines, and generators to be added to existing installations.

31. *FRUS*, 1946, VIII: 54.

32. Owen Lattimore, *Solution in Asia* (Boston: Little, Brown, 1945), pp. 186, 189.

33. *FRUS*, 1945, VI: 1006

34. SWNCC 236/12; *FRUS*, 1946, VIII: 488.

35. *Ibid.*, VIII: 509.

36. Memo of April 30, 1946. *FRUS*, 1946, VIII: 506.

37. Other targets included one-half of the machine tool industry, nine-tenths of ball- and roller-bearing works, all arsenals and private munitions plants, as well as airframe and aircraft engine factories, two-thirds of new shipbuilding capacity, 60 percent of the drydocks, 70 percent of the chlorine, and 60 percent of the caustic soda capacity, plus half the thermal power plants.

38. Radios W89351, May 28; WCL 46132, June 2; WCL 49908, June 16; and 251637Z, June 26, all 1946.

39. SCAPIN 1129–36; economic SCAPIN, pp. 242–62.

40. SCAPIN 629, January 20, 1946; *ibid.*, p. 96.

41. *Forrestal Diaries* (note 33, chapter 2), p. 177.

42. *FRUS*, 1946, VIII: 567.

43. *Ibid.*, p. 601.

44. *Ibid.*, pp. 490–91.

45. *Ibid.*, p. 493*n*.

46. *Ibid.*, p. 601.

47. *Ibid.*, pp. 573–75.

48. *NT*, November 18, 1946, p. 1.

49. *SCAP Monthly Summations*, June–September 1947.

50. George Kennan, in his *Memoirs* (Boston: Little, Brown, 1967), p. 410, charges that as of March 1948 ''masses of equipment were rotting, as we were told, on the docks of Shanghai and other Far Eastern ports.'' That was hardly possible. The shipments had just begun at that time, not to mention that machine tools don't rot.

51. According to General Patrick Tansey, SCAP Property Custodian, in *NT*, May 14, 1949, p. 1.

9. The Purge of Japanese Business

1. Comment on *Newsweek* article of January 27, 1947. (*PRJ*, II: 549.)

2. Interview with Walter Simmons, Chicago *Tribune*, quoted in *NT*, October 10, 1947, p. 1.

3. Home Minister Horikiri Zenjiro, Transportation Minister Tanaka Masao, Agriculture

and Forestry Minister Matsumura Kenzō, Education Minister Maeda Tamon, and Chief Cabinet Secretary Tsugita Ōzaburo.

4. Transportation Minister Hiratsuka Tsunejiro, Welfare Minister Kawai Yasunari, Justice Minister Kimura Tokutaro, Finance Minister Ishibashi Tanzan, and Commerce and Industry Minister Ishii Kōjiro.

5. Maeda Tamon, for having been *ex officio* chief of a prefectural branch of the Imperial Rule Assistance Association.

6. Suehiro Izutaro, former dean of Tokyo Imperial University Law School and leading drafter of the postwar democratic labor legislation, for having been a director of the Martial Arts Society.

7. "It may generally be assumed in the absence of evidence to the contrary that any persons holding such positions," that is, "important and key positions in national . . . civic and economic organizations; corporations in which the government has a major financial interest; industry; finance" and others, "are Nazis or Nazi sympathizers." (JCS 1067, September 25, 1944, Appendix A to Enclosure C, paras. 1a–i.)

8. Report on the 22d Session of the League of Nations Advisory Council on the Opium Traffic, June 12, 1939, submitted as testimony to the International Military Tribunal for the Far East on September 3, 1946. (*SCAP Monthly Summation*, September 1946, p. 35.)

9. Kennan, *Memoirs*, p. 410.

10. Justice Minister Suzuki Yoshi, writing in *Yomiuri*, December 5, 1947.

11. *PRJ*, I: 18.

12. *PRJ*, II: 561.

13. Conversation with Kades, November 1973, New York.

14. *NT*, August 31, 1946, p. 2.

15. Cresswell, a specialist on Japan, had participated in compiling a Japanese–English dictionary of military terms, published in 1932. But his judgment was questionable. As military attaché, he reported on October 20, 1941, that "general Tojo . . . is believed to have a breadth of vision which would seem to preclude the possibility of his taking extreme radical actions." (Sherwood, *Roosevelt and Hopkins*, note 47, chapter 4, p. 419.)

16. That was the way the official Government Section history, the *Political Reorganization of Japan*, I: 46–48, wrote it up. But it hardly squares with the formal assignment of missions by the Chief of Staff in November 1945, which allocated paras. 23 and 40 of JCS 1380/15 to ESS.

17. "Behind the Japanese Purge: American Military Rivalries," *Newsweek*, January 27, 1947, pp. 40–43.

18. Draft cable of June 16, 1947, to the War Department, prepared by the SCAP Antitrust Division in *TCP*.

19. *Forrestal Diaries* (note 33, chapter 2), p. 248.

20. *Newsweek*, June 23, 1947, pp. 36–43.

21. *Newsweek*, January 27, 1947, pp. 40–43.

22. Kennan, *Memoirs* (note 50, chapter 8), p. 409.

23. *PRJ,* II: 549.
24. *Ibid.*
25. *Ibid.*
26. *Ibid.*
27. That is, after the November 21, 1946, announcement by the Japanese Government. The estimate of the number of such resignations was made by Government Section's Major Jack Napier. (*PRJ,* I: 51.)

10. The Dilemma of the Great Inflation

1. From 30 billion to 50 billion yen.
2. For example, C. F. Thomas of the National City Bank, Norbert Bogdan of the J. Henry Schroeder Banking Corporation, and Frank Tamagna of the Federal Reserve Board, onetime adviser to H. H. Kung, Chinese Minister of Finance.
3. *SCAP Monthly Summation,* April 1946, pp. 214–16.
4. Memorandum for Major General W. F. Marquat from Theodore Cohen, July 21, 1946; subject: Labor Union Activities, in *TCP.*
5. Japan's southernmost main island.
6. *JES* #37, September 1949, p. 39. The year-end figure was 93 billion yen.
7. *JES,* #40, December 1949, pp. 3, 20.
8. The Cabinet Bureau of Statistics estimated that workers' take-home earnings had risen to only three times the 1941 level, while their cost of living had increased thirteen times. (*LDMR,* January 1946, paras. 13–14.)
9. About 837 yen in 1931. T. R. Havens, *Farm and Nation in Modern Japan* (Princeton, N.J.: Princeton University Press, 1974), pp. 149, 152.
10. In 1938, 5,519,000 farm families shared a total agricultural production of 4,073 billion yen. (*Orient Year Book,* 1942, p. 169.)
11. Roughly, the "exchange" rate between yen and dollars was about 100–1 in March 1947, 355–1 in March 1949 (see p. 365). The countrywide urban consumer index rose from 39.0 in March 1947 to 139.8 in March 1949. (*JES,* #39, November 1949, p. 1.)
12. In December 1948 the price paid by the Food Corporation to producers for rice was 1,810 yen per *koku. Staple Food Prices in Japan,* GHQ, SCAP, ESS Research and Programs Division, April 1949, p. 8. The average yield per *chō* was 20 *koku* annually, or 36,200 yen.
13. *NT,* October 1, 1946, p. 3.
14. In 1946, when government expenditures exceeded receipts by 67 percent, the Bank of Japan issue rose 69 percent and the consumer price index 60 percent. (*JES* #40, December 1949, pp. 1, 20.)
15. The peerage was officially abolished by the postwar Constitution, Article 14.
16. Kanō Hisaakira, *My Wartime Records* (Tokyo, 1956), privately printed.
17. A Labor Ministry was established for the first time during the Katayama cabinet (May 1947–March 1948) in September 1947.

18. *NT,* January 22, 1946, p. 3.

19. Tokyo Metropolis tripled the wages of 70, 000 workers on January 19, and Occupation workers' wages had been raised 20 to 60 percent in February (*LMDR,* February 1946, para. 19), but national workers had gotten nothing.

20. *LDMR,* January 1946, para. 7; *NT,* December 12, 1945, p. 1.

21. It seems that a CIC informant had reported that I had called Marquat "stupid," and General Willoughby had gleefully called this to Marquat's attention. The informant had been mistaken.

22. *Mission and Accomplishments,* 1950 edition, sec. II, p. 2.

23. *JES #39,* November 1949, p. 8.

Part IV. Journey into the Unknown:
The Occupation and the Japanese Labor Movement

11. Labor Emerges as a National Force

1. *LDMR,* December 1945, paras. 35 and 36; and June 1946, para. 36.

2. *LDMR,* May 1946, para. 1.

3. *Sanpō* was short for *Sangyō Hokoku-kai,* or Industrial Patriotic Society; Rōhō for *Rōmu Hōkoku-kai,* or Labor Patriotic Society. The former enrolled factory workers, the latter casual construction workers, stevedores, and so on. Both were organized along military lines, with foremen, department chiefs, and factory managers all carrying military ranks.

4. In 1929, 3.7 million out of a total nonagricultural labor force of 37.2 million.

5. Conversations with Takano Minoru and Katō Kanjū in 1973.

6. Conversation with Takano Minoru on April 19, 1973, in his house in Totsuka near Yokohama.

7. *"Dōmo, sumimasen."*

8. *NT,* October 13, 1945, p. 3.

9. *Ibid.*

10. John Emmerson, then in the Political Adviser's Office (later Deputy Ambassador to Japan), and Herbert Norman, then in Counter-Intelligence (later Canadian Ambassador to Japan), had interviewed him in Fuchū Prison and had even taken him in a U.S. Army sedan to Tokyo Headquarters for several hours of discussion. He was, therefore, adequately forewarned of his coming release. See Emmerson, *The Japanese Thread* (New York: Holt Rinehart & Winston, 1978), pp. 258–59.

11. April 16, 1917.

12. A total of 973 in 1936. Nakagawa Kenichi, *Shakai Seisaku Jōhō* (Social Policy Journal), March 1940, pp. 262–77.

13. *Japan Chronicle,* October 5, 1933, p. 436.

14. According to Hasegawa Kō, his comrade who had spent nine of *his* last fourteen years in prison, Tokuda worked as one possessed. In that fall of 1945, Hasegawa, who had been released a few days before Tokuda from another prison, labored long hours, never going to bed before one in the morning. But Tokuda, who was sharing his temporary quarters in Koganei, just outside Tokyo, never went to bed before two. Conversations with me on June 20 and 26, 1973, at the Sushiiwa Restaurant in Tokyo.

15. According to Hasegawa, in the June 1973 conversations, *ibid.* above.

16. Its first postwar editor, Shiga Yoshio, was released from prison together with Tokuda.

17. All according to Hasegawa Kō, who worked closely with him at the time. Hasegawa found certain aspects of Tokuda's behavior peculiar. For example, he attributed Tokuda's stubbornness on the Emperor issue—he was far more insistent on removing the Emperor than the rest of the Communist leaders—to the fact that Tokuda was an Okinawan and not a "true" Japanese.

18. Emmerson, *Japanese Thread*, p. 263.

19. *NT*, February 15, 1946, p. 3.

20. Credit unions (*shinyō kumiai*), cooperatives (*kyōdō kumiai*), neighborhood associations (*tonari-gumi*), import–export associations (*shutsunyū kumiai*), wholesalers associations (*tonya kumiai*), as well as labor unions (*rōdō kumiai*).

21. Report of the *Yomiuri* labor union. (*Yomiuri*, November 5, 1945.)

22. Statement to Shidehara, October 11. (*PRJ*, 11: 741.)

23. Anthony Costantino (Steel Workers), Charles Hicks (United Mine Workers), Leon Becker and Mark Starr (International Ladies Garment Workers), Richard Deverall (United Automobile Workers), Samuel Thompson (Radio Artists), and John Harold (Hotel and Restaurant Workers).

24. Kuroda Hisao, onetime member of the prewar Proletarian party (*Musan-tō*). Kuroda suggested that if I wanted him, I should have him arrested first.

25. *Keidanren*, the most powerful organization of Japanese "big business."

26. One *go* = .384 pints. Therefore, 6 *go* = 2.304 pints, and the ordinary ration of 2.5 *go* = .96 pints.

27. *LDMR*, March 1946, para. 34.

28. *LDMR*, January 1947, para. 9, and July 1947, para. 8.

29. *LDMR*, December 1946, para 23.

30. *Keieisha*, April 1948.

31. *LDMR*, April 1946, para. 16, and August 1946, para. 12.

32. *Nippon Rōdō-tō* (1925–26), *Rōdō Nōmin-tō* (1926), *Shakai Minshu-tō* (1926–32) *Nippon Rōnō-tō* (1926–28), *Musan Taishū-tō* (1928), *Nippon Taishū-tō* (1928–30), *Tokyo Musan-tō* (1929), *Nippon Musan-tō* (1929), *Shin Rōnō-tō* (1929–30), *Zenkoku Taishū-tō* (1930–32), *Zenkoku Minshu-tō* (1930), *Zenkoku Rōnō Taishū-tō* (1931–32), *Shakai Taishū-tō* (1932–39), and *Nippon Kokka Shakai-tō* (1932–39). Another *Nippon Musan-tō* (1936–38) was organized a few years later.

33. Raymond Aron, *The Opium of the Intellectuals* (London: Secker & Warburg, 1957).

34. Emmerson, *Japanese Thread,* p. 260.
35. In the Teachers' Union, Iwama Masao, a Communist, was president, but Kobayashi Tetsu, the secretary, was fraction leader. Similarly, in the *Sanbetsu* federation, the fraction leader, Hosoya Matsuta, was deputy secretary general, ranking below the president, two vice-presidents, five other executive board members, and the secretary general, all of whom incidentally were Communists.
36. According to Takano, in April 1973.
37. *Zenkoku Sangyō-betsu Rōdō Kumiai Kaigi.* The other three goals were the overthrow of the "Emperor system," a broad cooperative struggle of the masses with the Communist party as its center, and the establishment of a "people's republic." Masuyama Taisuke, "Dainiji *Yomiuri* Sōgi-shi" (History of the Second *Yomiuri* Strike), in *Senryō-ka-no Rōdō Sōgi* (Labor Strikes Under the Occupation), Rōdō Undō-shi Kenkyū No. 54 (Tokyo: Rōdō Jumpō-sha, 1972).
38. *Jiji Press,* May 15, Morning Edition, p. 1.
39. Kawazoe Takayuki, Kikunami's successor as head of the Newspaper Union, *Minpō,* May 21–22, 1947.
40. Kameda Tōgō of the Chemical Workers Union.
41. Yoshida Sukeji.
42. Tsutsura Wataru of the Coal Miners, Nakahara Junkichi of the Electrical Machinery Workers, Fukushima Fujio and Tatsuda Takashi of the Steel Workers, and Yamazaki Ryōichi of the Machinery Workers.

12. Help, but Hands Off! Labor and the Law

1. SCAP Monthly Summation, October 1946, p. 33, and April 1947, p. 46.
2. In accordance with articles 43, 44, 50, 52–55, 57, and 72–83 of the Civil Code and articles 35, 36, 37 clause 2, 126 para. 1, 137, and 138 of the Law of Procedure of Non-Contentious Cases.
3. *OJEPR,* pp. 194–95.
4. *FRUS,* 1946, VIII: 128, 138, 185–86.
5. Where, by this time, we had moved from the Daiichi Building.
6. *LDMR,* December 1945, para. 22.
7. The government owned the trunk lines, while the branch and secondary lines were left to private ownership.
8. *NT,* December 12, 1945, p. 1.
9. *NT,* December 14, 1945, p. 3.
10. *NT,* January 12, 1946, p. 2.
11. *NT,* January 19, 1946, p. 3.
12. *SCAP Monthly Summation,* June 1946, p. 159. In January, 80,000 workers were involved in labor disputes. Of these, 38,000 struck, 29,000 of them by way of production control.

13. Including the rice riots of 1919, when police guard boxes were burned down, and the Ashio copper mine strike of 1907, when the workers destroyed all the mine buildings above ground and troops had to be called out.

14. Led by Kagawa Toyohiko, the Christian social worker, the production control plan declared that the workers "would do our work at our respective workshops, ourselves assuming control of operations, until our demands are accepted." They pledged to turn out the same amount of work, although in two hours less a day, and proclaimed that any worker who disturbed the peace or impaired the efficiency of the plant would be dealt with by the union disciplinary committee. Text of the plan appeared in *The Nation*, October 26, 1921, p. 472.

15. *NT*, January 22, 1946, p. 3.

16. *NT*, January 24, 1946, p. 1.

17. *NT*, January 30, 1946, p. 3.

18. *NT*, February 3, 1946, p. 2.

19. "While looking forward to the development of labor unions with hope and favor, the Government regrets to witness cases of violence, coercion, and infringement of the rights of ownership in the labor disputes which have taken place of late. Such practices are definitely not to be resorted to by workers conscious of the responsibility of building a new Japan, and the Government, by no means ignoring them, will be compelled to take decisive measures on such unjust and unlawful actions. The Government earnestly desires that laborers will hereafter exercise full caution lest they commit such misconduct." (English translation from *NT*, February 2, 1946, p. 1.)

20. Interview with Kyōdō News Service, cited in *NT*, February 3, 1946, p. 3.

21. *Yomiuri Hōchi*, February 2, 1946.

22. *LDMR*, February 1946, para. 18.

23. *SCAP Monthly Summation*, May 1947, p. 159.

24. *Ibid.*, June 1946, p. 204.

25. *Ibid.*, July 1946, p. 173. "Trespass" in this case, the police decided subsequently, applied only to outsiders acting in groups.

26. Murakami Giichi.

27. *NT*, April 2, 1946, p. 3, and April 14, 1946, p. 2. In the latter case, the employees' union of the Coal Board called their own production control strike until Minister Ogasawara Sankurō did.

28. *NT*, February 9, 1946, p. 3.

29. *NT*, February 26, 1946, p. 3.

30. For the six months from October 1946 to March 1947, a period of intense labor–management confrontation, only 7 percent of the strikers resorted to production control. In the succeeding nine months, the percentage fell to five, and by December 1947, only one. (*SCAP Monthly Summations*, June 1947–February 1948, part III, section 8.)

31. Professor William MacPherson of the School of Industrial Relations, University of Illinois; Paul Stanchfield of the U.S. Labor Department; Leonard Appel of the staff of the National Labor Relations Board: Costantino; and me.

32. Dobashi asked me to repeat my statement, while two of his men furiously scribbled notes. Sure enough, in a few days Shiga came back to complain that I had "betrayed" him by divulging his disagreement with the "party line." I shook my head at him sorrowfully. It was hard to hate someone who had spent sixteen years in jail for his principles. "Haven't you discovered yet," I said, "that I'm on the other side? Don't confide in me, and your confidences won't be betrayed."

33. *NT,* July 12, 1946, p. 3.

34. *NT,* July 29, 1946, p. 1.

35. *NT,* August 7, 1946, p. 3.

36. *Rōdō Hyōron,* quoted in *NT,* November 9, 1946, p. 4.

37. Excerpted in *Newsweek,* December 1, 1947, pp. 36–38.

38. Including, additionally, wage payments, working hours, recesses, rest, annual vacations, safety, sanitation, women and child labor, vocational training, accident compensation, employment retirement, dormitories, inspection, posting of rules, and wage ledgers.

39. After graduating from university and joining the Home Ministry, he was accorded the usual diversified assignments from one end of the ministry to the other. It was in that service that he held police assignments from time to time.

40. Matsumura Kenzō.

41. Including the president of Nissei Spinning, the chairman of the Federation of Economic Organizations, the managing director of Ebara Pump, and the president of Furukawa Mining.

42. It prohibited discrimination because of nationality (mostly practiced against Koreans), creed, and social status (aimed at the *burakumin* untouchables), provided equal wages for men and women, forbade forced labor, set a maximum eight-hour day and forty-eight-hour week, required a month's advance notice for discharges, restricted dangerous work, banned child labor, protected apprentices against exploitation, specified factory safety measures, established scales of worker accident compensation, and set forth scores of other protective rules.

43. *NT,* August 7, 1946, p. 1.

44. Mitamura Shirō, the ex-Communist, told me in April 1951 that he was receiving a monthly police subvention to make available to the authorities his very extensive files on labor and leftist personalities.

45. Such as firemen, factory inspectors, air raid wardens, and clerks, who had not dealt with crimes or the maintenance of public order. We also excluded any police officer who could show that he had opposed labor repression prior to the end of the war. To those deemed temporarily essential, we granted nine-month postponements.

46. Aomori Prefecture, for example.

47. Nagano Prefecture.

48. And indeed, two years after the law's enactment, factory inspections reached 35,000 monthly and industrial accident claims 45,000. (GHQ SCAP, Labor Division, *Semi-Monthly Report #24,* 1949, p. 3, and *Labor Letter,* August 31, 1949, p. 5, both in *TCP.*)

49. *LDMR,* June 1946, para. 47.

13. *Travail of Newspaper: The Yomiuri Repels the Reds*

1. Economic and Scientific Section, Civil Information and Education Section, Civil Intelligence Section, International Prosecution Section, Office of the Political Adviser, and Press Relations Section.
2. At this writing, more than 8 million.
3. Ben Hibbs in the *Saturday Evening Post*, July 1946. The resident *Post* correspondent in Tokyo, Harold Noble, told me, however, that he had had nothing to do with the article.
4. *NT*, November 2, 1945, p. 1.
5. *NT*, November 13, 1945, p. 4, and November 28, 1945, p. 3.
6. Fifteen years later, when the paper was on its feet, he paid his surprised friends for the stocks they "practically forced" on him then. "They refused to take the money, but I made them take it," he asserted proudly long afterward. By 1939, he was sole owner. (Interview, *Chūō Kōron*, September 1960.)
7. Combined during the War with the afternoon *Hōchi* newspaper as the *Yomiuri-Hōchi*.
8. According to the reformists' version, *Yomiuri-Hōchi*, November 5, 1945.
9. *SCAP Monthly Summation*, September–October, 1945, p. 162.
10. *Yomiuri-Hōchi*, November 2, 1945. *Asahi*'s Murayama was "weak-kneed" and had only made trouble for other publishers, he stated.
11. *NT*, December 13, 1945, p. 3.
12. In Japanese, *shōnin*, or "acknowledgment."
13. Masuyama, "Dainiji" (note 37, chapter 11), p. 111.
14. The Nozaka buildup was not confined to Japan. In the United States too, brand-new party-lining books—Andrew Roth, *Dilemma in Japan* (Boston: Little Brown, 1945), Philip Jaffe, *New Frontiers in Asia: A Challenge to the West* (New York: Knopf, 1945)—had just hailed the hitherto unknown Comintern "international rep" under his Yenan alias, Okano Susumu, as Japan's "man of the hour." Where had they discovered him? It looked like an orchestrated international effort, and the *Yomiuri* editors were part of it.
15. *NT*, January 10, 1946, supplement, p. 4.
16. *NT*, December 13, 1945, p. 3.
17. Respectively, Suzuki Tōmin, Bannō Yoshio, Yamanushi Toshio, Katayoshi Satoshi, and Shiga Shigeyoshi.
18. Suzuki, Yamanushi, Bannō, Shiga, Iwamuro Michi, Miyamoto Tarō, and Masuyama Taisuke.
19. Particularly Suzuki and Masuyama.
20. Masuyama, "Dainiji," p. 125.
21. In July 1946, a SCAP Counter Intelligence Report noted that Suzuki "has been accused of having secret membership in the Communist Party," but "he describes himself as a 'republican' favoring a Swiss-type republic." (Memo for the Officer in Charge; subject: "The *Yomiuri* Dispute," drafted by Lieutenant C. H. Lande and approved by R. L. Gump, in *WP*.)

22. At a CIE–Labor Division meeting, June 26, 1946, stenographic record attached to C/N from CIE to Chief, ESS, July 3, 1946, in *TCP*.

23. Katayama Satoshi, "*Nippon Kyōsantō wa doko e yuku?*" (Where is the Communist Party Going?), *Shinsho*, No. 31, quoted in Masuyama, "Dainiji," p. 117.

24. Memo of Major Imboden, July 13, 1946, in *TCP*.

25. A set of regulations issued by SCAP directive on September 19, 1945, to ensure truth in reporting.

26. Of course, Suzuki had neglected to mention to Imboden that the secret Communist head of the composing room was probably submitting questionable editorials to Yoyogi Communist party headquarters for clearance and obtaining new copy from Yoyogi when necessary.

27. Masuyama, "Dainiji," p. 126.

28. The sad history of the incidents of *Yomiuri* defiance was recounted to me by Imboden in the June 26, 1946, meeting (note 22 above).

29. Para. 6: "News stories must be factually written and completely devoid of editorial opinion." Para. 7: "News stories shall not be colored to conform with any propaganda line."

30. Made up by Mutō Santoku, a leader of the anti-Communist faction on the union executive board, who, according to the Communists, had been rejected for party membership as untrustworthy. (Masuyama, "Dainiji," pp. 110–11.)

31. Baba told his side of the encounter at length in his *Jiden Tembyō* (*Autobiographical Sketches*). Masuyama, the Communist union official, gave his version in "Dainiji." My information at the time came from foreign correspondents, particularly Gordon Walker of the *Christian Science Monitor*.

32. Yasuda Shōji, Suzuki's replacement, took a less warlike view. Unaware of Suzuki's Communist ties, he sympathetically visited Suzuki at his apartment house the following night to gain his understanding—nothing personal, said Yasuda, he was only saving *Yomiuri* from the Communists—and offered him a lift downtown in the company car. Suzuki accepted the offer.

33. Deposition (undated) by Chief of the Criminal Affairs Bureau Nakanishi Hisao and Chief of 2d Criminal Investigation Section Masui Shōjirō, of the Metropolitan Police Board, re their meeting with "Lt. Col. Cowan" (they meant "Mr. Cohen") and Major Costantino on June 25, 1946, in *WP*.

34. "On 20th June, some violence was reported, but on 21 June . . . no violence took place." (CIS memo for OIC, July 12, 1946: "The *Yomiuri* Dispute," p. 3.)

35. The day after Baba fired the six, CIE Chief Nugent had telephoned to ask my concurrence to a SCAP statement that a free press meant freedom from domination by labor unions, among others. I agreed. But that was all.

36. The other two, including Suzuki, were at the War Crimes trials in Ichigaya, waiting to testify against the publisher Shōriki, and escaped the police operation.

37. It smelled even worse two weeks later when the Tokyo District Court acquitted the remaining four of trespass.

38. "The *Yomiuri* Dispute," p. 2, para. 9.

39. It was a dead-letter provision, originally copied from the German codes in the late nineteenth century, which I had looked up the day before.

40. Memo for the record by Major Imboden of conference with Messrs. Tachibana, Kinoshita, Mikawa, and Tamura, July 13, 1946, in *TCP*.

41. Nor did practically anyone else. Katō Kanjū thought Kikunami joined the party only in 1947. Hasegawa Kō, Tokuda's right-hand man, knew better; Kikunami got his party card in the spring of 1946, he told me later.

42. The nature of the Shōriki agreement, whether the six had been fired for union activities or for violation of editorial instructions, and whether a labor contract was enforceable when it ventured beyond the proper functions of a trade union as set forth in the Trade Union Law, namely, "maintaining or improving the conditions of work . . . and raising the economic standards of the workers."

43. Stenographic record of the June 26, 1946, meeting (note 22 above).

44. Deposition of Baba Tsunego to the Chief of the Marunouchi Police Station, dated July 25, 1946, in *WP*.

45. Memo by the CIE observer, Lieutenant Robert Pines: "Conference Report 29 June 1946," in *WP*, confirms these remarks. My written statement is in *TCP*.

46. Later, Baba was to say that he did not see how my statement applied to the *Yomiuri* dispute. On the contrary, as he recalled afterwards, "I sent . . . a deputation of *Yomiuri* reporters to Mr. Cohen [that is, subsequent to the meeting] and made him admit that the Press Code and Lt. Col. Nugent's statement regarding the determination of editorial policy by the owners of newspapers can override Japanese labor laws." Deposition of Baba Tsunego to the Chief of the Marunouchi Police Station, dated July 25, 1946, para. 11, in *WP*.

47. *Ibid.*, para. 11.

48. Deposition of T. Kiuchi, August 21, 1946, in *WP*.

49. CIS Memo for Information; subject: "T. Cohen," September 23, 1946, in *WP*.

50. The Communist Secretary of the *Yomiuri* union, Hosaka Kōmei, later revealed that far from giving up on the question of control of editorial policy, four days after the police raid (and three days before my meeting), the Party "Orgburo" had sent a special organizer to ensure that the *Yomiuri* printers would keep up the struggle. Masuyama, "Dainiji" (note 37, chapter 11), p. 152.

51. Against Baba, Suzuki's editorial successor, forty-eight other *Yomiuri* men (for interference with business, forgery, and complicity with violence), the Prime Minister and the police officials involved in the June 22 raid, and against Tokyo Procurator-General Kiuchi for libel. On this latter, see T. Kiuchi deposition, August 21, 1946.

52. From the movie workers to the Aoyama and Meguro car barn locals of the transit union, the Kameari branch of Hitachi, and the Tokyo local of Mitsubishi Steel.

53. Thirty-one barricaded themselves in the composing room, threatening to overturn the type trays onto the floor. With each of those trays containing thousands of Japanese characters, the paper would be out of business for days while they were being reassembled. Other strikers sprawled over floors and tables, refusing to allow anyone else to work. Draft Memo for the Record, July 25, 1946, by Theodore Cohen.

54. Memos are in *TCP*.
55. Report of the All-Japan Newspaper and Radio Workers Union, July 22, 1946, in *TCP*.
56. The worst case of SCAP interference was that of a hotheaded civilian named A. M. Thurston in Colonel Pulliam's Public Safety Division. He entered union headquarters on his own, told the puzzled staffers that the strike had been going on long enough, and declared that since the *Yomiuri* was located so close to GHQ, the strike had to be settled at once. In case of bloody violence, he warned, American MPs armed with machine guns and tanks would put down disorder. Report of the All-Japan Newspaper and Radio Workers Union, July 24, 1946, in *TCP*.
57. Checknote, ESS to C/S, August 2, 1946; subject: "Coordination of Staff Sections in Labor Relations," in *TCP*.
58. Reports attached to CIE checknote to G-2, August 20, 1946, in *WP*.
59. "He [according to Shibata Hidetoshi in a meeting with Costantino on June 28, 1946, memo in *WP*] has been the leader of the strike from the beginning. How can we accept a decision made by such a person?"
60. One deviation from American practice was the Committee ruling that only a union, not a person, could ask for redress. But considering the considerable potential for mischief on the part of outsiders in the circumstances, it was probably the wisest decision they could have made.
61. July 13, 1946, in *TCP*. When I objected hotly, Marquat amiably tore up the memo, and when I wrote my own formal reply (Memo for Brigadier General W. F. Marquat, July 21, in *TCP*), he prevailed upon me not to send it now that he had read it.
62. Checknote, ESS to C/S, August 2, 1946, in *TCP*.
63. According to Government Section sources at the time. I presume the information ultimately came from General Whitney.
64. Department of the Army Commendation for Meritorious Civilian Service, signed by General MacArthur personally.

14. Labor in Turmoil: The Fall of 1946

1. On October 31 and November 9, 1946. *NT,* November 2, 1946, p. 2, and November 9, 1946, p. 3.
2. Ishibashi argued that since the new harvest had reduced food prices, now was a good time to begin decontrol. When Sherwood Fine, General Marquat's economic adviser, pointed out that that was the first decline after seven consecutive months of 10 percent increases, that nonfood prices continued to soar, that Japan's basic food insufficiency remained with no certain remedy, and that if Ishibashi were wrong millions might starve, the supremely self-confident minister insisted that he was not wrong, he was a professional economist, and besides he knew his people, their capacity to endure, better than any foreigner. As it turned out, he was wrong. We were closer to the beginning than the end of the inflation, and, in any event, JCS 1380/15 required strict food controls, whatever Ishibashi thought.

3. Statement to the Budget Committee of the House of Representatives on August 5, 1946. (*NT,* September 18, 1946, p. 4.)

4. Later, when the year's end came, the workers still wanted their bonus and Marquat turned to me, "Didn't they already get their bonus?" My transparent device of June to get around budgetary restrictions had backfired, but by December the inflation justified special action anyway, and the General didn't object to a "second" year-end bonus.

5. *Minpō,* August 4, 1946.

6. Total expenditures, according to Satō, were about 10 billion yen. (*NT,* December 3, 1946, p. 2.) Discharging 130,000 at an average of 600 yen per month plus two months' bonus would have saved almost a billion yen a year; firing 60,000 at 300 yen per month only 237 million yen.

7. Rail freight tonnage in September 1946 totaled 9.5 million metric tons, coastal shipping only 300,000. (*SCAP Monthly Summation,* November 1946, pp. 189, 191.)

8. Ueno, Hachiōji, Omiya, and Mito.

9. *NT,* September 14, 1946, p. 3, and September 11, 1946, p. 1.

10. The best account of the entire affair, although slanted, was the memoir written by Ii Yashirō, who led the strike movement, "Kokutetsu Kyūgatsu Tōsō-to Ni-ichi Zenesuto" ("The Railway September Struggle and the February First General Strike"), *Senryō-ka-no Rōdō Sōgi* ("Labor Disputes Under the Occupation") Special Issue of *Rōdō Undō-shi Kenkyū,* No. 54, February 10, 1972, pp. 12 ff.

11. *NT,* September 13, 1946, p. 1.

12. The Seamen's Union promptly complied. Indeed, on September 10 they exempted all vessels working for the Occupation. *NT,* September 12, 1946, p. 2.

13. In *Rekishi-to Jinbutsu* (*History and Personality*), April 1973, pp. 177–83.

14. The account that follows is pieced together from the newspapers of the time plus Ii's memoir.

15. The newspapers and radio were struck. The workers of forty-six plants, laboratories, and offices of Tokyo Shibaura, the largest maker of electrical machinery, appliances, and equipment in Japan, walked out. And then the Hokkaidō coal miners left their jobs. As almost all of the nation's coking coal came from Hokkaidō, that threatened the steel industry. Panicky Commerce and Industry Ministry officials warned that the Hokkaidō newsprint mills, which furnished most of the country's supplies, would have to cut production for want of fuel, and newspapers would have to suspend publication one day a week. *NT,* November 4, 1946; p. 3. Twenty-one of the nation's largest machinery makers went on strike too, as did Hodogaya Chemical, Japan Cold Storage, parts of Nippon Steel Tube, a number of printing and publishing firms, plus the two biggest telecommunications manufacturers, Oki Electric and Nippon Wireless. One by one Japan's film studios followed suit until no movies, not even newspapers, were being made anywhere. The twenty-nine Tōhō chain theaters shut down, and so did the famous Takarazuka all-girls' troupe. Even hospitals were not immune, as the Nagano Red Cross Hospital and the Kyoto University Medical Department joined the movement.

16. *NT,* October 11, 1946, p. 4.

17. *SCAP Monthly Summation,* May 1947, p. 159.

18. Not one of the "capitalist" newspapers was shut down; the newspapermen elsewhere refused to defend the *Yomiuri* red cell. Only the independent Socialist *Minpō* and the Japan Broadcasting Corporation stopped operations, and then only for a few days. Kikunami, the national newspaper union president, had to resign. And once their strike petered out, the radio union had to listen to a severe fatherly lecture from the Corporation president, Takano Iwasaburō, himself an old socialist and one of the founders of the postwar Socialist party, on how a real union should behave.

19. *Shoki-kyoku Tsūshin* (*Secretariat Bulletin*) No. 37, October 26, 1946, *Tōshiba Strike Materials,* in *TCP.*

20. *Tōsō News* (Struggle News) No. 29, *Tōshiba Strike Materials,* in *TCP.*

21. *Tōshiba Strike Materials,* in *TCP.*

22. 419,000 tons instead of the programmed 360,000. *SCAP Monthly Summation,* November 1946, p. 122.

23. The rank-and-file insistence on sticking to their economic concerns was impressive. Even when the Youth Action Groups tried furiously to "intensify the struggle," they held out. One YAC leaflet proclaimed that "the Tōshiba dispute has now reached its peak. It is now a question of eat or be eaten!" *Tōshiba Strike Materials.* The Tōshiba YACs comprised two-thirds of the strike headquarters personnel. In the collective bargaining negotiations, they guarded the company president closely, even escorting him to the bathroom, and when he nevertheless escaped, they dispatched search parties throughout Tokyo. One YAC group near the Daiichi Hotel, an Occupation officers' billet, carried a sign in English: "Oh my dear boss Yamaguchi and President Tsumori! Will you now come to us without fleeting?" Photograph in *TCP.* The sign, alas, was not completely comprehensible to English-speaking Americans. Such escapades, however, had no wider political overtones. The most militant handbills might demand: "Democratize the workplace! Expel the reactionaries!" *TCP.* But that referred to the company. No one demanded the overthrow of the government.

24. *NT,* October 13, 1946, p. 1.

25. The cabinet would be authorized to designate critical industries with the help of an advisory committee of "thirty or forty" Diet members. Coal mining, electric power, and food distribution were to be named first, with others in due course.

26. *NT,* August 11, 1946, p. 1.

27. *Zen Nippon Denkō Shibu Tōsō News,* No. 4, October 23, 1946, *Tōshiba Strike Materials.*

28. On a 1932–36 base, *JES,* #41–47, IV, January–July 1950, p. 8.

29. *NT,* October 30, 1946, p. 2.

30. *NT,* October 21, 1946, p. 1.

31. In retaliation, ESB Director General Zen announced the government would be coming up with its own proposal, because the CLRC decision was too pro-labor.

32. Yoshida yielded to no one in his self-esteem. Once at a party, when I asked him the trick question of naming an active volcano in Tokyo Prefecture—the correct answer was Ōshima Island in Tokyo Bay—he replied that there were two: "one is in the Daiichi Building (that is, General MacArthur), and the other is me."

33. *NT,* January 26, 1947, p. 3.

34. *NT,* September 13, 1946, p. 2; November 7, 1946, p. 1; November 13, 1946, p. 2; and November 18, 1946, p. 4.
35. *NT,* December 2, 1946, p. 2.
36. *NT,* December 18, 1946, p. 1.
37. *NT,* November 18, 1946, p. 4.

15. Japan at the Precipice: The General Strike

1. Conversation of June 29, 1973, at Katō's apartment house in Meguro, Tokyo.
2. Education Minister Tanaka Kōtarō was the most receptive; Home Minister Ōmura Seiichi, the hard-bitten ex-chief of the Police Bureau, the least. Tanaka was one of Japan's leading Catholic intellectuals, formerly professor of law at Tokyo University, and then for ten years, between 1950 and 1960, Chief Justice of the Supreme Court. He ended his career as a Justice on the World Court.
3. An American civil service advisory mission was on the way to Japan for that purpose.
4. Several of the prime candidates were suddenly discovered to be subject to the Occupation purge, so government representatives told me, hence the delay.
5. Ii Yashirō, "Kokutetsu Kyūgatsu Tōsō to Ni-ichi Zenesuto" (The Railway September Struggle and the February First General Strike), *Senryō-ka no Rōdō Sōgi,* No. 54, February 10, 1972, p. 22.
6. *SCAP Monthly Summation,* February 1947, p. 255, and January 1947, p. 250.
7. Tōshiba workers had won a 1,000-yen-per-month average, the coal-pit workers 1,300, and the electric-power workers, many of whom did the same low-level administrative work as the government workers, 1,850 after taxes.
8. V. I. Lenin, *Collected Works* (New York: International Publishers, 1924), XVII: 142–45.
9. So we thought. But, as we learned later, the Communists had flattered and "stroked" him, assigning six men to watch him all the time, and brought him into camp. By November, he was a secret party candidate member, and he was busy filling union posts accordingly.
10. Labor Ministry (ed.), *Shiryō Rōdō Undō-shi, Shōwa 22-Nenban* (Documentary History of the Labor Movement, 1947), pp. 88–89. The representation was supposed to be according to membership, and the non-Communist Public Workers Union was as big as the Teachers.
11. Repeated at the May Day rally on the Imperial Palace Plaza and then again on May 19 at the Communist-inspired "Food May Day" demonstration.
12. According to Nozaka Sanzō in an Associated Press interview. *NT,* March 2, 1947.
13. Kenneth F. and Eloise P. Mailloux, *Lenin: The Exile Returns* (Princeton, N.J.: Auerback Publications, 1971), p. 88.
14. Especially the public utilities—communications, railways, and shipping. See Draft Memo for C/S, undated, but prepared in February 1947, in *TCP.*
15. Ōkochi Kazuō, "Interi to rōdō kumiai" (Intellectuals and Labor Unions), *Asahi Hyōron,* October 1947.

16. Forty percent of the government workers in whose name the Committee spoke—the quarter-million-man Occupation Forces Union, the Tokyo Transport Workers, the Finance Ministry's Tobacco, Salt, and Camphor Monopoly Workers, the Red Cross medical workers, the Municipal Workers, and so on.

17. According to Hasegawa Kō, Tokuda proposed to move from talk to action: a general strike at the end of January. The orators were fiery, none more than Tokuda. (As a matter of principle, Hasegawa said, Tokuda would never let anyone be more radical or audacious than he, at least in his speeches.) The principal uncertainty was SCAP. Tokuda assured the activist comrades: SCAP would have to stand aside, because the Far Eastern Commission's Principles for Trade Unions, issued only a few weeks before, permitted both strikes and union political activities. This was a little too facile for Hasegawa. In telling me the story many years later in 1973, he interrupted himself to ask me whether I thought Tokuda really believed the Occupation authorities would not intervene. I told him no. As usual, however, Tokuda's eloquence carried the day. Audacity and more audacity, he insisted. Look how far it had taken them already.

18. *NT,* January 9, 1947, p. 3; January 11, 1947, p. 3; and January 12, 1947, p. 1.

19. 1946–47 collections of 4.055 million kg. (ESS GHQ SCAP: *Staple Food Prices in Japan 1930–1948* [Tokyo, April 1949], p. 11.)

20. A total of 2.6 million workers earning an average of 1,800 yen for fourteen months, including standard two-month bonuses, plus 600 yen monthly for two dependents each, would have come to 84 billion yen in a year. 1946–47 revenues in the ordinary account totalled 77 billion yen. (*JES #39,* ovember 1949, p. 37.)

21. In one of his arguments with me in my office the last week of January, Ii readily confessed that even if the government tripled the government workers' wages, he would soon be back asking for more because "the present cabinet had neither the capacity nor the strength to solve basic economic problems." Verbatim record of the meeting of January 26, 1947, at 1 P.M. in my office, in the documents supplement in Saitō Ichiro, *Ni-ichi Suto ni taisuru Senryō-gun Kanshō no Kiroku* (A Record of Occupation Army Intervention in the February First General Strike) (Tokyo, Seifu Shoten, 1956), p. 332.

22. Their assertion that political strikes were protected by the Far Eastern Commission's December "Principles for Trade Unions," for example, and by General MacArthur's refusal to ban the railway strike in September.

23. Labor Division C/N to Chief ESS: "Strike Threat of Government Employees, 1 February 1947," File No. 004.07, dated January 15, 1947, in U.S. National Archives.

24. C/N, Chief ESS to Chief of Staff: "Strike Threat of Government Employees," 1 February 1947," dated February 16, 1947, in U.S. National Archives.

25. For example, the Iron and Steel Workers (110,000 members) for higher wages and a labor contract, and the labor union of the Nittsū Japan Express (trucking) Company (130,000 members) for democratization and improved working conditions.

26. The Electrical Engineering Workers Union (100,000), Machine Food Processors (160,000), Chemical Workers (130,000), Ship-building Workers (80,000), Coal Miners (100,000), printing and publishing workers (14,000), and the Harbor Workers (25,000). The Harbor Workers called their strike for February 5, but with the

railways and trams stopped, they would have been unable to get to work anyway on February 1.

27. Ii's memoir, "Kokutetsu Kyūgatsu" (note 10, chapter 14), p. 30, denies that I ever ordered him to call off the general strike on pain of GHQ intervention. That was just quibbling.

28. Once, in a Central Labor Relations Committee meeting in which both he and Tokuda were labor delegates, Nishio accused Tokuda of starting the general strike campaign, at which Tokuda stalked out in a well-simulated fury, but without denying the charge.

29. According to Takano in a conversation with me on April 19, 1973. The day after the meeting, however, the Communist newspaper *Akahata* (*Red Flag*) carried an interview with Tokuda in which he said, in answer to the question of whether a "people's cabinet" was possible as a result of the forthcoming strike, that the ministers and higher bureaucracy would have to be chosen from the appropriate unions, for example, the transportation minister from the Railway Union, the communications minister from the All-Communications Union, and so on. Both of those unions were, of course, controlled at the top by the Communists. Tokuda, clearly, was not going to be influenced by the mathematics of Diet representation.

30. Marquat had acted as deputy for him in presiding at the Allied Council's first few meetings.

31. I remember only one of my suggestions—that he make reference to MacArthur's record of protecting labor rights in the past and a determination to defend them in the future. He readily accepted it.

32. The government responded with an offer of a 42 percent average wage increase to the 700-yen level that the government workers had demanded as late as the beginning of December, plus the immediate activation of the heretofore moribund Wages Commission to consider further increases.

33. By interrupting national communications or transportation or curtailing the production of commodities necessary to prevent disease, unrest, and human suffering.

34. That was their second request; their first was to ask a postponement of their reply until the 25th, which Marquat readily granted.

35. The Communists later quoted me in one of their leaflets as advising the people of Japan to vote against Yoshida.

36. Years later, Ii reported discussing the incident with Iwama as they left the meeting. They agreed that we Americans just did not understand Japanese culture. We probably thought them barbarians and war lovers for using blood in signatures. (Ii Yashirō, "Kokutetsu Kyūgatsu," p. 31.)

37. A few months later, Iwama's Teachers Union had to consider the public uproar that followed the revelation that a sixth-grade teacher had made his pupils sign a pledge in blood to attend classes punctually. The president was not the only "barbarian" in the union. See *Jiji Press* dispatch from Kōchi, June 19, 1947.

38. One from the Communications Workers, one from the Research Section of *Sanbetsu,* and one from the non-Communist Government Administrative Workers Union. (Notation by Costantino on January 23, 1947, on the back of the carbon copy available for union representatives to look at in the Labor Division Office, in *TCP.*)

39. Saito, *Ni-ichi . . . kiroku* (note 21 above), documents, pp. 310–11.

40. *TCP*. The title of the handbill was: "Crush a False Rumor! This Is the Time."
41. While disparaging Marquat in one sentence, the leaflet cited his "support" in another, reporting him as saying that "you, members of unions, should note that this is a bad, demagogic response to Ii's complaints about the government's dilatoriness, that he could understand how the unions could be dissatisfied on this point in the past.
42. Also Sevelton Brown of the *Providence Journal;* E. Z. Dimitman of the *Chicago Sun;* Ralph Donaldson of the *Cleveland Plain Dealer;* and Thor Smith of the *San Francisco Call-Bulletin.*
43. Some of their control was based upon trickery and intimidation. In the Communications Union, for example, the YAC loaded and surrounded the Central Executive Board meeting that then decided to disregard Marquat's warning. In the Administrative Workers Federation, the messengers sent out to notify the Central Executive Board members were "unable" to contact ten of the eighteen unions represented. The others, less than half the board, voted five to three to support the strike.
44. "With [soldier's] field-service cap at a rakish angle," the Socialist party newspaper *Shakai Shinbun* later complained, "they shout invectives and accusations against the Socialist Party's supposed lack of zeal." (*NT*, February 16, 1947, p. 3.)
45. Tokuda was pictured in the press dancing happily with female party members at a dance at party headquarters on January 25. (*Shūkan Asahi*, April 7, 1978, p. 154.)
46. When Ii visited me the next day, I accused him of not bargaining in good faith. "Your answer today [that is, blaming everything on government insincerity] amounts to hanging yourself," I told him. He merely smiled. (Saitō: *Ni-ichi . . . kiroku*, p. 333.)
47. A distinguished professor of economics, later president of Hitotsubashi University.
48. Matsuoka of the Sōdōmei and Arahata Kanson, the left-wing Socialist, were the other labor representatives.
49. In fact, the government had already pledged to reduce or eliminate workers' income taxes, and General Marquat had personally attested to the pledge.
50. The *Yomiuri* (on January 23), the *Mainichi,* and the *Asahi* (on January 24), together having a combined circulation of 8.5 million, or two-thirds of the then national daily total.
51. He had once proposed a three-party coalition cabinet with the Socialists participating, but with himself, nevertheless, still prime minister. But when the Socialists said no, he reverted to his old conservative coalition cabinet, refusing to consider resignation.
52. Fortunately the record of the exchanges preserved by the union note-takers gives the import and flavor of those heated meetings and has refreshed my own memory of them.
53. Costantino, who as Labor Relations Branch Chief should have presided, was shunted aside, probably as the result of G-2's secret accusation against him as a "leftist." Marquat wanted no complications.
54. The notes taken by Sato Mitsuō of the Teachers Union, in Saitō, *Ni-ichi . . . kiroku*, pp. 337–43, confirm this account.
55. The new prime minister, it was said, would be Matsumoto Jiichirō, the left Socialist leader of the *burakumin*, or ex-untouchables, who advocated a Japanese republic and the end of the Emperor system, Communists Nozaka Sanzō as Foreign Minister, Itō

Ritsu as Minister of Agriculture, and Tokuda himself as Home Minister in control of the police. Many people have testified to those rumors, including Hakamada Satomi, a member of the Communist party Politburo, in his article "Watakushi no Sengoshi" ("My Postwar History"), *Shūkan Asahi,* April 7, 1978, p. 152. Matsumoto, a wealthy political boss from Fukuoka, was for a while considered the political leader of the *buraku* people, and in that capacity was elected to the House of Councilors in its first election, 1947, with the fourth highest number of votes in the "national constituency." He served as the Councilors' first Speaker until 1949, and thereafter he was reelected to the House two more times, serving as a member of the House of Councilors for eighteen years in all. Among his many plans was an early one to convert the Imperial villa at Akasaka (now used as the state guest house) into the national headquarters of the *buraku* organization. He was also well known for having refused to bow to the Emperor on the occasion of the Emperor's inauguration of the National Diet of 1947 and for insisting that he had the right to appear on public occasions without a necktie.

56. In his memoir, Ii says that about one o'clock in the early morning of the 31st, he received word that he was wanted at GHQ—apparently the 2 A.M. deadline had reached him in garbled form by an indirect route, and he thought it was something new—but when he arrived with his comrades, the windows of GHQ's Forestry Building were dark. No one was about but some Nisei guards who knew nothing of such a meeting. This provided him with additional proof that nothing further was to be expected from GHQ (in spite of a week of blunt GHQ warnings).

57. According to an NHK docudrama telecast in August 1947.

58. Although a five-to-eight-day supply of foodstuffs was stockpiled for the six biggest cities, a transportation strike would bring the supply down to "perilously low" levels in three days, as would be the case with charcoal and firewood. Public power reduction would immediately affect hospitals and continuous-process industries; private power in industrial plants depended upon coal, but coal supplies were spread very thin. If the docks were left unmanned, ships carrying relief food and vital raw materials might just bypass Japan, to return in weeks, if at all. Angry farmers might refuse to deliver the crops for the benefit of striking workers. This last struck me as unlikely. (Memo for the Supreme Commander, prepared for General Marquat's signature, but unsigned; subject: Emergency Economic Measures Required by the General Strike, dated January 31, 1947, in U.S. National Archives.)

59. For example, it warned of mass disemployment and the new unemployed asking for more free food; but Japanese factories never fired workers en masse so quickly, and certainly not without retirement allowances. Also, Colonel Ryder was not aware that the strike leaders had volunteered to Labor Division and General Marquat on January 30 to operate food trains.

60. According to Ii, the statement was brought by a news reporter and an ashen-faced Suzuki Mōsaburō, the left-wing Socialist (later head of the Socialist party for many years).

61. According to Hasegawa, June 27, 1973, in Tokyo.

62. Conversation with Hasegawa, June 27, 1973, in Tokyo. Hasegawa had heard the argument before the car drove off. Tokuda on his return had told Hasegawa that the matter was settled.

63. Ii gave two separate accounts of his own participation in these events. The first consisted of his remarks to his comrades at strike headquarters, taken down by a sympathetic listener and then filed by the *Sanbetsu* secretariat. The second was in his memoirs, published in 1972. There are striking contradictions between the two versions. The first described a humiliated, browbeaten Ii, the second the dauntless leader of the masses standing up to the arrogant might of the American military, as represented by General Marquat.

64. A photograph of him wiping his glasses appeared on the front pages of the dailies and also in the magazines and newsreels.

65. Watanabe Buntarō, "Lessons of the February First General Strike," *Fujin to Seiji* (*Women and Politics*), May 1947.

66. See note 6, chapter 16, below.

67. None of the speakers, for example, criticized the *Sanbetsu* or the Communist party in principle. All criticisms were confined to tactical or procedural issues. "Even if the methods used . . . were not exactly wrong," President Kikunami said, "they were not good enough." With that as the keynote, the other speakers delivered their remarks much along the same line. One speaker said that *Sanbetsu*'s leadership was too loose; he was contradicted by another who said it was too obstinate—it did not know how to surrender cleverly. The Electric Power Workers' Nakahara Junkichi, who in General Marquat's office had probed for loopholes in the strike ban, blamed the workers for the strike failure: They were "unenlightened" and needed more education in the class struggle. The Electric Machinery Workers' Ochiai took the same position: The fault was the workers' and they should undertake self-criticism. The meetings were held on May 10–12 and 14–15. See the reports in the independent Socialist newspaper, *Minpō*, May 21–22, 1947.

68. Among them the coal miners, newspaper and radio workers, and electric power workers.

69. Who told the story to Sherwood Fine.

Part V: The Limits of Democratization

1. January 1, 1948, *PRJ*, II: 776.

16. A Kind of Normality: SCAP Consolidates His Reforms

1. *Asahi, June 6, 1947.*

2. *Mainichi, August 21, 1947.*

3. *JES* #39, November 1949, p. 13.

4. ESS, GHQ SCAP, *Japan's Housing Requirements* (Tokyo, 1948), p. 3. By the end of December 1947, the number of housing units lost and not replaced—some 2.3 million destroyed, less half a million built during and after the war—was 1,771,728.

5. Report to the Diet, September 5, 1945, in *NT*, September 7, 1945, p. 1.

6. In the April 1947 House of Representatives elections, the Socialist party won 30.7 percent of the seats (with 26 percent of the votes). This made it the largest single party in the House, although very far short of a majority. It thereupon formed a coalition with two conservative parties, the Democratic party (26 percent of the votes, 26 percent of the seats) and the Cooperative party (7 percent of the votes, 6 percent of the seats). Together, the three parties formed a majority, overwhelmingly larger than the conservative Liberal party, which until then had formed the government. From May, the Socialists led the coalition, with Katayama Tetsu as prime minister. Then, in March 1948, the Democrats took over the coalition leadership, with Ashida Hitoshi as prime minister. Ashida's government, like Katayama's, was unable to effect any of its major programs, and that failure, along with serious scandals reaching up to the prime minister himself, brought the government down after eight months. Yoshida Shigeru, the former prime minister, took over the position once more. In the following elections, January 1949, the Liberals won a smashing victory—44 percent of the votes, 57 percent of the seats—and the coalition partners suffered a humiliating defeat: the Socialists dropped to 14 percent of the votes (10 percent of the seats); the Democrats to 16 percent of the votes (15 percent of the seats); and the Cooperatives to 3.4 percent of the votes (and 3 percent of the seats).

7. Statement of May 24, 1947, *PRJ*, II: 770.

8. On June 1, 1947. (*SCAP Monthly Summation*, May 1947, p. 28.)

9. *Japan Year Book*, 1947, p. 494.

10. The text of his letter of February 7, 1947 appeared in *NT*, February 8, 1947, p. 1.

11. The text is in *SCAP Monthly Summation*, March 1947, pp. 24–25.

12. New Year's statement, January 1, 1948, *PRJ*, II: 776.

13. SCAPIN 1741, July 3, 1947.

14. Letter to the prime minister, September 16, 1947. The text appears in *SCAP Monthly Summation*, October 1947, pp. 31–35.

15. October 7, 1946, *FRUS*, 1946, VIII: 332–34.

16. Message of February 20, 1947, *PRJ*, II: 763.

17. Interview with Russell Brines of AP, in *NT*, May 2, 1947, p. 2.

18. Whitney, *MacArthur* (note 6, "Personal Note"), p. 251.

19. Then Minister of State, Chief of the Economic Stabilization Board, and Chief of the Price Board.

20. *Missions and Accomplishments*, June 1950 edition, II, No. 2: 20.

21. *JES* #39, November 1949, p. 20.

22. Memo of the First Economic Section, Prosecution Bureau, Attorney General's Office, dated July 24, 1948, in *TCP*.

23. According to ESS Industry Division Chief Reday in a press conference on February 12, 1947, reported in *NT*, February 13, 1947, p. 1.

24. Economic Stabilization Board White Paper of July 3, 1947, Sect. II, 1B, gives the following percentages of black market to total rice consumed by urban families: October 1946: 25 percent plus; November 1946: 20 percent; February 1947: 43 percent; April 1947: 27 percent.

25. Only 550,000 metric tons in the period July 1, 1948–July 30, 1949, compared with a total rationed quantity of staple foods of some 7 million. (*JES* #39, November 1949, p. 50.)

26. *JES* #40, December 1949, p. 20, and *Mission and Accomplishments*, Sect. IV 3.

27. *JES* #40, December 1949, pp. 1, 17.

28. Monthly wages increased 188 percent from 2,231 to 6,423 yen, while consumer prices rose 61 percent, from an index of 71.9 to 115.9. *Ibid.*

17. Coal Mines and Kodan: Nationalizing in the Light and in the Dark

1. *PRJ*, II: 767.

2. In his victory statement of April 27, 1947. *NT*, April 28, 1947, p. 1.

3. *NT*, May 2, 1947, p. 2.

4. *NT*, June 21, 1947, p. 1.

5. First in 1950, when it was divided into a right and left Socialist party. After a brief reunion in 1958, it once again split permanently in 1960, the left Japan Socialist party, and the right Democratic-Socialist party.

6. *Forrestal Diaries* (note 34, chapter 2), entry for May 7, 1947, p. 273.

7. *JES* #78, February 1953, p. 18.

8. *JYB*, 1938, p. 343.

9. *LDMR*, November 1945, para. 8, gives the number at 130,000. A special report by Uemura Kōgoro, vice president of the Japan Coal Mining Company, reprinted in *NT*, September 20, 1946, gave the number at 140,000.

10. *Mission and Accomplishments*, sec. V, para. 1.

11. Total coal mine employment reached 286,000 in March 1946. *LDMR*, April 1946, para. 34.

12. Steel allocations for coal mines in the later war years, for example, were only a quarter of those at the beginning.

13. The Cabinet Planning Board allocated 160,000 tons of steel to mine operations and maintenance in 1941, 80,000 in 1943 and 40,000 in 1944. Uemura report.

14. *JYB*, 1948, p. 342.

15. Uemura report.

16. Mine employment as early as 1911, at 145,000, was already 55 percent of what it was to be in 1947. *Sekitan Rōdō Nenkan* (Tokyo, Sekitan Kōgyō Renmei, 1947), p. 237. In 1938, it had gone up to 263,000. (*JYB*, 1948, p. 342.)

17. Richard L. G. Deverall, then Chief of the Labor Division Field Liaison Branch, and Leon Becker.

18. According to Matsumoto Takeo, Chairman of the National Council of Coal Miners' Unions, in *Kyōdō News Service*, February 13, 1947, p. 3.

19. In September 1946, average daily wages were 22 yen, which at a quarter-ton produced per miner (including the surface workers) per day, worked out to a direct labor cost of 88 yen, but the official price was 216 yen per ton. (Uemura report.) The October settlement doubled wages and labor costs.

20. "Recent Situation in the Coal Mine Industry," *Ekonomisuto*, September 1947, cited in *Digest Service*, October 5, 1947, pp. 22–24.

21. *NT*, February 13, 1947, p. 1. Reday actually said that a million tons of coal had moved into the black market from Kyūshū in the last few months. Kyūshū's production was then running at 1.1 million tons monthly, or 3.3 million in three months.

22. Dated August 16, 1947, and signed by Obayashi Kanki, president of the National Council of Coal Miners' Unions, in *TCP*.

23. The prewar private utility companies still held shares in the monopoly generation and distribution companies.

24. Letter of September 17, 1947, in *SCAP Monthly Summation*, September 1947, p. 23.

25. Letter to J. H. Jipson, January 24, 1948, *PRJ*, II: 780.

26. *PRJ*, II: 770.

27. *Ibid.*, Bulletin No. 2, December 4, 1948, para. (a) (2), in *TCP*.

28. *Ibid.*, Bulletin No. 1, para. 1 in *TCP*.

29. The main outlines of the plan were revealed to *Jiji Shimpō* in June.

30. My memo of July 14, 1947, in *TCP*.

31. Socialist party memo of July 7, 1947, as reported in *ibid.*

32. "Plan of Temporary State Control of Coal Mines," submitted by the ESB to GHQ and dated August 1947, in *TCP*.

33. *Shakai Shinbun*, October 12, 1947.

34. *SCAP Monthly Summation*, August 1948, p. 38

35. Resolution of the National Council of Coal Miners' Unions, August 16, 1947.

36. *NT*, September 23, 1948, p. 1.

37. HCLC, "Illegal Diversion of Funds by Coal Companies," Bulletin No. 4, December 21, 1948.

38. "Revision (draft) of the State Control of Coal Mining Bill Desired by the Three Political Parties Supporting the Government," dated November 19, 1947, submitted to ESS Industry Division, in *TCP*.

39. *Minpō*, November 28, 1947, letter from Kanda Ryō.

40. From 2.1 million to 3 million metric tons. *JES* #40, December 1949, p. 12.

41. SCAP Monthly Summation, June 1947, pp. 25–31, contains the complete text as issued by the government in English.

42. Covering shipbuilding, industrial reconstruction, foreign trade, special Occupation Force procurement, price adjustment, and petroleum and solid fuels distribution.

43. JCS 1380/15, para. 25b(3).

44. The National General Mobilization Law of 1938, amended in 1941, and the Major Industries Association Ordinance of 1941.

45. Automobiles, cement, chemicals, coal, electric machinery, fibers, fuel gas, hides and leather, industrial machinery, iron and steel, light metals, nonferrous metals, mining other than coal, petroleum, railway and tramway, rolling stock, rubber, silk, and shipbuilding. (Memo for record, July 19, 1946, appended to SCAPIN 1108, Dissolution of Control Associations, dated August 6, *Economic SCAPINS*, p. 240.)

46. *SCAP Monthly Summation*, July 1946, p. 216.

47. Memo for the record, June 20, 1946, appended to SCAPIN 1037; subject: Dissolution of the Japan Lumber Company, Ltd. *Economic SCAPINS*, p. 217.
48. The Iron and Steel Control Association had dissolved itself in February 1946, and SCAP directives had abolished the Rubber Control Association and two of its satellites in May, and both the Automobile Distribution Control Company and the Japan Warehouse Control Company in July.
49. Memo for the record, October 16, 1946, appended to SCAPIN 1394, *Economic SCAPINS*, p. 343, ''The attitude of obstruction towards efforts to disestablish the control company device as a method of government-delegated control,'' Colonel Kupferer, Antitrust Division Executive Officer, commented, ''is not difficult to understand. . . . It is because of the complete control of every feature of production and distribution exercised by the men who have gained control of these companies that the Japanese have been able to mobilize small and medium-size industry during the war.''
50. SCAPIN 1934.
51. Memos for the record, November 1, 1946 for SCAPIN 1308 and October 17, 1946, for SCAPIN 1294, *Economic SCAPINS*, p. 318.
52. Memo for the record, July 19, 1946, appended to SCAPIN 1108, *Economic SCAPINS*, p. 239.
53. Frank Goodhue, reported in *NT*, August 14, 1947, p. 2.

18. The Normality of Scandal: The Japanese Army's Missing Supplies

1. *Shuppan Jōhō (Publishing News)*, June 1947.
2. *Jiji Press*, July 11, 1947.
3. *Asahi*, July 29, 1947.
4. *Shin-Hōchi*, May 13, 1947.
5. *Jiji Press*, January 24, 1948.
6. *Jiji Press*, July 8, 1947.
7. *Jiji Press*, June 25, 1947.
8. *NT*, November 16, 1947, p. 1.
9. *Jiji Press*, June 14, 1947.
10. *Shin-Hōchi*, May 27, 1947.
11. *Asahi*, December 15, 1947.
12. *Mainichi Shinbun*, May 17, 1947.
13. *Jiji Press*, May 12, 1947.
14. *Jiji Press*, July 23, 1947.
15. *Jiji Press*, July 30, 1947.
16. *Magazine Tokyo*, May 1947.
17. *Jiji Press*, June 24, 1947.
18. *Tokyo Shinbun*, July 29, 1947.
19. *Jiji Shinpō*, November 29, 1947.

20. *Sun Photo Times*, January 13, 1948.
21. *Jiji Press*, December 6, 1947.
22. *Jiji Press*, December 7, 1947.
23. In Nakanoshima, central Osaka.
24. *SCAP Monthly Summation*, May 1946, p. 41.
25. *SCAP Monthly Summation*, sections on Property Control up to October 1947. Some was owned by third governments (*SCAP Monthly Summation*, September–October 1945, p. 125), the rest by the Japanese Government.
26. Speech of May 24, 1947, before the Keizai Konwa-kai (Economic Discussion Society), a stenographic record of which appeared in *Jiyū Kokumin*, special number, July 1947.
27. Home Ministry, disposal lists furnished to me in late 1947, as I remember them, included 4 million tunics, 4 million trousers, 4 million pairs of shoes, 4 million caps, 8 million pairs of *tabi* socks, and 1 million hats. A Headquarters G-4 report, cited in *NT*, December 31, 1947, p. 3, declared that 5 million pairs of shoes, 21 million pairs of socks, and 7 million blankets were among Japanese Army stocks returned to Japanese civilian authorities by the Americans.
28. Report of House of Representatives Special Committee for Investigation of Concealed and Hoarded Goods, released December 20, 1947, hereinafter referred to as the Katō Committee Report, part II, para. 2. The verbatim report in English may be found in the *SCAP Monthly Summation* for December 1947, pp. 24–32.
29. *Ibid.*, para. 3.
30. *Ibid.*, para. 4.
31. Testimony of General Yoshizumi Masao, Chief of the Military Affairs Bureau under both the Suzuki and Higashikuni cabinets, before the House of Representatives Special Committee on Illegal Transactions, hereinafter referred to as the Mutō Committee, on October 18, 1948, as reported in the *Yomiuri*, October 19, 1948.
32. General Shimomura Sadamu, War Minister in the Higashikuni and Shidehara cabinets, testified before the Mutō Committee that the Americans told Kawabe this on August 23. That was wrong. The Japanese mission arrived in Manila on August 19 and was handed a packet of surrender documents, including General Order No. 1, immediately after their dinner. General Order No. 1, later to be officially reissued on September 2 as an attachment to Directive No. 1, stated in part (paragraph VI): "Responsible Japanese and Japanese-controlled Military and Civil Authorities will hold intact and in good condition pending further instructions from the Supreme Commander for the Allied Powers the following . . . (d) All factories, plants . . . and other material and property used by or intended for use by any military or para-military organization in connection with its operations." (*PRJ*, II: 443–44.) The story of the meeting is told in D. C. James, *Years of MacArthur* (note 39, chapter 4) II: 779. Lieutenant Colonel Frank E. Hayes, Special Adviser to General Whitney, in his report on "Government Aspects of Law Enforcement" in *PRJ*, I: 308, stated that General Order No. 1 was handed to Kawabe on August 20. *PRJ*, I: 308. In any event, Kawabe departed at 1:00 P.M. on August 20 for Tokyo and arrived late that night. (*NT*, August 23, 1945, p. 1.) He had to have received the orders before he left.

33. According to "Japanese sources," unnamed, referred to by Frank Hayes.

34. General Shimomura, in his testimony before the Mutō Committee, offered his guess that 60 percent of what had been removed was recovered, but that seems unreasonably optimistic without enforcement means. Other estimates were only 30 percent.

35. SCAPIN 53, September 24, 1945, Subject: Materials, Supplies and Equipment Received and to Be Received from the Japanese Armed Forces.

36. SCAPIN 629, January 20, 1946.

37. Testimony of Technical Captain Kawamoto Toshio, in charge of the Osaka Arsenal disposal program, before the procurators. (*Asahi Shinbun,* November 10, 1947.)

38. Before the Katō Committee, Report, part III, para. 5, finding six.

39. Furukawa Electric, Kobe Steel, Nippon Steel Tube, Fuso Metals, and Nippon Iron and Steel.

40. Katō Committee Report, part II para. 10. Memo for record by W. Thurman, Industry Division, April 30, 1948, attached to SCAPIN 1898, *Economic SCAPINS,* p. 429.

41. Calculated at 50 percent more than the price of steel scrap at that time. Copper and aluminum ingot sold for $330 and $270 per metric ton, and usable secondary products in all these categories were of course much higher.

42. Katō Committee Report, para. 1.

43. Japan Liberal party former president Hatoyama (later to become prime minister in 1954); Ōno Banboku; Gunma Prefecture Governor Kitano Shigeo; Democratic party secretary general Chizaki Uzaburō, State Minister Nishio Suehiro, Finance Minister Kitamura Tokutarō, ESB Director-General and Former Finance Minister Kurusu Takeo.

44. Chizaki, Nishio, and Kitamura were charged with not reporting political donations from private companies, Kurusu with bribery.

45. *PRJ,* I: p. 311.

46. No relation to prime minister Nakasone Yasuhiro.

47. *SCAP Monthly Summation,* June 1948, p. 35.

48. *NT,* June 23, 1948, p. 3.

49. At the Nakajima Propeller Company, *NT,* June 8, 1948, p. 3.

50. For fiscal 1942–43, national income was 45 billion yen, national budget expenditures 24.3 billion, defense expenditures 17.8 billion. (*Orient Year Book,* 1942, p. 1445.) For 1945–46, respective figures were 141 billion, 103 billion, and 87.55 billion yen. (*SCAP Monthly Summation,* September–October 1945, p. 121.)

51. Estimated 1945 national income of 141 billion yen times 4 = 562 billion yen for four years. If an average of half of this was spent on the war, it comes to 281 billion yen. Actual expenditures from the extraordinary military account from the China Incident of 1937 to the end of the war were 222 billion yen. (*NT,* October 14, 1945, p. 1.)

52. *NT,* August 20, 1947, p. 3.

53. In October 1945, the highest black market prices for consumer goods were from 2.5 to 266 times the official prices. (*SCAP Monthly Summation,* September–October 1945, pp. 112–13). A year later the ratios were much smaller, though still appreciable.

54. In 1947 industrial production is calculated at $2 billion on the basis of 38.3 percent (*JES* #68, February 1953, p. 9) of the $3.3 billion 1934–36 level (*Orient Year Book,* 1942, pp. 217, 289) and adjusted to 1947 dollars at 1.63 1947 dollars to one 1934–36 dollar.

55. 27.24 metric tons at the official price of 346 yen (or $1.82) per ton in the fall of 1947. *JES* #78, p. 18.

56. *JES* #76, December 1952, sec. II, p. 9, and Sherwood Fine, *Japan's Post-War Industrial Recovery* (Tokyo: Foreign Affairs Association of Japan, 1952), p. 36.

57. *SCAP Monthly Summation,* February 1948, p. 42.

58. *SCAP Monthly Summation,* March 1948, p. 35.

59. *NT,* October 3, 1948, p. 1.

60. In *TCP.*

61. By SCAPIN 1863.

62. Press release October 18, 1945, quoted in *NT,* October 19, 1945, p. 3.

63. ESS C/N #1, to G-2, February 3, 1948; subject: Concealed Goods. In *TCP.*

64. G-2 C/N #2 to ESS, February 13, 1948, in *TCP.*

65. Katō Committee Report, part II, para. 16.

66. *NT,* January 24, 1948, p. 3.

67. *NT,* February 26, 1948, p. 1, and *SCAP Monthly Summation,* February 1948, p. 42.

68. ESS C/N #1 to GS, May 12, 1948; subject: Removal of Mr. Shinobu Kinoshita as Deputy Director, Enforcement Bureau, ESB, and Memo of Mark Rosenfelt, May 10, 1948, both in *TCP.*

69. *JES* #40, December 1949, p. 8.

Part VI. The Last Targets: Oligarchs and Bureaucrats

1. *PRJ,* p. 765.

19. The Assault on the Zaibatsu

1. Composed by Paul Stanchfield of the Labor Division, poet laureate of the Occupation.

2. *FRUS,* 1945, VI: 826.

3. Douglas MacArthur, letter to Mr. J. H. Jipson, January 24, 1948, in *PRJ,* II: 780.

4. *NT,* October 17, 1945, p. 1.

5. See her account in "Personal Note," at note 8.

6. By SCAPIN 244. *Economic SCAPINS,* pp. 39–40.

7. Will Clayton, letter of October 31, 1945, in *FRUS,* VI: 811–12.

8. William C. Dixon, Samuel Neel, James MacI. Henderson, Robert Dawkins, Raymond Vernon, Benjamin Wallace, and Robert M. Hunter, respectively.

9. Including prohibition of intercorporate stockholdings, qualifications for directors, nondiscriminatory patent licensing, purging of former *zaibatsu* owners and managers, compensation for divested holdings, preference for trade unions and cooperatives in acquiring ex-*zaibatsu* securities, and corporate accounting methods.

10. FEC 230, para. 2, subpara. 3.

11. *Ibid.*, para. 2, subpara. 5. Italics added.

12. Draft cable of June 16, 1947, to the War Department, prepared by the SCAP Antitrust Division, but not sent, in *TCP*.

13. Memo for the record prepared by Irving T. Bush, Deputy Chief of Antitrust Division, March 5, 1946, appended to SCAPIN 813. (*Economic SCAPINS*, p. 141.)

14. Report of Major R. M. Cooper, Chief of Liquidations Branch, Antitrust and Cartels Division, to the ACJ, November 27, 1946. Cited in *FRUS*, 1946, VIII: 377. By October 1947, the number of dissolved holding companies was sixty-seven. (SCAP radio WARQSCAD Number C-56173, October 17, 1947, in *TCP*.)

15. SCAPIN 1741, "Dissolution of Trading Companies," July 3, 1947, and Memo for the record by E. C. Welsh, June 14, 1947, (*Economic SCAPINS*, p. 395.)

16. Checknote, GS to ESS, June 19, 1947, cited in memo from E. C. Welsh to Colonel Ryder, August 5, 1947; subject: Preparation of Proposed HCLC Law, p. 3.

17. Memo, Welsh to T. Cohen, August 12, 1947; subject: Proposed HCLC Law or Ordinance, para. 2a, in *TCP*.

18. A draft copy is in *TCP*.

19. Clifford L. James, assisted by Edward C. Welsh and Gordon Arneson, *Concentrations of Economic Power*, Temporary National Economic Commission of the 76th Congress, no. 10, (Washington, D.C.: Government Printing Office, 1940).

20. Letter from Y. Yoshida and eight other members, July 30, 1947, in *TCP*.

21. Para. 18, draft radio in reply to WDSCA 82082 of July 16, 1947, in *TCP*.

22. Memo of August 6, 1947; subject: HCLC in *TCP*.

23. Memo for General Marquat; subject: Deconcentration of Economic Power in Japan, October 20, 1947, p. 3.

24. Under the SWNCCFE number SFE 182 (later SWNCC 302).

25. WDSCA ECON to CINCFE, July 16, 1947, No. 82082.

26. Draft memo for Under Secretary of the Army William S. Draper; subject: Economic Mission of SCAP, October 1, 1947, in *TCP*.

27. MacArthur explained his stand to Senator Brien MacMahon a little later: "As the sources of origin, authorship and authority [of FEC 230] are all in Washington and my responsibility limited to the executive implementation of basic decisions formulated there, I am hardly in a position ten thousand miles away to participate in the debate." (Letter of February 1, 1948, *PRJ*, II: 783.)

28. With 14 percent of the shares, Libby-Owens-Ford was the biggest stockholder in 1951. *Kaisha Shiki-hō* (Corporation Quarterly Register), Keizai Shinpo-sha, 1951, p. 178.

29. He had me as a union organizer from New York University. I never belonged to a union and had gone to City College of New York. He alleged Japanese workers were receiving from 3,000 to 8,000 yen monthly instead of the 1,767 yen they were in fact

receiving (*JES* #37, September 1945, p. 16). He reported 10,000 GHQ officers and civilians earning between $5,000 and $10,000 annually instead of only 1,200. In September 1947 he blamed labor excesses on the Labor Standards Law, which had been enforced only since September 1. He never met me or, as far as I know, Sherwood Fine.

30. Part of Kauffman's report was published in *Newsweek,* December 1, 1947, pp. 36–38.
31. The wartime Office of Price Administration. (*Forrestal Diaries,* note 34, chapter 2, pp. 328–29.)
32. Kennan: *Memoirs* (note 50, chapter 8), p. 409.
33. *Forrestal Diaries,* p. 329.
34. WAR (CSCAD) to CINCFE, No. 88682, October 21, 1947.
35. SCAP to WAR (CSCAD) No. C-56173.
36. *FRUS,* 1946, VIII: 97.
37. CSCAD (Draper) to CINCFE (personal to MacArthur), No. 93502.
38. Seki Yoshinaga, managing director; Takasugi Shinichi, president; and Hirayama Kenzaburō, a "top flight engineer."
39. CSCAD PL (Draper) to CINCFE (MacArthur), No. 23520.
40. *NT,* January 8, 1948, p. 1.
41. Marquat radio to Draper, April 4, 1948, part 1, para. 1.
42. *NT,* December 24, 1947, p. 1.
43. *PRJ,* II: 776.
44. Radio Z-35682, January 18, 1947. *PRJ,* II: 778.
45. *PRJ,* II: 783.
46. Letter to J. H. Jipson, *PRJ,* II: 780–82.
47. *NT,* February 13, 1948, p. 3.
48. The radio was sent out on April 5. The draft is in *TCP.*
49. Satō was chief cabinet secretary from October 1948 to February 1949 in the Second Yoshida Cabinet. Thereafter he held a variety of party and cabinet posts until November 1964, when he became prime minister, a position he held until July 1972, the longest term in Japanese history.
50. *Asahi Nenkan,* 1967, p. 381.
51. *JES* #39, November 1949, p. 39.
52. *Missions and Accomplishments,* part XI, para. 2. The balance of 23 million shares was in companies that were liquidated.
53. Others included hair spray, electric massage vibrators, sytled men's ready-to-wear, vodka, home refrigerators, radar ranges, chocolate drops, copying machines, yogurt, disposable diapers, "infrared" cosmetics, cockroach spray, detergents, stainless-steel furniture, a hamburger fast-food restaurant (MacDonald's), air tours abroad, potato chips, facial tissue, electric typewriters, and farm machinery.
54. For example, a service combine like Tōkyū, with interests in suburban railways, bus lines, department stores, travel agency, "gold stamps," hotels (both domestic and international), and real estate. Significantly, former prime minister Tanaka's chief

financial backer, Osano Kenji, was not an industrial tycoon at all but a large-scale resort hotel owner, including several in Hawaii and California. (Tanaka Kakuei, the highly controversial prime minister, held the post from July 1972 until December 1974. At the moment of writing, he is still under indictment for allegedly accepting bribes from the Lockheed Aircraft Corporation, in return for favoring their jets over those of other manufacturers.)

55. Edwin O. Reischauer, in *The Japanese* (Cambridge, Mass.: Harvard University Press, 1977), states that "the American authorities held to the Marxist interpretation that the real villain behind Japan's imperialism had been the excessive concentration of industrial wealth and power in the hands of the *zaibatsu* . . . it led to a remarkable display of socialistic zeal on the part of MacArthur and his staff."

20. "Defeudalizing" the Civil Service

1. *PRJ*, I: 246.
2. Memo for Chief, Government Section, January 30, 1946; subject: Japanese Civil Service Reform, in *PRJ*, II: 578.
3. Letter of April 25, 1946, *PRJ*, II: 579.
4. Cabinet understanding of May 14, 1946, *PRJ*, II: 580.
5. W. Pierce MacCoy, Director of Personnel of the State Department; Manlie F. De Angelis, Chief of the Program Planning Staff, Civil Service Commission; and Robert S. Hare, Chief of Field Service Classification.
6. Herbert Passin, *Society and Education in Japan* (New York, Columbia University Teachers College Press, 1965), p. 129. The same educational elitism pervaded big business, where in 1963 Tokyo University accounted for 48 percent of the executives of the twenty-five largest corporations (p. 132) and politics, where in the first two Ikeda Cabinets, 1960–63, thirteen and eleven respectively of the twenty-one ministers came from the "big three" national universities (seven of them from Tokyo University, p. 146).
7. INS dispatch in *NT*, September 9, 1948, p. 1.
8. It remained for almost a year and then was converted *en masse* into a regular SCAP division.
9. All these ideas appear in Hoover's press statement of September 1948, in *TCP*.
10. All other penalties were dismissals, suspensions, and disbarments.
11. Including failure to testify before the National Personnel Authority, conspiring to strike, political activities like handing out leaflets on government premises, and so on.
12. *PRJ*, II: 583.
13. He was later to leave a trail of bureaucratic battle in his wake as U.S. Economic Aid Mission chief in Yugoslavia, Pakistan, Seoul, and finally Saigon (where he unsuccessfully tangled with Ambassador Henry Cabot Lodge).
14. In a memo of July 13, 1948, "Collective Bargaining and Government Service" (in *TCP*), Killen had proposed "the prohibition by SCAP [not the Japanese Government,

be it noted] of all acts of dispute in both administrative branches of government service and in those services operated by the government, deemed essential to the welfare and safety of the Japanese community.'' He had also proposed ''compulsory arbitration of unresolved issues.''

15. Draft of memorandum; subject: Program for Labor Relations and Personnel Policy in the Japanese Government Service, dated July 17, 1948, prepared for General Marquart's signature but unsigned, in *TCP*.

16. ''Mr. Killen's Remarks on the Denial of Collective Bargaining and Strike Rights of Japanese Government and Public Employees,'' prepared on shipboard on his way home in August 1948, in *TCP*.

17. As he was to write to the prime minister on July 22. 1948. (*PRJ*, II: 581–83.)

18. According to Bernarr Mazo, Assistant Chief of the Wages Branch, interviewed in February 1982 at his home in Los Angeles.

19. The ''poet laureate'' cited at the opening of chapter 19.

20. Conversation in Tokyo, June 18, 1973.

21. The Labor Relations Adjustment Law of September 1946.

22. According to Katō on June 29, 1973, at his home in Meguro, Tokyo.

23. Minutes of the House of Representatives, November 11, 1948, in *Official Gazette Extra,* November 12, 1948, p. 11.

24. Z-24312, September 27, 1948, last para., in *TCP*.

25. *NT,* December 2, 1948, p. 1.

26. In the 1947 elections, Katō ran from the Aichi First District. In 1949 he was defeated there, and in subsequent elections, from 1952 on, he ran from the Tokyo Second District, where his wife had won in the first two postwar elections. From 1952 until 1969, he won in five elections and was defeated in two, 1965 and 1963.

27. *NT,* January 26, 1949, p. 1.

28. Minutes of the Proceedings of the House of Representatives for November 13, 1948, in *Official Gazette Extra,* November 15, 1948, p. 5.

29. *NT,* January 26, 1949, pp. 1–2.

30. J. P. Napier, *A Survey of the Japan Communist Party* (Tokyo, *Nippon Times*, 1952), p. 55. Napier was Chief of the GS Public Administration Division at the time of the discharges.

31. Shimoyama Sadanori, whose body was found, run over by a train, on July 6, 1949, in the northern part of Tokyo. Two days earlier, dismissal notices had been sent out to 37,000 railway employees, the first batch of 102,000 discharges that had been scheduled.

32. On July 15, 1959, just nine days after the Shimoyama incident, an unmanned electric train derailed at the Tokyo suburban station of Mitaka and killed six people standing on the platform.

33. On August 7, 1949, a train was derailed, undoubtedly through sabotage, at the town of Matsukawa, Fukushima Prefecture, about 170 miles north of Tokyo. Three crew members were killed, and many passengers were injured. The best account of the three incidents will be found in Chalmers Johnson, *Conspiracy at Matsukawa* (Berkeley: University of California Press, 1972).

34. Tokuda had died in 1953 in Peking, China, where he had gone to escape the Occupation's purge order against Communist party Central Committee members.

Part VII. To Rescue the American Taxpayer

21. William Draper and the Marshallization of American Aid

1. Until recently, Tokyo's main international airport. During the Occupation, one section of it was reserved for the U.S. Air Force. In the 1970s it was displaced by the new (and controversial) Narita International Airport as the main entry point for international flights.
2. *NT,* September 28, 1947, p. 1.
3. *Ibid.*
4. *NT,* October 11, 1947, p. 1.
5. Department of State *Bulletin,* June 15, 1947, p. 1160.
6. His predecessors, Assistant Secretary of War John J. McCloy, Under Secretary Kenneth Royall, and Assistant Secretary Howard Peterson, were all lawyers, interested in principles and policies, not figures.
7. Sherwood Fine, *Japan's Postwar Industrial Recovery* (Tokyo: Foreign Affairs Association of Japan, 1952), p. 1160.
8. Forrestal (Dillon Read) as Secretary of Defense; Lovett (Brown Brothers Harriman), as Under Secretary and often Acting Secretary of State; and John Snyder (First National Bank of St. Louis) as Secretary of the Treasury. In contrast, Roosevelt had only one banker, Jesse Jones, in his cabinet in twelve years.
9. Dean Acheson as Under Secretary of State, John J. McCloy as Assistant Secretary of War, Averell Harriman, advising long-distance from his ambassadorial post in Moscow, and John Carter Vincent, director of State Department's Office of Far Eastern Affairs.
10. Radio to Secretary of State Byrnes, October 30, 1945. (*FRUS,* 1945, VI: 809.)
11. *NT,* October 14, 1945, p. 4.
12. *Forrestal Diaries* (note 34, chapter 2), pp. 251–52.
13. *Ibid.,* pp. 304–5.
14. *Ibid.,* pp. 536–37. Letter to Walter G. Andrews, December 13, 1948.
15. *Ibid.,* p. 282.
16. Taber, of New York, was chairman of the House Appropriations Committee, and Passman, of Louisiana, was one of the senior members.
17. Department of State *Bulletin,* June 15, 1947, p. 1160.
18. Cf. MacArthur's message for Congress on January 20, 1947, *PRJ,* II: 763–64, and his interview with reporters at the Tokyo Press Club on March 19, 1947, where he said, "I think Japan can pay back all the dollars we appropriate." (*PRJ,* II: 766.)
19. A year later, the ESS economists would revise the funds needed to $1.4 billion in a "Blue Book," but they still promised an end to U.S. aid by 1953. (Fine, *Japan's Post-War Recovery,* note 56, chapter 8, pp. 34–35.)

20. Radio of February 20, 1947, *PRJ*, II: 763.
21. Press release, July 13, 1947, *PRJ*, II: p. 774.
22. *Ibid.*
23. Percy Johnston (chairman), chairman of the Chemical Bank; Paul Hoffman, liberal president of Studebaker, then one of the world's big four automakers; Fred Williams, ex-president of Cannon Mills; Robert Loree, chairman of the Foreign Trade Council; Sydney Scheuer, a leading textile trader; and Herbert Feis, formerly adviser to the Secretary of State and now adviser to the Secretary of the Army.
24. NSC Directive 13/2, which ordered MacArthur to relax Occupation controls, took eight months to go through the mill.
25. *JES* #40, December 1949. The industrial activity index fell from 63.3 to 56.9 (p. 8) while real wages rose from 54.7 to 74.3. The real wage index is calculated on manufacturing wages (p. 17) divided by consumer prices in urban Japan (p. 1) with June 1948 = 100.
26. U.S. aid versus Occupation costs changed as follows:

A. United States Aid

	In Million $			In Billion Yen	
	Budgeted*	Arrived†	Yen per $‡	Budgeted	Arrived
1946–47	278	228	71	19.7	16.2
1947–48	333	520	200	66.6	104.0
1948–49	497	505	324	161.0	163.6

B. Occupation Costs in Japanese Budget (in Billion Yen)

	Total General§ Account	Occupation Costs		
		Budgeted¶	As Percent of General Account	As Percent of U.S. Aid Arrived
1946–47	119	46.6	39.2%	287.7%
1947–48	214	71.6	33.5	68.8
1948–49	410	104.2	25.4	63.7

*Fine, *Japan's Post-War Recovery* (note 56, chapter 18), pp. 33, 36.
†*JES* #76, December 1952, p. 9. (The figure for 1946–47 includes shipments from September 1945 and Army surplus not budgeted as aid.)
‡See Appendix A.
§For 1946–47, *Japan Year Book* 1948, pp. 192–93. For 1947–48, *SCAP Monthly Summation,* March 1948, pp. 265–66. For 1948–49, *ibid.,* July 1948, p. 273. The Japanese fiscal year was from April 1 to March 31, the American from July 1 to June 30.
¶See 4th footnote, above.

22. Washington Versus Tokyo: MacArthur Loses Control over His Occupation

1. *NT,* February 4, 1949, p. 1.
2. Omar N. Bradley, *A General's Life* (New York: Simon & Schuster, 1983), p. 526. MacArthur objected to the idea with a "blistering diatribe," Bradley said.

3. *Forrestal Diaries* (note 34, chapter 2), p. 328.

4. Kennan, *Memoirs* (note 50, chapter 8), p. 411.

5. *OJEPR*, p. 64.

6. *Ibid.*, p. 66.

7. *Ibid.*, p. 64.

8. *Ibid.*, pp. 66–67.

9. The index of industrial production was up 58 percent between November 1947 and March 1948; new housing starts up 40 percent over 1947; the 1947–48 official rice harvest 9.6 million tons, as against 9 million the year before and only 6 million in the first postwar harvest; the rice collections for the rationing system exceeded 1947 by 15 percent and 1946 by 25; the consumer price index rose only 3 percent from May to December 1948, as against 7 percent during the corresponding period in 1947; the Bank of Japan note issue, which had climbed 100 percent in the first eleven months of 1947, increased only 34 percent in the same period a year later; and export contracts quadrupled in the last months of 1948 over the year before. (On export contracts, see *JES* #39, November 1949, pp. 1, 8, 15, 17, 20. Export contracts usually take three to six months to ship out. Shipments in the first half of 1949 averaged $45 million monthly, as against $12 million monthly the year before.)

10. For example, an AP dispatch of August 26, 1948.

11. Whitney, *MacArthur: His Rendezvous with History* (note 6, "Personal Note"), p. 268.

12. *JES* #39, November 1949, pp. 1, 8.

13. Draper's account to Hata Ikuhiko on September 19, 1972. as reported in *Zaisei-shi News* (*Financial History News*), December 12, 1972. Cited by Richard Nanto, "The Dodge Line," in *OJEPR*, p. 47.

14. No. W81058.

15. From an average of 7 percent a month in the first four months to 5 percent in the middle four and only 3 percent in the last four.

16. Actually, the note issue was 161 billion yen at the end of November 1946, 321 billion yen in November 1947, and 624 billion yen in November 1948. The corresponding industrial activity indexes were 54.5, 55.6, and 83.0. (*JES* #39, November 1949, pp. 8, 20.)

17. *NT*, December 20, 1948, p. 1.

18. *NT*, March 18, 1949, p. 1.

23. Imperial Accountant: Dodge and Deflation

1. For example, *Mainichi*, December 14, 1948, p. 6.

2. A few years later I saw him with half a dozen companions in the rear of a small election campaign truck cruising in downtown Tokyo. He was appealing for votes through a bullhorn. This time, however, he was running not for the House of Representatives, to which he had been elected in 1947 from the Second Yamagata District,

but for the National Constituency of the less important "upper house," the House of Councilors. He won his election, and in fact he remained a member of the House of Councilors until 1962, but he never made minister again and never recovered from the night an irate Yoshida fired him.

Mrs. Yamashita, for her part, ran into her own political turbulence shortly after the incident. At a 6 A.M. farm wives' radio discussion, one of the farm women hesitantly reported that she had heard that Yamashita had also been drunk at the time. Interviewed subsequently on the subject, Yamashita indignantly denied that it was possible. She had had "only" one *shō* (about two liters) of saké, she affirmed. Besides, she added, anyone foolish enough to appear on radio as early as six in the morning could not be taken seriously. The hard-working farmwives in her rural Fukushima Prefecture constitutency, women who in summer rose at 3:30 or 4 A.M., voted her out of office the following January. In the next election after that, in 1952, she won her seat back, and in the 1953 elections she came in at the top of the list. She was finally defeated in 1960, never to run again.

3. Ikeda held the following cabinet posts:

> Minister of Finance (February 1949–October 1952, Third Yoshida Cabinet)
> Minister of Commerce and Trade (October 1952–November 1952, Fourth Yoshida Cabinet)
> Minister of Finance (December 1956–February 1957, Ishibashi Cabinet)
> Minister of Finance (February 1957–July 1957; First Kishi Cabinet)
> Minister of Commerce and Trade (June 1959–July 1960; Second Kishi Cabinet).

He was prime minister three times: from July 1960 to December 1960; from December 1960 to December 1963; and from December 1963 to November 1964, when his sickness, from which he soon died, rendered him unable to continue in office.

4. *OJEPR,* p. 68.

5. Audley Stephan, Duke Diehl, Paul M. O'Leary, and Rex Reed. Orville MacDiarmid joined them a few weeks later.

6. Later Foreign Minister, 1974–76, Finance Minister (1986–), and today, 1986, a leading candidate for prime minister, one of the three so-called New Leaders.

7. Letter from Dodge to Cleveland Thurber, December 1948. (Dodge Papers, Detroit Public Library, cited by Dick Nanto, *OJEPR,* pp. 18, 36.)

8. The Dodge quotations are from his two press conferences of March 7 and April 15, 1949, as reported in *NT,* March 8 and April 16, 1949.

9. GHQ, SCAP, ESS, "Program to Achieve Economic Stabilization in Japan Pursuant to the Interim Directive of the United States Government (Serial Number 96)," dated January 29, 1949, para. 4f, in *TCP.*

10. From 2,674 yen per *koku* wholesale for wheat in July 1948 to 3,807 yen. (*Staple Food Prices in Japan 1930–48,* ESS, GHQ, SCAP, April 1949, p. 14.)

11. *JES* #37, September 1949, p. 43.

12. *Ibid.*

13. *Mission and Accomplishments,* 2d Edition, 1950, II, no. 2: 40.

14. *JES* #40, December 1949, pp. 1, 20.

15. *NT,* March 26, 1949.

16. Industrial production, which had risen so much the year before, leveled off. Capital goods investment, certainly no indulgence in momentary consumer desires, slumped for the next seven months. Machinery production fell by fully 25 percent, while durable goods in general declined. (*JES* #40, December 1949, pp. 9–10.) Housing starts were cut by more than half from 50,600 to 23,400 in both October and November. (P. 13.) Even export contracts fell 5 percent. The results were to show up in smaller shipments in the second half of 1949 as compared with the first half from $261 million to $248 million. (*JES* #76, December 1952, p. 9.)

17. Memo for General Marquat from K. D. Morrow, chief, Research and Programs Division, dated July 27, 1949; subject: Finance Ministry Report, "State of the National Economy," in *TCP*.

18. *Mission and Accomplishments*, 1949 edition, II, no. 2: 3.

19. *OJEPR*, p. 69.

20. *Ibid.*, p. 68.

21. *JES* #76, December 1952, p. 43.

22. From $63 million in January–June 1950 to $172 million in July–December. (*Ibid.*, p. 88.)

23. See, for example, Dodge's letter to Martin Bronfenbrenner, June 12, 1950, in Dodge Papers, Detroit Public Library.

24. Labor's Disillusionment with America

1. Published in *NT*, December 20, 1948, p. 1.

2. *NT*, December 21, 1948, p. 1. Marquat reported the meeting to MacArthur that evening, and the General, by Marquat's account, considered Hepler's stricture "well put."

3. *Jiji Press*, December 25, 1948.

4. ESS memorandum; subject: "Progress Report on Program to Achieve Economic Stabilization," February 12, 1949, p. 8, in *TCP*. The particular labor paragraphs in the memo were supplied by Labor Division.

5. *NT*, March 27, 1949, p. 1.

6. *NT*, April 23, 1949, p. 2.

7. *NT*, June 11, 1949, p. 1.

8. *NT*, June 12, 1949, p. 1.

9. The Socialists declined by 3.06 million votes; the Communist gained by 1.99 million. A new left-wing party, Farmer-Labor, won 600,000, most of which may be presumed to have come from the Socialists.

10. After leaving the Occupation in 1949, Hepler joined the International Labor Organization in Geneva as one of its top officers.

11. Burati recounted the episode with relish to Professor Takemae Eiji almost thirty years later. (*Journal of the Tokyo College of Economics*, Nos. 97–98, 1976, p. 267.)

12. *NT*, April 19, 1949, p. 1. Among the scheduled dischargees were 95,000 railwaymen and 30,000 communication workers. (ESS memo: Labor Situation, July 6, 1949, in *TCP*.)

13. *NT,* June 5, 1949, p. 1.

14. According to Lieutenant Colonel Jack Napier, *A Survey of the Japanese Communist Party* (Tokyo: *Nippon Times,* 1952), p. 55.

15. A total of 2,819 employees out of 6,690. *NT,* April 30, 1949.

16. ESS Memo, July 4, 1949.

17. ESS, *Labor Division Report for 1949,* p. 4. Initial unemployment insurance claims in June 1949 were 30 percent higher than in May, and total weeks of unemployment insurance claimed within that month amounted to three times those of the preceding January. (GHQ ESS Labor Division, *Labor Letter,* Vol. 2, No. 2, July 31, 1949.)

18. *NT,* April 9, 1949, p. 3.

19. *NT,* April 22, 1949, p. 3.

20. In negotiating their new contract, for example, the metal-mining companies offered their workers a base pay of 4,300 yen ($12.00) monthly, a cut of more than 20 percent. (*NT,* April 1, 1949, p. 3.)

21. Requiring annual audits of union finances, annual union elections, majority strike votes, and employer bargaining in good faith; permitting a closed shop under certain conditions; excluding acts of violence from labor law protection; making union registration optional; and so forth.

22. *NT,* March 26, 1949, p. 1.

23. Napier, *Survey of Japanese Communist Party* (note 9 above), tabulates 9,514 in industry and 690 in press and radio (pp. 56, 58), but omits at least 650 in trucking.

24. Article 21.

25. Article 14.

26. Cited in Napier, *Survey of Japanese Communist Party,* p. 57.

27. The Fukuoka Court, for example, stated in its formal opinion: "The people in general have already deemed that there is a danger that the Communist Party may proceed to organized activity with the objective of violent revolution. This fact is also known from Gen. MacArthur's letters and messages."

28. *NT,* January 8, 1950, p. 1.

29. Tokuda disappeared from view, evidently having gone to China, from where his death on October 14, 1953, was reported.

30. The departure of the American troops for the Inchon landing in September 1950 was well known in the Japanese ports from which they sailed, but somehow or other the intelligence did not reach the North Koreans in time, or they misinterpreted its implications.

31. 12.7 million workers. (ESS *Labor Division Report for 1949,* p. 4.)

32. *JES* #40, December 1949, pp. 1, 17. The real wage rose from 113.4 (1948 = 100) to 126.6 in October and 137 in November.

33. James Killen, Paul Stanchfield, Samuel Romer, and Richard L.-G. Deverall, respectively. In the spring of 1949 Hepler, who had been both Chief of the Manpower Branch and of the entire division, left too.

34. Interview with Takemae Eiji, pp. 262–63.

35. Among other things, the convention rejected Mutō's proposed affiliation with the anti-Communist International Confederation of Free Trade Unions. The text of the

declaration may be found in *Nippon Rōdō Nenkan* (Japan Labor Year Book), 1953, p. 295.

25. The Balance Sheet: Stabilization, Economic Miracle, Broken Dialogue

1. Savings of 31 percent, according to the Economic Planning Agency's projection for 1979–82.
2. In 1936, 572 million yen was budgeted for the War Ministry, and 622 million yen for the Navy out of a national income of 13.676 billion yen, a percentage of 8.7. (*Orient Year Book*, 1942, pp. 126, 137.)
3. A friend of mine in Kutsukake, Nagano Prefecture.
4. Real wages in June 1950 more than doubled as against April 1948. (*JES* #41–47, January–July 1950, pp. 1, 17.) The Young mission's MacDiarmid estimated workers' consumption at the earlier date at 65 percent of 1934–36. *OJEPR*, p. 66.
5. Nissan's president Kawamata showed me the contract in 1953.
6. Edwin O. Reischauer, "Broken Dialogue with Japan," *Foreign Affairs*, October 1950.

Name Index

527